Baltic Sea

palacios

Miles

Koenigsberg

Danzig

EAST PRUSSIA

Novgorod

Grodno

Stettin

Bromberg

MAZURIAN LAKES
1914 BATTLE OF
TANNENBERG

Brest-
Litovsk

GERMAN - AUSTRO - HUNGARIAN LINES

Poznan

VISTULA R.

Warsaw

Rovno

Lodz

P O L A N D

R U S S I A

1916

BUG R.

Lublin

Prague

VISTULA R.

Cracow

Lemberg

G A L I C I A

CRESWELL UNION HIGH SCHOOL

RUSSIAN LINES

DNIESTER R.

Brünn

CARPATHIAN MTS.

1914

Kolomea

DANUBE R.

VIENNA

A - H U N G A R Y

Debreczen

Budapest

TISZA R.

RUMANIA

BUCHAREST

Szeged

Pécs

Agram
(Zagreb)

Fiume

SAVA R.

Luka

BELGRADE

Craiova

DANUBE R.

Sarajevo

S E R B I A

BULGARIA

MONTENEGRO

BOOKS BY JOHN DOS PASSOS

Historical Narratives

THE GROUND WE STAND ON
THE HEAD AND HEART OF THOMAS JEFFERSON
THE MEN WHO MADE THE NATION
MR. WILSON'S WAR

Contemporary Chronicles

CHOSEN COUNTRY
THREE SOLDIERS
MANHATTAN TRANSFER
THE 42ND PARALLEL
NINETEEN NINETEEN
THE BIG MONEY
THE MOST LIKELY TO SUCCEED
ADVENTURES OF A YOUNG MAN
NUMBER ONE
THE GRAND DESIGN
THE GREAT DAYS
MIDCENTURY

Mainstream of America Series ★

EDITED BY LEWIS GANNETT

MR. WILSON'S WAR

MR. WILSON'S WAR

by John Dos Passos

DOUBLEDAY & COMPANY, INC.

Garden City, New York, 1962

Wide World Photos: 1, 16, 26, 37, 47A, 47B, 47C, 47D, 47E
Culver Pictures: 3, 4, 5, 6, 7, 8, 9, 10, 11, 12, 13, 14, 15, 17, 18, 19, 20, 22, 23, 24, 25, 27, 28, 29, 30, 31, 32, 33, 34, 35, 36, 38, 39, 40, 41, 42, 43, 44, 45, 46, 48, 49, 50, 51, 52, 53, 54, 55, 56, 57, 58, 59, 61
The Bettman Archives: 2, 21, 60

Mr. Wilson's War by John Dos Passos

Acknowledgement is made to the following copyright holders:

The Bobbs-Merrill Company, Inc., for excerpts from *My Memoir* by Edith Boling Wilson. Copyright 1939 by Edith Boling Wilson. Reprinted by permission of the publisher.

Dodd, Mead & Company, for excerpts from *Leaves from a War Diary* by James G. Harbord. Copyright 1925 by Dodd, Mead & Company, Inc. Reprinted by permission of the publisher.

Harcourt, Brace & World, Inc., for excerpts from *Peacemaking, 1919,* by Harold Nicolson. Reprinted by permission of the publisher.

Ives Hendrick, for excerpts from *Life and Letters of Walter Hines Page* by Burton J. Hendrick.

Hillman Press, Inc., for excerpts from *The Second Division: American Expeditionary Force in France, 1917–19.* Reprinted by permission of the publisher.

Houghton Mifflin Company, for excerpts from *Journal of the Great War* by Charles G. Dawes. Reprinted by permission of Houghton Mifflin Company. *Letters and Friendships of Sir Cecil Spring Rice* by Stephen Gwynn. Reprinted by permission of Houghton Mifflin Company and Constable and Company, Limited.

J. B. Lippincott Company, for excerpts from *My Experiences in the World War* by J. J. Pershing. Reprinted by permission of the publisher.

The Macmillan Company, for excerpts from *Charles Evans Hughes* by Merlo J. Pusey. Reprinted by permission of the publisher.

Rachel Baker Napier, for excerpts from *Life and Letters of Woodrow Wilson* by Ray Stannard Baker.

Mr. Archibald Roosevelt, Mrs. Alice Roosevelt Longworth and Mrs. Richard Derby, for excerpt from Library of Congress collection of the Theodore Roosevelt papers.

Library of Congress Catalog Card Number 61–12612
Copyright © 1962 by John Dos Passos
All Rights Reserved. Printed in the United States of America

CONTENTS

PART ONE

The Search for Peace

Behold a republic, increasing in population, in wealth, in strength, and in influence, solving the problems of civilization and hastening the coming of a universal brotherhood—a republic which makes thrones and dissolves aristocracies by its silent example and gives light to those who sit in darkness. Behold a republic gradually but surely becoming the supreme moral factor in disputes.

—William Jennings Bryan
at Canton, Ohio, October 16, 1900

Chapter 1

T.R. AND THE YOUTH OF THE CENTURY

ONE hot dusty afternoon in the first week of September 1901 President William McKinley, accompanied by Mrs. McKinley and his two nieces, arrived for his official visit to the Pan-American Exposition in Buffalo. Amid the screeching of whistles and the jangling of chimes and the booming of a twentyone gun salute, the President and Mrs. McKinley were driven slowly around the grounds in a carriage drawn by four well-matched bays.

The next day had been designated President's Day. Mr. McKinley delivered an address from a platform decorated with the massed flags of all the American republics to a crowd which the newspapers described as "packed to suffocation" on the esplanade.

Mr. McKinley was a fine figure of a man, with a high broad brow and a roman nose flanked by searching gray eyes. Under the black neckcloth an ample piqué vest gleamed white between the folds of the long Prince

Albert coat. As he stood looking down into the enthusiastic faces, with the cheers and handclapping resounding in his ears, he couldn't help a feeling of confidence in his country's destiny and his own which amounted perhaps to complacency.

With the help of his friend Mark Hanna and "the full dinner pail" he had won re-election over William Jennings Bryan, nominee of Populists and Free Silver Democrats, by a plurality of over a million votes.

A new century was opening. The Spanish-American War was won. Expanding westward to include Hawaii and the Philippines, and southward to dominate Cuba and Puerto Rico, the United States had taken her place among the great powers in the world. After four years and a half of his administration, the nation rejoiced in unexampled prosperity.

". . . This portion of the earth" said Mr. McKinley, and struck a responsive chord in the listening crowd, "has no cause for humiliation for the part it has played in the march of civilization. It has not accomplished everything, far from it. It has simply done its best, and without vanity or boastfulness, and recognizing the valid achievements of others, it invites the friendly rivalry of all the powers in the peaceful pursuits of trade and commerce and will co-operate with all in advancing the highest and best interests of humanity . . ."

He spoke of the effect of railroads and swift steamships and of the Atlantic cables in knitting the world together: "Isolation is no longer possible or desirable. The same important news is read, though in different languages, in all Christendom."

He called for an increase in the merchant marine to spread the fruits of American prosperity—which he found so great as to be "almost appalling"—to less favored lands, and for increased intercourse with the Latin-American peoples to whom this exposition was dedicated. He demanded the immediate construction of an isthmian canal to join the Atlantic and Pacific oceans and the laying of a cable out into the far Pacific. He spoke with enthusiasm of the development of arbitration treaties between nation and nation which hopeful men were looking for to eliminate forever the causes of war: "God and man have linked the nations together. No nation can longer be indifferent to any other. And as we are brought more and more in touch with each other, the less occasion there is for misunderstandings, and the stronger the disposition, when we have differences, to adjust them in the court of arbitration, which is the noblest forum for international disputes."

After the speech the cheering crowd broke through the ropes and mobbed the stand. Smiling and dignified Mr. McKinley stepped forward and shook more than a hundred hands.

McKinley was a popular President. His enthusiastic reception wherever he met plain Americans man to man gave the lie to Bryan's oratorical denunciations of the Republican Party as the party of the trusts and of the oppressors of the working man and the farmer; and to the Labor Day rabblerousers who had been reviving the issues of the campaign.

Labor Day parades, animated perhaps by the news of the strike in Pittsburgh of seventy thousand steel workers who didn't seem to appreciate the fullness of their dinner pails, had drawn recordbreaking crowds.

In Kansas City, preaching to the text: "Muzzle not the ox that treadeth out the corn" William Jennings Bryan had castigated the interests that "would crucify mankind on a cross of gold" and deny a living wage to the working man.

McKinley's own Vice President, young Colonel Theodore Roosevelt, speaking at the opening of the Minnesota State Fair, with the glamor of his citations for bravery on San Juan Hill still about him, had, amid the whoops and yelps of his Rough Riders, called for "supervision and control" of the great corporations in the public interest.

Friday, September 6 was the last day of the President's visit. In the morning Mr. McKinley, accompanied by the ambassadors of the friendly nations south of the Rio Grande, journeyed to Niagara Falls in a private car. Everyone was captivated by the view of the falls from the International Bridge. After an excellent lunch the party returned to the exposition grounds for a presidential reception, in the old tradition of handshaking democracy, scheduled for four in the afternoon in the Temple of Music.

Still wearing his long Prince Albert coat, with what the reporters described as "a smile of dignity and benevolence" on his face, Mr. McKinley stood under a bower of greenery and palms at the end of a corridor hung with purple bunting so arranged as to reduce the incoming throng to a single file. Detectives, secretservice men, reporters and members of the diplomatic corps stood in a group behind him. The President was seen to rub his hands in pleased anticipation. Instead of an ordeal it was a pleasure for him to meet the common man.

When the doors were opened and the people poured in, the enormous organ installed in the building was still blaring forth a Bach sonata which was part of the afternoon concert.

The secretservice agents carefully scrutinized the men who filed in with outstretched hands. The reporter for the Baltimore *Sun* thought that one foreignlooking man whom he described as having a bushy black mustache, bloodless lips and a glassy eye, attracted their suspicion. They were so busy watching him that they hardly noticed a tall, boyishlooking smoothfaced fellow who wore his arm in a sling. The organ music had reached a crescendo when Czolgosz, offering his left hand to the President, shoved a pistol at him out of the bandage that swathed his right and shot him in the belly.

Mr. McKinley was assisted to a bench behind the purple bunting. The guards threw themselves on Czolgosz, who was with difficulty saved from lynching. He was quoted as saying that he was an anarchist and had done his duty. He came of a poor but respectable Polish family in Detroit. His head was said to have been turned by the theories of a young Russian Jewess named Emma Goldman who was inciting working people in Chicago to bring about the triumph of right and justice through anarchy.

The President was taken to a hospital and then to the home of friends where he was reported to be resting easily.

The Chicago police arrested Emma Goldman but the judge turned her loose for lack of evidence. Editorials demanded the deportation of foreign anarchists.

Senator Mark Hanna, who had first heard the news with stunned unbelief at the Union Club in Cleveland, hurried to the President's bedside, as did members of the Cabinet and Vice President Roosevelt. The early bulletins of the medical men were so reassuring that Colonel Roosevelt decided to take a few days off with his wife and children in the Adirondacks before returning to politics and to Oyster Bay.

He joined Mrs. Roosevelt and the children at the Tahawus Club up above Keene Valley in the headwaters of the Ausable River. When a messenger arrived announcing that President McKinley's condition had taken a sudden turn for the worse the Vice President was climbing in the mountains. A guide, set off in search of him, found him towards dusk on the trail down from Mt. Tahawus. He rode all night in a wagon and reached the railroad station at North Creek where his secretary was waiting with a special train to rush him to Buffalo.

When he reached Buffalo towards midday he found that Mr. McKinley was dead and was immediately sworn in as President of the United States.

T.R.

Theodore Roosevelt was the youngest man ever to be President. When he moved into the Executive Mansion, which he preferred to call the White House, he brought with him the romping uninhibited family life of Sagamore Hill, where politics and amateur boxing and a passion for wild creatures and wild country mingled with jingo enthusiasms and a real taste for history and for certain kinds of literature. Since Jefferson, whom T.R. acutely disliked, no American president had exhibited such varied interests, or shown himself so completely to the manor born.

He was the descendant of six generations of eminent New Yorkers. From his mother, a southern gentlewoman from one of the great plantation homes in Georgia, he absorbed the conviction so general among the daughters of the defeated Confederacy, that if the human race had an aristocracy they belonged to it. This established preconception made for social selfconfidence, and enabled him to deal with King Edward or the Kaiser or Manhattan wardheelers or the cowhands on his ranch or his sparring partners from the Tenderloin, on a basis of courteous give and take between equals. The foundation of his personal magnetism was an ardent fellow feeling for all sorts and varieties of men. A man who could be friends with Sir Cecil Spring Rice and John L. Sullivan at the same time could really boast that nothing human was strange to him.

In his autobiography he described himself as having been "a rather sickly rather timid little boy very fond of desultory reading and natural history, and not excelling in any form of sport." As a child he suffered terribly from asthma. Very early he was fascinated by the animal kingdom. He used to say that it was the feeling of romance and adventure he got from the sight of a dead seal laid out on a slab of wood outside of a Broadway market that started him on his career as amateur taxidermist and zoologist.

His parents worried about his nervousness and timidity, but when he found other kids beating him up he took to developing his muscles with dumbbells and exercises. His father arranged for lessons in boxing and wrestling.

As he grew older he developed a ferocious energy. Overcompensation with a vengeance. In spite of extreme nearsightedness he became a fair shot. He took to long walks and mountainclimbing. He acquired a good seat on a horse.

Though he loved life outdoors he had a bookish streak. He wrote fluent and expressive English. While still at Harvard College he started, probably under the influence of his mother's brothers who had both been officers on the blockaderunner *Alabama,* a highly technical history of American seamanship in the War of 1812.

The fall after graduating from college he married a Chestnut Hill girl named Alice Lee whom he had fallen desperately in love with during a country walk. The couple settled down at his mother's house in New York so that T.R. could study law at Columbia, but he was more interested in the assorted characters he met at the local Republican Club. He took up ward politics as he took up boxing, just to prove that he could do it.

At twentythree as a representative of the "better element" he found himself elected to the state legislature from the Twentyfirst Assembly District, known as the Diamond Back District, one of the few safely Republican districts in New York. In spite of the embarrassment of a Harvard drawl, dundreary whiskers and pincenez anchored by a black ribbon, he made such an impression on the assemblymen that he was soon being talked of as a possible minority leader. He was beginning to make a name for himself by exposing a stockjobbing scandal in connection with the financing of one of the new elevated railways when he suffered a crushing blow.

Hurrying joyfully home from Albany one winter weekend to greet his firstborn child he found his Alice dying and his mother desperately ill with typhoid fever. "There is a curse on this house" his brother Elliott cried. Their mother died during the night and Alice the next afternoon. ". . . as a flower she grew and as a fair young flower she died . . . when she had just become a mother, when her life seemed to be just begun, and when the years seemed so bright before her," Theodore wrote in a memorial which he circulated among the family, "the light went from my life for ever."

T.R. was no man to let grief get him down. Spring Rice once described his friend Theodore as "pure act." After finishing up his duties with the legislature as best he could, he headed for the wild west. His father had left him a moderate income. As he put it, he had the bread and butter but he must earn the jam. His first effort to make himself some money was to invest in a Dakota ranch. In his bereavement he decided to give cowpunching his personal attention.

He stopped off in Chicago to attend the Republican convention. The nomination of James G. Blaine, whom he considered somewhat less than honest, to run against Grover Cleveland, thoroughly disgusted him. When he was asked whether he was going to make ranching his business he said no but it was the best way to avoid campaigning for Blaine.

The last thing T.R. wanted was to lose himself in the western wilderness. Immediately an item appeared in *The Bad Lands Cowboy*, a recently established newspaper in the recently established tanktown of Medora: "Theodore Roosevelt the young New York reformer made us a very pleasant call Monday in full cowboy regalia."

T.R. took to the cowhands and the cowhands took to him. He was affectionately known as Four Eyes. He didn't drink or smoke. He couldn't shake off his Harvard drawl. His profoundest cussword was By Godfrey, but his energy and nerve and knack for leadership won him the amazed admiration of the whole countryside.

He was made a deputy sheriff and helped round up some horsethieves and was asked to run for Congress. He lost every cent of the sixty thousand dollars he invested in cattle but he wrote a successful book on his experiences called *Hunting Trips of a Ranchman*. The frontispiece was a photograph of Theodore Roosevelt in sombrero hat, beaded buckskin shirt, chaps and boots with silver spurs: the greatest showoff of his generation.

Not many months later he was in England marrying Edith Carow at St. George's, Hanover Square. Cecil Spring Rice, then a sprightly young fellow just out of Oxford whom T.R. had taken a shine to on the boat, was best man. Theodore and Edith had been playmates in Gramercy Park when she was a little girl and he was a small boy. Probably she had been a motherly little girl. All their lives it was to be Mrs. Roosevelt who would watch over Theodore along with the other children, seeing that he got the proper meals and didn't spend his money foolishly and changed his clothes when he came home drenched from a hike in the snow.

After one of those European honeymoons popular with wealthy Americans in the nineteenth century the couple settled at Sagamore Hill, in the house Theodore had been building on some family property at Oyster Bay and was wondering how he would pay for. Private life was repugnant to him. He missed the admiring throng. He was an industrious writer but writing wasn't enough. Right away he was back in Republican politics.

With the election of Benjamin Harrison came an appointment in Washington to the new Civil Service Commission. "I rose like a rocket," wrote T.R. President Harrison's comment on T.R.'s activities was: "He wanted to put an end to all the evil in the world between sunrise and sunset."

When, twelve years later, he took over the presidency T.R. carried with him to Washington all the enthusiasms of the grubby little blueeyed sandyhaired boy who had filled the house with the smell of formaldehyde and with the pelts of dead animals; and all his adolescent joys in hunting and warfare and naval tactics and history and literature; to which, with burgeoning virility, had been added the naturalborn leader's passion to make other people do what he wanted them to do, and a type of bullheaded moralizing which was entirely his own. His friends complained that Theodore never would grow up.

No man ever enjoyed being President more.

The New Nationalism

When T.R. took the oath of office at the age of fortytwo on September 14, 1901, at his friend Wilcox's house in Buffalo, he was thought of as a jingo with a knack for personal publicity, a political embodiment of Kipling's theory of Anglo-Saxon supremacy. It was characteristic of his complex personality that the first scandal he caused was by inviting Booker T. Washington to dinner at the White House. It was typical too, of the less attractive side of him, that he tried to explain the story away by giving out that the Negro president of Tuskegee had merely been invited to lunch on the spur of the moment.

However the incident was twisted around in the war of words that followed, the fact remained that social or racial snobbery had no place in T.R.'s gentleman's code. He didn't need to put himself out to make Jews feel at home. It never occurred to him that he couldn't ask a man he admired to dinner because he happened to have a dark skin. In his correspondence with his dear friend and passionate admirer, Owen Wister, whose head was a roost for all the snobberies acquired in undergraduate days at Harvard, T.R. showed more understanding of what men of diverse races and traditions had to face before finding acceptance by the then dominant Anglo-Saxon elite than any other public man of the day. For T.R. 'a man was a man for a' of that.'

Conservation of national resources and of the beauties of nature were among his many passions. He instigated enforcement of the antitrust laws. He cudgelled the mine operators into arbitrating their differences with John Mitchell's United Mine Workers. For the miners it was the first step out of serfdom to the coal companies.

Coming into conflict with financial barons whom he dubbed "malefactors of great wealth" he found himself adopting, as time went on, planks from the platform of "Messrs. Bryan, Altgeld, Debs, Coxey and the rest," whom he'd lumped together when he was fighting free silver during McKinley's first presidential campaign, as "strikingly like the leaders of the Terror in France in mental and moral attitude."

By the time T.R. was ready to go on the stump for a second term he had managed to appropriate a large part of these gentlemen's following. This was a generation that read Henry George and Bellamy's *Looking Backward* and listened to young Debs, the impassioned spokesman for the railroad workers. The more distant reaches of the cornbelt abounded in enthusiasts eager to make the nation over in accordance with their aspirations for a perfect democracy. Populists, freesilver men, greenbackers, pacifists, nonresisters, utopian socialists vied with each other for the speakers' platforms in the raw middlewestern towns.

The century was new. When the frontier reached the Pacific some of its backwash rolled back to invigorate the entire nation. Americans were ready to discover the globe. Beyond the oceans lay lands benighted, open to adventure. The heathen must be taught the ways of Christian self-government. If only the grip of corrupt politicians and greedy businessmen could be loosened at home the great example of American democracy was ready to set all mankind on the path of progress.

In spite of the New York Republicanism of his background T.R. managed, with his cowboy gear and his whooping escorts of Rough Riders, to appear as a Lochinvar off the western plains. He channelled the hopes and plans of the westerners for reform into his thoroughly personal program for justice and fair play. He spoke out with so much zest that soberer and older men found themselves following in his trail.

The Peerless Leader

The Democrats made Roosevelt's task easy. For eight years the ardent and active wing of the party had been swayed by William Jennings Bryan's silver tongue. At their convention in St. Louis in 1904 the gold-standard men took over and nominated as their candidate, amid the indignant groans of the westerners, an estimable but politically colorless New York judge named Alton B. Parker instead of the peerless leader.

It was Bryan's ironical fate, in spite of his gift of eloquence, twice to clear the path that was to lead another man into the presidency. Bryan's oratory helped arouse the enthusiasms that Theodore Roosevelt took advantage of in 1904, and in 1912 it was Bryan's prestige as leader of the forces of righteousness in the Democratic party that assured Woodrow Wilson's nomination.

Bryan was nurtured on righteousness from the cradle. His father, a Democratic politician in southern Illinois, who served a number of terms in the state legislature and prospered in later years as a judge of the circuit court, was a "praying Baptist."

His mother, though the most dutiful of wives, clung to the Methodist faith she'd been brought up in. Bryan in later life explained in his memoirs how much he had been the gainer: as a boy he had doubled his "Sunday school opportunities" by attending both churches.

His parents were stern in their upbringing. Their boys shirked no chores. The young Bryans got their education between McGuffey's Reader and the Holy Bible continually elucidated at prayer meeting and Sunday school. William Jennings studied law in Jacksonville, Illinois, married and moved his family out to Nebraska in search of opportunity.

Opportunity was not far to seek. He was an agreeably handsome young man with an extraordinarily resonant voice. One day when the speaker didn't turn up for a Democratic rally Bryan volunteered to pinch hit. His speech was so successful that when he reached home he woke up his wife and told her, "I found I had power over the audience. I found I could move them as I chose . . . God grant I may use it wisely." He knelt down by the bed and prayed.

He was soon recognized as the best speaker in the state and a few years later, although a teetotaller, he was backed by the Lincoln liquor interests who trusted him to oppose prohibition when he ran for Congress. The Republicans teased him with the nickname of "Boy Orator of the Platte." Proudly bearing that title he arrived in Washington to represent his district in the Fiftysecond Congress.

He immediately let himself be heard from with a successful speech against the protective tariff. Adopting the "free and unlimited coinage of

silver" as his personal plank, he was renominated in Nebraska and returned to Congress with the frenetic support of the populists. Operators
of silver mines were glad to furnish his campaign funds.

Another successful oration in the House almost took the Democratic
leadership away from Grover Cleveland, representing gold and the economic creeds of the Wall Street bankers, who as President was the party's
titular head. Bryan earned obloquy in financial circles and near deifica-
tion from the western insurgents by following it up with a demand for a
tax on the incomes of the rich. He was only thirtysix when in 1896 he
joined the Nebraska delegation to the Democratic National Convention
in Chicago.

A few days before, as correspondent for the Omaha *World-Herald* in
St. Louis, where the Republicans were convening, he had seen the free-
silver men go storming out of the hall amid cries of "Take the Chicago
train." He had already tried out in the halls of Congress his peroration
that was soon to be so famous: "I shall not help crucify mankind upon a
cross of gold . . . I shall not aid in pressing down upon the bleeding brow
of labor this crown of thorns."

He had been experimenting for months with other booming passages
of the great speech he was planning, at meetings in his home state and
in private to his wife. Bryan was an orator who left nothing to chance.

His name had for some time been bruited about as presidential timber.
His opportunity came when, in a conclave even more sharply torn than
the Republican convention, but this time by antiplutocratic factions, he
was called upon to speak. That speech was the climax of his career.

Edgar Lee Masters wrote down his recollections of the scene in the
Colosseum: "Suddenly I saw a man spring up from his seat among the
delegates, and with the agility and swiftness of an eager boxer hurry to
the speaker's rostrum. He was slim, tall, pale, raven-haired, beaked of
nose . . . as this young man opened his great mouth all the twenty thousand persons present heard its thunder . . . He was smiling. A sweet
reasonableness shone in his handsome face . . ."

Men and women present in the hall that day never tired of telling all
who would listen of the magical effectiveness of the Cross of Gold speech.
Bryan's nomination for President followed. To the tune of Sousa's "El
Capitan" march, his oratory swept the country. Mark Hanna and the
Wall Street "interests" had to strain every dollar to carry McKinley's
election.

Finding himself even in defeat one of the country's great men and
with the dignity of a presidential candidate to support, young Bryan had
to find some suitable way of making a living. He had no taste for the
drudgery of the law. He and his wife produced a book: *The First Battle,*
which did well enough to clear up the debts of the campaign. As a per-

manent source of income he took up lecturing on the Chautauqua circuit.

When they moved to Nebraska the Bryans joined the Presbyterian Church. He soon became an elder. His speeches were lay sermons. A favorite was on reading the Bible. He tried to live the Christian life.

Although as a practicing Christian he deplored war, as a proselyting democrat he couldn't help being stirred by the struggle for selfgovernment in Cuba that gave the American expansionists an opportunity to flex their youthful muscles by declaring war against the decrepit empire of the Spanish Bourbons.

"Universal peace cannot come until Justice is enthroned throughout the world," Bryan declared to a shouting crowd at the Trans-Mississippi World's Fair in Omaha. "As long as the oppressor is deaf to the voice of reason, so long must the citizen accustom his shoulder to the musket and his hand to the saber."

The "young man eloquent" modestly enlisted as a private in the militia. Thereupon the governor of Nebraska commissioned him to raise a regiment and, after a summer spent with his troops fighting fever and mosquitoes in a Florida swamp, he emerged from the six weeks war as Colonel Bryan.

In uniform he had suffered acutely from what he called military lockjaw. His experience confirmed his inherent suspicion of the military way of doing things, and made him more than ever an opponent of the imperialism which was luring the youth of both parties away from the set-our-own-house-in-order-first creed of the reformers.

In the congressional debate over the disposition of Spain's overseas empire, Bryan's anti-imperialism took a turn which both his friends and his enemies found hard to explain. Ratification of the treaty by which the United States would assume sovereignty over the Philippines was bitterly contested in the Senate. In spite of remonstrances from such hearty pacifists as Andrew Carnegie and David Starr Jordan, Bryan used his influence among Democratic senators to "enthrone justice" in those distant islands by placing them under American rule. His supporters failed by a single vote to put through the justifying amendment he lobbied for desperately which would assure the Filipinos eventual independence.

The peerless leader was left impaled on the dilemma. The explanation, that the treaty, if ratified, would give the Democratic opposition to overseas expansion a better talking point in the coming campaign, never quite held water. His loss of a large part of the anti-imperialist vote had something to do with his defeat by McKinley in 1900.

After his defeat and his mistyeyed retirement from presidential politics Bryan made up for past inconsistencies by the increased ardor of his advocacy of the cause of peace. During the campaign he had been painting a picture of America as arbiter of the world's disputes.

"Behold a republic," he declaimed in President McKinley's home town of Canton, "increasing in population, in wealth, in strength, and in influence . . . Behold a republic gradually but surely becoming the supreme moral factor in disputes."

The Laird of Skibo

Bryan was not alone in these hopes. Peace by arbitration had been one of the themes of McKinley's last speech. The world over, thoughtful men looked forward into the new century with the hope that at last they would see an end to the curse of war.

Andrew Carnegie, whom many good Bryan supporters had been excoriating as the plutocratic villain of the industrial warfare round Pittsburgh, was dedicating his vast fortune and his very considerable ability as a publicist to the cause of peace between nations.

Carnegie had early promulgated the theory that a businessman should spend half his life making money and the other half distributing his wealth "for the improvement of mankind." He was as good as his word. After selling out his interests in steel and iron and coke to U. S. Steel for what was reputed to be the sum of two hundred and fifty million dollars in five percent gold bonds, the laird of Skibo Castle kept himself busy writing exhortatory letters to those in authority, accompanied by the relevant checks, in furtherance of the great cause.

Carnegie was the personal embodiment of the mythology of nineteenthcentury capitalism. Coming from a family of learned Scottish artisans, he was brought up in desperate poverty, since his father who was a weaver had lost his livelihood to the factories. America was the escape. The undersized towheaded boy, already a mighty reader, reached New York with his family on the old whaling ship *Wiscasset* in 1848.

Starting as bobbinboy at thirteen in an Allegheny textile mill, he worked as messenger for the telegraph office, then as telegraphist and private secretary to a railroad man who became Assistant Secretary of War in charge of transportation during the Civil War. When Scott retired from the railroad, Carnegie took over his job. Innovations were the air he breathed. As superintendent of the Pittsburgh division of the Pennsylvania Railroad he introduced the first Pullman cars. Still a young man he went into steel and imported the Bessemer process. He promoted some of the first oilwells and became dizzyingly wealthy.

His first benefaction was a public bath for the stony ancient capital of Scotland, Dunfermline, where he was born and had his schooling. He gave away libraries, bought a string of newspapers to promote republicanism among the English and engaged a large staff of wellpaid smoothies to talk peace at all seasons.

Prince of Peace

Arbitration had been in the air for a decade. The British and American governments had successfully arbitrated a dispute over the boundary between Colombia and Venezuela which had once seemed a *casus belli*. There had followed a long negotiation between the two governments for a permanent arbitration treaty. This treaty, in spite of urgent appeals from outgoing President Cleveland and incoming President McKinley, failed in ratification in the Senate in the spring of 1897. The short war with Spain, an unnecessary war if there ever was one, proved the need for renewed activity by the advocates of peace.

In 1899 they were much heartened by an appeal from Czar Nicholas of all the Russias to the principal powers to meet at The Hague to discuss the limitation of armaments, and to impose a humane code on nations that did have recourse to war. Out of this conference came a few rules of war more honored in the breach than the observance, and the Hague Tribunal. Carnegie furnished an endowment that housed the Tribunal in a handsome palace in the Dutch capital.

Bryan, having retired from the political battlefield like the sulking Achilles, kept his name and admonitions before the public by publishing a weekly magazine from his home in Lincoln "with the purpose to aid the common people in the protection of their rights, the advancement of their interests and the realization of their aspirations." He named it *The Commoner*. The magazine found immediate circulation.

Through *The Commoner* and constant lecturing on the Chautauqua platform he remained in touch with the aspirations of the mass of the American people. From the response of his audiences he gathered that next to fair play in the economy their most ardent desire was for international peace.

The peerless leader was now assured of an income. The Bryans built themselves a new home named Fairview on a hill overlooking the state capitol. Mrs. Bryan desired the broadening influence of travel. After a couple of short peeks into Mexico and Havana, Bryan made an article writing arrangement with Hearst that paid for a nine weeks European tour.

The Bryans, as uninformed about foreign lands as any of Mark Twain's *Innocents Abroad*, visited the British Isles, France, Germany and Italy and even Russia. Everywhere he was received as a great American. The Pope gave him an audience, and he was allowed to compliment Czar Nicholas to his face on the establishment of the international court at The Hague.

The high point of the trip was his visit to Tolstoy at Yasnaya Polyana.

The venerable old Russian noble-in-peasant's-clothing held forth on non-resistance and the power of love. Though Bryan followed Christ's teachings literally indeed, he seems to have taken the doctrine of "turn the other cheek" with a grain of salt.

"Not long ago," wrote Tolstoy soon after, "I read . . . that my recognition of the principle of nonresistance is a sad and partly comical error, which, taking into consideration my old age, and some of my deserts, one may pass with condescending silence. Just such an attitude . . . I met in my conversation with the remarkably clever and progressive American, Bryan." Tolstoy had found more cleverness than Christianity in his visitor. "Bryan certainly does talk a lot," he added.

Bryan regarded the interview with Tolstoy as one of the great moments of his life. His enthusiasm for nonresistance grew with the telling. "I am satisfied," he wrote in *The Commoner* of the author of *War and Peace*, "that, notwithstanding his great intellect, his colossal strength lies in his heart more than in his mind . . . Love is the dominant note in Count Tolstoy's philosophy . . . It is his shield and sword. He is a deeply religious man."

Later in a lecture on peace by arbitration, trying to put the thing in practical terms for his audience, he used Tolstoy as an example: "There he stands proclaiming to the world that he believes that love is a better protection than force; that he thinks a man will suffer less by refusing to use violence than if he used it. And what is the result? He is the only man in Russia that the czar with all his army dare not lay his hand on . . . I believe that this nation could stand before the world today and tell the world it did not believe in war . . . that it had no disputes it was not willing to submit to the judgment of the world. If this nation did that, it not only would not be attacked by any other nation on earth, but it would become the supreme power in the world."

After he had come reluctantly to the support of Judge Parker in the 1904 campaign, Bryan used his Tolstoyan convictions to belabor the Rough Rider from Sagamore Hill. "This is an exalting of the doctrine of brute force," he said of T.R.'s New Nationalism, "it darkens the hopes of the race . . . It is a turning backward to the age of violence. More than that it is nothing less than a challenge to the Christian Civilization of the world."

In the years that followed peace and social justice were *The Commoner's* chief themes. Peace was the theme the silver tongue wove into the resonant orations that thrilled farmers and their families, seated on the hard chairs of Chautauqua tents; and small business men and schoolteachers and working people in crowded halls in the middlewest. Barred from high office by the vicissitudes of home politics the peerless leader aspired to become peacemaker to the world.

The Big Stick

Theodore Roosevelt won handily in the election of 1904. He regarded his victory as a mandate from the American people to continue in the role which he had been playing with so much zest. The United States was too small a stage. With McKinley he believed that "no nation can longer be indifferent to any other." He was the first American President to exercise a personal influence in the international drama.

Though an admirer of Admiral Mahan and an enthusiast for a powerful navy, and almost as fond as the Kaiser was of appearing in a military uniform and talking of "the fighting edge," T.R. used his influence as President pretty successfully for world peace. He had an able assistant in his Secretary of State.

Querulous and whimsical old John Hay, who started public life as Abraham Lincoln's private secretary, had given his country, under various administrations, a lifetime of discriminating public service of a sort unusual in America. Though one of the Americans most drenched in Europe of his generation, he never forgot that, like Mark Twain, he spent his boyhood in a Mississippi rivertown. He wrote graceful verse. The worshipful life of Lincoln he and Nicolay worked on for many years did much to enshrine the figure of the brooding emancipator in the mind of the nation. He wrote a novel on industrial strife and, from a diplomatic post in Madrid, travel sketches of a charm to rival Irving's. McKinley brought him back from the Court of St. James to head the State Department.

John Hay and Henry Adams from their twin Richardson houses on Lafayette Square presided over the cultivated literary society of the national capital, which in T.R.'s day included, for once, the White House. Now in his late sixties Hay was an ailing, crotchety, disinterested and wise old man. Relying on his great experience in practical diplomacy T.R. steered the country through a period of competition and intrigue among European powers that kept the world on tenterhooks.

The victory over Spain, however much it distressed anti-imperialists in the United States, enhanced American prestige abroad. The President's unique combination of athletics with statesmanship, together with his literary flair, made his grinning countenance with the buck teeth and the eyeglasses loom large in the European chancelleries. Here was an American politician at home in the world of books and ideas, which meant culture and refinement and status to European statesmen. His flamboyant costumes, the frontier pose, the impudence with which he led members of his "tennis cabinet" and unsuspecting visitors on breakneck hikes through Rock Creek Park, his endless stream of amusing conversation at the dinnertable, his knack for launching pat phrases which became the catchwords of the era, gave a special quality to his personality. As dissimilar Europeans as James Bryce and Kaiser Wilhelm found T.R. irresistibly attractive.

The diplomatic corps respected the professional skill with which he conducted his policy of "walk softly and carry a big stick." After he had averted possible warfare by inducing the Germans and the British to arbitrate their quarrel over the collection of debts from the Castro who was then dictator of Venezuela, T.R. was admitted to their international club by the world's potentates.

When they made their moves on the chessboard of power such highbinders as the Kaiser and Czar Nicholas and the imperialists of the Third French Republic could no longer disregard the United States.

The Panamanian Revolution

Even the somewhat scandalous methods by which T.R. made possible the building of the Panama Canal caused more amusement than protest. The need for an isthmian canal had been dramatized for Americans by the length of time it took the battleship *Oregon,* plowing at full steam round South America and through the Straits of Magellan, to join the Pacific fleet in 1898. Opinion was about evenly divided on the merits of a canal through Panama and a canal through Nicaragua. Interested parties buzzed like scavenger flies about both projects.

For a century the isthmus had been the stamping ground for freebooters and adventurers. Ever since the failure of the French company its debentures had been the playthings of speculators and bluesky operators on the Paris Bourse. T.R. plunged in where other statesmen had feared to tread. To his death he considered the canal his greatest achievement.

Through John Hay he secured from the British a revision of the fifty-yearold Clayton-Bulwer treaty according to which any such canal was to have been built jointly. Having made the decision to continue the French project in Panama, he induced Congress to put up forty million dollars to pay off the investors in the old company. He looked on with amused approval when Monsieur Bunau-Varilla, de Lesseps' chief aide,—who'd spent his life promoting the Panama route and was thick with various adventurers on the isthmus—, and a Mr. Nelson Cromwell of New York, representing a group of densely anonymous American investors, took their plot from an O. Henry short story, and backed a cast of comic opera characters in the establishment of an independent Republic of Panama.

The revolution was carried out in a rain of gold. When the Colombian authorities sent troops to prevent the secession of the freedom mad Panamanians, the colonel in charge received a handsome retainer. A couple of

American warships were ordered to stand by to see that nobody played it rough. The United States Government thoughtfully paid for the transport of the pacified colonel's troops back to Cartagena on one of the Royal Mail Steam Packet Company's liners. A Colombian general and an admiral each received whopping sums. Even the enlisted men got fifty dollars a head.

Amid the popular rejoicings that resulted from the distribution of this flood of baksheesh, the republic was proclaimed in November of 1903. An American officer was so indiscreet as to be seen hoisting the new Panamanian flag up a flagpole. When one of the sudden tropical downpours typical of the climate drove the demonstrators indoors, the founders of the new republic expressed their patriotic enthusiasm by pouring bottle after bottle of champagne over the head of defecting Colombian General Huertas, who now became commander of the Panamanian Army. Next day Monsieur Bunau-Varilla, with a cable appointing him Minister of the Republic of Panama in his pocket, called on John Hay. A few days later Washington recognized Panama as independent and sovereign.

"The haste with which the government at Washington acted was regrettable," wrote one student of diplomatic protocol from the serenity of the Cosmos Club twenty years later. "President Roosevelt apparently could not be restrained."

"If I had followed traditional, conservative methods I should have submitted a dignified state paper of probably two hundred pages to the Congress and the debate would have been going on yet," T.R. blurted out to a California audience, "but I took the Canal Zone and let Congress debate, and while the debate goes on the canal does also."

The Peace of Portsmouth

T.R. was nothing of a pacifist, but he worked hard to stave off wars. In his first administration he took up the cause of the arbitration treaties which had received such a setback when the Senate failed to ratify the Hay-Pauncefote Treaty under McKinley. He proved his good faith by submitting to The Hague court a complicated dispute with Mexico over the disposition of the funds of the ancient California missions.

Arbitration won a victory in Europe with the signature of the treaty between Britain and France in 1903. The following year President Roosevelt through his State Department suggested a fresh meeting of the powers at The Hague.

Taking the Anglo-French agreement as a model he signed arbitration treaties with France, Germany, Portugal and Switzerland, and was promoting negotiations with Great Britain, Italy, Mexico, Russia, Japan and a number of other countries when the Senate dropped a monkeywrench in the works by insisting that no arbitration should go through without specific senatorial approval in each case.

"I think that this amendment makes the treaties shams," T.R. wrote his good friend Senator Lodge, the stickler for senatorial privilege who had proposed the amendment, "and my present impression is that we had better abandon the whole business rather than give the impression of trickiness and insincerity which would be produced by solemnly promulgating a sham."

The outbreak of war in the Far East made it necessary to postpone the second Hague conference to a more propitious time.

Russia and Japan had been bickering over which of them should exploit Manchuria and bring the blessings of civilization to what was then called the hermit kingdom of Korea. When negotiations broke down in the winter of 1904 Japanese Admiral Togo made an unannounced attack on the Russian ships anchored at Port Arthur.

From then on the Japanese held the offensive. They crossed the Yalu River in the face of entrenched Russian positions. They outfought the Russians on land and sea, and knocked out the eastern section of their navy.

Early in the following year, the Russian Baltic fleet, which had distinguished itself by mistaking some British trawlers off Dogger Bank for enemy torpedoboats, and letting fly a salvo that killed a number of peaceful fishermen and added to the unpopularity of the czarist government among the Western nations, arrived in Japanese waters. Togo's crack squadrons promptly swept the Baltic fleet off the map.

The Russians were driven back into Siberia but the war cost the Japanese lives and money that they could ill afford. Both sides were ready to negotiate a peace.

President Roosevelt, who was already dabbling in mediation between clashing European imperialisms in North Africa, let it be known to the German ambassador that he would favor an arrangement that would give Korea to Japan, and neutralize Manchuria (under German management) in return for a German engagement to respect the "open door" policy in China and not to meddle in the Philippines or other islands in the Pacific, which since the annexation of Hawaii had become necessarily an American sphere.

When the Imperial Foreign Minister forwarded this report to the Kaiser he added a note: "The President is a great admirer of Your Majesty and would like to rule the world hand in hand with Your Majesty, regarding himself as something in the nature of an American counterpart of Your Majesty." Kaiser Wilhelm, who was not without humor in those days, scrawled in the margin: "One must not divide the hide of a bear before he has been shot."

From this seed sprang suggestions to Czar Nicholas in one direction and to the Mikado's foreign office in the other, that President Roosevelt would be just the man to mediate between them. A few days after the Battle of the Sea of Japan destroyed Russian seapower it was announced that plenipotentiaries were on their way to Washington.

John Hay, already very ill, who had been in Europe trying to recoup his health at one of the spas that were considered so restorative, wrote T.R. ". . . the big news was of your success in bringing Russia and Japan into conference. It was a great stroke of that good luck which belongs to those who 'know how' and are not afraid."

John Hay died the first of July. His death dealt a fatal blow to the curious little Washington circle which had grown up round Lafayette Square. T.R. felt it keenly. Hay was replaced in the State Department by Elihu Root, a dignified New York lawyer who was already one of the elders of the Republican Party.

Throughout Hay's last illness T.R. had been conducting arbitration in his own way. When Washington got too hot for the negotiators, who had gone into a deadlock on the question of indemnities and of Sakhalin Island, T.R. suggested that the seabreezes would refresh them at Portsmouth, New Hampshire. For two months the beautiful old New England seaport was the center of all the power politics of the world. T.R. watched the proceedings from Sagamore Hill, cajoling, advising, remonstrating, until in early September Russia and Japan came to the agreement that ended the war.

Roosevelt the Arbitrator

Immediately the President put his enhanced prestige to work to try to unravel the tangle of discords between the French, the British and the Germans over spheres of influence in North Africa. If they did nothing more the negotiations at Algeciras postponed the showdown in Europe for a number of years.

His efforts in that direction came to a head in his proposal for limitation of armaments to the second Hague conference sponsored again by Czar Nicholas in 1907. Campbell-Bannerman, a convinced anti-imperialist, was Prime Minister in England. Andrew Carnegie had hopes of inducing Sir Edward Grey, who was already Foreign Minister, to back T.R.'s plan.

T.R. understood the difficulties he was facing. "I do not want this new Liberal government with which in so many matters I have such hearty sympathy, to go to any maudlin extremes at The Hague conference," he wrote Whitelaw Reid, U. S. ambassador in London. "It is eminently wise and proper that we should take real steps in advance towards the policy of minimizing the chances of war among civilized people . . . but we must not grow sentimental and commit some Jefferson-Bryan-like piece of idiotic folly such as would be entailed if the free people that have free governments put themselves at a hopeless disadvantage compared with military despotisms and military barbarisms."

The proposals put forth at The Hague proved no panacea, but they bettered the peacemaking machinery. T.R.'s faith in arbitration, at least between nations of similar background, continued a modest growth. After he'd left the presidency he wrote Admiral Mahan, "I am prepared to say . . . I think the time has come when the United States and the British Empire can agree to a universal arbitration treaty . . . and that no question can arise between them that cannot be settled in judicial fashion."

This first decade of the century was a period of great hopes. Progressiveminded men looked forward to a golden age of peace. As civilization became established throughout the world, democratic institutions as they had developed in America and in Great Britain and her dominions would serve as a model for other nations. People were beginning to speak of the twentieth as the Anglo-Saxon century.

In foreign affairs T.R. did his best to avoid what he called shams, while he sought the peaceful solution in his own peculiar way. When the Japanese seemed to be allowing their victory over the Russians to go to their heads a little, he walked softly with them. At the same time he sent his new white fleet around the world to show off its gunpower and practice its marksmanship on a goodwill tour.

On the domestic stage he became more and more the radical leader. He had early stolen the thunder of the populists and the reformers. The demagogue in him made him adapt his slogans to the demands of his audience. He got the wildest applause when he lambasted "malefactors of great wealth."

Fighting Bob

The voter was in revolt. From the Atlantic to the Pacific righteous men were speaking out against political corruption and the highhanded behavior of captains of industry. Reform leaders were convinced that the cure was to make the machinery of selfgovernment more effective.

The first reform had been the adoption of the secret or Australian ballot. In Oregon U'Ren's People's Power League passed a corrupt practices act, put through a referendum borrowed from Switzerland, instituted the recall of public officials, popular election of U. S. senators and a system of preferential primaries for the nomination of presidential candidates

which it was hoped would take the party conventions out of the hands
of the bosses. In Ohio there was an epidemic of reform mayors. In Colorado Judge Ben Lindsey and his friends fought the utilities. In California
the Lincoln-Roosevelt League was gradually shaking the state Republican
Party loose from the hired men of the railroads.

It was the day of the young firebrands in politics. From the governor's
mansion in Madison Bob La Follette was proclaiming the Wisconsin
idea.

Born in a sure enough log house five years after his family moved out
from Indiana in covered wagons to take up a tract of farmland some
twentyfive miles out from the state capital, La Follette grew up with the
country. His people were literate hardworking borderers, farmers and
schoolteachers of Huguenot and Scotch-Irish stock. His father made the
farm succeed but died while Bob was still an infant. His mother, who had
been brought up a Baptist, married a Baptist deacon reputed to be the
leading citizen of the little town of Argyle. The deacon was an opinionated old man who didn't believe in sparing the rod, or the rawhide whip
either.

His mother's remarriage when he was seven left little Bob very much
on his own. He worshipped the image of his father. He picked up some
skill at carpenter work by using his father's set of tools, helped out the
family by huckstering produce from house to house in Madison. His stepfather mismanaged the farm, kept petitioning the court to sell off strips of
La Follette land; his business ventures failed.

Bob had to pay for his own schooling. At an early age he learned to
shave and to cut hair and picked up a little money acting as barber at the
Argyle hotel. He was a smart wrestler and a clever mimic, the darling of
the elocution teachers. Even his stepfather said he had a career ahead of
him. He early developed a knack for public speaking.

Already the farmers were in revolt against railroad barons, and the
lumber barons who strangled their market in a network of monopolies.
Bob La Follette listened eagerly to speeches of Grangers and agrarian
radicals. He read Henry George. He cut his teeth on the Shakespearean
style.

When he was seventeen his stepfather died and left him the head of
the family. He was a wiry handsome youth with lustrous dark eyes full of
ambition to forge ahead. He couldn't decide whether he wanted to be an
actor or a lawyer.

Determined to go to college, he rented the farm to his brotherinlaw
and moved the family into Madison. His schooling had been so sketchy
he had to take preparatory courses for a year at the Wisconsin Academy.
He never did learn to spell. He taught school. He coached debaters. He
edited and mostly wrote *The University Press*, the college paper, which
he distributed at enough profit to pay for his college course. All this, and

acting in amateur plays, kept him so busy his grades weren't of the highest.

When he fell in love with Belle Case he won over her family by his readings from *Hamlet*. His graduation would have been doubtful if he hadn't won first prize in an interstate contest by a speech on the character of Iago which for years was the pride of midwestern oratoricals.

Probably his fiancée influenced him towards studying law. He'd hardly passed his bar exam before he was running for district attorney. Riding from house to house with horse and buggy, the way he'd sold vegetables as a boy, he became an irresistible campaigner.

He stood for the people against the interests.

In 1884 he ran for the House of Representatives and at twentynine became the youngest member of the Fortyninth Congress. Belle and her small children moved with him to Washington. He served three terms, learned everything there was to know about the lawmaker's profession. In a day when politicians were supposed to serve business for retainers his independence made him enemies. In 1890 he was defeated. The opposition of the state Republican machine threw the election to the Democrats. He went back to the practice of law but politics was his world.

New forces were stirring in the Republican Party. He became friends with T.R. but McKinley was his chosen leader. In 1896 La Follette and Roosevelt were McKinley's two most effective campaigners. While Bryan thundered for the common man among the Democrats, Progressivism raised its voice among the Republicans.

In 1900 La Follette was elected governor of Wisconsin. With a large following, based on the student body at the university and on the farmers he visited on his famous horse and buggy circuits, or harangued from a spring wagon at country fairs, he started a systematic restoration of the processes of selfgovernment. If the people knew, he passionately believed, the people would vote right.

The Animated Feather Duster

In New York the sword of righteousness which T.R. had brandished as police commissioner and then as governor, fell into the hands of an austere young man named Charles Evans Hughes.

Born in a tiny frame house in Glens Falls in the spring of 1862, the man who was to be reform governor of New York was the only son of a ravenhaired Welshman, who emigrated to the United States in the middle fifties eager to do God's work. By dint of preaching and teaching he managed to dig himself out an education in Latin, Greek and Hebrew, and to find himself a blueeyed bride from an upstate farming family. Raised a Baptist Mrs. Hughes soon convinced her husband that the

Baptist faith was nearer to the primitive religion of Christ's disciples to which they both aspired, so it was as a Baptist that they brought up their son.

Young Charles was precocious. His parents started training him for the ministry from the time he started to read at the age of three and a half. He was literally raised in church, because there was no one to leave him with at home while his father was preaching and his mother was playing the organ.

At fourteen Hughes was ready for college and was sent to board at the Baptist seminary in Hamilton, New York, which later developed into Colgate University. "Pray for me," he wrote back to his doting parents, then living on Great Jones Street, in Manhattan, where the Reverend Hughes was secretary of the American Bible Union, "that I may be a useful servant in God's vineyard."

Already secular interests were crowding into God's vineyard. As a precocious youngster living in the heart of Boss Tweed's New York Hughes came to know something of the savagery and sin of the old brick seaport where masts and yards and steamboat funnels crowded in a forest about the wharves at the end of each crosswise street.

He honed to strike out on his own. He argued theology with his father in his letters home. In spite of their differences in points of doctrine his father loyally helped him transfer to Brown University where he obtained a small scholarship and, as a minister's son, had his room free of rent.

At Brown his horizons broadened. He found he had inherited a Welshman's flair for public speaking. He helped edit the magazine. For pocket money he tutored the duller students or occasionally wrote their themes for them for a price. He graduated in 1881, a slight, lively, smoothfaced lad of nineteen, the youngest in his class and third in scholastic standing.

A generation earlier he might well have been attracted to a career in the ministry, but growing up into the bustling moneymaking confident eighties, the law appeared to be the avenue to success for an able and impecunious young man.

Eking out the slender allowance his parents were able to spare him with teaching jobs and clerking, he passed his bar examination with record high marks at twentytwo, and was taken into the office of a successful attorney named Walter S. Carter. Not many years went by before Hughes, with the boss's enthusiastic consent, was marrying the boss's daughter.

During his college years he had missed out on many a good teaching job on account of his youthful and beardless appearance. Now he encouraged a bushy mustache and soon supplemented it with a neatly trimmed beard.

He worked himself down to skin and bone. He was so thin no company would give him life insurance. When Cornell offered him a professorship in law he jumped at the chance.

Hughes enjoyed teaching. He liked the country life and the walks over the hills overlooking Lake Cayuga. He gained weight. The life insurance company no longer turned him down for a policy. His courses were popular with the students.

A new baby was born. Responsibilities were multiplying. He hadn't been able to sell his New York house and the mortgage payments were a drain. In spite of a heavy teaching load and a new course in international law he was induced to undertake, all Cornell could offer him for a salary was three thousand a year. Hughes loved Ithaca; he stoutly turned down an offer of five thousand from the New York University Law School; but at last his fatherinlaw's cajoling letters and firm promise that by 1900 the business would be netting a hundred thousand dollars a year decided him to go back to New York . . . "if there is anything in this big moneymaking world I can win I'll win it for wife and babies," he wrote his wife. "I have no business to be out of the great rush."

He taught the young men's Bible class at the Fifth Avenue Baptist Church, and was elected a trustee. This was different from the impoverished meeting houses he had known as a boy. John D. Rockefeller was president of the board of trustees.

His work was all absorbing. He was the lawyer's lawyer. Attorneys and even judges consulted him on knotty points. Outside of his profession he was unknown. "My dear," he told his wife, who was complaining that though all the other lawyers' names were mentioned in connection with a notorious lawsuit she couldn't find her husband's in any of the papers, "I have a positive genius for privacy."

It wasn't until after his fatherinlaw's death when he was heading the Carter lawfirm that Hughes suddenly emerged into the light of the front pages as counsel for a committee of the state legislature which was investigating the gouging of the public by the company that furnished the city's gas.

The early nineteenhundreds were the heyday of muckraking. In a moment of annoyance at the scandalmongering which had become habitual in newspapers competing desperately for the public's pennies, T.R. had pulled the term out of a quotation from *Pilgrim's Progress*.

The "better element" had worried for decades over the corruption of boss rule in the cities, but now the general public took up the cry. The exposure of corruption became profitable. S. S. McClure was presenting Lincoln Steffens' *The Shame of the Cities* in his magazine. Ida Minerva Tarbell's *History of the Standard Oil Company* was bringing home to people the political and economic power inherent in vast aggregations of capital. Muckrakers rose to fame and fortune. Pulitzer and Hearst sold their penny newspapers to hundreds of thousands by exposing the malefactions of the politicians in cahoots with unscrupulous businessmen. Every editorial page had its David slinging his pebbles at the Goliaths of the vested interests.

Skillfully and decorously Hughes began pulling such a story of corruption and extortion out of reluctant witnesses that the featurewriters were delighted.

Reporters, who at first had complained of his austerity and of the chilly personality they found behind his whiskers, now fell over each other to make a public figure of him. The *Evening Mail,* the house organ of the Roosevelt Progressives, described him as "a large man, not burly but with the appearance of one who is built on broad lines. He looks strong. His shoulders are square, his limbs solid, his teeth big and white and his whiskers thick and somewhat aggressive." Pulitzer's New York *World* described his whiskers as being "broader, braver, bigger, bushier" than they appeared in the cartoons . . . "In action they flare and wave about triumphantly like the battleflag of a pirate chief."

He was invited to run for mayor on a reform platform. Instead he went mountainclimbing in Switzerland with the children, but soon he let himself be called back for a new investigation, this time of the life insurance companies. By the time he had grilled a choice assortment of capitalists and revealed the highhanded way in which the men who ran the companies paid off the politicians and handled the public's funds as if they were their own, Hughes was a national hero.

Legislation followed which cut the insurance companies down to size. Ida Tarbell gave him the accolade: "Charles E. Hughes is engaged in a passionate effort to vindicate the American system of government."

Even though Hughes had given the chief financial backer of T.R.'s presidential campaign, George W. Perkins, a bad quarter of an hour, forcing him to admit that in a four million dollar bond deal he had represented both New York Life, which was the buyer and J. P. Morgan and Co., which was the seller, Theodore Roosevelt began quietly pushing Hughes as a Republican reform candidate for the governorship of New York.

The *World* proclaimed that he had "restored faith in legislative committees as a means of bringing the truth to light," and described him as a man "who has a service of the highest order to give to the public and who can be neither intimidated or betrayed." "Why not make him governor?" asked Ida Tarbell in the *American Magazine.*

To run against him Boss Murphy, who had been much bespattered by the reformers, put up William Randolph Hearst. Hearst had all the money in the world to spend and was a reformer, an extremely noisy one, to boot. It was an exciting campaign.

T.R. wrote Hughes from Washington . . . "You are an honest fearless square man, a good citizen and a good American first and a good republican also . . . If I were not president I'd be stumping New York from one end to the other for you."

Hughes turned out an unexpectedly effective campaigner. His election put the quietus on William Randolph Hearst's political career. He successfully served two terms as governor and became one of Taft's chief assets in his campaign for the presidency in 1908.

Billy Possum

William Howard Taft had been Roosevelt's Secretary of War. In the Cabinet he was the President's most faithful lieutenant. Such was T.R.'s prestige at the end of his second term that he was able to impose Taft's nomination on the Republican Party in spite of the big man's mumbled protest that as a Unitarian he could never be elected. Roosevelt considered Taft the man most certain to carry out his progressive policies.

It was only when T.R. saw his dear friend, in spite of innate modesty, willynilly taking the center of the Washington stage as President-elect that his enthusiasm for him began to cool. Now he talked as if Governor Hughes, whom in impatient moments he'd scornfully referred to as "that animated feather duster," might be the man on whom the mantle of his strenuous Republicanism would fall when he disappeared from the Washington scene. To distract himself from the acute pain it gave him to leave the White House he was planning a public massacre of the lions and leopards and elephants of the African wilds.

In Taft's inaugural parade, beset by a famous blizzard that almost froze out the proceedings, Governor Hughes reached the peak of his political popularity. In silk hat and frock coat he risked pneumonia by riding at the head of the New York militia.

"Thinking an overcoat too clumsy," Hughes wrote in his notes, "I had protected myself with a chamois vest. But my hands inside my gloves were very cold and I had to dig them into the horse's flesh to keep from freezing. As we came down the hill from the Capitol our horses almost slid on the icy street. My horse had always been in the ranks and it was with some difficulty he could be persuaded to take his place at the head of the procession. But with the cheers of the crowd as we came to the large stands, he seemed to realize that this was his day and he went along at the head, proudly arching his neck and acting his part as a well trained horse of the Commander in Chief should. I made my bows with all the grace I could command and managed to get through without mishap. I dismounted," he added, "with a keen sense of relief."

Mr. Hughes was being modest. The Washington Post reported that he had aroused the wildest enthusiasm. According to the New York Tribune "a continuous roar of applause . . . greeted him from one end of the avenue to the other."

When Hughes stepped down as governor, Taft gratefully appointed him to the Supreme Court.

Once the ex-President was off harrowing the great carnivores in Africa, Taft, though he showed almost pathetic eagerness to carry out T.R.'s instructions, found himself straying from the straight path of progressivism. No continuous roar of applause greeted his administration.

President Taft was a corpulent humane slowmoving man with a sharp streak of intellectual honesty that made public life far from easy for him. He had the judicial temperament to a high degree and seems to have been forced to undergo the hazards of politics largely because he was a Cincinnati Taft and because his wife and the family expected it of him.

Politics with the Tafts was an avocation. The President's father, Alphonso Taft, moved out to Ohio from Vermont in the early eighteen hundreds to grow up with the country. He served as Secretary of War and then as Attorney General in Grant's cabinet and, in his declining years, as American minister to the courts of Vienna and St. Petersburg. He left the family not only rich but leaders of a group of literate and cultured people who early made Cincinnati one of the intellectual centers of the middlewest. President Taft's older halfbrother Charles started schools and endowed his home city with an art gallery and a symphony orchestra. The Tafts were the embodiment of public spirit.

Like his father, William Howard Taft graduated at Yale. He studied law in the lawschool his halfbrother founded in Cincinnati. He was early elected to an Ohio judgeship which he reluctantly gave up for the post of Solicitor General in Benjamin Harrison's administration. Then for six years he served as a federal circuit judge. The class war was heightening. Some of his decisions were considered antilabor but few of them pleased the vested interests.

In 1900 McKinley appointed Taft to the Philippine commission. Serving as their first civil governor he showed real friendship and understanding in his dealings with the various inhabitants of that barely pacified archipelago. He made himself such a reputation in Manila that Theodore Roosevelt brought him home for the job of Secretary of War. He gave a good account of himself in Washington.

As President, Taft, innately a conservative man, lost touch with the ebullient progressives in the east and with the western radicals accustomed to the strong drink of T.R.'s or La Follette's public speeches. The resurgent Democrats took over the House of Representatives in 1910 and filled the welkin with their outcry against entrenched privilege and the Payne-Aldrich tariff. With his soupstrainer mustache and his elephantine girth Taft was the very picture of the Mr. Moneybags of the radical cartoonists. "Politics makes me sick" was a phrase that appeared oftener and oftener in his private letters.

Taft was not a popular president. T.R.'s campaign managers had made so much of his totem, the teddybear, that they enshrined it in the hearts of generations of American children. All the Republican committees could dream up for Taft was the drowsy opossum. Billy Possum never caught on. Taft left the White House after one term, a much misunderstood man.

Lion Hunter

The American public was not kept in ignorance of their hero's prowess during T.R.'s months in the African wilderness. A steady stream of articles poured out from his tent on safari. Photographs filled magazines and Sunday supplements. Museums were embarrassed by the great shipments of pelts and skeletons and skulls representing every conceivable species that piled up in their storerooms.

On the way out and on the way home T.R. tracked as many lions in the courts of Europe as he did on the Kapiti plains. On his way home he was appointed by President Taft, anxious to apply healing unction because he knew T.R. was mad at him for falling out with T.R.'s friends, the Pinchots, to serve as his personal representative at the funeral of King Edward VII.

T.R. never tired telling stories about what was to prove to be the last assemblage of the crowned heads of Europe in their antique glory. He bubbled over with delight at hobnobbing with the heads of states. At tea at the American Embassy before going to the reception and banquet which preceded the interment he horrified Whitelaw Reid, who was grooming him for appearance at the court of St. James, by chuckling delightedly in his shrill voice: "I'm going to a wake tonight; I'm going to a wake."

It was said that it was only Mrs. Roosevelt's firm no that prevented him from wearing his Rough Rider uniform.

Appearing in plain evening dress amid all the gold lace and orders and decorations at Buckingham Palace he found himself the target of every eye. George V played host. The monarchs clustered around the bearhunter and lionslayer who represented to them everything that was most amusingly mad and wild west about the American myth.

Completely at his ease T.R. lectured them roundly. "I would never have taken that step at all if I had been in your place, Your Majesty," he'd say clenching his fist; or, "That's just what I would have done," clapping the back of his right hand into the hollow of his left: "Quite right."

"Before the first course was over, we had all forgotten the real cause of our presence in London," was how T.R. told the story when he got home. "I have never attended a more hilarious banquet in my life. I never saw quite so many knights. I had them on every side. They ran one or two false ones on me, and each had some special story of sorrow to pour into my ear."

During a visit to Germany a short time before, T.R. had found the Kaiser cordial and excessively voluble. The cordiality was mutual. "I do admire him," T.R. said of Wilhelm II, "much as I would a grizzly bear."

At Buckingham Palace T.R. described the Kaiser as acting the drillmaster to the lesser monarchs. All evening he tried to monopolize the Rough Rider's conversation. When the parvenu Czar of Bulgaria started pouring the tale of his troubles in the Balkans in Roosevelt's ear, Kaiser Wilhelm dragged him away: "That man is unworthy of your acquaintance," he said in a loud voice.

"Kings and such like are just as funny as politicians," T.R. would explode into laughter when he told the story back home.

Try as he would to settle down to writing for the *Outlook*, and leading the life of an elder statesman at Sagamore Hill, he couldn't help slipping back into politics. Out of sheer exuberance, when he got home, he helped ruin his old friend Taft's political career, snatched the Progressive movement away from La Follette, who as senator was attaining a position of national leadership, and acted, as he liked to boast with a toothy grin and a flash of his glasses "like a bull in a china shop."

Chapter 2

THE SCHOOLMASTER IN POLITICS

THE result of T.R.'s Bull Moose rampage was a split in the Republican Party that assured the Democrats a return to power if only they could find a leader who would appeal to both town and country wings of the party. New Jersey, the state which for years had furnished a convenient mailing address for every unsavory trust in the Union, where politics was considered safely under the thumb of the railroads and the utilities, had seethed with reform for a decade. The New Jersey reformers found themselves the leader the Democratic Party needed in a smoothvoiced lecturer on history and government who had since 1902 been president of Princeton.

Although Woodrow Wilson was two years older than T.R. and six years older than Hughes, politically he was a newcomer. Like Hughes he entered politics fullblown from another profession. He was fiftythree when he resigned as president of Princeton to run for governor of New Jersey on the Democratic ticket. Almost immediately he developed into one of the most skillful political operators in the history of American statecraft. It began to be said of him that his whole career had been a preparation for the White House.

Like Hughes, Woodrow Wilson was a clergyman's son. He was a Presbyterian by birth and rearing. His grandfather Wilson was a Scotch-Irish printer and journalist who, emigrating to Philadelphia as a very young man, worked on Duane's famous old *Aurora* and then moved to the Ohio country to edit a newspaper of his own in Steubenville. There he raised numerous progeny.

The youngest son, Joseph Ruggles Wilson, turned out to be a scholarly boy with a gift for public speaking who took his degree in divinity at Princeton. He was teaching at the Steubenville Academy when he met the daughter of Thomas Woodrow, a Scottish minister who had made a name but no money for himself preaching in Carlisle in the North of England and had been forced to move to America in search of a living that would support his family. The Woodrows came of a long line of Presbyterian divines. Woodrow Wilson liked to speak of his forebears as troublesome Scotchmen, hardbitten and opinionated, calvinists and covenanters.

X Born in the year of Buchanan's election at the manse in Staunton, Virginia, Woodrow Wilson was still a babe in arms when his handsome preacher father, who was becoming famous for the high style and fine delivery of his sermons, was called to Augusta, Georgia, to become pastor of the First Presbyterian Church there.

Though the father and mother were both Ohiobred they absorbed the politics of their parishioners. Dr. Wilson became an ardent secessionist. The assembly that split the denomination in two was held in his church and he became permanent "stated" clerk of the Southern Presbyterians.

For the first ten years of his life Tommy as he was known was the only boy in a family of girls. His parents destined him for the ministry as a matter of course. It was a trial to Dr. Wilson, who was a passionate reader of books with a palate for the modulations of English style, that his son learned to read slowly and that he had difficulty in mastering the Shorter Catechism. Dr. Wilson had a sharp Scottish tongue. His sarcasms lashed the dull student. "Whom the Lord loveth he chasteneth." At the same time tales were handed down in the family of most unministerial frolickings when Dr. Wilson roughhoused with the children in the garden of the manse.

When Tommy was fourteen the father was called to a chair at the theological seminary in Columbia, South Carolina's inland capital which Sherman had so thoroughly laid waste during the war. Dr. Wilson had a salary from his teaching and another from one of the principal pulpits in the town, and Mrs. Wilson had come into a legacy from a brother in the North who had died without issue. Amid the general impoverishment of the ruined South, all this meant opulence unusual for a minister's family. They built themselves a brick house. The Lord was indeed providing. The children grew up steeped in righteousness and drilled in admiration of good English prose.

X In the summer of 1873 Thomas Woodrow Wilson, with two other boys from the Sunday school, (according to the church register) "after free confession during which they severally exhibited evidences of the work of grace, were unanimously admitted to the membership of this church."

Woodrow Wilson never wavered in his strict adherence to the Presbyterian creed. He prayed on his knees. He wore out Bibles reading them. "The Bible," he said, "reveals every man to himself as a distinct moral agent responsible not to men, not even to those men he has put over him in authority, but responsible through his own conscience to his Lord and Maker." So far as religion was concerned, he told Cary Grayson years later, argument was adjourned.

X He loved his mother but so long as Dr. Wilson lived his father ruled his life. A warm, admiring, almost reverent affection grew up between father and son. Even so Tommy Wilson's ambitions strayed early from the ministry. As a boy he'd read deep of Cooper's and Captain Marryat's seastories. Before he ever saw the sea he had drawn plans of frigates and entertained the phantasy of being admiral of an American fleet pursuing pirates in the Pacific. When his father accepted a call to a large church in Wilmington, North Carolina, young Wilson had his first sight of real seagoing ships. The story is told that it was only his mother's supplications that kept him from shipping before the mast.

Meanwhile a new daydream intervened. His father subscribed to the *Edinburgh Review* and to Godkin's *Nation*. Tommy began to read of debates in the British House of Commons. These were the years of the great liberals. England was in a period of fervid parliamentary activity. The slender shy awkward lad—"an old young man" the Wilsons' colored butler called him—began to throw all his youthful passion into imagining himself a Cobden or a John Bright thundering from the opposition benches under the hallowed rafters of St. Stephen's. Instead of drawings of fullrigged ships a portrait of Gladstone appeared above his desk.

When at sixteen he was sent to Davidson College near Charlotte he began to show an aptitude for hard work. He made good marks in his courses. He taught himself shorthand. In deportment his score was perfect.

He worked so hard at Davidson that he began to show signs of acute dyspepsia—all his life his nerves were too taut for good digestion—; he was ordered home to Wilmington for a rest and began to tutor in Latin and Greek for the entrance examinations at Princeton.

At nineteen he entered Princeton as a freshman carrying a letter from his father, which he was too shy to present, to that notable Scottish divine the Reverend James McCosh, who was president. Dr. McCosh was a scholar and a speaker famous for force and wit. In the Darwinian controversy then raging through schools and pulpits he had the courage (as did Tommy's scholarly uncle Professor James Woodrow who fell into hot water with the Presbytery because of it) to take the side of science: "If it is found to be true," Dr. McCosh affirmed, ". . . it will be found that it is consistent with religion."

At Princeton young Wilson paid enough attention to the curriculum to get through with moderate honors, but his real interest was in reading and debating about politics, statesmanship and constitutional law. He devoured the witty accounts of the debates in British parliament he found in the library in bound volumes of *The Gentleman's Magazine*.

Debating was popular with undergraduates at Princeton in those days. He joined the Whig Society, which was still operating under a constitution devised by James Madison, and became its star debater. Not content with that he founded a new society: The Liberal Debating Club, modelled on the British parliament, for which he himself furnished the constitution. He showed a lively interest in campus affairs generally, served as president of the Athletic Committee and of the Baseball Association and as managing editor of the *Princetonian*.

He found himself associating with a generation of young Americans who were beginning to think that they should emulate the English gentry and take politics away from the wardheelers. Among a gang of friends, mostly members of an eating club known as the Alligators, who used to meet in eachother's rooms in Witherspoon Hall, there appeared a comic tag line to break off a discussion: "When I meet you in the Senate I'll argue that out with you."

Tommy Wilson went so far as to put his name on some visiting cards as "Senator from Virginia."

With the Utica boy who later went to Congress from upstate New York he entered into one of those youthful compacts that do so much to mould men's lives.

"I remember forming with Charlie Talcott, a class-mate and very intimate friend of mine," he wrote in reminiscent vein, "a solemn covenant that we would school all our powers and passions for the work of establishing the principles we held in common; that we would acquire knowledge that we might have power; and that we would drill ourselves in all the arts of persuasion but especially in oratory (for he was a born orator if ever man was) that we might have facility in leading others into our ways of thinking and enlisting them in our purposes."

He saw himself as part of the procession of the great parliamentarians. He read Macaulay with rapture; he tried to model his style on Bagehot's.

Greene's *Short History of the English People* delighted him so that he planned to follow it up with a *History of the American People*. He decided to be a writer as well as a talker. He wrote his father excitedly that he had discovered he had a mind. In vacationtime down at Wilmington, on days when the church was empty, he practiced oratory by reciting Burke's speeches from his father's pulpit.

He was obsessed with the beauties of the British parliamentary system. By his senior year he had produced an article on "Cabinet Government in the United States" which was printed in *The International Review*, then the foremost American journal of theoretical politics. He used the same theme for his commencement address when he graduated.

He carried some of the aura of that publication along with him when he went to the University of Virginia to study law. "The profession I chose was politics; the profession I entered was the law. I chose the one because I thought it would lead to the other," he explained in a letter to his fiancée a few years later.

He hated the law but he plugged away at it. He had done well at Princeton, but at Charlottesville he was almost fulsomely admired. He had a good clear tenor voice; he sang in the glee club and in the chapel choir. He was described as having "rare charm and courtesy of manner"

and as carrying himself "with an air of quiet distinction." He was developing a sense of humor. He was in demand whenever a graceful speech
was called for at some public function.

He was filling long arduous days with the law, with debating, with reading, with warm college friendships and with the unsuccessful courtship
of one of his Woodrow cousins who attended the Female Seminary at
Staunton, when he broke down again with what was still described as
dyspepsia. Again the doctor told him to go home and take it easy. For a
year and a half he let his mother nurse him back to health while he read
law in the comfortable Wilmington manse.

The whole family connection had gone to work to find the most suitable
place for Tommy Wilson to practice when he was strong enough to take
his bar examination. He settled on Atlanta in partnership with a friend
from the university. At twentyfive he was a seriousappearing young man
with a mustache and sideburns. He had dropped the childish Tommy and
signed himself Woodrow Wilson.

Woodrow Wilson was not cut out for the life of an attorney at law. He
wanted a political career but, raised as he was among women, in the
protective cocoon of his father's affection, he didn't have the brash energy
needed to break into politics at the local level as Theodore Roosevelt did
in New York. He was too shy and aloof and selfcentered for the rough
moneygrubbing Atlanta of reconstruction days. He gave up his lawfirm, which had hardly picked up a client, and went to Johns Hopkins,
then in its first heyday as a great graduate school, to study for a Ph.D.
The life there just suited him. At Hopkins he wrote his first and best
book: *Congressional Government.*

Meanwhile he had fallen in love again. On a trip to Georgia to attend
to some lawbusiness for his mother, he met Ellen Axson, the daughter of
the pastor of Rome's First Presbyterian Church, a quiet earnest girl of
great charm. Her friends spoke of her "flowerlike" freshness. Their up-
bringings were so similar they might have been brother and sister.

The Axsons like the Woodrows came of a line of Scottish clergymen.
Her grandfather had been known to his Presbyterian parishioners in
Savannah as "the great Axson."

Ellen Axson had been planning herself a career as a painter. She convinced Wilson that he must finish his work at Hopkins and that she
must have a year studying at the Art Students League in New York before their marriage. Both families seem to have been overjoyed by the
engagement. Ellen Axson's brother Stockton became one of Woodrow's
most intimate friends.

It was as if they had known each other all their lives. They wrote almost daily. "You are the only person in the world," he told her, "except

the dear ones at home—with whom I do *not* have to act a part; to whom I do *not* have to deal out confidences cautiously . . ."

As usual he was working himself too hard: "One must dig in books," he wrote from Baltimore, "he can't find history anywhere else: he can't understand present experience unless he knows the experience bound up between the senseless covers of ponderous books or recorded on the faded faces of old manuscripts . . . so that he must focus all his senses in his spectacles, and strive to forget he was not meant to sit all day in a hard chair at a square table . . . It's quite as necessary for a Christian to work as for him to be glad."

He was critical, in his letters, of the dryasdust quality of American scholarship even in the brilliant assemblage Professor Adams had collected in his Historical Seminary: "Style is not much studied here; ideas are supposed to be everything—their vehicle comparatively nothing. But you and I know that there can be no greater mistake . . . and style shall be, as under my father's guidance, it has been, one of my chief studies. A writer must be artful as well as strong."

From earliest boyhood his father had been drilling him in the niceties of English prose. Years later in an address to a teachers' association he told of his father's saying to him: "When you frame a sentence don't do it as if you were loading a shotgun but as if you were loading a rifle. Don't fire in such a way and with such a load that you will hit a lot of things in the neighborhood besides; but shoot with a single bullet and hit that one thing alone."

From the prolix academic style of the period Woodrow Wilson did manage to develop a way of writing suited to the purpose for which it was intended; but his real gift was for public speaking. He seized every opportunity to address an audience. Primarily he was training himself for a career as a college lecturer, afterwards, who knew? "Oratory," he wrote Ellen Axson, "is not declamation, not swelling tones and an excited delivery, but the art of persuasion, the art of putting things so as to appeal irresistibly to an audience."

He described to her his joy in speaking "as an intellectual exercise. That is the secret," he added, "undoubtedly of what little success I've had as a speaker. I enjoy it because it sets my mind—all my faculties aglow: and I suppose that this very excitement gives my manner an appearance of confidence and self-command which arrests the attention. However that may be I feel a sort of transformation—and it's hard to go to sleep afterwards."

Woodrow Wilson and Ellen Axson, as wellmatched a pair as ever said "I will," were married in a Presbyterian manse in Savannah, Georgia, in June of 1885.

The following September Wilson settled down to academic life at Bryn

Mawr as Associate Professor of History with a salary of fifteen hundred dollars a year. The young couple's board and lodging would cost them twenty dollars a week. It was slim pickings.

Particularly after the first baby appeared it was essential for him to find means of increasing his income. The great work he was planning on the philosophy of politics had to be put aside for a textbook on government. He was beginning to manage to get articles into *The Atlantic Monthly*. It seemed as if he would have indefinitely to postpone his political ambitions. In the fall of 1886 he wrote his friend Charlie Talcott, who had gone home to upstate New York to practice law and was already city counsel in Utica, explaining why he wasn't getting ahead with their project to reform the government of the United States: "After my winter had been hurried away by the unaccustomed, therefore arduous duties of the classroom, my summer vacation was swallowed up by work on a textbook . . . But Mrs. Wilson could tell you how, meanwhile, my thoughts have constantly reverted to our old compact.

"I believe, Charlie," he wrote, "that if a band of young fellows (say ten or twelve) could get together (and by getting together I mean getting their *opinions* together, whether by circular correspondence or other means) upon a common platform, and, having gotten together good solid planks upon the questions of the immediate future, should raise a united voice in such periodicals, great or small, as they could gain access to, gradually working their way out, by means of a real understanding of the questions they handled, to a position of prominence and real authority in the public prints and so in the public mind, a long step would have been taken towards the formation of such new political sentiment, and party, as the country stands in such pressing need of,—and I am ambitious that we should have a hand in forming such a group."

The "arduous duties of the classroom" occupied Woodrow Wilson's life for the next twenty years. His academic career was notably successful. The years at Bryn Mawr were the dullest. No one could have been less enthusiastic over the education of earnest young women. It was lecturing rather than teaching that interested him. He complained that if he got off a joke in class his girls copied it solemnly down in their notes.

Externally he was himself a solemn young man. "I am quite used to being taken for a minister," he admitted to a friend. When his classmate Robert Bridges, who was making himself an editorial career in New York, arranged for him to give a talk at an alumni gathering there, he produced such an austere harangue on the duty of the colleges to prepare men for government service that people kept slipping out and only returned to their seats to roar with laughter when Chauncey Depew, who followed him, poked fun at the lanternjawed young professor with the eyeglasses.

He was happier at Wesleyan. Middletown was one of the loveliest places in Connecticut. He found New Englanders congenial. Students crowded into his classes. He established a debating club on the English model which he named The House of Commons. The club managers stayed in office only so long as they could secure votes of confidence from the floor.

Already he was the popular professor. He led a movement to break up the fraternity cliques and get men accepted, in athletics at least, on their merits alone. Though not athletic himself he was an enthusiast for college sports. An alumnus told one of his biographers of seeing Professor Wilson dash out from the bleachers in slicker and rubberboots at an edgy moment in a hardfought football game played in the rain against a heavier team from Lehigh to lead the Wesleyan cheering with his umbrella.

Among the colleges his reputation was building. Johns Hopkins invited him to give a course of lectures. He was elected president of the Alumni Association, honored by Phi Beta Kappa, given an honorary degree, which was to be the first of many, by Wake Forest in North Carolina. James Bryce, whom he'd met at a Baltimore lecture, commended his *Congressional Government* in a new edition of *The American Commonwealth*. By 1889 his friends of the class of '79 didn't find it too hard to put through this outstanding alumnus' appointment to a professorship at Princeton.

At Princeton he passed pleasant years. The pay was far from ample but Ellen Wilson was an excellent manager. She set a hospitable table. She made most of her own dresses and the dresses for their three little girls and cut out paper dolls for them to save buying toys. She worked the flower garden, did embroidery, drilled the girls in the Shorter Catechism and even found time for a little painting. Hers were the crayon enlargements of portraits of Burke, Webster, Gladstone, Bagehot and of Professor Wilson's own father that hung in the study. She acted as occasional secretary and helped him read proof. The professor was not a handy man around the house but with grim determination he tended the coal furnace in winter. He once was seen mowing the lawn.

His students loved his lectures. Year after year he was voted the most popular professor. He was much in demand as a public speaker. His articles were published in the leading magazines. He reviewed books for *The Atlantic Monthly*.

At home he was the center of a group of admiring females. The Wilsons' house was always full of relatives who joined the family as a matter of course in the oldtime southern way. There were Ellen Wilson's brothers and sisters and nieces, Woodrow and Wilson cousins, distantly related students they were helping through college.

Meals were on the dot, breakfast at eight, lunch at one. The professor led the conversation from the head of the table. Only his wife dared contradict him. "Oh Woodrow, you don't mean that," she would sometimes say. "Madam I was endeavoring to think that I meant that," he would answer with a sarcastic smile, "until I was corrected."

Though he made warm friends and fervent supporters among the faculty he remained a shy standoffish man. He was reluctant to meet strangers.

It was only at home that he relaxed from the cold intellectual stance. At home he made puns, recited limericks, told dialect stories. Evenings he read aloud from Dickens or Macaulay or Matthew Arnold. He enjoyed charades and sometimes said he wished he'd been an actor. To amuse the little girls he'd pull the loose skin of his long face into odd shapes, or act out little skits. The town drunk or the affected Englishman were favorites with the children. He is even described as having been seen dancing a jig with his silk hat cocked over his eyes. He rode to his classes on a bicycle.

His health was uneven. There was a consistent history of breakdowns from overwork. When in the spring of 1896 he finished his *George Washington* he was so crippled by "writers' cramp" that he had to start learning to write with his left hand. The doctors advised a change. Since there wasn't money enough to take the whole family Ellen Wilson urged him to leave for a solitary English holiday. He sailed on one of the economical Anchor Line boats to Glasgow.

Princeton's foremost political theorist, who remained a Democrat though he deplored the populist heresies that the Boy Orator of the Platte was arousing in the cornbelt, spent the summer of Bryan's free-silver campaign bicycling through Scotland and England.

The sight of the Gothic colleges at Oxford sent him into ecstasy. He read Wordsworth at Tintern Abbey. After an afternoon with the Rembrandts and the Reynoldses and the Turners at the National Gallery he wrote his dear Ellen that he felt quite guilty looking at them without her.

He picked up travelling acquaintances. On the *Ethiopia* going over he became so cosy with a South Carolina lawyer and his wife that they chummed up for the whole trip. He unbosomed himself of his ambitions to them. They parted with the halfhumorous understanding that when he was President he'd make Mr. Woods a federal judge. Years later he fulfilled this pledge to the letter.

Around the turn of the century higher education in America was in the throes of one of its periodical soulsearchings. Hadley at Yale and Eliot at Harvard were much in the news. The Princeton trustees, reinforced by ex-President Grover Cleveland and several other prominent alumni who had chosen the pleasant village for their residence, were getting tired of having their college known as a rural resort for wealthy young loafers. In the fall of 1896 Professor Wilson, fresh from his visit to Oxford, at the ceremonies incidental to the formal changing of the name of The College of New Jersey to Princeton University, called for a sound rigorous classical education to train up young men in conservative principles for the service of the state. The speech made an impression. When Dr. Patton resigned as president in 1902 Professor Wilson found himself elected by unanimous vote of the trustees to serve in his stead.

That was the end of a plan he had been forming to take sabbatical leave and to give his girls the advantages of travel in Europe while he devoted himself to his project for a philosophy of politics which would be the Novum Organum of nineteenthcentury liberalism.

His inauguration was a great occasion. Ex-President Grover Cleveland and Governor Murphy of New Jersey led the academic procession. Friends remarked on Woodrow Wilson's slim erect keenfaced appearance under the mortarboard. Henry van Dyke the poet preacher, Booker T. Washington, Hadley of Yale, Lowell of Harvard, Butler of Columbia added their varicolored hoods to the train. The participants were astonished by the size of J. Pierpont Morgan's nose. There was Mark Twain whitemaned in his invariable linen suit, and William Dean Howells. Plughatted Colonel Harvey and Walter Hines Page followed in the rear as the faithful publishers of the professor's books.

The new president's inaugural speech was received with acclaim. Only Grover Cleveland is said to have muttered under his mustache: "Sounds good. I wonder what it means."

Dr. Joseph Wilson, bowed down by the years, had taken to his bed for his last illness, but a visitor downstairs told of hearing his singing, "Crown him with many crowns," at the top of his voice. He said it was the best day of his life. He lined up his three little granddaughters at the foot of his bed and told them never to forget what he was going to tell them: their father was the greatest man he had ever known.

Woodrow Wilson was fortysix years old when he moved from the cosy stucco house in the fashionable halftimbered style which he and his wife had built for themselves on Library Place into the grandeurs of Prospect, the official residence.

As president of Princeton he was a talkedabout and writtenabout man. He began a drive for funds. He hired fifty new tutors to superintend the students' studies according to the preceptorial system he had admired at Oxford and Cambridge. He made plans to abolish the snobbish eating clubs which took the place of the forbidden fraternities and to divide the university into colleges in the English manner, where students and tutors would eat their meals together. He tightened up the curriculum. Sons of wealthy alumni found themselves flunking out.

"He's spoiling the best country club in America," groaned the old grads, but for a while they went along, even in the face of a drop in enrollment. Led by Grover Cleveland and M. Taylor Pine, wealthy Princetonians began to make really sizeable contributions. Ralph Adams Cram was designing the new quadrangles in the Tudor Gothic style dear to the hearts of the anglophiles.

These were the years of Theodore Roosevelt's New Nationalism. The president of Princeton, who was described as fighting the entrenched snobbery of privileged wealth in the colleges, was greatly in demand as a speaker. His campaign for equality of opportunity for education for the service of the commonweal was closer to the theories of the Republican progressives than to what was considered in the East as the rabblerousing appeal of William Jennings Bryan. But even to him the word democracy was taking on an egalitarian tone. Professor Wilson who had previously been a Hamilton man began to interest himself in the ideas of Thomas Jefferson.

In the winter of 1905 his health broke down again. A hernia operation followed by phlebitis forced him to take five weeks off in Florida to recuperate.

His reforms at Princeton had at first clear sailing, but now opposition was raising its head. He ran up against another Presbyterian, equally enthusiastic for a great future for Princeton, but with somewhat different ideas as to how to bring it about.

Andrew West was dean of the Graduate School. At first he and Wilson agreed as to how this school, which they were both promoting, should fit into the new scheme. Indeed Dean West was induced to refuse the presidency of Massachusetts Tech in order to assist with the good work.

Differences of opinion as to details turned into a personal contest of wills. The rancors of the presbytery began to work in both men. Once Woodrow Wilson had formed an opinion it became to his mind the cause of righteousness. If you disagreed you were either a knave or a fool. He decided Dean West was both.

Political omens "barely the size of a man's hand" had begun to appear in the Democratic sky. Talk was beginning of Woodrow Wilson as a standardbearer to whom conservative Democrats might rally. "Don't you pity me," he wrote Robert Bridges, then editor of *Scribner's Magazine*. "With all my old political longings . . . set throbbing again."

After a speech on Americanism in Charleston, South Carolina, the influential *News & Courier* spoke of him as the most promising southern candidate for the presidency. Introducing him to a dinner held in his honor at the Lotos Club in New York, George Harvey, the hardbitten Vermont publicist and political wirepuller who had been entrusted by the Morgans with the reorganization of Harpers' publishing firm and who personally edited *Harper's Weekly*, formally nominated him to be the Democratic candidate in the next election:

"As one of a considerable number of Democrats who have become tired of voting Republican tickets, it is with a sense of rapture that I contemplate even the remotest possibility of casting a ballot for the President of Princeton University to become President of the United States."

Wilson quoted Tennyson in reply and declared he had learned more about statesmanship from the poets than from the politicians. He affected to make light of Harvey's suggestion, but his political longings were indeed set throbbing. He began to see his battle for righteousness at Princeton as the preliminary skirmish in a greater campaign to reform the nation.

His mail increased. He travelled all over the country to speak. He drove himself hard. There was research to do for his *History of the American People*. He was handling an enormous amount of paperwork with only the help of his wife and an occasional student. He did all his own typing. It would have been a strenuous enough life if his plans for Princeton had gone unopposed. He could never reconcile himself to opposition.

One morning in the spring of 1907 he woke up to find that he couldn't see out of his left eye. It was only then that he admitted to his wife that he had been suffering severe pain which he described as neuritis in his left shoulder and leg. His friend Professor Hibben hurried him to Philadelphia to consult a specialist. The specialist reported that he had a severe case of hardening of the arteries and must immediately give up all activity and spend the rest of his life as an invalid.

Outwardly Woodrow Wilson bowed to the verdict. He cancelled his speaking engagements and secured leave of absence from the university. Meanwhile he shopped around for other physicians who might see his predicament in a less drastic light. A doctor was found who considered that the symptoms were not so alarming after all and promised him complete recovery after a three months rest.

Here was an opportunity to take Ellen and the girls on an outing to England. Sitting in a chair Woodrow Wilson packed the family trunks, as he always did. Ellen Wilson brought along her paints. They rented a cottage (from a Mrs. Wordsworth who had married some descendant of Wilson's favorite poet) in the English lake country for the summer, and were completely happy there.

Wilson had the knack of resting when he had to. He could sleep for hours on end. He took great pleasure in the sluggish green Cumberland countryside. He found entertaining friends, sat on a bench outside the local pub chatting with the northcountry characters, took walks between showers and read Browning and the lake poets to the girls or sang college songs after supper. Reverently he attended Sunday services in the little stone church where Wordsworth lay buried. In the fall he returned to Princeton in roaring health and ready for battle.

Though he had started his campaign with the trustees on his side, now the board, like the faculty, had split into warring camps. The university seethed with backbiting. Wilson showed no ability to meet disagreement halfway. Whoever wasn't for him must be against him. Associations were disrupted. There were charges and countercharges. Old friends crossed the street to avoid speaking.

Even his dear Jack Hibben, whom he had made acting president during his absence, turned against him at a faculty meeting when he brought his "quad plan," which would abolish the eating clubs, to a vote. Wilson's propositions were defeated. "Nobody can make a gentleman associate with a mucker," said a prominent alumnus.

For the first time in his life Woodrow Wilson failed to get his own way. He wrote a friend, "I have got nothing out of the transaction but complete defeat and mortification."

After his illness the university furnished him an assistant to take some of the routine work off his hands. President Wilson was away from Princeton a great deal now, lecturing about the country, conferring with publisher friends and political sponsors in New York. He took winter holidays in Bermuda where a charming American hostess named Mrs. Peck collected prominent and amusing people at little dinners for his entertainment. Academic life began to pall. He was being taken up by the great world.

The conflict at Princeton had settled down to a tug of war between the advocates of a new graduate school under Dean West and Wilson supporters who wanted first to go ahead with his undergraduate quadrangles. There was not enough money in sight for both projects. Then an old grad named Wyman suddenly died, in May 1910, leaving several million dollars in his will for a new graduate school. So that there would be no mistake as to his intentions he appointed the dean as executor. This meant victory for Andrew J. West.

The eating clubs were to remain as exclusive as ever. Trustees began to speak hopefully of Wilson's coming resignation.

President Wilson wasn't as afflicted by his defeat as his friends had expected. He had lost interest in Princeton when he found he couldn't have his own way there. His ambitions had settled on a higher goal. He was planning to become President of the United States, nothing less.

When friends suggested that he didn't know enough about practical politics he pointed to his rows with the Princeton faculty. "Professional politicians," his daughter Eleanor quoted him as saying, "have little to teach me; they are amateurs compared with some I've dealt with in the Princeton fights."

Kingmaker from Vermont

Colonel Harvey, looking forward with relish to the role of president-maker, noted Woodrow Wilson's disenchantment with academic life. He was planning to run him for governor of New Jersey as a preliminary to the Democratic Party's nomination for the presidential race in 1912.

George Harvey knew his way around in New Jersey politics. Having started life clerking in a Vermont country store he'd served his apprenticeship in journalism with the Springfield *Republican* and covered the Garden State for the New York *World*. A sharp pen, an acid tongue with a touch of the old crackerbarrel style combined with a convivial streak to carry him far in New Jersey. He was somewhat of a dandy. One governor, who wanted to make his administration a fashionable success, made young Harvey a colonel on his staff to handle the entertaining at the summer mansion at Sea Girt and provided him with a sinecure in the Department of Banking and Insurance. For a while he edited the Newark *Journal* and at the age of twentyeight was picked by Pulitzer to be managing editor of the New York *World*.

From the time when at fifteen he managed to attend the Democratic state convention in Vermont he kept a shrewd eye on the political pot. He backed Grover Cleveland in 1892 and made such a killing in Wall Street that he was able to buy *The North American Review*.

Dabbling in New Jersey banks and streetcar companies along with his wealthy and politicalminded friends William C. Whitney and Thomas Fortune Ryan he became associated with another convivial gentleman who had started life clerking in a store, Senator James Smith, Jr.

Senator Smith was undisputed boss of Democratic state politics in New Jersey. He was as popular with the poor and downtrodden as he was with the public utilities. He was a tall and handsome man. His pink and white face under the silk hat was described as being as innocent as a child's. A lavish entertainer, a free spender of his own and other people's money, he was known as a prominent Catholic layman. It was said of him that not a day passed that he didn't attend a funeral.

Muckraking was in the air. Reform was sweeping out of the West. Newspapers were saying hard things of a swarm of lobbyists known as the Black Horse Cavalry that infested the statehouse at Trenton. Stirred out of their torpor by echoes of Teddy Roosevelt's hue and cry against the control of politicians by malefactors of great wealth, the voters of New Jersey were beginning to yearn for righteousness.

Senator Smith had three boys at Princeton. He had met President Wilson. He had heard him spoken of as being opposed to federal regulation of corporations, to woman's suffrage, to the closed shop and to other bugaboos of men of means. The professor had even written kindly of political machines. Colonel Harvey invited Smith to a magnificent lunch at the private dining room he maintained at Delmonico's for the benefit of the Harper publishing firm. There he managed to convince him that Woodrow Wilson as governor would head off the radicals and dress the state up with a few harmless reforms.

The senator did take the precaution of sending an underling to ask "the Presbyterian priest" as he called Wilson, whether if he were elected he would set about "fighting and breaking down the existing Democratic organization." President Wilson looked the man straight in the face with the grayeyed ingenuousness which was his greatest asset and said certainly not, "the last thing I should think of would be building up a machine of my own."

Boss Smith was convinced but Wilson continued to play hard to get. He was spending the summer with his family in a boarding house at a painters' colony at Old Lyme that Ellen Wilson loved. At various conferences with the politicians he made no commitments whatsoever. Meanwhile he was asking the advice of such college friends as had stuck to him through the battles at Princeton and of his old cronies who had become opinionmoulders through editorial positions in New York magazines.

Ellen Wilson's counsel was sought at every step. The Wilsons went through weeks of agonizing indecision. There wasn't any question that Woodrow intended to be President. The question was would the governorship of New Jersey be the best steppingstone. Finally Ellen Wilson, that smart little lady who, on top of her other virtues, was developing a discriminating political sense, told him to go in and win.

So it came about that the day before the Democratic convention met in the Trenton opera house on September 15, 1910, Colonel Harvey and Senator Smith went to work, operating from the boss's suite at the adjoining hotel, to railroad the nomination through. They were up all night arguing with the delegates. They had a rough time of it. All the liberal and progressive elements were opposed to the bosses' candidate. Wilson was unknown to the political stalwarts of his own Mercer County. In important elections he hadn't even voted. When his name was placed in nomination there were cries of "accredit him to Virginia, he's not a Jerseyman."

Boss Smith said later it was one of the toughest nights in his career. With the help of the machine bosses of Hudson County he finally put Wilson's name before the convention and bludgeoned the delegates into voting for it.

William Inglis, Harvey's handyman, to whom the colonel entrusted the mission of fetching Professor Wilson over to Trenton, told of the embarrassment of waiting with the candidate at the Trenton House. Inglis had been instructed on no account to let his charge be seen until the nomination was a certainty.

He ushered him into a stuffy little Victorian parlor reserved for ladies waiting for their escorts and closed the door. There they sat for two hours. Inglis was on tenterhooks but the professor was cool and seemed entirely relaxed. Inglis kept offering him a drink or a cup of tea. No he didn't care for any. It wasn't till after five in the afternoon that a delegate from Atlantic County rushed in, white as a sheet and all out of breath, to announce that the nomination had been made unanimous.

A Leader at Last

The convention was still in a sullen mood when Professor Wilson appeared on the stage of the opera house. James Kerney of the Trenton *Evening Times* who had not yet seen the candidate, described him as ". . . wearing a dark gray business suit with a sack coat, a type which he used almost exclusively. He had a dark felt hat with a narrow brim, with a knitted golfjacket under the coat. It was a bangup Democratic outfit.

"Wilson looked the part of one of the romantic figures of American politics as he stood before that convention. He was in the pink of mental and physical condition, fresh from the golf-links, with all the color of the outdoors upon him, and a general appearance of having been battered by life and of having given it somewhat of a battering in return. Behind him was the background of teacher, writer, historian and educator. Here was the beginning of the 'schoolmaster in politics.'"

"As you know," Wilson told the delegates, "I did not seek this nomination . . ." Not only had no pledges of any kind been given but none had been proposed or desired. The future was not for parties playing politics but for measures "conceived in the largest spirit, pushed by parties whose leaders were statesmen, not demagogues, who loved not their office but their duty and their opportunity for service."

It was his manner of speaking more than what he said, his air of cool determination, the flash of the gray eyes behind his noseglasses. Stockton Axson, the professor's brotherinlaw listening from the wings, saw one wardheeler poke another with his elbow: "God, look at the man's jaw," he said. The smalltime lawyers and partyworkers and local officeholders who made up the delegations, sodden and blearyeyed from a night of wrangling, were carried away. "A leader at last. The Big Fellow was right," men whispered hoarsely in each others' ears. "Boss Smith knew what he was doing." They cheered at every pause in Wilson's short speech of acceptance. "Go on, go on," they shouted.

Wilson cast his eyes up at the flag above the platform and delivered himself of a carefully prepared peroration: "When I think of the flags our ships carry, the only touch of color about them, the only thing that moves as if it had a settled spirit—in their solid structure—it seems to me I see alternate strips of parchment on which are written the rights of liberty and justice and strips of blood spilled to vindicate these rights, and then —in the corner—a prediction of the blue serene into which every nation may swim which stands for these great things."

Young Joe Tumulty who had been bitterly opposed to the nomination had wormed his way from the back of the hall and was standing beside the band in front of the speakers' stand. He used to tell how the men around him had tears streaming down their faces. He himself fell like Saul on the road to Damascus. An old progressive from Atlantic City named John Crandall was trying to fight off the spell. The drum was beating. Men were cheering at the top of their lungs. Finally he started wildly waving his hat and cane. "I'm sixty-five years old and still a damned fool," he yelled.

Four days later when Kerney went over to Prospect with Smith and James R. Nugent, the conservative city counsel of Newark, to plan the campaign, he noted that the boss seemed awed by the quiet sweep of the green lawns, the flowerbeds, the airy stateliness of the big house. "Jim," he whispered to Kerney, "can you imagine anybody being damn fool enough to give this up for the heartaches of politics?"

Jim Kerney who was thick with the reform element had been as opposed as Tumulty to Wilson's nomination. When the professor came out to usher them into his booklined study Smith introduced Kerney as a troublesome progressive editor. Wilson shook hands warmly and said something about having Irish blood himself in his veins. Right away they were all bits of the old sod together.

"The manner in which he grasped every suggestion" as to how to win over the local Mercer County partyleaders "was a revelation," wrote Kerney admiringly. At the same time "he had his own notions about things . . . He did not favor the handshaking, house to house, Roosevelt style of whirlwind campaign and was against all day tours . . . One big evening speech in each county was his idea of the way of conducting the fight."

It fell to Nugent to arrange the practical details. He confided in Kerney that the professor was devilish hard to manage. It was Nugent who enlisted the services of irrepressible young Joe Tumulty who had already made a name for himself as an orator during his three years in the state legislature. Tumulty's job was to keep the candidate in touch with the rank and file. They had been horrified to discover how ignorant Professor Wilson was of local issues.

The only newspaper he read was Oswald Garrison Villard's New York *Evening Post*. According to Kerney they told off a man named St. John to slant articles in the *Evening Post* especially for the political education of Woodrow Wilson.

The Democratic leaders held their breath when the professor stepped out to open the campaign before a rough and tumble audience in St. Peter's Hall in Jersey City. His first story fell flat, he fumbled and hesitated. Then all at once he caught the feel of his hearers. Taking advantage of his bad beginning he explained, in a simple man to man tone, that up to then he had asked audiences to accept ideas and principles . . . "and now I find myself in the novel position of asking you to vote for me for Governor of New Jersey."

Why shouldn't he be embarrassed?

He went on to outline his principles of independence from political and financial interests in a rather general way, but in such a sincere and personal tone that the whole hall was captivated. "Something new in stump speeches" commented the Trenton *True American*.

Reform in the Jerseys

The Republicans were running a reform campaign. Their aspirant for governor was a good man. On the whole the New Jersey reformers had come more from among the Republicans than from the tightly ruled Democratic organizations. Republican progressivism was greatly stimulated in 1906 when, during a furious campaign, La Follette cut a tornado path across the state. He made seventeen speeches in six days. "If in this eastern country," announced the apostle of the Wisconsin Idea, "where the money power is strongest, I could do something towards bringing down the lightning, it would be more effective than anything I could do."

One of the reasons La Follette came into the state was that his friend and admirer, the prince of muckrakers Lincoln Steffens, had written up the reform movement in Jersey City in the magazines.

Reform in Jersey City was the work of an Irishman named Mark Fagan. By profession an undertaker he had been raised in the machine. As a youth he read Henry George and was excommunicated by the Church for joining the Anti-Poverty League. He was a warmhearted simple sort of man with a great deal of the common touch. When he was elected mayor he tried "to make Jersey City a pleasant place to live in." He even said, "I'd like to make it pretty."

His corporation counsel and general mentor was a tall shambling lawyer, so obsessed with the character of Abraham Lincoln that his friends claimed he was getting to look like him, named George L. Record. Record came from Maine. He had worked his way through Bates on jobs in a shoefactory and as carpenter's helper and had come to the New York area to study law and make his fortune. Although originally a Democrat he was attracted by the progressive ideas of the Jersey Republicans. He and Fagan between them founded the Equal Taxation League which worked to cut the excessive tax reductions enjoyed by the railroads and utilities which threw the support of municipal government on the small home owners.

Record had little success when he tried to run for office himself, but his influence was great as a lobbyist for progressive measures. He had put through a senatorial primary law. Now he was agitating for a corrupt practices act, for the sort of control of corporations which Hughes had put through in New York, for employers' liability and other measures out of the progressive textbook as set forth in Oregon and Wisconsin. Record's word carried great weight with reform elements in both parties. When he described Professor Wilson's speeches as "glittering generalities beautifully phrased, but having nothing to do with the political campaign in New Jersey," Wilson's backers were dismayed. Record challenged Professor Wilson to debate the issues.

To the consternation of the old pros running the Democratic cámpaign, who considered George Record a radical too dangerous even to speak to, Wilson accepted. The campaign committee pointed out that the professor was falling into a trap. Wilson announced, with the greatest air of innocence, that he still would be glad to debate with Mr. Record if the Republican committee would designate him as their spokesman. The Republican committee, who thought of Record as a son of the wild jackass, would do no such thing. In terms of sweet reasonableness Wilson suggested an exchange of letters.

Record promptly fired off a long list of questions. Wilson's nomination had been steamrollered through by bosses Nugent and Smith; how did he propose to abolish boss control in politics?

"By the election to office of men who will refuse to submit to it . . . and by pitiless publicity," Wilson replied. He answered the nineteen questions frankly. Sometimes he agreed with Record. Sometimes he didn't.

By the time election day came around Woodrow Wilson had appropriated a large part of George Record's progressive platform: state control of utilities, workingmen's compensation, a corrupt practices act and even the direct election of United States senators. In every speech he was drawing cheers from the crowds by attacking the privileges of entrenched corporations and by harrying the political bosses.

He had been developing his flair for carrying day to day politics up into the epic sphere:

"We have begun a fight that, it may be, will take many a generation to complete," he announced in his ringing tenor voice that so effortlessly filled the hall during his address that closed the campaign at New-ark. "No man would wish to sit idly by and lose the opportunity to take part in such a struggle. All through the centuries there has been this slow painful struggle forward, forward, up, up, a little at a time, along the en-tire incline, the interminable way . . ."

Listening to his candidate's speeches Boss Smith seems to have been torn between admiration for the "Presbyterian priest's" political skill and dismay at what he was saying. When his friends shook their heads he called it confidently "great campaign play." He thought he had the pro-fessor in his pocket.

Wilson was elected by a majority of almost fifty thousand. To every-one's amazement he carried with him a Democratic majority in the lower house of what had been considered a firmly Republican legislature.

Every successful politician learns from his audiences. Wilson had been learning fast during the campaign. One thing he learned was that the bosses needed him more than he needed the bosses. The reform tide was rising.

He meant exactly what he said when, in the final speech at Newark, he announced in the vibrant voice that stirred listeners to the marrow of their bones: "If I am elected governor I shall have been elected leader of my party . . . If the Democratic Party does not understand it that way, then I want to say to you very frankly that the Democratic Party ought not to elect me governor."

Part of his agreement with Smith when Wilson accepted his tender of the nomination had been, so Wilson's supporters claimed, that Smith, who had left Washington in bad odor after his previous term, should not try to get the legislature to elect him to the Senate again.

A reform enactment, part of the nationwide campaign for the direct election of United States senators, had established a senatorial primary in New Jersey. The designate was a gentleman known as "Farmer Jim" Martine, an old tubthumper in the Bryan style whose name was put on the ticket largely because no one else thought it worthwhile to run.

Now after Wilson's victory, the Democrats were sure to elect whom-ever they picked for senator. So James Smith changed his mind and an-nounced that the primary didn't mean a thing and that he would run for election. Meanwhile he suggested, pointedly, that the professor needed a rest after a strenuous campaign. Why didn't he go back to Old Lyme for a vacation?

The professor did no such thing. Instead he travelled about the state, dropping in on his newfound friends, the progressives, and asking them whether he ought to come out for Martine or let Smith have his way. He found young Tumulty, who had been such a help in the populous eastern counties, acting as Martine's campaign manager.

Jim Kerney and the whole band of progressive newspapermen who had become Wilson's warmest adherents admitted that Martine was a fool, but claimed that, since he'd been nominated by popular vote, if they believed in their principles as true Democrats they had no choice but to send him to the Senate. They urged Wilson to come out against Smith.

The governor-elect made quite a show of calling on the party bosses at their homes to try to argue them out of supporting Smith's candidacy. The bosses answered that they had given Smith their word. Wilson went to see Smith himself and argued with him for two hours.

The conversation was civil, because Smith was a civilspoken man, but he insisted he wanted to go to Washington. He'd left a bad impression last time. This time he'd do better. He wanted another chance for his boys' sake. He laughed off Wilson's threat to come out against him. They parted political enemies.

Wilson issued a dignified statement against Smith and promptly invaded the machine's own bailiwick in Jersey City. Before an uproarious meeting he described the political bosses as warts on the body politic. "It is not a capital process to cut off a wart. You don't have to go to the hospital and take an anaesthetic. The thing can be done while you wait . . ."

Wilson's speeches were widely reported by the New York press, and reprinted by local newspapers from Texas to California. Martine's campaign for senator became a national issue.

The senatorial election was the new legislature's first business. The whole country was watching to see who would come out on top, the schoolmaster in politics, only inaugurated in his first political post a week before, or the man who had bossed New Jersey for years.

Using all the old blarney, with the brass knuckles hidden under the kid glove Boss Smith confidently mobilized his troops. While Smith's henchmen poured out whiskey for the faithful in the famous old room 100 of the Trenton House, Wilson and Tumulty sat up all night keeping tab on their supporters from the executive offices. Their only weapon was the telephone.

On the day of the vote Smith's cohorts paraded through Trenton with a brass band and were reviewed by the Big Fellow himself from the steps of the hotel. Everybody who could be reached had been reached. Smith was confident.

When the two houses voted separately Martine lacked one vote of a majority. Next day he was elected in joint session. Only three men voted for Smith.

"I pitied Smith at the last," Wilson wrote his friend Mrs. Peck, with whom ever since Bermuda he had carried on a brisk and, later slanderers to the contrary, platonic correspondence. "It was plain he had few real friends, that he held men by fear and power and the benefits he could bestow, not by love or loyalty or any genuine devotion. The minute it was seen that he was defeated his adherents began to desert him like rats leaving a sinking ship. He left Trenton, (where his headquarters had at first been crowded) attended, I am told, only by his sons, and looking old and broken . . . It is a pitiless game . . . —and for me it has only begun."

The Pitiless Game

Wilson was proving himself, for an amateur, remarkably adept. Turning the tables on Boss Smith did him more good politically than all the "glittering generalities beautifully phrased" of his campaign speeches.

Bryan Democrats and progressive Republicans were alike smarting over their failure to attain national leadership. Bryan had beaten his head against a wall. Roosevelt had gone off to Africa and let his party fall back into the hands of the reactionaries. La Follette was tied to the middlewest. Hiram Johnson was local to California. Here was a reformer stepping down from the high sphere of academic wisdom. He seemed to mean what he said. The muckraking journals applauded him from coast to coast.

The professionals, to be sure, saw Governor Wilson in a less favorable light. When he heard of Smith's misadventures old Boss Croker of New York is reported to have growled: "An ingrate in politics is no good."

The Wilsons were rapidly becoming professionals themselves. Ellen Wilson struck up a friendship with Joe Tumulty who was already the indispensable adjutant. Between them they kept the governor informed on local politics. She subscribed to all the papers and began to keep a scrapbook of clippings that had to do with her husband's presidential candidacy.

It wasn't easy for her after the pleasant academic years to become a politician's wife. Moving out of Prospect into cramped quarters at the Princeton Inn was a wrench. The girls hated hotel life. Of course what Woodrow wanted Ellen wanted but she couldn't help repining a little. She confided in Jim Kerney that she feared it was the end of the "happy home days" when she would play the piano evenings while her husband sang college songs with the girls. "That kind of joy is largely over for us."

Wilson was oblivious of everything except the task in hand. He had to make himself a record as a modern liberal and he had to do it fast. Up to now his liberalism had been distinctly of the Manchester school. He had preached in his courses the beauties of the English Constitution.

Along with the great Britishers he'd admired as a young man he had been for free trade and against wars of aggression and for limiting the powers of government. Like Bright and Cobden he had been suspicious of government interference in such things as the wages and hours of labor. In the name of Southern chivalry he had scoffed at women's suffrage. Now the word liberal was beginning to be applied to a set of tenets that would have made Gladstone's hackles rise.

Wilson was going to school with the progressives. For the first time in his life he had discovered the people. The vested interests, as represented by the wealthy Princeton alumni who had opposed his plans, had given him a hard time. Now he found great exhilaration in addressing halls full of plain uneducated people right off the streetcorners. They thrilled to his words; he thrilled to them. The people must rule.

He made a friend of George L. Record. He set himself to learn about the legislation the reformers hoped would take local and state governments, and eventually the national government, away from the vested interests and their hired politicians, and restore control to the voters. These measures were already being tried out. Hadn't James Bryce written, somewhat puzzled, after a recent trip through the United States, that rapid changes were causing him to revise some of his views of American government? These were currents of day to day life that the professor had ignored during his years in the academic backwater.

The day before his inauguration Wilson attended a meeting that George Record organized at the Hotel Martinique in New York for progressive assemblymen of both parties to map out a program for the coming session. Record read the project for an election law setting up direct primaries as a means of ridding New Jersey of boss control. He outlined a stiff corrupt practices act, a law to regulate public utilities such as Governor Hughes had put through in New York and a workingmen's compensation act. By the time Governor Wilson took the train to Princeton that night he had made Record's program his own.

In an extraordinary burst of activity, the new governor, taking advantage of the mantle of invincibility he had worn since the defeat of Boss Smith, rammed the most important items through the legislature in three months. Record furnished drafts of the bills and Wilson and Tumulty sat in the executive office and saw to it that the assemblymen did the right thing.

The oldtimers were aghast. Smith was so shaken he stayed home. When Nugent, who had worked so hard for Wilson's election, tried to stack the cards against the new legislation in a Democratic caucus, the governor announced that as leader of the party he had the right to attend. He lectured the Democratic legislators for three hours on civic duty. Boss Smith threatened to have him impeached, but Wilson had convinced the assembly that the voters expected reform. He threatened to expose to public wrath any man who stood in the way of the people's will. With Record and his friends doing the paperwork, in spite of a continuous outcry from Boss Smith's personal press and collusion between the Republican and Democratic machines, the bills were drafted and passed.

Getting them approved by the state senate was a fresh problem. The senate was still in Republican hands. Wilson used all his charm, all his humor, all his felicity of phrase to woo the state senators as he had wooed the undergraduates at Princeton. He invited them to his office, he attended their banquets.

In a letter to Mrs. Peck he described himself as joining one senator in a cakewalk. "We pranced together to the content of the whole company. I am on easy and delightful terms with all the Senators. They know me for something else than an ambitious dictator." By April 23, 1911, he was able to write her: "I got absolutely everything I strove for—and more besides . . . Everyone, the papers included, are saying that none of it could have been done, if it had not been for my influence and tact and hold upon the people . . . The result was as complete a victory as has ever been won, I venture to say, in the history of the country."

The news of Governor Wilson's performance at Trenton spread over the nation's newsstands. William Jennings Bryan who, in spite of his three defeats for the presidency, still considered himself leader of the popular wing of the Democratic Party, wrote to inquire how such things could be. How could a man sponsored by Colonel Harvey, whom Bryan considered an errandboy from the Morgan office, turn out a progressive? To try Governor Wilson's sincerity, he suggested that he endorse the constitutional amendment for a federal income tax. Governor Wilson promptly obliged with a special message to the legislature. The Commoner was "gratified."

The Commoner

Bryan at fifty was a disappointed man. In spite of Mrs. Bryan's leavening good sense, a shrewish tone was creeping into his exhortations to righteousness. His religious fundamentalism, his ranting against the demon rum, and war, and imperialism, and high finance, and vested privilege, began to pall even on the Chautauqua circuits. The great speeches had been so often repeated they had lost their savor. The voice was losing its resonance. But, even in his decline William Jennings Bryan remained the embodiment of the aspirations of the plain people, and the most powerful single factor in Democratic politics.

The situation was ticklish. In his academic days Professor Wilson had hardly let pass an opportunity to hold the crude notions of the cornbelt demagogue up to ridicule. He had once refused to share a platform with him. The two men had never met. Bryan had to be conciliated.

Ellen Wilson, who was using all her gentle housewifely guile to advance her husband's political fortunes, made the first move. When she discovered that Bryan was coming to Princeton to deliver an address on Faith to the theological seminary, she invited him to dinner and wired Woodrow, who was off lecturing in Georgia, to come home at once.

The evening was a success. Bryan, whose lips never touched liquor, was a colossal trencherman. The Princeton Inn did its best. Instead of talking politics the men swapped stories. The Commoner announced himself afterwards as charmed by the governor's gaiety and nimblemindedness and captivated by Mrs. Wilson. The governor wrote Mrs. Peck that he found in Bryan force of personality and sincerity and conviction. Tumulty who had been hovering in the lobby rushed up to Mrs. Wilson after the guests had left, his blue eyes popping. "You've nominated your husband," he said. She smiled and answered that she hadn't done a thing.

When, three weeks later, both men appeared on the same platform at Burlington, Wilson paid Bryan a handsome compliment: "It is because he has cried 'America awake' that other men have been able to transform into action the doctrines he so diligently preached."

Professor Wilson's Travelling Fellowship

The presidentmakers were buzzing. A Princeton graduate from Arkansas named William McCombs, who practiced law in New York and dabbled in Tammany politics, opened a small office on lower Broadway to nourish the Wilson boom. Wilson insisted on calling it his literary bureau. McCombs was financed by Cleveland Dodge, Walter Hines Page, the publisher, and a few other of Wilson's old admirers from Princeton days. Between them they organized a western lecture tour for the governor right after the windup of that first triumphant session of the New Jersey legislature. The Schoolmaster in Politics must be shown to the country.

Wilson, who had never been west of Colorado, spent the month of May lecturing in the mountain states and on the Pacific coast. In Kansas City, on the way out, he was so carried away by the progressive atmosphere that he came out for the initiative, referendum and recall, and talking to newspapermen, barely stopped short of the recall of the judiciary. Some of his eastern backers set up such a doleful clamor at the news that he promptly dropped these inflammatory expressions from his vocabulary.

He spoke in Denver on a Sunday. Since he had scruples against talking politics on the Sabbath, he harangued twelve thousand people in the auditorium on the Holy Bible and sent them away so fired with enthusiasm that when next morning the first long distance phone connections were opened between New York and Denver, and the *Times* reporter asked what the news was, the answer came that the town was wild over Woodrow Wilson and was booming him for President.

Wilson was applauded in Los Angeles and San Francisco. He hobnobbed with the progressive leaders of the Northwest. He travelled eight thousand miles and delivered thirtyfive speeches. The facile enthusiasm of western audiences warmed his heart. He began to admit publicly that indeed he was out for the presidency.

On the long trainride east to Minneapolis he told the reporter for the Baltimore *Sun* that he had been waiting to weigh the results of this trip. Now he felt that the response was such that if he could get the nomination he could surely be elected: "It's an awful thing to be President of the United States . . . I mean just what I say. It means giving up nearly everything that one holds dear . . . In spite of what I said to you I do want to be President and I will tell you why: I want this country to have a President who will do certain things . . . I am sure that I will at least try to the utmost to do them."

His final address, at Lincoln, Nebraska, in William Jennings Bryan's home bailiwick, was a rousing appeal to businessmen to forget their own selfish interests and to work for the public good. Men jumped to their feet and clapped and cheered. Charles Bryan, the Commoner's banker brother, came across with a check to help defray the expenses of Governor Wilson's campaign.

Back in Trenton the governor discovered, with some chagrin, that an article in the state constitution, which he hadn't had time to peruse, made it impossible for the state controller to pay him his salary for the days he had spent out of the state. The president of the senate, sworn in as acting governor in his stead, had received his paycheck. The senator generously endorsed the check back to Wilson and continued to do so during all the many absences from duty made necessary by his new career as presidential timber.

It was a period of money worries for the Wilsons. The governor's salary was only ten thousand dollars. They had a few savings from Princeton days and occasional royalties from his books, but Mrs. Wilson had to pinch every penny.

The main business of the summer, which the Wilson family spent at the official residence at Sea Girt, was gaining control of the state Democratic committee. James R. Nugent, who by this time hated Wilson with a bitter personal hatred, was chairman. The report that Nugent on a champagne drunk at a nearby summer resort had publicly toasted the governor as an ingrate and a liar was seized on by Wilson supporters. They made it a pretext for forcing Nugent's resignation. His successor was a Wilson man.

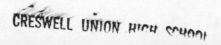

The immediate result was a split in the New Jersey Democracy which resulted in the loss of the legislature to the Republicans. Just as at Princeton Wilson lost interest in university affairs, when opinion began to turn against him after the first flush of enthusiasm for his setting everything to rights, so now the executive offices at Trenton began to lose their glamor. He was always away lecturing. The New York *Sun*, a Republican paper continually yapping at his heels, took to describing the governorship as Professor Wilson's travelling fellowship.

He did press through a batch of laws, known to the newspapers as the Seven Sisters, which made New Jersey less the promised land for the incorporation of outofstate trusts and holding companies, but his lack of interest in the local problems of the people of his home state was becoming painfully evident.

His veto of the bill to force the railroads to start eliminating grade crossings came as a disappointment to supporters in both parties. Kerney told the story that when the bill was returned to the state senate with the veto message the senators found a letter to the governor from a railroad official which had slipped into the engrossed copy by mistake. The letter was couched in terms strangely similar to the terms of the veto message. Such was Woodrow Wilson's prestige that the senators, although bitterly disappointed by the veto, returned the letter to Wilson instead of tipping off the newspapers, in order not to damage his prospects of the presidential nomination.

Woodrow Wilson was becoming the center of a political cult, but personally he remained a lonely man. His craving for love and admiration was insatiable. His home was full of doting female relatives but that was not enough. He missed his friendships among the Princeton faculty. No one had taken the place of Jack Hibben as a daily and approving companion since their bitter break in the row over the quadrangles. Then one day in late November, 1911, Governor Wilson paid a call, at the suggestion of his literary bureau, on a gentleman from Texas. He found, right in the world of politics where he most needed a crony, a sympathetic friend, who like himself had spent a lifetime cultivating the arts of power.

Chapter 3

THE SILENT PARTNER

EDWARD Mandell House was two years younger than Wilson. He was born and raised in Texas. His first memories were of living in a whitepillared redbrick mansion set among oleanders in an orange grove near the beach in Galveston. The roof was crowned with a cupola where his father, a trader and shipowner who had run away from England as a boy and fought the Mexicans with Sam Houston, spent a good deal of his time searching the horizon with a telescope for federal gunboats. T. W. House invested heavily in blockaderunners. Sometimes he lost, but when he won he deposited his winnings in gold with Baring Brothers in London. The end of the war found him a very wealthy man. In reconstruction times a man with gold sovereigns could buy almost as much of Texas as he wanted.

House liked to tell of those murderous days when he was one of a band of guntoting youths running wild in Houston. He told Arthur Howden Smith, who became his biographer, that he used to spend hours practicing the quick draw before the mirror. His mother died when he was twelve. The same year he suffered a severe concussion falling out of a swing onto his head. In later life he attributed to the brain fever and to the severe bouts of malaria that followed, his continued poor health and his inability to stand hot weather.

His father sent him north to a rundown school in Virginia and then to New Haven where it was hoped he might matriculate at Yale. There he made friends with another young scapegrace, the son of Oliver P. Morton, Republican senator from Indiana, who aspired to the Republican presidential nomination in 1876. The pair of them decided to tutor for Cornell instead of entering a preparatory school for Yale.

"Both Morton and I were more bent on mischief than books," House wrote in his memoir, "and while the mischief was innocent it made us poor students. We were both filled to the brim with interest in politics and public affairs."

House was an enthusiastic Democrat and Morton was an enthusiastic Republican but they were thick as thieves, nevertheless. During the convention in 1876 instead of studying at Cornell they hung around the telegraph office on Union Square in New York. When Rutherford B. Hayes was nominated instead of Morton's dad they were equally disappointed. In the breathtaking suspense of the winter of the disputed election they dropped their studies completely and moved in with the Morton family at the Ebbitt House in Washington. As the Mortons were friends of the Grants, the boys had the run of the White House, and even managed to squeeze into the old Supreme Court Chamber in the Capitol for the sessions of the Electoral Commission which eventually awarded the election to Hayes, in spite of Tilden's popular majority.

House used to speak of these bloodheating days as "an education in representative government." It left him, so he said, with no ambition to hold office or taste for public speaking but with an insatiable appetite for the machinery of politics. "Yet I have been thought without ambition. That I think is not quite true. My ambition has been so great it has never seemed to me worth while to try to satisfy it."

When his father, whom he adored, suffered a stroke a couple of years later, he went home to Houston to nurse him. Meanwhile he read up on American government. Back at Cornell he had eagerly studied de Tocqueville. After his father's death he pitched in with his brothers to help manage the widespread holdings the elder House had left to his children.

When at twentythree young House married Miss Loulie Hunter of Hunter, Texas, he felt himself well enough off to take a year's honeymoon in Europe with his bride.

Advising and Helping

Back home in the early eighties he found himself in the thick of a new generation growing up in Texas on the heels of the empirebuilders. His father, a humane man who had manumitted his slaves as fast as they learned a trade, taught him to admire character and initiative more than money and social position. It came natural to him to side with the people against the magnates.

When his friend James S. Hogg became governor House joined in his campaign to free Texas politics from the domination of railroad and financial interests. House used to say he considered Hogg the greatest Texan after Sam Houston. It was Governor Culberson who made House a colonel on his staff. House used to tell in his deadpan way how much his colored coachman enjoyed wearing the uniform.

House devoted three years of his life to promoting the Trinity and Brazos Valley Railroad on capital furnished by Thomas Jefferson Coolidge of Boston. He used to boast that this was one honest railroad, honestly financed and honestly built.

After that he seems to have felt he was as well off as he wanted to be. He and his wife built themselves a fine house with broad verandas in

Austin, where they lived lavishly, and entertained outofstate visitors. They interested themselves in the university. They were friendly with the professors. Their home was the center of the intellectual life of Austin. Without ever running for office himself the colonel became the guide and philosopher of several generations of Texas politicians.

"So in politics," he wrote, "I began at the top rather than at the bottom, and I have been doing since that day pretty much what I am doing now; that is advising and helping wherever I might." In Austin if you wanted to accomplish some reform Colonel House was the man to see. He never wanted anything for himself. His pleasure was in making the wheels go round.

When Joseph D. Sayers became governor House was consulted on every detail of the administration. "I lay upon a large lounge in our living room, for I was in anything but good health, and gave my opinion as to the best man for each office . . . I had long made it a rule not to visit and it was understood that if anyone desired to see me it must be at my home. I did this not only to conserve my strength but because it enabled me to work under more favorable conditions . . . Those days and those guests are among the pleasantest recollections of my life."

Bryan's freesilver campaign in 1896 failed, but it taught House, who was beginning to fancy himself as a political weatherprophet, how much talent and how many resentments could be marshalled in behalf of a Democratic revival. He became interested in trying out on the national stage the techniques of behind the scenes manipulation he had developed at home.

His appetite for national politics was heightened by the appearance of the Bryan family in Austin one winter during McKinley's first administration. House and ex-governor Hogg arranged for the Bryans to rent a house adjoining theirs. House started spinning his webs, hoping that Bryan would fall under his influence as easily as his Texas friends. "I found Mrs. Bryan very amenable" he wrote, "but Mr. Bryan was as impracticable as ever . . . I believe he feels his ideas are God-given." Bryan, he said, was the most opinionated man he'd ever met.

The Confidential Colonel

House was convinced he couldn't stand the Texas summers. Heat prostrated him. He took to spending more and more time in the North or in European spas. Going and coming to and from Europe in the spring and fall he and his wife would stay several weeks in New York. He began to cultivate the more respectable Democratic politicians. He was spoken of as searching, like Diogenes with his lantern, for a Democrat who could be elected President.

Colonel House was described in those days as a slight grayish almost mousily quiet man with high cheekbones and a receding chin. There was something pebblelike about the opaque blue of his eyes. He wore a close-clipped colorless mustache. His speech was meticulous with a slight Texas drawl. A good listener, he had a way of punctuating a visitor's outpourings with exclamations of "True, true."

People remarked on his soundless tread when he came into a room. In conversation he was master of the meaningful silence. He continuously wore the air of having just left a conference where men of importance had been concerned with transcendant events. The impression he gave was that he knew more than he let on. At the same time he was incurably confidential. "Just between you and me and the angels" was a favorite expression.

Talk at the Gotham

The meeting between Woodrow Wilson and Colonel House had not gone unprepared. Wilson had for some months been in communication with friends of the colonel's in Texas. That October he delivered an address at the state fair in Dallas which set the forwardlooking politicians to discussing him favorably. His friend Harvey urged him to get in touch with House. Congressman Burleson of Texas wrote describing House as "a good politician, a wise counselor, able and unselfish . . . I think he can help you."

A couple of letters were exchanged on questions of party regularity and it was arranged, through the young men of the literary bureau, that Governor Wilson would take it upon himself to call on Colonel House.

It was a great day in both men's lives.

"He came alone to the Gotham promptly at four and we talked for an hour," House noted portentously in his diary. "From that first meeting I have been in as close touch with Woodrow Wilson as with any man I have ever known."

Years later, talking to Arthur Howden Smith, he described that first interview:

"We talked and talked. We knew each other for congenial souls from the very beginning . . . We exchanged our ideas about the democracies of the world, contrasted the European democracies with the United States, discussed where they differed, which was best in some respects and which in others . . . I remember we were very urbane. Each gave the other the chance to have his say . . . The hour flew away. It seemed no time when it was over."

Wilson was engaged to confer with a California Democrat and had to leave when the hour was up. They arranged to dine together a couple of days later. After a few more ardent meetings at the Gotham, House remembered having remarked to Wilson one day as he was about to leave, "Governor, isn't it strange that two men who never knew each other before, should think so much alike?"

Woodrow Wilson answered, "My dear fellow, we have known each other all our lives."

This pair of middleaged politicians, family men both, were as excited about each other as two schoolgirls developing a crush.

Here was a man, House confided to Senator Culberson "one can advise with some degree of satisfaction." "He is not the biggest man I ever met," he wrote Sidney Mezes, his brotherinlaw who taught government at the University of Texas, "but he is one of the pleasantest, and I would rather play with him than any prospective candidate I have seen . . . From what I have heard I was afraid that he had to have his hats made to order: but I saw not the slightest evidence of it . . . Never before have I found both the man and the opportunity."

To Ameliorate the Condition

House was ill a great deal that fall and winter. From his bed he kept in touch by letter and telephone with all the political skirmishing preliminary to next June's Democratic convention. At the same time he was engaged in putting down on paper a fantasy in the style of Bellamy's *Looking Backward*, which does a great deal to explain the remark in his memoir: "My ambition has been so great it has never seemed to me worth while to try to satisfy it."

This fantasy, a daydream remarkably boyish to be the work of a man of fifty, was eventually published, anonymously of course, by Ben Huebsch under the title of *Philip Dru, Administrator.*

A quotation from Mazzini on the title page expressed the political creed House was hoping to put into effect, by advice and cajolement, during the Democratic administration to come:

"No war of classes, no hostility to existing wealth, no wanton or unjust violation of the rights of property, but a constant disposition to ameliorate the condition of the classes least favored by fortune."

The dedication restated the theme in his own words: *"To the unhappy many* [he must have remembered Stendhal's 'happy few'] *who have lived and died lacking opportunity, because, in the starting, the worldwide social structure was wrongly begun."*

It is a rather awkward story, set ten years forward in the nineteen-twenties, of a civil war between progressive and reactionary forces in the United States. The hero is a lithe young West Pointer named Philip Dru whose army career is cut short by a case of heat prostration contracted while riding out in the Mexican desert with a highly imaginary young lady named Gloria. During his convalescence the hero lives over a hardware store on the lower East Side of New York and absorbs the mystique of the coming European revolution from a Jewish idealist who escaped from Polish pogroms to take refuge in America. Meanwhile Gloria, who has taken up settlement house work, tells him of a Senator Selwyn's conspiracy, backed by a fund raised by a thousand multimillionaires, to take over the United States Government in the interest of the rich.

Senator Selwyn bears a more than accidental resemblance to Senator Nelson W. Aldrich of Rhode Island who, as sponsor of the Payne-Aldrich Tariff so hated in the south and west, was the bugbear good Democrats and Progressives used to frighten naughty children with. Senator Aldrich, able, ruthless, and thoroughly convinced of the Godgiven right of the moneymen to rule, led the standpat forces which had taken over Taft's indecisive administration. In the story, House, as a science fiction touch, has his Senator Selwyn imprudently dictate his conspiratorial plans into a dictaphone. Dru, who has become a journalist for the muckraking press, gets hold of the guilty cylinder and forms a committee to fight for freedom and right. With Gloria raising money from the Pinchots and Walter Perkinses among the millionaires, Philip Dru becomes the leader of outraged democracy. Civil war breaks out. Transformed into a general of Napoleonic scope, he defeats the army of capitalist privilege and marches on Washington.

Wearing Dru's fictional cloak, House simplifies the legal code and repeals unnecessary laws. He institutes a graduated income tax. He borrows a land tax on unimproved land from Henry George. He centralizes government administration, takes the currency out of the hands of the bankers, regulates public utilities and bans holding companies.

For the benefit of the workingman he sets up state employment agencies, old age insurance, workingmen's compensation for accidents. Labor is to be represented in management and to share in the profits of industry.

He institutes cooperative financing and marketing for the farmer.

He rewrites the Constitution. The President with a ten year term becomes a mere head of state but an Executive is chosen by the House of Representatives and is responsible to the House. Party government in the English style. Senators are elected for life subject to recall every five years.

Having reformed the government to Colonel House's satisfaction the hero resigns his powers and fades away in a rosy haze with the beautiful Gloria.

The few intimate friends House allowed to see the manuscript were impressed. In a naïve way it expressed the hopes and frustrations of a good many reformers disheartened by the slow working of the progressive panaceas. Sidney Mezes urged him to rewrite the book as a serious exposition of his ideas. E. S. Martin, who edited *Life,* in those days a New York counterpart of the London *Punch,* offered to help in revamping the story. "I had no time, however, for such diversions," wrote House. "I was so much more interested in the campaign than I was in the book . . . that I turned it over to the publisher as it was."

The Candidate Switches Colonels

It was becoming evident that the split between Roosevelt and Taft supporters amongst the Republicans was so irreconcilable that for the first time in years the man the Democrats were going to pick at their convention in June would have a real chance to be elected. Woodrow Wilson was beginning to understand that taking over the progressive platform would serve him even better in national politics than it had in New Jersey. The reformers of the South and West had a superstitious horror of Wall Street. To establish himself in the running against such dangerous radical contenders as Roosevelt and La Follette he had publicly to kick away the stool which had offered him his first foothold.

Colonel Harvey's *Harper's Weekly,* published by the old New York publishing house which the Morgans were known to control, was carrying at the head of its editorial column a rubric: "For President, Woodrow Wilson." To the West that meant Wall Street's blessing.

The ministrations of the mercurial Harvey, which a few short months ago had seemed so congenial, were becoming an embarrassment. There were rumors that Harvey himself, though he pretended to cantankerous independence, shared the misgivings of his financial associates.

Colonel House before enlisting wholeheartedly in the Wilson campaign, had to discover how the winds blew on Franklin Square. A few days after House's first meeting with Wilson, the two colonels conferred.

Next day House wrote Bryan, undoubtedly coloring his narrative a little to suit the Commoner's prejudices:

"I took lunch with Colonel Harvey yesterday. It is the first time I have met him. I wanted to determine what his real attitude was towards Governor Wilson, but I think I am left as much in the dark as ever.

"He told me that everybody south of Canal Street was in a frenzy against Governor Wilson and said they were bringing all sorts of pressure upon him to oppose him. He said he told them he had an open mind and that if they would convince him he was a dangerous man he would do so.

"He said that Morgan was particularly virulent . . ."

House ended diplomatically by asking Mr. Bryan's advice as how best to meet these attacks from entrenched privilege.

The day after Colonel House left for Texas to make sure of his state delegation, Wilson and Colonel Harvey met at the Manhattan Club as guests of another honorary colonel, a Kentucky one this time, Henry Watterson who edited the Louisville *Courier-Journal*. Marse Henry, the "grand old man" of Southern journalism, had been a Wilson backer since the early days. The conversation seems to have been about where to go for campaign contributions.

Just as Wilson was leaving, Colonel Harvey, maybe stung by some carefully barbed remark Colonel House dropped on purpose in his ear, or from a tactless communication from a Wilson enthusiast from the literary bureau, asked Wilson whether there was anything left of the cheap talk about Harvey's promoting him on behalf of the "interests"!

"Yes, there is," Wilson blurted out sharply: some of his supporters felt that Harvey's backing was having a bad effect in the West.

Harvey bristled. "Is there anything I can do except to stop advocating your nomination?"

Wilson shook his head. "I think not," he said.

Harvey replied, "I shall sing low." According to Harvey, Governor Wilson left the room abruptly.

Next week "For President, Woodrow Wilson" was no longer seen at the head of Harvey's editorial column. The candidate had switched colonels.

The incident made a great flurry in the press. The Republican papers blew it up as another instance of Wilson's ingratitude.

On the other hand Tumulty's publicitymen managed to make political hay by circulating the tale that what had really happened was that Wilson had righteously turned down insidious offers of contributions to his campaign by Thomas Fortune Ryan and other malefactors of great wealth who thought they could buy the Democratic Party. Marse Henry announced that this version was not in accord with the facts. Wilson countered with the statement that Colonel Watterson was "a fine old gentleman," implying that his memory was not to be trusted, and became touchy with the reporters whenever they brought the subject up.

On the whole the Wilson men had the better of it. The impression left in the public mind was that Wilson had simply told the truth when asked a direct question, like the good honest oldtime Presbyterian schoolmaster that he was.

The loss of the New Jersey colonel as a political handyman made the acquisition of the urbane Texan, with whom Wilson had so much more in common, all the more agreeable. The correspondence between the two became affectionate to a degree.

The Grand Dress Parade

While House was in Austin laboring to get just the right men picked
for the Texas delegation Wilson's campaign had to take another hurdle.
Just before the Jackson Day dinner in Washington in January 1912 a
corporation lawyer whom Wilson had tangled with as a Princeton trustee
during the quadrangle row, turned over to the New York *Evening Sun*
a letter Wilson had written him five years back (when they were still
good friends) suggesting that something be done "at once dignified and
effective, to knock Mr. Bryan once for all into a cocked hat."

Fortunately for Democratic harmony Bryan was stopping off with
Josephus Daniels in North Carolina when the reporters poked this bit
of news under his nose and asked for comment. Daniels was a liberal
newspaper editor who genuinely believed in both Bryan and Wilson. He
exuded good nature. His Raleigh home was famous for easy hospitality,
good conversation and crisp fried chicken. He urged Bryan not to go off
halfcocked and was delighted when the Commoner growled out the comment that the *Sun* had been trying to knock him into a cocked hat for
years and hadn't succeeded yet.

The "cocked hat" letter threw Wilson's literary bureau into a panic.
Everybody knew that he could never be nominated against Bryan's op-
position. Even Wilson himself felt that his presidential aspirations hung
by a thread. On the train down to Washington on his way to the Jackson
Day dinner he gave vent to his feelings in a letter to the sympathetic
Mrs. Peck:

". . . The banquet in the evening is to be a grand dress parade of
candidates for the presidential nomination . . . I hate the whole thing
but it is something 'expected' of me by my friends and backers . . . There
is a merry war against me. I am evidently regarded as the strongest
candidate at present, for all the attacks are directed against me . . . this
rain of small missiles makes me feel like a common target for the malicious (by the way nearly all the darts are supplied by Princetonians who
hate me), and somewhat affect my spirits for a day at a time (the
strongest nerves wince under persistent spite); but for the most part I go
serenely on my way. I believe very profoundly in an overruling Providence and do not believe that any real plans can be thrown off the track.
It may not be intended that I shall be President—but that would not
break my heart—and I am content to await the event, doing what I hon-
orably can, in the meantime, to discomfort mine enemies."

That night Wilson discomforted his enemies by a speech which combined candor with tact. He made no attempt to deny that he had disagreed with some of Bryan's policies in the past, but proclaimed that he

had ever been in accord with his underlying principles. He ended by turning to the Commoner, who sat near him at the speaker's table, with what the politicians round about described as "a chesterfieldian gesture": "Let us apologize to each other that we ever suspected or antagonized one another; let us join hands once more—all around the circle of community of counsel and of interest which will show us at the last to have been indeed the friends of our country and of mankind."

Applause drowned out the last words. Bryan's face, we are told, was "a study." Afterwards he confided to a friend that it was the greatest speech in American political history. The New York *World* summed up the situation next day with a headline: WILSON LEADS IN CLASH OF BOOMS.

La Follette's Blunder

Three weeks later Wilson won another oratorical victory. At the annual banquet of a publishers' association in Philadelphia he spoke on the same program with the redoubtable Bob La Follette who for months had been campaigning for the Republican nomination as ardently as Wilson had for the Democratic. Wilson started by poking a little gentle fun at publishers: he used as a writer to be afraid they wouldn't publish him, and now, as a public figure, he was afraid when they did. He frothily outlined some of the principles of what was soon to be known as the New Freedom, and sat down amid great applause.

La Follette arrived late. He was suffering from indigestion and overwork. He had been drinking. He was desperately worried because his daughter was in hospital and was to undergo a dangerous operation next morning. He brought with him one of those bulky and closely reasoned manuscripts with which he was accustomed to flagellate the United States Senate. It was a long denunciation of the evils of the kept press. It may be that he'd taken a shot of whiskey too many in an effort to settle his stomach before he came.

He spoke for two hours with more than usual asperity, shaking his finger in the faces of the newspapermen opposite him. He lost his place in his manuscript, repeated himself, lost his temper at some hecklers and ended with his audience slinking off to the rathskeller below. "There go some of the fellows I've been hitting," he shouted. According to Owen Wister he shook his fist after them. "They don't want to hear about themselves." The speech was the worst failure of his life.

The toastmaster, representing the publishers who had sponsored the function, felt called upon to apologize to the audience for the speaker's rudeness. La Follette rushed to the washroom immediately after he finished speaking and was taken with a fit of vomiting. His soninlaw hurried him back to Washington in a nervous collapse.

Meanwhile the embittered newspapermen were scattering throughout the country to fill their columns with the news of his failure. The headline in The Philadelphia *Record* ran: WILSON HERO OF BIG FEAST.

The Baltimore Convention

The spring of 1912 was a time of political tension in both parties. Among the Republicans the standpatters were closing ranks round Taft as a reluctant leader. La Follette's collapse at Philadelphia gave T.R. the cue he was waiting for to throw his Rough Riders' felt hat into the ring as Progressive candidate.

Among the Democrats there were even more contenders for the throne. Hearst was mobilizing his newspapers and his millions in support of Champ Clark of Missouri, the speaker of the House of Representatives, a rustic figure in black slouch hat and frock coat whose campaign ditty was "You got to quit kickin' my dawg around." Senator Underwood and Governor Judson Harmon, Ohio's favorite son, each had more organization and money support behind him than Wilson had. Bryan was still keeping his thin lips clenched in stony silence when asked whether he would try for the nomination.

Only Texas and Pennsylvania were surely for Wilson. Colonel House came north in early April with assurances that the Texas delegation was solid; and, in Pennsylvania, Vance McCormick, A. Mitchell Palmer and William B. Wilson of the anthracite miners' union had the conservative machine on the run. But as spring advanced Wilson's hopes took a bad beating in the state primaries. When the delegates gathered in Baltimore in the midst of a ferocious heat wave Wilson's chances of nomination looked slimmer than at any time since his campaign began.

The day the convention was called to order, Colonel House, having written Wilson: "I have done everything I could up to now to advise and anticipate every contingency," embarked on the Cunarder *Laconia* for his customary summer trip to Europe. He was proving his detachment by planning a tour that would take him to Sweden and Finland and as far afield as Moscow. He had done his best, now he must care for his health.

William Jennings Bryan arrived in Baltimore fresh from the press gallery of the Republican convention in Chicago. There he had seen, with some satisfaction, Taft's nomination steamrollered through against the sullen opposition of the progressives, with the result that more than three hundred delegates turned in blank ballots and surged into Orchestra Hall to form the Progressive Party under the lash of Theodore Roosevelt's sibilant exhortations: "We stand at Armageddon and battle for the Lord."

The Commoner was convinced that the reforms for which he had so long cried in the wilderness were at last just under the horizon. If the Democrats nominated a candidate who might be labelled a reactionary T.R. would scoop up the progressive votes of both parties and might very well win. It was Bryan's business to keep the "interests"—typified in his mind by Whitney and Hearst and Thomas Fortune Ryan—from taking over the convention. During the long sweaty days and tumultuous nights in the Baltimore Armory it was Bryan's grizzled fringe of hair and craggy nose and wide lipless mouth, clenched above a continually beating palmleaf fan, that dominated the proceedings.

While the delegates braved heat prostration in Baltimore, Woodrow Wilson, at the governor's mansion at Sea Girt, was amazing his wife and daughters by his coolness and amusing them with imitations of T.R. in Chicago threshing his arms and whooping it up for Armageddon. "Good old Teddy," he would chuckle, "what a help he is."

Tumulty had a direct telephone line to campaign headquarters at the Emerson Hotel. The first problem his campaign manager McCombs put up to Wilson was whether to back Bryan in his fight for a progressive as chairman. McCombs wanted Wilson to hedge in the interests of harmony. As Eleanor Wilson tells the story, her father and the girls went up to her mother's bedroom to consult. Her mother was often poorly these days. They were already worried about her health. "There must be no hedging," was Mrs. Wilson's advice. "What's the use of having a principle if you don't stick to it," had always been her motto. Sitting on the edge of his wife's bed Wilson wrote out a telegram to Bryan: "You are quite right . . ."

All night Tumulty clung to the telephone, clocking the cheering that followed the nominating speeches. The Wilson crowd yelled for twenty minutes longer than Champ Clark's but when the balloting began Champ Clark was ahead. His strength increased until it was only the twothirds rule that kept him from the nomination.

Only Texas and Pennsylvania stood firm for Wilson. The galleries were all for Wilson; Wilson telegrams were pouring in; the Baltimore *Sun*, which was the first newspaper that came to the delegate's hand every morning, talked nothing but Wilson; but Clark still had the majority vote.

Bryan turned the tide. He early announced that he would oppose whatever candidate Tammany and the financial magnates stood for. After Boss Murphy had delivered his Tammany votes to what seemed to be a stampede for Clark, Bryan got to his feet and asked for the floor. His Nebraska delegation had been instructed for Clark and he had dutifully been voting for Clark. Now he declared he would cast his vote for Nebraska's second choice: Woodrow Wilson.

Still the Champ Clark forces seemed to be in control. Saturday morn-

ing McCombs called Governor Wilson to the phone. "The jig is up," Mc-
Combs said, and told Wilson to release his delegations. Wilson drafted a
telegram. Mrs. Wilson and the girls comforted each other by promising
themselves a long quiet summer on the English lakes.

It was William Gibbs McAdoo, the energetic promoter of the first
Hudson River tube, who had been promoting Wilson as energetically as
he had under river transportation, who first got wind of the telegram.
He bawled out McCombs and snatched for the telephone. He begged
Wilson not to quit; he assured him there was no conceivable way Clark
could get twothirds of the vote.

The convention went on and on. The Sunday that ended the first week
was a day of smoky hotel rooms, of finagling and palaver. It's hard to
imagine that Bryan was not still hoping against hope that maybe his
would be the name to break the deadlock.

On the Jersey coast the Wilsons went quietly to a little country church
at Spring Lake. In the afternoon the governor read Morley's life of Gladstone aloud to the family.

Meanwhile, according to the reporters, "the plain people of the hills"
were making their views felt. Telegrams kept coming in disclaiming any
candidate controlled by Tammany or Hearst or Thomas Fortune Ryan.

Monday morning the New York *World* ran an editorial saying that the
nomination of Wilson was the only way to save the election from Roosevelt. On the sixth day and the thirtieth ballot Wilson's total passed Champ
Clark's for the first time. Wilson told the newspapermen he was receiving the news with a riot of silence.

On the fortysixth ballot he was nominated.

At the governor's mansion at Sea Girt pandemonium ruled. Brass bands
played "Hail to the Chief" and "The Conquering Hero Comes." Every
room swarmed with reporters and with hoarse veterans of the Baltimore
Armory, each telling how singlehanded he had snatched Wilson's nomination out of the hands of the Wall Street interests. The ladies of the
family, whom Wilson liked to keep in what he considered a decent seclusion, were persecuted by featurewriters and photographers. Eleanor
Wilson told of finding her mother in the clutches of a peculiarly hard-
faced female journalist.

" 'Have you some sort of prejudice against jewelry Mrs. Wilson?' the
woman was asking. I realized how impossible it would be for her to understand why mother had no jewelry," Eleanor Wilson wrote in retro-
spect: "Mother, who had sacrificed for us, so that father might have the
books he needed, and the vacations; that we might study art and singing;
that there might be always room in the house for relatives and friends.
I thought of her rigid economy, her perennial brown dress and hat . . .
Mother said 'No, I have no prejudice against it. We just haven't any.' "

Chapter 4

In the campaign that followed all Governor Wilson needed to do was to address the throngs the faithful Tumulty marshalled on the lawn at Sea Girt, charming them with his calculated otherworldliness and with the "glittering generalities" that had disquieted George Record, while the Republicans tore each other to pieces.

For the Republicans it was a spite fight. La Follette excoriated T.R. T.R. excoriated Taft. Taft, who had been heard to growl that even a rat would fight if cornered, fought back. The occasional haymakers T.R. delivered in the direction of the Democratic candidate, whom he had not yet begun wholeheartedly to detest, went wide of the mark.

Liberty for the Oppressed

The dramatic moment came in October in Milwaukee when a crazy man put a bullet into T.R. as he was about to step out of an automobile to enter the hall where he was going to speak. His life was saved by the fact that the bullet was deflected by his glasses case and by the thick wad of the manuscript of his speech in his inside pocket. One of the doctors who examined him and found the bullet lodged next to a lung remarked that the heavy chest muscles T.R. had spent his life developing had helped too. Having done his best to protect the assassin from the frantic crowd T.R. strode up to the platform and before he allowed anything to be done about the wound hoarsely delivered his speech. He waved the perforated manuscript before the crowd and cried: "It takes more than that to kill a bull moose."

Woodrow Wilson's magnanimous gesture in calling off speaking engagements until Theodore Roosevelt's recovery was assured brought him wide acclaim.

As was the custom the campaigns culminated in Stanford White's Madison Square Garden in New York. Fresh from his hospital bed, T.R. delivered a speech which expressed better than anything any of the candidates said the aspirations of a people stirred by ten years of crusading against privilege and corruption:

"We are for human rights and intend to work for them. Where they can best be obtained by the application of the doctrine of states' rights, we are for states' rights. Where in order to obtain them, it is necessary to invoke the power of the Nation, then we shall invoke to its uttermost limits that mighty power. We are for liberty. But we are for the liberty of the oppressed, and not for the liberty of the oppressor to oppress the weak."

The standpat Republicans feared T.R. more than they feared Wilson. While their papers poured out abuse on Theodore Rex, as they called him, they gave the mild laissez-faire liberalism of the Schoolmaster in Politics respectful attention. In spite of the hymnsinging zeal of his followers it was already obvious that T.R.'s hastily improvised party could not win. The odds on Wall Street were six to one on Wilson.

The papers described the Madison Square meeting as a last salute to their leader from those about to die. Even the liberal New York *Evening Post* characterized T.R.'s final exhortations as a speech such as Custer might have made to his scouts when he saw the Indians coming.

On the night after the Roosevelt rally Wilson's joint managers McCombs and McAdoo, whose bickerings had been no help to his campaign, were able to work together long enough to foment an ovation when their candidate entered the hall that lasted one hour and four minutes. The Bull Moosers had worn themselves out after yelling fortyfive minutes for T.R. Wilson was able to exchange glances of happy triumph with his wife who sat in the box in front of him as he coolly proclaimed to an audience almost mad with enthusiasm: "All over the country, from one ocean to the other people are becoming aware that in less than a week the common people of America will come into their own again."

When the ballots were counted the result was Wilson (Democrat) 6,286,214; Roosevelt (Progressive) 4,126,020; Taft (Republican) 3,483,922 and Debs (Socialist) 897,011. The Democrats carried the Senate and the House. Wilson's 435 votes in the electoral college against Roosevelt's 88 and Taft's 8 constituted a record, but uncommitted commentators noted that Wilson had received a minority of the popular vote. The majority vote was a vote for reform. Almost half as many voters again voted for Eugene V. Debs as in 1908. It was a vote, in T.R.'s words, "for the liberty of the oppressed."

A few days after the election Senator La Follette expressed the yearnings of the reform element in an article in *La Follette's Weekly Magazine:* "Oppressed and heartsick, a nation of ninety million people, demanding plain, simple justice, striving for educational, political and industrial democracy, turned to Woodrow Wilson as the only present hope."

Four Years' Hard Labor

The governor's election disrupted the Wilsons' family life. Deserving Democrats in shoals converged on Princeton. "Our little house was a terrible mess" wrote daughter Eleanor, "and mother, for the first and only time in her life, walked through rooms pretending she didn't see the confusion and disorder . . . Even the tables and shelves in the studio were piled high and the easel was pushed aside to make room for efficient young women and their typewriters."

William F. McCombs, who considered himself the first Wilson for President man and felt he should be rewarded for his services by being made Secretary of State at least, was one of the first to appear. During the campaign Wilson had been disgusted by his erratic behavior, his drinking and his chumming up to the political bosses.

It was the businesslike McAdoo who had endeared himself to the Wilson family; so much so that, although he was twice her age and a widower with grown children, he had already fluttered the heart of daughter Eleanor.

According to McCombs' own story Woodrow Wilson told McCombs off in no uncertain terms and sent him away an enraged and frustrated man, to die a few years later, so his friends claimed, of a broken heart. "Before we proceed," he remembered Wilson as saying as soon as they were alone, giving him a cold gray stare through his eyeglasses, "I wish it clearly understood that I owe you nothing. Remember that God ordained that I should be the next President of the United States."

Fifteen thousand letters and telegrams poured into the little house on Cleveland Lane. McCombs was only the first of the parade of office-seekers. The Democrats had been out of office for twenty years. The Democrats were hungry.

Ten days after his election Wilson hurried his ladies aboard the *Bermudian* for a month's rest on his favorite island. He took along a single secretary and the now inevitable secretservice men. Only he and his wife knew how frayed his nerves were. His digestion was out of kilter. He was suffering from his old neuritis. He had to have quiet.

"As soon as I knew I had been sentenced to four years hard labor my first thought was to get away to Bermuda and enjoy my liberty while I might," he told the British official who greeted him at the dock. He begged the reporters and photographers to leave him alone. How tense he still was was shown by his blowup when he caught a photographer outside of the family cottage about to snap one of his daughters coming back hot and dusty from a bicycle ride, garbed, it was whispered, in bloomers. "You are no gentleman" he shouted at the astonished photographer. "If you want a good thrashing keep that up."

When his ship docked in New York the President-elect was met by prophets of doom. McCombs brought a rumor that the financial community was so alarmed by the prospect of a Democratic administration they were about to precipitate a panic. The bosses were filtering back into the State House at Trenton.

In a speech before the Southern Society the night after he arrived Wilson lashed out at "some gentlemen in New Jersey" who were counting the days until they could get rid of him. "I informed them today that they were not going to get rid of me." He was going to remain governor until the last moment. Of the rumors of panic on Wall Street he said, pushing out his sharp jaw in cold fury, "A panic is merely a state of mind . . . Frankly I do not believe there is any man living who dares use that machinery for that purpose. If he does, I promise him, not for myself but for my countrymen, a gibbet as high as Haman."

The Republican papers made a lot of the hanging high as Haman remark. The *Sun* printed a cartoon: "Lord High Executioner Wilson." Many of Wilson's supporters felt he had gone too far, but the Schoolmaster in Politics had let it be known that he intended to keep order in the classroom.

Founding an Administration

There was one haven of refuge from the importunities of the politicians and the clamors of party stalwarts trying to tell him whom he should appoint to his cabinet. That was Colonel House's quiet apartment in the Murray Hill section of New York. The colonel was discretion itself. No visitors were allowed to intrude. No telephone call got past the switchboard downstairs. With the colonel Wilson could talk over the pros and cons of cabinet appointments without feeling that something was being put over on him. Already he had expressed his trust in his Texas friend by offering him any office except Secretary of State.

House disclaimed any interest in holding office. "My reasons were," he noted in his diary, "that I am not strong enough to tie myself down to a cabinet department . . . I very much prefer being a free lance, and to advise with him concerning·matters in general, and to have a roving commission . . ."

"Take my word for it," a senator is quoted as having said of Colonel House, "he can walk on dead leaves and make no more noise than a tiger."

The President-elect's advisers mostly agreed that Bryan should be Secretary of State. Wilson owed his nomination to Bryan's steadfast opposition to Champ Clark. Bryan was the leader of progressive Democracy. Then too, as Finley Peter Dunne put it in his "Mr. Dooley" column: "With a brick in his hand he's as expert as a rifleman. An' I'd rather have him close to me bosom thin on me back."

McAdoo was to have the Treasury. Lindley M. Garrison, an able and uninspiring lawyer who presided over the chancery court of the state of New Jersey, became Secretary of War. Josephus Daniels, the genial social leveller and prohibitionist for whom Wilson felt real friendship, got the Navy. David F. Houston, an old friend of House's who had been president of the University of Texas, was to be Secretary of Agriculture. Another Texan, Albert S. Burleson, a professional of politics who led the Texas delegation in Baltimore, disposed of the presidential patronage as Postmaster General.

Among the lesser planets were Franklin K. Lane, a cheerful and garrulous San Francisco conservationist whom Daniels used to say reminded him of Humpty Dumpty, in the Interior; William Redfield, whose main claim to fame was that he was the last man in American politics to wear sidewhiskers, in the Department of Commerce; and William B. Wilson, who had come up out of the coalpits to become secretary-treasurer of the United Mine Workers under John Mitchell, filling the new post of Secretary of Labor. It was a cabinet heavily weighted with southerners and westerners. These were men more given to shirtsleeves than to frock coats.

Tumulty, who had served Wilson ably at Trenton, became the President's secretary. Talkative, warmhearted, somewhat scatterbrained in the violence of his party feelings, he became an effective buffer between the aloof President and the reporters and politicians who besieged the executive offices.

The Wilsons in the White House

The inaugural weather proved good. Wall Street remained calm. The threatened panic did not materialize. Except for the loss of a trunk containing the President's nightwear, the Wilson family, with its abundance of female relatives in attendance, was successfully transferred from the modest dwelling on Cleveland Lane to the great spaces of the White House.

When Woodrow Wilson turned towards the crowd after taking the oath on the Capitol portico, he saw the police pushing people back to clear a place in front of the stand. "Let the people come forward," he called in his clear tenor voice. Then looking into the upturned faces in front of him, he began: "My fellow citizens, there has been a change of government . . ."

The address was short and wellreceived. Lyman Abbott's *Outlook* hailed it as "the call of a prophet to a Nation to repent of its sins and return, not to the methods, but to the spirit of the Fathers."

The day after the inauguration the Wilsons entertained the entire Woodrow connection, with a few old friends mixed in, for lunch; and the Wilson cousins, to the number of twentyfive, for dinner. During the afternoon the President shook hands with one thousand, one hundred and twentythree persons at a public reception and received, in the Blue Room, with the punctilious assistance of Mr. "Ike" Hoover, the chief usher—who had been conducting such ceremonies ever since he was called to the White House to help install the first electrical wiring in Benjamin Harrison's day—the ambassador of Great Britain.

Ambassador James Bryce was a wiry ruddyfaced little man with white hair and beard and an energetic manner of speaking. For many years Bryce had been one of the idols of Woodrow Wilson's life. Of similar Scotch Presbyterian lineage, Bryce too had come a long way since Wilson, as an impecunious graduate student, heard him lecture at Johns Hopkins.

It was a career such as young Wilson dreamed of for himself in those days. Bryce had not only won fame as a writer on constitutional law and democratic government and as traveller and mountainclimber, but had become one of the voices of the nonconformist conscience in England in the agitation against Turkish oppression of the Armenians, of which he had personal experience while on an expedition to ascend Mount Ararat. He sat in Parliament, served in Gladstone's last cabinet, was president of the Board of Trade and occupied the uneasy eminence of Secretary for Ireland under Campbell-Bannerman. He twice refused a peerage.

Sent to Washington during T.R.'s second term he had negotiated with the United States one of those arbitration conventions liberalminded men hoped were the forerunners of the rule of law in the civilized world. Now his chief preoccupation was the friendly settlement of the problem of tolls in the Panama Canal which was soon to be open for traffic. No Britisher alive was better suited by temperament and training to hit it off with Woodrow Wilson.

If Bryce looked forward to a renewal of the easy hospitality of the Roosevelt days, when he found the White House the center of the best brains and the most amusing conversation in Washington, he was to be disappointed. The new President, though he had his charming moments and was quite a wag in the privacy of his family circle, was to prove singularly lacking in the social graces.

In the White House even more than at Princeton, Wilson took refuge from the racket and glare of public life, which T.R. had frankly enjoyed and Taft had goodhumoredly tolerated, in the inner circle of his wife and daughters and admiring female cousins. He was desperately determined that his fireside should be his own.

Tumulty's domain stopped at the entrance to the presidential suite. Colonel House was admitted but very few others from the outside world. Dr. Grayson was the exception.

Like Ike Hoover, Cary T. Grayson, a navy surgeon with rank of lieutenant, had been a White House familiar for some years. As a young man he was one of the party on T.R.'s breakneck ride to Warrenton and back in one day. He was a friend of the agreeable Archie Butt who was Roosevelt's and then Taft's military aide and perished on the *Titanic*. He served Taft as medical aide. Taft took a fancy to him. Entertaining the incoming President at their last White House tea, the Tafts recommended him warmly to the Wilsons.

Then when President Wilson's sister Mrs. Howe fell on the steps and cut her forehead in the scramble of inauguration day Lieutenant Grayson tended her so assiduously that the Wilsons were captivated. Grayson was a Virginian. The President liked his Culpeper County accent and his selfeffacing demeanor. Immediately he asked Josephus Daniels to attach him permanently to the White House. Dr. Grayson found himself coping with a fit of dyspepsia and sick headaches into which the President had been thrown by the strain of the inaugural festivities. Instead of going to church his first Sunday in the White House Dr. Grayson ordered him to stay in bed and rest. It was good advice.

Woodrow Wilson was desperately trying to keep his head in the turmoil. "At least Washington and Jefferson had time to think," he remarked bitterly.

The President on Capitol Hill

His opinion of the position of the President had changed with the times. Before his inauguration he wrote A. Mitchell Palmer, a fervent supporter in the Pennsylvania delegation at Baltimore who was carried into Congress on the crest of the Wilson wave: "The President is expected by the Nation to be the leader of his party as well as the Chief Executive officer of the Government, and the country will take no excuses from him. He must play the part and play it successfully or lose the country's confidence. He must be prime minister, as much concerned with the guidance of legislation as with the just and orderly execution of the law, and he is the spokesman of the nation in everything even in the most momentous and delicate dealings of the Government with foreign nations."

Wilson had hardly been installed in the White House before he let it be known that he was going to use the President's Room at the Capitol to confer with congressional leaders on important legislation. Since Jefferson had given up reading the President's messages in person no President had appeared in the legislative chambers. Shocked horror and cries of "Federalism," "tawdry imitation of English royalty," and the like, met his announcement that on April 8 he would deliver in person his first message to the special session of Congress he had immediately called to consider revision of the tariff.

This breaking with a centuryold tradition assured the new President a breathless crowd in the galleries and the attention of the entire nation when he walked in to address the joint session. Friends noticed his pallor, a certain constraint about his erect figure. He took his place at the desk of the reading clerk, just below the speaker's chair. The atmosphere was tense. Southern congressmen particularly were fidgety about this reckless innovation.

The moment he began to speak the strain was relieved. His voice was beguiling. He spoke with just a trace of humor of "verifying for himself the impression that the President of the United States was a person, a human being trying to cooperate with other human beings in a common service."

He spoke for only ten minutes. He spoke of squaring tariff duties with the actual facts: "We must abolish everything that bears even the semblance of privilege . . . and put our business men and producers under the stimulation of a constant necessity to be efficient, economical, and enterprising, masters of competitive supremacy, better workers and merchants than any in the world."

The speech was received with resounding applause. Driving back to the White House down the Mall, Ellen Wilson, delighted with the success of her husband's defiance of tradition, said it was "the sort of thing Theodore Roosevelt would have liked to do if only he'd thought of it."

The President laughed. "Yes I think I put one over on Teddy."

The Most Momentous and Delicate Dealings

Foreign affairs had been T.R.'s personal playground during his presidency. Taft, trained in the Philippines and as Secretary of War, tended to see the world as a whole; in his quiet way he supported every move towards peace by arbitration. Although careful listeners could already detect the ticking of the time bomb in Europe, Woodrow Wilson had ignored all mankind outside of the borders of the United States in his pronouncements during the 1912 campaign. A few found it odd. In the four months between his election and his inauguration, many an unwanted foreign fowl came home to roost.

Twentyfive years after the French project ended in pestilence and bankruptcy the Panama Canal was nearing completion. T.R.'s manner of achieving it had left problems for his successors. The secession of Panama was admittedly a farce, but the brazenness of its buffoonery left hurt feelings. There was the little matter of Colombian sovereignty which T.R. had laughed off as the delusion of greedy Latin politicos. Taft had been trying to put a legal face on the proceedings by negotiating a treaty as a form of heart balm for the government in Bogotá. Three weeks before Wilson's inauguration Colombia rejected the Taft proposals.

When Ambassador Bryce called on the newly elected President he may not have mentioned tolls, but he surely had tolls on his mind. The Hay-Pauncefote Treaty between Great Britain and the United States, replacing the earlier treaty calling for joint management of some future isthmian canal, had stipulated that all nations were to have equal treatment, but Congress had lightheartedly passed a bill exempting American coast to coast shipping from paying any tolls at all. The Foreign Office sent Bryce to Washington with the idea of using his unique prestige among Americans to secure the repeal of that measure. After that he was planning on retirement.

Roosevelt's diplomacy had been all his own, a mixture of aggressive nationalism and shrewd sense. Under Taft the flag had followed the dollar. Now Wilson and Bryan were determined to extend the blessings of democratic justice to all the world. How to go about it?

Wrongdoing abounded abroad and at home. The California legislature was passing exclusion acts against the Japanese. President Wilson had hardly settled at his desk in the executive office before the Japanese ambassador appeared to present a protest. Since defeating the Russians the Japanese were in no mood to accept discrimination.

Western ideas were stirring in the Far East. In China a republic had been proclaimed. Wilson's first conversations with his newly installed Secretary of State dealt with the terms of a loan the European powers were trying to force on the backward Chinese.

The Caribbean was uneasy. Trouble was popping everywhere. In Mexico a revolution was on the march. Rifles bristled out of every adobe hut. Two weeks before Wilson's inauguration, Francisco Madero, whom American Democrats had hailed as a kindred spirit when he displaced the old Mixtec dictator, Porfirio Díaz, a few months before, was shot full of lead by a new strong man named Victoriano Huerta. The reform wave that had swept the United States was agitating the Mexicans, but south of the Rio Grande the revolt against the vested interests took the form of arson and murder.

"It would be the irony of fate," Wilson told a Princeton friend when he heard the news, "if my administration had to deal chiefly with foreign affairs."

The Tariff for Revenue Only

In spite of storms brewing on every frontier Wilson's first duty was to his campaign commitments. In a rare burst of legislative energy, Congress, under the President's skillful prodding, passed two basic measures during the first nine months of his administration.

Tariff for revenue only had long been a Democratic motto. The Underwood Tariff Act, pushed through the two houses during the summer, accomplished the first thoroughgoing downward revision of import duties since 1846.

For years the reformers had dreamed of an income tax to syphon off the guilty profits of the rich. A small progressive income tax, made possible by a constitutional amendment ratified by the states a couple of years before, was included ostensibly to make up for the loss of revenue. The bill was ready for signature by October 3.

"I have had the accomplishment of something like this at heart ever since I was a boy" the President cried out exultantly to the assembled cabinet members, congressmen and reporters who packed into the executive office to see him affix his Woodrow Wilson with two gold pens, "and I know men standing around me who can say the same thing, who have been waiting to see the things done which it was necessary to do in order that there might be justice in the United States."

The Federal Reserve

At the same time a far more intricate and controversial measure was in the works.

Breaking up what Bryan and his followers called the money trust was a shibboleth of the southern and western uprising against Wall Street which had landed the new administration in Washington. The management of the currency of the United States, and consequently of credit and finance, was admittedly chaotic and outdated. Conservatives and progressives agreed that the state of affairs where some seven thousand banks could issue money under the vague direction of a Comptroller of the Currency was a breeder of panics. For some years Senator Aldrich, heading a committee that sought the guidance of the New York bankers, had been working for legislation which would centralize the banking system. Nobody denied the need. The question at issue was who would run the new system, the bankers or the representatives of the people.

The construction of the Federal Reserve Act out of a welter of conflicting interests and conflicting dogmas was one of the great successes of the congressional system.

It would never have come to pass if Woodrow Wilson had not managed to make himself the leader of the whole Democratic Party, instead of merely its progressive wing; and if he had not shown, during that first summer of his administration, an unexpected ability to learn by doing. Finance was not his special province, but he eagerly soaked up information from such men as the reforming Louis D. Brandeis, who was then considered a dangerous firebrand by the conservatives, and from banker friends McAdoo smuggled into the White House when Bryan wasn't looking. It was the President himself who suggested the Federal Reserve Board, which made control in the public interest a workable proposition.

At first the bare notion of such a board horrified both sides. Bryan's followers claimed it would create "an oligarchy of boundless wealth . . . to govern the financial destiny of the nation, operating under governmental protection." Conservatives were equally revolted. The New York *Sun* described the President's project as "the preposterous offspring of ignorance and unreason . . . The provision for a government agency and an official board to exercise absolute control over the most important of banking functions is covered all over with the slime of Bryanism."

Virginia Representative Carter Glass, who, starting from a printshop in Lynchburg, became publisher and owner of his smalltown papers, and developed into the southern congressman best qualified to deal with fiscal matters, steered the bill through the House. Robert L. Owen, a stockman and banker from Oklahoma, who had been a careful student of European banking systems, steered it through the Senate. Secretary Bryan did yeoman service keeping his radicals in order once the President had convinced him the measure was the nearest thing to public control of banking that could be achieved at that time. Secretary McAdoo, meanwhile, whose promotion of the Hudson tubes had won the admiration of the business community, cajoled the conservatives.

Throughout the hot summer and the long fall the President managed to simulate an air of coolness and equanimity while he conducted the general strategy from the White House. In private he blew off steam:

"Why should public men, senators of the United States, have to be led and stimulated to do what all the country knows is their duty—" he wrote Mrs. Peck, finding it hard, as usual, to imagine that any man in his right mind could honestly disagree with him on any topic whatsoever. "Why should they see less clearly, apparently, than anyone else what the straight path of service is? To whom are they listening? Certainly not to the voice of the people, when they quibble and twist and hesitate . . . A man of my temperament, and my limitations will certainly wear himself out on it . . . the danger is that he may lose his patience and suffer the weakness of exasperation."

The Carabao

When President Wilson did lose his patience "and suffer the weakness of exasperation" his wrath found an unexpected target. There existed in Washington a branch of an organization of veterans of the Philippine insurrections know as the Military Order of the Carabao. The Carabao's annual celebrations were bibulous affairs with skits and spoofing of public officials in the spirit of the Gridiron dinners conducted by the press. They were accompanied by the singing of old warsongs like "There's Many a Man Been Murdered in Luzon," and "Damn Damn Damn the Filipinos." No one had ever taken their jollifications seriously until one December morning while the tug of war over the Currency Bill which was to set up the Federal Reserve was still undecided on Capitol Hill, the Schoolmaster in Politics read a facetious account of the antics of the local corral of the Carabao in his morning paper.

He was not at all amused. He decided to give the military a lesson.

Wilson's policy towards the Philippines was a cautious advance in the direction of selfgovernment and his pronouncements on the subject had been received with jubilation in Manila. The oldtime jingos of the regular army viewed independence for the little brown brethren with derision.

Though not a prohibitionist himself Wilson had appointed two prohibitionists to his cabinet. Bryan was refusing to allow wine to be served at his state dinners and Josephus Daniels would soon go so far as to cut off the Navy's traditional grog.

Here was a bunch of army officers poking fun at the Democratic Party's Philippine policy, insulting the Filipinos with slanderous ditties and holding Secretary Bryan's grape juice suppers up to ridicule. Wilson went after them like a college president cracking down on student pranksters. It was all Daniels and Garrison could do to argue him out of hauling the general officers involved up before a courtmartial. They compromised on a reprimand.

The President administered the chastisement personally in a letter which, to the embarrassment of all concerned, he gave to the press. "What are we to think of officers of the Army and Navy of the United States who think it fun to bring their official superiors into ridicule and the policies of the government . . . into contempt? If they do not hold their loyalty above all silly effervescences of childish wit, what about their profession do they hold sacred?"

The Days Go Hard with Me

Wilson had stuck to his desk for nine solid months with only a few short breathers in the country. His nerves were taut to the breaking point. During the summer he poured out his feelings in a letter to Mrs. Reid, another of the sympathetic matrons he liked to tell his troubles to:

"The days go hard with me just now. I am alone. My dear ones went away almost at my command. I could not have been easy about them had they not gone; and we have found a nest for them in New Hampshire . . . where they have just the right airs, a beautiful country around them, and most interesting neighbors . . . These are stern days, and this all but empty house fits well with them. My secretary [Tumulty] is living with me and the young naval doctor who is of my staff [Grayson] . . . I work hard of course (the amount of work a President is supposed to do is preposterous) but it is not that that tells on a fellow. It's the anxiety of handling such 'things' as that scoundrel Huerta . . . I play golf every afternoon—[this was part of Dr. Grayson's regime of 'preventive medicine']—because while you are playing golf you *cannot* worry and be preoccupied with affairs . . . I have myself well in hand. I find that I am often cooler in my mind than some of those about me. And of course I find a real zest in it all . . . So far things go very well and my leadership is most loyally and graciously accepted even by men of whom I did not expect it. I hope that this is in part because they perceive that I am pursuing no private and selfish purposes of my own. How could a man do that with such responsibilities resting on him!"

Two days before Christmas the President had his reward. He triumphantly signed the Federal Reserve Act in the presence of the ladies of the family in their billowing frocks and of the Speaker of the House and members of the congressional committees and his cabinet officers, with tall giraffenecked McAdoo towering above them grinning in his tight stiff collar. There was the usual distribution of gold pens to the deserving. Wilson spoke modestly of his satisfaction ". . . that I played a part in completing a work which I think will be of lasting benefit."

This was statebuilding as he had dreamed of it. The New York *Times* reporter spoke of the look of radiant happiness on Mrs. Wilson's face. She had reason to feel exultant. The establishment of the Federal Reserve system was possibly the most lasting achievement of her husband's career.

The New Freedom Abroad

Immediately after the ceremony the Wilson family embarked on a private car for a much needed holiday at Pass Christian on the Gulf of Mexico. They had hardly time to enjoy their Christmas tree and to wish each other a Happy New Year before the President became thoroughly preoccupied with new complications in his campaign to oust "that scoundrel Huerta" from the presidency of Mexico. His disinterestedness was not appreciated south of the Rio Grande. The Mexican politicians were not accepting his leadership as "loyally and graciously" as did the Democratic politicians on Capitol Hill.

On January 2, 1914, the cruiser *Chester*, after dashing at full steam across the Gulf from Vera Cruz, dropped anchor off Gulfport, Mississippi. Under conditions of considerable secrecy the President went out on a launch to confer for some hours with a large blond civilian on board the warship. This gentleman was the Honorable John Lind, Swedishborn retired governor of Minnesota, Bryan supporter and deserving Democrat, who had been chosen for no reason that anyone could imagine, unless his ignorance of Spanish and his lack of any Mexican experience qualified him as unprejudiced, to be the President's personal representative in Mexico. At that conference Mr. Lind and Mr. Wilson decided to back the northern Mexican revolutionaries against Huerta. For a pacifist John Lind had remarkable faith in the efficacy of arms.

Ever since the inauguration the President had been carrying out a policy described as of "watchful waiting" towards the revolutions and counterrevolutions in Mexico. To implement that policy he had been using every possible means to bypass the Embassy in Mexico City. Wilson was even more suspicious of professional diplomats than of professional military men.

In this case there was some justification for his suspicions. When the unfortunate Madero called on General Huerta, who had grown up as a career man in Díaz's army, to suppress a *cuartelazo* engineered by members of the old regime, Huerta joined with Díaz's nephew Felix, to suppress Madero instead. This act of treachery was carried out with the blessing of Taft's ambassador, Henry Lane Wilson. In fact the written agreement between the two counterrevolutionaries was known as "the pact of the Embassy."

Neither Wilson nor Bryan had personal experience with any but Englishspeaking people. Their Mexican policy consisted of trying to find Americanstyle reformers in the Democratic tradition among the warring bands which Madero's assassination and Huerta's assumption of power had launched on the warpath.

There was Zapata pillaging the haciendas of the sugar barons in the south under the banner of "land and schools for the peons."

In Chihuahua, Francisco Villa, recent convert from professional banditry to revolutionary idealism, was showing a genius for guerrilla fighting and building himself a small empire out of the ruined holdings of the *científicos*.

In Coahuila, Venustiano Carranza, *maderista* governor, whose long white beard added respectability to his cause, proclaimed himself First Chief of the constitutionalist forces pledged to reestablish law and order and to continue Madero's program of rational reform. After talking to Lind, Wilson decided that Carranza was his man.

"That scoundrel Huerta," idolized as chief by the regular army, held the capital and central Mexico and the railroads to Vera Cruz and to the oil port of Tampico. He had the support of most of the foreign powers, and the sympathy of Mexican and American business interests. Seventeen nations had recognized his government. Particularly the British looked to Huerta to protect their investments and keep order as old Díaz had for forty years.

The British had reason to be anxious about Tampico. His Majesty's fleet had recently switched from coal to oil and Mexico was its main source of supply. With such support Huerta remained unmoved by admonitions from Washington to retire and hold free elections.

When Huerta did announce elections he got ready for them by dissolving the largely maderista congress and arresting a hundred and ten of its members. For Wilson this was the last straw. Forcing out Huerta became an obsession.

The Foreign Office was amazed; but Sir Edward Grey was willing to make sacrifices to keep the good will of the new administration in Washington. The British began to intimate in their sly unspoken way that they might reconsider their support of Huerta in exchange for the President's help in doing away with the exemption of American shipping from paying tolls in the Panama Canal which, in spite of landslides in the Culebra cut, was well on its way to completion.

Bryce had retired with his aim still unachieved, and T.R.'s old friend Cecil Spring Rice was slated to replace him. Meanwhile Colonel House brought Foreign Minister Grey's private secretary Sir William Tyrrell to call on the President at the White House.

"We all spoke with the utmost candor and without diplomatic gloss," House noted in his diary. "If some of the veteran diplomats could have heard us they would have fallen in a faint," the Britisher confided to House after they left the executive office.

The British washed their hands of Huerta. From that moment on the Mexican problem was in Uncle Sam's lap.

Mr. Bryan's Thirty Treaties

Bryan was only too glad to leave the day to day administration of foreign affairs to the President. As Secretary of State he felt that his historic function was to negotiate arbitration treaties. He was convinced he had found an infallible remedy for war.

Back in 1905 in an article in *The Commoner* he had suggested that all the differences between nations should be submitted to a court of arbitration. If nations could agree to a year's cooling off period while some sort of neutral factfinding commission investigated their causes of friction, declarations of war would be postponed long enough to let hot tempers cool.

He explained his plan more in detail in an address to the Interparliamentary Union in London in the summer of 1906. James Bryce called it "certainly splendid." The English press reported the project with enthusiasm. Arbitration was officially endorsed by the Interparliamentary Union and by the Liberal government. Bryan's evangel appealed to the nonconformist conscience then in the ascendant in Britain. Great hopes were raised.

After Roosevelt failed to induce the Senate to ratify his arbitration treaties, Bryan, who was drumming up his plan before Chautauquas and at peace conferences all over the country, urged Taft to try again. At a meeting with Taft and Elihu Root he convinced them that his plan was practical and that it would find popular backing in Great Britain and at least in the smaller European countries. Taft's arbitration treaties met the same fate as T.R.'s.

As soon as Bryan was installed as Secretary of State he went to work. He used all his skill in political manoeuvering and all his powers of persuasion. Before he accepted the office he showed a sample treaty to Woodrow Wilson for his approval. One of his first acts was to call together the entire diplomatic corps and ask them to submit his proposals to their governments.

The warmth of his dedication to the cause of peace melted the icy scepticism of the professional diplomats. Using the arts of compromise and cajolement he had acquired working with platform committees at many a party convention he allowed the treaties to be worded to suit the individual prejudices of the various governments. While trying to save the spirit he conceded the letter. Starting with San Salvador and the Netherlands he negotiated a first batch of eighteen arbitration treaties, and took them in person to the Senate. Germany was one of the few countries that refused.

Bryan had a knack with politicians, and especially with senators. "I

remained in the office of the Clerk of the Senate two days while the treaties were being discussed, answering questions as they arose," he wrote.
While the treaties were being drafted he had taken the precaution of
consulting the Senate Committee on Foreign Affairs in advance on every
provision. Where the two previous Republican administrations had failed,
Bryan, by his conciliatory manner and his personal prestige with Democratic politicians, blarneyed the Senate into ratification.

Bryan's chest swelled with pride under his piqué vest. For years he had
been throwing all the organ notes of his voice into his favorite oration,
which he called "the Prince of Peace."

At the celebration of the hundredth anniversary of the signing of the
Treaty of Ghent that ended the War of 1812, his optimism rose to the
point where he dared exclaim: "We know of no cause today that cannot
better be settled by reason than by war. I believe there will be no war
while I am Secretary of State . . . I hope we have seen the last great war."

At the formal signing of a large batch of the treaties, amid the whir of
motion picture cameras and the jostling of journalists, a lifesized oil painting was unveiled of Mr. Bryan with an arbitration treaty in his hand.

The Secretary had induced his friend Secretary of the Navy Daniels to
have a set of paperweights made for him from some old steel swords at
the Navy Yard. They were cast in the form of a plowshare and engraved
with two quotations: one the soothing words Mr. Bryan himself used when
the Japanese ambassador complained about the treatment of his nationals in California: "Nothing is final between friends"; and the other the
more familiar phrase from Isaiah about beating swords into plowshares.
These he distributed to the signatory diplomats as mementos of the
occasion.

Chapter 5

THE RED MAN

WHILE Bryan was happily signing arbitration treaties and assuring Chautauquas and summer conferences that the triumph of peace was at hand, more wary observers of the international scene were expressing misgivings. A few months after the inauguration of Wilson's administration, T.R.'s friend Spring Rice—then representing the British in Stockholm —wrote Henry Adams asking for his impressions of "the professor's victory." He went on to describe the mounting tension in Europe.

In a sort of code used by the intimates of Henry Adams' and John Hay's twin houses on Lafayette Square the spirit of militarism was in those days called "The Red Man." "Isn't it curious," Spring Rice wrote Uncle Henry, as he called him, "that we are all supposing ourselves to be standing on the edge of the most terrific disaster (for Europe) which has ever taken place. Even the hardened dip. looks a little solemn when the subject is alluded to at dinner. The appearance of the Red Man in a particularly realistic manner, in the middle of the cocked hats and laced coats, had had rather a calming effect"—he was talking about the latest outbreak of war in the Balkans, which he feared might be the beginning of something worse— "We shall have some red spots on our white kid gloves. But this isn't yet the real thing. Austria may have given the order which may lead Europe to a several-years' war"—he was referring to Austrian efforts to keep the southern Slavic nations from getting a port on the Adriatic—"but it is singular to think how tremendous are the calamities that may be brought about at any moment by one slight act, based on what look to you the meanest motives. As a matter of fact it is a peoples' question, the struggle for existence between races; and this struggle has been going on for ages and perhaps the moment for the decisive struggle has come."

The Dragon's Teeth

The Red Man was indeed at large. In Mexico and in the Balkans armed bands fought and murdered and raped and burned. While the armies of civilized Europe marched and countermarched in more and more realistic

manoeuvers, the "hardened dips" of the foreign chancelleries cooperated
with Bryan and his aides in the State Department as they would humor
some child's game. Perhaps it eased their consciences a little to mutter
little prayers for peace at a time when every move they made on the
chessboard of power politics brought war nearer.

Woodrow Wilson, sitting long hours at his solitary typewriter upstairs
in the White House, was conducting the relations of the United States
with the Mexican revolutionists in such a way as to keep the diplomats
thoroughly puzzled.

At the end of January 1914 Spring Rice, who was just settling down at
the British Embassy in Washington, described the situation in a letter to
Sir Edward Grey's secretary:

"The President has maintained and rather increased his influence in
Congress and in the country, but he is as mysterious as ever. When he
summons the newspaper men he talks to them at length and in excellent
language, but when they leave his presence they say to each other, What
on earth did he say? When he sees the members of Congress he reads
them a lecture and tells them what he thinks is good for them to know,
which appears to them to be very little. He asks the advice of no one."

In Mexico armed men kept springing up from the blood of the dead
Madero. His mystique of democracy spread in strange forms to even the
remotest hamlets where Spanish was hardly spoken, much as the reforming zeal of the Theodore Roosevelt era infected the North American
backlands with a yearning for righteousness. In the United States the reforms took legal shape according to the ancient traditions of Anglo-Saxon
comity; but in Mexico the young men who trooped out of the mountain
cornfields and the dry maguey plantations and the irrigated sugarcane
to make a revolution, found themselves slaves of the only social formation
they knew outside of the communal village and the hacienda: the robber
band under a chieftain who enforced his will with the gun.

The Mexicans remained puzzling to Woodrow Wilson to the last.

A Constant and Intolerable Annoyance

He had family perplexities too. Right along he had hated the idea of
his daughters having beaux. At Princeton his sarcasms tore to pieces the
young men the girls occasionally ventured to bring home to meals. Jessie
managed to win her father's approval of a college professor and married
him. "The pang of it is still deep in my heart," the President wrote Mrs.
Peck after the wedding.

Now Eleanor, after an effort to keep her engagement secret for fear of
her father's wrath, was about to marry his Secretary of the Treasury. The

press, inevitably nosy about the doings of nubile young women in the White House, was filling the society pages with rumors of Eleanor's and Margaret's engagement to this man and that. One day the President betrayed his underlying tension by lashing out at the newspapermen Tumulty worked so hard to keep in a cosy frame of mind.

"I am a public character for the time being," he announced at a press conference, his sharp jaw jutting and his eyes flashing behind his noseglasses, "but the ladies of my household are not servants of the government and they are not public characters. I deeply resent the treatment they are receiving at the hands of the newspapers . . . It is a constant and intolerable annoyance . . . If this continues," he glowered into the embarrassed faces assembled in front of his desk, "I shall deal with you, not as President, but as man to man."

The men trudged out of the oval office like schoolboys who had been tonguelashed by the headmaster.

It was hard for Wilson to keep his serenity amid so many worries. His greatest anxiety was about his wife. Ellen Wilson's health was worse. She had a fall in her room one day, but she wouldn't stay in bed. She laughed off her symptoms, appealing from their father to her daughters. "This goose keeps worrying about me for no reason at all."

She was busy with a private project. While her husband worried about the Colorado mine strike, and the need to send troops to the Mexican border to keep the bandits from spilling over into United States territory, and busied himself piloting antitrust legislation through Congress, Ellen Wilson was lobbying for a bill of her own. As a southerner she had been raised to look out for the wellbeing of Negroes. Now in Washington she found families living in back alleys under conditions she felt were a disgrace to the national capital. She joined the group of social workers to get through a bill to clean up these conditions. All her ebbing strength, all her quiet charm and winsome ways, went into backing her housing bill.

In April the President stole a few days off to take his wife to White Sulphur Springs. He was trying to believe that the change of air would do her good. A nurse went along.

The Dignity of the United States

The presidential party had hardly settled at the Greenbrier before a dispatch from Secretary Bryan appeared on Wilson's breakfast table. Huerta's commander at Tampico had arrested a navy paymaster and the crew of a ship's boat flying the American flag. The detention was short but Admiral Mayo, in command of the American fleet hovering off the

Mexican coast, was demanding the punishment of the guilty Mexicans and a twentyone gun salute in apology for the insult to the flag.

The President hurried back to Washington. For a week the cables back and forth to the chargé d'affaires, who replaced the recalled ambassador in Mexico City, resounded with that twentyone gun salute.

Huerta was sorry. His officers were sorry. It had all been a mistake. Huerta offered to arbitrate the dispute at The Hague.

The President refused. Arbitration would mean recognizing the blood-stained old drunkard. Instead he delivered himself of an ultimatum, giving Huerta until April 19 to salute the American flag. "People seem to want a war with Mexico," he told his daughters when they brought their mother back from the springs, "but they shan't have it if I can prevent it."

To Wilson this seemed the chance he'd been looking for to put the Mexican dictator out of office. To Huerta it looked like a chance to rally the Mexican people behind him. Already his prestige was rising so that wealthy Mexicans were subscribing to a loan to be used to buy munitions for his army.

When the news reached Washington that a shipment of arms was about to be landed at Vera Cruz from the Hamburg-America steamer *Ypiranga,* Wilson went before the two houses of Congress and obtained a joint resolution empowering him to use the army and navy to enforce his demands. The yellow press was all for cleaning up "the mess in Mexico." Western senators even talked of taking over Central America clear to the Panama Canal.

Meanwhile Bryan and Wilson decided that, since no state of war existed and they didn't intend it should exist, it would be most incorrect to seize the cargo off a friendly ship on the high seas. They must wait until the shipment was unloaded and seize the arms on Mexican soil.

At eleven in the morning on April 21, 1914, a thousand marines landed from the American fleet off Vera Cruz and occupied the customhouse. The Mexicans fought back. Another three thousand men had to be landed next day. Before quiet was restored in Vera Cruz a hundred and twenty-six Mexicans were dead and the American forces had lost nineteen dead and seventyone wounded.

President Wilson was very profoundly shocked.

Some good came of the affair. The sanitary methods which had proved successful in Cuba and in Panama were applied to the area occupied by American troops to the lasting benefit of the *veracruzanos,* and the dreadful old fortress prison of San Juan de Ullúa was opened to the light of day and its miserable victims turned loose.

The violation of Mexican soil, if it didn't unite the warring factions in support of Huerta, at least gave unanimity to their hatred of the gringos. American consulates were burned, American property was looted, Americans were murdered. The cry of indignation resounded throughout Latin America and found a selfrighteous echo in the London press.

Sober opinion in the United States, particularly among the reforming element the President depended on for support, was almost wholly against him. In one of his moments of selfdeception he had told the reporters the day before the landing that the purpose of the naval demonstration was not to eliminate Huerta but "to compell the recognition of the dignity of the United States . . . I have no enthusiasm for war but I have enthusiasm for the dignity of the United States."

The President became entangled in his own contradictions. There was a general outcry against going to war over a mere matter of prestige. Andrew Carnegie's was one of thousands of messages of protest. He reminded Wilson of Gulliver's adventures in Lilliput: this was like "the fabled war of two kings to decide which end of the egg should first be broken."

The incident ended with the flight of Americans from Mexico, and a cordon of troops spread along the Mexican border. The Administration renewed the embargo on arms to the constitutionalists. Except for Villa, who tried to curry favor in Washington by pretending to be delighted, the constitutionalists were protesting even more vigorously than their enemy Huerta against the Yankee invasion.

An initiative, which had the bland encouragement of Colonel House, from three Latin-American ambassadors, Naon of Argentina, de Gama of Brazil and Suarez Mújica of Chile, gave the Administration a chance to retire from an impossible position. The three ambassadors offered to mediate between the various Mexican factions and between the Mexicans and Washington.

The Mexican problem was taken behind closed doors at one of the resort hotels at Niagara Falls. The mediation of the "A.B.C." powers, if it did not do much to alleviate the anarchic situation in Mexico, at least did something to convince the rest of Latin America that the United States was not planning an invasion. United States citizens could once more venture out on the streets in Latin-American towns without having stones thrown at them.

To Die in a War of Service

On May 11, 1914, three days after his daughter Eleanor's marriage to Secretary McAdoo, President Wilson rode in the New York funeral procession of seventeen of the navy men killed at Vera Cruz. Enormous crowds packed Broadway under the halfmast flags. In front of the Marine Barracks at the Brooklyn Navy Yard the President delivered an address to serve as their funeral oration.

It would have been disgraceful to die in a war of aggression, he said, but "to die in a war of service is glorious." In landing at Vera Cruz Americans had been performing a service for the Mexican people. "I never was under fire but I fancy it is just as hard to do your duty when men are sneering at you as when they are shooting at you . . . The cheers of the moment are not what a man ought to think about but the verdict of his conscience and the conscience of mankind."

It was a very hot day. The sun beat down on the ranks of bluejackets and marines at parade rest. A crowd of ten thousand people broke through the police lines and milled around on the Navy Yard. Nineteen women fainted and several small children narrowly escaped being trampled. Members of the official party noticed that the President's face showed deep emotion when he looked down on the seventeen guncarriages and the flagcovered coffins: it was by his orders that these young men had gone to their deaths.

That evening the President and Dr. Grayson dined in the seclusion of Colonel House's apartment at 135 East Thirtyfifth Street. Wilson was in a relaxed frame of mind. Public speaking always made him feel better. After supper Wilson read some of his favorite poems out of Wordsworth and Matthew Arnold and Keats aloud to the small company. Grayson tactfully took his leave. "When he finished reading," noted the colonel, "I took up my budget."

Though there was class war in Colorado between miners and mine-owners to talk about, and Mexico still seethed south of the border, most of the colonel's budget dealt with Europe.

The Great Adventure

Colonel House was preparing to sail on the first of his missions as the President's personal representative. Woodrow Wilson was about to take a hand in European affairs. He was about to try, as Theodore Roosevelt had tried, to talk, quietly behind the scenes, some sense into the heads of the great powers. Behind his poker face and deferential manner the colonel felt the excitement of a schoolboy who's just been elected captain of the football team. In the privacy of his diary he wrote of the coming trip as The Great Adventure.

He went first to Germany. The Germans put themselves out for him. Since the days of T.R. American prestige had been high with the Kaiser. House found a worse state of affairs than he possibly could have imagined. After a talk with Admiral Von Tirpitz he reported to the President by diplomatic pouch: "It is militarism run stark mad. Unless someone acting for you can bring about a different understanding, there is some day to be an awful cataclysm. No one in Europe can do it. There is too much hatred, too many jealousies . . . It is an absorbing problem . . . I wish it might be solved, and to the everlasting glory of your Administration and our American civilization."

The colonel had learned that, like Oscar Wilde, President Wilson liked his flattery to be gross.

The literalminded Germans couldn't get it into their heads that President Wilson's representative was only an ersatz colonel. They gave him the military whirl. At the aviation field they let him see "all sorts of dangerous and curious manoeuvres," such as looping the loop performed in a new style airplane by a young Hollander in the German service named Fokker. "I was glad when he came down, for I was afraid his enthusiasm to please might result in his death."

On June 1, Colonel House and Ambassador Gerard were entertained at Potsdam by the Kaiser at a very special military festival called the *Schrippenfest*. The colonel was placed among the generals right across the table from the Kaiser. The meal was served in a famous hall with walls made entirely of seashells which Gerard described as probably the ugliest room in the world. House noted that the food was delicious and, approvingly, "the meal not long, perhaps fifty minutes."

After lunch His Majesty took House out on a terrace and talked to him, tête à tête, while Ambassador Gerard and Herr Zimmermann, the acting Secretary for Foreign Affairs, waited deferentially out of earshot. "I found he had all the versatility of Roosevelt with something more of charm, something less of force . . . He declared he wanted peace because it seemed to Germany's interest. Germany had been poor, she was now growing rich and a few more years of peace would make her so . . . I asked the Kaiser why Germany refused to sign the 'Bryan treaty' providing for arbitration and a cooling off period . . . He replied Germany would never sign such a treaty. 'Our strength lies in being always prepared for war at a second's notice. We will not resign that advantage and give our enemies time to prepare.'

"I told him that the President and I thought an American might be able to . . . compose the difficulties here and bring about an understanding . . . He agreed . . . I talked to the Kaiser on the terrace for thirty minutes and quite alone . . . Gerard told me afterwards that all Berlin was talking of the episode and wondering what the devil we had to say to each other for so long and in such an animated way."

Colonel House left for Paris the same day. He couldn't get anywhere with the French. President Poincaré was preparing for his state visit to St. Petersburg which was to put a public seal on the Russian alliance. The cabinet was in crisis. The wife of one of the ministers had brought a long political feud to a head by shooting Gaston Calmette, the editor of *Le Figaro*, who had been calling her husband a traitor. The papers were

full of the trial and acquittal of Mme. Caillaux. Among the politicians
there was nobody home but the concièrge.

When House called at the Embassy he found Ambassador Myron T.
Herrick in a whirl over T.R.'s carryingson at dinner the night before. T.R.,
fresh from his explorations of the Amazon basin which had nearly been
the end of him, was rearing to get back into politics. Herrick predicted
he would give the Democrats an unhappy time when he got home.

In England things were different indeed. The weather was delightful.
It was the height of one of the most brilliant seasons in London's history.
Everybody who was anybody was everywhere. Right away Walter Hines
Page had Colonel House to lunch with T.R. at the Embassy. House found
himself the toast of the town. Since the repeal of the tolls exemption any-
body connected with Woodrow Wilson was popular with the leading
Britishers.

House had cosy chats with Bryce, who had signalized his retirement
from active politics by accepting elevation to the peerage as Viscount
Bryce of Dechmont. Sir Horace Plunkett and Sir George Paish couldn't do
enough for the confidential colonel. While waiting for Ambassador Page
to get hold of Sir Edward Grey for lunch he had a talk with Henry James
and renewed acquaintance with John Singer Sargent, at dinner with a
wealthy art collector on Piccadilly.

Not a word of international tension, not a word of the ticking of the
time bomb across the channel. The Irish question and the hysterical behavior of the suffragettes were the topics of conversation, and society . . .
"I found here everything cluttered up with social affairs," House wrote his
dear friend in the White House, "and it is impossible to work quickly. Here
they have their thoughts on Ascot, garden parties, etc. etc."

Lunch with the British foreign minister was a great success. Sir Edward was "visibly impressed" when the colonel told him of his conversation with the Kaiser. He shied off, however, when House suggested that
the pair of them go right over to Kiel where the Kaiser would be attending
the yacht races and where there might be opportunities for private talks.
That sort of thing was just not done. Sir Edward had to think of the Russians and French. No it was not an alliance, merely an entente, but feelings had to be spared.

House seems to have baited Sir Edward a little by telling him that the
Kaiser had said the British Foreign Secretary couldn't understand Germany because he had never been in Europe. Sir Edward answered, come
now, he had crossed the continent once on his way to India, and he'd
been in Paris only recently with the King.

To tell the truth Sir Edward was one of the most stayathome foreign
ministers in English history. The birds of Britain and tennis and flyfishing

and the broad dialect of his Northumberland constituents interested him more than travel among foreigners.

They agreed to meet again as soon as Sir Edward could consult his colleagues. The next lunch lasted two hours, and included Haldane, the former war minister, now Chancellor of the Exchequer, and Sir William Tyrrell. "Sir Edward was in a delightful mood and paid you a splendid tribute," House wrote Wilson.

Colonel House spent six pleasant weeks in England. He had talks with Tyrrell and Spring Rice about the possibility of setting up an international consortium to furnish loans at decent rates to underdeveloped countries such as Mexico. He had a long talk with Prime Minister Asquith after the ladies had left the table at dinner at 10 Downing Street. He breakfasted with Lloyd George.

"I feel that my visit has been justified," he jotted in his diary, "even if nothing more is done than that already accomplished. It is difficult for me to realize that the dream I had last year is beginning to come true. I have seen the Kaiser and the British Government seem eager to carry on the discussion."

In Washington Bryan was working on a second batch of peace treaties. The State Department exuded optimism. That scoundrel Huerta had given up the fight and fled from Mexico leaving the A.B.C. powers to arrange a peaceful transfer of power to Carranza's *constitutionalistas*. New Freedom policies were triumphing all over the world. Peaceful mediation in Europe would be another laurel wreath for the Wilson administration. The President had virtually endorsed ahead of time anything that House might do.

"House," he wrote, "is my second personality. He is my independent self. His thoughts and mine are one. If I were in his place I should do just as he suggested . . . If anyone thinks he is reflecting my opinion by whatever action he takes they are welcome to the conclusion."

That One Slight Act

While House, in the character of Woodrow Wilson's alter ego, was being wined and dined in London and weekending at country houses with leaders of the ruling party, there occurred that "one slight act" which Spring Rice had spoken of with apprehension in his letter to Henry Adams.

A young enthusiast for the liberation of the southern Slavs shot a number of holes through the somewhat unpopular heir to the Hapsburg throne and his morganatic wife, while the couple were on a state visit to the Bosnian capital of Sarajevo.

There followed a strange lull while the Austrian authorities investigated the rumor that the Serbian Government had instigated the murders.

The Kaiser went about his projected cruise to Norway as if nothing had happened.

In St. Petersburg the Czar Nicholas continued to show Monsieur Poincaré the sights of the Russian capital amid all the splendor and pageantry the court of the Romanoffs could afford.

In London, the members of Asquith's cabinet took their minds off the threatened civil war in Ireland long enough to give the nod to Sir Edward Grey's cautious approbation of President Wilson's plan as embodied in the suggestions of Colonel House.

On July 3, in the course of an affectionate letter, House wrote:

"Tyrrell brought me word today that Sir Edward Grey would like me to convey to the Kaiser the impressions I have obtained from my several discussions with this government, in regard to a better understanding between the nations of Europe and to try to get a reply before I leave. Sir Edward said he did not wish to send anything official or in writing for fear of offending French or Russian sensibilities . . . He also told Page he had a long talk with the German ambassador here in regard to the matter and that he had sent messages by him directly to the Kaiser."

During the next few days House composed, with the help of one of the counsellors at the Embassy, who advised a stilted and ceremonious style of address in which, the colonel noted, he did not feel at home, a letter to the German Kaiser. In peroration he quoted an enthusiastic statement from President Wilson: "Your letter from Paris, written just after coming from Berlin, gives me a thrill of deep pleasure. You have I hope begun a great thing and I rejoice with all my heart." If the Kaiser would join President Wilson in the effort, European peace was assured.

House sailed for Boston on July 21. By the time he arrived at his summer place at Prides Crossing on the North Shore the Austrians, having discovered that the Serbian Government was indeed implicated in the murder of the Hapsburg heir, had served their ultimatum on Serbia and the Russians were mobilizing to back up the Serbs. House's letter lay on the Kaiser's desk in Potsdam while he cruised through the Norwegian fjords. August 1, Herr Zimmermann wrote House from the German foreign office that the Kaiser had received his letter but that now it was too late.

Years later the Kaiser in rueful exile at Doorn confided in George Sylvester Viereck that Wilson and House by their offer of mediation very nearly managed to avert the war. Spring Rice propounded the opposite theory: that the war party was so alarmed by the prospect of the Kaiser's being talked into peaceful negotiations, that they precipitated the crisis in Wilhelm II's absence.

However it happened, during the first days of August 1914, the Germans answered the Russian mobilization by putting into effect their plan for the invasion of France that had been so long on the drafting board. That meant a violation of the neutrality of the innocent states of Belgium and Luxembourg. "Necessity knows no law," Chancellor Bethmann-Hollweg announced to a special session of the Reichstag. "We have broken the law of nations . . . The wrong—I say again—the wrong we have done we will try to make good as soon as our military objectives have been reached. He that is threatened as we are threatened thinks only of how he can hack his way through."

Americans heard the news with stunned disbelief. Ambassador Page had gone down to Bachellor's Farm in Surrey for the weekend. "I walked out in the night a while ago," he noted in his diary. "The stars are bright. The night is silent, the country quiet, quiet as peace itself. Millions of men are in camp and on warships. Will they have to fight and many of them die to disentangle this network of treaties and alliances and to blow up the huge debts with gunpowder so that the world may start again?"

When he got back to London he found his embassy besieged by panicky American tourists.

"Upon my word!" he confided in his friend Woodrow Wilson, "if one could forget the awful tragedy, all this experience would be worth a lifetime of commonplace. One surprise follows another so rapidly one loses all sense of time: it seems an age since last Sunday."

On August 4 Page entered in his diary: "At 3 o'clock I went to see Sir Edw. Grey." Grey was a tall gaunt, rawboned man with jutting cheekbones and a powerful nose. "He rehearsed the whole situation in a calm, solemn, restrained way, sitting in a chair with both hands under his jaws, leaning forward eagerly. 'Thus the efforts of a lifetime go for nothing. I feel as a man who has wasted his life,' and tears came to his eyes . . .'"

"I shall never forget Sir Edward Grey telling me of the ultimatum while he wept," he wrote the President, "nor the poor German ambassador who has lost in his high game . . . almost a demented man; how the King as he declaimed at me for half an hour and threw up his hands and said 'My God, Mr. Page, what else could I do?' Nor the Austrian ambassador weeping and wringing his hands and crying out 'My dear colleague, my dear colleague.'"

Prince Lichnowsky, a liberal Polish nobleman in the service of the German foreign office, had accepted his assignment to London as an official endorsement of his campaign for a peaceful settlement and had been immensely encouraged by the Kaiser's interest in House's suggestions. He took the German declaration of war as a personal affront.

"I went to see the German ambassador in the afternoon," Page wrote. "He came down in his pyjamas, a crazy man. I feared he might literally go mad. He is of the anti-war party and has done his best and utterly failed. This interview was one of the most pathetic experiences of my life . . ."

Before signing the letter typewritten on his embassy stationery, Page scribbled some further details in the margin:

"The servant . . . who went over the house with one of our men came to the desk of the Princess Lichnowsky, the ambassador's wife. A photo of the German emperor lay on the desk face down. The man said she threw it down and said 'This is the swine that did this' and she drew a pig on the blotting pad wh. is still there . . ."

Page wrote with some pride that he had stationed a naval officer at the German Embassy, and hung the letters U. S. on the door to protect it. He took a deep breath and ended with high emotion:

"And this awful tragedy moves on to what? We do not know what is really happening, so strict is the censorship. But it seems inevitable to me that Germany will be beaten after a long while, that the horrid period of alliances and armaments will not come again, that England will gain even more of the earth's surface, that Russia may next play the menace; that all Europe (as much as survives) will be bankrupt, that relatively we shall be immensely stronger—financially and politically—there must surely come great changes—very many yet undreamed of. Be ready, for you will surely be called on to compose this huge quarrel. I thank heaven for many things—first the Atlantic ocean; second that you refrained from war in Mexico; third that we kept our treaty; the canal tolls victory I mean. Now when all this half the world will suffer the incredible brutalization of war, we shall preserve our moral strength, our political power and our ideals.

God save us!

Yrs faithfully,
WALTER HINES PAGE"

As the news of the breakdown of the European peace came item by item into the White House during those muggy desperate days of late July and early August, Woodrow Wilson's face became taut and gray. Overseas, civilization was cracking in pieces. At home his family, which he relied on so for shelter and comfort, was full of wretchedness. Ellen Wilson's secretary, their dear cousin Helen Bones, was ill. Cousin Mary Smith had been taken to the hospital stricken with appendicitis. And at last he admitted it to himself: his dear one could not live: Ellen was dying.

When the news came of Austria's declaration of war his first thought was that his daughters must not tell their mother. They were at lunch. Their mother's place was empty. He put his hand over his face. "I can think of nothing, nothing when my dear one is suffering."

Dr. Grayson had done his best. The consultants he brought in diagnosed Bright's disease, complicated by tuberculosis of the kidneys. August 2 was a Sunday. From the sickroom they could hear the newsboys calling the extras that announced the German ultimatum to Belgium. Woodrow Wilson's old classmate Dr. Davis had come from Philadelphia. He had no hope to offer. Telegrams were sent to her brother, to her nearest relatives. On one of the last days the girls brought her the news that her housing bill had passed through Congress. She smiled contentedly. The last thing her daughter Eleanor heard her say was "Is your father looking well?" Then she whispered to Dr. Grayson, "Promise me you will take good care of my husband." Not long after she was dead.

PART TWO

Trying to be Neutral

For nineteen hundred years the gospel of the Prince of
Peace has been making its majestic march around the world,
and during these centuries the Philosophy of the Sermon on
the Mount has become more and more the rule of daily life.
It only remains to lift that code of morals from the level of the
individual and make it real in the law of nations, and this I
believe is the task that God has reserved for the United States.

—William Jennings Bryan
in his oration: "The Prince of Peace"

Chapter 6

THE FREEDOM OF THE SEAS

THE shattering of the forty years of peace so often acclaimed as the heyday of European civilization was at first hardly believable. Americans
had for generations held devoutly to the creed that progress was inevitable. How to reconcile progress with these monstrous crimes? What was
the use of Christianity if after twenty centuries it had not taught men
better? Many a man's faith in God was shaken.

Americans in those years particularly, when almost a third of the population was of European origin, were a people of refugees, brought up in
revulsion against the Old World's wrongs; but during the sunny years of
the century's first decade, the educated classes had been inventing a
nostalgic geography of civilized and cultured Europe where existence
was conducted on a higher plane than the grubby materialism of American business.

Travel in Europe, particularly for the wife and children, was one of the rewards of success: Paris, the crossroads of civilization, city of boulevards and the Eiffel Tower, magnet of American artists and millionaires, was where good Americans went when they died.

Culture was only to be had on the old continent. The Rhineland, Heidelberg, Göttingen, Munich, Bayreuth were hives of the world's scholarship and the world's music. Kensington, the English lakes, the Cotswolds were redolent with the fame of the great Victorians. Rome and Florence, with their domes and colonnades and towers and their dark cypress gardens, were cities of refuge for men of letters fleeing the yammer of moneymaking.

To Europeans too the peace had seemed unbreakable. While rich Americans dreamed of Europe poor Europeans dreamed of America. In those peaceful years each could try for the fulfillment of his hopes. While the British Navy assured peace on the seas, the European order overflowed the globe. With time and money a man could travel anywhere, except for a few blank spots where the natives were unruly, or the dominions of the Czar and the Turk where passports were required, secure in life and property, without any official's by your leave. The poorest cobbler in Przemysl or Omsk only needed the price of a steerage passage to Ellis Island to try his luck in the Promised Land.

"If you didn't know the world before the war," old men told their sons, "you've never known what it is to live."

Armageddon

During that last July of the old order only the most sophisticated students of European affairs had any inkling of the rancors and hatreds and murderous lusts fermenting behind those picturesque façades. Realization of the extent of the calamity came slowly. The assassination of the archduke was shrugged off as a continuation of the Balkan disturbances that had been relegated for years to the back pages. When the Czar's armies were mobilized in the name of Slavic brotherhood it could be explained away as a measure to distract the downtrodden Russians from the manifold wrongs and oppressions they lived under. But when the Kaiser answered by alerting his generals and the French called their citizens to the tricolor it was plain that Europe had gone raving mad.

In extras and fourinch headlines Americans read breathless: BELGIUM INVADED. When England declared war on Germany it seemed that every ruling group had made the decision that now was the time to settle old scores. No war could last on such a scale, the wellinformed told one another; one short summer campaign and the nations would see the folly of mutual suicide and start negotiating peace.

It was with a certain grim satisfaction that Americans watched the bestlaid plans of the general staffs go awry. Although the French, true to their military dogma of *toujours l'offensif,* did just what the deceased von Schlieffen had planned for them to do by pushing up into Lorraine, the enormous flanking sweep of German armies through the northern plains of Flanders and of France, which the great strategist had imagined, failed to win the promised "victory in eight weeks."

General von Moltke, the lesser nephew of the von Moltke who had broken the Second Empire at Sedan, allowed himself to be distracted by the defense of Antwerp and by the Czar's "steamroller" advance into East Prussia. He allowed armies which were supposed to make his extreme right flank invincible to be detached for service in the East.

With the first roar of the German guns against the Belgian fortresses the French Chamber of Deputies virtually abdicated its powers. One third of the membership was called to the colors. Northern France was turned over to military government. Paul Painlevé and his cabinet pinned all their hopes on General Joseph Jacques Césaire Joffre, who had been dredged up out of obscurity by the Radical Socialists, largely because he was the best general they could find who had the right politics. He was a republican and a Freemason. Already known as Papa Joffre, he was a florid bespectacled stout man of fiftynine with the air of a *bon bourgeois* which appealed to the anticlerical voters of the French left. The son of a cooper in the eastern Pyrenees, his army career had been distinctly humdrum. His only distinction was having, as a young officer, successfully conducted a small expedition against Timbuctoo. He was reputed to know about railroads and fortifications. His first contribution to the strategy of the war was his conviction that the German offensive was a colossal feint and should be countered by an attack in the direction of Metz.

Joffre's offensive came to grief at Morhange, but the very speed of the German advance, once resistance was beaten down along the Meuse, wrecked the Schlieffen plan. Armies lost contact with their supply and with each other. Instead of enveloping Paris they drove east along the Marne and gave the brilliant military governor of the city, General Gallieni, the chance to hurry Maunoury's troops out, some of them in Paris taxicabs, to attack the German flank. In spite of the sluggishness of the French command under Joffre and the inadequacy of the British expeditionary force, which landed under the navy's protection, without the loss of a man to be sure, but only in time to join in the general retreat, the Germans were beaten back in five days to the line of the Aisne. Winter found both armies digging entrenchments which no general staff had planned.

In the East the Russian masses poured triumphantly into East Prussia only to be trapped by the Germans under von Hindenburg in the region of the Mazurian Lakes. They were butchered there by the tens of thou-

sands in a battle which the Germans named Tannenberg after an engagement the Teutonic Knights fought centuries before. Romanoff prestige
never recovered from the blow, even though to the south, against the
Austrians, their armies were tolerably successful.

Meanwhile the Austrians three times invaded Serbia and three times
were driven back to the Danube. The Austro-Hungarian empire was already showing signs of the strains and stresses which were to destroy it.
The Serbs successfully routed the invaders but their country was left a
ruin where typhus ruled.

The war along the western front, from neutral Switzerland to the sea,
became a business of trenches, deep shelters, barbed wire, mining and
countermining. Instruments of oldtime siege warfare like the hand gre-
nade and the mortar were reinvented. With the increased use of machineguns the odds turned in favor of defense. This wasn't war as it had been
taught in the military schools.

Vast advances and retreats left homeless populations, fleeing from
burnedout towns and villages, a prey to starvation and pestilence.
Densely settled regions in Belgium and northern France were left a ruin.
The summer months of 1914 saw the prosperous European order turn into
all the abominations of the Apocalypse. Every newspaper reader had his
eyes stuffed daily with horrors. There was created in the American mind
an anguished new geography of massacre. Unfamiliar names in small
letters on the map were outlined in blood. The refugee became the symbol
of the age.

A Southerner in the Treasury

Through all the anguish of his wife's last illness, Woodrow Wilson went
on, with haggard face and firmset jaw, meeting the problems that poured
across his desk. The cool promptness of his decisions amazed the people
around him.

The first thing he had to face was the threat of a panic on Wall Street.

The United States was still a debtor country. Europeans held something
like two and a half billion dollars in American stocks and bonds. They
held paper for some four hundred and fifty million dollars worth of obligations due or about to come due during the balance of the year.

In that crazy last week of July, when European banks and exchanges
were closing their doors, Europeans began to sell their dollar holdings. In
spite of large shipments of gold to Europe, the franc rose from 19 ⅓ cents
to 23½ cents and the pound from $4.89 to $7.00. Thursday, July 30, the
stock market had its worst day since the panic of 1907. Early Friday the
news came over the Atlantic cable that the London Stock Exchange had

suspended operations. Brokers' offices were stacked high with selling orders for overseas customers.

That same morning J. P. Morgan, Jr. telephoned Secretary of the Treasury McAdoo before officehours at his home to tell him the governors were meeting to decide whether or not to close the New York exchange. What was his advice? "If you really want my judgment," his wife Eleanor heard McAdoo answer in a firm tone, "it is to close the exchange."

Sunday morning, when the newsboys were yelling "Belgium Invaded" through the rainwet streets, Mac, as he was known to the Wilson family, went early to his office at the Treasury, while Eleanor rushed to the White House to be near her dying mother. President Woodward of the Hanover National, who had been appointed one of the directors of the Federal Reserve Bank which was scheduled to open in the fall, called McAdoo from New York. The Clearing House Committee was in session and wanted his advice. McAdoo suggested that they come to Washington, but was told there wasn't time. They expected a run on their banks when they opened for business Monday morning. They needed millions in extra currency if they were to hold off a disastrous panic. McAdoo said he would have to consult the President.

All Woodrow Wilson knew about finance was what he had learned during his campaign for the enactment of the Federal Reserve Act. He had confidence in his soninlaw's financial acumen. He told him by all means to go to New York immediately. The Secretary had already taken the initiative by shipping fifty million dollars of the new currency he was authorized to use in emergencies to the subtreasury in New York. Taking Eleanor along to keep his spirits up he left on the afternoon train.

Having Mac in the family and in the administration was proving a real boon to the sorely beset man in the White House. McAdoo's success with the Hudson tunnels had won him prestige among New York businessmen. They believed that his hunches were sound. A dourfaced sixfooter, his stringy mountaineer look had endeared him to the Wilsons. Ellen, whose shrewd feminine judgments the President had come to rely on more and more, had taken to him with real affection as a soninlaw.

He was the Wilsons' kind of man. He came of similar Southern Presbyterian stock. His father, another very tall man, was a Tennessee lawyer who had fought in the Mexican War and served as attorney general of his state. When Tennessee, against the wishes of so many of her citizens, seceded from the Union, he took the Confederate side.

Mac's boyhood was spent in Milledgeville, Georgia, in the ruined heartland of the Confederacy. As a Confederate officer his father was disfranchised and barred from the practice of law. There were seven children and no money. He tried farming and smalltown journalism. When his mother was paid fifty dollars for a novel she wrote about gentlefolk among the magnolias, Mac remembered that the money was spent in a single day buying shoes and clothes for the family.

When Mac's father was offered fifteen hundred dollars a year to teach history and English at the University of Tennessee it seemed like opulence. It was a chance for the children to get some education. The elder McAdoos were cultivated people, full of a literary nostalgia that made it hard for them to fight their way in the harsh reconstruction world. When young William Gibbs went to bed, worn out with fights at school, and selling papers and doing odd jobs for storekeepers, he dreamed of money.

He started to study law as deputy clerk in the United States District Court in Chattanooga and reading nights with a friendly attorney. He was a hard worker with a mind fertile in expedients. By the time he was admitted to the bar at twentyone he had tried his hand at Democratic national politics and dabbled in various speculations and investments. He married a Georgia girl and immediately started to make money buying and selling Chattanooga real estate.

He risked his first twentyfive thousand in a project to apply electric power to the muledrawn streetcars of Knoxville. It was a little too soon for rapid transit. The company went into receivership and young McAdoo, who had accumulated mostly debts for his pains, went north to hang out his shingle in downtown New York.

It was a long hard struggle. When the lawbusiness was slack he sold bonds and securities. He studied railroad finance. He got the notion of bringing railroad trains into New York by tunnelling under the North River. One company had already gone broke, but a tunnel had been built halfway across about ten years before. He started promoting a company to finish that tunnel. He had a knack of convincing other men that his hunches were sound. By the time Woodrow Wilson became governor of New Jersey the tunnels were completed and profitable. William Gibbs McAdoo had become one of the great names of American enterprise.

Mac first met Woodrow Wilson when he went to Princeton to see his collegeboy son who was laid up with diphtheria at the infirmary. He was captivated by what he called Wilson's Jeffersonian humanism.

Mac was a born promoter. There wasn't much left to do in promoting the Hudson River tunnels so he took to promoting Woodrow Wilson. His promotion was so successful that he found himself promoting the United States Treasury.

In his autobiography McAdoo tells of pestering his father, when he was a tenyearold boy, to tell him exactly how many polecats Vera Cruz smelt like when the United States troops landed there in the Mexican War. His father had told him Vera Cruz smelt worse than a crowd of polecats. "Did it smell worse than a thousand million polecats?" "Listen son," his father had said to him, "you have a bad habit of dealing with uncomfortably large figures."

When as Secretary of the Treasury on August 2, 1914, he sat with his wife in the drawing room of the New York train, faced with a panic that might wreck half the banks in the country, Mac was jotting down on a yellow pad propped on his knees what his father would have called "uncomfortably large figures."

Years afterwards Mrs. McAdoo remembered the haggard look of the financiers that met their train at the Pennsylvania Station. "I was startled by their white faces and trembling voices," she wrote. "Could these be America's great men?"

The Secretary of the Treasury was hustled over to the Vanderbilt Hotel where a group of bankers was anxiously awaiting him. McAdoo with his long stride and his selfassured somewhat rustic manner, exuded confidence. The news that fifty million dollars in fresh currency was already in New York quieted the bankers' nerves, but they complained its use was restricted by the present law. New legislation was needed. No sooner said than done. By midnight McAdoo was back on the sleeper to Washington sketching out the necessary bill on his yellow scratchpad.

At breakfast he brought the President up to date. At his news conference that morning Wilson took the reporters into his confidence with the friendly reasoning man to man tone he could assume when he needed to: "It is extremely necessary . . . that you should be extremely careful not to add in any way to the excitement . . . So far as we are concerned there is no cause . . . America is absolutely prepared to meet the financial situation and to straighten everything out without any material difficulty. The only thing that can possibly prevent it is unreasonable apprehension and excitement . . . I know from . . . the Secretary of the Treasury . . . that there is no cause for alarm. There is cause for getting busy and doing the thing in the right way . . ."

While Woodrow Wilson transmitted soothing balm to the press of the nation McAdoo hurried to the Capitol to confer with the chairman of the Senate committee on banking. Senator Owen of Oklahoma was a member of the team that had put over the Federal Reserve Act. He understood immediately that what was needed was stopgap legislation to tide over until the reserve system was operating. The Treasury must be authorized to increase the amount of emergency currency issued under the Aldrich-Vreeland Act. Congress, under his direction, "did the thing in the right way" so expeditiously that the bill went through both houses and was at the White House ready for signature on the following day.

The run on the banks stopped immediately. There were few extraordinary withdrawals and only five small bank failures.

The next job was to staunch the drain on gold. The chief New York banks had already made an agreement among themselves to ship no more out. Later in the week McAdoo called a meeting of international bankers and exporters at the Treasury. A nationwide gold pool was established to meet obligations as they fell due. The amount was oversubscribed right there.

The mere gesture had the effect of reducing the drain. Only some hundred million dollars' worth of gold bullion left the country.

Already war orders were coming in. By fall the exchange situation had reversed itself completely, and American bankers were talking about extending credits to the English and the French. In January 1915 the gold pool went out of business for lack of customers.

A few months before the bankers had been viewing national control of the moneymarket with all sorts of apprehensions. Now they were calling for the help of the federal reserve system before its organization was complete. Meanwhile, American victims of the breakdown of European banking were sending out desperate appeals for help. Congressmen, state governors, cabinet members were bombarded with cables. Stranded American travellers swarmed around every embassy and consulate in Europe. They couldn't cash their letters of credit. They couldn't change their money. In London the hotels wouldn't give change for a five pound note for fear of having to give up gold currency. At the same time hotelkeepers and restaurants were demanding immediate cash payment for everything.

On Monday August 3 after the President had spent the first part of his day quieting the panicky financiers in New York, he shut himself up in his office with Secretary Bryan to decide what to do to help the frightened tourists. They decided to allow embassies to countersign travellers' checks and letters of credit and to urge representatives abroad to use their own judgment in affording what relief they could. Within a couple of days Congress responded by appropriating several million dollars. Before the end of the week the warships *Tennessee* and *North Carolina* were steaming for Europe laden with currency for the relief of stranded citizens.

Casting about for shipping to bring Americans home from the zones of war the President and Secretary Bryan came up against the fact that the United States had no merchant marine. Of around five and a half million tons under American registry the great bulk operated on inland waterways or in the coastwise trade. Only fifteen ships flew the American flag on transatlantic or transpacific routes and of those all but six were passenger liners with little cargo capacity.

The United States was one of the great exporting nations, though still mostly of raw materials, but her exports were customarily carried on foreign bottoms.

Right away grain from recordbreaking harvests of wheat and barley and oats began to pile up at the railheads and in the warehouses. Wharves became glutted with products that could find no outlet. Democratic congressmen began to prophesy immediate ruin for the South, which was still in the straightjacket of a onecrop economy, if some way couldn't be found to market the cotton crop which promised to be enormous.

The economic structure of the southeastern states was based on credit. When a man planted an acre of cotton he borrowed the money for the seed and fertilizer and often for food for himself and his mule, and cash to pay the pickers, from his broker; in the fall the broker took the cotton and sold it and paid the farmer the balance. The broker financed the operation by borrowing from the bank and so on up into the financial hierarchy. The sudden extinction of a market for cotton meant that the whole house of cards would come tumbling down.

A man didn't have to be a financial genius to see that something had to be done. The President and his advisers were southerners. They felt tenderness for the cottongrower. Immediately Secretary McAdoo began to make currency available to southern banks and to cast around for some way of inducing private financiers to form a syndicate to advance loans on the freshly harvested crop. His aim was to establish a floor under cotton prices.

Republicans in Congress bristled, particularly the New Englanders. The textile manufacturers felt they were being cheated of an opportunity to buy cotton cheap. The opposition, which in the first daze of the European calamity had been tamely accepting Wilson's leadership, began to harden.

The Shipping Bill

Both sides agreed that, if the American economy were not to strangle in its own productiveness, vessels had to be found to replace the German and Austrian shipping immobilized in neutral ports and the Allied shipping deflected to military uses. But how? The problem kept McAdoo awake nights. "One morning at dawn," he wrote, "I was lying in bed thinking about the matter when it occurred to me I might as well write out a tentative draft of the shipping bill which would embody the idea of a government owned corporation." He was thinking of Theodore Roosevelt's purchase of the Panama Steamship Company which was still being managed by the War Department. Wilson and McAdoo had privately agreed to buy the idle German ships and operate them under the American flag.

At the thought of the government in the shipping business the New

York financiers raised a storm. Shipowners' lobbyists arrived in Washington on every train. Rank socialism was the cry.

At the same time another of McAdoo's bills was having smooth sailing. Nobody cried "socialism" when he suggested the formation of a Bureau of War Risk Insurance in the Treasury. The professional underwriters were scared to death of war risk insurance. Let the government take the loss. McAdoo's war risk insurance agency surprised everybody when its affairs were wound up at the end of the war, by showing seventeen million dollars of profit.

The First Republican Filibuster

McAdoo's shipping bill furnished the first battleground between Wilson's progressive Democrats and the Republican opposition which the Schoolmaster in Politics was soon to be excoriating as the forces of darkness.

Investors were in a fever over the profits to be made owning ships. Tramp steamers were clearing their cost in a single voyage. Oceangoing freighters were bringing in clear profits of from three to five times the money invested in them. As soon as the measure was introduced in the House, Republican papers described the government's entrance into the shipping field as a menace to private enterprise. One of the Morgans called at the Treasury and lectured the Secretary on the hazards and difficulties of transatlantic shipping in wartime. He wanted no government interference. "As for being a menace," wrote McAdoo, "I could not see that the government's ships would menace anything but the absurdly high rates of private shipping concerns."

The bill passed the House against vigorous opposition. In the Senate it was stalled by the Republican minority led by two of T.R.'s old associates from the imperial era of the "tennis cabinet," Elihu Root, the learned New York corporation lawyer, who had been Roosevelt's Secretary of State after John Hay's death, and Henry Cabot Lodge.

Senator Lodge of Massachusetts held the powerful position of chairman of the Senate Committee on Foreign Affairs. Since the very considerable Republican gains in the House and Senate in the fall elections in 1914 he had become a leader of conservative Republican opposition to the Democratic administration's legislative program.

Lodge was partisan to the marrow. He came of the purest codfish aristocracy. His father was a Boston shipowner and his mother was a Cabot. He had been a friend of T.R.'s since, as a rising historian, an associate of Henry Adams on the *North American Review,* he'd been interested in the young New Yorker's project for a naval history of the War of 1812. They had shared a romantic navalism and all sorts of literary enthusiasms since Harvard College days, even while they differed politically. Lodge swallowed part of the New Nationalism but he looked on the New Freedom with a bilious eye.

When the Democrats, in spite of the loss of several southern conservatives who voted with the Republicans, were able to marshal enough voices to pass the measure with the help of three Republican progressives from the Middle West, the Republican minority, ably marshalled by Lodge and Root, talked it to death in one of the longest and bitterest filibusters yet recorded. The Sixtythird Congress adjourned March 4, 1915, without the shipping bill's being brought to a vote in the Senate. The Administration introduced it again in the next Congress.

The chief objection voiced by the two scholarly conservatives was that if the government bought the German ships and Great Britain did not recognize the transfer of registry, there would be immediate danger of war with the Allies. Lodge seems to have convinced himself, furthermore, that the bill would legalize a gigantic deal by which McAdoo, working through Kuhn, Loeb and Co., would buy up idle German shipping at great personal profit. In their speeches they both decried government in business as state socialism and the end of individual liberty.

McAdoo claimed to be merely motivated by the practical consideration of reducing the cost for American shippers. He used to say that the Republican filibuster cost the American people a cool billion dollars. He insisted that he believed in private enterprise "as a theory, but economic theories, I have observed, often fail in practice. Private initiative becomes extremely timid in times of peril and uncertainty . . . Shipowners were making so much money . . . that they were satisfied . . . More ships would mean lower freight rates and less profit . . . When the bill was first introduced, ships might have been bought or constructed at the cost of about forty dollars a ton. But when the measure was finally enacted, eighteen months later, they were selling at prices that ranged from one hundred and fifty to three hundred dollars a ton."

The President was grimly stimulated by the opposition of the "entrenched interests." It was the Princeton quads all over again. He never could understand how reasonable men could honestly disagree with him.

In a speech in Indianapolis during the congressional campaign that fall he violently attacked the leaders of the Republican filibuster: "These gentlemen are now seeking to defy the nation and prevent the release of American products to the suffering world which needs them more than it ever needed them before." His violence shocked his supporters.

Writing to his friend, Mrs. Toy, who had remonstrated with him, he apologized a little ruefully for letting himself be carried away by the "psychology of the stump" but added to his own defense: "I think you cannot know to what lengths men like Root and Lodge are going, who I once thought had consciences and I now know have none . . . We are fighting as a matter of fact the most formidable (covert) lobby that has stood against us yet in anything we have attempted; and we shall see the fight to a finish."

The Peacemaker in the State Department

William Jennings Bryan, who sat dreaming of peace in ducktails and crash suits under the high dark ceilings of the old War and State Building, couldn't for the life of him understand why Wilson and McAdoo wouldn't allow a clause to be inserted in their shipping bill ruling out the purchase of ships from the belligerents. He assured the President that this would satisfy the southern conservatives who shared the misgivings of Lodge and Root about government operation of Austrian and German ships. Never strong on practical details it did not occur to him that these were the only ships to be had.

For two years he had loyally squandered his personal influence in behalf of every administration measure but his heart wasn't in the shipping bill. As a practicing Christian he observed the letter of the Ten Commandments. War was murder. He couldn't quite convince himself that war trade wasn't complicity with murderers.

He believed passionately in neutrality. His first thought was for a sort of Jeffersonian embargo on any dealings with the warring nations. In the early weeks of the war he almost managed to convince President Wilson that American bankers must not be allowed to make loans to the belligerents. Money was the worst kind of contraband. Personally, as a private man, he was in favor of cutting off the shipping of munitions. Impractical as he was he had to recognize that the economic wellbeing of the country depended on exports.

Though the American people, in spite of widespread indignation at the German violation of Belgian neutrality, were as anxious to keep out of the war as their Secretary of State was, the geography of the conflict early forced them into an undeclared and somewhat unwilling partnership with Great Britain and France. Britannia ruled the waves. While armies fought to a stalemate along the Aisne, the British Navy swept German commerce off the seas and bottled up the German fleet behind the fortified island of Heligoland. An Order in Council of August 20 established a blockade of Germany and Austria modelled on the blockade which a hundred years before had brought Napoleon to his ruin. Neutral ships were intercepted and escorted into British ports to be inspected for contraband of war even if they were bound for neutral countries. Contraband was just about any class of goods the British authorities decided might give aid and comfort to the enemy.

Secretary Bryan, with the President's fervent backing, at first tried to enforce the old American theory of freedom of the seas. Early in the war he dispatched notes to all the belligerents asking them to conform to the Declaration of London. This was a set of rules affirming the rights of neutral shipping in wartime drawn up by an international conference in the winter of 1908 and 1909. Unfortunately the Declaration of London had not been ratified either by Great Britain or the United States.

These rules would have greatly benefited the neutral nations and would have made impossible the starving out of Germany which was developing as the basic British strategy of the war.

The British showed no interest in giving up any of the advantages which came to them from their mastery of the ocean. There followed a prolonged wrangle between the State Department and the Foreign Office, kept somewhat within bounds by the terms of Bryan's arbitration treaty. The British pressed for as much blockade as they could get without completely alienating American sympathies, and the United States pressed for as much freedom of the seas as could be had without playing too much into the hands of the Central Powers.

Bryan was often absent from his desk. He had accepted the office with the understanding that he would lecture for part of the year. He must be allowed to make his living. His position in Washington as second fiddle to the President fed his rather innocent vanity and enabled him to entrench himself in the party leadership by finding jobs for deserving Democrats, but his heart was on the Chautauqua circuit. He loved money and he loved applause. When hostile newspapers blamed him for such undignified behavior as lecturing for money he struck back: "Mingling with the multitude is not a cause for reproach . . . The forum is not below the level of official life. It is not stepping down to go from the desk to the platform."

Happier stirring the hearts of the plain people than knitting his brows over problems each more insoluble than the last that kept appearing on his desk he left the day to day paper work to his counsellor, Robert Lansing, who acted as Secretary of State when he was away. Lansing was a rather solemn, steelyhaired upstate New Yorker, now in his early fifties. His old associates from Amherst College days and from the Watertown bar still addressed him affectionately as Duke. He had made himself a career in international law and married into diplomacy by his union with the daughter of John W. Foster, the respected Secretary of State under Benjamin Harrison. Lansing reported directly to the President.

Madison's Dilemma

The President's chief adviser, private negotiator, and, particularly since Mrs. Wilson's death, most intimate friend, was Colonel House. House and Lansing were often at cross purposes, and House and Bryan, although outwardly on terms of backslapping friendship, almost always so. Since Bryan's mind was fixed on the sonorous generalities, decisions, even on small details, were up to the already overtaxed President.

House's relation to Wilson was that of a star reporter to his city editor. House did the legwork. In Washington and New York he gloried in a modest omnipresence. He was on fair terms with the sceptical Jusserand, the squarebearded professorial diplomat who represented the French. He was cosy with the German ambassador, dressy Count von Bernstorff. He was even more at home with Sir Cecil Spring Rice, the old Washington hand, whom Sir Edward Grey had sent over to take the place of the prodigious Bryce.

War trade with Europe grew from week to week. After the stunning effects of the first blow wore off American businessmen began to discover that the war was a bonanza. The Europeans had to have American products regardless of cost. Meatpacking and coppermining boomed. The price of wheat rose. War was lamentable but what an opportunity to make money!

The British were devising their own rules of contraband. American shippers had no problem with goods destined to England and France. Exports destined for Germany, mostly through neutral ports, were even more profitable, but neutral ships suffered under detentions, delays, seizures and from the arbitrary behavior of British prize courts.

A stream of protests and complaints found its way to the President's desk. Woodrow Wilson, like most literate Americans, was prejudiced in favor of the British by the whole course of his education, but he had freedom of the seas in his blood. He smarted personally under the indignities suffered by American shipping. In private he made no bones of his exasperation.

"While we were discussing the seizure of vessels by Great Britain," House jotted in his diary one day in late August 1914, "he read a page from his history of the American people telling how during Madison's administration the War of 1812 was started in exactly the same way as this controversy is opening up . . . The President said: 'Madison and I are the only two Princeton men that have become President. The circumstances of the War of 1812 now run parallel. I sincerely hope they will not go further.'"

House hurried over to the British Embassy with the tale, and added that Lansing was preparing a stiff note of protest.

Spring Rice described the conversation in a somewhat peevish tone to Sir Edward Grey: "I had suspected for some time that something was up among the lawyers in the State Department, but I could extract no hint of what was intended. The only indication was a rather unfriendly atmosphere." (Spring Rice and Lansing never did get along.) He retailed House's account of the President's state of mind. "He then told me he happened to be sitting with the President when a large package was brought in from the State Department. The President was very tired and did not want to look at it; he was told it was to go off by mail the next morning. He read it and to his astonishment it was a sort of ultimatum . . . which really would have convulsed the world if it had got out . . . The two men were astonished, the more so as the Secretary of State had been away for some time, tired with his exertions in procuring peace treaties, and was at that moment at a distant watering place with his wife. The President said that the document though signed, could not go at once . . . The President was very much impressed by the gravity of the question because it touches the pockets and the prejudices of so many of the people. It happens to be just the sort of question which takes the popular fancy and also enlists the monied people as well."

Spring Rice then passed on Wilson's remark about the War of 1812. For the ambassador's benefit House had quoted him as adding, "I hope I shall be wiser."

Sir Edward Grey professed sympathy and understanding of the President's position. The Lansing note was sent to London after considerable editing by House and Spring Rice, who put their heads together over it in private. The Foreign Office promised a new Order in Council and at the same time soothed the sensibilities of the southern Democrats—and possibly of Colonel House himself as a Texan—by somewhat illogically allowing cotton, which as an ingredient of most of the explosives in use was certainly a contraband item, to be shipped direct to Germany. During the fall of 1914 and the winter of 1915 a million and threequarters bales of Southern cotton were unloaded at Hamburg and Bremerhaven.

The new Order in Council, in spite of a few conciliatory expressions, laid out a longer list of contraband items than the first one. The State Department grumbled but acquiesced. Freedom of the seas was temporarily shelved.

The U-Boats

The controversy between Washington annd Westminster would have been carried to greater lengths if the Germans, who all along were showing a characteristic knack for putting themselves in a bad light, had not decided that their safety lay in the submarine.

As soon as it became apparent that the German high seas fleet was no match for the Royal Navy, submarine construction was stepped up to fever pitch. The Germans entered the war with about twenty gasoline-burning coast defense submarines of about five hundred tons each and a few new diesels. The diesel motor immediately proved its superiority. The Germans started building diesel submarines of a thousand to two thousand tons. Many of the Kaiser's advisers were still unconvinced of their usefulness.

The torpedoing of H.M.S. *Pathfinder* on September 5 and two weeks later the sinking by a single U-boat of the three old British cruisers, *Aboukir, Hogue* and *Cressy,* on patrol off the coast of Holland, with the loss of fourteen hundred trained men, gave a fillip to submarine enthusiasts among German officialdom.

The British answered by a raid on Heligoland Bight which wrecked three light cruisers and a destroyer and cost the Germans a thousand lives and much damage to the fleet. Both sides went to work to increase their minefields. The British declared the whole North Sea a warzone only to be navigated by neutrals on courses laid down by the Admiralty.

By this time Admiral von Tirpitz, who headed the German naval office, was convinced that the use of submarines as commerce destroyers could turn the tables on the British blockade. In November he tipped his hand by crying out in an interview with Karl von Wiegand of the United Press: "America has not raised her voice in protest . . . against England's closing of the North Sea to neutral shipping. What will America say if Germany declares submarine war on all the enemy's merchant ships? England wants to starve us. We can play the same game. We can bottle her up and torpedo every English or allies' ship which nears any harbor in Great Britain."

The German fleet was showing dash and bravado, but at sea it was hopelessly outnumbered. Its heavy cruisers brought the war home to the islanders by shelling Scarborough and Hartlepool and killing a hundred or more helpless civilians on England's North Sea coast. In the South Pacific von Spee seriously mauled a British formation. By December the Royal Navy had manifested its lumbering superiority by knocking off the few German cruisers on the rampage in outoftheway oceans and by sinking, in a battle off the Falkland Islands, von Spee's dangerous little squadron. In German governing circles the advocates of the U-boat carried the day.

End of the First Round

The year 1914 ended in a stalemate slightly favorable to the Allies. Britain cleared the seas and began a leisurely takeover of the German colonies. The Germans had neither been able to master the French in the West nor the Russians in the East.

Turkey's entrance into the war on the side of the Central Powers cut off Russia from the munitions she had to have to keep her armies in the field, but the advantage to the Germans of the Turkish alliance was largely offset by the fact that the stubborn Serbs still occupied a long stretch of the railroad to Constantinople, that German expansionists dreamed of as the first leg of the Baghdad-Bahn which was to link them with the oil and the markets of the Middle East.

In the Far East Bryan's State Department failed to induce the British and their Japanese allies to preserve the *status quo*. Japan was moving in on the German "leased territory" of Kiaochow and establishing herself as a power in Chinese affairs. There as elsewhere Germany lost far more than she had gained.

Chapter 7

NEUTRALITY IN THOUGHT AND DEED

EVER since the Battle of the Marne, Bryan had been trying to induce the belligerents to cry quits. A remark dropped by von Bernstorff at dinner with some New York bankers gave the Secretary hope that an offer of mediation might be acceptable to the Kaiser. "Even a failure to agree will not rob an attempt at mediation of all its advantages," Bryan wrote eagerly to his ambassadors in Paris and London, "because the different nations would be able to explain their attitude, their reasons for continuing the war, the end to be hoped for and the terms upon which peace is possible. This would locate responsibility for the continuation of the war and help mould public opinion."

The last thing any of the warring governments wanted was to locate responsibility. In the face of the overwhelming pacifism of American public opinion none of them wanted to be charged with willfully prolonging the war. But none of them wanted to make the first move towards negotiations. Each hoped to win a better bargaining position from some coming move on the chessboard of battle.

Spring Rice, who kept carefully in touch with what was being said and thought in the middlewest, went so far as to write Bryan in early October: "It may be that some people at first spoke lightly of your idea. No one who has studied the diplomatic history of the events leading to the present disastrous war can ever speak lightly of your idea again. For it is abundantly manifest that even one week's enforced delay would probably have saved the peace of the world."

To Stop the War

In theory broadminded men among all the ruling circles in Europe were still in favor of Bryanstyle arbitration, but practice was another matter.

House made an effort to get Spring Rice, Jusserand and von Bernstorff together in one of the private confidential chats he had such a flair for. He was afraid Bryan's loud mouth would spoil his game.

"The President," he confided in his diary, "said that he, Mr. Bryan, did not know that he, the President, was working for peace wholly through me, and he was afraid to mention this fact for fear it would offend him."

House's suggestion of mediation seems to have been taken seriously at least by the civilians among the Kaiser's advisers. So much so that he received a personal letter from Arthur Zimmermann at the Foreign Office.

"The war has been forced upon us by our enemies," Zimmermann wrote; "and they are carrying it on by summoning all the forces at their disposal, including Japanese and other colored races. This makes it impossible for us to take the first step . . . it seems to me worth while seeing how the land lies in the other camp."

House rushed to Washington with the letter. Wilson agreed with him that it offered a basis for negotiation. House must go to Europe to see what he could do. The situation was embarrassing because Secretary Bryan had been making it clear that he felt he was the man to go to Europe to stop the war.

His methods were oratory on the stump and daily publicity through the newspapers. By public discussion he would make the misguided belligerents see reason.

It was largely because Bryan had been so preoccupied with stump speaking during the fall campaign—which hadn't turned out too successfully for the Democrats—that he'd let the mediation negotiations get out of his hands. He couldn't help showing a certain pique on discovering that the supple colonel had taken the business into his own back room. In the end he generously acquiesced. So long as he was in the cabinet his attitude was: "The President knows best."

The Colonel's Reconnaissance

The President decided to send House abroad on the pretext of investigating war relief. "Our single object is to be serviceable," he wrote in a private letter House carried to show to Sir Edward Grey and to Zimmermann, "if we may, in bringing about the preliminary willingness to parley which must be the first step towards discussing and determining the conditions of peace."

"We are both of the same mind," House quoted the President as telling him in their final interview before he left for New York to board Britain's queen of the seas, the fast fourstack liner *Lusitania*. The details of the negotiations were left entirely to the colonel.

The President insisted on driving him to the Union Station in his own car: "The President's eyes were moist when he said his last words of farewell," House wrote in his diary. "He said 'Your unselfish and intelligent friendship has meant much to me' . . . He declared I was the only one in all the world to whom he could open his entire mind. I asked if he remembered the first day we met, some three and a half years ago. He replied 'Yes, but we had known each other always, and merely came in touch then, for our purposes and thoughts were as one' . . . He got out of the car and walked through the station and to the ticket office and then to the train itself, refusing to leave until I had entered the car."

As drenched in noble sentiments as any pair of Knights of the Round Table the two cronies parted. The colonel wrote from New York in an exalted vein. "Goodbye dear friend and may God sustain you in all your noble undertakings . . . You are the bravest wisest leader, the gentlest and most gallant gentleman and the truest friend in all the world."

The trip was stormy. "Just after passing the Banks," House entered in his diary, "a gale came shrieking down from Labrador and it looked as if we might perish. I have never witnessed so great a storm at sea . . . the *Lusitania*, big as she was, tossed about like a cork in the rapids. This afternoon as we approached the Irish coast the American flag was raised. It created much excitement."

Next day he entered an explanation: "Captain Dow had been greatly alarmed the night before . . . He expected to be torpedoed and that was the reason for raising the American flag. I can see many possible complications arising from this incident. Every newspaper in London has asked me about it, but, fortunately, I was not an eye-witness to it and have been able to say I only knew it from hearsay."

House found the London of the winter of 1915 so different from the London he'd known before that it might have been in another world. The stolid British were under siege. They had laughed off the Zeppelin bombings as a futile gesture of German frightfulness; they were treating as a victory the action off Dogger Bank where the British fleet took considerable punishment stopping a sudden new raid by German heavy cruisers, but the tight little island no longer felt safe from invasion.

On February 4, a couple of days before House landed in Liverpool, the German Admiralty, with twentyfour modern U-boats in commission, announced a submarine blockade of the British Isles: any Allied merchantman found in British waters would be sunk without warning. It was undoubtedly a radio report of that threat that caused the skipper of the *Lusitania* to break out the Stars and Stripes.

House was struck by the grim mood he found. England was settling down to war as a way of life. His kindly friend, Walter Hines Page at the Embassy, was subtly imbued with the war spirit. House, a man extremely sensitive to such influences, no sooner saw Sir Edward Grey than he blurted out to him that he had no intention of pushing the question of peace, not right now, "for in my opinion it could not be brought about before the middle of May or the first of June. I could see the necessity for the Allies to try out their new armies in the spring . . ."

The Foreign Office was all in a tizzy about how to deal with Mr. Wilson's confidential colonel. Even the humblest clerk knew that the Foreign Secretary was busy night and day tempting the Italians, the Greeks and the Romanians into the war on the Allied side with promises of hunks of Austrian, Hungarian and Turkish territory, and that the American Secretary of State's formula for peace on the basis of the *status quo ante* was thoroughly unwelcome.

Astonished at Colonel House's sweet reasonableness Sir Edward Grey wrote enthusiastically: "I found combined in him a rare degree of the qualities of wisdom and sympathy. In the stress of war it was at once a relief, a delight, an advantage to be able to talk to him freely . . . He had a way of saying 'I know it' in a tone and manner that carried conviction both of his sympathy with and understanding of what was said to him."

From London, House travelled to Paris, where he found the French icily preoccupied with their own ideas, and then through Switzerland to Berlin. He arrived in a March snowstorm. The civilians in the German administration were as cordial as before. They pointed out, however, the rising bitterness among the German people against American persistence in selling munitions to the Allies, while acquiescing in the blockade which was starving German women and children. House chummed up the waters by calling for inclusion of freedom of the seas in the eventual peace terms. "I have sown this thought of the Freedom of the Seas very widely since I have been here," he wrote the President, "and I think I can already see the results . . . I think I can show England that, in the long run . . . it is as much to her interest as it is to that of the other nations of the earth."

Back in Paris, he found the French, as usual, harder to talk to than the British and the Germans. The French politicians were obsessed with the idea that the President was privately pro-German. "I find your purpose badly misunderstood," House wrote him. For Secretary Bryan whom he made a point of soothing with vague communications, he summed up his mission, "Everybody seems to want peace but nobody is willing to concede enough to get it."

From Paris he returned to London where he found British ruling circles more warlike than ever. The very word "Peace" was getting a pro-German sound to their ears. Page gave vent to the pervading mood: "Peace talk . . . is yet mere moonshine—House has been to Berlin from London, thence to Paris, thence back to London again—from Nowhere (as far as peace is concerned) to Nowhere again."

The colonel remained optimistic. He seems to have taken it for granted that the expedition in preparation against the Dardanelles would knock Turkey out of the war, that the Balkan nations and Italy would come in on the Allied side and that then the Germans would be willing to negotiate. The English politicians he talked to gave him no inkling, if they knew it themselves, of the effectiveness of the U-boat war on shipping. In February and March a hundred and thirty thousand tons of Allied shipping was sunk.

Meanwhile in Washington discussions were going on continuously between the President, Secretary Bryan and Counsellor Lansing on how to preserve American neutrality. They were in agreement on the note to Great Britain protesting against the misuse of the American flag and on the note to Germany declaring that the German Government would be held strictly accountable for damage to American property and loss of American lives from submarines. Bryan was urging the President to use this opportunity to demand that both governments call off their blockades. He had been encouraged by von Bernstorff and by a note from the Foreign Office. He saw cancelling the two blockades as a first step towards inducing the belligerents to accept the Declaration of London.

Blockade and Counterblockade

The Secretary's hopes received a setback when, in spite of soothing phrases from the Foreign Office, the British in the middle of March announced a total embargo on trade with Germany. This last order in council resulted in an outburst of popular indignation in the United States led by the Hearst press. Powerful lobbies for cotton and copper were aroused. The German propaganda machine was encouraged to step up its agitation for an embargo on the shipment of munitions of war. In this the Irish societies in the east and good Bryan Democrats in the middlewest sympathized vigorously with the German-American bunds. Sentiment against war profits was growing. A steel company operating what was known as The Golden Rule Plant in St. Louis was one of a number of manufacturers to announce that they would sell no war materials whatsoever.

The President wrote House a sharp letter urging him to bring home to Sir Edward Grey the state of sentiment in America. Secretary of the Interior Lane wrote him too: "Notwithstanding all the insults of Germany, he (the President) is determined to endure to the limit . . . And the English are not behaving very well . . . We have been very meek and mild under their use of the ocean as a tollroad . . . You would be interested, I think in hearing some of the discussion around the Cabinet table. There isn't a man in the Cabinet who has a drop of German blood in his veins, I guess. Two of us were born under the British flag. I have two cousins in the British army and Mrs. Lane has three. The most of us are Scotch in our ancestry, and yet each day we meet we boil over somewhat, at the foolish manner in which England acts. Can it be that she is trying to hamper our trade? . . . If Congress were in session we would be actively

debating an embargo resolution today." The people had more confidence
in than love for the President he went on to say. Then he added: "I am
growing more and more in my admiration for Bryan each day. He is too
good a Christian to run a naughty world and he doesn't hate hard enough,
but he certainly is a noble and highminded man, and loyal to the President to the last hair."

Before American indignation had a chance to build up a proper head
of steam against the British, the exploits of the U-boats turned the popular fury against the Germans. Although the German U-boat commanders
were instructed to spare neutral ships, mistakes were inevitable. On
March 28 an American mining engineer named Leon C. Thrasher, bound
for a job in South Africa, was drowned when the British liner *Falaba* was
sunk by a German submarine.

The argument over poor Thrasher brought the differences of opinion
inside the administration to a boil. Lansing called the sinking "an atro-
cious act of lawlessness" and wanted vigorous action. Bryan put forth the
theory that Americans travelling on belligerent ships in wartime did so
at their own risk.

Wilson was of two minds. In every speech he made he was campaigning for "neutrality in thought and deed." Having convinced even Bryan
that the export of arms and ammunition was consistent with neutrality,
the President tended to Lansing's view on the need for a firm protest to
Berlin on Thrasher's death. Bryan was profoundly disturbed.

He wanted every dispute with the belligerents put up for arbitration.
"Nearly nine months have passed," he wrote the President, who preferred mulling over the arguments in writing rather than coping with
them during the hasty give and take of cabinet meetings, ". . . and after
the expenditure of ten billion dollars and the sacrifice of several millions
of the flower of Europe the war is at a draw. Surely the most sanguinary
ought to be satisfied with the slaughter. I submit that it is this nation's
right and duty to make, not a secret, but an open appeal for the acceptance of mediation . . . As the greatest Christian nation we should act—
we cannot avoid the responsibility."

Arbitration: the principle was so clear to him he could not understand
the President's hesitations. "Mary, what does the President mean?" he
asked his wife in agony of mind. "Why can't he see that by keeping open
the way for mediation and arbitration, he has an opportunity to do the
greatest work a man can do? I cannot understand his attitude."

The Lusitania

The German authorities were encouraged by American resentment against the British to step up their submarine war. While the President and Secretary Bryan were arguing over whether the Thrasher case was a fit subject for arbitration, news of new outrages poured in. A German airplane attempted to bomb the American ship *Cushing*, and the tanker *Gulflight* out of Port Arthur, Texas, was sunk without warning by a submarine in the Irish Sea. The skipper died of a heart attack and two sailors, who jumped overboard in fright, were drowned.

May 1, the same day that the *Gulflight* was sunk, there appeared in the newspapers of eastern seaboard cities an advertisement signed by the Imperial German Embassy warning prospective passengers against travelling through the warzone on British or Allied ships. The *Lusitania* was sailing from New York with an unusually large passenger list. Of the many passengers warned by anonymous telegrams and by strangers who whispered to them on the street, only one man, a clergyman from Bennington, Vermont, changed his passage to the American liner *New York*.

In London on May 7 submarines were on everybody's mind. Driving out to Kew on a flowery May morning Colonel House talked about the submarine war with Sir Edward Grey. "We spoke," he wrote in his diary, "of the probability of an ocean liner being sunk and I told him . . . a flame of indignation would sweep across America." Later in the day at a private audience with King George at Buckingham Palace their talk revolved around the same subject. "Suppose," said His Royal Highness, "they should sink the *Lusitania* with American passengers aboard?"

At lunchtime the same day, the *Lusitania*, steaming slowly on the straight course for Liverpool, as if there were no submarines in the world, was hit by a single torpedo fired by the U-20, Kapitan-lieutenant Walter Schwieger in command. In spite of watertight compartments the *Lusitania* rolled over and sank in eighteen minutes. Of the passengers and crew seven hundred and sixtyone were rescued and eleven hundred and fifty-three drowned, among them a hundred and fourteen American citizens including women and children.

May 9 Colonel House sent the President a cable: "I believe an immediate demand should be made upon Germany for assurance that this shall not happen again . . . America has come to the parting of the ways."

"We shall be at war within a month," he told Ambassador Page.

Before any reply came from the President, House stepped out on a London street one morning and read a newspaper headline advertized by a sandwichman: WILSON: TOO PROUD TO FIGHT.

The Lusitania Fury

In Washington, the President had just returned from a pleasant trip to Williamstown, Massachusetts, for the christening of his first grandson, Francis Woodrow Sayre, when he received the news. The cable was handed to him as he came out from a cabinet meeting.

In the face of the explosion of indignation in the newspapers that followed Wilson gritted his jaw. He had Lansing examine the manifest of the *Lusitania* and discovered the cargo was mostly food but included four thousand two hundred cases of cartridges and one thousand two hundred and fiftynine cases of unloaded steel shrapnel shells. The impression at the State Department was that the ship was armed. Secretary Bryan's opinion was that "England," as he put it to his wife, "has been using our citizens to protect her ammunition."

Wilson's secretary, Tumulty, although as anti-British as a professional Irishman could be, was profoundly shocked by the horror of drowning innocent noncombatants. He could not understand the President's grim detachment. He let the President know that his coolness surprised him. "'I suppose you think I am cold and indifferent,'" Tumulty quoted him as replying, "'and a little less than human, but, my dear fellow you are mistaken, for I have spent many sleepless hours thinking about this tragedy. It has hung over me like a terrible nightmare.' . . . I had never seen him more serious and careworn," added Tumulty.

In public, in the face of denunciations from Theodore Roosevelt, who was beating the wardrums now in every speech, Wilson was determined to continue on his neutral course. Addressing a group of recently naturalized citizens in Philadelphia on May 10, he told them: "The example of America must be the example not only of peace because it will not fight, but of peace because peace is the healing and elevating influence of the world and strife is not. There is such a thing as being too proud to fight."

The words "too proud to fight" sounded fine in Secretary Bryan's ears, but to the growing horde of pro-Allied partisans, outraged almost to madness by new tales of German brutality in the daily press, they had a hollow sound. To the British they seemed the denial of every decent feeling.

The Bryce Report

It was an accident that the Bryce report was published five days after the sinking of the *Lusitania,* but a most timely one. All that winter Viscount Bryce had been acting as chairman of a committee appointed by

Prime Minister Asquith to sift the truth out of allegations by the Belgians of unnecessary atrocities by the German troops occupying their unhappy country. The public had been made receptive to a gruesome diet by the wave of horror that swept through the Allied nations after the first gas attacks during the fighting at Ypres in April. Propaganda agencies were filling the newspapers with stories of enemy frightfulness. The Germans were Huns; they had crucified a Canadian officer, they cut the breasts off women; the Kaiser had personally instructed his troops to crucify Belgian babies on the doors of barns.

The wildest tale, later admitted to have been a hoax, was of the German corpse factories. General Charteris, a British intelligence officer in France, snipped off the caption of a German photograph of dead horses being taken to a rendering plant and pasted it on a photograph of a trainload of human corpses being removed from the front for burial. The German explanation that the word *kadaveren* in their language only referred to animal corpses made no impression on the Allied press.

Soberminded Americans had so far been a little leery of British and French atrocity stories. German treatment of the Belgians was brutal enough, in all conscience; there was no doubt about the German burning of Dinant and Louvain and the shooting of indiscriminate masses of civilian hostages; but, after reading the appendix to the Bryce report, opinion-moulders in newspaper offices and rectories and colleges were ready to believe anything. Viscount Bryce had a worldwide eminence that matched that of almost any living Englishman. Literate Americans revered him as a god. Whatever he put his name to must be true.

The fact that the evidence was collected not by the eminent members of the committee but by "thirty barristers" working anonymously, that the witnesses were not sworn, and that their names were not given, and that no effort was made to make an on the spot check of atrocity stories through neutral investigators, made scant impression at the time. The columns of American newspapers were filled for weeks with accounts of the hideous brutalities of the German soldiery.

For the British it was a propaganda victory. The sufferings of the brave Belgians quite drowned out pleas for neutral rights coming from levelheaded professionals in the State Department.

Mr. Bryan's Last Stand

Against this background of mounting hysteria Bryan manfully held his ground for arbitration, mediation and peaceful solutions. Lansing, who now had the President's ear, rebuffed his suggestion that ships carrying war munitions be forbidden to carry passengers. Bryan wanted Americans at least to be warned against travelling on belligerent ships, and for some means to be found to put off dangerous issues for arbitration after the war was over. He admitted the need to protest to Germany, but he asked for a simultaneous protest to England against Allied treatment of neutral shipping, to show Germany "that we are defending our rights against aggression from both sides."

Lansing's draft of a severe note to Berlin telling the Germans they would be held to "strict accountability" for the loss of American lives became, in spite of Bryan's protests, the basis for the document the President wrote out on his own typewriter, as usual all alone in his study. At the last moment Bryan induced Wilson to prepare a statement to the press to be issued at the same time, emphasizing the ancient friendship between the American and German peoples, and suggesting again the postponement until peacetime of conflicts that could not be settled by diplomatic means.

When Tumulty saw Secretary Bryan's press release the excitable Irishman had a fit. He alerted several members of the cabinet and pointed out to his boss that taking the sting out of the note this way would only encourage the Germans to sink more ships. The President, who had confidence in his secretary's popular touch, was convinced. Most of the cabinet members whom Wilson consulted agreed. When Tumulty joined Secretary of War Garrison for lunch at the Shoreham after his bout with the President he was still pale and shaking. "I've just had the worst half hour of my life," he said. Garrison told him he ought to have a medal of honor for his good work.

By this time President Wilson had decided that the country demanded a stiff protest even at the risk of breaking off relations with Germany. Bryan was not convinced. Not a man to keep his ideas to himself, in an expansive moment he assured Dr. Dumba, the Austro-Hungarian ambassador, that the United States had no intention of going to war, but only wanted a German assurance that ruthless submarine warfare would stop.

Dumba, a bald, stooping, mustachioed figure, whom Lansing found to be "the most adroit and at the same time the most untrustworthy of the diplomatic representatives of the Central Powers," immediately transmitted these soothing words to his government via the German radio station in Berlin.

There U. S. Ambassador Gerard was dramatizing the importance of the *Lusitania* note by making sleepingcar reservations for his wife and himself to Switzerland. Zimmermann, who had been given a copy of the radiogram before it was forwarded to Vienna, read it out triumphantly to Gerard as a proof that President Wilson's *Lusitania* note was merely for home consumption. Gerard cabled the news to House. House cabled the President and the fat was in the fire.

Secretary Bryan called in Dumba to his office. Dumba admitted that the language of his message had been misconstrued, and Bryan issued a repudiation of the whole interview to the press. The Peacemaker was editorially tarred and feathered by the eastern newspapers.

Meanwhile in Berlin the advocates of ruthless submarine warfare were quoting Bryan's words as proof that no amount of frightfulness would bring the United States into the war. As a result the German foreign office dispatched a highly unsatisfactory reply to the American note. House in London, who had been working for just the sort of mutual abatement of the two blockades that Bryan wanted as the first step towards a mediated settlement, gave up his mission in despair. He returned home, accompanied as usual by his wife and his secretary, Miss Denton, who coded and decoded his private messages. This time House's little group sailed on the *St. Paul* of the American Line.

The pro-Allied press was in a fever against Bryan and his pacifism. The Republicans, in New England especially, now committed to intervention on the Allied side, poured out their scorn on the ineffectiveness of President Wilson's stream of notes. Theodore Roosevelt called the *Lusitania* sinking an act of piracy and made it clear that if he'd been President none of this would have been allowed to happen.

The Peacemaker Resigns

Bryan's position in the administration was becoming impossible. His pacifism and his arbitration treaties were the laughingstock of editorial writers. At a cabinet meeting called to discuss the German answer to the *Lusitania* note, which Frank Cobb described in the *World* as "the answer of an outlaw who assumes no obligation towards society," the Secretary of State seemed, as Secretary of Agriculture Houston recalled it, "to be laboring under great strain, and sat back in his chair most of the time with his eyes closed." Suddenly he snapped out, "You people are not neutral. You are taking sides."

The President was nettled. With a cold flare in his gray eyes he said in the voice which he could make so icy, "Mr. Secretary, you have no right to make that statement. We are all honestly trying to be neutral against heavy difficulties."

The Germans were claiming that they had a right to sink the *Lusitania* as an armed ship carrying munitions of war. Counsellor Lansing got up an elaborate brief refuting the German contentions point by point, but as Woodrow Wilson revised it, his chief theme became "the sinking of this passenger ship involves principles of humanity which throw into the background any special circumstances of detail."

Wilson was seeing the drowned bodies of women and children washed up on the Irish coast. Bryan was sending him copious messages meanwhile begging for mention of arbitration and asking for a parallel note to England. To Wilson, as to most Americans, the quarrel with England, about the money value of goods and seized cargoes and the technicalities of contraband, was in a different category from the quarrel with Germany, which involved human lives. He wrote Secretary Bryan "with the warmest regard and with a very solemn and by no means self-confident sense of deep responsibility," that he could not agree with him. Bryan decided he would have to resign.

It was a Saturday. Bryan went around to see McAdoo, whom he considered the member of the cabinet closest to the President. Perhaps he thought McAdoo might help him argue the President around to his point of view.

McAdoo set to work to talk Bryan out of the idea of resigning and right after lunch drove over to see Mrs. Bryan. Everybody had confidence in Mrs. Bryan's level head. Mrs. Bryan came right out with it. Her husband felt that Colonel House's opinions were given more weight than her husband's. Lansing furnished the background. The President wrote all the state papers. The Secretary of State was playing the part of a figurehead.

Then she went on to tell of her husband's sleepless nights, his agony of mind. McAdoo begged the Bryans to think it over for a day or two and suggested she take her husband out to the country for the weekend. The Bryans jumped at the suggestion and drove out to a friend's house in Silver Spring. The magnolias were in bloom, mockingbirds sang through the moonlit June night but Bryan could get no repose. Sunday he took a long walk. That night Mrs. Bryan got a doctor to prescribe a sleeping powder. Monday morning he woke up refreshed but with his determination unshaken.

The Bryans were hardly back in their house on Calumet Place Monday morning, when McAdoo came in with fresh arguments. Bryan would be accused of having resigned to embarrass the Administration. His career would be ruined. "I believe you are right," Bryan answered solemnly. "I think this will destroy me . . . it is merely the sacrifice one must not hesitate to make to serve his God and his country."

At the State Department Lansing sought the Secretary out and begged him not to resign, but Bryan had become suspicious of Lansing's sincerity in his regard. He drove to the White House for an hour's quiet talk with the President. The President was convinced the *Lusitania* note was right. The Secretary was convinced it was wrong. Bryan became agitated. His hands shook so that when he tried to pour himself out a glass of water he spilt it on the table.

"Colonel House," he said, "has been Secretary of State, not I, and I have never had your full confidence."

He went back to his office and wrote out his resignation. The President accepted it immediately.

At the cabinet meeting next day the President announced that Mr.

Bryan had resigned but suggested he be asked to attend anyway. Throughout the meeting Bryan, his face white and haggard, sat back in his chair as his habit was when he was disturbed, with his eyes closed.

After the President had retired Bryan asked the members of the cabinet to lunch with him. In a private dining room at the University Club he told the five men who went along that he felt a second note meant war. He said he knew the President wanted to avoid war as much as he did. "I believe I can do more on the outside to prevent war than I can on the inside. I think I can help the President more on the outside."

"You are the most sincere Christian I know," blurted out cheerful plump Secretary of the Interior Lane. Tears glistened in his eye.

Bryan broke down. "I go out into the dark," he said huskily. "The President has the prestige and power on his side." Then he added, "I have many friends who would die for me."

The scene remained so vivid to several of the men present that they described it at some length in their memoirs.

Chapter 8

THE LONELY MAN IN THE WHITE HOUSE

COLONEL House sailed home convinced that war with Germany was inevitable. He told his friend and T.R.'s, the half-Americanized instigator of the Irish cooperative movement, Sir Horace Plunkett, who was at this stage his liaison man with the Asquith government, that he was going home to persuade the President "not to conduct a milk and water war, but to put all the strength, all the virility, all the energy of our nation into it so that Europe might remember for a century what it meant to provoke a peaceful nation into war."

Before House left London, Plunkett arranged for him to visit some members of the new coalition cabinet Asquith was organizing in an effort to meet public criticism of the lag in the supply of shells for the artillery in France. He had talks with the Chancellor of the Exchequer; with Lloyd George, the oratorical Welsh leader of the radical wing of the Liberal Party, who was applying his great energies to the Ministry of Munitions; and with Arthur Balfour, the philosopher of conservatism, now First Lord of the Admiralty. They were all delighted by his belligerent views.

The life of Mr. Wilson's confidential colonel seemed so precious to the Allied cause that the Admiralty furnished the *St. Paul* with a convoy through the danger zone.

House was pleased by the two destroyers but regretted that they made themselves conspicuous by steaming right alongside the American liner. "Much as I appreciate this attention," he wrote in his diary, "I have many misgivings as to what the American press may say, and also whether it might not lessen my influence as intermediary of the President."

The destroyers threw the American press into a hubbub of speculation. Hearst's New York *American* referred to mysterious dispatches Colonel House was bringing home with him. The dispatches were mostly in the confidential colonel's head.

When Dudley Field Malone, whom House had helped obtain the appointment of Collector of the Port of New York, came out on the revenue cutter to meet him off Ambrose Lightship, his news was that the colonel would be the next Secretary of State. A smile creased the small jaw under the neatly clipped mustache. House shook his narrow head. He could be more useful doing what he was doing, he told Malone, in a tone that resounded with untold secrets. When the reporters met him at the dock he confused them thoroughly. "I did not talk peace," he said, "that was not my mission."

Colonel and Mrs. House stopped off to see their daughter and her family on Long Island and then repaired to their summer place at Manchester, Massachusetts. Sir Cecil Spring Rice had a house at Prides Crossing nearby. The upstate North Shore village became the center for many portentous comings and going.

The President and his confidential colonel were communicating only by letter and telephone during this period. It was understood that Colonel House must never be asked to Washington during the hot weather. Now Wilson let him know that, much as he wanted to press the hand of his affectionate friend, for fear of comment in the newspapers he thought it wiser not to call on him on his way to Cornish. He had taken for the summer the ample mansion which the American author Winston Churchill built himself out of the earnings of his novels, in New Hampshire, on the edge of the White Mountains. Margaret Wilson who was working hard on her singing in preparation for a concert tour in the fall, and Helen Bones and several other of the relatives who hovered about the President in hopes of relieving his widower's solitude, were already there. The President planned a full two weeks vacation from the nagging decisions and the sultry heat of the executive office.

The President was holding House at arm's length for a while. Perhaps he was waiting for the influence of Sir Edward Grey to wear off. He had decided not to appoint Walter Hines Page whom House seems to have then favored for Secretary of State. The President thought his old publisher friend too much under the influence of the beguiling English and appointed Lansing instead. Wilson was determined to keep foreign affairs in his own hands and he felt that Lansing had just the right training in the language of international law to give legal underpinning to his own ideas.

He was still fond of the colonel but he didn't need the company of a confidential crony as much as he'd needed it during the past winter. He had acquired a new crony of a much more attractive sort.

Mrs. Galt

The President was in love with a Washington widow.

It was the congenial Dr. Grayson who first met Mrs. Galt, at the Mount Kineo House on Moosehead Lake in the summer of 1914, while he was courting a younger friend of hers, a Virginia girl named Altrude Gordon, whom he was later to marry. Mrs. Galt favored the match. The doctor found her charming and introduced her to Eleanor McAdoo and to Helen

Bones. The ladies struck up a friendship, and one fine March day, after a walk in Rock Creek Park, Helen Bones invited Mrs. Galt to tea at the White House. Dr. Grayson and President Wilson happened to come back from golf just as the ladies were beginning their tea. The President invited himself to the party and became unusually animated and amusing.

Edith Bolling Galt was born and raised in Wytheville, Virginia. Her father was a rural judge of some standing, who served on the board of visitors of the University. She was seventh in a family of five boys and four girls. Like so many southern families in the postbellum period the Bollings made up for their lack of this world's goods by enlarging abundantly on the family's past glories. The Bollings traced their ancestry to Pocahontas.

It was considered quite a comedown when beautiful buxom vivacious Edith Bolling consented to marry a tradesman. Norman Galt was a very nice man and welloff, but he ran a retail jewelry business in Washington. The business did have a most fashionable clientele. With that complete confidence in her own brilliance, intelligence, charm, attractiveness to the male which characterized her generation of southern belles, Mrs. Galt held her head high.

As the wife of a tradesman her existence was not recognized by the ladies and gentlemen unsullied by toil who were written up in the newspapers as the capital city's social leaders. She gave out that social life bored her. The marriage was childless. She devoted herself to her husband's business interests, and when he died untimely, she took a hand in the management of the jewelry store.

After the first black crepe period of mourning was over Mrs. Galt discovered that purple was becoming. The broad picture hats of the period brought out her dark hair and flashing eyes and fine teeth. She surrounded herself with Virginia relatives and kept a certain air of mystery about her. She was pointed out as one of the most beautiful women in Washington.

Edith Galt needed a husband as badly as Woodrow Wilson needed a wife. She shared his southern prejudices. She was a good listener with that knack possessed by many women of her peculiar upbringing of appearing more knowledgeable than she really was. She was good company. She had a certain stylish dash. She bought her clothes at Worth's in Paris and liked to wear an orchid pinned on her left shoulder.

Before long the President was sending her flowers daily and passing on state documents for her comments. His attentions to Mrs. Galt left little time for the usual affectionate epistles to Colonel House.

"I never worry when I don't hear from you," House wrote the President. "No human agency can make me doubt your friendship and affection. I always understand your motives."

The Colonel's Callers

The Houses had hardly settled in their Manchester home before a stream of callers started. First it was Attorney General Gregory who described the scene of Bryan's resignation and brought the colonel up to date on the cabinet gossip. The next day it was Spring Rice.

Wartime strains were telling on Sir Cecil. He was worried about his family and friends in England exposed to bombings from the air. He knew enough to see through the optimistic communiqués published in the British and American press. He knew that the Gallipoli expedition, which was to have opened up the Black Sea for the Russians and blocked off the Central Powers from the Middle East, was a costly failure; that Italy's entrance into the war was not bringing the hoped for advantages; that the Russians were on the run in Poland; that the Allied offensives on the western front were proving to be an inconclusive butchery of brave men by the tens of thousands. His health was poor and he felt a peevish irritability that occasionally showed itself in public tantrums.

Secretary Lansing, who disliked Sir Cecil, described him about this time in his private notes, as looking and acting like "a foreign office clerk" with his small pointed gray beard, his pepper and salt sack suits baggy at the knees, and his pockets always bulging with documents. Known as an intimate of T.R.'s old Washington circle, the President suspected him of being in cahoots with the Republican opposition.

House found him wellinformed. Though he disparaged his effectiveness as a diplomat, as a man he enjoyed talking to him. This time he raked Sir Cecil over the coals a little for having allowed himself to be heard to complain that the President was pro-German. He knew better. He was as bad as Jusserand. "I advised him," wrote the colonel, "in the future to say nothing upon the subject or to maintain that the President was observing strict neutrality."

The next day von Bernstorff appeared in Manchester. The natty Prussian with the kaiserlike mustaches, who was already boasting to his superiors how easy it was "to hold off" Colonel House, couldn't have been more cordial. Unfriendly observers noticed something unpleasant about the writhing of von Bernstorff's full lips under his mustache when he desired to be particularly ingratiating. Von Bernstorff talked sympathetically about the treaties of 1785 and 1799 between the United States and Prussia, and the possibility of getting the U-boats to conform to the rules therein laid down for cruiser warfare. Germany would suspend her submarine blockade if the British allowed Germany to import food. The count claimed to envisage a possible peace settlement, with Germany evacuating Belgium and northern France on a basis of no indemnities, no reparations. House observed in his notes that he talked like a neutral: "If he's not sincere, he's the most consummate actor I've ever met."

The German ambassador had reason to be in high spirits. Germany was winning the war. American opinion, which he felt he had some part in forming, was building up against the munitions trade.

The German ambassador spent as much time at the Ritz Carleton in New York, which was his propaganda headquarters, as at the Embassy in Washington. The campaign for an embargo on arms shipments was eliciting support. William Jennings Bryan, thrilling great crowds with his demand for an immediate negotiated peace to be enforced by an embargo on arms to the belligerents, was unwittingly helping the German cause. Ample funds were available to subsidize German and Hungarian daily newspapers and weeklies in the various slavic languages of the Hapsburg Empire. In spite of all Spring Rice could do, the very vocal Irish populations scattered over the country refused to be convinced that Britain would not default on her promise of home rule for Erin.

Outside of the east coast, peace sentiment was overwhelming. The Republicans had inaugurated their League to Enforce Peace on June 17 at Independence Hall in Philadelphia with many notables in attendance and ex-President Taft ponderous and benign in the chair. Taft aroused more applause when he talked about peace than when he talked about enforcement.

Von Bernstorff's mission was to keep America neutral. He was looking forward to success with a reasonable amount of confidence, until, a few days after his talk with Colonel House, the whole fabric of German propaganda began blowing up in his face.

The Year of the Bombs

Nineteen fifteen was a year of bomb scares. Persons who confessed to being anarchists were caught attempting to explode what the newspapers described as an infernal machine in St. Patrick's Cathedral in New York. A bomb went off in the new Bronx courthouse. A mansion belonging to Andrew Carnegie was damaged by a similar explosion. Now on July 3 readers of the morning papers the country over read with amazement and horror that the afternoon before a bomb had shattered a reception room in the Senate wing of the Capitol at Washington.

That same morning Spring Rice breakfasted with the J. P. Morgans at Glen Cove, their Long Island place, where he was spending the weekend. Jack Morgan, as his friends called him, since old J. Pierpont Morgan's death the year before the war broke out, was chief ruler of the financial empire of the Morgan banks. Brought up in England, English in tastes and sympathies, he became the kingpin of the Franco-British wartrade in the United States.

The British ambassador was quietly chatting with Mr. and Mrs. Morgan over the coffee and newspapers when he heard the butler shouting "in a most fearful voice" to Mr. Morgan to go upstairs.

The party went scuttling about the upper floors looking for a fire. On their way back down the front stairs they ran into the butler being backed up step by step by a thinfaced man with a revolver in each hand. "So you are Mr. Morgan," the assassin said, raising his pistols. As the man reached the upper hall Morgan and his wife both jumped at him. A powerful heavyset man like his father, Jack Morgan pinned the man to the floor. As he fell the man discharged both pistols. By this time the butler had found some firetongs and started beating the man over the head with them. Other servants came with ropes and trussed him up.

"I see that the thing to do is to close at once with the assassin and not let him put his hands out," Spring Rice wrote Mrs. Henry Cabot Lodge, deprecating any assistance he'd been able to give; "Morgan was really a trump and so was she."

Morgan, bleeding from a wound in the thigh and an abdominal wound that might have been fatal, walked stolidly to the telephone, called his office in New York and told them to send out the best physician they could find. Then he lay down on the bed.

It turned out that one bullet had merely creased the skin of his belly while the other had gone through a fleshy part of the thigh. He was on his feet in a few days.

The assailant on being taken to the Mineola jail gave his name as Frank Holt. He was identified as a Ph.D. who taught German at Cornell. He claimed he had not intended to kill Mr. Morgan but merely to hold his family as hostages until Morgan gave orders to suspend the shipment of munitions to Great Britain. On further questioning he boasted of having planted the bomb in the Capitol the day before. He refused all food, tried to slash his wrists and seemed in a state of complete nervous collapse. He was obviously a man of education and at times was quite coherent. Always he came back to his determination to stop the shipment of munitions.

Widening investigation turned up an extraordinary tale. The man was a German. His real name was Erich Muenther. An instructor in Germanic languages at Harvard, he had vanished a few years before from Cambridge with the dead body of his first wife, on being questioned by the police over her death from arsenic poisoning. Professor Hugo Muensterberg, the famous psychologist and stout defender of the German cause, admitted that he'd known Muenther and threw a hedge of scientific terminology about the proposition that Muenther had been mad all along.

The same day the newspapers printed the story of Holt's past, they reported his suicide. In some unaccountable way he had been allowed to escape from his cell and was said to have killed himself plunging head first from the upper tier of cells above to the concrete floor below. The jailer's first story was that he'd blown his head off by chewing on a percussion cap. Spring Rice claimed Muenther was murdered by an accomplice.

This news had hardly hit the headlines before a message came from Holt's present wife in Texas warning the police that Holt had written her that he'd planted time bombs on a number of eastbound liners. Searches were carried out on several ships in vain, but sure enough, a few days later, there was a violent explosion on the *Minnehaha* of the Atlantic Transport Line bound for England with a cargo of munitions.

Dr. Albert's Briefcase

While these events were holding the front pages, a tale even more fantastic was being unfolded by Secretary Lansing and his assistants for the private ear of Woodrow Wilson, still happily vacationing at Cornish in a house full of adoring relatives with Mrs. Galt as house guest.

In early July Lansing received a letter from a young lady of his acquaintance who was spending the summer at a fashionable hotel at Kennebunkport, Maine, saying that she had information of vital importance which she didn't dare put in writing. Lansing sent up his assistant Chandler Anderson who hurried back to Washington with her story.

An aristocratic young German who spoke perfect English and seemed thoroughly at home in the highest circles in England and America had lost his head so completely in his enthusiasm for the young lady's charms that he had confessed to her that he was the secret German agent who had given the order for the sinking of the *Lusitania*.

The Department of Justice checked on the story and discovered that the gentleman was Franz Rintelen von Kliest, an intelligence officer on the staff of the German Admiralty, sent to America on a Swiss passport with many millions of dollars at his disposal to try to get the Welland Canal destroyed; to hire underworld characters to blow up munitions ships and piers; to stir up strikes against the loading of arms for the Allies and to finance a counterrevolution in Mexico by the ousted Huerta, who was lurking on the United States side of the Mexican border, against the Carranza government.

The story was corroborated again when British Intelligence lured Rintelen aboard a Europebound liner by a message in the supersecret German Admiralty code which the British had broken. They arrested him when they searched the ship off Dover.

A couple of weeks before Rintelen stepped into the British trap, Dr. Heinrich Albert, commercial attaché of the German Embassy, a privy counsellor and a gentleman of great prestige in Germany, was indiscreet enough to forget his briefcase on an elevated train in New York.

Secretary McAdoo's treasury agents had been interested in Dr. Albert for some time. Besides being commercial attaché he had an office on lower Broadway with vast bank accounts, where no visible business was transacted. Dr. Albert's briefcase came into McAdoo's hands through a series of happy accidents.

Two secretservice agents were dogging the footsteps of George Sylvester Viereck, editor of *The Fatherland* who was suspected, it turned out, rightly, of being in the pay of the German Government. Following him one Saturday afternoon from the offices of the Hamburg-Amerika Line to the Rector Street station of the Sixth Avenue El, they noticed that he was being very deferential to a large germaniclooking gentleman carrying a heavily stuffed briefcase who accompanied him.

One of the agents followed Mr. Viereck when he left the train at Twentythird Street, the other, Frank Burke by name, stayed aboard to watch the stout gentleman, whom he'd now decided must be the portentous Dr. Albert.

Dr. Albert, who was reading a paper, almost missed his stop at Fiftieth Street and jumping up shouted to the guard to hold the train. In his excitement he left his briefcase on the seat.

Frank Burke just had time to snatch it up and make away with it before Dr. Albert came storming back into the car. After a chase Burke managed to elude the stout German and get the briefcase into the hands of William J. Flynn, the head of the Secret Service. "A glance at the contents of the bag," he noted in his report, "though much of it was in German, satisfied me that I'd done a good Saturday's work."

The documents in Dr. Albert's briefcase dealt with the subsidizing of newspapers and motion pictures and lecture tours, with the bribing of labor leaders to foment strikes in munitions plants and to agitate for an arms embargo. ("I am morally convinced," McAdoo noted when he described the incident in his memoirs, "that the British were doing the same thing, but we had no documentary proof.") With Teutonic thoroughness every detail was set down of the measures being taken to get control of the Wright Airplane Company, to rig the cotton market, to corner chlorine and to purchase munitions to keep them away from the Allies.

Flynn immediately jumped on the Bar Harbor express to take the mass of material up to Secretary McAdoo who was at North Haven, Maine, with his family. McAdoo drove over to Cornish to show the President the documents.

Wilson told him to get Lansing's and Colonel House's advice as to whether they should be published. The three of them, House, Lansing and McAdoo, decided to give copies to Frank Cobb who, promising to release no inkling of their origin, started publishing them in the *World* as a great scoop on August 15. It was generally believed that British Intelligence furnished the documents.

House as usual gave his opinion to the President in writing: "It may . . . even lead us to war, but I think the publication should go ahead. It will strengthen your hands enormously and will weaken such agitators as Mr. Bryan . . ."

Personal Diplomacy

Every new disclosure of German intrigue deepened House's conviction that the United States would be drawn into the war on the side of the Allies. He wanted American involvement to come about in such a way that the United States could dictate the terms of the peace that had to follow.

In his talks with Sir Edward Grey in London, he had already broached the idea of an alliance of nations to keep the peace. But first the war had to be brought to an end. To dictate a rational peace in a world where only force was respected the United States had to have at least a potential army. Josephus Daniels, with the help of the Navy League and other powerful congressional lobbies, was doing a good job building up the fleet. The army was Saturday's child.

In his letters to the President, House was trying, through suggestions phrased with oleaginous tact, to bring his friend around to an understanding of the need for preparedness. Wilson still shied off from the word. Preparedness had taken an evil connotation in his mind because Theodore Roosevelt, whom he was coming to consider his archenemy, was calling for it in every speech he made.

Early in August the retired Chief of Staff called on Colonel House in Manchester. Major General Leonard Wood was a New Englander who had gone into the army from the Harvard Medical School. A vigorous broadshouldered man, full of enthusiasm for frontier life, he found while serving in the campaign against Geronimo that he was more interested in soldiering than in doctoring. It was Wood who helped T.R. organize the Rough Riders and who was in command at San Juan Hill. As military governor of Cuba he backed Walter Reed in his investigation of the causes of yellow fever. In the Philippines he helped pacify the Moros.

Wood was the living examplar of the New Nationalism. No more given to keeping his opinions to himself than his friend T.R., his army career proved stormy. Taft appointed him to the newly instituted post of Chief of Staff. Now he was organizing officers training camps to prepare for the war he was sure would come. Since the Democratic administration furnished him with no funds, the students paid their own way. He wanted House to convince the President that the regular army should immediately be raised to full strength. He was talking up universal military service on the Swiss model.

The immediate aim of his visit was to urge House to argue the President into letting him go to the western front for a while as an observer. He promised to do it without publicity. He pointed out that American officers had no idea of how the war was actually being fought.

House couldn't have agreed with the general more wholeheartedly. He passed on Wood's suggestions to Wilson at Cornish but got no reply. Perhaps it was enough for the President that Wood was a friend of T.R.'s.

Wilson remained the man of words. He was working long hours at his solitary typewriter trying to find just the right words that would convince the Germans on the one hand and the British on the other that they must bind themselves to respect neutral rights at sea. Considerations of power politics failed to hold his attention. On problems of action he liked to have his mind made up for him. But how could he trust any other man's judgement? He was getting a somewhat petulant attitude towards all his various advisers and passing on the carbons of their reports on White House flimsy to Mrs. Galt with derogatory remarks pencilled in the margins.

Only Edith Galt thoroughly understood his lonely dedication to doing the right thing. He had already told his daughters of their approaching engagement. The daughters approved.

While the President was taking Mrs. Galt and the ladies of the family on summer automobile rides to show them his favorite views over the New Hampshire lakes, he was letting Colonel House bear the brunt of a new tangled dispute with Great Britain over cotton. The President was making no bones of the fact that as soon as he extorted a satisfactory agreement from the Germans on the *Lusitania* sinking he was going to turn his attention to the highhanded conduct of the British blockade.

During Sir Edward Grey's much needed vacation, watching his birds and enjoying the North Country dialect of his farmhands at Falloden, Asquith's coalition cabinet decided that, come what might, they had to take cotton off the free list. The British were detaining more neutral ships than ever. They had already seized two hundred thousand bales of American cotton consigned to Rotterdam; but, to avoid bringing the issue to a head, were paying for them at prevailing market rates.

The South, where so many good Democrats lived, was in an uproar again at the prospect of cotton being declared contraband. Lansing was

issuing preliminary warnings through Ambassador Page. It was up to
House, who had won the British Foreign Minister's private esteem, directly and working through Spring Rice, to convince the British that only
by generous treatment of the cotton interests could they avoid agitation
in Congress for that embargo on the export of munitions which the German propagandists were working so hard to obtain.

House put the dilemma clearly in two cables, coming as authorized by
the President, to Sir Horace Plunkett in mid July. He frightened Spring
Rice with the picture of an aroused South shouting for an embargo.

The British Cabinet saw reason and put into effect what became
known as the Crawford plan, since it was finally formulated by Sir Richard Crawford, their embassy's commercial adviser, with the advice of
prominent cotton brokers and of the governor of the New York Federal
Reserve Bank. The British Treasury would send agents into the exchanges in Liverpool, New York and New Orleans to support the price
of cotton. The United States Government would submit, at least tacitly,
to cotton's being declared absolute contraband. It might cost the British
twenty million pounds, but it would be a fair price to pay to stave off
the arms embargo.

House and Spring Rice conferred almost daily. Officially the President
was supposed to be in the dark on these negotiations, but practically he
gave his approval of each step through the confidential colonel.

As soon as von Bernstorff got wind of the Crawford plan he rushed
into the State Department with a German offer to buy three million bales
at the market price if the United States would guarantee their transport
to Germany. Blockade was outbidding blockade in the cotton exchanges.
The cotton interests began to take heart. Wilson, in high righteousness,
denounced the German plan as an attempt to bribe the American people.

The British had barely reached a happy solution of the cotton imbroglio before a new crisis began to loom. The pound sterling that had
ruled world finance for a hundred years was in trouble. The British were
running out of credit.

McAdoo, who saw at once that American war prosperity depended on
Allied credit to finance the munitions trade, was trying to talk the President into reversal of his earlier attitude, assumed under Bryan's influence,
that the financing of warloans would be an unneutral act.

While McAdoo, to whom as a moneyhungry southerner the soaring
stockmarket, high wages, boom prices for cotton and wheat were the
chief consideration, worked in Washington, J. P. Morgan wrestled with
the financial community in New York, which still harbored many neutral
and even pro-German elements. Little by little regulations against dis-
counting Allied paper through the Federal Reserve banks were relaxed.

The German submarine command gave the pro-Allied bankers a hand by sinking on August 19, just as their foreign office seemed about to talk turkey on the *Lusitania* protests, the British liner *Arabic,* of fifteen thousand tons, outward bound out of Liverpool for New York. There were fortyfour casualties, and two Americans among the killed. The news threw the President into an agony of indecision. "I greatly need your advice what to do in view of the sinking of the Arabic," Wilson wrote House.

"The President has put it up to me and I have not flinched in my advice," House noted proudly in his diary. ". . . No citizen of the United States realizes better than I the horrors of this war, and no one would go further to avoid it, but there is a limit to all things. Our people do not want war," he wrote the President, "but even less do they want you to recede from the position you have taken . . . Your first note on the Lusitania made you not only the first citizen of America but the first citizen of the world. If by any word or act you should hurt our pride of nationality you would lose your commanding position overnight."

The President didn't like the last sentence. "All this is true, only too true," he scribbled on the copy he sent Mrs. Galt. "I wish he had not put in the sentence I have marked in the margin. It is not how I will stand that I am thinking, but of what it is right to do. You see he does not advise," Wilson added pettishly. "He puts it up to me."

The colonel was advising him all right. Indeed the President found an ingenious way to follow the colonel's advice without committing himself too far. He inspired a news report: if the facts of the sinking of the *Arabic* proved to be what they seemed to be from the first accounts, the United States Government would break off diplomatic relations with Germany. The result was headlines in the press and the immediate collapse, in Wilhelmstrasse at least, of German obduracy.

On September 1, von Bernstorff appeared, all smiles, in Secretary Lansing's office at the State Department. His Foreign Office he announced cheerily, was about to yield. Lansing insisted on a written statement. An hour later von Bernstorff was back with the assurance in the form of a letter: "Liners will not be sunk by our submarines without warning and without safety of the lives of noncombatants provided that the liners do not try to escape or offer resistance."

The President and Mrs. Galt were happy indeed. The White House desk was buried under letters and telegrams congratulating the President. Editorial writers hailed the German assurance as the diplomatic triumph of the age.

The Colonel's Misgivings

In the uneasy days that preceded the President's victory in the argument over the *Arabic* it may have occurred to him that he'd been neglecting the confidential colonel. The newspapers, as happened every August when news was thin, were full of speculation on the possibility of a break between Wilson and his "silent partner."

On August 31 the President wrote House:

"My dearest friend,

Of course you have known how to interpret the silly malicious lies that the papers have been recently publishing about a disagreement between you and me, but I cannot deny myself the pleasure of sending you just a line of deep affection to tell you how they have distressed me."

Eager as he was to keep the country out of war Wilson was coming around to House's way of thinking. On September 3 he gave to the press letters which he had written six weeks before to Secretary of War Garrison and to Secretary of the Navy Daniels instructing them to put their staffs to work on plans for "adequate national defense" for presentation to the Congress which would convene in December.

He had at last convinced himself that the country must be ready for eventualities in case German assurances on their use of the submarine turned out not to be in good faith. At this point, though House felt that von Bernstorff was doing his best, there was a growing suspicion among the President's advisers that the German Admiralty would not honor the *Arabic* pledge. Smoldering suspicions were fanned by new revelations of intrigue.

While the Dutch liner *Rotterdam* was calling at Falmouth at the end of August, in searching the cabin of an American correspondent named Archibold, who was known to be a propagandist for the Central Powers, agents of British Intelligence found that he was carrying, under the protection of his U. S. citizenship, diplomatic correspondence for the Hapsburg foreign office. Copies were immediately transmitted to Ambassador Page who cabled the highlights to the President.

Dr. Dumba was boasting of his campaign to foment strikes among workers in armament plants through his agents who financed a large part of the foreign language press. In a personal letter to Fritz von Papen's wife, which the Austrian had allowed to be included with his own dispatches, the German military attaché in Washington let himself go: "I always say to these idiotic Yankees that they had better hold their tongues."

British propagandists lost no time in spreading excerpts from these dispatches through the nation's press. The President, Secretary Lansing and Colonel House agreed on the course to be taken. A cable went off to Vienna demanding Dr. Dumba's immediate recall.

Dr. Dumba had a nasty scene with Lansing, who could be crusty when he was on his high horse; but his parting with the confidential colonel, who had assumed the position of father confessor to the whole diplomatic corps, could hardly have been more cordial. "As to the unfortunate incident which is the cause of my departure," Dumba wrote House, "I was certainly wrong because I made the mistake of being found out."

In September, Colonel and Mrs. House stopped for a few days at Roslyn with their daughter and her husband on their way into New York, where they had taken a new apartment on East Fiftythird Street. Entertaining the President, even privately, was a taxing business. Woodrow Wilson, like Haroun al Raschid, was fond of dropping in on his friends without notice.

House was worried. A new Mrs. Wilson offered a real challenge to his influence. He had reason to fear that she would not be so understanding of his usefulness to the President as was her beloved predecessor. He had been suggesting that the best way of countering newspaper gossip about a break between himself and Wilson was for them to be seen together more often. On September 24 he allowed the reporters to catch him calling at the White House.

There was reason for the colonel's misgivings. When Edith Wilson published *My Memoir* it came out that she was already suspicious of the President's advisers. She attributed the publication of certain malicious rumors about the President's relations with his Bermuda friend, Mrs. Peck, to an intrigue by House and McAdoo to break up her romance.

House's papers, to the contrary, show him to have been anxious to assure his dear friend of his approval of the match. There had been disagreement among the President's intimates as to whether his early remarriage would hurt him or help him in the campaign for re-election coming up in 1916. House wrote that he had made a tactful canvass of political friends and that the decision was that remarriage would not hurt the President politically. More important, because the opinion of the ladies counted heavily in these matters, was that House's wife Loulie agreed with them.

"I have a plan," added the confidential colonel, "by which you may be able to see each other as much as you wish without anybody being the wiser."

On October 7 the New York *Times* appeared with the headline: PRESIDENT TO WED MRS NORMAN GALT INTIMATE FRIEND OF HIS DAUGHTERS ALSO COMES OUT FOR WOMAN'S SUFFRAGE.

The same day the President again took a public stand in favor of preparedness.

When questioned by the newspapermen Mrs. Galt couldn't have been more tactful: she hedged on woman's suffrage. She was whispering to her closest friends that she halfhoped Woodrow would be defeated for re-election; she wanted to marry the man not the President.

At the White House an extra force of clerks had to be taken on to handle the congratulatory mail.

Colonel House was assiduous in his attentions to the betrothed couple. The day after their engagement was announced he had them both to dinner at his New York apartment. This dinner was far from being conducted in the privacy customary to the colonel's little affairs. After arriving on the Pennsylvania train in the afternoon the President and Mrs. Galt took a drive up and down Manhattan Island. Their car was followed by nine cars full of secretservice agents and newspapermen. Wherever they went they were cheered from the sidewalks. The photographers were given every opportunity.

The President's party consisted of Mrs. Galt and her mother, Mrs. Bolling, both in wide dark hats, and Helen Bones and Dr. Grayson and Joe Tumulty. The ladies stayed at the St. Regis. The police had to make a lane for them as they entered and left the hotel.

They were joined at dinner by the colonel's daughter and soninlaw Mr. and Mrs. Gordon Auchincloss. It was a festive occasion. Flowers and asparagus fern were everywhere. Reporters were previously given a glimpse of large framed portraits of Mr. Wilson and Mrs. Galt bowered in roses on a table in the colonel's newly decorated library.

After dinner the colonel took his guests to the theatre. Though the President, who didn't care for the serious drama but loved comedy, had already seen the play, he wanted Mrs. Galt to see *Grumpy*, which was the laughprovoking hit of that season, with Cyril Maude in the lead. When the party filed into their boxes the audience rose and applauded.

During the months of his engagement President Wilson became less accessible than ever. No matter how important their errands, few visitors got further than Tumulty's office. Whenever he could spare an hour from his official correspondence he took Mrs. Galt out driving, always along the same roads. The White House chauffeur was restricted to an established series of drives. Number one, number two, number three. Each drive had to follow its customary track: the President hated change in his routine.

Days when he couldn't see her he wrote her copious letters. Ike Hoover, the White House usher, remarked that the President was continually calling up the Library of Congress to check on the correct wording of some poem he wanted to quote. He had a direct telephone line installed between Mrs. Galt's house on Twentieth Street and his private study.

It was during the summer and fall of the President's courtship that a note of disillusion began to appear in House's diary: "I am afraid the President's characterization of himself as 'a man with a onetrack mind' is all too true . . . I say this regretfully because I have the profoundest admiration for his judgement, his ability and his patriotism." Or later: ". . . He dodges trouble. Let me put something to him that is disagreeable and I have great difficulty getting him to meet it. . . . The President, as I have often said," House complained again, "is too casual and does the most important things sometimes without reflection."

The Beginning of Relief

One result of the President's absorption in his private life with his bride to be was that, more and more, people who needed to keep in touch with the Administration were taking their problems to Colonel House in New York. Early in November it was Herbert Hoover calling to say goodby before returning to his relief job in London.

Hoover was the engineer who formed the American Refugee Committee to help the Consulate and the Embassy in London finance stranded Americans during the first August days of the war. From this he was drawn into relief work for the Belgians, who were threatened with starvation by the German refusal to guarantee the subsistence of civilians after their invasion. He now found himself heading the hugest charity the world had ever seen.

Although British Naval Intelligence at one point suspected him of being a German spy, the story was reported by Ambassador Page in his letters to House and the President, that the British were so impressed by Hoover's efficiency in handling Belgian Relief that they offered him citizenship and a place in the cabinet if he would join in their war effort. Hoover was said to have answered that as soon as he became a British subject he'd lose his Yankee drive.

A plumpfaced man with a hick curl to his hair and a California accent, he was still known in his early forties as young Hoover. He had packed a great deal of successful adventuring and prospecting into a few years. Coming from a family of impoverished Iowa Quakers, he was left an orphan at the age of eight and raised by an uncle in the Willamette Valley in Oregon. With a hundred and sixty dollars saved up working as officeboy in his uncle's landoffice he enrolled in the new university being launched under the presidency of David Starr Jordan at Palo Alto. He put himself through the course in mining engineering by working summers as a geologist. In the geology laboratory he met Lou Henry whom he married a few years later. He showed his budding administrative ability by managing first the baseball team and then, senior year, the whole athletic program of Leland Stanford.

When he graduated as a mining engineer the best job he could get was pushing a car in a Nevada goldmine for two dollars a day, but it wasn't long before he was working on the staff of one of the most brilliant engineers in San Francisco. At twentythree he was hired by a British firm as an expert in California methods to reorganize production in their mines in western Australia. At twentysix he was in China prospecting coal deposits for the same firm. As he was making twenty thousand a year he felt he was welloff enough to marry.

Lou Henry adopted the Quaker faith. The young couple had hardly been in China a year before they were besieged, with a small band of Europeans, in the neighborhood of Tientsin by Chinese troops during the Boxer uprising and barely escaped with their lives.

Hoover returned to London with such valuable information on the Chinese coal deposits that Berwick Moreing and Co. made him a partner. At thirtyfour he set up for himself, with offices in San Francisco, London, Paris and St. Petersburg, as a mining consultant, and administrator of ailing properties. His troubleshooting carried him to every raw new region of the globe.

The Hoovers already had as much money as they needed. They were raising their two boys on the Stanford campus. They had a house in London. Herbert Hoover had a certain scholarly bent in his own field. With the help of his wife, who was a good latinist, he made the first usable translation out of the Renaissance Latin of Agricola's *De Re Metallica*. Being a Quaker he couldn't keep from public service. As a trustee of Leland Stanford he was one of the mainsprings of the university.

The outbreak of the war caught him in London promoting the Panama Pacific Exposition to be held in California to celebrate the opening of the Panama Canal. He threw all his talent for administration, first into getting Americans home, and then into the incredibly difficult task of feeding occupied Belgium. The food had to be bought, the food had to be shipped through warring blockades, the food had to be distributed in territory occupied by enemy troops. "I did not realize it at the time," he wrote in his memoirs, "but on Monday August 3rd my engineering career was over forever. I was on the slippery road of public life."

In the summer of 1915 he was back in America mending his fences. The relief was originally planned merely to tide the Belgians over the first winter. About thirtyfive million dollars of Belgian government funds was spent and fifteen million was raised by contributions from Belgians living abroad and from private sources in America and in the British Empire. But now there was no telling how long the war would last. The situation in Belgium and Northern France was worse than ever. The population was being trampled into the mud by the contending armies. Almost three million people were destitute. The original plan had been to sell food to those who could pay for it, but, as the economic paralysis continued, that became less and less feasible. Money, a great deal of money, must be raised in America.

Ambassador Page in London was cooperating loyally with Hoover's re-lief work. It was at his table that Hoover and House first met. The colonel supported him from the beginning, but now House had let Hoover know that his project was in danger in America. A discharged and disgruntled associate was filling the lobbies of Congress with talk of Hoover's high-handed negotiations with the warring governments. It was claimed that Belgian Relief was operating like a sovereign state. Senator Lodge was out for Hoover's scalp and threatening prosecution under the Logan Act.

As soon as he arrived in America, House arranged for Hoover to see the President. Hoover found him completely sympathetic. The fact that Lodge was on Hoover's trail was in his favor. The President publicly com-mended the work of the Belgian Relief Commission and helped select an advisory committee of prominent New Yorkers to raise funds.

When T.R. heard of Hoover's difficulties he invited him to lunch at Oyster Bay and talked his ear off. "Mr. Roosevelt kept me all afternoon —making havoc of several appointments." When Hoover told him of a frigid interview with Lodge in Boston, T.R. almost laughed himself sick. He said Lodge could see involvements in Europe under every bush. "I'll hold his hand," he said.

On this American trip, by which he assured the continuation of Belgian Relief, Hoover's last interview, like his first, was with House. For the con-fidential colonel, he was becoming an important source of information on the realities of the war.

Hoover's work carried him back and forth across the battlelines. He was one of the few Americans who could appreciate the blind unreason-ing hate the brutalities of warfare aroused in both camps. The execution of Edith Cavell, an English nurse who helped smuggle Belgian and es-caped British prisoners out of Brussels, had thrown the Allied peoples into a fresh paroxysm of anger. Yet House and the President persisted in thinking these warmad populations could be made to listen to reason. Hoover felt this hope was unrealistic, at least for the present. House urged Hoover to dissuade the Germans from any more Zeppelin bomb-ings of London. Hoover had little that was encouraging to say along that line. As soon as he brought House up to date Hoover drove straight to the Holland America Line pier where he was catching the *Rotterdam*, sailing at noon.

Pacifism's Last Gasp

To cross the Atlantic in those days was like moving to a different planet. Peace and war were two worlds. Only determined idealists like Jane Addams, the queenbee of Chicago settlement house workers, who had been presiding at a women's peace congress at The Hague, came back hopeful. She and a number of other pacifist ladies pestered House all summer to induce the President to appoint delegates to join with other neutrals in a permanent commission seated at The Hague to keep on making peace proposals until one was accepted.

House told the ladies, tactfully of course, that they were misinformed. The President knew better than they did what the best methods were to promote peace.

The peace agitation would not down. Peace societies were proliferating over the country. Herbert Hoover's old preceptor, David Starr Jordan of Stanford, who headed the American Peace Society, turned up in House's study asking for an appointment with President Wilson to present the resolutions passed at a congress in San Francisco. A few days later it was David Starr Jordan's secretary, a popeyed and voluble young man named Louis P. Lochner, who took up an hour of the colonel's time to talk permanent mediation. With him was none other than Henry Ford.

Henry Ford was in his heyday. Model T's were chugging along every dirt road in the country. Ford's mass production had revolutionized transportation. He had turned the tables on the bankers and learned how to finance his own concerns. Ford's five dollars a day had laid the foundation for the highwage economy. Millions were pouring in faster than he could find a use for them.

Ford's formation was that of a rural mechanic. To the mind of a simple rural mechanic from the American middlewest war was plumb madness. Why couldn't these crazy Europeans be made to see reason: give up murder and destruction and go to work. If they spent the billions they were throwing away into massacre and destruction on useful production they could make more money in a year than any of the odd lots of real estate they were fighting for was worth.

Lochner and an ardent Hungarian lady named Rosika Schwimmer had talked Ford into backing Jane Addams' plan for permanent mediation. Suppose it cost a couple of million dollars to send a committee to Europe to end the war. How better could he advertise Tin Lizzie?

House complained in his notes that young Lochner wouldn't let Mr. Ford get a word in edgewise: . . . "just as soon as I got him discussing his great industrial plant at Detroit and the plans for the uplift of his workmen, the young man would break in. . . . Ford I should judge is a mechanical genius . . . who may become a prey to all sorts of faddists who desire his money." House found Ford's ideas about peace "crude and unimportant."

Instead of letting the confidential colonel dash cold water on Lochner's scheme, which was to charter a steamship to take a peace commission to Europe, Ford brashly suggested that House come along. House couldn't be induced to consider it. For fear German propagandists might get hold of the idea he immediately wrote Ambassador Gerard in Berlin disclaiming any connection with the peace pilgrims. "Of course there's no need to tell you that the Government are not interested in it, either directly, indirectly, or otherwise."

The Ford Peace Ship turned out a saturnalia for the press. The word peace was already as unfashionable among up to date people in America as it was in England. Wiseguy reporters found plenty to poke fun at.

The expedition consisted of eightythree delegates, including one state governor; the wellknown reformer and judge of the juvenile court in Denver, Ben Lindsey; Ben Huebsch the New York publisher, and the lovely suffragist Inez Millholland Boissevain. There was an assortment of clergymen, professionals of the peace associations and plain crackpots.

The secretarial staff amounted to fifty. Among them were publicitymen from the Ford organization instructed to watch over the Old Man. The press was represented by S. S. McClure, fiftyfour reporters and three movie photographers. Eighteen college students were invited along for the ride. A Western Union messengerboy named Jake stowed away and was allowed to join the technical staff. As the *Oscar II* was about to sail somebody let loose two squirrels on the deck.

Ford, a tonguetied man who spoke in bunches, aroused the sophisticated risibilities of the press a few days before he sailed by blurting out to his interviewers: "We'll get the boys out of the trenches by Christmas . . . The main idea is to crush militarism and get the boys out of the trenches . . . War's nothing but preparedness. No boy would ever kill a bird if he didn't first have a slingshot or a gun."

"Do you actually expect to get the boys out by Christmas?" a reporter tried to pin him down. Ford gave him his famous grin. "Well there's New Year's and Easter and the Fourth of July, isn't there?"

Ford's great disappointment came when his dear friend Thomas Edison refused to sail with him. Jane Addams pleaded illness. John Burroughs the naturalist, another of Ford's cronies, came to see him off, his mane of white hair flowing in the breeze, but said he was too old to go.

William Jennings Bryan, who had at first seemed willing to go along, delivered a moving address instead on the Hoboken dock. He was still insisting he would join the delegation in Holland. He made a point of shaking every individual pilgrim by the hand. A pair of the pilgrims added to the gaiety of the scene by getting themselves married in the firstclass saloon before the ship sailed.

The crowd was immense. One of the Ford publicitymen, a bigmouth named Bingham, led pacifist cheers through a megaphone. "Get together all you friends of peace," he'd shout.

He led cheers for Henry Ford, for Jane Addams, for Rosika Schwimmer, for Thomas Edison and for Judge Lindsey. As the final whistle blew Henry Ford was seen at the rail with an armful of red roses which he threw down one by one to his friends on the dock below. A man named Ledoux was so moved that he jumped overboard after the *Oscar II* left the pier and tried to swim after the ship.

Preparedness

The same day that the newspapers carried rollicking stories of Henry Ford's Peace Pilgrims sailing out of New York on the "peace ark" they carried the news that Captain Boy-Ed the German naval attaché and Fritz von Papen were being recalled from Washington at the request of the United States Government. It was Wilson's answer to the sinking in the Mediterranean, with heavy loss of life, of the passenger liner *Ancona* in disregard of the German pledges in the *Arabic* case.

The peculiarly brutal circumstances of the sinking of the *Ancona*, the shelling of the liner and its torpedoing before there was any opportunity to lower the boats, sent a shudder through the newspapers, but there was as yet little real war spirit. The President sensed a demand for a sterner stance. In his public speeches he was beginning to take the word "preparedness" away from the warhawks.

He had been particularly stung by some remarks T.R. made offhand to the reporters after delivering a speech to Leonard Wood's amateur cadets at their Plattsburg camp. Asked about the administration slogan "We must stand by the President," T.R. squeaked out: "The right of any President is only to demand public support because, if he does well, he serves the public well, and not merely because he is President."

His next statement rankled so Wilson never forgave him; or Leonard Wood either, for having sponsored T.R.'s appearance: "To treat elocution as a substitute for action, to rely on highsounding words unbacked by deeds is proof of a mind that dwells only in the realm of shadow and of shame."

Wilson's answer came in an address before the Manhattan Club in New York: "We have it in mind to be prepared, but not for war, but only for defense." The word "prepared" brought down the house.

At the same time preparedness meant something quite different to the President than it did to the pro-Allied fanatics who wanted the United States, by immediately backing up the French and British, to ensure Germany's defeat. Wilson was turning over in his mind the prospects opened up by an intimation from Sir Edward Grey through his confidential colonel:

". . . To me," the British Foreign Secretary wrote, "the great object of securing the elimination of militarism and navalism is to get security for the future against aggressive war. How much are the United States prepared to do in this direction? Would the President propose that there should be a League of Nations binding themselves to side against any power which broke a treaty? I cannot say which governments would be prepared to accept such a proposal, but I am sure that the Government of the United States is the only government that could make it with effect."

A tentative plan, gradually forming in discussion between Colonel House and the President, was to intervene on the side of the Allies, if, when the moment came, Germany refused to accept mediation. Thus without too much bloodshed, the Administration could force a negotiated peace on the basis of limitation of armaments, freedom of the seas, arbitration and the sanctity of treaties.

Colonel House, in the high style of his daydreams when he was writing *Philip Dru, Administrator,* was building for the President an image of himself as peacemaker to the world. "This is the part," the colonel wrote him from New York on the very day of his farewell interview with Herbert Hoover, "I think you are destined to play in this world tragedy, and it is the noblest part that has ever come to a son of man. This country will follow you along such a path, no matter what the cost may be."

House meanwhile had been trying for some sort of a commitment from Grey. All he could get out of Spring Rice was a stream of complaints about how American insistence on neutral rights was hurting the Allied cause. Sir Edward Grey's last letters were so full of gloom over Allied failures in Gallipoli, Russian failures in the east and the rising butcher's bill in the stalemated entrenchments in the west that he seemed to have forgotten the mirage of a League of Nations he'd been dangling under the colonel's nose.

According to House, Page too was in a blue funk. All Page could write of was the growing unpopularity of Americans in England. The British seemed to be blaming every new fumble in their military strategy on the failure of the American public to get sufficiently aroused about German atrocities. Meanwhile von Bernstorff, in a panic since the dismissal of von Papen and Boy-Ed, was assuring House that the German Government would welcome a peace emissary from the President.

Like Noah from the Ark President Wilson decided to send out one more bird of peace from Washington. Maybe this time he'd come back with an olive branch.

The colonel went abroad as the President's accredited though unofficial representative. His trip was paid for out of executive funds. House and his party carried their first passports. To keep tabs on travelling Americans who might be acting as agents for the belligerents the State Department was now demanding that American citizens carry passports abroad.

On December 28 fully equipped with diplomatic documents, Colonel and Mrs. House and the intrepid Miss Denton drove down to the Holland-America Line dock to tempt the wintry seas, by now dangerously infested with floating mines. Among the ship's company was Brand Whitlock, the man of letters, ex-political reformer and mayor of Toledo who was the very emotional U. S. minister to Belgium (and a thorn in the flesh of brusque and businesslike Hoover), and Captain Boy-Ed, travelling home under a British safeconduct.

"When we reached the pier," House noted in his diary (dutifully typed by Miss Denton), "there was the greatest array of newspapermen with cameras and moving-picture machines I have ever seen. There must have been fifty of them ranged up to do execution. I was perfectly pleasant, acceding to their demands, and posing for them something like five minutes . . . Before leaving the pier, the General Manager of the Holland-America Line had our things moved from the cabin we had engaged to the cabin-de-luxe, consisting of a sitting-room, two bedrooms and two baths."

Copious reports of what Colonel House had said and not said appeared in the papers next morning. No, the colonel was definitely not going to transmit the President's orders to his ambassadors abroad. He had no instructions to work for mediation, nothing to say about peace. He would make no demands on the British or on the Germans. No that wasn't what the President had in mind. Under a cloud of denials the colonel retired to his deluxe cabin as the ship's siren started booming. An enterprising journalist added to the confusion by printing a composite picture showing Boy-Ed, Minister Whitlock and Colonel House engaged in what seemed to be friendly conversation.

A Washington Wedding

Ten days before House and his party sailed for Falmouth, the President and Mrs. Galt were married in Washington. They were married at eight o'clock in the evening at Mrs. Galt's narrow brick house on Twentieth Street.

It was a cold day, gusty after rain. Only members of both families were present, but that made up a group of forty or fifty. Mrs. Galt wore a black velvet gown. The ceremony was performed by their two favorite ministers under a bower of maidenhair fern studded with orchids, which had been constructed by the gardeners from the White House conservatory in Mrs. Galt's livingroom. Pyramids of American beauty roses virtually filled the small house.

After cutting the cake, while their families were eating supper, the President and Mrs. Wilson slipped out into a waiting car with drawn curtains and were hurried to a small platform between Washington and Alexandria. There a private car awaited them attached to the train which would take them to the Homestead at Hot Springs, Virginia. Meanwhile the White House limousine with the presidential seal, also with curtains drawn, left ostentatiously in another direction to be followed by car after car full of reporters and photographers.

The little ruse arranged by Tumulty and Ike Hoover was completely successful. Except for a few secretservice men to watch over them, the President and his bride were able to embark unobserved on their honeymoon train.

They would not be unobserved for long. Nor would they want to be. "No matter how accustomed one grows," wrote Edith Wilson in *My Memoir,* "to the deference paid the great office of the Presidency, it never ceases to be a thrilling experience to have all traffic stopped, the way cleared, and hear acclaims from thousands of throats."

Chapter 9

INTERMEDIARY TO THE PRESIDENT

THE Woodrow Wilsons returned to Washington after a little chilly golf and some wintry mountain walks around the Hot Springs, very much refreshed. With the family life which was the prime necessity of his existence re-established under the new Mrs. Wilson's firm management, he could turn all his energies to getting himself re-elected for a second term.

It was not going to be easy. The prospects for the Democrats in 1916 were far from good. The Republican tide which made itself felt in the congressional elections of 1914 was still running strong.

Outside of banking and industrial circles immersed in the munitions trade, and a few eastern college professors and publicists already hypnotized by the British propaganda deftly piped in through New York by Sir Gilbert Parker's opinionmoulders at Wellington House, the country was for peace at almost any price.

The American people still thrilled to the terms of President Wilson's address in Indianapolis early in the preceding winter: "Look abroad upon a troubled world," he told his audience. "Among all the great powers of the world only America saving her powers for her own people . . . Do you not think it likely that the world will one day turn to America and say: 'You were right and we were wrong. You kept your heads when we lost ours.'"

Under the flattering stimulus of House's proddings and insinuations, Wilson was beginning to see himself, like House's own Philip Dru, as the leader to whom a sick world would turn; not for his own glory, he would tell himself when he prayed on his knees by his bedside night and morning in the stillness and agony of selfappraisal, but because it was a duty ordained by the living God to serve mankind.

To lead the world, he had to go on leading the United States. To lead the United States he had to be elected for a second term.

Looking Abroad Upon a Troubled World

As the year 1916 got underweigh the American people could look into their future with a certain complacency. The period of low wages and unemployment which fed the fanatical hatreds of anarchists and I.W.W.'s was turning to boom. Wartime industries paid the highest wages ever. Cotton prices were good. Wheat was high. The stock market was optimistic. Shipping, meatpacking, steel flourished. Gold imports for 1915 reached an alltime crest of four hundred and eleven million dollars. The favorable trade balance was estimated at nineteen billions as against eleven billions in 1914. The risks of wartime trade were great but so were the profits. New York was eclipsing London as the center of world finance.

Looking across the seas towards Europe, Americans could see everywhere "the deep-wrought destruction of economic resources, of life and of hope" which Wilson described in his Indianapolis address.

The war was going badly for the Allies. Not all the censors' scissors clipping bad news out of the mail, nor the rosy veils the propagandists managed to drape over the military communiqués, could disguise the fact that on the western front the British had lost half a million men and the French nearer two million, with the gain of only an occasional thousand yards of shellpocked mud on the Flanders front.

It was costing the Germans somewhat less in blood and munitions to defend their entrenchments across northern France and Belgium, while the bulk of their forces slaughtered the Russians and captured prisoners by the hundreds of thousands in the east.

Virtually all Poland was German territory. Along the Danube the Germans and Austrians, with the help of the Bulgarians, who had come into the war on the German side just at the moment when the Allied diplomats thought they had them tied up in an agreement to come in on the Allied side, had destroyed the Serbian Army. British ships were picking up its pitiful remnants in the Adriatic ports and carrying them to Corfu to refit. The Italians weren't doing much more than hold their own along the Isonzo.

The dream of Mittel-Europa had come true. The Germans dominated a great belt of territory, rich in raw materials, from Warsaw and Vienna clear through to Constantinople and the Near East.

Meanwhile the British scored their one success by the efficient way they evacuated the beaten Allied troops from impossible positions on the Gallipoli Peninsula.

Their forces in Salonika, while they managed to keep neutral King Constantine quiet in Greece, were suffering as great losses from malaria as from the bullets of the Turks.

Further east General Townsend's expedition, intended to keep the oil of Mesopotamia out of German hands, was badly knocked about amid the ruins of ancient Ctesiphon and driven back to the barely defensible mud huts of Kut-el-Amara.

On the seas Britain ruled to be sure. The short range German fleet was still cooped up in the fortified harbors back of Heligoland. An enormous shipbuilding program was keeping the Allies supplied with fresh bottoms, but the loss of an average of two hundred and fifty thousand tons a month to the U-boats was hard for even the sanguine English to laugh off.

"Our armies had everywhere been either checked or beaten and they needed to be reorganized before any new effort could be demanded of them," was Joffre's summing up of the year.

On the parade grounds of the United Kingdom Lord Kitchener was training the finest batch of young recruits his drillsergeants had ever seen, in the military methods that had built the empire during the nineteenth century. At the War Office they hoped great things would come from the substitution of the silent lowland Scot, Sir Douglas Haig, for the voluble Sir John French as British commander in the field.

In France they were calling beardless young new classes to the colors.

In Germany the junkers were working Russian prisoners on their estates while Prussian farmboys learned the goosestep. Next spring would bring victory. "The year 1915 had opened gloomily," wrote an Austrian historian, "but it ended with a spectacle of military success on a scale such as Europe had not seen even in Napoleon's time."

The Colonel's Mission

For two months House haunted the European chancelleries. In London he was lunched and dined by the members of Asquith's cabinet. In Paris he penetrated for the first time the closed circle of French politicians by ingratiating himself with the then Premier, Aristide Briand, a man of considerable intellect but of a disenchanted indolence that ruined his career.

During his stay in Berlin, the confidential colonel remained under Ambassador Gerard's wing at the Embassy for fear of finding himself at the same table with Admiral von Tirpitz, whom he considered the fountainhead of frightfulness on the high seas. From Bethmann-Hollweg down, the civilians in the imperial government put on their best drawingroom manners when they called on Colonel House. At this point, so far as they could without changing their plans, all the European leaders wanted to make a good impression on President Wilson's representative.

By letter and cable, using, with Miss Denton's help, the private code House and Wilson had worked out for themselves to avoid the leaks to the press through the State Department that had been so bothersome during Bryan's regime, the colonel kept in touch with the White House. The President and the new Mrs. Wilson laboriously decoded his messages, all by themselves upstairs in the President's study.

"I am trying to impress upon both England and France," House wrote from Paris by diplomatic pouch, "the precariousness of the situation and the gamble that a continuance of the war involves."

His talking point with the French was that Russia might be forced into a separate peace which would allow the Germans to throw all their forces into a breakthrough on the western front. For the first time the French were beginning to admit, under the hush of the profoundest secrecy, that peace might not be a treasonable word. The French press treated the colonel's silences with respect; he was the sphinx in the slouch hat.

Back in London, House dined with Asquith, Grey, Balfour and Lloyd George at Lord Reading's. "The conversation," he noted, "was general while dinner was being served . . . When the butler withdrew there was a general discussion of the war, the mistakes that had been made, and possible remedies."

The colonel dropped a private bomb by suggesting that the Germans were getting ready to attack Verdun. (His intelligence was good: a week later the German barrage began along the Meuse which heralded the most desperate fighting so far in the history of war.) "My theory is," House remarked in his diary, "that the Germans are still at their highest point of efficiency, and if they could strike a decisive blow, break through and capture either Paris or Calais, it might conceivably end the war."

This was what he told the British Cabinet. ". . . My whole idea in leading the conversation in this direction was to make them feel less hopeful and to show them as I have often tried to do, what a terrible gamble they are taking in not invoking our intervention."

"It was 10:30," House went on, "before we got down to the real purpose of the meeting. Lloyd George began . . . I interrupted him . . . and said: . . . 'Sir Edward and I in our conference this morning thought it would be impossible to have a peace conference at Washington, and I have promised that the President will come to The Hague if invited, and remain as long as necessary.'

". . . It was now twelve o'clock, and the Prime Minister made a move to go. While the conference was not conclusive, there was at least a common agreement reached in regard to the essential feature; that is, the President should, at some time to be later agreed upon, call a halt and demand a conference. I did not expect to go beyond that, and I was quite content."

House was in his heyday. He was so content that he allowed Laszló, a fashionable portraitpainter, to do a halflength oil of him, wearing the noncommittal smile under his mustache that delighted the London reporters, and the gray felt hat that so intrigued the French. Sir Edward Grey went so far as to incorporate the gist of their conversations in a memorandum.

The battle for Verdun had already lasted five days when Colonel and Mrs. House and Miss Denton sailed for New York by the Dutch line. The British cabinet thought the contents of House's briefcase so valuable that they sent along a secretservice agent from Scotland Yard, entered on the passenger list as his valet, especially to guard it.

The colonel's silences so impressed the reporters who swarmed aboard when the ship reached New York that even the Republican *Tribune* wrote: "House managed to be both elusive and significant . . . His glance showed that his silence covered a great deal of humor. He succeeded so well in the difficult task of being both taciturn and agreeable that he was even popular with the newspaper reporters when he told them nothing. Clearly one of the shrewdest of men."

As soon as Colonel House arrived in Washington the President and the new Mrs. Wilson took him out for an automobile ride. "During this time I outlined every detail of my mission." On the way back the White House car dropped him off at the State Department, where he gave Lansing an hour to bring him up to date.

Next day the President confirmed the tentative agreement with Sir Edward Grey. He himself worded a cable for House to send. "After some discussion the President took down in shorthand what he thought was the sense of our opinion," wrote House, "and then went to his typewriter and typed it off." The President authorized House to say he agreed with Sir Edward Grey's memorandum of his talks with Colonel House. He preferred to insert in one line the word "probably." ". . . If such a conference met, it would secure peace on terms not unfavorable to the Allies; and if it failed to secure peace, the United States would probably," insisted the President, "leave the conference as a belligerent on the side of the Allies, if Germany was unreasonable . . ."

The colonel felt thoroughly justified. He had been telling the French and British governments that "the lower the fortunes of the Allies ebbed, the closer the United States would stand by them." Talking to his dear friend in the White House, he repeated what he'd written him from Europe: the time for mediation was not far off. "I am as sure as I ever am of anything that by the end of the summer you can intervene."

Feeling that he had accomplished his mission, House took the train back to New York. There he had his cable to Sir Edward Grey coded in the private Foreign Office code and transmitted to England. Writing his memoirs years later Lloyd George insisted that it was Wilson's insertion of the word "probably" that ruined House's scheme for mediation.

Villa's Raid

The President was leaving his project for the re-establishment of peace in Europe in the hands of his confidential colonel. He had other anxieties than the coming election. In Congress and in the newspapers he was beset with criticism by Bryan's pacifists on the one hand and by Roosevelt's interventionists on the other. Mexico was a thorn in the flesh.

The Woodrow Wilsons had hardly unpacked their bags at the White House before the Mexican imbroglio, which had seemed laid to rest by the mediation of the A.B.C. powers and the constitutionalist success in destroying Villa's army near Saltillo the September before, exploded into the headlines. Mexican guerrillas, presumably on Villa's orders, took sixteen American mining men, who were travelling under a safe conduct from Carranza, off a train near Chihuahua, stripped them and robbed them and shot them dead.

A roar for immediate intervention went up from Republicans and Roosevelt supporters, and even from a good many Democrats. The President kept the State Department busy sending notes of protest to Carranza.

At the same time Wilson was engaged in a speaking tour, talking up cautious preparedness to enthusiastic audiences through the middlewest where the pacifist spirit was strongest. The plain people made him feel that they believed in him. Letters poured into the White House commending his moderation. "You are keeping us out of war, Mr. President. We believe in you."

He had been trying to convince his Secretary of War, Lindley Garrison, that the Administration could not move faster towards military preparations than the people moved, but Garrison saw things differently. He underlined his stand for immediate universal military service by sending in his resignation. Assistant Secretary Breckenridge resigned with him.

A few days later, Ida Tarbell, who had been writing laudatory articles about the New Freedom in the large circulation magazines, was invited to dinner at the White House. She remarked to the President that it was an anxious time. "No one can tell how anxious it is," answered the President in a taut voice. "I never go to bed without realizing that I may be called up by news that will mean that we are at war. Before tomorrow morning we may be at war."

The President's words proved only too prophetic when, a few days later, the "Red Man" struck close to home. Before dawn on March 9, Villa led several hundred mounted men on a raid on the U. S. Army post, several miles inside the border at Columbus, New Mexico.

Villa had been in a fury against gringos since the Administration al-

1. *T. R.*

2. *Big Game*

3.
The Peerless Leader

4.   *The Genial Mr. Taft*

The Kaiser and His Generals

The Popular Professor

7. *Kingmaker from Vermont*

8. *Congenial Sou[l]*

The Woodrow Wilsons

10.   *Mac*

11.   *Leaders of Democr*

12,   *President Wilson with Joe Tumulty at His White House Desk*

13. *Kaiser Wilhelm II*

14. *Papa Joffre*

15. *The Peacemaker in State*

16. *Colonel and Mrs. House*

17. *Page at the Court of St. James*

18. *The President's War Cabinet*

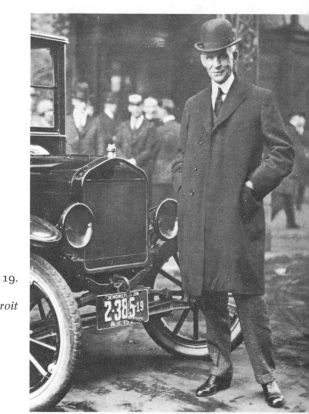

19.

Mr. Ford of Detroit

20.   *The Beguiling Widow*

21.

The Faithful Physician

22.

*Roosevelt and Wood
on the Warpath*

23.   *Black Jack Pershing*

24.
*The
Republican
Candidate*

5. *Vote for Wilson*

26. *Newton D. Baker*

27.

Briand's Goodbye

The Dapper Von Bernstorf

. *Casualty*

30. *The Ingenious Nivelle*

31. *Dollar a Year Men*

lowed *carranzista* troops he was fighting to cross United States territory by train. After a series of defeats he had to do something to restore his prestige among the revolutionary armies.

His attack was carefully planned. American officers were pinned down in their houses by snipers. While the guard under the officer of the day was fighting off one bunch of Mexicans another detachment attacked from the rear. The obsolete American machineguns jammed. Their gunners were killed. Villa held the town for an hour, looting and burning stores and shooting at anything that moved, before he was driven off and pursued (against strict War Department orders) into Mexico by two troops of the 13th Cavalry.

Eight soldiers and eight civilians were killed in Columbus, and a number wounded. The army reported finding sixty dead Mexicans in the streets of the gutted town.

A Pacifist in the War Department

What to do about Villa's raid was the first problem that met Wilson's new Secretary of War when he turned up at his office to be sworn in. Looking about for a loyal Democrat to put in Garrison's place Wilson picked a man after his own heart. Newton D. Baker was a progressive reformer and a Wilson man from long before Baltimore. He was reputed to be an ardent pacifist.

He came from a prominent West Virginia family. Though most of his people were Union, his father fought for the Confederacy but lived to tell his son he was glad the North had won. Dr. Baker was a popular physician and had a large circle of friends in Martinsburg where the Bakers were first settlers. Hearing one of Huxley's lectures in the early days of Johns Hopkins he decided that that was where he wanted his boy to go to college. In Baltimore young Newton roomed in the same boarding house with Woodrow Wilson, then an instructor in history and government. He kept a little of the student to professor attitude towards Wilson all his life.

Baker studied law and was settling to a comfortable practice in Martinsburg when he was invited to a job in the Post Office Department in Washington by a friend of his father's who was Postmaster General under Grover Cleveland.

Caught up in the progressive movement he went to the city of Cleveland as solicitor for Tom Johnson's reform administration. When Johnson died Baker succeeded him as mayor. Wilson was so pleased with the able support Baker gave him in his presidential campaign in Ohio and at the Baltimore convention, that, in 1913, the Schoolmaster in Politics offered his pupil a cabinet post. Baker preferred to remain as mayor of Cleveland to install the municipal electric plant which had been his promise to the voters.

When, eventually convinced he must serve the Administration, he turned up at the Secretary's office in the old War State and Navy Building to take his oath, he was still, at fortyseven, a neat trim boyish little man. He disarmed craggy old General Hugh Scott, the Chief of Staff who was acting Secretary, by telling him, "I am an innocent. I don't know anything about this job. You must treat me as a father would his son."

Planning an expedition against Mexican bandits was indeed a far cry from reforming the administration of a middlewestern city. In spite of his reputation as a humanitarian of the somewhat mollycoddle type, Baker had no qualms about convincing the President that Villa must be punished. The first decision to be made was the choice of a commander. The ranking general officer, Major General Funston, would remain in command of the entire border. The old military heads around the War Department with one accord told the new Secretary that Brigadier General Pershing was the man.

Black Jack

John Joseph Pershing was raised in a hard school. He was born the year before the Civil War began in a railroad boarding house near LaClede, Missouri. His father was section foreman at the time on the Hannibal and St. Joseph Railroad. During the war the elder Pershing did well for himself as regimental sutler with the 18th Missouri Infantry. With the proceeds he started a general store which he lost in the panic of 1873. After that he travelled as a salesman for a readymade clothing concern and engaged in all sorts of not too successful speculations. He was a man of some standing in his community, nonetheless; was president of the school board and a charter member of the LaClede Methodist Church. He believed the children should work for their education.

Jack Pershing's first ambition was the law. At seventeen he started earning a little money teaching a Negro grade school, to pay his way through the state teachers college. All his life he had a way with Negroes. A silent hardworking dour sort of lad he planned to earn his living by teaching until he could save up enough to study law.

When the local congressman, who, as a greenbacker and a Baptist, believed in equality of opportunity, announced he would give his West Point appointment to the boy who passed the best examination, Jack Pershing jumped at the chance of a free education. He studied hard. When he came out on top over eighteen competitors he still felt he was unprepared to enter the academy and eked out his scanty funds to study for a year at a military school at Highland Falls on the Hudson. He was almost twentytwo before he entered West Point as a plebe.

Though far from brilliant in his studies, Jack Pershing was known for his good riding, his inflexible deportment and his erect stance. His final year he was senior captain of the cadet corps. After graduation he served against the Apaches and the Sioux.

When the plains Indians were quieted the army took advantage of Lieutenant Pershing's training as a teacher by sending him to instruct in military science at the University of Nebraska at Lincoln, where his family had finally settled and where, as usual, his father was prominent in the affairs of the Methodist Church and of the Y.M.C.A. Pershing fulfilled his old ambition by completing his law course there.

Later he taught tactics at West Point. During the Spanish War he served in Cuba with the Negro 10th Cavalry and was breveted a captain for gallantry at Santiago. He came back from Cuba with the nickname of "Black Jack."

During the first Roosevelt administration Pershing, now a major, helped put down the Moro insurrection on Mindanao. He was one of the few American officers who learned the Moro language. T.R. was so delighted by the crisp style of his reports he recalled him to work on the General Staff.

Pershing's army career had been all hard sledding. He'd had no time for women. During his stay in Washington at the age of fortyfive he wooed and married the daughter of Senator Warren. This marriage to the daughter of an influential congressman who had been governor of Wyoming in territorial days and was now chairman of the Senate committee on military affairs, did Major Pershing's career no harm. Soon after he was sent as attaché to observe the strategy of the Russo-Japanese War. President Roosevelt jumped him over eight hundredodd names to make him a brigadier general.

Returned to the Philippines as governor of Moro Province, he was recalled, when the Mexican troubles began, to take command on the border. Since service there was expected to be of short duration Mrs. Pershing and the children remained in the residence that had been allotted them in the Presidio at San Francisco. On August 27, 1915, the general was called to the telephone in El Paso to be told that his wife and three small daughters had burned to death in the fire that swept the military post. His baby son, Warren, was saved by a maid.

Pershing had always been a silent grimfaced man. After that he was more silent and grimmer. His hair from grizzled became gray.

For an ambitious meticulous soldier there was little solace to be got from the Mexican campaign. Of all the assignments an American general ever had the pursuit of Villa was the most heartbreaking.

The population was sullenly hostile. There was the problem of transport. The expedition penetrated two hundred and fifty miles into the desert state of Chihuahua without being allowed the use of the railroad. The old army muletrains were too slow. Trucks had to be hired and bought. Their maintenance had to be improvised.

There was the problem of intelligence. As the expedition penetrated deeper into the country, *villistas* and *carranzistas* joined to excoriate the gringo. Although the constitutionalists were glad to see Villa's forces scattered they wouldn't lift a finger to help the Americans.

Wherever they went the Americans were met with treachery and deceit. It had been thought that airplane reconnaissance would be useful in tracking down armed bands. The few airplanes the army had proved incapable of anything more arduous than exhibition flights at a county fair.

At the War Department, however, Secretary Baker, whose appointment had been greeted with dismay in regular army circles, was showing a capacity for quick decisions. His speed in dictating wore out the army stenographers. The military discovered with relief that he was shaking off his humanitarian inhibitions. Get the job done was his motto. When the Quartermaster Corps claimed that there was no appropriation for motor trucks he said buy them anyway. "Mine is the responsibility."

Pershing failed to catch Villa, but his embarrassingly futile marches and countermarches proved a valuable training school for the regular army. The problem of supplying ten thousand men in hostile country taught the War Department and Newton D. Baker things they had never dreamed of about procurement and logistics.

The Sussex Correspondence

While American troopers were sweating out their lives trailing false rumors through the scorched deserts of northern Mexico, where every nopal hid a skulking rifleman, the President was knitting his brows over the freshly puzzling behavior of the Germans. Though von Tirpitz's resignation and von Bernstorff's protestations to Colonel House seemed to proclaim a new reasonableness, the imperial government's announcement in early March that it would treat armed merchantmen as ships of war held threatening possibilities.

The Allies were discovering that an agile gun crew could do considerable damage to a submarine that surfaced to give warning. They were trapping the submarines with innocentappearing freighters that turned out to be heavily armed. In America the peace organizations were echoing Bryan's demand that Americans be prohibited from travelling on armed merchantmen. The argument had reached a hysterical pitch when the newspapers, the morning of March 25 carried news of the *Sussex* disaster.

The *Sussex* was a Calais-Dover ferry with women and children on board and was known to be unarmed. An explosion blew the bow off the ship right under the white cliffs of Albion. There were eightyodd casualties. It was taken for granted that Americans were among the dead, though it turned out later that there were none. The State Department was in a rage. Lansing wanted to give von Bernstorff his passport right away.

Though Colonel House was indulging in one of his bouts of illhealth he hurried to Washington with advice. He agreed with the Secretary of State. He found the President preoccupied and evasive. "From the way he looked at me," he confided to his diary, "I am inclined to believe that he intends making excuses for not acting promptly in the new submarine crisis . . . He does not seem to realize that one of the main points of criticism against him is that he talks boldly, but acts weakly."

The argument about what to do about the *Sussex* went on for weeks. The President listened to Lansing and to Counsellor Polk. He called in Baker and other members of the cabinet, separately and collectively. House's advice was considered so important that the confidential colonel took up his residence at the White House for a while.

At last the State Department transmitted a note, of which the final version was as usual painfully typed out by the President himself on his own solitary typewriter, curtly warning the German Government that unless their submarines gave up attacking unarmed merchant ships the United States would break off relations.

Largely at von Bernstorff's insistence the German foreign office replied that their government would "do its utmost to confine the operations of war for the rest of its duration to the fighting forces of the belligerents." They went on to demand that, in return, the United States bring pressure on Britain to restore freedom to the seas. Wilson accepted the first part and ignored the rest. The Germans were outdebated. They clumsily accepted responsibility for the *Sussex* attack and offered to pay an indemnity for any American losses. The result, for the American press at least, was another diplomatic victory for the President.

Chapter 10

HE KEPT US OUT OF WAR

THE *Sussex* correspondence brought forth new outbursts from Theodore Roosevelt. In preparation for the conventions of the Bull Moose and Republican parties slated for early June in Chicago, T.R., refreshed by a trip to the West Indies which had improved the chronic bronchitis that his bullet wound had left him with, was on the rampage in the middle-west. Dorcas was willin'. Too astute a politician to have any real hope of the nomination, he couldn't help being affected by his friends' plans for Chicago. The inner circle of Bull Moose was hoping to bring about a stalemate in the Republican convention to be followed by a dramatic merging of the two conventions with T.R. acclaimed as the only man who could heal the schism and defeat Woodrow Wilson. It would take a miracle but miracles could happen.

The project filled T.R. with the old zest. At breakfasttime at the Planters Hotel in St. Louis he jumped on a couch in the crowded lobby and in an impromptu speech attacked hyphenated Americans. There were no English-Americans or Irish-Americans or German-Americans, he shouted in his squeaky voice while his arms flailed the air. There were only Americans.

At the City Club he leapt on the speaker's table and accused President Wilson, who had come around to advocating preparedness and military training for those who wanted it, of using weasel words, words that had the content sucked out of them, the way a weasel sucks the yolk out of an egg. "Teddy oh Teddy, there's nobody like you," somebody chanted in the audience.

St. Louis was a center of German *vereins* and German beer and had a truculent Irish population, to boot, infuriated by Britain's bloody suppression of the Easter rebellion, but the throng at the City Club cheered T.R. to the rafters. He returned to Sagamore Hill hoping against hope.

Something of the Heroic

A couple of days later the news of the sea battle off Denmark pushed local politics off the front pages. GERMANS ACCLAIM JUTLAND VICTORY BUT ENGLAND IS CALM announced the New York *Times*.

The losses were enormous on both sides and the decision was doubtful. When propaganda exaggerations were sifted out it became known fairly accurately that the British lost three heavy cruisers, five light cruisers and eight destroyers: a total of one hundred twelve thousand tons with six thousand eight hundred men killed and wounded, while the Germans lost a firstclass battleship, a new heavy cruiser, three light cruisers, and five destroyers: sixty thousand tons and three thousand men. The German armor plate and artillery and particularly their armorpiercing shells proved superior, but their fleet, badly battered, limped back into its protected anchorage.

The British were at sea again in two days. It was a virtual victory, the London papers said; the Germans suffered a greater relative loss. In America Jutland proved a sobering blow to German and Allied supporters alike.

The grim news, indicating that no conclusion to the European war could be expected in the foreseeable future, was swallowed up in the indigenous distractions of the presidential campaign.

The first week in June Chicago hummed like a beehive. The hotels were crowded with Republican and Bull Moose delegates. The Loop resounded with the brass bands of a "preparedness" parade that filled the streets for eleven consecutive hours. Ten thousand women tramped through the rain in behalf of woman's suffrage.

The same morning that the Republican convention came to order in the Coliseum with Senator Warren G. Harding of Ohio in the chair, the Progressive Party, with less bunting, but more shouting, started proceedings in the Auditorium. The Bull Moose leaders, deep in private negotiations with a committee appointed by the Republican regulars, wanted to keep their excitable delegates from blowing the lid off and nominating Roosevelt prematurely. At the first mention of his name they cheered for ninetythree minutes. T.R. heard the roaring over his private wire to Sagamore Hill. In spite of the enthusiasm of the crowd he already knew in his heart that this time there would be no miracle.

In March he had cabled from Trinidad to the New York *Evening Mail,* "It would be a mistake to nominate me unless the country has in its mood something of the heroic, unless it feels not only like devoting itself to ideals, but to the purpose measurably to realize these ideals in action."

No one knew better than T.R. that by coming out flatfootedly for a war program he had alienated great segments of his supporters. The reformers who had responded to his leadership in earlier campaigns now had very different ideas about how to "realize their ideals in action." The rural and western Progressives, led by La Follette in Wisconsin and Hiram Johnson in California, were either outright pacifists or sceptical of any headlong involvement in European quarrels. Only the wellconnected Bull Moosers from the financial and industrial centers in the east were for war on the side of the Allies, and they were hard to distinguish from the elements who were working for the nomination of Charles Evans Hughes on the Republican ticket.

The Reluctant Justice

Hughes was sincerely reluctant to allow his name to be placed before the Republican convention. He was so conscientious about keeping the Supreme Court out of politics he had even given up voting. Chief Justice White, a frank and garrulous old man in feeble health, had been telling Hughes he would retire soon and that he expected him to be his successor. President Wilson, whose daughters were on friendly terms with the young people of the Hughes family, made it quite clear that if Hughes kept out of the presidential race, and if Wilson were re-elected, he would be the next Chief Justice.

Ex-President Taft's letters played a large part in convincing Hughes that it was his moral duty to run. It was to Taft that Hughes was beholden for his appointment to the supreme bench. Taft knew that Hughes was a conscientious party man in much the same spirit as he was a conscientious member of the Baptist church.

". . . The Democratic party," Taft wrote him, "is what it has always shown itself to be—the organized incapacity of the country. I am no partisan but I cannot escape this conclusion. The Republican party was split in two in 1912. The great body of Progressives have enrolled themselves again in the party. To retain them however and to win over the others, we must have a candidate who will . . . stimulate the enthusiasm of both elements and give them confidence in victory . . . Mr. Roosevelt is thundering. He is a genius. In certain ways he commands my admiration more than he ever did for his genius . . . But I cannot think it is on the cards for him to win."

Taft insisted that after his first disappointment T.R. would have to come out in support of Hughes: ". . . he has put himself in a position which makes it absolutely necessary for him to support you if you are nominated."

Taft was not alone. From all segments among the Republicans came earnest pleas that shook Hughes' determination to continue the aloof and carefree life which he so much enjoyed. All the political augurs echoed Taft's statement: "You will certainly be elected if you accept the nomination."

Mrs. Hughes, who never concealed her conviction that her husband was a man of destiny, said she wanted to see him President. Hughes felt his resolution slipping, but he knew what the presidency might mean.

"When you see me in my coffin," he told Mrs. Hughes with some bitterness, "remember that I didn't want to take this burden."

The End of Bull Moose

Voting started on the third day of the conventions. Hughes, who had no personal organization, no throwaways, no badges, no banners, rolled up 253½ votes on the first ballot against Roosevelt's 65 among the old guard Republicans at the Coliseum. At the Auditorium the Progressive managers wore themselves out trying to stave off a premature nomination. The "peace committees" trying to reach an agreement behind the scenes were at a deadlock.

When the conventions adjourned the night of June 9 with Hughes still 170 votes short, the Justice, who had been in his study keeping up the pretence of working on his Supreme Court cases, said rather snappishly to his wife, "That settles it. I shall not be nominated. I'm going to bed."

Next day the regular Republicans put his nomination through. Hughes resigned from the Supreme Court with a note Woodrow Wilson felt was unnecessarily curt, and accepted. The Progressives in desperation nominated Roosevelt.

From the end of his private wire at Sagamore Hill T.R. stalled. He wouldn't say yes and he wouldn't say no. He made his refusal of the nomination conditional on the acceptance by Hughes of certain principles.

The convention heard his evasions with "anger, derision and groans." The New Nationalism falling in ruins about them, Roosevelt's reformers and conservationists and social workers left Chicago in a bitter mood. Many of them, like Mark Twain's lawyerfriend Bainbridge Colby, eventually supported President Wilson. Bull Moose was dead.

Blessed Are the Peacemakers

The Democrats meanwhile were assembling for their convention in St. Louis. Woodrow Wilson had been taking a leaf out of T.R.'s book and attacking hyphenated Americans. The national committee planned to make Americanism the keynote of the campaign. Words and music of all the patriotic songs were furnished to the convention bands. Arrangements were made to wave Old Glory at every opportunity. To the amazement of the backroom leadership their delegates rose to quite different bait.

The Honorable Martin H. Glynn, onetime governor of New York, delivered the keynote address. He had planned to open with an apology for the concessions Woodrow Wilson was forced to make to keep the peace and then to bring the audience to its feet with the eagle screaming for the red, white and blue. He enumerated some ticklish situations, involving American lives and American property, under Washington, Jefferson, Adams, Van Buren, Franklin Pierce . . .

"When Grant was President a Spanish commander in cold blood shot the captain of the *Virginius*, thirtysix of the crew and sixteen of the passengers . . . But we didn't go to war. Grant settled our troubles by negotiation as the President of the United States is trying to do today."

To Glynn's surprise the crowd cheered. Every time he tried to lay aside his list of precedents for peace by arbitration there were shouts of "Give us more." Glynn warmed to his task. He brought up crisis after crisis. "What did we do?" people roared. "We didn't go to war," their voices echoed.

William Jennings Bryan, sitting in the press gallery, was so moved he burst into tears. When he was invited to the platform at the opening of the night session he got almost as much applause as Woodrow Wilson's name when it was first mentioned. Like a good party man he eulogized the President. In spite of their differences about ways and means, their aims were the same. The President had kept the peace.

Ollie James of Kentucky was permanent chairman. Senator James was a large loud man. A reporter from the New York *Times* described him as having "the face of a prizefighter, the body of an oak and the voice of a pipe organ." He opened up with "Blessed are the peacemakers for they shall be called the children of God."

The words were met with a wild scream of excitement.

He described the long lonely struggle of the man in the White House to keep America neutral and to restore peace to the warring nations of Europe. "If that be evil and vacillating may God prosper it and teach it to the rulers of the world."

"The delegates did not rise to their feet," wrote the *Times* reporter, "they leaped. 'Keep it up Ollie, keep it up,' they shouted."

The senator described the President's victory in the Sussex case: "Without orphaning a single American child, without widowing a single American mother, without firing a single gun or shedding a drop of blood, he wrung from the most militant spirit that ever brooded above a battlefield the concession of American demands and American rights."

"Repeat," the crowd shouted.

Ollie James boomed out the sentence again. They made him repeat it a second time. Then they cheered for twentyone minutes which was one minute more than they had given Woodrow Wilson's name.

Late that night Wilson's nomination, which was a foregone conclusion, was carried with but a single dissenting vote. When the platform was put together next day someone, no one ever remembered who, inserted the phrase that became the keynote of the campaign: "He kept us out of war."

A Bloody Summer

While the Democrats were shouting for peace in St. Louis events in the world were taking a more and more warlike turn. Earl Kitchener, the British war leader, went down on the *Hampshire* that hit a mine off the Orkneys. The German armies were pressing, with men and metal, on the fortresses of the Verdun salient, where the French were defending their positions with desperate courage. The British were preparing to take the pressure off Verdun by squandering the recruits Kitchener's drillmasters had trained in a reckless offensive on the Somme.

In Mexico, Carranza, egged on, it was whispered, by German agitators, was trying to unite all factions in a holy war against the gringo. Daily he called on Pershing to take his troops off the sacred soil of the Mexican republic.

Attacks on Americans, from Mazatlán to the Gulf of Mexico, became so threatening that the President instructed the state governors to call out the militia. On June 22 a group of Negro troopers from Pershing's 10th Cavalry was ambushed at Carrizal by carranzista forces. The Mexican general who laid the trap was killed. Three American officers were dead or missing and twentythree troopers and a Mormon scout were captured and taken to Chihuahua.

Daily notes passed back and forth between Washington and Mexico City. The National Guard, now enlisted under federal orders, started taking up positions on the border. Peace societies and South American diplomats offered their good offices. On June 29 Carranza backed down and telegraphed his people in Chihuahua to turn loose the captured Americans. The twentyfour men were placed on a train for El Paso.

A couple of days later, while the news of the petering out of the Verdun offensive was encouraging Allied supporters, German prestige in America received a great boost with the appearance in the Chesapeake of a German merchant submarine. The *Deutschland,* loaded with dyes, had crossed the Atlantic unarmed and unscathed in spite of the British blockade.

I Wouldn't Give a Dollar

Wilson's campaign made a slow start. The President's health was bothering him. Daily problems tied him to his desk in the White House. Vance McCormick, retired mayor of Harrisburg, Pennsylvania, and like

Newton D. Baker a grassroots reformer from the progressive wing of the party, took the place of the petulant McCombs as campaign manager. Wilson described him glowingly as a steam engine in boots, but he had trouble finding campaign contributors. Betting in New York was still two to one on Hughes.

Henry Morgenthau, the wealthy real estate promoter and financier who had been the leading Wilson man in moneyed circles ever since a speech of Wilson's had set tears streaming down his face years before, was back on leave from his embassy to Turkey to serve as treasurer; but, in spite of the help of Bernard Baruch who was rising like a new comet on the Wall Street sky, he was having tough going. Men of means favored Hughes.

Josephus Daniels used to tell an amusing tale in later years of how he was called in as a friend of Edison's and Henry Ford's to try to induce these gentlemen to part with some folding money. Both men were invited to lunch at Vance McCormick's suite at the Biltmore in New York. No alcoholic beverages were served, but, when McCormick and Daniels tried to edge up to the topic of campaign contributions, the two great mechanical innovators became exceedingly skittish.

There was a gas and electric chandelier above the table with large groundglass globes. Henry Ford suddenly cried out to Edison, "I'll bet you anything you want to bet that I can kick that globe off that chandelier."

Though only the first course had been served, the table was pushed aside and Edison began limbering up his legs in the middle of the room. Daniels' story was that the electrical wizard made the highest kick he'd ever seen and smashed the globe to smithereens. Ford missed by a fraction of an inch.

Through the rest of the lunch Edison was busy crowing over Ford: "You are a younger man than I but I can outkick you."

It wasn't till the arrival of the icecream that McCormick could get his guests' attention back to the needs of the Democratic campaign. All his pretty speeches about the President's great work for peace were of no avail. Ford was a little leery of the word since the razzing he'd taken over the fiasco of his "peace ark" the winter before. "All this campaign spending is the bunk," he said. "I wouldn't give a dollar to any campaign committee."

In the end he was induced to run a series of newspaper advertisements which kept Ford products in the public eye at the same time as they gave reasons why people should vote for Woodrow Wilson. All McCormick got out of Edison was a catchy statement: "They say Wilson has blundered. Perhaps he has but I notice he usually blunders forward."

The Eight Hour Day

One reason why money was shy was Wilson's appointment of a Louis-villeborn Boston lawyer named Louis D. Brandeis to the Supreme Court. Brandeis, a scholarly product of the Harvard Law School, had made his career in the harrying of monopolies and trusts in the interests of the consumer. Bigness was his bugaboo. He was the knight errant of the small man. Conservatives looked with suspicion upon his glittering pronouncements. Even Taft, broadminded as he was, considered his appointment "the worst possible," and every conservative voice in the country was raised against him in the bitter battle for approval of his appointment in the Senate.

Another reason was the La Follette Act establishing improved working conditions for American seamen, and greatly increasing the cost of operating merchantships under the American flag, which business blamed the President for conniving at. A third was the amendment to the Clayton Act exempting laborunions from the antitrust laws. A fourth was the Adamson Law establishing an eight hour day and arbitration procedures for railroad labor. To most of the business community the eight hour day was still a red flag to a bull.

The Adamson Act was passed as an emergency measure in the muggy dogdays of a summer session of Congress to stave off a strike of railroad workers which threatened to involve four hundred thousand men and all the important railroads in the country. A general strike had been brewing for months against working conditions and low wages. It was part of labor's demand for a share in war profits.

At a time when the railroads offered the only means of transport, outside of the inland waterways, for food and fuel and necessities, a prolonged stoppage was a terrible prospect. The President grew gray and haggard haggling with committees from the brotherhoods and from management, while he tried to induce both sides to arbitrate their differences.

The union leaders refused to be convinced. "I was shocked to find a peculiar stiffness and hardness about these men. When I pictured to them the distress of our people in case this strike became a reality, they sat unmoved and apparently indifferent," he told Tumulty. "I am at the end of my tether."

Disgusted with the union leaders he tried to reason with the railroad executives. A committee from various railroad managements was assembled in the heavily curtained Blue Room in the White House. After they had been sitting for some time in sullen obscurity on rows of little gold chairs, a curtain was pulled open at the end of the room and the President appeared freshfaced and eager in his white suit in the stream of sunlight that poured through the long windows behind him.

"I have not summoned you to Washington as President of the United States to confer with me on this matter," he said, in what Tumulty considered one of the most moving appeals he ever made, "for I have no power to do so. I have invited you merely as a fellow-citizen to discuss this great and critical situation. Frankly, I say to you that if I had the power as President I would say to you that this strike is unthinkable and must not be permitted to happen . . . A nation-wide strike at this time would mean absolute famine and starvation for the people of America . . . They will not quietly submit to a strike that will keep these things of life away from them. The rich will not suffer in case these great arteries of trade and commerce are temporarily abandoned, for they can provide themselves against the horror of famine and the distress of this critical situation. It is the poor unfortunate men, and their wives and children, who will suffer and die. I cannot speak to you without a show of emotion, for, my friends, beneath the surface in America there is a baneful seething which may express itself in radical action, the consequences of which no man can foresee . . ."

He stepped forward and continued in his most confidential, man to man manner. "The Allies are fighting our battle, the battle of civilization, across the way. They cannot 'carry on' without supplies and means of sustenance which the railroads of America bring to them . . . Who knows, gentlemen, but by tomorrow a situation will arise where it will be found necessary for us to get into the midst of this bloody thing? . . . I know that the things I ask you to do may be disagreeable and inconvenient, but I am not asking you to make a bloody sacrifice. Our boys may be called upon any minute to make that sacrifice for us."

"What the hell does he mean?" one railroad director asked another when the President left the room.

"I suppose he means it's up to us to settle the strike."

Neither side made a move to settle, so Wilson appealed to his Democratic supporters in Congress, and with extraordinary speed a bill was drafted by Representative Adamson of Georgia giving the railroad workers their eight hour day and setting up machinery for the arbitration of grievances. The Adamson Law went through Congress like lightning and was upheld a few months later by the Supreme Court.

The College Professor's Village Habit

As perplexities and crises piled up on his desk Woodrow Wilson retired more and more into isolation. He conferred less frequently with his cabinet officers. Everything had to be sent in to him in writing. Mrs.

Wilson was with him constantly. Together they pored over pardons, bills before Congress, over the texts of projected notes or the first drafts of speeches and statements.

Dr. Grayson, preaching fresh air and exercise as preventive medicine, urged a little horseback riding. He insisted on the daily golf at the Kirkside Club. Mrs. Wilson took up the game to keep her husband company. There were never enough hours in the day. Often they got up at five, and worked through, except for the family meals and necessary public appointments, until eleven or twelve at night.

Walter Hines Page, called home for consultation from England, arrived in Washington on a steaming August day when the railroad crisis was at its hottest. House and the President had long agreed that Page needed a spell at home in America to get the London warfever out of his system. The ambassador, remembering his long almost affectionate association with Wilson over the years, arrived bubbling with phrases he hoped would make the President see the English point of view. He was primed for a long heart to heart talk. He was bursting with a private message from Sir Edward Grey.

"The President was very courteous to me, in his way," Page wrote in his journal. "He invited me to luncheon the day after I arrived. President; Mrs. Wilson, Miss Bones, Tom Bolling, his brotherinlaw, and I . . . not a word about England. Not a word about a foreign policy or foreign relations. He explained that the threatened railroad strike engaged his whole mind."

It was agreed that Page should take a few days rest and come back when the President had time to listen to him.

Two weeks later Page was again invited to lunch at the White House. He found his old friend redeyed from having been up all night working over a special message he was to deliver to Congress that afternoon. Wilson had just come from his appeal to the railroad executives. There was no time for a word on European affairs. Page found himself talking to the ladies of the family, reinforced by some extra cousins from New Orleans. Mr. Sharpe, the ambassador to Paris, who was there on the same sort of errand, got no chance either to put in a word about European politics.

After hurrying through luncheon the party was bundled off to the Capitol to hear the President address both houses to ask for immediate passage of the Adamson bill. Page didn't even have a chance to bid his old friend goodby.

"There's no social sense at the White House," Page wrote in his disgruntlement. "The President has at his table family connections only . . . It is very hard to understand why so intellectual a man doesn't have notable men about him. It is the college professor's village habit I dare say . . . Mr. Wilson shuts out the world and lives too much alone, feeding only on knowledge and subjects he has already acquired and not getting new views and fresh suggestions from men and women."

"The President," Page wrote his friend Laughlin in the State Department, after he'd cooled his heels at the New Willard for another couple of weeks, "dominates the whole show in a most extraordinary way. The men about him (and he sees them only on business) are very small fry, or worse—the narrowest twopenny lot I've ever come across. He has no real companions. Nobody talks to him freely and frankly . . ."

Page still hadn't had a private talk. His explanations of why the British had cooled to House's peace proposals were stale by now, but still he was determined to have his say. "I'm not going back to London," he insisted, "till the President has said something to me or at least until I've said something to him . . . if he does not send for me, I'm going to his house and sit on his front steps till he comes out."

Finally, after an insistent letter, Page received through Tumulty an invitation to "Shadow Lawn." Shadow Lawn, near Long Branch, was the great rambling seaside summer mansion with wide verandahs and a cavernous living room, ornamented, like the lobby of a summer hotel, with a gilt piano and statuary, which Wilson was using as his headquarters because he had scruples about conducting a political campaign from the White House. After a family dinner the President listened to his old friend's explanation of the deep rift he believed the President's policies were producing between America and England.

Page tried in vain to interest Wilson in a medal the British had struck off to commemorate the *Lusitania* outrage and solemnly repeated his oral message from the British cabinet: the Germans were using the campaign for mediation for their own purposes: if the Germans proposed an armistice on the President's terms, the British would refuse.

The President was polite but unimpressed. All he seemed interested in, Page noted rather naïvely in his diary, was ending the war.

Page left after breakfast next morning feeling that Wilson was completely out of touch with the thoughts and feelings of daily life. Their last handshake was final. The old confidence and friendship was gone. They never met again. "I think he is the loneliest man in the world," Page told his son.

The Labor Vote

At Shadow Lawn Wilson at last found time to let himself be formally notified, in Senator Ollie James' booming periods, of the Democratic nomination, and to make his speech of acceptance.

The partyworkers were uneasy. Tumulty was in the dumps. He saw Hughes running away with the woman's suffrage issue and attacking the

Adamson Law as submission to blackmail. The Republicans would get the German-American vote. Maine, on September 11, went even more solidly Republican than usual. Tumulty begged for more action. The President refused to be flustered. "The moment is not here," he told his secretary soothingly. "Let them use up their ammunition and then we'll turn our guns upon them."

That September the President was preoccupied with a new private grief. His sister, Mrs. Howe, died. For a few days the Wilsons gave all their attention to her funeral at the old Wilson home in Columbia, South Carolina.

He got back to Shadow Lawn to find Tumulty and his friends in great distress. Judge Westcott, the devoted Wilson supporter who made the nominating speeches in both conventions, had been defeated in a New Jersey senatorial primary.

The President kept his confident attitude. "I believe that the independent vote," he wrote his brother in Baltimore, "the vote of the people who aren't talking and aren't telling the politicians how they are going to vote, is going to play a bigger part in this election than it ever played in any previous election and that makes the result truly incalculable."

Though the President refused to allow the photographers to take pictures of his and Mrs. Wilson's private life, he allowed Tumulty to arrange press conferences. Trainsful of supporters trampled the grass at Shadow Lawn every Saturday afternoon. When one man asked Wilson what he thought of Hughes' campaign he replied, "If you will give that gentleman enough rope he will hang himself."

"Never murder a man who is committing suicide," was how he put it to Bernard Baruch. "Clearly this misdirected gentleman is committing suicide slowly but surely."

In October he did allow himself to be induced to tour the midwest, delivering speeches to enthusiastic crowds in Omaha and Indianapolis and Cincinnati. "He kept us out of war," was the slogan of all the introductions by local politicians. The crowds were wild for it. Woodrow Wilson tried not to work it too hard. "I can't keep the country out of war. They talk of me as if I were a god," he said in private. "Any little German lieutenant can put us into the war at any time by a calculated outrage."

This time Woodrow Wilson's hunches sized up the political situation better than the calculations of the professionals. Hughes didn't have his heart in the campaign. He found it hard to heckle the President over policies with which he basically agreed. His clumsy mishandling of his personal relations with Hiram Johnson lost him muchneeded Progressive votes in California. His speeches gave the impression of quibbling over details. People began to say "Oh he's just a Wilson with whiskers."

T.R.'s plumping for Hughes not only alienated the Progressives, but his wartalk produced many a Wilson vote. The crowds laughed and hooted when he jeered at "Nice Mr. Baker, he knits" and described Wilson as "kissing the bloodstained hand that slapped his face," but working people and farmers made it clear that they were going to vote for the eight hour day and keeping out of war. When T.R.'s campaign train stopped at Gallup, New Mexico, he bounced out on the rear platform to greet a crowd of ranchers and section hands. Gallup had been a recruiting station for the Rough Riders and was strictly Roosevelt territory. The railroad workers waved pictures of Wilson under his nose. "I think the world of the colonel, but I love the President," shouted a voice.

"I love no one too proud to fight," T.R. snapped back.

"You're a grand man," came another voice, "but me for Woodrow Wilson."

The final rally of the campaign was held as usual in Madison Square Garden. The national committee was planning it as the greatest ever.

"Final touches were given this afternoon," noted House in his diary, "for November 1. I hope everything will work out as planned, though there is a danger it will not—for much will depend on luck, as matters are supposed to happen spontaneously which are really prepared far in advance. For instance, the head of the parade must be down at Thirty-fourth Street and Fifth Avenue at 8:30. At twenty minutes of nine the President must come out of the Waldorf Hotel and start for the Garden, stopping at Thirty-fourth Street and Madison Avenue for ten minutes to receive the cheers of the crowd and review the parade . . . Glynn is to commence his speech at the Garden at fifteen minutes of nine . . . The President must walk on the speaker's platform just as it ends, in order to receive continuous applause for Heaven knows how many minutes."

Next day the colonel found his affectionate friend suffering from campaign jitters: "The President arrived promptly at nine o'clock. McCormick and I met him and went with him to the *Mayflower* which is anchored in East River. We talked to him for an hour and a half and it was the most acrimonious debate I have had with him for a long while . . . He thought New York 'rotten to the core' and should be wiped off the map . . . He thought McCormick and I had New Yorkitis and that the campaign should be run from elsewhere. He was absolutely certain of the election without New York.

"I have heard the story so often from candidates that it makes me tired. They go about receiving adulation everywhere, hearing the people declare that they look upon them as their savior, until they begin to look upon themselves in that light.

"It is true we have organized wealth against us, and in such aggregate as never before. On the other hand we are pitting organized labor against it and the fight is not an unfair one. I feel it good sport to fight with the odds against us, for the United States is normally Republican."

In the privacy of his diary House couldn't help being a little scornful of Wilson's peevishness: "The President reminds me of a boy whose mother tells him he has ridden long enough on his hobbyhorse and he must let little Charlie have a turn . . . His attitude is not unlike that of T.R. who has never forgiven the electorate for not continuing him directly in the White House."

The President was undoubtedly edgy. He seemed to be blaming House and McCormick for the fact that the New York papers that morning ran sixteen columns of ads for Hughes to one and a half for his candidacy. "However before he left," added House, "he put his arms around us both and expressed appreciation for what we were doing."

That night the colonel walked around the streets. When he got home he made his entries in a more cheerful frame of mind. He had found "as much precision as could be expected in the circumstances . . . After the President had passed down the Avenue, I returned to the Garden to find it packed to the doors and the streets beyond. I merely looked in to hear the cheering and to find that everything was going as planned, and then left for home. All reports say it is the biggest demonstration of the kind ever given a President or a candidate for President in the city of New York."

Sweeping Victory for Hughes

Election day, November 7, 1916, dawned mild and clear. The newspapers forecast a recordbreaking vote. Everywhere the voters lined up early at the polls.

Hughes voted in New York. The bearded former governor, still wrapped in some of the dignity of his recently doffed black robe, was photographed at 7 A.M. on the way to cast his vote in a small laundry on Eighth Avenue. His ballot was number 13. "This is a lucky omen," he said to the reporters.

Later he attended a luncheon at the Harvard Club in honor of William R. Wilcox, the Republican National Chairman, who it was admitted later had made a hash of his campaign. Returning in midafternoon to Republican headquarters at the Hotel Astor, Mr. Hughes was told that the first precinct in the nation to register complete returns had given him a clear majority over President Wilson. It was New Ashford, Massachusetts. The figures were Hughes 16, Wilson 7. The candidate was reported to have expressed satisfaction over the Republican trend in New England.

At virtually the same moment, in the temporary executive offices in

Asbury Park, New Jersey, Joe Tumulty was discovering a Democratic trend in the same figures. He was pointing out to reporters that several more Wilson votes had been cast in New Ashford than in 1912.

As the day wore on, Mr. Hughes, the public was told, was so gratified by growing Republican majorities, that he took Mrs. Hughes for a drive in the park before returning to what partyworkers were beginning to call the presidential suite for a late afternoon nap. He was completely fagged from the smiling and the travelling and the speaking and the waving and the handshaking. He was hoarse as a crow.

At Shadow Lawn the President shook himself out of bed at five that morning, stropped his razor on his old razorstrop and shaved; and after an early breakfast drove, with Mrs. Wilson on the seat beside him, over to Princeton to vote. Mrs. Wilson had to wait outside of the old firehouse while he voted; woman's suffrage was not yet on the statute books in New Jersey. When he came out a group of students gave him the Princeton cheer.

Although he had spared himself as much as possible the campaign had tired him, too. Washington had been even hotter than usual. After the arduous summer, though public speaking usually refreshed him, the campaign speeches had been a punishing strain. Mrs. Wilson was worried about the blinding headaches he complained of.

After voting the President drove directly home to Shadow Lawn. There he sat at his desk keeping tally on a sheet of paper of the figures Tumulty reported over the telephone. The instructions were that he wasn't to be bothered with scattering returns.

As always Wilson was trying to keep politics at arm's length from the closed circle of his family life. In spite of all he could do there was a hush of expectation about the house. As they passed on the stairs, the ladies of the family exchanged comments on Woodrow's composure in admiring whispers.

The day passed slowly. When there was nothing else to do the President could always while away the time signing documents. A host of papers, including every commission and every promotion in the army and navy, had to have the President's personal signature. Sometimes it amounted to thousands of signatures in a single week. Signing papers filled every spare moment. Edith Wilson helped by arranging the papers neatly in a pile and handing them to him in an endless chain.

As the fine seaside afternoon wore on Joe Tumulty's voice grew boyishly confident over the phone. Maybe the east was doubtful but the middlewest looked increasingly good. Colorado and Kansas were sure.

The shock came at dinnertime. Tumulty's voice lost its resonance. Hughes would carry Illinois and New York.

Around nine that night the reporters broke into Tumulty's office in Asbury Park to find him sitting with his son staring glumly out of the window. They brought in a bulletin for him to comment on. The New York *World* had conceded defeat. The *World*, edited by a personal friend, Frank Cobb, was Wilson's most fervent supporter among eastern newspapers. Tumulty kept his dukes up with an optimistic pronouncement. "Wilson will win. The west has not yet been heard from."

Tumulty's heart was in his boots. As soon as he could get rid of the reporters he called Shadow Lawn.

The President had already heard the bad news from Grayson. "Well Tumulty, I guess we've been badly licked," was all he would say.

Grayson had been trying to console him by prophesying a comeback like Grover Cleveland's. Wilson replied with a favorite story about a Confederate veteran who reached home after Appomattox. He walked with a limp. He had his arm in a sling. His house and barns had been burned, his fences were down, his stock driven off, his family scattered. "I'm glad I fought," he said, after surveying the ruins, "but I'm damned if I'll ever love another country."

In New York at the Hotel Astor Mr. Hughes was awakened from his afternoon nap with the news that he would be the next President. The *Times* searchlight was flashing a Republican victory. A skysign on the roof of the hotel spelled out HUGHES in electric bulbs. Marchers from the Union League Club appeared with a band in Times Square calling on Mr. Hughes to claim election. At Oyster Bay, Theodore Roosevelt was already declaring that the Republican victory was "a vindication of our national honor."

Charles Evans Hughes was a careful man and a decorous man. There was a lot of rural upstate New York in his makeup. Against his own better judgement, he had allowed himself to be cajoled into resigning from the Supreme Court to run against Wilson. He wasn't going any further out on that limb. He insisted that he would make no claims until the count was completed in California.

Meanwhile, over at the Biltmore, a victory banquet which had been arranged for the Democrats, with Henry Morgenthau at the head of the table, was falling flat. Colonel House refused to attend. "While I did not expect defeat"—House's promise to Wilson of 230 electoral votes for sure left him needing only 35 more to be picked up in the heat of battle—"I did not wish to be at such a gathering without knowing whether the President was successful." Morgenthau told House afterwards that "there never was such a morguelike entertainment in the annals of time."

Instead of going to the Democratic banquet Colonel House walked around with Attorney General Gregory to the Bar Association Library to look up the federal statutes on the subject of the President's resignation.

The outcome of the war in Europe seemed to teeter on a knife edge.

The moment was too dangerous for an interregnum in Washington. Wilson had decided to resign at once if he failed in re-election.

The idea appealed to him as a political theorist as well as a practical politician. He was convinced that the American government must be made more responsive to the popular mandate, more like the English party government by a responsible ministry. He had talked it over many times with House. Resigning would turn defeat into a constitutionally constructive gesture.

So that nobody could say he was acting in a fit of pique, two days before the election he outlined his plan in a letter to Secretary of State Lansing.

"Again and again the question has arisen in my mind, What would it be my duty to do were Mr. Hughes to be elected? Four months would elapse before he could take charge of the affairs of the government, and during these four months I would be without such moral backing from the nation as would be necessary to steady and control our relations with other governments . . . Such a situation would be fraught with the gravest dangers . . . The course I have in mind is dependent upon the consent and cooperation of the Vice President; but if I could gain his consent to the plan I would ask your permission to invite Mr. Hughes to become Secretary of State and would then join the Vice President in resigning."

As the law then ran, the Secretary of State would be next in succession to the presidency.

It was a gesture planned in the grand style. "It seems," House wrote in his diary, "that during the uncertain hours of Tuesday night . . . both the President and Mrs. Wilson were cheered, as I was, by the thought of the dramatic dénouement we had in mind in the event of defeat."

The letter, sealed with sealingwax and addressed in Woodrow Wilson's own hand, with "most confidential" underlined on the envelope, was entrusted to Frank Polk, a crony of House's who was counsellor at the State Department. He handed it to Secretary Lansing when they met at Democratic headquarters, where Lansing arrived on his way from voting at his home in Watertown, to the Balthasar's feast, as Henry Morgenthau was calling it, at the Biltmore.

Wilson supporters went disconsolately to bed. SWEEPING VICTORY FOR HUGHES, read the headlines in their own New York *World*. Conservatives who distrusted theorists and innovators and pro-Ally fanatics in the eastern cities, turned in contentedly: the country was in good hands.

Colonel House was between the sheets by eleven. "I believe I can truthfully say I have not worried a moment," he confided in his diary. "If I had I could not have stood the strain. It was not that I was altogether certain of the result, but I never permit myself to worry over matters about which I have no control."

The colonel admitted that he woke at five. By daybreak he was hanging onto his bedside phone. The far west was going Democratic. He immediately called the despairing watchers at party headquarters and urged that they telephone the county chairmen of every doubtful state telling them to pay no attention to press reports that Hughes was elected. As soon as he decently could he had Attorney General Gregory up and worrying about federal measures to protect the ballotboxes wherever the vote was in doubt.

California was the crucial state; in southern California the vote was expected to be particularly close.

"I did not close my eyes all night," Meredith Snyder, the reform Democrat who was mayor of Los Angeles told Josephus Daniels in reminiscent vein some years later, "until the result of the election was declared. Shortly after the polls closed I ordered that every ballotbox be sealed and stationed policemen in every booth with orders to shoot any man who should lay the weight of his hands on the ballotbox. With associates I went from booth to booth all night. We kept vigilant watch and a staunch Democrat was assigned as watcher in every booth. Nothing was left undone to see that there was no tampering. I knew that the fate of the Presidency in the next four years would be settled in those boxes, and I staked my life that the votes should be counted as cast."

All over the country Democratic watchers and wardheelers were frightening each other out of a year's growth with the tale of a mammoth Wall Street plot, financed by millionaires, to steal the election for the Republicans.

"We lost no State I had placed in the certainties," Colonel House boasted to his diary. "I regard this with some degree of pride. The President was skeptical regarding the value of organization. I wonder whether he is now . . ."

On the morning of November 8, while Woodrow Wilson was shaving, his daughter Margaret knocked on the bathroom door with the news that the New York *Times* was about to run off an extra announcing that the election was in doubt. Wilson thought she was pulling his leg. "You tell that to the marines," he called back through the door.

At Asbury Park, Tumulty had been comforted in his unhappy vigil by telephone calls from an unknown supporter who claimed to be calling from Republican headquarters. The Republicans were worried, the strange voice kept saying. "Don't concede."

To get some fresh air the President went out with Grayson for a few holes of golf. "How is your game today, Mr. President?" asked an acquaintance on the links. Wilson is quoted as having answered, with a wave of the hand, that Grayson had him three down, but he didn't care, he was four states up over yesterday's returns.

The Democratic column kept building on the tallysheets. Everything depended on the outcome of the close race in California. It wasn't until November 10 that Vance McCormick dared wire his county chairmen to buy red fire and celebrate.

A telegram came into Shadow Lawn from Wilson's runningmate. Vice President Thomas R. Marshall was a professional Hoosier, fond of classical quotations and pokerfaced statements in the crackerbarrel style: "T'is not so deep as a well, nor so wide as a church door," he wired, "but t'is enough. T'will serve."

A story went through the corridors of the Pulitzer Building that a reporter who tried to get into the Hughes suite early that morning for a statement was told, "The President can't be disturbed."

"Well when he wakes up tell him he's no longer President," replied the reporter. "Wilson's re-elected."

PART THREE

The Birth of Leviathan

In the sense in which we have been wont to think of armies, these are no armies in this struggle. There are entire nations armed . . . It is not an army that we must shape and train for war; it is a nation.

—Woodrow Wilson's statement
accompanying his draft proclamation,
May 18, 1917

Chapter 11

THE END OF MEDIATION

As the immediate consequence of Villa's raid Congress ordered an increase in the regular army to some five thousand officers and a hundred and twentythree thousand enlisted men. The states were instructed to raise their militia units to full strength and the President was authorized to take them into the federal service at his discretion as the need arose. The entire National Guard was estimated at sixtyseven thousand men in March 1916 but many regiments mustered barely half their theoretical numbers. Although the navy was fast catching up with Germany's, the American military establishment on land was proportionately smaller than Holland's. Recruits were needed and fast.

Little Newton D. Baker, just beginning his David and Goliath contest with the gigantic lethargy of the War Department, hired a publicityman to produce leaflets and posters extolling the military life. One of those groups of enthusiasts for improving the behavior of their fellow citizens which abounded on the American scene was sponsoring the national tour of a trainful of exhibits to warn people against the reckless driving of automobiles and industrial accidents generally. A recruiting sergeant was placed on the Safety First Train.

The National Guard

Enlistments in the regular army lagged. Seven years looked like a long time in the land of opportunity. Munitions plants were offering good wages. Farmers were looking forward to high prices. American young men showed every sign of preferring safety to soldiering.

On the other hand Leonard Wood's and Theodore Roosevelt's campaign for preparedness stimulated enthusiasm for enlistment in the militia. The Plattsburgtype camps and the R.O.T.C. were proving attractive to college men. The war spirit was rising among them. Citizen soldiers were not entirely unprepared for the shock when, on June 18, a few days before the humiliating ambush at Carrizal, President Wilson started calling out the state militias for service on the Mexican border.

The colleges and highschools had closed down for the season. American youngsters were curious about war. As they turned to the sports page in the newspapers it was hard quite to ignore the daily headlines. Young men dropped their search for summer jobs and hurried to enlist. Armories filled up with confused youths called in some cases all of a sudden from their beds. Many guardsmen with wives and young families gave up positions they had staked their future on.

The officers knew no more of soldiering than the enlisted men. Probably the outfit best prepared was an Illinois regiment which had been acting out wargames for the benefit of a motion picture company.

Equipment was lacking or thoroughly out of date. Most of the militia regiments were issued woolen o.d. uniforms impossible in the arid heat of the border country. Rifles and ammunition were in short supply. Machineguns were rare and mostly of unworkable types. For the purposes of logistics most units depended on the old Civil War wagon train. The army mule was still considered the proper means of military transport. The Quartermaster General in Washington was supposed to fill in deficiencies in the equipment of the state militias, but the War Department was ensnarled in requisition systems which had proved faulty in the campaign against Geronimo and almost fatal in the Spanish War.

The feeding and equipping of the national guard regiments was left largely to the good will of state officials and to the ingenuity of officers and noncoms yanked suddenly out of civilian life. Camps were improvised out of fairgrounds and on back lots, cook shacks and bath houses built, latrines dug. By guess and by God trainloads of excited young men found their way to the border.

Accustomed to think of themselves as volunteers, the militiamen were unexpectedly faced with the federal oath. Regular army officers supervised the grim ceremony. Their orders read: "If any man refuses to step forward and answer to his name when it is called, or refuses to raise his hand and take the oath, he is to be jerked out of line and placed under arrest pending courtmartial."

Henceforward the militiamen were subject to the Articles of War. Overnight they found themselves in the straightjacket of a military caste system which ran counter to all the habits of democracy. Officers were superior beings, enlisted men coolies who must learn to obey orders with automatic alacrity.

The manual of arms. Close order drill. Atten'shun. Eyes front. Left dress. Wipe that smile off your face. Forward 'arch.

By midsummer a hundred thousand men sweltered under tents from Brownsville to San Diego. Boys who dreamed of marching on Mexico City found themselves standing guard among the dusty mesquite and the pricklypears. The sun beat down with the weight of a sledgehammer. Duststorms or "sand devils" blinded sentries on watch or snatched up hats or loose bits of clothing to whirl them out of sight into the air. Most of the time the country was dry as an oven but as summer advanced cloudbursts would wash out campsites and leave the desert a sea of slippery mud. There were continual latrine rumors of greasers sniping across the border and now and then a fulldress alarm when companies would throw themselves on their bellies and open fire into the dark. Like as not the alarm would turn out to have been caused, not by raiding bandits but by some sulky old Indian on a burro trying to sneak across the border to sell his watermelons.

The one universal gripe was the attitude of civilians towards enlisted men. Girls turned up their noses at anything less than a second loot's gold bars. The first fruits of twenty years of fanatical agitation for prohibition was that the canteens only sold 2½% beer. Thirsty privates had to buy rotgut at fancy prices in blind tigers. On leave they were persecuted by military police and sheriff's deputies. At Ysleta near El Paso the owner of a dance hall put up a sign:

DANCING FOR LADIES AND GENTLEMEN

SOLDIERS AND DOGS NOT ALLOWED

Building the canal in Panama and fighting yellow jack in Cuba and campaigning against the insurrectos in the Philippines, the Medical Corps had learned to cope, as no other army service in history, with the problems of military health in torrid regions. Sanitation was excellent. Outside of sunburn, heat prostration, cracked lips from the dry air and occasional outbreaks of venereal disease, the health of the troops was good, better, the public health men said, than it would have been at home.

Reports of the military aptitude of the militia were less favorable.

After the national guard units were mustered out in the late fall of 1916 the Militia Bureau of the War Department published the results of an inquest on efficiency:

"As to the present degree of readiness and fitness for field service of organizations of infantry, the answer in 89% of the reports was either 'fair,' 'poor,' 'unfitted,' 'not ready,' 'wholly unprepared,' or the like; 46 reports out of 102 said that under the most favorable conditions it would require 6 months in the field to have the regiment meet an inferior enemy, and 2 years to meet trained troops; 10 reports stated that it was doubtful if organizations inspected would ever become efficient under their present officers.

"Of the cavalry, one third of the reports indicated that it would require from 6 to 9 months to make the organizations fit for service against an inferior enemy, and approximately from 2 to 3 years against trained troops. In 6 other reports 4 to 6 months was considered the time needed to make them ready for active service.

"In the field artillery there were 30 inspections—6 of regiments, 8 of battalions and 16 of separate batteries. In 17 the organizations were reported as 'unfit for field service' . . . None of the engineer organizations was reported as fit for field service . . ."

The regular army, though superior in the manual of arms, was not much better off in equipment than the militia. Testifying before a congressional committee during the following winter, the ranking U. S. Major General, Leonard A. Wood, pointed out that the regular army totally lacked hand grenades or instruction in their use, or the trench mortars which were proving so important in the fighting in Europe. There were virtually no machineguns or signal apparatus; no searchlights or antiaircraft weapons or usable airplanes for that matter. Field artillery was inadequate, small arm ammunition was in short supply. Nothing had been done to expand production of muchneeded automatic rifles. Coast defense guns lacked fire control systems. The few modern light guns the army had had been bought from a firm supplying the British, and American ammunition didn't fit them.

Wood's revelations were brushed off as "politics" at the War Department. He was not a West Pointer. Who ever heard of a commanding general coming up out of the Medical Corps? He was known to be deep in the councils of the Bull Moose wing of the Republican Party. When a friend pointed out that he was damaging his army career by his outspoken criticisms he answered:

"I realize that I cannot give information I am sometimes called upon to give without appearing to criticize those who have the power to remove me, but I am so sincere in my belief that I am on the right line that I am perfectly willing to run the risk of hurting myself with the heads of departments, if that is the price I must pay in my effort to teach the men of this country how to defend themselves."

To Define the Terms

Woodrow Wilson returned to Washington after the 1916 campaign convinced that his mandate from the nation demanded the immediate formulation of peace terms which must somehow be forced on the warring powers.

Physically he was worn out. His sick headaches continued to worry Edith and Dr. Grayson. His head still spun with the clamor of political oratory. He had to collect his thoughts.

As soon as he settled at his desk he wrote out a memorandum to Tumulty: "Please say to *all* that the President is so engrossed just now with business of the most pressing sort that it is not possible for him to make appointments unless the business *cannot* be postponed."

The President knew he had to act quickly before the rash shot of some German submarine commander forced him into the war. He felt that British and French dependence on American supplies and American credit might give him a whip hand over the Allies if he could only find how to apply it. One third of the world's gold supply was already piled up in the vaults of American banks. "We can determine to a large extent who is to be financed and who is not to be financed," he had told an audience gathered at Shadow Lawn during the campaign.

He summoned the confidential colonel to the White House to resume his last winter's intrigue for mediation. For once House balked. He was convinced the United States should already have intervened on the side of the Allies. Peace now could only be to Germany's advantage: "I argued again and again that we should not pull Germany's chestnuts out of the fire."

They broke up late. Neither man would budge from his position.

Next morning Woodrow Wilson did not appear for breakfast. "The President was unusually late which bespoke a bad night," House entered in his diary. "I was sorry, but it could not be helped. I dislike coming to the White House as his guest and upsetting him to the extent I often do."

House's point was that the Germans now wanted mediation and were holding the threat of a renewed submarine campaign over the world's head to obtain a victorious peace. "In my opinion," House noted again, "the President's desire for peace is partially due to his Scotch Presbyterian conscience and not to personal fear, for I believe he has both moral and physical courage."

Like any oldtime Covenanter Wilson believed in the efficacy of the word. By the right word men could be brought to see the light. For days, while cabinet members and the faithful Tumulty handled the government business as best they could without him, the President wrote and rewrote, on his own typewriter in his study, a fresh note to the belligerent powers.

The war was making the position of neutrals intolerable. "My objects," he jotted down in shorthand before typing out his notes, "to stop the war before it is too late to remedy what it has done:

"To reconsider peace on the basis of the rights of the weak along with the rights of the strong, the rights of peoples as well as the rights of governments:

"To effect a league of nations based upon a peace which shall be guaranteed against breach by the common force and an intelligent organization of the common interest."

After the first phrases, disconnectedly jotted down, his periods began to swell into the long balanced sentences he found so effective in public speaking. This time, instead of the United States Congress or a crowd in Madison Square Garden, he was addressing the parliament of the world.

He pointed out that the warring nations were all fighting, so they claimed, "to be free of aggression and of peril to the free and independent development of their people's lives and fortunes . . . Must the contest be settled by slow attrition and ultimate exhaustion?" he asked. "An irreparable damage to civilization cannot promote peace and the secure happiness of the world.

"I deem myself clearly within my right," he went on, ". . . as a representative of a great neutral nation whose interests are being daily affected . . . I do most earnestly urge that some means be immediately taken . . . to define the terms upon which a settlement of the issues of the war may be expected."

All through late November and early December the wording of the President's note was hashed and rehashed to make it palatable to the British and French. House and Lansing and Polk at the State Department conspired to tone down its more startling expressions.

By the time they finished their work of revision events in Europe had already blunted any effectiveness the note might have had.

The Mincing Machine

Neither side in the European war was yet fully aware of its own weaknesses. Both sides were still hopeful of victory. In the east Brusilov's offensive had shattered the fighting power of the Hapsburg empire. At the same time, by encouraging the Czar's government to force Romania into the war, the Russian successes, won at a cost which no one had yet calculated, were instrumental in handing the Germans another victory.

On August 27, 1916, the Romanian Government declared war on the Central Powers. By December 6 von Mackensen's armies were in Bucharest. The richest oilfields in Europe and the food producing plains of the lower Danube lay open for the replenishment of the German population and of industries starved for raw materials by the British blockade.

In the west 1916 was the year of Verdun. In spite of Joffre's mistaken decision that Vauban's old forts were useless in modern war and the fact that the French had only one road and a rickety line of narrow gauge, and these partly under shellfire, to supply their armies, while the Germans had thirteen lines of railroad to supply theirs, the French held out against a series of desperately fought and carefully planned attacks.

The fighting lasted throughout the year. Joffre made up for his stupidity by his paternal imperturbability. He put Pétain in charge of the Verdun salient. Pétain did an extraordinary job in organizing supply but it was a General Nivelle who got the credit for two skillful and not too costly operations which in the fall recaptured the forts of Vaux and Douaumont and nullified the German effort. The score ran around half a million casualties on either side.

The gray battered old walled town and the *Voie Sacrée* that led to it became the symbol of everything the French held dear. After such sacrifices they would accept no terms but victory.

Sir Douglas Haig, the lowland Scot who commanded the British expeditionary forces, was a perfect product of his nineteenthcentury military training. Like a good chronometer his routine mind performed exactly the same operations at the same time every day of his life. An innocent godly man, no new idea was ever allowed to penetrate his head. In his youth he had been a great polo player. He retained a touching belief in the efficacy of cavalry.

To take the pressure off the French at Verdun he squandered the troops Kitchener had trained in a bloody series of assaults on the heights on the north bank of the Somme. When tanks, which were that year's British contribution to the science of warfare, made their first blundering efforts in the Albert-Bapaume sector in September, Haig failed to understand that tanks were the cavalry of the twentieth century.

Instead of holding the favorable positions his men had captured on the heights, Haig drove them on till his armies ended the year floundering in the deadly mud of the plains beyond. He had pushed the Germans back to be sure, at the cost of four hundred thousand irreplaceable casualties, but only to positions more easily defended than those they had given up. So confident were the German generals that the British had no striking power left, that early in the fall they began to pull their best divisions out of the lines for service on the eastern front.

As division after division came back mangled from the mincing machine of Verdun a clamor arose in France for more discretion in the government. Briand reshuffled his cabinet and removed slow Joffre from his command. Retired as Field Marshal, Joffre became the propagandists' embodiment of the miracle of the Marne. Lyautey of Moroccan fame, now Minister of War, placed great hopes on Nivelle. Nivelle had saved Verdun. Nivelle, repeating his lucky coup on a larger scale, would drive the Germans off French soil.

In England the Asquith cabinet, confronted with the butcher's bill from the Somme, collapsed in despair. Lloyd George, who had been stirring the enthusiasm of the crowd with talk of a knockout blow, took over. His first job as Prime Minister was to hurry to Paris to a meeting of Allied political leaders which was held concurrently with a meeting of the commanding generals and their staffs at nearby Chantilly. Everybody was urging unity of command but nobody knew how to attain it.

Premier Briand arrived late for the first session. Lloyd George found him oddly inattentive. He was so ruffled and preoccupied he could hardly follow the agenda. It turned out that he had that moment emerged from a conference with the Chamber of Deputies' permanent committee on the conduct of the war. The angry old man who was chairman of that committee had given him a bad quarter of an hour. The old man's name was Clemenceau.

Peace Without Victory

Three days after the fall of the Romanian capital, the German foreign office, in an aggressive mood since the resignation of the moderate von Jagow, offered, in terms which their enemies considered insolent, to join in conference for a negotiated peace. To the Allied chancelleries, confused by the falsehoods of their own propaganda, Wilson's note, coming ten days later, seemed a mere echo of the German proposals. To French and British ears the words "negotiated peace" smacked again of defeatism and treason.

Still, London and Paris were distressingly conscious of the fact that they had to keep on good terms with Washington: enormous new credits had to be obtained, and soon.

Sir Robert Cecil, who had taken over the Foreign Office from Sir Edward Grey, immediately went around to Grosvenor Square to sound out Ambassador Page. Page was by this time so saturated with the war spirit that he had lost all patience with the President's efforts for the peace. He told Sir Robert that accepting the proposals of the German note would be buying a pig in a poke and led him to believe that most of Washington thought so too. Page continued writing the State Department what scurvy knaves the British thought the Americans were for keeping out of the war.

It was a time of jangled nerves. In Washington, Spring Rice went into one of his tantrums in the Secretary of State's office. Lansing was, as usual, defending the American theory that the seas must be free to neutral commerce. The question that touched off what Lansing described in his diary as "a distressing scene" was whether British gun crews on merchantships should be considered naval or civilian personnel.

In the midst of a legalistic discussion of the sort that Lansing enjoyed, Sir Cecil cried out, "You propose to prevent our guns from being properly served." The little man was suddenly white and shaking.

Lansing did not answer. Both men got to their feet.

"If you follow this course, sir, of doing nothing while helpless people are murdered and put in open boats three hundred miles from land . . . you will be held personally responsible," screamed Sir Cecil. "Yes, you and the President will be held personally responsible."

"I was looking in his face," wrote Lansing, "when he uttered these words and probably was not able to conceal my amazement and indignation at this outburst . . . I said nothing . . . then finally: 'Mr. Ambassador I advise you to sit down and to think over carefully what you have just said to me.'"

Lansing, exuding from every pore his consciousness of the impeccable correctness of his own attitude, sat glowering behind his desk.

The British ambassador's mouth trembled above the skimpy vandyke. His eyes turned down. Lansing thought them suffused with tears. His hands kept nervously opening and shutting.

The little man began to apologize profusely, embarrassingly. "I am so sorry . . . I should not have said what I did. I did not mean it. I can hardly endure it when I think of these inhuman beasts of Germans sinking our ships. Why my wife might be on one."

No man to let a defeated opponent off too easily, Lansing remarked grimly that it would be hard to forget Spring Rice's words. Yet, like all the rest of Wilson's cabinet, Lansing agreed with the British ambassador. A few days later he made this entry in his diary: "War cannot come too soon to suit me because I know it must come at last."

President Wilson was still telling his intimates he would go to any lengths to avoid war. Like Jefferson planning his embargo he was dreaming of some better way of enforcing the nation's will. Determined to make one final effort he went back to his solitary typewriter. His final pro-

posals were launched into a quicksand more treacherous than either he
or his advisers knew.

Among ruling circles in Germany the Allies' rejection of their offer to
negotiate carried the day for the resumption of fullscale submarine warfare. The admirals and generals, far better informed of the importance of
Allied shipping losses than Wilson's advisers, were convinced Britain
could be brought to collapse in a few months. American military fumbling
along the Mexican border had been carefully noted. If the Americans did
not have the strength to keep a few bandits from raiding their territory
and murdering their citizens, they certainly were not to be feared in
Europe, four thousand submarine-infested miles away from their shores.

While Wilson agreed with House that the Germans were "a slippery
lot" he had become deeply distrustful of the Allied leadership. He was
daily irritated by the blacklist of neutral firms suspected of having dealings with Germany, through which the British authorities assumed a virtual dictatorship over American overseas trade. More sincerely neutral
than ever he was struggling to live up to the unsought slogan: he kept us
out of war.

He went to work on a new declaration of principles. This time he would
appeal to the peoples over the heads of their governments.

Before the American President had finished putting his principles on
paper, decisions in Europe made it certain that his words would fall on
deaf ears. On January 9, 1917, Kaiser Wilhelm, with due secrecy, distributed a message to the German fleet: "I order that unrestricted submarine war be launched with the greatest vigor on the 1st of February.
You will immediately take all the necessary steps, taking care however
that this intention shall not prematurely come to the knowledge of the
enemy and the neutral powers."

On January 15, using the facilities of the American Embassy in Berlin,
which had been put at von Bernstorff's disposal to facilitate the transmission of peace proposals, Chancellor von Bethmann-Hollweg in a coded
message notified his American ambassador of the Kaiser's decision. Von
Bernstorff, though he still chattered sweetly about a negotiated peace to
Lansing and House, immediately went to work to carry out the German
plans. He notified the skippers of German ships interned in American
ports to get ready to wreck the engines of their vessels at a moment's
notice, and he transmitted, again using the cable facilities of the U. S.
State Department, a telegram to the German minister to Carranza's administration in Mexico City:

Washington, January 19, 1917

"German Legation,
   Mexico City.
   No. 130 (code used)

"Foreign Office telegraphs January sixteenth:
   Number 1. Strictly secret. Decode yourself.

"We intend to begin unrestricted U-boat warfare on February first. Efforts will be made notwithstanding this to keep the United States neutral. In the event that we shall not be successful in this, we propose alliance to Mexico upon the following basis: To make war together; make peace together; generous financial support; and agreement on our part that Mexico shall reconquer the formerly lost territory in Texas, New Mexico, Arizona. Arrangement of details to be left to your honor. You should disclose the following to the President (Carranza) in strict secrecy as soon as outbreak of war with the United States is certain and add the proposal to invite Japan to immediate spontaneous concurrent effort and at the same time use his good offices between us and Japan. Please call the President's attention to the fact that the ruthless employment of our U-boats offers the prospect of forcing England in a few months to peace. Acknowledge receipt. Zimmermann. End of telegram."

British Naval Intelligence, which had broken this particular German code, intercepted the message almost as soon as it was received in Mexico City, but for reasons best known to themselves, the authorities in London took their time in transmitting the news it contained to Washington.

On January 22 the President was ready to produce the declaration he had been carefully preparing. At the last moment he decided to make his appeal in the form of an address to the Senate. No President had appeared before the Senate alone since George Washington retired in a huff from a heated discussion with that body during his second administration. Historian Wilson was again breaking with precedent to lend emphasis to what he had to say.

It was a Monday morning. The Senate convened at twelve. The White House gave only an hour's notice of the President's visit.

"On the eighteenth of December last," Wilson told the Senators in his mellow tenor voice, "I addressed an identical note to the governments of the states now at war requesting them to state . . . the terms on which they would deem it possible to make peace."

Though it demanded some stretch of the imagination, he declared that the terms of his note had been accepted, in principle, by both parties. ". . . We are that much nearer a definite discussion of the peace which shall end the present war . . . Such a settlement cannot be long postponed. It is right that before it comes this government should frankly formulate the conditions upon which it would feel justified in asking our people to approve its formal and solemn adherence to a league for peace. I am here to attempt to state those conditions.

"The present war must first be ended . . . The treaties and agreements which bring it to an end must embody terms which will create a peace that is worth guaranteeing and preserving . . . There must be not a balance of power but a community of power: not organized rivalries but an organized common peace."

He had assurances from each group of belligerents, he said, that they did not intend completely to crush their antagonists. He must now make clear to all parties the implications of these assurances:

"They imply first of all that it must be a peace without victory . . . Only a peace between equals can last . . . The equality of nations . . . must be an equality of rights . . . No peace can last or ought to last which does not recognize and accept the principle that governments derive all their just powers from the consent of the governed . . .

"I am proposing, as it were, that the nations . . . adopt the doctrine of President Monroe as the doctrine of the world: that no nation shall seek to extend its polity over any other nation or people, but that every people should be left free to determine its own polity, its own way of development, unhindered, unthreatened, unafraid . . ."

His final words were moving: "I am proposing government by the consent of the governed; that freedom of the seas which in international conference after conference representatives of the United States have urged . . . and that moderation of armaments which makes of armies and navies a power for order merely . . . These are American principles, American policies . . . They are the principles of mankind and must prevail."

The first senator to jump to his feet and applaud was La Follette of Wisconsin. Democrats and Progressives joined in an ovation. Some Republican regulars were so carried away that they had to explain later that they applauded the President's eloquence rather than his proposals.

The phrase "peace without victory," which was to float as a banner over the aspirations of the liberals both in Great Britain and the United States, was culled from an editorial in *The New Republic*, a New York weekly financed by a wealthy Progressive named Willard Straight, where a group of ardent young optimists was at work reweaving the frazzled strands of the New Nationalism and the New Freedom into the New Liberalism.

Herbert Croly, then editor, wrote that hearing the President pronounce those words was the greatest moment of his life. Lowes Dickinson in England called the speech "perhaps the most important international document in all history." Woodrow Wilson's leadership of collegebred idealists throughout the Englishspeaking world was assured from that moment.

Count von Bernstorff's Regrets

The last day of January, while editorial approval of the President's sentiments re-echoed through the American press, Ambassador von Bernstorff called up the State Department at ten in the morning to make an appointment with Secretary Lansing for that afternoon. Earlier still he had transmitted an order to the crews of interned German ships to disable their engines. He had on his desk Bethmann-Hollweg's note announcing the new German effort to blockade Great Britain.

Lansing carefully told the story of the interview in his memoirs:

"That afternoon I was working on a letter to the President in regard to the arming of merchant vessels on the ground that Germany was undoubtedly preparing to renew vigorous submarine warfare . . . Before I had completed the letter the German Ambassador was announced . . . I noticed that, though he moved with his usual springy step, he did not smile with his customary assurance. After shaking hands and sitting down in the large easy chair by the side of my desk he drew forth from an envelope . . . several papers . . . He asked me if he should read them to me or if I would read them myself before he said anything about them. I replied that I would read the papers, which I did slowly and carefully for . . . I realized that it . . . would probably bring on the gravest crisis which this government had had to face . . . The note announced the renewal on the next day of indiscriminate submarine warfare."

Lansing remarked that he viewed the situation with the utmost gravity but preferred not to make any immediate comment. Von Bernstorff stammered out his private regrets.

"I believe you do regret it," answered Lansing, "for you know what the result will be." He added that he wasn't blaming the German ambassador personally.

"'You should not,' he said with evident feeling. 'You know how constantly I have worked for peace.'"

Lansing answered drily he did not care to discuss the matter further. Von Bernstorff shook hands and left "not at all the jaunty carefree man-of-the-world he usually was. With a ghost of a smile he bowed as I said 'Good afternoon' and, turning, left the room."

When the Secretary of State arrived at the White House after dinner that night he found the President agitated. Wilson was still of two minds. He believed that von Bernstorff's protestations that Germany still wanted a negotiated peace must represent some sector of civilian opinion in the governing circles about the Kaiser. Did this note mean that the militarists were completely in the saddle?

Lansing set forth his arguments for an immediate break. As usual the President listened attentively. He would call a meeting of the cabinet. It was Lansing's impression that Wilson was waiting for some overt act.

The Secretary went home to bed in a frustrated state of mind. "Has the blood of patriotism ceased to throb in American veins? . . . Have we forgotten that our heritage of liberty was sealed with the lives of Americans and that it is a sacred trust which we must hold unimpaired for the generations to come?" he had written in his private diary after the *Lusitania* sinking. The President's temporizing brought on a new storm of resentful thought. Robert Lansing's sleep was fitful that night.

On February 1 the German note drove everything else off the front pages. Atlantic shipping was paralyzed. House's friend Dudley Field Malone took it upon himself to close the port of New York. Reports came in of glutted dockside warehouses and of goods piling up at the railheads. The stockmarket slumped. While Allied partisans stormed in the east coast newspapers, pacifist groups held meetings urging the President not to submit to provocation. Editorials were full of uneasy conjecture on what the German-American societies might do in case of war. Would the United States face a situation akin to the Easter rebellion?

Colonel House was reported to have escaped a throng of reporters waiting for him in the Pennsylvania Station by having himself smuggled by a back stairway into his stateroom on the night train to Washington.

The confidential colonel found President Wilson "sad and depressed . . . The President said he felt as if the world had suddenly reversed itself; that after going from east to west, it had begun to go from west to east, and that he could not get his balance . . . The question we discussed longest was whether it was better to give Bernstorff his passports immediately or wait till the Germans committed some overt act. When Lansing came this discussion was renewed, and we all agreed that it was best to give him his passports at once."

The argument his advisers used to convince the President was that breaking off relations might bring the Germans to their senses. Lansing was sent back to his office to write out an explanatory note.

Even then the President was insisting to House that he would not allow the break to lead to war. He spoke of Germany as "a madman to be curbed." House asked if it was fair to the Allies to let them do all the curbing. "He noticeably winced at this," said House when he dictated his private notes to the indispensable Miss Denton.

The colonel described the events of the next day with some gusto in his diary: "We sat listlessly during the morning until Lansing arrived . . . The President nervously arranged his books and walked up and down the floor. Mrs. Wilson spoke of golf and asked whether I thought it would look badly if the President went out on the links. I thought the American people would feel that he should not do anything so trivial at such a time.

"In great governmental crises of this sort the public have no conception of what is happening on the stage behind the curtain . . . When the decision has been made nothing further can be done until it is time for the curtain to rise . . . Meanwhile we were listlessly killing time . . . The President at last suggested that we play a game of pool." House used to tell his friends afterwards what poor poolplayers both he and the President were. Towards the end of the second game, Lansing was announced.

"The President, Lansing and I then returned to the study. Lansing was so nearly of our mind that there was little discussion. He read what he had written and we accepted it . . ."

In the cabinet meeting that afternoon the President went into all the arguments pro and con once more. The cabinet members were edgy. Houston and McAdoo wanted action. Jolly Franklin K. Lane wrote a friend: "He comes out right but he's slower than a glacier and things are mighty disagreeable whenever anything has to be done."

Lansing sat quiet. Since his talk with the President and Colonel House that morning he was convinced that the President had made up his mind. "I slept soundly that night," he noted in his diary, "feeling sure that the President would act vigorously."

A Little Group of Wilful Men

Next day the President addressed the two houses of Congress to explain why he had to give von Bernstorff his passports. He was applauded. Only the Progressives were mum.

The President's relations with Congress had been deteriorating all through the winter. Though the Senate was still safely Democratic, the House was split 213 to 213. Even his most loyal supporters were losing the unity of purpose of the happy days of the New Freedom. The Republican regulars were grouped in a bitter phalanx around Senator Lodge of Massachusetts. The Progressives, formerly so cooperative, were balky.

In mid-January after months of White House pressure, which Tumulty was adept in masking under a velvet glove, President and Mrs. Wilson learned with relief that the appointment of their dear Dr. Grayson as Rear Admiral was finally approved by the Senate. His promotion jumped him over a list of a hundred and one names. The fight went on for months. Satisfying this presidential whim caused Wilson's legislative managers many a sleepless night. The Grayson appointment left bitter feelings in the Senate.

Wilson seized on Lansing's suggestion of arming merchantships and letting them fight their way across the sealanes as a way of emulating the "armed neutrality" policies of the Scandinavian countries during the Napoleonic wars. The President believed he already had the authority as Commander in Chief of the armed forces but he wanted congressional endorsement of his plan. The Armed Ship Bill was introduced.

Though it passed the House, the Armed Ship Bill became entangled in the political strategy of the Republicans, panting for a return to power in 1920. The Republican leadership had no intention of giving the Democratic administration a free hand after the President's second inauguration. They wanted to force a special session. The Progressives in the Senate, who had stood by the President in the long fight for public ownership of emergency shipping, opposed the plan to arm merchantships as the first step towards war against Germany in the interests of British trade and the New York banks. It was putting the dollar sign on the American flag said Norris of Nebraska.

La Follette of Wisconsin seized on the arming of merchantships as the dramatic issue in the struggle for peace. As usual, once he had made up his mind, black was black and white was white. When it became obvious that the bill had enough votes to pass, his passionate denunciation turned into a filibuster. Twelve men, in spite of the crescendo of vituperation raised up against them by the war spirit now sweeping the country, decided to hold out until the Sixtyfourth Congress expired on Inauguration Day.

The filibuster produced vast bitterness. According to Capitol gossip, Ollie James of Kentucky at one moment advanced threateningly toward La Follette across the Senate floor, with his hand on his gunpocket. The filibustering senators were excoriated in the press as "flirting with treason," as "knaves who betrayed the nation," or as "La Follette and his little group of perverts." La Follette was hung in effigy by the students at Massachusetts Tech. He was denounced by professors at Columbia. Even at home in Wisconsin old supporters turned against him.

Public indignation was exacerbated by the publication of the Zimmermann telegram. On February 25 a translation was handed to Page in London. He promptly cabled it to Washington where Polk and Lansing originated a search for the original cypher message in the telegraph company's files. The versions matched. Lansing hurried to the White House to show the President the telegram.

Lansing reported in his diary that Mr. Wilson "cried out, 'Good Lord,' several times in the course of its perusal." His first thought was that it might be a forgery. It was hard for him to swallow having been taken in by fast talking von Bernstorff.

As soon as he was convinced that Zimmermann's message was genuine, the President decided that the State Department should leak it to the press. The head of the Washington bureau of the Associated Press was sworn to secrecy as to the origin of the text and on March 31 it was spread over the front pages of the nation's newspapers.

The Zimmermann telegram, which the German foreign office, with characteristic German bluntness, soon admitted to be genuine, proved a great help to President Wilson in his difficulties with Congress over the Armed Ship Bill. It turned La Follette's filibuster into a futile gesture. "Fought it through to the finish" the old warrior for righteousness wired his wife after the Sixtyfourth Congress disbanded on Inauguration Day. "Feeling here intense. I must take the gaff for a while."

The Red Man had won.

In his heart Woodrow Wilson still felt as great a loathing for war as the senators he now denounced as "a little group of wilful men representing no opinion but their own." He had consistently held in check the "preparedness" campaigns that were whooping up the warfever. He even tried to discourage the War College from making plans for some possible eventual campaign in Europe. As late as early January 1917 he was telling House, "This country does not intend to become involved in this war . . . it would be a crime against civilization for us to go in."

In his agony of mind in the final hour he got his old friend Frank Cobb up from New York and talked to him through most of the night.

"It would mean," he told the editor of the New York *World*, "that we would lose our heads along with the rest and stop weighing right and wrong. It would mean that a majority of people in this hemisphere would go war mad, quit thinking, and devote their energies to destruction . . . Conformity will be the only virtue. And every man who refuses to conform will have to pay the penalty . . . Once lead this people into war and they'll forget there ever was such a thing as tolerance . . . If there is any alternative for God's sake let's take it."

We Will Not Choose the Path of Submission

The German authorities were doing their best to make any alternative to war impossible. They lost no time in presenting the American public with overt acts to force the President's hand. During the month of February the U-boats sank seven hundred eightyone thousand five hundred tons of shipping, including two American ships warned in time to allow the crews to escape. When the Cunard liner *Laconia* was torpedoed two American women lost their lives.

March 12 the U.S.S. *Algonquin* went down off the Scilly Islands. On March 19 the news reached Washington of three American steamers torpedoed on a single day. On the *Vigilancia* fifteen seamen were lost.

The President called a special session of the Sixtyfifth Congress for April 2.

Colonel House arrived the day before on the night train from New York. Reaching the White House in time for breakfast he found the President and Mrs. Wilson up betimes and getting ready to play a little golf. Woodrow Wilson's night had been sleepless. Again he was complaining of headaches.

While the President and his party were out on the links Colonel House was pestered by cabinet members calling up to ask what the President was going to say in the speech he was planning to deliver as soon as the two houses had finished organizing.

Since Colonel House didn't know himself, he held them off with noncommittal murmurs. It wasn't till after lunch that the President got around to going over his manuscript with the confidential colonel. "No address he has yet made pleased me more than this one," noted House. Though others considered the President unnaturally calm, House noted signs of nervousness as the afternoon dragged on. "Neither of us did anything except kill time until he was called to the Capitol."

After the usual family dinner the presidential party drove to the Capitol. It was a night of gusty rain with fitful flickering of lightning on the heavy clouds. Secretary Baker had ordered out two troops of cavalry to protect the President. The wet Washington streets were crowded with sightseers come to see him drive by in this hour of emergency. The House galleries were filled early and thousands stood in the occasional splatters of rain, looking up at the dome of the Capitol which was lit by floodlights from below, while the President asked Congress for a joint resolution declaring that a state of war existed between the United States and the Imperial German Government.

Except for La Follette, who stood with his arms crossed and the lines deep and grim about his bulldog jaw, almost every congressman and even the Supreme Court justices wore a little American flag in the lapel.

The President's entrance was greeted with cheers and handclapping. In tones clearer and cooler even than usual, he described his efforts to keep the peace against Germany's everincreasing provocations. He described the possible reactions short of war that were left to him. "There is one choice we cannot make, we are incapable of making: we will not choose the path of submission."

At that moment Chief Justice White dropped the soft felt hat he was holding, raised his arms above his old white head and brought them together with a resounding slap. The rest of the sentence was drowned in shouts, with the Chief Justice holding his arms above his head like a cheer leader.

We would be fighting, the President went on "for the ultimate peace of the world and the liberation of its peoples . . . The world must be made safe for democracy . . ." The cheers within the Capitol were echoed by the crowds outside, standing under the dripping trees in the rainy gardens of the Hill.

"To such a task we can dedicate our lives and our fortunes, everything that we are and everything that we have, with the pride of those who know that the day has come when America is privileged to spend her blood and her might for the principles that gave her birth . . . God helping her, she can do no other."

President Wilson received the greatest acclamation of his career. Even Senator Lodge wrung his hand. When he finally shook himself loose from the handshakes and congratulations of the Capitol lobbies he was driven back to the White House along streets lined with yelling throngs. All down Pennsylvania Avenue they cheered him.

Back in the White House he sat down at the end of the long table in the Cabinet Room. Tumulty, who was the only one with him, remembered his sitting a long while silent and pale.

"Think of what it was they were applauding," he said at last. "My message today was a message of death for our young men. How strange it seems to applaud that."

Then he began telling Tumulty that all along he'd seen the futility of neutrality, that he couldn't move faster than the American people moved. "Our life till this thing is over . . . will be full of tragedy and heartaches."

In a broken voice he began to read his secretary clippings from newspaper editorials approving of his course. A letter from the editor of a paper in Springfield, Massachusetts, touched him particularly . . . "after all the political experience and conflicts of the past few years, I am conscious of a very real yet peculiar feeling of having summered and wintered with you, in spite of the immeasurable and rather awful distance that separates our respective places in the life and work of our time."

"That man understood me and sympathized," were the President's words as Tumulty remembered them. "As he said this, the President drew his handkerchief from his pocket, wiped away great tears that stood in his eyes, and then laying his head on the cabinet table, sobbed as if he had been a child."

Chapter 12

ORGANIZING TO THE UTMOST

THE day the United States entered the war, though the situation in Europe was so obscured by censorship and propaganda no one in Washington knew exactly what it was, the fortunes of the Allies were approaching their lowest ebb.

Brusilov's great offensives had worn out the Russian armies. They had no striking power left. During the winter the progressive breakdown of the Romanoff regime kept easing the military pressure against Germany from the east.

Russians of all classes were crying out against the incompetence, the corruption and the callous brutality of the management of the war. The Russian soldiery had reached the point where men felt they had a better chance to save their lives by fighting their own government than by fighting the Germans.

The Anniversary Revolution

The outbreak began with a printer's strike in Petrograd on the January anniversary of the abortive revolution which resulted from Russian failures in the war against Japan. Incapable of making up his own mind, the Czar turned to almost anybody for advice. First he was induced to assemble the Duma, which was little more than a consultative assembly of notables, in the hope of regaining some popular support. From the Duma there arose an immediate clamor for the elimination of traitors and embezzlers from the imperial court. Spontaneous strikes paralyzed Petrograd. The imperial household was thrown into a panic and the Duma was promptly dissolved.

All the Czar's advisers could think of now was to induce him to call in the same General Ivanov, by this time a flabby and peevish old man, who had put down the popular uprising in 1905. As a result regiments of the imperial guard rose in revolt. Troops recalled from the front, even the everfaithful Cossacks, joined the insurrection. The Czar's authority melted with the snows under the spring sun.

The striking workingmen elected a soviet, or general council, to represent them. The Baltic fleet took up the revolutionary cry. Singing the "Marseillaise" in memory of the Bastille, sailors led in the storming of the prison fortress of Peter and Paul. Jails were opened, political prisoners freed, exiles called home. Soviets sprang up in factories, in provincial towns, in Moscow. Russia became a vast debating society. In the country districts peasants were busy staking out their landlords' fields. Whole army divisions disbanded, arrested their officers and trooped into the cities.

By the middle of March the Czar had abdicated. The imperial family was confined in their summer palace. What central government survived was in the hands of a provisional committee of the dissolved Duma, with an oratorical young lawyer named Kerensky as Minister of Justice.

The revolution started to the tune of the "Marseillaise." Liberty, equality, fraternity. Russia would pattern itself on the western democracies.

The liberal press in France and Great Britain and the United States greeted these February events with enthusiasm. The one flaw in the theory upon which democratic propaganda was based, that the Allied and Associated nations were fighting for selfgovernment and the rights of man against the Kaiser's military autocracy, was that their Russian ally represented the most brutal and backward of all autocracies. With parliamentary government triumphing in Russia the war could be carried on with a clear conscience.

The German authorities were even more pleased. For them the revolution was the climax of the corruption and decay of the Czar's regime which had served them so well at the front. It meant that they could transfer muchneeded troops to the west, where for all their superior techniques and superior positions the Kaiser's divisions were being worn thin by the war of attrition. They needed to make sure that the disorganization of the Russian military machine should be immediate and complete.

The Sealed Train

Free Switzerland had for years furnished a haven where the planners of the new society, which was to eliminate want and injustice from the world, developed their programs of mass subversion and mass leadership. The Russian exiles who offered the most drastic program for the destruction of existing institutions were grouped around a newspaper named *The Social Democrat,* published in Zurich by V. I. Ulianov and his wife. They represented the segment of the socalled majority wing of the old Russian Social Democratic Party which had been driven into exile after the revolutionary failure in 1905. These "Bolsheviks" had split off from the "Mensheviks" in one of the numerous embittered splinterings that characterized the international socialist movement. Ulianov's articles were of a trenchant clarity; he was considered by the powers that were one of the most dangerous of revolutionaries. He signed his articles by the code name he used in the party's underground manoeuvring: Lenin.

From January on Lenin was in a fever to get back to Russia. When the Allies refused him a visa to some Scandinavian country, he accepted the offer a German agent made him to cross the Fatherland in what was for ever after described as "a sealed train." True to their doctrine of military frightfulness the German authorities wanted the social overturn in Russia to be as thorough as possible. As they would turn firebugs loose on their enemies' wheatfields, they turned a batch of revolutionists loose on the collapsing Romanoff empire. To make sure that there would be plenty of discord they sent in an opposition group under the Menshevik, Martov, a month later.

On April 3 (according to the old Russian calendar), a thickset trimbearded man with high cheekbones under large gray eyes, set far apart in a very large head, stepped from an incoming train at the Finland station in Petrograd. He was met by a crowd of delegates from the various revolutionary committees that filled every block of Peter the Great's old capital with wrangling voices. An incongruous bouquet of flowers was thrust into his arms and he was led into the gaudy salon which a short month before had served as waiting room for members of the imperial family.

He hardly listened to the speeches of welcome; his eyes were on the crowds he saw through the windows.

He replied in the formalized phraseology of socialist oratory. He greeted the Russian revolution as the beginning of the rise of the international proletariat against its exploiters and its butchers. He denied any Russian patriotism, or interest in any war except the class war, and he hailed "the world wide socialist revolution."

The raw air off the Neva tasted sweet in Lenin's nostrils as he looked about at the cheering soldiers and sailors and the students and factory workers and the convoy of armored cars they had brought to protect him. This was the moment he had been training for all his life. He would see to it that the "Marseillaise" would give place to the "Internationale." Immediately he set to work to seize power.

Nivelle's Plan

In France and England the year 1917 began in a spirit of optimism. Lloyd George, the proponent of the knockout blow, hurried from the winter meeting of Allied political leaders in Paris, to a meeting in Rome, and back to London again. Lloyd George was sanguine. At last the

French had found a commander with a plan for a breakthrough on the western front.

Robert Georges Nivelle, the hero of the recapture of the forts at Verdun, was a dapper man with slit eyes and a slender mustache. He was brought to Lloyd George's compartment to be introduced as his train crossed France. The British Prime Minister approved of the glib general at first sight. Nivelle was a Protestant and his mother was English. He hardly seemed a foreigner at all. He was fluent in both languages. "At last a general whose plan I can understand," said Lloyd George.

Nivelle's plan was to repeat the Verdun *coup de main* on an enormous scale against the German line along the Aisne. The British were to swing with their left at Arras and the French would follow with a right Sunday punch east of Soissons. In fortyeight hours the front would be breached. The first phase would be the pinching off of the Arras-Soissons salient. In four days the Huns would be rolled back on the Meuse. Invited to London, Nivelle described his plan to the British cabinet, then to "several persons of both sexes," as the British Chief of Staff put it, at lunch. Lloyd George was so captivated he promised Nivelle to put Haig under his orders.

Both the British Chief of Staff and Sir Douglas Haig were pained by this news to the verge of resignation. They were cajoled into following Nivelle's instructions for this one operation. In his diary Haig referred to one of Nivelle's communications as the type of letter which no gentleman could have drafted. Sullenly but loyally the British command went along.

Nivelle's plan had meanwhile become entangled in French party politics. It was discussed in the Chamber and in the newspapers. The German generals hardly needed to be further informed, when, on February 15, they captured a sergeant with a divisional order in his pocket which outlined a great part of it. On March 3 they captured Nivelle's entire memorandum, which, to be sure there would be no misunderstanding, was being distributed widely among French commanders at the front.

Ten days after the capture of the French plans Ludendorff began an orderly and carefully planned retirement from the salient in question to a much shorter line which the Germans named for their mighty Hindenburg.

The code name of the movement was Alberich after the malicious dwarf in the *Niebelungenlied*. As the German troops retired they tore up the railroads, wrecked every house, poisoned every well, exploded mines at every crossroad. Fruit trees were cut down, cattle destroyed. Wherever a house was left standing it contained some kind of a booby trap.

So preoccupied were the British and French commanders with Nivelle's plan that they allowed the German withdrawal to continue unhindered.

The British engineer corps was kept busy reopening roads through the area of unexampled destruction the Germans left behind them.

In spite of cautious protests from British generals, in spite of Briand's fall and the advent of the eightyyearold Ribot as head of the government in Paris, and in spite of the scepticism of Paul Painlevé, the new Minister of War, Nivelle managed to keep the politicians bemused. When it was pointed out that the German withdrawal had left no salient to pinch off, Nivelle shrugged and replied that the breakthrough would be that much easier.

It was a late spring. Cold rain alternated with sleet and snow. From day to day the offensive was postponed on account of bad weather, giving the Germans time to multiply the concrete pillboxes for Ludendorff's newly conceived defense in depth. In the ravines of the limestone plateau north of the Aisne they dug tunnels or enlarged natural caves for gun emplacements. There was never an army better prepared to meet an offensive.

On April 6, the day the United States declared war, the Germans captured the detailed orders for Nivelle's Fifth Army which was to lead off the attack. Preparations at French headquarters continued undisturbed. Nivelle was so hypnotized by the perfection of his plan he refused to change a single detail.

On April 9 the British began with their part of the show in front of Arras. After one of the greatest bombardments in history (eightyeight thousand tons of shells were thrown into the German positions) and a punishing gas attack, the British advanced with twelve divisions and sixty tanks. The Canadians captured Vimy Ridge, which had so long been fought for; but otherwise the British armies were stopped dead by the German pillboxes.

Haig, who had grudgingly allowed the tanks to see what they could do, brought up his beloved cavalry to exploit a breakthrough. Only a few squadrons saw combat. Haig's attacks were continued, long after there were worthwhile gains to be made, as interference for Nivelle. The British lost eightyfour thousand men against a German loss of seventyfive thousand.

April 16, on a day of sleet and rainsqualls, Nivelle's offensive took off. Continual delays had given the Germans time to bring in eighteen fresh divisions from the eastern front. The French air reconnaissance was poor. By some incredible miscalculation hundreds of Nivelle's pilots were still at Le Bourget waiting to be issued new planes. French tanks floundered in the mud.

The attack was a disaster from the first. The Senegalese troops, of which much had been hoped, shivered and ran. The French divisions fought with their usual bravery. The first day they gained six hundred yards. Nivelle had predicted six miles. Instead of a breakthrough the operation settled down into a step by step slugging match. By the first of May the French after a loss of a hundred and eighteen thousand men had a foothold on the high ground of the Chemin des Dames.

By this time Painlevé had screwed up his courage to the point of demanding Nivelle's resignation. Nivelle demurred. Old Ribot kept driving up and down behind the front in a tizzy, asking all the generals British and French what they thought of Pétain for a successor. At the French G.H.Q. at Beauvais such a yelling match took place between Nivelle and his subordinates, Gouraud and Micheler, all heroes of Verdun, that their recriminations were heard by the orderlies outside. It wasn't till May 15 that Nivelle could be removed from his command.

Nivelle's failure shattered the morale of the French armies. The Russian revolution was filling the newspapers with fine phrases about the rights of man. Socialists and syndicalists began to remember the old watchwords of the first of May, forgotten in the patriotic frenzy of the war's beginning. All at once the French *poilu* had enough of letting himself be marched into German machinegun fire *pour la patrie*. Infantry regiments refused to attack. Red flags appeared. Military police ordered to suppress the mutinies were savagely slaughtered. In one camp behind the lines they hung gendarmes on the meathooks in the abattoir.

Companies deserted en masse. Even crack fighting units elected councils and drew up lists of demands. Woodrow Wilson's call for a negotiated peace, echoed by the Petrograd Soviet and by socialists in neutral countries, was reiterated in the demands of the French troops. Besides that they begged for regular periods of leave, better living conditions and rational planning by the G.H.Q.

President Wilson dreamed of appealing to the people over the heads of their governments. The people had heard.

By the end of May fiftyfour divisions, something like threequarters of a million French soldiers, were involved in the mutinies. The censorship, which had not been able to keep secret the plans for Nivelle's offensive, was successful in keeping knowledge of the mutinies from the Germans and from their Allies and from the French themselves. To those in the know the French Army seemed finished as a fighting force. With a heavy heart, Haig, who hadn't any confidence in foreigners anyway, took upon his troops the punishing job of keeping the Germans busy for the rest of the summer.

Henri Pétain, who succeeded Nivelle, had also made his reputation at Verdun. He was known to have been opposed to the Aisne offensive from the first. A chilly aloof sort of man, an ardent Catholic, he belonged to the traditionalist antidemocratic sector of the officer corps, but he was enough of a soldier to understand the needs of the fighting man.

Some had to be shot, as Napoleon put it, *pour encourager les autres,* but courtsmartial were instructed to hear both sides of the story. While the courtsmartial were in progress two hundred and fifty of the mutineers considered most dangerous were sent to a quiet sector and annihilated by their own artillery. Units particularly noisy in singing the "Internationalc" were placed in exposed posts where the German machineguns disposed of them. A hundred alleged ringleaders were banished to the colonies. Only twentythree mutineers were condemned to death, and led out publicly before firing squads, with the drumrolls and the panoply of military justice.

Pétain spent the summer months driving from division to division, talking to officers and men, making promises, which he promptly carried out, of better conditions, more frequent leave. There would be no more random butcheries. The Americans were coming. Tanks were the instruments of victory. He reassured everybody: "We must wait for the Americans and the tanks."

When Greek Meets Greek

News of the coming declaration of war found Theodore Roosevelt fishing for "devilfish" in the Gulf of Mexico, in the company of a congenial Virginia tobacco trader named Russell Coles, whose hobby was sharks and rays. Coles had a houseboat anchored among the keys that fringe Charlotte Harbor as a base for fishingtrips after shark and manta. The giant rays occasionally seen off the Florida coast were known as mantas to the watermen, but T.R. found it more exciting to astonish the reporters by calling the ugly monsters "devilfish." Boarding the launch that was to take him out to the fishing grounds from Punta Gorda he delivered himself of a tirade against pacifists.

The outing was a success. T.R. managed to thrust his harpoon a full two feet through the hard cartilage of one monster's slippery back. The barbed iron held. After the launch had been towed a half a mile the four "twohanded" men of Cole's crew hauled the thrashing batlike creature in to the point where it could be dispatched, amid great splashing and lunging and outpouring of greasy blood into the brine, by hacking and poking with a sharp steel lance specially designed for the purpose. When thoroughly dead the giant ray was found to measure sixteen feet eight inches from fin to fin. "Good sport but not the sort of thing to recommend to a weakling," T.R. told his newspaper cronies.

After a few days of such relaxations, the politician in T.R. mastered the fisherman, and he decided it was time to head back into the theatre of action.

On the train that carried him north he had two pieces of news to ponder. Woodrow Wilson was asking Congress for a declaration of war against Germany. That was all to the good.

The second piece of news boded ill for T.R.'s fondest hopes. Wilson's Secretary of War was depriving his dear friend Leonard Wood of command of the Eastern Department where he'd done yeoman's work organizing the Plattsburg camps, and getting the units under his command as ready for war as he could with the skimpy equipment at his disposal. He'd gone so far as to set some companies drilling with broomsticks when the War Department could not furnish rifles for them.

Wood, although publicly muzzled, had been second only to T.R. in private denunciations of the "peace at any price" policies of the President. Now the Administration was striking back by dividing General Wood's command into three and suggesting that Manila, notorious as the repository for superfluous officers, might be a suitable field for his talents. Wood, as the ranking major general in the army, insisted on being given command of the new South-Eastern Department, with headquarters at Charleston, South Carolina, where he could at least go on training troops.

The meaning of this move was obvious. Wood was not to be considered for the command of an expeditionary force in Europe.

This shelving of the most popular military leader in the country threatened the scheme to raise a volunteer division, to which T.R. had been devoting his energies ever since the German announcement of unrestricted submarine warfare. Men from all walks of life including crowds of retired army officers had answered his call. One division wouldn't hold them all. Now he was planning four.

The old dream of military glory had become an obsession. San Juan Hill wasn't enough. Although not quite fiftynine T.R. had to admit that the fevers he contracted in the Amazon Basin and the bullet near his lung had damaged his old robust health. If he wasn't well enough for field service he could at least infect others with his enthusiasm. He couldn't help seeing himself, in spite of everything, leading one last charge, as a fitting climax to the strenuous life, and ending in a burst of glory with the flag planted on one last shelltorn hill.

On the train north T.R. determined on a personal interview with the President. He stopped off in Washington and called unannounced at the White House. The President was in a cabinet meeting. T.R. chatted for a while with his old friend the chief usher and then, before catching his New York train, drove up to the Hill to drop in on Henry Cabot Lodge.

The occasion of the call was to congratulate the other "scholar in politics" upon a successful bout of fisticuffs which the newspapers had reported as taking place in a Senate corridor, with a young pacifist who, in the course of an altercation about war policies, called the Massachusetts senator a coward. Lodge, though a far older man than T.R., hauled off and knocked the pacifist down. New England cheered. The pro-Allied press blew up the incident to heroic size.

Lodge himself was keeping mum about the affair. He did mutter something to a friend about how after a lifetime of public service "the public suddenly discovers I'm a great man when I commit a breach of the peace."

"The dear old Brahmin," T.R. exclaimed to one of his "newspaper cabinet," "that's just like him. The scholar in politics simply couldn't bring himself to say he had indulged in a fist fight."

The President and his advisers put their heads together as to what should be done about T.R. After exhaustive consultations with Baker and the Chiefs of Staff, Wilson had already decided to pass over Wood, and appoint John J. Pershing as commander of any American expedition that needed to be sent to Europe. Though Pershing stood in a poor light in the public press as a result of the failure of his efforts to catch Villa, it was well understood in the War Department that he had risked his military reputation through punctilious obedience to orders from Washington. To Wilson, Pershing looked like his man.

So long as Wood remained in the army he was subject to discipline, but T.R. was not only an ex-President and the most popular leader of the war party, but a possibility for the Republican nomination in 1920. He must be shelved, but gently. Wilson had to think of the support he needed in Congress to get his war measures through, particularly conscription, sure to be unpopular in many quarters. An interview was arranged.

A few days later T.R. reappeared in Washington. He put up at his daughter Alice Longworth's house. As wife of a prominent member of Congress, and as a woman of sharp wit and spirit, her home constituted a last redoubt of the old Washington society of the days of John Hay and Henry Adams. Immediately the Longworth house became the center of political conjecture.

On April 10 at twelve o'clock Theodore Roosevelt appeared at the front door of the White House. He was in his usual gusty spirits. Tumulty met him in the Blue Room. He slapped Tumulty on the back and congratulated him on being the father of six. He was immediately ushered into the President's office. Woodrow Wilson and Theodore Roosevelt talked alone for fortyfive minutes. As he left T.R. was heard kidding Tumulty about having a staff job for him at his divisional headquarters in France, though it wouldn't be a dangerous job; he could assure Mrs. Tumulty and the six children of that. Tumulty jokingly answered he had half a mind to accept.

On the White House steps T.R. found thirty waiting reporters surrounded by a crowd of some three hundred people. He flashed his teeth and his glasses and puffed out his chest for the photographers. He declared the interview was bully. The President was most courteous and attentive.

T.R. had assured Woodrow Wilson that the past was buried and that in this emergency he was giving him his complete support. He plead to be allowed to raise his division. He tried to be disarmingly jocose. If the President would let him go he'd promise not to come back. In any case, he declared he was in favor of the administration conscription bill, and would go right to work to see it was put through Congress.

He stopped himself, and turned to Tumulty, who was listening attentively to every word. "If I say anything I shouldn't be sure and censor it," he said waving his arms. Then addressing the reporters he added, "I'm already under orders."

"I congratulated him upon his war message," he continued later, in an off the record chat, "and told him it would rank with the world's great state papers . . . if it were made good . . . And I told him I wanted a chance to help make it good . . . If Tumulty came along," he let his voice drop in a hoarse aside, "it might be as a sort of watchdog to keep Wilson informed. I'll have a place for him but it won't be the place he thinks."

"If any other man than he talked to me as he did I would feel assured," he told the friends gathered to meet him at his daughter's house, "but I was talking to Mr. Wilson . . . He has however left the door open." Interested parties lost no time in reporting these remarks to the White House.

That afternoon and all next day T.R. kept open house at the Longworths'. Newton D. Baker was the first to call. He listened politely to everything T.R. had to say. "I had a good time with Baker," T.R. told his newspaper friends. "I could twist him around my finger if I could have him about for a while . . . He will do exactly what Wilson tells him to do, he will think exactly as Wilson wants him to think . . . He has the blindest faith in the General Staff and the graduates of West Point. He doesn't realize that a muttonhead, after an education at West Point, or Harvard, is a muttonhead still."

It was like the old days. The ambassadors called, with Jusserand and his dear Spring Rice, old members of the "tennis cabinet," in the lead; and Senator Lodge; and people from the Council of National Defense; and congressmen from the military affairs committees of the Senate and House. He lectured them all on the need for conscription and for four divisions of volunteers for immediate action, to be raised by himself and trained and led by General Wood.

Roosevelt's Lost Division

When Congress passed the conscription act T.R.'s four divisions of volunteers were, in spite of vigorous pressure from the White House, incorporated in it. The provision was added that these divisions should be activated at the President's discretion. Wilson lost no time in announcing that this was a war for professionals and not for amateurs.

General Wood, who had been acclaimed as a hero throughout the South as he travelled about inspecting campsites, couldn't help confiding to his friends that the War Department was playing politics with him. T.R. stormed at Sagamore Hill, but issued a statement that he was bowing to superior authority, and releasing the men who had volunteered to serve under him.

Pershing, as soon as he was notified that he was chosen to lead the first troops to France, intimated privately to the Secretary of War that neither Wood nor Roosevelt would be acceptable to him overseas. Troublemakers. Physically unfit. Baker's underlings in the War Department began spreading tales about how T.R.'s bronchitis would never support the French climate and how Leonard Wood had a hole in his head.

Tumulty, who feared a voters' revulsion against the shelving of the two most popular military figures, argued long and valiantly on the other side. He begged his boss to let some sort of ornamental posts at least be found for them.

Joffre, when he arrived on his mission to Washington, gave out that he wanted volunteers at once. Pétain, from France, begged for volunteers. Clemenceau wrote specially to the President pointing out the morale value of a Roosevelt mission. Bryce added his plea.

Wilson had made up his mind. Once he had made up his mind there was no altering him.

"The real truth," wrote T.R. to an Arizona friend, in the bitterness of his disappointment, "is that Wilson is bent on making this merely a war to advance his own personal fortunes from a political standpoint. He has always been more interested in preventing Wood and myself from being of service to the nation than he has of rendering himself such service."

A great many people from both parties agreed with T.R. One of the more prominent Roosevelt volunteers, John M. Parker, a New Orleans cotton factor and a progressive Democrat who had performed as a mighty man of valor during Wilson's campaigns in the South, made it his business to tell the President so.

"Mr. President," said Parker, who pulled too much political weight to be denied an interview, "you preach against autocracy and today in the civilized world there is no greater autocrat than Woodrow Wilson."

Wilson's treatment of General Wood and Colonel Roosevelt was destroying confidence in his conduct of the war, Parker went on. "You should realize that you are simply an American citizen, exalted for the time being by the votes of your people to the President's chair. As a man who gladly gave his own time and money touring the country to support you,

I feel I have the right to criticize, because you are my hired man, just as you are the hired man of the people . . . remember it is their money, their sons who are making this fight . . . I beg you not to play politics."

According to Tumulty the President kept his temper:

"Sir," he replied, "I am not playing politics. Nothing could be more advantageous to me than to follow the course you suggest."

He pointed out that the British had used Kitchener, their most famous general, for training troops. "General Wood is needed here. Colonel Roosevelt is an admirable man and a patriotic citizen but he is not a military leader."

After fifteen stormy minutes Parker took his hat and went back to the Shoreham Hotel to write down every word that had been said. Meanwhile Roosevelt, smouldering with frustration at Sagamore Hill, was including in almost every letter of his enormous correspondence a phrase that tickled him: "Fighting this war under Wilson is like fighting the Civil War under Buchanan."

Selective Service

Congress passed the conscription bill on May 18. The next day President Wilson issued a proclamation based on a draft Newton D. Baker had sent over from the War Department early in the month.

The proclamation quoted section five of the act which the President's signature had just made law: "That all male persons between the ages of 21 and 30 inclusive shall be subject to registration in accordance with regulations established by the President: And upon proclamation by the President and other public notice given by him or by his direction stating the time and place of such registration it shall be the duty of all persons of the designated ages, except officers and enlisted men of the army, the navy and the National Guard and Naval Militia while in the service of the United States, to present themselves for and submit to registration under the provisions of this act."

Failure to register was a misdemeanor punishable by a year in jail followed by compulsory registration.

Woodrow Wilson went on to develop some characteristic variations upon the theme of "selective service," the euphemism for conscription which had been hit upon as being most palatable to the American public:

"The whole nation must be a team in which each man must play the part for which he is best fitted . . . To this end Congress has provided that the nation shall be organized for war by selection: that each man shall be classified for service in the place to which it shall best serve the general good to call him."

He was preparing the public for the exemption of farmers and railroadmen and seamen and essential workers in war industries.

"The day here named is the day upon which all shall present themselves for assignment to their tasks. It is for that reason destined to be remembered as one of the most conspicuous moments in our history."

This was the historian Wilson speaking. He clearly understood that the Selective Service law, supplemented by the espionage bill Congress had in the works, would give him more power than any President had enjoyed before him.

The lag in recruiting during the past year of war prosperity and high wages had combined with what they read of the failure of recruiting in Britain to convince Wilson and his War Department that the only way an army large enough to make its weight felt in the present war could be raised was by some sort of compulsory military service. A large body of moderate Republican opinion led by William Howard Taft, whose pulpit was the League to Enforce Peace, had for some time been calling for universal military training on the Swiss model. Long before the declaration of war, the Judge Advocate General, a skinny little Missourian named Enoch Herbert Crowder, had been at work on a conscription bill.

Conscription was a bitter dose for Wilson's Democrats to swallow. A draft army had long been as anathema as alcohol to Bryan and his supporters. Champ Clark, the Speaker of the House, declared as the debate opened that in his opinion a conscript was the next thing to a convict.

While, with the help of the Republicans, Crowder's bill was being rammed down the throats of reluctant congressmen, the Judge Advocate General's office was in a fever of activity. The most original feature of the bill, by which registration and selection for the draft would be in the hands of the same civilian boards that handled registration for voting, was largely the contribution of Crowder's assistant, Major Johnson, an irrepressible young cavalry officer who, like his boss, had studied law in leisure moments of his military career. Hugh Johnson was making it his business quietly to alert the state governors, and the sheriffs of about ten thousand counties, as to what would be expected of them when the moment came. He found them almost universally cooperative. At the same time he attended to the printing, in secret and before the money to pay for them had been appropriated, of some ten million registration cards at the government printing office.

Secretary Baker had convinced the President that, so that there should be no opportunity for opposition to organize, as little time as possible should be allowed to elapse between the passage of the law and registration day. They both spent sleepless nights remembering the bloody riots against Lincoln's draft in the Civil War. They dreaded the reaction of the large enemy alien population enrolled in German *vereins* and foreign language societies. The Irish were unpredictable. The Socialists, though their votes had diminished in the last election and their leadership was split on the war issue, were still to be reckoned with. Trouble was expected from women's peace leagues and from the pacifist fringe of the labor movement, from the I.W.W. and from foreignborn anarchists stirred to frenzy against capitalist war by such agitators as Emma Goldman.

The Judge Advocate General's office worked fast. Before the ink was dry on the President's proclamation the machinery for registration was well on the way to completion. Crowder was appointed Provost Marshal General to administer it.

The Power to Curb

At the same time the Department of Justice, without waiting for the additional powers to curb free speech which administration lawyers were incorporating in the espionage bill Congress was hotly debating, mobilized a force of special agents to nip anticonscription agitation in the bud. Attorney General Gregory made the announcement from Washington that, "Any spoken or written word, uttered or written for the purpose of interfering with the purpose of the Selective Service Act, will result in prompt arrest of the person or persons responsible."

In New York two Columbia students and a Barnard girl were taken into custody for getting up a protest against conscription. In Columbus, Ohio, some more students and a printer were arrested for preparing an antiwar poster and charged with treason. A Socialist meeting was raided in Topeka, Kansas. In Kansas City the three Browder brothers were arrested, along with several other persons, for declaring in public that they would refuse to register. In Wichita Falls, Texas, the members of a Socialist group, calling themselves the Farmers and Laborers Protective Union, were hauled off to jail. Eight prospective draftdodgers were picked up in Cedar Rapids, Iowa, and several in small towns in Wisconsin.

In New York the police overawed the disloyal and the foreignborn, and the youthful radicals who packed to overflowing mass meetings held by an Anti-Conscription League in Madison Square Garden, and at Hunts Point Casino in the Bronx. The President found it necessary to issue a fresh proclamation warning draftdodgers who were trying to leave the country, and agitators against registration, that they would run afoul of the Selective Service Act.

Enthusiastic citizens began to take the law into their own hands. Soldiers and sailors attended pacifist meetings to howl down the orators. Many a man lost his job because he spoke English with an accent. In Racine, Wisconsin, the employees of a tin plant made a machinist, heard to mutter against conscription, crawl across the floor on his knees to kiss an American flag. In Omaha a young man suspected of being a socialist was chased by a mob, and only escaped by outrunning them.

On Capitol Hill a battle raged over censorship of the press. Wilson was insisting that a clause be inserted in the espionage bill giving him power to censor the newspapers. This was too much even for his most faithful adherents among the nation's journalists. Letters and telegrams against censorship piled up on Tumulty's desk. He was reminded of the bad odor the Alien and Sedition Laws had left in the history books. Even the warmongering New York *Times* published editorials against censorship. Tumulty, who as usual had his ear among the grass roots, formulated his opinion in writing. "I know how strongly you feel on the matter of a strict censorship, but I would not be doing my full duty to you . . . if I did not say . . . that there is gradually growing a feeling of bitter resentment against the whole business."

When the House voted censorship down Wilson, hoping it might be restored to the bill in the Senate, invited some of his most energetic opponents among the Republican old guard to the White House. Henry Cabot Lodge, after spending two hours talking to the President, along with Senator Gallinger and Senator Knox, made an entry in his diary: "The President has at last discovered that without the Republicans he would not and could not get his legislation . . . He was most polite and talked well, as he always does so far as expression goes. We discussed revenue, food control and censorship chiefly. The two latter were his objects." . . . Lodge added selfrighteously: "We told him perfectly pleasantly some truths which he ought to have heard from those who surround him."

In spite of the agreeable way the President conducted the interview, Lodge still hated the man. "I watched and studied his face tonight as I have often done before—a curious mixture of acuteness, intelligence, and extreme underlying timidity—a shifty, furtive, sinister expression can always be detected by a good observer . . . The man is just what he has been all along, thinking of the country only in terms of Wilson."

In the end the President had to content himself with an Espionage Act shorn of specific powers of press censorship. As it turned out the powers conferred on the presidency by the mass of wartime legislation were so extensive that censorship was hardly needed. So long as the war lasted most of the news that appeared in the newspapers was piped to them through the administration's Bureau of Public Information.

Section three of the Espionage Act contained a clause which could be interpreted by the courts to prove an effective curb on free speech in wartime: ". . . and whosoever, when the United States is at war, shall willfully cause or attempt to cause insubordination, disloyalty, mutiny or refusal of duty in the military or naval forces of the United States, or shall willfully obstruct the recruiting of enlistment service of the United States, to the injury of the service of the United States, shall be punished with a fine of not more than $10,000 or imprisonment for not more than twenty years, or both."

Once Lead This People into War

Registration Day passed off quietly. Throughout the nation men lined up at precinct polling places with no more concern than if they were voting in an election. The Census Bureau had estimated that there were something more than ten million men of draft age in the country. When all returns were in it turned out that more than nine million six hundred thousand had registered. The slackers, announced the Department of Justice, would be rounded up in due course.

The administration press hailed the turnout as a plebiscite in favor of the Wilsonian policies. The Republican papers joined in the flagwaving.

The editions that came out on the morning of June 6 had few exceptions to note to the general calm. In Butte, Montana, a small riot was caused by the parade of an Irish society. A radical Finn made a speech which nobody could understand. The mayor, addressing the troublemakers from the roof of a house, induced the crowds to disperse before shooting began. A report from Flagstaff, Arizona, alleged that the Navahos had chased the officer who appeared to register them off their reservation. In New Mexico the governor of the Santo Domingo pueblo was arrested for refusing to produce a list of his people's names. In Ignacio, Colorado, the Utes took to the hills at the first rumor of a draft and were reported to have furnished themselves with liquor and to be performing war dances and bear dances. At Phoenix three hundred Russian Doukhobor settlers politely but firmly explained to the sheriff that their religion would never allow them to register for war.

With these few exceptions the young men of America stood up to be counted. With registration the war spirit spread. "Once lead this people into war and they'll forget there ever was such a thing as tolerance," Woodrow Wilson had told Frank Cobb. His words proved prophetic.

The Secret Government

From being one of the drowsiest of capitals, Washington, as the summer of 1917 advanced, took on an air of bustle. Fresh faces daily filled the great waiting room of the newly constructed Union Station. As the government departments proved incapable of coping with enormous wartime demands new agencies had to be created. Each new agency imported clerical workers. The government kept taking over apartment houses for offices without providing living accommodations for the people who were going to work in them. A housing shortage developed. Hotel rooms were all taken. Industrialists come to help had to live in their private cars lined up in the railroad yards. Every boarding house was full. Editorials in the newspapers implored respectable residents to do their bit by renting spare rooms to young women secretaries.

TEN THOUSAND NEW CLERICAL WORKERS EXPECTED THIS SUMMER, ran a headline in the *Evening Star*. According to the Census Bureau the population of the District increased by forty thousand in a year.

The dilatory habits of the federal government died hard. The War Department proved especially incapable of coping with its problems. Civilians had to be called in. Pushing business executives invaded leisurely bureaus where, in high old rooms shuttered against the heat, ailing colonels, often relics of the Indian wars, had for years shuffled yellowed foolscap under slowmoving ceiling fans, with the secretarial assistance provided, as often as not, by needy gentlewomen of Confederate families, who spoke of themselves with some pride as being "in office," and were loath to be hurried; and offices closed for the day at four in the afternoon. One man, on loan from a busy New York corporation, called in to explain to the Chief of Staff how some problem of procurement could be solved, after having worked his whole office force through several nights to get up the facts and figures, went back to his associates appalled: the elderly general, halfway through the explanation, fell asleep in his chair.

One of the chief wonders of the European war, as seen by American men of affairs, was the effectiveness of German industrial mobilization. For years advocates of preparedness had been calling for the creation of some sort of skeleton agency which might, if the need came, establish contact between the War Department and the industries capable of producing war materials. The navy already had a civilian consulting board, figureheaded by Thomas A. Edison and engaged in a survey of all possible sources of munitions.

So strong was the feeling against military measures of any kind in the Wilson administration and on Capitol Hill that the first moves to create a Council of National Defense had to be almost surreptitious.

Dr. Hollis Godfrey, a Massachusetts engineer and writer of books for boys, who was president of the Drexel Institute in Philadelphia, had been propounding a plan for industrial mobilization under such a council ever since, on a trip to England in 1906, he found Campbell-Bannerman and young Winston Churchill in the throes of organizing a war council for the empire.

With the worsening of relations with Germany, Dr. Godfrey's plan began to assume more than hypothetical importance. He went to work with fresh zest and managed to interest Secretary of War Garrison, who was wearing himself out trying to move the Wilson administration towards preparedness. The chairmen of the Senate and House committees on military affairs approved the project and Elihu Root, who as McKinley's Secretary of War tried to centralize the administration of the army under a General Staff, drafted a bill. Secretary Baker took time off from the confusions and frustrations of the campaign against Villa to revise the plan and gave it his endorsement. General Wood and T.R. were loud in its favor.

Bringing the projected Council of National Defense to the attention of the President was a ticklish matter. Anything endorsed by Leonard Wood smelt of Wilson's tormentors in the Republican press. It was deemed advisable that Dr. Godfrey should call on Colonel House at his New York apartment. House approved the plan, revised it again, and, when he judged the time was ripe, presented it to the President. He used such discretion that Woodrow Wilson is reported to have exclaimed, "This is extraordinary, this composite work . . . It is exactly the putting of this theory of education into government. I am heartily for it."

The Council of National Defense had to be handled even more gingerly by its sponsors in Congress, for fear of touching off pacifist oratory. A clause was quietly inserted in the National Defense Act giving the President powers towards the mobilization of industry and transportation in case of war. The same act assuaged the suspicions of the antimilitarists by throwing a spoke into the wheels of central military planning. The General Staff was reduced in numbers and more than half its members were forbidden to be stationed in Washington at any one time.

The subsequent Military Appropriations Act set up a Council of National Defense to consist of the Secretaries of War, Navy, the Interior, Agriculture, Commerce and Labor. Provision was made for unpaid advisory commissions of businessmen, manufacturers and technicians. A small appropriation was made for hiring a permanent staff.

McAdoo, who had a good deal to do with the scheme at this point, kept the Treasury off, claiming with some justice that he already had more work than he could handle. It was McAdoo who suggested the appointment of Walter S. Gifford, an inconspicuous young Harvard man from Salem, Massachusetts, who had risen by quiet brains to the post of chief statistician of the American Telephone and Telegraph Company by the time he was thirty, as director, and of Grosvenor B. Clarkson as secretary. The setting up of this novel federal agency met with little comment in Congress or in the press.

The President described the council as maintaining "subordinate bodies of specially qualified persons . . . capable of organizing to the utmost the resources of the country." He added that these commissions would be nonpartisan. Secretary Baker, who contributed his mouselike presence to the first meetings as permanent chairman, seems to have seen to it that they remained so.

When Clarkson, who was a Republican, wrote up his history of the vast organizations that developed out of these vague beginnings, he went out of his way to state with some solemnity that he was unable to "recall a single instance in which Mr. Baker or the council requested him to make an appointment or take an administrative action on a personal or partisan basis . . . a demonstration of nonpartisanship in a crisis that the writer would not have deemed possible before going to Washington . . . The credit," he added, "is no less due to Mr. Baker by reason of the fact that this attitude reflected the policy of the President . . . politics simply did not enter into the makeup of the American war machine."

The Council of National Defense, in itself formal and inert, proved, under the continually increasing demands of the war machine, to be the fertile parent of a series of commissions that, acting by rule of thumb, without theory or legal basis, organized American industry, as the President put it "to the utmost," for the war effort.

First came the Advisory Commission. On December 7, 1916, a group of somewhat bewildered tycoons was brought together in a Washington hotel room. In their derby hats and overcoats, they were photographed with the appropriate cabinet officers on the steps of the War Department. Besides Dr. Godfrey who fathered the scheme, there was Daniel Willard of the Baltimore and Ohio Railroad; Howard E. Coffin of the Hudson Motor Company, a champion of preparedness so energetic that his colleagues described him as giving the impression of a gale of wind when he came into the room; shy Julius Rosenwald of Sears, Roebuck and Co., who as much as Henry Ford was an energumen of mass distribution; Dr. Franklin Martin of the American College of Surgeons; the canny old cigarmaker Samuel Gompers who had created the American Federation of Labor in his own image, and Bernard Baruch. When a reporter asked Baruch what his business was he answered tersely: "Speculator."

When the journalists began to catch on to the scope of the activities of the chairmen of the various commissions spawned by the Council of National Defense they tagged the commissioners "dollar a year men," taking a hint from the President's words: "They serve the government without remuneration, efficiency being their sole object and Americanism their only motive."

The War Department's separate procurement agencies, following time-honored procedures in the name of the Signal Corps, or the Engineers, or the Medical Corps, were proving incapable of serving even the needs of the force of around a hundred and thirty thousand men that existed before the passage of the National Defense Act. The Quartermaster Corps had a staff of about sixty. Many of their methods dated from the Civil War.

With the taking over of the National Guard, and the prospect of a greater army to come, agencies had to be improvised if the troops were to have shoes and uniforms and guns. The Advisory Commission kept bringing fresh groups of businessmen to Washington to create them.

As a disgruntled Republican congressman, George Scott Graham of Pennsylvania, investigating in 1919 what he called "the secret government of the United States" reported after reading the records of the Advisory Commission: "An examination of these minutes discloses the fact that a commission of seven men chosen by the President seem to have devised the entire system of purchasing war supplies, planned a press censorship, designed a system of food control and selected Herbert Hoover as its director, determined on a daylight saving scheme, and in a word, designed practically every war measure which Congress subsequently enacted; and did all this behind closed doors, weeks and even months before the Congress of the United States declared war on Germany."

Grosvenor Clarkson considered these words such a handsome tribute to his organization that he quoted them in his *Industrial America in the World War.*

The Dollar a Year Men

"Reference and deference are the curse of bureaucracy" wrote this same Mr. Clarkson when he became their historian after acting as secretary of both the formal Council, which functioned merely to endorse with the majesty of the presidential mandate the acts of the subsidiary commissions, and of the allimportant Advisory Commission. The administrators who crowded into Washington hotels and hall bedrooms to man the subcommissions that kept separating off from the parent body had one thing in common: a fear and hatred of bureaucratic methods.

They were raised in the school of getting things done. Their system was to find a man who could do a job and let him do it no matter how and no questions asked. "My notion of organization," Herbert Hoover told the President, when he was called to Washington from his Belgian Relief to head the Food Administration which grew out of one of the projects of the Advisory Commission, "is to size up the problem, then send for the best man or woman in the country who has the 'know how,' give him a room, table, chair, pencil, paper and wastebasket—and the injunction to get other people to help, and then solve it."

All through the frustrating summer of 1917 executives who had come to Washington at real personal sacrifice sweated long hours in airless offices laying, amid confusion and heartbreak, the groundwork for the efficient procedures of the following year. Already in the Advisory Commission they were talking of an army of a million men.

The first efforts had to go towards changing the methods of procurement already established. The army, navy and the allied purchasing commissions must be kept from bidding against each other for scarce supplies. Every method from patriotic appeal to brute force had to be used to curb the catastrophic rise in prices. A system of priorities had to be invented, and a clearing house established, where the needs of the various services and of the Allies could be appraised. Communications had to be kept open between Washington and the local committees of the various industries and chambers of commerce. The railroads had to be induced to drop competitive systems favored by the Sherman Act. Ships, wooden ships, steel ships, concrete ships—anything that would float—had to be built on a scale and at a speed never before imagined.

It was inevitable that duplications and conflicts should arise. Each commission tended to struggle with its own problems without reference to the work of its neighbors. "We used the words coordination and cooperation until they were worn out" wrote Herbert Hoover of this period. "We surrounded ourselves with coordinators and spent hours in endless discussions with no court of appeal for final decisions."

The President had become almost unapproachable in the White House. Tumulty could always be reached, but he never pretended to understand industrial problems; politics was his field. Even the faithful secretary's private opinions had to be transmitted by letter. All he could do was lay documents on the President's desk.

The Secretary of War was engrossed with the complications of the expanding army. McAdoo at the Treasury took a broad view of the needs of the war machine, but, although still Mac, and a member of the family at White House meals, he was not listened to as carefully as in the past: Edith Wilson suspected him of having been opposed to her marrying the President.

There remained the roundabout method of approach through the good offices of the confidential colonel in his New York apartment, but House's visiting hours were limited; and sometimes even he had to wait for days for the privilege of visiting the President in his study.

It was inevitable that out of the welter of jostling commissions, striving to bring order out of the chaos of production and supply, certain agencies should assume primacy over the rest. Bernard Baruch of the Advisory Commission's subcommission on raw materials developed extraordinary talents as coordinator of coordinators. Before long the commission he headed became the War Industries Board and central in the organization of supply.

Bernard M. Baruch had no administrative training whatsoever. At fortyseven he had accumulated a fortune which Wall Street estimated in the tens of millions as a lone speculator on the stock exchange. Although flatterers called him a financier, he showed neither pride nor shame in his career as speculator.

Un Prince d'Israel

Baruch was the son of a German Jewish doctor who had emigrated to America as a very young man and served as a surgeon in the Confederate Army. His mother, known in the family as Miss Belle, came of a prominent Sephardic family long established in the South. He was born and spent the first ten years of his life in Camden, South Carolina, where his father, a wellread man of varied interests, practiced medicine and carried on agricultural experiments that were more prophetic than profitable. Miss Belle gave music lessons.

When Bernard was eleven, Dr. Baruch, who wasn't making much of a go of it in Camden, moved his family to New York. Bernard went through the public schools and the City College. He grew up a tall slender active youth. A blow from a bat in a ballgame that ended in a scrimmage left him permanently deaf in one ear. Although his parents wanted him to be a professional man he couldn't decide what career to take up.

About the time he graduated his father became resident physician at a summer hotel on the Jersey coast. Bernard, who had already shown more interest in poker than in his studies, became a habitué of the Monmouth track. He had a good memory and an analytic mind. He devoted himself to gambling with singlehearted devotion. An adventurous spirit carried him out to Cripple Creek. There he did surprisingly well playing poker, but when he invested his winnings in mining stock, he lost every cent. He came home broke and took a job as a customers' man in a brokerage house at twentyfive dollars a week.

Twentyfive dollars a week was considered good pay for a young man in the nineties. Baruch had presence. His ebullient charm was mingled with a certain unassuming personal dignity. He never lost his pleasant South Carolina manners. *Un prince d'Israel*, Clemenceau was to call him.

With his savings out of his paycheck he began to speculate in earnest. His retentive memory and his knack for analyzing every factor of a business situation stood him in good stead. He paid no attention to Wall Street gossip but made it his business to know what was behind every stock he traded in.

At twentyseven he married, and bought himself a seat on the New York Stock Exchange.

His associates and customers were in the higher brackets. He traded in tobacco with Thomas Fortune Ryan. At the outbreak of the Spanish War, he got to a cable before any of the other brokers, and made a killing in the London Stock Exchange. His specialty was playing the bull market. At thirtyfour he was a millionaire and already somewhat disgusted with moneymaking. He had friends in every walk of life. Garet Garrett kept telling him he ought to turn his great abilities to the public service.

From the days when he was a small boy in Camden he'd loved to shoot quail. He bought himself one of the great South Carolina plantations, known as Hobcaw Barony, near Georgetown. There he entertained lavishly. He indulged his taste for racehorses.

A congenital Democrat, and known to be openhanded with his money, he was much sought after by the politicians. Democratic chairman Mc-Combs introduced him to Governor Wilson at a fundraising dinner in 1912.

Immediately Baruch became a devoted adherent of Woodrow Wilson's. The feeling was mutual. Wilson liked Baruch, he found him learned in matters pertaining to finance and industry on which he himself admitted ignorance. Here was a financier from wicked Wall Street who had no pride in his money bags, who liked to talk about human values, who listened with reverence to Wilson's plans for the country. He called Baruch "Dr. Facts."

In the dark days of the 1916 campaign Baruch was a solace. He brought his aging parents to Shadow Lawn to tea. He became a family friend. McAdoo esteemed him highly. Mrs. Wilson liked his humorously deferential manner. He shared with Grayson a passion for horseflesh. Though the recently appointed admiral was a notoriously bad shot, he was often invited to hunting parties at Hobcaw Barony.

When Baruch went to work with the Advisory Commission his colleagues marvelled at how little he exploited his "in" at the White House. Already he was being talked of as the man to head a general purchasing agency. The multimillionaires who dominated steel and iron and copper and tin listened to Baruch as one of themselves. At the same time he'd made his money in such a way that he had no ties with any particular industry. He'd taken advantage of them all, playing the rise and fall of Wall Street's tides. His knack for sizing up the potentialities of the various industries, which had made him a master speculator, prepared him for the worldwide trading operations of procurement for war. He had zest for the work, and the shrewdness needed to pick good subordinates and to back them up unreservedly so long as they did what he considered a good job. Being new at administration he had no bad habits of "reference and deference" to overcome.

Only to the President did he defer. With a boyish sort of heroworship he tried to anticipate Woodrow Wilson's every wish. Whenever he arranged a set of purchases or dug out a piece of information, he made Woodrow Wilson feel that he was doing it for him, personally.

Baruch had at that point no legal authority to corner raw materials. His operations depended on cajolement and the patriotic appeal. His associates worried themselves sick during the summer and fall of 1917, wondering why he didn't ask the President directly for the powers he needed to enforce his demands; why he allowed Secretary Baker, who distrusted him, to build a rival agency in the War Department under Stettinius of J. P. Morgan and Co. As Secretary Lane liked to say, Woodrow Wilson moved slowly as a glacier. Perhaps he was afraid of stirring up Democratic oratory in Congress by appointing a Wall Street man.

Finally, when McAdoo tried to enlist Baruch for a Treasury post, Wilson revealed his intentions: "I'm mighty sorry but I can't let you have Baruch for the Finance Corporation," he wrote his soninlaw. "He has trained now in the War Industries Board until he is thoroughly conversant with the activities of it from top to bottom, and as soon as I can do so without risking new issues on the Hill I am going to appoint him chairman of that board."

That strenuous summer of 1917 saw the beginning of the proliferation of federal agencies that grew into the leviathan of years to come. Since nobody in government had the ability to run them, they had to be run by businessmen who signed on for the duration.

Chapter 13

THE TURNING POINT

In April 1917 Allied prospects were if possible worse at sea than they were on land. The British Grand Fleet, to be sure, kept the Kaiser's navy in a coop back at Heligoland, but the U-boats fulfilled the German admirals' wildest hopes. At the most there were never more than a hundred and thirty largesize submarines in commission at any one time, besides the small coastal types that harried British commerce with the Scandinavian countries. They were based on the inland port of ancient Bruges in conquered Belgium, and slipped out into the North Sea through the shipcanals to Ostend and Zeebrugge.

The first onslaught of the U-boats was appalling. A fourth of the merchantmen leaving British ports that April never returned. In thirty days the Allies lost almost nine hundred thousand tons of cargo space.

To Keep the Sealanes Open

Optimistic British propaganda, filling the American newspapers with accounts of imaginary victories, so overreached its aims that nobody in authority in Washington knew the extent of the peril. President Wilson had a general inkling of the situation, but from another angle.

Like so many Americans, his knowledge of naval warfare stemmed from boyish enthusiasm for American successes in the War of 1812. He saw American merchantships fighting their way across the Atlantic in the name of the freedom of the seas. He was much preoccupied with the arming of merchantmen. Obviously the first prerequisite for keeping the sealanes open was close cooperation with the British Admiralty.

From what reports he could get the British Admiralty seemed opposed to the idea of conveying merchantships. Ambassador Page, who had cried wolf so long that there was a tendency at the State Department to write off his messages as wartime hysterics, sent a particularly urgent cable on the shipping situation. This time it was listened to.

"The main thing," the President was writing Josephus Daniels as early as March 24, "is no doubt to get into immediate communication with the Admiralty."

The wordy North Carolinian, whom some naval officers claimed was more interested in saving his sailors from the Demon Rum and improving their educational opportunities than he was in the problems of combat, reluctantly picked the head of the Naval War College at Newport, recently appointed Rear Admiral Sims, as the man most likely to get along with the Britishers. According to some accounts it was the aristocratic young New York politician, Franklin D. Roosevelt, serving in the post of Assistant Secretary of the Navy, which had furnished his famous cousin Theodore a springboard into national politics, who urged Sims' appointment.

Sims had the reputation of being a desperate anglophile. He was called to Washington, warned against letting the British pull the wool over his eyes, and ordered to proceed to London immediately. Since war had not yet been declared, the admiral must travel incognito. He was not even to take his uniform.

On March 31, entered in the passengerlist under the name of Mr. V. J. Richardson, with his aide disguised under another alias, Admiral Sims sailed for Liverpool on the U.S.S. *New York* of the American Line. The captain and crew were immediately aware that there was something special about this loquacious civilian. The last man in the world for a secret mission, Sims had the reputation of being the most indiscreet officer in the American service. He had a smiling manner that kept belying the dignity of his neatly trimmed gray beard, of the type affected by flag officers in the Royal Navy, and the impressiveness of his massive physique. Now a handsome genial outgoing man of fiftynine, he had managed throughout a stormy career to get away with saying what he thought and more than he thought, on every topic under the sun.

Sims of the Flotilla

Like General Pershing, Admiral Sims was a discovery of Theodore Roosevelt's.

William Sowden Sims was the son of a Canadian engineer who moved to Pennsylvania as superintendent of a coal and iron company, and became a United States citizen. Young Sims grew up a goodlooking highspirited youth, with more taste for practical jokes than for organized study. When the local congressman, in some way beholden to his father, offered him an appointment to Annapolis, he barely scraped his way in after a couple of tries at the examinations.

In 1876 the navy was still in the period of transition from sail to steam and from wooden ships to ironclads. Only an intermittent student, Willy Sims had a sharply inquiring mind. Seaduty gave him time to read. As a subaltern he plunged into Buckle and Darwin and Huxley.

He became an enthusiastic student of Henry George. For publicspirited Americans it was an age of reform. Everybody must pitch in to make a better world. The reforming zeal that carried T.R. into state and national politics carried Sims into the study of naval organization and the new techniques of warfare on the seas.

His first cruise as a cadet was on the old frigate *Constellation*. He served on the *Swatara*, described as a thirdrate shiprigged sloop of war, when she still had muzzleloading smoothbore guns. His first ironclad was the four thousand ton *Philadelphia* of the "Great White Fleet." In the late eighties, as a lieutenant junior grade, he took a year's leave to board in a Paris pension and study French. He read French books and haunted the theatre and took fencing lessons. He returned to seaduty with a reputation for dandyism and breadth of culture.

He first attracted notice at the Navy Department by the excellence of his reports while on the China station during the Chinese-Japanese War in 1895.

When the Intelligence Department sent him to the Paris Embassy as naval attaché, he spent two years investigating every navy yard in Europe. Theodore Roosevelt was Assistant Secretary in those days. The department sent Lieutenant Sims a formal appreciation of his report. At the bottom of it was scrawled "Not perfunctory. I wish to add my personal appreciation of it. T.R."

Sims went back to seaduty as a full lieutenant on the China station convinced that the American Navy had much to learn about the construction of ironclad fighting ships and was dangerously backward in gunnery. In Hong Kong he struck up a friendship with a Britisher who was applying Sims' sort of inquiring mind and a talent for invention to the improvement of marksmanship in the Royal Navy.

In a series of reports on the British advance in the art of gunnery, Sims tried to puncture the complacency of the bureaus at the Navy Department. The reformer was on the rampage. When his reports brought no action he risked his career by writing directly to Theodore Roosevelt, whom Czolgosz's bullets had recently made President.

T.R. was not a man to worry about channels. Instead of turning young Sims in to his superiors, he wrote him a frank reply saying he doubted if things were as bad as Sims thought. When months passed and nothing further happened, Lieutenant Sims, who was passionately convinced of the rightness of his position, wrote the President again. All of a sudden ordered to report to Washington, he returned home full of forebodings of a courtmartial for insubordination. Instead he found himself appointed inspector of target practice for the Bureau of Navigation.

He hadn't been too long in Washington before he was lunching at the White House. Sims was a great talker. He had a sailor's fund of stories and anecdotes. There was an innocent candor about his conversation as there was about his personal life. An active and muscular man he delighted in feats of strength. He and T.R. were two of a kind. They hit it off immediately.

With the President's backing Sims was able to impose his theories of central fire control on the Bureau of Navigation. After the Russo-Japanese War he plunged into a controversy with another friend of T.R., Captain Mahan, the historian of seapower. Mahan interpreted the accounts he'd read of the Battle of the Sea of Japan as proof of his contention that guns of mixed caliber gave a ship more firepower than the all big gun ordnance Sims and his friends in the Bureau of Navigation were advocating. The British put an end to that argument by producing the *Dreadnaught*. Sims reported to the Navy Department that the *Dreadnaught* made all the navies of the world obsolete from the day she was launched.

Captain Mahan, who was far from being a small man, admitted that his information on Japanese ordnance might have been faulty. Sims became known, in British and American circles, as one of the men who'd guessed ahead of the Admiralty on the *Dreadnaught*. The British civil lord asked permission to have Lieutenant Commander Sims' report published in *Blackwood's Magazine*.

Sims, who had a way of chumming up to his English friends whenever anything new was in the works, managed to turn up in England. In spite of the fact that the Admiralty was wrapping the *Dreadnaught* in portentous secrecy, Sims got himself smuggled on board in civilian clothes and was shown every detail of construction and ordnance. When he came home President Roosevelt appointed him his naval aide.

Meanwhile at fortyseven Sims married a young lady whom he'd met years before on his diplomatic tour of duty in Europe, when her father was minister to St. Petersburg, and followed his friend T.R.'s example by rapidly producing a large family: three pretty little girls and two handsome boys. Whenever he wasn't at sea the commander devoted himself to their upbringing.

One of T.R.'s last acts, before so reluctantly handing the presidency over to William Howard Taft, was to see that Sims was given command of a battleship. A skillful and popular commander, his ship became known as the "cheer-up ship."

In the course of his duty on the *Minnesota* the Atlantic fleet made a fraternal visit to England. Officers and enlistedmen were entertained at Guildhall by the Lord Mayor of London. The officers sat on a dais and drank champagne while the men drank beer at deal tables in the body of the hall.

The luncheon culminated in toasts and speeches extolling the kinship between the two great branches of the Anglo-Saxon race. Full of the spirit of the occasion, Commander Sims sent his cap sailing into the middle of his crew and called for a cheer that would raise the roof off old Guildhall.

Then, in his speech of thanks to the Lord Mayor and City of London for the entertainment, he declared that if ever the integrity of the British Empire should be seriously threatened, the English could count on the assistance of every man, every ship, every dollar and every drop of blood of their kinsmen aross the sea.

Commander Sims' speech, received in England as no more than was due, raised a storm in the American press. The German language papers roared. President Taft was besieged with demands that Sims should be courtmartialed. Enemies in the Navy Department were out for his hide. The President agreed with his Secretary of the Navy that Sims was too valuable an officer to cashier. He let him off with a public reprimand.

When his tour of duty on the battleship came to an end Commander Sims was relegated to the academic calm of the Naval War College at Newport.

Newport gave him leisure to study and think on naval tactics. He became passionate for destroyers. Leaving Newport with the rank of captain he was put in charge of the Atlantic destroyer flotilla. With the outbreak of war in Europe the words of his Guildhall speech were beginning to seem more and more prophetic. Sims threw himself into the practical management of destroyers under combat conditions at sea. As usual he was idolized by his command. The flotilla became "Sims' Flotilla."

In January 1917 Sims went back to the War College as president with the rank of rear admiral. In spite of Josephus Daniels' conviction that he was too pro-British, when war became imminent, the controversial Admiral Sims was the obvious man to represent the United States with the Board of the Admiralty in London. His orders were merely to find out what was going on and to report.

An American on the Board of the Admiralty

Sims arrived in England three days after Congress declared war. He had his first taste of the noisy side of the business when the *New York* ran into a floating mine in the Mersey and was considerably damaged.

The passengers were taken off by an excursionboat full of drunken vacationers from the Isle of Man. The Britishers weren't letting the war interfere with the Easter Bank Holiday.

A flag officer met Sims at the dock and hurried him to London by special train. He was immediately taken to the Admiralty to see his old friend John Jellicoe, now a full admiral and, as first Sea Lord on the Board of the Admiralty, in direct charge of naval operations. With hardly a word Jellicoe handed him a paper with the actual figures of the sinkings by submarine. Sims, who'd been reading the newspapers, was, as he put it, "fairly astounded."

"It looks," he said, "as if the Germans were winning the war."

"They will win, unless we can stop those losses," said Jellicoe.

Sims spent the next few days rooting the facts out from reluctant officials. At the beginning of the war the Allies could dispose of twentyone million tons of shipping, six million tons more than was considered absolutely essential for the supply of the British Isles and the armies in the field. Up to February of 1917 shipbuilding had been not quite keeping up with losses. Now in February and March onethird of the margin of safety had been wiped out. If sinkings kept up at the present rate, by October there would be less tonnage available than was necessary to carry on the war.

It was generally agreed that the best weapon against the submarine was the fast torpedoboat destroyer. Ever since the Japanese sneak attack by destroyers on the Russian fleet in Port Arthur the innovators in the Royal and the United States navies had been begging for more destroyers.

Against submarines, destroyers were almost the perfect weapon. Their speed and shallow draft made them almost immune to torpedoes. The destroyers' torpedoes could be more quickly aimed and had longer range than those on the submarines. If the submarine was caught on the surface the destroyer could ram it with its sharp heavily reinforced bow. Even the oldest types had great firepower.

The development by the Royal Navy of effective depth charges greatly added to the destroyers' efficiency against submarines. These ashcans, as they were called, were mines set to be exploded by the pressure of the water at any desired depth. They could be dropped over the destroyer's stern. Within a radius of a hundred feet they were usually fatal, but even when they exploded at much greater distance they could damage fragile machinery or at least give the submarine crew a shaking up they never forgot.

When Sims asked the Britishers why more destroyers couldn't be detailed to protect merchant shipping they explained patiently that there just weren't enough destroyers. Their antisubmarine patrol was pieced out with converted yachts, trawlers, drifters, tugs, anything that could keep afloat long enough to drop an ashcan when a U-boat was sighted or suspected.

The Grand Fleet at Scapa Flow had first priority for destroyer protection. Then came hospital ships. Sims learned of the ingenious devilment that lay behind the German announcement that they would sink hospital ships. The Germans knew that the British would not face abandoning sick and wounded men to drown. Destroyers needed to protect valuable cargoes had to be detailed to the hospital ships. The third priority went to the Channel crossings where by continuous patrol an immune zone had been created where no submarine dared venture. Fourth was the lifeline to India through the Mediterranean.

Well, the American asked, if convoys worked in the Channel, why wouldn't they work in the Irish Sea, and on the Atlantic approaches? Just weren't enough destroyers, the Britishers repeated. In spite of a speededup building program there were only ten or fifteen destroyers left to protect the merchantmen that brought in the food, the petroleum products, the rubber and the munitions on which Great Britain's survival depended.

Destroyers were constantly in need of repair. Steaming at twentyfive knots through heavy seas they took a terrible pounding. The crews had to have rest. At times there were only as few as four at sea to patrol the whole region. Too bad, Sims was told, but convoys were impracticable.

Sims was a stubborn fellow. His reasoning was that the Grand Fleet was continually protected by destroyers, wasn't that a convoy? Although at first sight it might seem that a mass of ships steaming slowly together would prove an easier target for a submarine than ships proceeding singly at top speed, in practice the opposite had turned out to be true.

Sims began to point out that when ships steamed in convoy the submarine commander had to come where the patrol ships were. Otherwise, no matter how carefully you divided the sea into squares, he could always be where the patrol ships weren't.

The area to be patrolled amounted to something like twentyfive thousand square miles. It would take a destroyer to a square mile to do a proper patrol job. Where would they get twentyfive thousand destroyers?

"Is there no solution to the problem?" Sims asked Jellicoe.

"Absolutely none that we can see now," Jellicoe answered without the slightest expression on his smooth round face.

The Convoy System

When Sims began to ask questions among the lesser ranks in the Admiralty offices at Whitehall he found solutions aplenty. There was a Commander Reginald Henderson who had directed the shuttle service of colliers carrying English coal to France. His day to day experience had proved to him that convoys worked. The younger officers backed him up.

The final argument of the admirals, who'd be damned if they'd convoy merchantmen, was that the merchant skippers wouldn't stand for it. These crude old salts would never be able to steam all night in formation without lights, just hadn't had the training for that sort of service. What with the bad coal they were getting and the fact that the Royal Navy had taken all their best officers and engineers, they would never be able to keep their engines throttled down to a set speed. Ships that made twelve knots would be endangered by having to wait for ships that only made six or eight. There would be collisions in the dark. A submarine coming up in the middle of a great huddle of freighters could sink as many as she pleased.

Sims was a crusader. He traded on the respect the British admirals had for him as one of their own kind, a dreadnaught man before dreadnaughts and a fire control man before fire control. Though he affected the blunt old seadog who said the first thing that came into his head, when need be he could be pretty tactful about what he blurted out. Admiral Beatty was a convoy man but it was mostly Sims' influence that made it possible for the Sea Lords to execute a dignified retreat.

He found himself teaming up with Lloyd George who had been talking convoys for some time. Forever optimistic, the Prime Minister was for trying everything. He already suspected he might have guessed wrong about Nivelle's offensive, although the disastrous consequences of that wrong guess were not yet apparent. He was all for giving convoys a try. "We shall get the best of the submarine, never fear," he told Sims, with a cheerful wave of the hand that the American found bracing amid the prevailing gloom.

At Lloyd George's insistence Henderson was allowed to prepare a memorandum. On April 30 the Prime Minister, threatening to overrule them in their own sanctuary, called on the Sea Lords at the Admiralty. That night, meeting Sims at dinner at the Waldorf Astors', the Prime Minister gave him the news that the Sea Lords had consented, oh so reluctantly, to let a single convoy be tried out. "You are responsible for this," he told Sims.

While he was crusading for convoys in the handsome old salons of the Admiralty, where he was shown the long table where Nelson had sat and the windvane over the fireplace he'd kept his single eye on, Sims was crowding the Atlantic cable with pleas for destroyers from America, destroyers right away. Page, happy at last to find a man who saw the peril as he saw it, backed him up valiantly.

On May 4 the first division of six destroyers from Sims' old flotilla steamed into Queenstown. The Germans, who seem to have known the date of their arrival before Sims did, were ready for them with a string of mines across the harbor entrance, but the sweepers managed to clear a channel.

The first convoy from Gibraltar arrived in British ports May 20 without the loss of a ship. The next day the Admiralty appointed a board to set up a convoy system. Overnight practical shipping men were converted to convoys. The merchant skippers picked up the knack of steaming a zigzag course in convoy with very little trouble. Proceeding at night without lights lost its terrors. Shipping losses for the month of May dropped to roughly six hundred thousand tons. In June, they rose again, but after that the decrease was continual.

The Command under Admiral Sims

The spring of 1917 was unusually cold and stormy. May was a bad month on the Atlantic. The men on the U. S. destroyers, based on the York River in Virginia and on Guantanamo Bay, were in a storm of excitement. Crews had been weakened during the preceding months by the detaching of gunners for service on merchantships. New men fresh from the farm kept turning up who had to be trained.

In every navy yard destroyers were being overhauled for distant duty. Orders would come giving some ship four days to put to sea. Navy yard workers, accustomed to taking their time, were flustered by the sudden wartime pressure. Accidents occurred. In Philadelphia the hasty scaffolding shoring up two destroyers in drydock collapsed and the destroyers fell in on each other and crushed like a bug a little tender being repaired between them. Somehow, higglety pigglety, destroyer after destroyer was readied for seaservice. Under sealed orders they steamed out of the great estuaries of the Atlantic coast. Usually the commander was instructed to open his orders at some point off Cape Cod.

Proceed to Halifax for instructions from the British Admiralty as to Atlantic crossing to Queenstown Ireland to join the command under Admiral Sims.

As Admiral Sims' name went through the narrow ship lurching over the long rollers, in the cramped wardroom and the crew's skimpy quarters, spirits rose. Admiral Sims was considered a great man to serve under.

When the destroyer, cruising at fifteen knots to ease the strain of the huge Atlantic seas, reached the danger zone pulses quickened. The newly rigged crow's nest and observation points were manned. Lookouts were told to keep their eyes peeled.

Like as not it would be rainy and there would be fogbanks off the land. These were crowded waters. Smoke smudges were always on the horizon. A freighter would go lumbering through the surging seas or a twostack liner would be seen streaking for safety under full steam. Every oddlooking foreign sailing ship might be a submarine in disguise.

Wreckage aplenty. To heated imaginings every floating bottle or drifting spar would seem a periscope, a hatchcover would be a conning tower. A porpoise breaking the surface of a wave might set off the alarm for battle stations. Many a destroyer wasted ammunition on a whale.

On the bridge the officers would be edgy. As dusk dimmed the great expanses of tossing waves under the cold lash of rainsqualls men would doubt their own judgement. Were they reading right the position of the minefields on the chart they'd been furnished in Halifax? The coast was shadowy. Through a rent in the mist the far hills broke away. Was that the harbor entrance? A lighthouse with no light in it.

The commander would ring the engine room for full speed. Forts and patrol boats had a way of firing on ships attempting to enter harbors after sunset. At last they were following a patrol boat that showed a tiny light astern to an indicated anchorage. The anchors plunked. As the engines quieted the deck stopped shaking. It was silent in the smooth bay. All around them through the gloaming they could see the dim green hills of Ireland.

Old Frozen Face

The first thing the Americans discovered was that instead of being under Sims' direct command they were under the command of Vice-Admiral Sir Lewis Bayly and, in fact, part of the Royal Navy.

Admiral Bayly had the reputation of knowing his destroyers, but was a martinet of the old school. He was reputed to hate Yankees, particularly. He'd once been Naval Attaché in Washington and had left there, virtually by request, imbued with a profound distaste for everything American. Since the war began he had been further embittered by being removed from command of the first battle squadron of the Grand Fleet, where he'd flown his flag on the superdreadnaught *Marlborough*. Detailed to the Channel fleet he had the humiliation of losing the *Formidable* by torpedo to a submarine, while engaged in routine target practice off the Devon coast, and had been relegated to the antisubmarine patrol at Queenstown.

Winning Admiral Bayly's heart for the American destroyer crews was as important a victory for Sims as was his putting over of the convoy system.

Their relationship couldn't have started out worse. Bayly was ordered to London, where he was at odds with most of his superiors, to meet Sims when Sims first arrived; and so Sims put it, the old tartar "was as rude to me as one man can be to another."

Sims swallowed his pride and went to Queenstown full of honeyed words to prepare for the American destroyers which were already on their way. Sims admired Bayly for his seamanlike qualities: he told all and sundry that personal feelings must be subordinate to the needs of the service.

The two admirals "walked around each other for three days." Then Bayly growled to his niece, who kept house for him at glum old Admiralty House on a hill overlooking the harbor, "That man is on the square."

Bayly, a childless old bear, had one soft spot in his heart, and that was for the spinster niece whose loving care offered him what few amenities his life contained. Sims, who had as much of the blarney as any Irishman, managed from the first to get into the good graces of Miss Violet Voysey and of her little spaniel Patrick. Soon Miss Voysey was declaring that she loved Americans, and particularly her American admiral. The two of them began to club together to rescue Uncle Lewis from the results of his own churlishness.

Back in London Sims put it up to the Admiralty board that Bayly was one of the ablest men in their navy as well as one of the most snappish. At that he had just gripes. He hadn't had a leave since he'd undertaken the particularly worrisome and exacting command of the antisubmarine patrol, and he was treated as a subordinate by the naval authorities in London.

The First Lord, Sir Edward Carson, eventually agreed. Bayly got his independent command and immediate leave. Bayly made the retort courteous by asking Sims to take over his command when he went off for his short rest late in June. Sims flew his flag from the destroyer tender *Melville* and, for five days, personally directed the patrol work, in which convoy protection was little by little taking the place of the old hit or miss system.

When Sims went back to the Admiralty, where he had virtually become an additional Sea Lord, he left his own right hand man Captain Pringle as Admiral Bayly's Chief of Staff. Captain Pringle knew as much about destroyers as Sims did and he was even more adept at fitting square pegs into round holes. Captain Pringle, Admiral Sims and Miss Voysey became a sort of triumvirate to keep old Bayly's rude remarks from ruffling the feelings of the men under his command; and also to keep from Bayly's ears the fact that the Americans called him "old Frozen Face."

By midsummer there were thirtysix American destroyers, tendered by two motherships and assisted by a group of converted yachts, operating out of Queenstown. Similar bases for antisubmarine and convoy work were established at Brest and Gibraltar. From the supreme menace to Allied hopes the German submarines were gradually being reduced to a dangerous nuisance.

As early as June 8, Page, whose letters accurately reflected the state of morale among ruling circles in England, was writing the President: "Praise God our destroyers are making the approach to these shores appreciably safer . . . Admiral Sims is the darling of the kingdom."

Hunting Hornets All Over the Farm

Meanwhile Woodrow Wilson, beset with everincreasing problems he felt no man could handle but himself, stewed with impatience whenever he thought of the great British fleet, lying idle it seemed to him, at Scapa Flow, under the protection of flotillas of destroyers that would be better employed defending the merchantships that were the lifeline of the armies in France. July 5 he let his impatience show in a confidential message to Sims.

"From the beginning of the war I have been greatly surprised at the failure of the British Admiralty to use Great Britain's great naval superiority in an effective way. In the presence of the present submarine emergency they are helpless to the point of panic. Every plan we suggest they reject for some reason of prudence. In my view this is not a time for prudence but for boldness even at the cost of great losses. I would be very much obliged to you if you would report to me, confidentially, of course, exactly what the Admiralty has been doing, and what they have accomplished, and add to the report your own comments and suggestions . . . Give me such advice as you would give . . . if you were running a navy of your own."

The President had immediately backed up Sims in the matter of convoys, but he didn't yet feel satisfied with the results. He wanted more protection for merchantmen. He was looking forward to the execution of a project for fencing the U-boats into the North Sea with a barrage of mines across its entrances which he and Franklin Roosevelt, the increasingly active Assistant Secretary of the Navy, spent hours conferring about during the summer months. Most especially Wilson wanted an attack on the German submarine bases in Heligoland Bight and back of Ostend and Zeebrugge.

Early in August he stole a weekend from his overloaded desk to slip out of Washington on the *Mayflower*, in the company of Edith Wilson and some of her Bolling relatives, for a private visit to the Atlantic fleet. The trip was strictly off the record. The ships were forbidden to fire the twentyone gun salute. He addressed the fleet's officers collected for the purpose on the flagship *Pennsylvania*. Those who heard his speech likened it to a pep talk the coach might deliver to his team between the halves at a football game:

"This is an unprecedented war and, therefore, it is a war in one sense for amateurs. Nobody ever before conducted a war like this and therefore nobody can pretend to be a professional . . . Now somebody has got to think this war out. Somebody has got to think out a way not only to fight the submarine but to do something different from what we are doing.

"We are hunting hornets all over the farm and letting the nest alone
. . . I am willing to sacrifice half the navy Great Britain and we together
have to crush out that nest, because if we crush it the war is won. I have
come here to say that I do not care where it comes from, I do not care
whether it comes from the youngest officer or the oldest, but I want the
officers of this navy to have the distinction of saying how this war is going to be won . . . I am ready to put myself at the disposal of any officer
in the Navy who thinks he knows how to run this war . . . We have got
to throw tradition to the winds . . . Every time we have suggested anything to the British Admiralty the reply has come back that virtually
amounted to this, that it had never been done that way, and I felt like
saying: 'Well nothing was ever done so systematically as nothing is being
done now.'

"America . . . is the prize amateur nation of the world. Germany is
the prize professional nation. Now when it comes to doing new things
and doing them well, I will back the amateur against the professional
every time, because the professional does it out of the book and the
amateur does it with his eyes open upon a new world and a new set of
circumstances . . . Do not stop to think about what is prudent for a
moment. Do the thing that is audacious . . . because that is exactly the
thing the other side does not understand . . . So gentlemen, besides coming down here to give you my personal greeting and to say how absolutely
I rely on you and believe in you, I have come down to say also that I
depend upon you, depend on you for brains as well as training and
courage and discipline."

Convoy Service

No such novelties in naval warfare as the President was hoping for
appeared; but, as the summer advanced, the destroyers proved themselves.

Destroyer service in the Irish Sea and the adjacent Atlantic was a
punishing business. Fine weather was rare. Often the wind blew half a
gale lashing up steep and spiteful seas. The rain never seemed to stop.
The narrow little ships driven at such speed by their powerful engines
pitched and lurched continually. Half the time decks were awash. Salt
water sloshed down companionways and seeped into bedding. To eat
men had to prop themselves in corners. A coffee mug set for a moment
on a table would be tossed in the air. Many a night the ship plunged
and shook so that there was no sleeping. It was all a man could do by
bracing himself carefully to stay in his bunk.

Repairs were endless. Steering engines jammed. Generators died. Guns
and torpedo tubes needed continual attention. Every operation was made

twice as difficult by the vibration of the hull slamming through the great weight of the seas.

Action when it came was short. Something that might be a periscope, seen through the heavy rain, would broach ahead. Battle stations would sound and the destroyer would bound at full speed over the waves. Over would go the ashcans at the place where the periscope was figured to have been. While the ship cruised in a circle every eye would search the waves for an oil slick or bits of wooden deck that might indicate a hit.

"Sept 7 Real excitement at 5:30 PM" a young lieutenant on the U.S.S. *Cummings* entered in his diary. "The alarm went off and we headed for a perfect periscope and conning tower awash and apparently under way at 6000 yards on the starboard bow. We opened fire with #1 gun and fired about 14 shots making 2 hits. #2 gun fired once and #4 which is on the fantail fired once and made one hit. We were only 500 yards away when we discovered it was a capsized wreck with the spar sticking up through the bottom. Everybody terribly disappointed."

Convoy service would have been a hopeless game of blind man's buff if the wireless room hadn't furnished the ships with ears. There skinny young men in earphones, with cigarettestained fingers and a look of strain on their faces, spelled out the dots and dashes of the Morse code. Their scribbled flimsy kept the officers on the bridge informed of every event over a great radius of stormy seas. Through the newly invented radio direction finder, Sparks could spot, with some accuracy, the part of the ocean his messages came from. An SOS, the last stutter from the wireless of a sinking merchantman; reports of hairbreadth escapes or frustrated engagements were retailed from wireless room to wireless room. The news seeped down through the ships until the lowliest oiler in the engine room knew the location of the latest sighting of a periscope. To many a destroyer crew Sparks was the most important man on board.

Night and day the warzone was full of stuttering communications. German submarines particularly kept up an incessant chatter back and forth from ship to ship and with the Admiralty back home. Perhaps it relieved the desperate solitude of their crews, but the urge to communicate proved many a submarine's undoing.

Allied wireless operators got to know the commanders, Old Hans or Fritz or Franz von this and that, as well as if they'd met them in a pub. Some were decent fellows who gave the crews of sunken ships a break by reporting their position even at risk to themselves. Others were murderous swine who shelled open boats.

At Whitehall a special intelligence room was devoted to sorting out the reports that came in night and day, in code and out of code, from escort ships and convoys. British Naval Intelligence kept track of the departure of submarines from Bruges, and out between the long jetties at Ostend and Zeebrugge. The movement of U-boats became predictable. Since their speed was known, once a submarine was approximately located even an unprotected convoy could be detoured out of its way.

The direction of the whole system was centered in what became known as the Convoy Room at the Admiralty in London. The position of assembling merchantships was plotted on a huge chart on the wall where each convoy was represented by a wooden cutout of a ship. Timetables like railway timetables were instituted, and trunk lines through which the converging ranks of ships were routed for protection as they approached the danger zone. Convoys left New York every eight days, Hampton Roads every sixteen days. Others were dispatched from Gibraltar or Dakar or Halifax or Sydney, Nova Scotia. Ocean traffic was handled the way freight trains were handled in a railroad system. Little circles showed the position of every submarine known to be at sea.

Each convoy sailed under a convoy commander who received code messages giving his ships their instructions. At his command they began their zigzag course: fifteen minutes thirty degrees to port, fifteen minutes thirty degrees to starboard, fifteen minutes straight ahead on the indicated course. He alone knew the latitude and longitude of the spot in the ocean where their escorts would meet them. The eastbound convoys were timed to meet the escorting ships that had just brought out the westbound ships.

Under varying conditions of wind and sea on the stormy Atlantic there was no avoiding occasional failures in the timetable. The dangerous moments came when convoys had to cruise around waiting for their destroyers. Then sinkings were inevitable; but the U-boats had to fight for every ship they got, and rarely escaped without a chase from an escort ship dropping ashcans, now made more effective by the American invention of the Y-gun, which made it possible to shoot them overboard in pairs at either side of the destroyer's wake.

By August 1, ten thousand ships had been convoyed in and out of the British Isles with a loss of only one percent. The odds had changed. Thirtysix extra American destroyers were enough to tip the scales. U-boat crews began to lose their verve. The blockade of Germany continued. The blockade of Britain had failed.

Late in the fall of 1917, even after Jellicoe had retired, a wornout and disappointed man; long after subordinates, assisted by American officers, and by practical steamboat men from the Ministry of Shipping, had proved the success of the convoy system, the Sea Lords, sitting at the long table in the Admiralty boardroom where Nelson had sat, would occasionally discuss the question of whether convoys were really a proper protection for merchantmen against submarines.

Chapter 14

INNOCENTS ABROAD

At the beginning of May 1917 Major General John J. Pershing was still in command at Fort Sam Houston, grimly busy with the unrewarding daily chore of keeping the peace along the Mexican border. Pershing at this stage of his career was not a happy man. Intimates told of his staring for minutes on end every morning, with fixed expressionless face, at a photograph of his dead wife and the little girls. Though a stiff somewhat unapproachable officer, and in his late fifties, he still betrayed occasionally the frustrated yearning for female companionship his fellows had noticed when he was a West Point cadet.

Perhaps ambition kept him going. Up to the day when the declaration of war against Germany gave fresh impetus to his military aspirations, he had toyed with the notion of resigning from the service and taking up the law or business, so that he might really amount to something in the world.

A letter from Major General Bell, under whom he had served in the Philippines, gave his ambition a sharp spur. The rumor was already abroad in army circles that if the President decided to send an expeditionary force to Europe, out of the five commissioned major generals, it was Pershing who would be picked to command it. In spite of his being Pershing's senior in rank, his old friend Bell was asking for an assignment under him in France.

General Pershing's French

Pershing had hardly read Bell's letter before a wire came in from Senator Warren. Their mutual bereavement had tightened the bond between the two men, and Pershing knew that his fatherinlaw, who was still chairman of the Military Affairs Committee, would do anything possible to further his career. The wire asked how well Pershing spoke French. It was followed by an explanatory letter. Secretary Baker had invited the senator to drop in to his office the other morning and asked him, in an elaborately offhand way, if he happened to know whether Pershing spoke French. The senator, to gain time to find the right answer, said he wasn't sure but he was sure his wife would know. He'd ask her and report back.

Even before Pershing could wire the senator that he'd studied the language in France for several months ten years before, a coded message from General Hugh Scott, Chief of Staff in Washington, was placed on his desk, ordering him to pick regiments to form a regular army division for service in France.

A few days later he was in Washington standing rigid in his khaki uniform with its stiff choker collar before Secretary Baker's desk in the War Department. "I was surprised," Pershing wrote, "to find him much younger and considerably smaller than I expected. He looked actually diminutive as he sat behind his desk, doubled up in a rather large office chair."

When the little man started to speak the impression was different. In a few short sentences Baker told Pershing he had given the subject of a commander in chief in France careful thought and had chosen him upon his record. "I left Mr. Baker's office with a distinctly favorable impression of the man . . ."

Very Difficult Tasks

Immediately the general settled into a small room in the War Department to assemble a headquarters detachment to take to France. To head his staff, in spite of his conviction that only West Pointers could make really good officers, he chose Major James L. Harbord, who had risen from private to first lieutenant in the 10th Cavalry at a time when promotions from the ranks were hard to come by. He combed the army bureaus for talented young men. According to civilians called in later to activate the moribund services of the War Department, he carried off every army officer with brains in Washington City.

He knew he owed a debt of gratitude to Colonel Roosevelt. To sooth T.R.'s hurt feelings he promised to find posts in France for his three sons who were rearing to go overseas. He held at arm's length a mass of applications for service from all sorts and conditions of men.

Before the month was over Pershing discovered that he was expected to command, not merely the 1st Division, but the entire expedition to France. The question of general officers immediately arose. Hugh Scott and Tasker Bliss admitted they were too old for service in the field. His friend Bell, he decided reluctantly, was not in good enough health. Leonard Wood he did not want for reasons too numerous to mention. As the only ranking regular army general with the troops abroad Pershing would be in a position to run his own show.

One afternoon Secretary Baker took him to the White House to call on President Wilson. The President was so preoccupied with a discussion of the shipping situation he hardly seemed to notice Pershing at first. Then he gave him a sharp gray glance through his noseglasses and his pale lips smiled. "General," he said, "we are giving you some very difficult tasks these days."

Pershing answered stiffly that difficult tasks were what West Pointers were trained to expect. It was disappointing, he noted afterwards, that the President didn't outline his policy in relation to the demands for manpower for their own armies that the French and British missions in Washington were already making. Talk lagged. The general was instructed to convey the President's best wishes to the heads of state in England and France. The time had come for him to take his leave. He rose and made another set speech: he appreciated the honor and realized the responsibilities entailed. He would do his best.

"General," the President, who was always a little ill at ease with militarymen, answered with equal formality, "you were chosen entirely upon your record and I have every confidence that you will succeed; you shall have my full support."

The President was as good as his word. When Secretary Baker sent Pershing his formal orders, the general found himself designated "to command all the land forces of the United States operating in continental Europe and in the United Kingdom of Great Britain and Ireland, including any part of the Marine Corps which may be detached for service there with the army . . . You will establish, after consultation with the French War Office, all necessary bases, lines of communication, depots etc., and make all the incidental arrangements essential to active participation at the front . . ."

The fifth paragraph assumed particular importance in the minds of Pershing and his staff: "In military operations against the Imperial German Government, you are directed to cooperate with the forces of the other countries employed against that enemy; but in so doing the underlying idea must be kept in view that the forces of the United States are a separate and distinct component of the combined forces, the identity of which must be preserved."

That was Newton D. Baker's answer to the campaign the British and French missions under Balfour and Joffre were conducting to have American levies drafted as replacements into their own war machines. When the general appeared in the Secretary's office to say goodby, Baker, so Baker remembered later, said he would give him only two orders, one to go to France and the other to come home; but that in the meantime his authority in France would be supreme. "If you make good, the people will forgive almost any mistake. If you do not make good, they will probably hang us both on the first lamppost they can find."

The Baltic *Contingent*

At noon on May 29, a rainy blustery day, General Pershing and fifty-nine officers, sixtyseven enlisted men and thirtysix field clerks, accompanied by five civilian interpreters and two newspaper correspondents, embarked on a ferryboat from Governor's Island and headed through the Narrows into Gravesend Bay. There, after tossing around for some hours in a choppy sea, they were picked up by the White Star liner *Baltic*.

Although submarines and death by drowning were on every man's mind, the trip was uneventful. The officers attended French classes, and were lectured on the problems of maintaining an army in France by various British authorities on board. Their medical men vaccinated them and shot them full of injections against typhoid and paratyphoid A and B. On the tenth day the *Baltic* zigzagged into the Mersey.

Pershing's plan had been to slip through England and to set up his headquarters in France as secretly as possible, but a fulldress military welcome awaited the little detachment when the *Baltic* warped into the Liverpool dock. There was a British admiral, a lieutenant general, a delegation from the Imperial General Staff, the Lord Mayor of Liverpool and the Royal Welsh Fusileers with its band drawn up at attention to meet them, complete with the regimental mascot, a stately old white billygoat. In the background was a swarm of newspapermen and photographers. British propaganda was evidently blowing up the arrival of American troops for all it was worth. Stiff as ramrods, with polished puttees and uniforms pressed to the nines, the American officers marched down the gangplank to the tune of "The Star-Spangled Banner."

They were conveyed to London on a Royal train. The officers were put up at the Savoy as guests of the nation and the enlistedmen housed among the Beefeaters in the Tower. The general and his staff were received at Buckingham Palace. They attended services at Westminster Abbey. They were greeted by Lloyd George and wined and dined at the War Office. After a dizzy round of receptions, luncheons and state dinners, they found themselves one dewy June morning boarding the channel boat for France.

"At Boulogne wharf," Major Harbord wrote in his diary, "a drove of French officers, a few Britishers (for Boulogne is a British debarkation port), scores of newspaper men, and a regiment of French soldiers with their funny little steel helmets, and whiskers of various types . . ." The band played "The Star-Spangled Banner" and the Americans stood at attention "for several days," it seemed to Major Harbord, "while they played it over and over. Even the General who stands like a statue growled at the number of times they played it." Next came the

"Marseillaise," "and then, our hands having broken off at the wrist, we stood up to the gangway while a dozen fuzzy little Frenchmen came up. Each saluted the General and made a little speech and then sidestepped and was replaced by another until each little man had made his speech."

The last was a French brigadier with a sweeping mustache that hid great scars on his chin. His right arm was gone below the elbow. This was General Pelletier, who, having lived two years in San Francisco, was detailed, on account of his knowledge of English, to Pershing's staff.

"He is a brave, simpleminded, gallant old fellow," noted Harbord, "now rapidly becoming an embarrassment to us, his rank having to be constantly considered . . . He has a bunch of attachés, for, like the British cousins, many French officers are keen to serve with the Americans. A Lieutenant Colonel Comte de Chambrun, great grandson of Lafayette, and husband of Nicholas Longworth's sister, is one of them. He is an artilleryman and speaks good English, and a great deal of it."

Though eager to reach Paris and go to work, Pershing and his little group were detained in Boulogne all morning. As a matter of course they were taken to visit the ancient castle on the hill. In Europe the past was still present. At every pause somebody made a speech about it. Like good Americans most of them had never given a thought to history. Now they found the word *historique* ringing in their ears. They were returning, a hundred and forty years later, the visit of Rochambeau and Lafayette. Their arrival was *un moment historique.*

They finally discovered the reason for the delay. Their train was being held so that they could make their entry into Paris after working hours, when the streets would surely be crowded. The French, too, were out to squeeze every bit of propaganda value out of the arrival of Pershing's tiny detachment. Pétain had been telling his troops: we must wait for the Americans. The Americans were here.

Worn out with oratory the general closed himself in his compartment for a nap while the members of his staff sat, in the unfamiliar compartments with their crocheted headrests, jiggling with the rhythm of the rails, looking out of the grubby train windows at the gray skies, the great stone walls, the thatched and slate roofs, the lacy steeples, the ancient towers encrusted with lichen and moss, and the green fields, the carefully tilled gardenplots, the parklike hills of northern France. Red poppies bloomed everywhere. It seemed a picturebook world, with only an occasional string of brown British lorries, or field guns on the move, or a staffcar cruising along poplarlined stone roads to give a hint of war.

As they drove out of the Gare du Nord, after endless delays while the French protocol officers decided who would ride with whom in which car or carriage, they were met by a storm of cheers.

"The acclaim that greeted us," wrote Pershing, "as we drove through the streets en route to the hotel was to me a complete surprise. Dense masses of people lined the boulevards and squares. It was said that never before in the history of Paris had there been such an outpouring of people. Men, women and children absolutely packed every foot of space, even to the windows and housetops. Cheers and tears were mingled together and shouts of enthusiasm fairly rent the air. Women climbed into our automobiles screaming 'Vive l'Amerique,' and threw flowers till we were literally buried. Everybody waved flags and banners. At several points the masses surged into the streets, entirely beyond control of the police."

When they arrived at the Hôtel de Crillon, General Pershing was forced to appear again and again on his balcony to salute the enormous crowds massed in the Place de la Concorde. He let himself be carried away by the enthusiasm of the moment to the point of endeavoring to address the French journalists, crowding into the lobby of his suite, in their own language. The journalists had trouble hiding their smiles behind their notebooks. "After a sentence or two I concluded in my mother tongue," noted the general. Pershing's French became a byword among the irreverent.

He was putting himself out, sometimes awkwardly because it went against the grain, to make a good impression on the French public; as when, at his chief of staff's suggestion, he spoiled a new pair of gloves by shaking hands, for the benefit of the photographers, with the engineer and the fireman of the train which had brought him into Paris. But he was determined not to be taken in, no, not by anybody.

"I guess our man will hold his own," noted Harbord, just after seeing him off on a visit to the front with General Pétain and Minister of War Paul Painlevé, who were repeating the arguments Joffre had used in Washington to induce him to send in American units as replacements into French divisions. "He knows the probable attempt in advance and he has his teeth set."

The General Organization Project

General Pershing's first care, on arriving in Paris, was to find quarters where he could put his outfit to work. Two dwelling houses were rented on the rue Constantine opposite the vast buildings of the Invalides, where Foch had his niche as chief of the French general staff; and the fusty old rooms were fitted up as improvised offices. There the field clerks were installed at their desks. Benches were dragged into the halls for the enlistedmen who were to serve as orderlies and messengers and guards. Cubbyholes were partitioned off for the colonels and majors and captains and lesser fry on whom would fall the detailed work of inventing an army, a staff system, and supply services capable of conducting a campaign four thousand miles from the home base. It was an operation without precedent in the annals of war.

For his own quarters Pershing, whose uniform was about to be embellished with the four stars of a lieutenant general, so that he might keep his head up amid the panoply and glitter of the European military, accepted from Ogden Mills, a wealthy scion of New York society who was serving as a captain of infantry, the loan of his Paris residence. This was a magnificent Left Bank mansion set in gardens dating from the early years of Louis XV. The Americans were to learn to live in the European style.

In spite of a punishing calendar of official calls: on the President of the Republic, and on Marshal Joffre, and on General Foch, and on a long list of generals whose stars were rising or falling in response to the complicated manoeuvres of French military politics; and on Pétain, whom all described as the man of the hour; and dinners to attend and luncheons and toasts to be responded to, and gala performances at the Opèra and the Opèra Comique and the Comèdie Française, and interallied concerts at the Trocadèro which the American officers had at least to appear to enjoy; and troops to review and field headquarters and picked spots on the front to visit, Pershing and his assistants went to work with extraordinary dispatch to draw up the scheme for an American expeditionary force.

Pershing knew it was up to him. The War Department had made no preparations. The officers at the War College had been trying to work up a sketchy sort of plan for the supply of troops abroad during the winter, but General Tasker Bliss, alternating as Chief of Staff with the old Indian negotiator Hugh Scott, who was more interested in Indian sign languages than in administrative problems had, the day before Pershing sailed on the *Baltic*, written on the War College memorandum: "General Pershing's expedition is being sent abroad on the urgent insistence of Marshal Joffre and the French mission that a force, however small, be sent to produce a moral effect . . . Our General Staff has made no plan (so far as known to the Secretary of War) for prompt dispatch of reinforcements to General Pershing, nor the prompt dispatch of considerable forces to France . . . What the French General Staff is now concerned about is the establishment of an important base and line of communication for a much larger force than General Pershing will have. They evidently think that having yielded to the demand for a small force for moral effect, it is quite soon to be followed by a large force for physical effect. Thus far we have no plans for this."

During his first days in France Pershing learned that he would have to deal not only with procrastination in Washington but with deepseated, if tactfully expressed, opposition among the French and British commands. The French and British wanted American recruits to use—as the British were using the Canadians and Australians and New Zealanders, and as the French were using their colonial troops—to ease the drain on their own manpower in fighting a war of attrition.

If Pershing had been a more imaginative man he would have been appalled by the difficulties of his position. Being a man of single mind he managed to ignore the pressures and embarrassments and hindrances that lurked under the torrents of fair words with which the Allied authorities greeted him on every hand. This was his opportunity to realize the ambitions which had been instilled in him when he entered West Point as a raw young rural schoolteacher without a prospect in the world. His orders were to lead an American Army against the Germans and he intended to carry them out to the letter.

Le Bassin de la Briey

His first business was to pick an objective. Where could an American army be used most effectively "to carry on the war," in the terms of Secretary Baker's orders, "vigorously . . . and towards a victorious conclusion"?

Except for small French and Belgian forces defending the fraction of Belgian soil left free from German occupation, the British under Haig held an entrenched line that stretched south from the channel coast to St. Quentin. Their General Plumer had, early in June, managed somewhat to offset Nivelle's defeat on the Aisne by a successful mining operation, through which he captured the high ground the Germans held in front of the Flemish village of Messines. Messines was to the right of Ypres, where Haig, on whose patient shoulders the whole weight of holding the Germans back now rested, was planning great efforts for later in the summer. Since the fizzle of the Nivelle plan there had been no further effort to unify the French and British commands.

From St. Quentin east the French armies, riddled by defeatism and mutiny, had tenuous hold—how tenuous the Germans, fortunately for the Allies, did not know—on the trenches and fortifications leading through Soissons to Rheims and Verdun, and on past Nancy to the Swiss border.

It didn't take Pershing long to discover from his talks with Pétain that the French had no offensive plans on a large scale whatsoever. The most Pétain hoped for was to restore morale to the point of undertaking a local attack of limited risk in the Verdun sector.

Searching the map with fresh eyes Pershing found what he hoped might turn out to be a weak spot in the German position. That was the salient east of Verdun that thrust deep into French territory with its apex at St. Mihiel. Behind that salient was the old French fortress of Metz in Lorraine, which the Germans held as part of their spoil from the Franco-Prussian War.

To the northwest of Metz was a region known as the Bassin de la Briey where the iron ore was mined upon which the Germans depended for a great part of their steel production. To the northeast was the Saar valley which furnished most of their coal. The railroad lines that linked the sources of German raw materials ran roughly east and west. An Allied breakthrough into the Bassin de la Briey would deal German industry a fatal blow. From the moment that General Pershing circled the St. Mihiel salient with his pencil on the map the course of the American campaign in France was decided.

Other considerations entered into the choice of the Lorraine front. It was the only region where lines of supply could be established independent of the French communications which all centered on Paris, and of the British, which radiated out from the channel ports. Accordingly Pershing arranged with the French to set up American ports of entry at St. Nazaire at the mouth of the Loire, at La Pallice a little further south on the Bay of Biscay; and at Bassens, across the Garonne river from Bordeaux in the estuary of the Gironde. American money would have to be spent and American labor imported to improve docking and warehousing facilities and to modernize the railroad line which ran up from St. Nazaire and La Pallice to Tours and thence crossed south of Paris in an easterly direction to Chaumont and Neufchâteau, which were small towns near enough the front to furnish staging areas. Another line would feed into the American sector from Bassens and Bordeaux through Issoudun and Bourges. If the need should arise a third route could be utilized up from Marseilles, France's principal Mediterranean port, through Lyon and Dijon.

"The low morale and worn condition of the Allied armies," wrote Pershing in the final summing up of his plans, "suggested that they might be unable to protect their communications, and therefore it was essential that we should have our own independent system."

On June 28 General Pershing went down to St. Nazaire to meet the advance guard of his 1st Division. To everybody's amazement, the fourteen merchantmen converted to troop transports slipped past the U-boats without a casualty. At lunch aboard the flagship Seattle, Admiral Gleaves, who commanded the convoying cruisers and destroyers, could only attribute their safe arrival to the hand of Providence.

The Yanks Are Coming

The general, who had been lecturing all and sundry on the need for strict censorship of the news of military movements, was considerably put out by finding detailed descriptions of the landing of the American troops, including names of units and numbers of men, in the British and French newspapers next morning.

He was further disturbed by his inspection of the port facilities at St. Nazaire. Though they were reputed to be among the best in Europe, Pershing found the docks archaic. There was no warehouse space. Each freightcar shunting out from the loading area had to be turned by hand on a turntable. Neither the longshoremen nor the railroad workers nor the port officials showed the least intention of giving up their leisurely ways. Frenchmen just would not be hurried. American officers handling cargo were in despair. "All of us" wrote Pershing, philosophically, "were destined to experience many discouragements before the end of the war, in our efforts to improve conditions, both here and elsewhere."

He set the marines to helping a detail of Negro stevedores handle cargo. Somehow the railroads were put in motion. By the time the distractions and celebrations of the Fourth of July interrupted the labors of his staff at Paris headquarters, the *quais* of the old port of St. Nazaire were humming with unaccustomed activity and something like twelve thousand troops were on their way in French boxcars (forty men eight horses) to a training area at Gondrecourt in the bleak Burgundian hills north of Chaumont. The smartestlooking detachment that could be found was routed through Paris to be shown to the Parisians on Independence Day.

Although the battalion chosen from the 16th Infantry contained a good many raw recruits, the tall khakiclad Americans in their broadbrimmed campaign hats made a brave show when they paraded through the Court of Honor at the Invalides between ranks of helmeted French troops in horizon blue. General Pershing made a fine appearance. ". . . the shouts outside and the stirring of the crowd told that the American was approaching," Harbord wrote in his diary, "and in came Pershing followed by a single aide. He was cheered to the echo. It is too early to say what the General will do in the war . . . But whatever the future holds for him, General Pershing certainly looks his part since he came here. He is a fine figure of a man: carries himself well, holds himself on every occasion with proper dignity; is easy in manner, knows how to enter a crowded room, and is fast developing into a world figure. He has captured the fickle Paris crowd."

The tall American general with his sharp cleanshaven chin strode along the ranks of men at "present arms" beside dumpy bearded little Poincaré in his frock coat and tricolor sash, who had to waddle to keep up with him. Orders rang hoarse. Rifle butts clanged on the flagstones. There were presentations of battleflags. The bands played.

"It was a tremendously moving scene," Harbord noted when he returned to his quarters that night. "Perhaps twice in her history foreign troops have entered that old Cour d'Honneur; once in 1815 after Waterloo; again after Sedan in 1870, and violated that inner shrine of French history; but never before has an ally with armed men violated that holy of French holies. It certainly meant much for France, much for Germany, and I believe a new era for America: and no American could look on it without a thrill and the tears starting to his eyes."

After the ceremony at the Invalides the Americans in columns of fours marched three miles across Paris to Lafayette's tomb in the Picpus cemetery. They marched in a storm of flowers. "Girls, women, men crowded into the street, linked arms with the flank men of the fours and swept on down the avenue in step with American music. The roar of applause rose and never died away."

A luncheon followed at the American Chamber of Commerce; and a reception at the Embassy (privately known to Major Harbord and his friends as "the house of the stuffed shirt"); and a stately dinner of interminable courses with their appropriate wines, presided over by General Foch at Armenonville in the Bois de Boulogne. Speeches, speeches, speeches.

It was a wonder to the men on Pershing's staff that the chief could get any work done at all. When his time wasn't taken up with military festivities or conferring with French generals, groups of freshly arrived Americans pre-empted his officehours. "Almost every day some different American mission turns up," wrote Harbord bitterly. "Apparently there is no one who applies to the powers who is not sent over, unless he be a soldier wishing to join an expedition."

Paris in its time of crisis was more than ever the center of Europe's ancient civilization. In spite of wartime restrictions life there held great fascinations. Americans swarmed about the city like flies about a ciderpress.

All had good causes. There were groups from the Red Cross eager to combat the French war depression by deluging the soldiers' families with American charity. A committee from the Y.M.C.A. was out to protect the morals of the American boys in khaki. There were railroadmen come to tell the French how to run their railroads, lumbermen to tell them how to cut their forests, commissions of chemists attempting to standardize weights and measures, engineers with plans for rebuilding the French ports.

The commission which had to be handled with the greatest care was the board of officers Baker sent over from the War Department to help Pershing plan the war. He solved that problem by taking them over to the rue Constantine and putting them to work with his staff.

By July 6 Pershing's staff and the War Department board had reached certain conclusions. Pershing cabled Washington that day: "Plans should contemplate sending over at least 1,000,000 men by next May."

Estimates kept rising. Five days later a joint session of his staff and War Department board adopted what became known as the General Organization Project. This was forwarded to Washington accompanied by a preliminary statement by the Commander in Chief:

"It is evident that a force of about 1,000,000 is the smallest unit which in modern war will be a complete well-balanced and independent fighting organization. However, it must be equally clear that the adoption of this size force as a basis of study should not be construed as the maximum force which will be needed in France. It is taken as the force which may be expected to reach France in time for an offensive in 1918, and as a unit and basis for organization. Plans for the future should be based, especially in reference to the manufacture etc. of artillery, aviation, and other material, on three times this force—i.e. at least 3,000,000 men."

Weekending with Sir Douglas

Pershing and his staff were so busy working on plans for the future and getting acquainted with the French that it was late in July before they could accept the British invitation to visit the general headquarters of their expeditionary force. Pershing and Harbord drove out from Paris, through beautiful rolling country, along roads bordered by great trees, to the walled town of Montreuil in the Pas de Calais which was the administrative center for the British. They were much impressed by the complicated hive of headquarters organization. In every office they found a general. The size and blondness of the British generals struck Harbord. Pershing who stalked like a giant among the stumpy French found himself a small man beside them. Poor Harbord still only a lieutenant colonel, although Chief of Staff, felt himself thoroughly outranked.

The British adjutant general turned out to be an acquaintance of General Pershing's from the Russo-Japanese War, when they had both been among the group of foreign observers with General Kuroki's staff who had such an interesting time watching Japanese operations in Manchuria. After a full day studying the workings of the G.H.Q. and a remarkably good lunch at the mansion where this General Fowke had his mess, they drove to Blendecques. There in a stately pile, Sir Douglas Haig had his quarters throughout the war.

"It was almost dusk," wrote Pershing, "when we arrived at an old châ-teau, halfhidden in a magnificent grove of chestnut trees." They found the Commander in Chief a remarkably handsome man, perfectly accou-tered, almost the painted model of a wooden soldier, with his regular features, his keen gray eyes, his carefully clipped mustache. His greeting to the Americans was surprisingly cordial. His staff made them at home in the château.

Haig seems to have been taken with Pershing. "I was much struck with his quiet gentlemanly bearing—so unusual for an American," he wrote in his diary. "Most anxious to learn, and fully realizes the greatness of the task before him. He has already begun to realize that the French are a broken reed."

Haig was still smarting at the way Lloyd George had bullied him into taking a subordinate position to Nivelle during the preparations for Ni-velle's great fiasco.

At dinner the talk was mostly about guns and the difficulty of keeping them supplied with ammunition. The British averaged a piece of artillery to every twentyfive yards of front and still the Germans outgunned them. Haig spoke disparagingly of Nivelle's plan. He had felt from the begin-ning it was no go. "His remarks," noted Pershing, "entirely confirmed the belief I had long since held that real teamwork between the two armies was almost totally absent."

After dinner they drank coffee on the lawn under the trees. Pershing noted that nothing disturbed the quiet of the place save the sound of distant guns "wafted in from the front by the evening breeze." Harbord, whom Haig described as "a kindly soft looking fellow with the face of a punchinello," noted that the guns sounded to him like an artillery battery rumbling across a high bridge, punctuated by explosions of blasting in a quarry.

The British Commander in Chief, for all his aplomb, must have sat lis-tening to their roar with a certain trepidation. The sound meant that the preliminary bombardment had already started for the great offensive he was planning, to offset the French disasters and to roll the Germans back from the Channel coast. He was already unpopular with the politicians in Lloyd George's cabinet. His reputation hung on the success of this of-fensive. When the generals retired to their respective quarters at eleven the artillery was still pounding the night sky.

Pershing noted that the theory of winning by attrition, with isolated attacks on various fronts, "which was evidently the idea of the British general staff," did not appeal to him. "Moreover their army could not afford the losses in view of the shortage of men which they themselves admitted."

On Sunday while General Haig was attending the Church of Scotland service, listening devoutly to the Reverend George Duncan preaching to the text out of St. Paul "By hope are we saved," the Americans were visiting the Royal Flying Corps, and discovering how little they knew about military aviation. Major General Trenchard, now fortyfive, who admitted that he had only been flying for five years, was in command. He carried Pershing and Harbord off their feet with his cheery enthusiasm as he showed them around the repair shops and salvage shops, and the rooms where watchmakers were adjusting flight chronometers, or where tailors were cutting linen for wing coverings, or where wireless specialists were tinkering with their machines. The British were working on the problem of supplying oxygen to their pilots. Their ceiling was already twentyfive thousand feet.

"We went to the squadron airdrome where dozens of the planes are stabled," wrote Harbord, "and famous pilots were all about us, slight, modest, handsome English boys nearly all of them . . . Many were working around their machines painting devices on them etc., hovering over them as one might rub off a much prized race horse." A flier took his plane up to show General Pershing how he could loop the loop and spin down in a nose dive. "Scarcely anything during this visit impressed me more with our unpreparedness," noted Pershing.

That night they dined again with Sir Douglas at his château in the company of the Reverend George Duncan, the Archbishop of York, a Bishop Gwynne, and the Imperial Chief of Staff, Sir William Robertson, another Scot who was somewhat of a marvel in the British Army because he'd started life as a stable boy and worked his way up from the ranks.

Neither Pershing nor Harbord, in their accounts of the weekend, remarked on a certain tenseness that must have been in the air due to the strain of great decisions pending. They may have heard a few remarks in conclusion of an earlier conversation between Sir Douglas and the Archbishop on the need for amalgamation of the various churches in the United Kingdom. Sir Douglas had suggested a great Imperial Church. He believed Church and State would have to unite "and hold together against those forces of revolution which threaten to destroy the State." But of the indecision in the British cabinet they heard not a word.

Though the Americans got no inkling of it, Robertson, on his way to an interallied military conference, was bringing Haig the formal though reluctant approval by Lloyd George's cabinet of the offensive for which he had already started the artillery preparation.

The terrible butcher's bill at Arras had alarmed Lloyd George, who was, furthermore, trying to get together forces to stiffen the Italian front. In spite of the Italian General Cadorna's successes against the Austrians he suspected things might go wrong there at any moment. The delay in obtaining approval, for what he considered his most important operation of the war, exasperated Haig. Only in his private diary did he express his feelings.

"After dinner we discussed the situation"—Haig and Robertson—"he agreed with me as to the danger of sending forces to Italy. I urged him to be firmer and play the man; and if need be resign should Lloyd George persist in ordering troops to Italy against the advice of the General Staff. I also spoke strongly on the absurdity of the Government giving its approval now to operations after a stiff artillery fight had been going on for three weeks . . . I requested to be told whether I had the full support of the Government or not."

The next morning, after one of the buffet style breakfasts they were becoming accustomed to with their British friends, the Americans drove, along roads encumbered with convoys of trucks moving supplies up for the coming offensive, to the Flanders front. Airplanes were busy overhead keeping German reconnaissance out of the sky. The roar and grinding of trucks never stopped, but it was occasionally blotted out by the thunder of nearby batteries of great naval guns.

Flanders was in a rare spell of dry weather. Vehicles moved under a pall of chalky dust. Faces, uniforms, guns, trucks were coated with it. Dust filled men's eyes, caked their lips. "Belgium," wrote Harbord, "for we were in that unfortunate kingdom, looked badly and tasted worse."

At Fifth Army headquarters they were greeted with enthusiasm. The Fifth Army, under General Gough, was cast for a leading role in the coming show. The Americans were shown, with some pride, a large scale model in high relief of the terrain to be captured in the first three days. From photographs taken from airplanes the enemy's entrenchments had been reconstructed. The scale was large enough so that men could walk around in them. Beyond some indication of the shattered buildings of Ypres, and its canal that had to be crossed on treacherous bridges, were the German lines bending back to Messines, on their flank, which the British had captured that June.

The British artillery had already pounded the trenches along the swampy Steenbeeke River to dust, but beyond were the heights, merely comparative in that flat land, from which the Germans dominated this Ypres salient so desperately held at such bloody cost by the British since the first weeks of the war. On the heights were the remnants of the villages of Gheluvelt and Passchendaele. From Passchendaele the railroad ran due north to Bruges, where the submarines nested in protected pens, and to the Channel ports which were the campaign's objective.

It was a most interesting morning for the American officers. When they lunched with General Gough at his headquarters they found him in good spirits and "true to his Irish blood, most hospitable, jolly and friendly." During lunch he entertained his guests with the skirling of bagpipes. All through the meal an Irish band, with pipes and drum, walked back and forth in front of the house playing "The Campbells Are Coming," "The Harp that Once through Tara's Halls" and other martial airs.

General Pershing, who had a weakness for dancing, admitted in his diary that the marches were so stirring they made him want to stir his dogs in a jig or a clog. After lunch the Americans motored back towards Paris. They were glutted with impressions. "And we have a firm respect for the British Army," Harbord jotted in his notes.

Somewhere in France

On September 1 Pershing moved his G.H.Q. to a French army barracks in Chaumont. Chaumont was a provincial town situated at the headwaters of the Marne, on the boundary between the ancient dukedoms of Champagne and Lorraine. It was conveniently placed on the rail line from Troyes to Nancy behind the St. Mihiel salient where the general's hopes were fixed for a breakthrough in the summer to come. Since their positions there had stabilized during the early months of the war neither the French nor the Germans had shown much interest in the Lorraine front that stretched from St. Mihiel to the Swiss border. The French generals picked it as the sector where the zany Americans could do the least harm.

Pershing at once instituted such elaborate precautions to keep the whereabouts of the American headquarters a secret that, while the doings at Chaumont were common knowledge in France and Germany, the only identification vouchsafed to the American public was "somewhere in France."

Establishing his own headquarters was an important step in Pershing's struggle to keep his American Army free from interference by the French. He had often envied friends who made themselves successful careers in business; here was his opportunity to set up an army headquarters according to the principles of modern business efficiency. Chaumont, for all the uniforms and the saluting and the "military courtesy," observed with the more punctilio because officers and men were mostly new to the business, became a little fragment of the Chicago Loop or of downtown New York in the green fields of France. British and French liaison groups reported with delighted surprise on the New World atmosphere as they would report on one of Buffalo Bill's Wild West Shows. Before the first week had gone by the general was expressing his satisfaction by an entry in his diary: "Surroundings give relief after depression of Paris."

The August Attack

While the noncoms and junior officers of the headquarters detachment sweated and strained, during the weeks before the move to Chaumont, to Americanize the bleak buildings, Pershing was Pétain's guest for what became known as the Third Battle of Verdun. Along with regular leaves, better service from the field kitchens and increased rations of wine and grog, Pétain had promised, in his campaign to soothe the mutinous feelings of his troops, successful offensives on a limited scale which would not be too costly in lives. To show what he could do, he was planning to recapture two hills on the west bank of the Meuse that had been dealing out death and destruction to the French positions to the left of Verdun ever since the Germans captured them in their spring offensive the year before.

General Pershing duly reported to the headquarters of the French commander in chief at Compiègne and was taken aboard Pétain's own private train. Next morning they found themselves on a siding at Gondrecourt, where the doughboys were being trained for combat in the open with bayonet and rifle. Jointly they reviewed the French infantry division, detailed to help train the green Americans, as a reward for severe losses and good conduct in the lines. Pershing was impressed by the solemn ceremony of decorating various officers and men for gallantry and the smart style the ranks showed when the men marched past the generals to the heartening strains of "Sambre et Meuse."

Next they visited the American billets, in barns and farmyards and haymows and open fields, where groups were practicing with hand grenades and shooting the French automatic rifle. Pétain questioned the men about their quarters, and showed interest in the American cuisine. It was traditional for a French general to taste the soup when he visited a mess.

As they travelled from gray village to gray village with cobbled courts and manure piles under the windows, Pershing noted with some envy the reception which the sparse civilian population that remained gave Pétain. Strings of flags and green boughs arched the streets. Occasionally Monsieur le Maire appeared in his tricolor scarf. Little girls in pigtails advanced with bouquets. In this Germanic region most of them were blonde. Paternally the general would press his broad grizzly mustache against each rosy cheek. He was the hero of Verdun.

They lunched at Souilly on the Verdun road at the headquarters of the French Second Army. There, over the brandy and cigars, General Guillaumat, who was in charge, had his chief of staff describe to Pershing in detail the plan of the offensive to be conducted against the heights of Mort Homme and Hill 304 by twelve divisions on a fifteenmile front that straddled the Meuse. Already like distant surf, the pounding of the guns could be heard from beyond the hills to the northward.

For four days guns of all calibers had been pouring steel and lyddite into the German trenches. Proportionately to the area, Pershing was told, more shells were fired than in any engagement in the war. The American general figured the cost of the preliminary barrage at seventyfive million dollars.

While waiting for the attack to develop, Pershing, whose mind ran on the problem of supplying the two thousand guns and the hundred and eighty thousand men involved in the operation, had himself driven back to the sorting station at St. Dizier, where rations, clothing, construction supplies, fuel and arms and ammunition were stored in bulk in great warehouses, to be shipped out in daily trainloads consigned to the various divisions. Convoys of trucks took the supplies from the railheads as near to the front as they dared venture. From there supplies were pushed on small carts, or on mule or donkeyback to the deep dugouts near the command posts from which they were distributed into the trenches.

Less interesting to Pershing were the civilities he had to exchange with Monsieur Paul Painlevé, the Minister of War, and with Monsieur Albert Thomas, a socialist orator whom Pétain told him was just back from fraternizing with the revolutionists in Petrograd. Thomas was Minister of Munitions. The politicians had come out from Paris to see the show. The two generals agreed that the less civilians poked their noses into the warzone the better. Pétain could clothe himself with an icy chill when he talked to politicians.

After lunch the generals drove out the Voie Sacrée, the single road which, along with a single line of narrow gauge railway known as *le Meusien,* supplied the Verdun salient during the ferocious fighting of the preceding spring, to the command post of the XVI Corps, on high ground overlooking the valley of the Meuse. Pershing spent one of the most interesting afternoons of his life watching through the glasses the wavering lines of French advancing over the shellpocked hills. The slopes were gouged with entrenchments and churned by shellfragments until they had a puttycolored powdery look as one might imagine the surface of the moon. Groups of tiny moving specks advancing with erratic jerky motion from shellhole to shellhole were pointed out as elements of the Foreign Legion, which Pershing remembered having read of in his youth in Ouida's *Under Two Flags.* As the sun was at their back visibility was perfect from the command post. It was a rare privilege, especially in such a war as this, to have a panoramic view of a battlefield.

Things were going well. The French officers were in high spirits.

A chance encounter added to the pleasure of the afternoon. Major General Corvisart, who was running that particular part of the show, turned out to be another old acquaintance of Pershing's from the group of young

European officers who tagged along after General Kuroki during the Russo-Japanese War. They went over the names of the lighthearted crowd they had travelled with in Manchuria. Pershing had seen General Fowke a few days before. Sir Ian Hamilton was another mutual friend: what a mess he'd made at Gallipoli. Jolly Captain Hoffmann was earning a name for himself now that he was Ludendorff's successor as German chief of staff on the Russian front. What had happened to Major von Etzel? General Corvisart burst out laughing and pointed into the valley before them. "I have just beaten him today. He is commanding a division opposite me."

The Attack Was a Success

The attack, the French told Pershing, was a complete success. They described the losses as minimal. Their troops had already overrun most of Mort Homme. Hill 304 was proving a tough nut, but the German grip on it was loosening.

Driving away from the front to board Monsieur Painlevé's train back to Paris, Pershing was shown gray columns of captured Germans moving to the rear. The wornout men shuffling through the mud gave off a sour smell. The enemy's smell. Four thousand he was told. By the time he read the communiqués the number had mounted to ten.

General Pétain was in a rarely expansive mood. He was pleased by Pershing's frank marvelling at the enormous convoys of trucks, and at the numbers of men engaged in all kinds of supply behind the lines. Pétain was pointing out with pride the work he had done on the road, and boasting of the courage of his troops, and of the enormous losses they suffered during the fighting at Verdun the year before. He rubbed his hands over the lightness of the casualty lists so far reported in today's operation. He fell to his favorite sport of flaying the politicians and congratulated Pershing on being far enough away from home to be out of their reach.

As they got on more familiar ground Pétain asked Pershing how many times he'd sat for his portrait. The American modestly admitted that a man named Jonah had just done one for *L'Illustration*. "Don't let them publish it!" cried Pétain. "Every officer whose portrait by Jonah has appeared has been relieved of his command."

General Pershing in his *My Experiences in the World War* disclaimed any superstitious feelings: "Quite the contrary, but I immediately forbade the publication of the portrait."

The men parted on very good terms. Pershing came away full of admiration for Pétain's careful planning and for his good work in stimulating the morale of his troops. What he'd seen of the complicated coordination needed to supply divisions in the front line steadied his conviction that communications and shipping were the first thing to work for before starting to lay the plans for an American offensive. He must impress that on the minds of the staff officers he was to confer with in Paris in the morning.

While General Pershing and the liaison officers and the ministers and their attachés trundled towards Paris getting what sleep they could in the jiggly blue light of their compartments, on the slopes of Hill 304 and at the crest of Mort Homme, from Avocourt Wood to Bezonvaux on the east bank of the Meuse, the fighting continued.

As usual it was the German counterattack that caused the casualty list to mount.

The heavy artillery went on shattering men's eardrums. There was the sharp slamming of seventyfives. Machineguns kept up their ratatatat. Minenwerfers annihilated the night with their crunching roar; or, in some moment of comparative silence, when the storm beat far away, men crouching in the muck in the lee of some pile of stones, with their fingers on the triggers of their rifles, would hear from the trenches behind them the sound of the klaxon that warned of a gas attack.

The lucky ones who had managed to crawl into a dugout or deep shell-hole would huddle in the corners trying to catch a little sleep while their faces seemed to turn to slime under the sleazy gasmasks.

Dawn would bring a certain calm. Stretcherbearers would start gingerly dragging the wounded into dressing stations. In deep shelters doctors would do their best with gauze and splints and blessed morphine as long as it held out. Men, moaning through their gasmasks on the stretchers, would be inched up the uneven stairways and shoved into some motor ambulance backed up to the entrance; and the long jouncing journey over washboard roads, here and there gouged into pits by high explosives, would start—past wrecked guns and broken equipment drowned in mud, and dead men lying in quaint attitudes where they had fallen. When higher ground was reached the gasmasks would be pulled off to make it easier to vomit, and men who had lived through the night would breathe the morning air and look back down at the gasinfested mist, greenish like spewed up bile, in the hollow ruins below.

Going would be smoother on the main roads to the rear, past the bloated bodies of mules killed days before, and carcasses of wrecked trucks dragged out of the way. Smartly dressed military police would be handling the traffic. Ambulances with their cargo of groans and bloody bandages would line up to let by fresh halfdrunk detachments with doom on their faces, shambling in as replacements, or strings of the invaluable seventyfives.

Unloaded from the ambulance outside the field hospital the wounded would look around, with the big eyes of suddenly awakened children, at green leaves and undestroyed houses, and perhaps at cabbages growing in a prettily tilled field. The first duty of the admitting officer was to sort out the cases that could be helped from the hopeless bellywounds and the too drastic amputations and the too abundant hemorrhages. The stretchers of the men too far gone to take up the surgeons' time would be laid out in the shade. Some orderly would try to make them comfortable with such narcotics as were available, or at least, if a man still had breath in his lungs and a mouth to smoke with, light a cigarette and place it between his lips.

General von Hutier's Experiment

The same September 1 that Pershing set up shop in the old army barracks at Chaumont, the Kaiser's generals tried out a novel method of attack on the Russian lines in front of Riga on the Baltic. In spite of their conquest of the broad middle band of Europe through the Danube Valley to the Black Sea, Germany was feeling the pinch of the British blockade. Food was short. Manpower was short. Steel and chemicals for munitions were short. The enormous losses on the western front were beginning to tell. Some style of attack more economical in men and munitions than the mass offensives of the past year had to be invented.

Credit for working up a new plan went to General von Hutier who commanded the troops facing the Russians on the east Prussian border. Von Hutier seems to have studied with some care Nivelle's success at Fort Douaumont and his failure on the Aisne. Though the textbooks extolled it as the most important element in warfare the principle of surprise had been neglected by both sides on the Western Front. Von Hutier began to prepare for surprise attack on the Russian lines in front of Riga. He moved his troops only at night and took the greatest care that his concentrations should be kept secret from the enemy. He was planning to attack a limited section of the lines with overwhelming force, after a short but extremely violent artillery bombardment, and then to exploit the breakthrough by pouring trained divisions into the enemy's rear.

While he drilled his troops in the new tactics, the High Command kept him waiting for the opportune moment when disorganization in Russia should reach its maximum. They did not want to shock the Russians into unity by premature action.

Mission to Petrograd

Wilson's administration in Washington had as great hopes of the Russian revolution as did the German general staff, but where the Germans saw disintegration and ruin by which they expected mightily to profit, the Americans saw the rise of a sister democracy in the image of their own. The United States was the first country to recognize the Provisional Government. Every American leader from T.R. and Taft to Gompers and Debs cheered the abdication of the Czar Nicholas. Ink and oratory were lavished on the new democracy. To Woodrow Wilson, and his propaganda mouthpiece, George Creel, it was a relief to be able to conduct the war "to make the world safe for democracy" without having to explain away their alliance with the blackest autocracy in Europe.

It wasn't long before the President began to feel some misgivings. Instead of waging the war for democracy with renewed vigor the liberated Russians seemed to be calling for peace at any price. His ambassador in Petrograd was an agreeable old gentleman in whose judgement Wilson felt little confidence. Early in May he decided he must send a mission of his own, headed by some eminent figure.

McAdoo and Lansing, who were trying to get bipartisan support for the war effort, suggested Elihu Root as the eminent figure. Woodrow Wilson for years had considered Senator Root a hidebound reactionary, but his name was somewhat sweetened by a speech he made soon after the declaration of war wholeheartedly backing up the Administration. Mr. Root, who was seventyone, confided in his wife that the last thing in the world he wanted to do was travel ten thousand miles to Petrograd; but that, at a moment when young men were being asked to risk their lives, he felt he could not refuse any service required of him.

Elihu Root was no more ignorant of Russia than anybody else. No man of any political prominence could be found who spoke the language. The few men Lansing was able to consult who had visited the country felt that, with encouragement from the United States and a sizeable loan, the Russians would develop in due time into a proper democracy.

The President's desk was piled so high with pressing problems he could not give the Russian situation much thought. He did considerable worrying about Socialist representation on the commission. Socialistic agitators were said to be swaying the Russian masses, so he decided that an American Socialist must be sent along to talk to them in their own language. The trouble was that most of the men suggested turned out to be unabashed pacifists. This, in the present mood of the Administration, was equivalent to being pro-German. After a good deal of correspondence, a wellmeaning magazine writer named Charles Edward Russell, who had taken the Woodrow Wilson line in the split which destroyed the American Socialist Party at its spring convention, was invited to go along.

Secretary Baker, possibly feeling that the Chief of Staff's knowledge of the Indian sign languages would be more useful in Russia than it was proving to be in the War Department, was quite willing to relinquish the services of General Hugh Scott. There was added an admiral; Cyrus Mc-

Cormick, the grandson of the inventor, whose International Harvester Company was reputed to be popular in the Russian wheatbelt; a vice president of the A.F. of L., a banker, and an inspirational expert from the Young Men's Christian Association.

These gentlemen received a formal sendoff from the White House and embarked on a special train to Seattle. Mrs. Root saw that two hundred gallons of Poland Water, two cases of Haig & Haig and two hundred and fifty of his favorite cigars packed in a tin box were included in the senator's baggage, along with some provision of the gargle he used for his sore throats.

To prepare their way Secretary Lansing cabled Ambassador Francis to assure the Provisional Government that: ". . . the High Commissioners of the United States will present themselves in the confident hope that the Russian Government and people will realize how sincerely the United States hopes for their welfare and desires to share with them in their future endeavours to bring victory to the cause of democracy and human liberty."

After the train crossed the Missouri River General Scott, who hated desk work at the War Department, was in his element. He listened eagerly as a boy to the wise adages on politics and statesmanship that fell from the lips of Senator Root; and, as the train puffed up the steep grades in the valley of the Yellowstone River, pointed out with shining eyes his old campsites during the Indian wars.

At Seattle, after an ovation from the local patriotic organizations, they put to sea on the old cruiser *Buffalo* which had been hastily converted into a troop transport. The skipper steered the great circle course so religiously that the *Buffalo* nearly capsized in the rough waters north of the Aleutians and Mr. Root was thrown out of his bunk. General Scott, who was suffering from seasickness, only clung to his with the greatest difficulty. Finally, after a great detour to avoid an unexpected iceflow off Kamchatka, the *Buffalo* staggered into the Sea of Japan and, after a fruitless search for a pilot, steamed unannounced into the harbor of Vladivostok.

As no port authorities came out to greet them, the commission went ashore in the *Buffalo's* whaleboat and landed with some difficulty on a cobbly beach. There they were met by a gang of rumlooking fellows who claimed to be the port's revolutionary committee. It was all the commission's two interpreters could do to convince them that the Americans should be allowed to land. Eventually a Russian general of the old regime appeared and explained that these were eminent guests of the Russian people and that the Czar's own imperial train was waiting to carry them to Petrograd.

They spent just enough time in Vladivostok to note the universal indecision and disintegration that paralyzed all business. Quantities of war material, paid for out of American loans, was piled up on the docks. There were hundreds of locomotives waiting for mechanics to put them in commission and eight thousand automobiles still in their original crates.

The commissioners spent ten days on the Trans-Siberian Railroad.

General Scott marvelled at the great quantities of waterfowl he saw and wished for a bird dog and shotgun. He enjoyed trying to communicate with the various types of aborigines that crowded the platforms during the long waits in distant stations. He had a knack with primitive peoples. "I'm a firm believer in democracy," said Mr. Root after walking around one village, "but I don't like filth."

It was the middle of June before they reached Petrograd. They were welcomed politely by members of the Provisional Government. Senator Root and General Scott were housed in Catherine the Great's state apartments in the Winter Palace.

Crowds everywhere, soldiers, sailors, workers. No work going on. Wild inflation of the currency. Food getting scarce but no violence. Speeches. "There is no governing power but moral suasion," Root wrote his wife, "and the entire people seem talking at once."

Senator Root and the rest of them added to the flow of oratory in a forlorn effort to counter the pacifist propaganda, spread, so they claimed, by thousands of German agents. Among other material, the Germans were distributing cartoons out of the Hearst press that ridiculed Senator Root himself as an old mossback.

Meanwhile General Scott was taken on an inspection tour of military installations. He was horrified by what he saw. The barracks of even the crack regiments of the imperial guard were rough and dirty. The men had no bedding but the single blanket they carried as part of their equipment. Discipline was gone. At the Putilov arms works the manager who was showing Scott around was not allowed into a section of the plant barricaded off for a mass meeting.

General Scott went as far as Tarnopol in Galicia to view the offensive which Kerensky, the loquacious young Socialist lawyer now in complete control of the Provisional Government, ordered Brusilov to attempt, largely to impress the American mission. Scott stumbled around through the wheatfields deafened by the heavy artillery and saw thousands of Austrian prisoners being herded to the rear. The offensive he was told was a success.

Back in Petrograd he noted that the disorganization of the city was worse. Mr. Root was complaining that he couldn't get a response from Washington to his plea for a hundred thousand dollars to set up an American propaganda agency. Scott found the members of the mission bubbling with enthusiasm for young Kerensky's energy and magnetism. "Too radically inclined to suit me" was the general's comment.

Petrograd was being organized but not according to the hopes of the American Mission. They learned that Lenin and Trotsky, two German agents, as they were described, were influencing the soldiers of a machinegun regiment and the workers of the Putilov plant. Already they were said to control most of the workingclass quarters of Petrograd. Senator Root's advice to Kerensky was to arrest Lenin immediately. "Any government would have arrested, tried, imprisoned and executed him," he complained in a letter home. General Scott agreed. Kerensky would have been very glad to arrest Comrade Lenin but he couldn't get his hands on him.

The American Mission did not wait to see the outcome of the Brusilov offensive. They all piled back into the Czar's special train and were trundled across Siberia to Vladivostok again. The last news they had was that Brusilov had advanced forty miles towards Lemberg and that Lenin's attempted insurrection—the July days of the Russian revolutionary legend—had failed. By early August they were back in Washington telling President Wilson and the State Department that Kerensky was the man who would not only promote democracy in Russia, but continue to fight the Germans.

Lansing was unconvinced. "I am astounded at their optimism," he wrote in his neatly kept diary on August 8. "When I expressed doubts as to Kerensky's personal force and ability to carry through his plans in view of the strong opposition developing against him, they assured me everything would come out all right . . . and that Russia would continue the war. I presume they know more about it than I do, and yet in spite of what they say I am very skeptical about Kerensky."

Exit Kerensky

The Eastern experts on the German general staff, meanwhile, were biding their time. By the end of July Brusilov's army was buckling under clever German counterattacks. These, combined with lack of supply from the rear, produced a sudden and complete collapse. Whole divisions turned around and started for home. The Galician front was no longer defended.

The moment had come to let von Hutier try out his experiment in front of Riga. After a three hour bombardment his army advanced in a spearhead behind a rolling barrage, crossed the Dvina River on pontoons and broke through the strong Russian positions on the eastern shore.

By September 3 the Germans had captured the city of Riga. From Riga they sent small expeditions to occupy some of the Baltic islands as a method of increasing the confusion among the Russians. They had no intention of risking large forces in an expedition into Russia proper. The aim of von Hutier's experiment was to bring down Kerensky's pro-Allied government. In that aim it was completely successful. Within two months the Bolsheviks had established the Soviet power.

Chapter 15

TRAINING and supply were General Pershing's chief preoccupation during the summer and fall of 1917. "It was one thing," he wrote in his *Experiences,* "to call one or two million men to the colors, and quite another thing to transform them into an organized instructed army capable of meeting and holding its own in battle against the best trained force in Europe with three years of actual war experience to its credit."

At home General Wood had already laid down a preliminary system of training. Sixteen cantonments each to accommodate approximately fortyeight thousand men were being planned by the War Department for the instruction of the national draft army, and an equal number of camps under canvas for the reinforced National Guard.

In France, Pershing's immediate problem was to get his 1st Division in fighting trim. Next, a system of instruction had to be set up for the reinforcements to be landed in France during the summer by the navy's transport service, which under Admiral Gleaves had so successfully brought the first contingent across the Atlantic without loss.

Schoolteacher Pershing

Pershing started as a schoolteacher. He taught military subjects at the University of Nebraska and at West Point. He had confidence in the school method of teaching. Even before he moved his headquarters away from the beguilements of Parisian life, he set up a special section of his staff to supervise army schools. He and Harbord were impressed when they visited the British armies by their methods of instruction in trench warfare. One of the fruits of Pershing's weekend at Blendecques was that Haig assigned to him a lieutenant general, and a group of officers for one reason or another incapacitated for frontline service, to help train his raw Yanks. Pétain did the same. In the end Pershing had to train his own teachers.

The trouble with the British and French instructors from the American general's point of view was that their minds were bogged in trench warfare. "Therefore in large measure the fundamentals so thoroughly taught at West Point for a century were more or less neglected . . . It was my opinion," he continued, "that victory could not be won by the costly process of attrition, but it must be won by driving the enemy out in the open and engaging him in a war of movement."

Drive the squareheads out of their trenches and knock 'em off with rifles, was his plan. He wanted his men trained in marksmanship, rapid riflefire, the use of the bayonet, and oldfashioned field tactics. He claimed that handgrenades, machineguns, mortars, and trench artillery were all right for specific purposes, but he clung passionately to the dogma that the welltrained infantryman with rifle and bayonet would eventually emerge as master of the field.

Before he could train an army he had to train his staff officers. He opened a General Staff College with a three months course in the old walled town of Langres a little south of Chaumont. Separate from that, he established a network of schools for corps, divisional and regimental staffs, for unit commanders, for noncoms, for recruits and replacements, for specialists in everything from bridgebuilding to the warehousing of o.d. uniforms. Most important in the early months were the schools for training teachers to teach in all these schools.

The Problem of Supply

While the troops were being trained arrangements had to be made for their supply. As soon as Pershing had dispatched his General Organization Project to Washington he set his staff to work to plan a line of communications to the American ports. Almost every day he cabled for fresh personnel. He needed railroadmen to run and recondition the worn-out railroads the French were placing at his disposal, canalboat men to operate the canals, trucking experts to handle shipment by road, carpenters, muleskinners, warehousemen, stevedores.

Most of his supply would have to come from America. Everything depended on shipping. Food and shells and powder and small arms ammunition produced in the States had to be shipped across the Atlantic. The British were proving closefisted about letting go any ships of their own. Not enough ships were being built to make up for the U-boat sinkings. In Washington a Shipping Board had been established and enormous new shipyards were in the blueprint stage. No new ships could be expected until the following year. There was a list of materials as long as your arm that Pershing needed right away.

To ease the strain on shipping he decided to set up a purchasing agency in France. To head it he picked Charles G. Dawes, a friend of many years standing whom he'd helped procure a commission in the Engineers. When as a lieutenant he taught military science at the University of

Nebraska he'd known Charley Dawes as a fledgeling lawyer there. With a certain amount of envy he'd watched Dawes, who came of an Ohio family already firmly entrenched in railroad finance and banking, become wealthy and eminent in financial Chicago. Herbert Hoover tried to commandeer Dawes for his Food Administration but Dawes managed to slip through his fingers and to get himself sent overseas. He was hardly established as a major with an engineer regiment from Alabama reconstructing the docks at St. Nazaire when Pershing called him to Paris.

Major Dawes put up at the Ritz and hurried around to Pershing's office. The general said at once he wanted him as General Purchasing Agent. "It's a man's work," wrote Dawes in his diary, "but I am thankful beyond words that it is work that will count for my country in its hour of greatest trial."

To make sure that the record he decided to keep of his trials and achievements with the A.E.F. should not fall into the wrong hands, he trotted across the Place Vendôme to the Morgan Harjes bank and rented a safedeposit box. Whenever he had a spare moment he sat in one of the little rooms they furnished their customers to cut coupons in, to jot down the events of the day.

". . . Dear fellow and loyal friend," he wrote of the general in an access of gratitude. "I hope I do not fail him. We have both passed through the greatest grief which can come to man . . ." He was thinking of the loss of his son Rufus drowned some months before Pershing lost his wife and daughters. These tragedies were a bond between them. His first day in Paris when Pershing and Dawes were being driven to the general's quarters for lunch "there occurred an instance of telepathy which was too much for either of us. Neither of us was saying anything but I was thinking of my lost boy and of John's loss and looking out the window, and he was doing the same thing on the other side of the automobile. We both turned at the same time and each was in tears. All John said was 'Even this war can't keep it out of my mind.'"

Dawes was accustomed to the millionaire's life, but he liked to recall the days when he and John Pershing used to eat fifteen cent lunches together at the lunchcounter of a certain Don Cameron. He was flabbergasted by the Hôtel de Lannes. "As I looked around me I said 'John, when I contrast these barren surroundings with the luxuriousness of our early life in Lincoln, Nebraska, it does seem that a good man has no chance in the world.' To which John meditatively replied, 'Don't it beat hell?'"

The Education of Charles G. Dawes

The first problems Pershing put up to his purchasing agent were lumber and coal. He needed lumber immediately to build cantonments at Chaumont, where his staff was already outgrowing the barracks building they started with. American units were bidding against each other for scarce French supplies. The French were stuffy about cutting their national forests.

Coal was needed to heat the cantonments and offices and for the railroads that were to supply the A.E.F. There was plenty of coal in England, but the British were stuffy about parting with colliers to bring it across the Channel for their American allies. Dawes set his operatives to scouting the Great Lakes for freighters, he requisitioned tramp steamers.

He suggested to the French that American miners might teach them to increase production in their own mines but was told that was impossible; the trade unions would never allow it. The officials shrugged: *"Les syndicats . . ."*

Dawes began to learn that there were subtle shadings to war in Europe. Politicians had connections that crossed the frontiers. Certain places were never bombed. Certain ships were never sunk. In the business world certain tolerances and understandings had grown up between enemy states despite the daily massacre on the front lines.

Warweariness was the prevailing mood. Even the German Reichstag had passed a resolution urging a peace of understanding and the permanent reconciliation of the peoples. The call for a peace without annexations or indemnities, continually broadcast over the wireless by the firebrands of the Petrograd Soviet, re-echoed Woodrow Wilson's old slogan: peace without victory. Socialist visionaries meeting in Stockholm hammered on the theme. The people of Europe were pricking up their ears. In France it wasn't only the army that was mutinous. Alarmists kept whispering that unless sufficient coal could be found for heating in the coming winter the civilian population would rise in revolution.

"Everybody, Germany included, except America, seems 'fed up' as the British say," Dawes put down somewhat dolefully in the privacy of his diary. The men on Pershing's staff seemed to fear their war might be taken away from them before they could show what they could do.

Dawes worked like a beaver. He had set up his office in Paris in early September. By the first week in October he could tell the general with some confidence that coal was on the way. He had agents established in Switzerland and Spain for purchasing a long list of scarce items obtainable in those countries. Sitting in the quiet of Morgan Harjes' one Saturday he found the leisure to note a few general deductions from his experience so far: "When the source of main military supply is so far distant from the point of use, as is the case with the United States and its army in France, the importance of coördination increases in proportion to its difficulty."

The principle that Pershing and his staff were trying to inculcate in the War Department was that the flow of supplies should be managed and controlled from the point of use, which meant the headquarters of the A.E.F. "Priority in shipments, route of shipment (ports of disembarkation), and relative necessity of material should be, barring exceptional emergency, determined here and not in America," wrote Dawes. "If we fail . . . in this war it will be because we do not coördinate quickly enough. Pershing and all of us see this. We are working for it night and day."

Two days later Dawes was able to note that the first of his coal was actually being loaded on a requisitioned ship at an English port.

"The war has resolved itself in a large degree into a freight tonnage situation for the present." His optimism overflowed. While "the mighty work of American preparation," in which he was so happy to have a part, went on, "Great Britain is making a splendid offensive."

The Splendid Offensive

Haig's great offensive, glowingly described as a series of victories in the dispatches of gullible war correspondents schooled by the same General Charteris who invented the story about the German corpse factory —Charteris was Haig's Intelligence officer—was forcing the Germans to concentrate divisions in Flanders, but at the cost of enormous expenditure of munitions and men.

The operation started just a week after Pershing visited the Fifth Army, and was shown the relief map of the terrain to be captured, and lunched to the sound of bagpipes with jolly General Gough. It had been planned for early in the summer, but Lloyd George's opposition, the hesitations of the French and the complications of supply, caused it to be put off from week to week. It was a race with the treacherous Flemish weather. Zero hour came the day the short dry season ended.

Haig's delays gave the German general staff time to organize a defense in depth and to prepare troops fresh from the walkaway on the Russian front for the sharp counterattacks on which they relied so heavily. "I had a certain feeling of satisfaction when this new battle began," von Hindenburg reminisced in his memoirs. ". . . It was with a feeling of absolute longing that we waited for the wet season . . . great stretches of the Flanders flat would then become impassable."

The wet season began the very day of the attack. In spite of the threatening sky Haig ordered his Fifth Army to go over the top anyway. The weeks of bombardment had so pitted the swampy ground in front of Ypres it would have been difficult to negotiate in dry weather. In rain it proved impassable. The tanks bogged down. The German pillboxes proved impregnable. The slight gains made to the north of the city merely brought the British troops into a dangerous salient where they were enfiladed by artillery fire from the higher ground between Passchendaele and Gheluvelt. By noon of the first day it was obvious to everyone except Haig and his staff that the offensive was a failure.

The Commander in Chief, who was making his advanced headquarters in a railway car, went over to visit General Gough. It was raining heavily. "This was a fine day's work," Haig noted in his private journal. "I told Gough to carry out the original plan."

"Heavy rain fell this afternoon and aeroplane observation was impossible," he added later. "The going also became very bad and the ground was much cut up. This has hampered our further progress and robbed us of much of our advantage due to our great success."

The younger officers were doubtful about the quality of this success. After three days of struggling to force men and equipment into machinegun and artillery fire, through mud so deep the wounded often drowned in it, the attack was called off. The Fifth Army was so badly shattered that the attacks on Passchendaele Ridge which followed had to be entrusted to General Plumer's Second Army. The hoped for breakthrough to the Channel ports was no more spoken of at G.H.Q.

Haig reverted to the old step by step methods which were supposed to be wearing down the German will to fight. By the end of August the British and French had lost seventyfour thousand men on the Flanders front with only occasional gains of a few hundred yards. General Charteris reported a hundred thousand German casualties. The British and American press was completely bemused. On August 25 the London *Spectator* in its weekly summary proclaimed, "This has been for the Allies the greatest week of the war."

In spite of what the newspapers printed disillusionment was spreading in England. The wounded men's stories could hardly be said to gibe with the journalists' reports. Hospital trains began to be routed into London late at night so that the stretcher cases could be hustled away to hospitals before they were seen.

When the weather improved in mid September the Australians and New Zealanders advanced nine hundred yards along the Memin Road. Twentytwo thousand casualties. Another victory. When someone inquired where the German prisoners were General Charteris replied, "We are killing the enemy, not capturing him."

A few days later in Polygon Wood on the edge of the Passchendaele Ridge seventeen thousand men were lost with small gains. On October 4, after suffering twentysix thousand casualties, Plumer's army achieved a slippery foothold on the ridge in front of what was left of Passchendaele village. This was the occasion of the entry in Dawes' diary about Haig's splendid offensive. Pershing sent Haig a message congratulating him on this magnificent answer to "weak kneed peace propaganda."

The rain had started again. On October 9 a new attack was attempted. Once more Plumer's army was pinned down in the mud by enfilading

fire from German pillboxes. ALL HAIG'S OBJECTIVES GAINED was
the headline in the New York *Times*. The London *Times* had the British
troops in sight of Bruges.

"G.H.Q. could not capture the Passchendaele Ridge but it was determined to storm Fleet Street and here strategy and tactics were superb,"
was Lloyd George's scornful comment.

By this time it was taking fourteen hours to evacuate a wounded man.
German planes were strafing the bogged British with machineguns. German mustard gas was producing a new type of casualty. Shell shock was
the order of the day. Supplies could only be moved up on duckboards.
Tanks, trucks, mule trains wallowed in slime. Entrenchments filled with
water to the brim. Field guns buried themselves by the force of their
recoil each time they were fired.

Only the rats thrived; bloated rats swam through the muck feeding on
the dead in the flooded trenches.

"Imagine a fertile countryside," wrote Gough in justification, "dotted
every few hundred yards with peasant farms and an occasional hamlet;
water everywhere, for only an intricate system of small drainage canals
relieved the land from the ever-present danger of flooding; a clay soil
which the slightest dampness turned into clinging mud . . . Then imagine
the same countryside battered beaten and torn by a torrent of shell and
explosive . . . a soil shaken and reshaken, fields tossed into new and fantastic shapes, roads blotted out from the landscape, houses and hamlets
pounded into dust so thoroughly that no man could point to where they
had stood . . . and the drainage system utterly and irretrievably destroyed . . . Then came incessant rain (the wettest August for thirty
years). The broken earth became a fluid clay; the little brooks and tiny
canals became formidable obstacles, and every shell hole a dismal pond
. . . Still the guns churned this treacherous slime . . . Every day became
worse. What had once been difficult became impossible."

On October 23 in response to Haig's urgent request that he do something to relieve the German pressure, Pétain had his General Maistre
conduct a small operation against the village of Malmaison a little to the
west of the Chemin des Dames. The attack was made with the help of
the French light tanks on a ten mile front. In spite of a six day preliminary bombardment the Germans were caught by surprise and lost
their last foothold on the Craonne Plateau north of the Aisne. The French
took twelve thousand prisoners and two hundred guns and resisted the
usual violent counterattacks. Following Mort Homme, Malmaison did
more than all Pétain's pleading to restore the morale of the French Army.

November 6 the occupation of Passchendaele Ridge was announced by Haig's headquarters as complete. Lloyd George sent him a telegram of congratulation. The Allied newspapers trumpeted the victory. German morale they said was broken: a German general was reported to have called it a disastrous day for the German Army.

After that the fighting in Flanders subsided in drizzle and sleet. Relieved of their onerous duties coordinating the staff work, generals from headquarters visited the front. Lieutenant General Sir Launcelot Kiggell, Haig's chief of staff, as he looked out over the boggy mess which he was seeing for the first time, is reported to have exclaimed, "Did we really send men to fight in that?"

Return to Open Warfare

The German strategists were so pleased by the success of von Hutier's experiment at Riga that they determined to repeat it. While his armies in Flanders were in their death grapple with the British in the mud around Ypres, von Hindenburg was supervising the formation of a new German-Austrian Army formed to break the stalemate between the Austrians and the Italians in the mountains north of Venice.

Military surprise plus civilian demoralization had been the formula for success in the north. German agents were reporting civilian warweariness and a mutinous spirit among Italian conscripts exasperated by scanty food, and by tales of warprofiteering in the rear, and by the fact that their officers were rarely, if ever, seen in the front line. An army under General Otto von Bulow was readied in the mountains for a sudden push across the valley of the Isonzo.

The Italian Intelligence reported the arrival of German units to the headquarters of their Commander in Chief General Cadorna. General Cadorna was said to have given orders for a defense in depth, but the general in charge of the Italian Second Army was absent from his command and no preparations were made. A serious gap between the defenses of two Italian armies was allowed to remain unfortified. The Germans struck at that gap.

After three hours of intensive shelling of the Italian network of communications and a saturating gas attack, in a dim dawn of mist and rain which was turning to snow in the high mountains, the German spearhead broke through at the village of Caporetto, crossed the Isonzo and outflanked the Italian line.

Though other units held until forced into orderly retreat the Italian Second Army broke and ran. The panic crossing of the Tagliamento, thirty miles to the rear, became a byword for defeat. It was largely because the unexpected extent of their gains threw the German and Austrian armies off balance that the Italians, under new generalship and stiffened by

British and French reinforcements, were able in the first days of November to establish a line of entrenchments along the Piave, sixtyfive miles to the south on the dank Venetian plain.

In Paris, sitting on November 3 in the quiet of the Morgan Harjes bank, Dawes, groggy from his struggle to free shipping space for essential items, described the Italian reverse as sobering. He noted that eightyfive thousand British and French troops were speeding to the Piave. He had just lunched with Pershing, whom he found both depressed and stimulated by the Italian news. Dawes' nephew, who was a private, drove the two friends out to a secluded place where they could take a long walk on a country road together. Their conversation was solemn.

"To help the Commander in Chief, my dear friend carry this his burden, to help my country in this time of need . . ." wrote Dawes, "all this is my weary but happy lot. But it is not difficult to be happy when one feels the sense of progress . . . With the latitude John gives me I feel as if I were exercising the powers of one of the old monarchs. To negotiate singlehanded with governments comes to but few men."

Pershing, while shaken by Caporetto, felt privately stimulated, as a professional of warfare, by the German successes at Riga and on the Isonzo. It seemed to foretell the end of trench warfare. Here was convincing proof of the correctness "of the doctrine of training for open warfare . . . It simply proved that nothing . . . had changed this age-old principle of the art of war."

Tanks at Last

About ten days after the Austro-German advance into Italy had settled down to a war of waiting along the Piave, the correctness of Pershing's doctrine on the art of warfare received fresh confirmation, this time from the British. On November 20 the British tanks broke through the German lines at Cambrai and led the infantry on a four mile advance with casualties light indeed for the western front.

The eager young officers of the British tank corps had been much chagrined by their failure to score any gains during the first days of the offensive at Ypres. Almost tearfully they had tried to point out, while the battle was still in the planning stage at G.H.Q., that the terrain there was impossible for tanks. They had prepared careful maps indicating the most dangerously flooded areas and had been told to forget that nonsense. Now in front of Cambrai, between Lens and St. Quentin, on hard rolling ground which had not been made impassable by constant shelling, they were given a chance to see what they could do.

The British and French had been developing armored vehicles independently. In England the idea seems to have started when the official army reporter, a Colonel Swinton who signed his reports "Eyewitness," remembered having read a story a dozen years before in the *Strand Magazine* called "Land Ironclads." Of course it was by H. G. Wells. He confabulated with some young fellows of the Royal Naval Air Service who had been impressed by the performance of the armored motor cars they improvised for use on the roads around Dunkirk during the first battle of the Marne. They got hold of an American Holt caterpillar tractor and called in the help of various engineers to see how it could be developed into a selfmoving armored gun carriage, the land ironclad of Wells' science fiction. At that point the Sea Lords announced that the Royal Navy would have no part of a contraption that cruised on land and the program was transferred to the army.

Winston Churchill, being an imaginative fellow, was struck with the idea of landships from the first moment he heard of them. When Lloyd George became Minister of Munitions he followed up Churchill's suggestions. In September 1916 General Haig allowed some Mark I tanks to be deployed on the Somme, to bolster morale he somewhat apologetically explained. Of fortynine primitive types on hand only thirtysix reached the scene of the engagement before breaking down.

At that time the fastest speed tanks could make was four miles an hour. Even so, a couple of the clumsy vehicles made a name for themselves. The first tank to go over the top flushed out a pocket of German resistance before a shell put it out of business. Another, followed by a company of infantry, captured a trenchful of startled Heinies. Their greatest achievement came later in the Somme campaign when a pair of tanks, although hopelessly stuck in the mud, forced the surrender of four hundred men.

At Cambrai the tank corps rejoiced in the possession of three hundred tanks of their latest improved model. The tanks were hidden from the enemy in an undamaged piece of forest. When they took off before dawn, in spite of their slow motion, the surprise was complete. Advancing in groups of twelve followed by infantry, they flattened the barbed wire entanglements and crossed the concrete trenches of the Hindenburg Line with the greatest ease. Two German divisions were routed and a hundred and twenty guns and seventyfive hundred men were captured.

The catch came when it was discovered that the only preparations made by Haig's G.H.Q. for following up a breakthrough was the deployment of some units of Haig's beloved cavalry. German machinegunners from their pillboxes slaughtered the horses and their riders. A few days later German counterattacks wiped out the British gains.

The success of their counterattack proved to the satisfaction of the German High Command that tanks were a failure. For the benefit of German civilians the cumbersome machines were ridiculed as unmanly devices of the degenerate English and unworthy of the brave Teutonic soldier.

Pershing was present at the headquarters of General Byng who commanded the Cambrai show during the first part of the engagement. His staff was already at work on arrangements for the furnishing of French light tanks and British heavy tanks to the American troops, but nothing that he said or wrote indicated that he felt H. G. Wells' "land ironclads" in any way threatened the infantryman with rifle and the bayonet, whom he trusted to dominate the war of movement he looked forward to in the coming year.

The Bridge of Ships

Meanwhile the buildup of the A.E.F. continued with gradually increasing tempo. By the end of November something like a hundred thousand men had been landed in France. Brest became the chief disembarkation port. A little more than half the American troops crossed the Atlantic on British ships, a small percentage on French and Italian ships, and the rest on transports officered and convoyed by the U. S. Navy.

Early in the summer the destroyers had learned to refuel at sea. That meant that even the smaller types could make the full voyage to Europe with their convoys instead of having to turn back halfway.

The first few convoys reached home ports intact in spite of continual forays by U-boats off the Brittany coast and in the far Atlantic in the latitude of the Azores. On the eastbound course not a ship was lost during that year.

A day out of Brest on the return voyage in mid October the small transport *Antilles* was hit square in the engineroom by a torpedo. The ship sank in six and a half minutes, but due to carefully worked out abandon ship routines only sixtyseven men were lost out of two hundred and thirtyfour on board. The radio electrician stuck to his wireless room and continued sending out SOS signals until the ship sank and he drowned. The skipper who insisted on being the last man off the ship was saved by a hair.

In spite of very rough seas, the converted yachts of the escort picked up the survivors and took them back to Brest. The rules were that as soon as a ship was attacked the merchantmen in the convoy should scatter and that only shallow draft yachts and destroyers, which were poor targets for torpedoes, should engage in rescue work.

Back in Brest, the crew and passengers from the *Antilles* were placed on the *Finland*, which had just unloaded and was preparing for the return trip. They had poor luck. The *Finland* was hardly out of Brest before a torpedo struck her under the bridge.

These transports had civilian crews. The crew of the *Antilles*, described by the naval officers as "the sweepings of the docks, a low class of foreigners of all nationalities," had come on board in a state of shock from their previous experience. They communicated their terrors to the civilian crew of the *Finland* with the result that there was a general panic when the torpedo hit, which the officers had to quell revolver in hand. In the rush boats were lowered carelessly, some capsized. Men jumped overboard.

"The engineroom and fireroom crews left their stations and rushed on deck, which was contrary to orders," wrote Admiral Gleaves. "These men were finally driven below, with the aid of a revolver and a heavy wooden mallet, and the engineers' stations again manned."

When discipline was restored it was found that only one cargo hold was flooded. The men in the water were picked up and the *Finland* made her way back under her own steam through the submarine nets into the harbor of Brest.

Officers and crews were learning that the submarine was not an unbeatable foe. As the autumn advanced coordination kept improving between merchantships and their escorts.

The great day for the American destroyers came in November when the U.S.S. *Fanning* was escorting a tardy merchantman to its position in the westbound convoy out from Queenstown. The coxswain sighted the small "finger" periscope of a submarine which seemed to be taking aim on one of the larger merchantmen. No sooner seen than gone. The *Fanning* took a wide turn to pass over the spot where the periscope had vanished. At the same moment her companion destroyer the *Nicholson* bore down on the spot from the other side of the convoy. They both dropped depth charges.

Nothing happened. They cruised around hopefully for fifteen minutes. No oil, no timbers. They were about to rejoin their positions in the convoy when all at once the stern of a submarine broke the water between them. The stern rose so high that the men could see the rear torpedo tubes.

Soon the whole submarine lay on the surface, seemingly without a scratch. The destroyer crews could read the inscription: U-58. Both destroyers were shelling it when the conning tower trap opened and out popped a German officer with his arms in the air crying "Kamerad" at the top of his lungs. He was followed by the crew, all with their arms in the air. Fearing it was a trick both destroyers approached queasily with their machineguns trained on the men. The *Fanning* went alongside and threw the Germans a line. At that moment the submarine sank. The Germans had opened the seacocks. The Americans had a job saving the crew. One kraut was so exhausted that he died.

When the German commander was hauled out of the water, all dripping as he was he clicked his heels and saluted Lieutenant Carpender

who was in command of the *Fanning*. He explained in tolerable English
that he was a minelayer. The ashcans had wrecked his motors, jammed
his rudders and broken the fuel lines. He was sinking so fast there was
nothing to it but to blow his ballast tanks and surface, and take his chance
with the Americans.

The Germans were given dry clothing and fed and placed below under guard. According to the crew of the *Fanning* what impressed the
captured squareheads most was their soap. It was the first soap they had
had in three months.

The Policy of the Wedge

Colonel House spent the hot months of the summer of 1917 as usual
on the North Shore of Massachusetts. His summer home at Magnolia constituted a port of entry for the stream of European envoys such as Northcliffe, the English press lord, Tardieu, the French High Commissioner,
and Sir William Wiseman, the very astute head of the British secret service. All of them were trying to thaw their way through the ring of ice
that surrounded the President in Washington.

Besides being liaison man with Paris and Westminster the confidential
colonel was trying to keep what he and Wilson referred to jokingly as
his friend's "one track mind" from concentrating too exclusively on military efforts "to knock the Kaiser off his perch."

House had to remind the President that the purpose of war was peace.

House wanted to prepare for the day when Woodrow Wilson would
be in a position, like Philip Dru setting the troubled republic to rights
as Administrator in his fantasy, to dictate to the prostrate nations of the
world a peace which would inaugurate a golden age.

House well knew that through all the massacres and countermassacres
of that summer's campaigns, the word peace would not down. The people of Europe were tired of being killed. Peace was the slogan that
toppled the autocracy in Russia. All the revolutionary parties there sympathized fervently with the aims of the conference of the world's socialists
which the Second International, recovering from the paralysis into which
it had been thrown by the martial ecstasy of the early years of the war,
had called in Sweden. Wilson's answer to the Stockholm convocation,
like that of the British and French governments, was to refuse passports
to the Socialist leaders invited. Bakhmetief, Kerensky's envoy to Washington, had been camping on Colonel House's doorstep in Magnolia in
an effort to convince him that Mr. Wilson was making a grave mistake.

A similar agitation for peace was stirring the Catholic Church. The
Reichstag resolution of July 17 was sponsored by the German Catholic
Center party. This was followed on the first day of August by an appeal

from Pope Benedict XV to the belligerents to negotiate a peace without victory, on approximately the terms laid down in Woodrow Wilson's speeches before America's entrance into the war. Associated with the Pope's appeal, at least in the minds of Wilson's advisers at the State Department, was the attempt by Count Czernin, the Austrian foreign minister, to use the new Emperor Charles' brotherinlaw Prince Sixtus of Bourbon, then serving in the Belgian Army, as his private gobetween in preliminary conversations between the French, the Germans and the Italians. Wilson's first thought was that he was too busy waging war to pay any more attention to the Pope's appeal than he did to the mistaken exhortations of the socialists.

On August 17 Colonel House wrote from Magnolia begging him to reconsider:

"Dear Governor,

"I am so impressed with the importance of the situation that I am troubling you again . . . I believe that you have an opportunity to take the peace negotiations out of the hands of the Pope and hold them in your own. Governmental Germany realizes that no one excepting you is in a position to enforce peace terms. The Allies must succumb to your judgment and Germany is not much better off. Badly as the Allied cause is going, Germany is in a worse condition. It is a race now of endurance with Germany as likely to go under first as any of the Entente Powers.

"Germany and Austria are a seething mass of discontent. The Russian Revolution has shown the people their power and it has put the fear of God into the hearts of the Imperialists . . . A statement from you setting forth the real issues would have an enormous effect and would probably bring about such an upheaval in Germany as we desire . . . You can make a statement that will not only be the undoing of autocratic Germany, but one that will strengthen the hands of the Russian liberals in their purpose to mould their country into a mighty republic.

"I pray that you may not lose this great opportunity.
                              "Affectionately yours,
                              "E. M. House."

The President's reply was to mail House the text of a note, prepared with the usual agonizing care and typed as usual on his own typewriter. The gist of it was that although he refused to believe that the word of the present German Government could be trusted, he hoped to help negotiate with some eventual German Government which really represented the German people, an equitable peace.

"The object of this war," Wilson wrote, "is to deliver the free peoples of the world from the menace and the actual power of a vast military establishment controlled by an irresponsible government." The enemy was not the German people but their "ruthless masters."

The night after House received the President's rough draft he confided to his diary that this had been one of the busiest and most important days of the summer. "I did not receive it until twelve o'clock and . . . I succeeded in reading, digesting and answering it in time to mail on the Fedderal Express." With one of his portentous looks he turned his packet of typescript over to the Boston postmaster, who had providentially come to call. The postmaster, much flattered, promised to convey it to Washington in a special pouch, or if necessary to take it there himself. House noted that the man "would have been even more impressed had he known that he had in his possession what at the moment was the most interesting document in the world."

President Wilson's reply to Pope Benedict was published by the State Department on August 29. In America it effectively cut the ground out from under such "wilful" senators as Borah and La Follette and the Socialist agitators who were risking jail under the Espionage Act by demanding a clear statement of war aims. Furthermore it reassured German-American opinion, which though muffled was still influential, that German-Americans who backed the President in his war against the Kaiser's generals were not fighting the German people. It was the beginning of the politics of the wedge.

The Inquiry

After the note was spread over the press House wrote the President, amid a torrent of praise: "You have again written a declaration of human liberty," and signed his letter "your devoted." Wilson had written him: "I think of you every day with the deepest affection."

They had not seen each other for several months and the newspapermen were coming up with their usual summer crop of stories about a break between them. House joked the reporters about these stories. Weren't they rather late this year? They usually came at midsummer along with the seaserpents.

The President's next letter to House was written from the *Mayflower*. The Wilsons and a group of Mrs. Wilson's relations were spending a weekend anchored out in Hampton Roads to escape what the President was beginning to call the madness of Washington. The following week he promised House he would get away for a longer time. "Do not be alarmed about my health. I need rest, and am growing daily more conscious that I do: but I am fit and all right. All join," he added significantly, "in affectionate messages."

In the same letter he made an important suggestion. It was following a train of thought that House had been gently urging all summer. The time had come, he suggested, to prepare American peace terms. He knew that the British and French had their preparations already made in case the war should come to a sudden end. "What would you think," he wrote House, "of quietly gathering a group of men about you to assist you to do this? I could, of course, pay all the bills out of the money now at my command. Under your guidance these assistants could collate all the definite material available and you could make up the memorandum by which you should be guided."

House went to work with enthusiasm. He asked his brotherinlaw, Sidney Mezes, who was president of the College of the City of New York, to head up an organization which came to be known as The Inquiry. Glib young Walter Lippmann of *The New Republic* was made secretary. The eminent Dr. Isaiah Bowman of the American Geographical Society gave the researchers working space in the society's rooms in New York and put his mapmaking facilities at their disposal.

The aim of The Inquiry, so Dr. Mezes wrote the President, would be to collect information 1. "about Europe's suppressed, oppressed and backward peoples," 2. about international business, 3. about international law, 4. to analyze what serious proposals could be uncovered for an organization to insure peace, 5. to make suggestions as to the restoration of war damage in France and Belgium.

In answer the President immediately called for a further investigation of the needs of the larger states such as Russia, Germany and Austria, for access to the sea and to raw materials. "Of course," he wrote, "what we are seeking is a basis that will be fair to all and which will nowhere plant the seeds of such jealousy and discontent and restraint of development as would certainly breed future wars."

Wilson wanted facts he could trust. He knew something of England at first hand but he was only dimly aware of the particulars of the tangled ambitions, congenital hatreds, and crass conflicts of interest that he knew would confront him when the time came to straighten out continental Europe and put its congeries of peoples on the path to freedom and democracy and peace. He wanted The Inquiry to give him facts to base his theory on.

Although everybody connected with the enterprise was enjoined to secrecy, the newspapers got wind of it. The New York *Times* ran a headline: AMERICA TO SPEAK IN HER OWN VOICE AT THE PEACE TABLE.

The President was indignant. "I think you newspaper men can have no conception of what fire you are playing with when you discuss peace now at all," he wrote David Lawrence, pointing out that Germany had achieved the hegemony of middle Europe from Hamburg to Baghdad and would be at a great advantage should negotiations start from that basis. "It is my stern and serious judgment that the whole matter ought to be let alone." As a result the operations of Colonel House's inquirers were swathed in as much secrecy as if they had been working on a high explosive or a new poison gas.

Colonel House's Letter of Marque

On September 9 House noted in his diary: "Around seven o'clock the Navy Yard of Boston called me over the telephone to say they had a wireless stating that the Mayflower would be in Gloucester Harbor at two o'clock. Loulie and I went over to meet the boat, boarded it, met the President and Mrs. Wilson, and motored along the shore for two hours or more. We stopped first at our cottage and then went over to Mrs. T. Jefferson Coolidge's house to look at her prints, china etc., which have been inherited from Thomas Jefferson." As they motored around the shore drive Wilson described himself as "a democrat like Jefferson with aristocratic tastes."

Next morning the President played nine holes of golf and lunched with Colonel and Mrs. House. "Once or twice during the conversation," House noted, "I threw the President off his line of thought by interpolations, and he found it difficult to return to his subject. He smiled plaintively and said 'You see I am getting tired. This is the way it indicates itself.'"

The *Mayflower* steamed back around Cape Anne and into Massachusetts Bay. Passing through the Cape Cod canal the presidential party seated on deck watched the great groups of people gathered along the banks to cheer him. Schoolchildren waved little flags and sang. The President was much moved. Edith drank in the adulation of the distant crowds. Her husband was at the peak of his personal popularity. Every day there came, in the mail she often helped him cope with, photographs of babies and scrawled letters from the proud parents explaining that their latest had been named Woodrow or Wilson.

After a short visit to the Sayre family on Nantucket to see the grandchildren, where they were greeted again by cheers and the piping songs of schoolchildren let out of class for the occasion, the *Mayflower* conveyed President and Mrs. Wilson and their friends and relatives smoothly through the Sound, around the humming manywindowed promontory of Manhattan and came to anchor opposite Grant's Tomb in the North River. The Wilsons went to the Belasco Theatre that night to see a popular comedy called *Polly with a Past*. As soon as the President was recognized the entire audience rose and cheered vociferously.

Next morning they called on Admiral and Mrs. Grayson at the St. Regis and attended divine services at the Fifth Avenue Presbyterian Church. Edith Wilson's mother and sister went on board with them for Sunday dinner, and so did the discreetly smiling Colonel House.

House was braving the September heat to meet the Marquess of Reading, Chief Justice of England, the son of an East End fruit merchant, risen by brains and tact and skill in the law to the Privy Council, who had just arrived in New York. Reading was one of the Liberals closest to Lloyd George, and after much correspondence with House and Northcliffe, the Prime Minister had picked him as the man most likely to get along with Baruch of the War Industries Board in coordinating the war effort and in bringing home to the Americans the dreadful urgency of the situation the Allies faced on the western front as the result of the Russian collapse. Then too he had to arrange a fresh credit. The British were out of funds again.

Before the meal was served on the *Mayflower* the colonel managed to buttonhole the President long enough to show him a letter from Lloyd George to House which Reading had brought, suggesting that Wilson send a personal representative to join in the councils of the Allies and that that representative should be House himself. Wilson held the suggestion at arm's length, and they rejoined the party waiting to sit down at table.

The President returned to Washington by train so as to be at his desk Monday morning. A few days later Lord Reading called by appointment and presented another personal letter from Lloyd George, this time addressed to Wilson directly, urging with some vehemence that the President of the United States be represented at the next interallied conference.

In the first place the decisions made there would directly affect the American Army . . . "But another reason weighs still more strongly with me," wrote the Prime Minister. "I believe that we are suffering today from the grooves and traditions that have grown up since the war . . . Independent minds, bringing fresh views . . . might be of immense value in helping us to free ourselves from the ruts of the past." The wily Welshman ended with an encomium of the President's public statements. "They have recalled to many the ideals with which they entered the war, and which it is easy to forget amid the horrors of the battlefield and the overtime and fatigue of the munitions shops. They have given to the bruised and battered peoples of Europe fresh courage to endure and fresh hope that with all their sufferings they are helping to bring into being a world in which freedom and democracy will be secure, and in which free nations will live together in unity and peace."

The President's desk was bombarded in the days that followed with similar requests from the French and the Italians. In early October he asked House to come to Washington to discuss them. House found the President still set against letting what he called "the center of gravity of the war" be transferred to Europe. At the same time he had come reluctantly to the conclusion that he must be represented at the next interallied meeting.

House was the only man he could trust to protect his liberty of action. House must head the delegation, which they now decided should be a fulldress affair, including General Bliss, the Chief of Staff, Admiral Benson, Chief of Naval Operations, and important figures in the administration who could discuss authoritatively the problems of finance and supply, and the allimportant embargo on German trade through neutral nations. Two cruisers and a destroyer would be furnished for transportation. All expenses would be paid through the State Department. As usual the colonel's instructions were vague.

Without keeping a copy, or sending one over to the State Department for the record, the President wrote out for House what the colonel slyly called his letter of marque. It was a private letter endorsed to the premiers of Great Britain, France and Italy, whom Wilson addressed simply as "gentlemen." He stated that he had "asked his friend Mr. Edward M. House, the bearer of this letter, to represent me in the general conferences presently to be held by the governments associated in war with the central powers or in any other conferences he may be invited and think it best to take part in."

On second thought it was decided to ask Lansing to send formal notification of the dispatch of an American mission to the governments involved.

"I shall think of you and dear Mrs. Wilson constantly while I am away," wrote House from New York where he was hastily assembling his delegation, "and I shall put forward the best that is in me to do the things you have intrusted to me . . ." He begged the President to take care of his health . . . "You are the one hope left to this torn and distracted world. Without your leadership God alone knows how long we will wander in the wilderness . . ."

"I hate to say good by," the President answered. "It is an immense comfort to me to have you here for counsel and for friendship. But it is right that you should go. God bless and keep you both. My thoughts will follow you all the weeks through, and I hope it will be only weeks that will separate us.

"Mrs. Wilson," he added significantly, "joins in all affectionate messages."

Since the mission was turning out to be such a numerous affair, House felt he was entitled to take his family along. He appointed his soninlaw Gordon Auchincloss secretary to the commission. Loulie went as a matter of course, and the indispensable Miss Denton, who was so adept at the private code House and Wilson had worked out between them for their personal communications.

Sir William Wiseman was a very shrewd fellow. He had become an intimate of the House apartment on Fiftythird Street, where he found the richest field for the intelligence on American affairs it was his business to transmit back to Whitehall. Now he was taking every precaution to see that the Americans should be made comfortable when they arrived in the tight little isle: "House is very insistent on not having any public banquets or lunches," he cabled. "He is not strong physically and has a perfect horror of public functions . . . May I remind you that Americans hate cold houses, and it is important that the places should be steam-heated as they do not think fires are enough."

House was privately quite aware that there was something incongruous in this sort of preparation for the comfort and convenience of the topdogs whose mismanagement had brought civilization to such a grievous pass, while the underdogs who were in no way to blame suffered and froze and died in the mud and misery of the trenches. One day amid the fluster and botheration of the commission's preparations for departure he paused long enough to make a quaintly ruminative entry in his diary: "It is to be hoped that the people of all nations will some day notice that those in authority who are largely responsible for wars and those who fan public opinion to white heat, are seldom hurt. Where among the crowned heads of Europe do we find a fatality? Where among Cabinets and members of parliaments has the war caused a death? Where among the great editorial writers, politicians and public orators has one suffered death on the field of battle?"

The American mission proceeded by train to Halifax and was safely conveyed across the Atlantic, arriving in Plymouth on November 7.

In London they found long faces. House had no sooner digested the full story of Caporetto, with eight hundred thousand Italians killed, wounded or prisoner, when the news came of the collapse of Kerensky's middleclass government and the seizure of power in Petrograd by Lenin's Bolsheviks in the name of the workers and soldiers and peasants. One of their first public acts was to demand an armistice from the German High Command.

Lloyd George was already at Rapallo, meeting with Painlevé and the Italian Premier Orlando to form a Supreme War Council with sufficient authority to stem the tide of defeat. Such was the uproar against him in England that it was doubtful whether the Prime Minister could face Parliament when he came home without a vote of no confidence. From France came reports that the Painlevé cabinet was doomed. The Allied politicians were snatching in panic at the President's confidential colonel. "Never in history" cabled the New York *Times* correspondent from London, "has any foreigner come to Europe and found greater acceptance or wielded more power."

Lloyd George had House to dinner alone the day he got back to London from Rapallo. Right away, he explained, he needed a statement that would assure the House of Commons that he, Lloyd George, had full American support for his Supreme War Council. Asquith's supporters, egged on by Lloyd George's enemies on the General Staff, were out for the Welshman's head. He had to give the impression that American participation in the Supreme War Council was a sort of victory. House cabled the President asking for a statement.

"To House: Take the whip hand. We not only accede to the plan for unified conduct of the war, but we insist on it," were the words that Wilson wrote on his private memorandum pad.

Mrs. Wilson helped the President code a message to that effect in his private cipher which was transmitted to House through the State Department. House, who didn't want to be accused of meddling in British politics issued a statement in general terms that he had received a cable from the President to the effect that "the Government of the United States considers that unity of plan and control between all the Allies and the United States is essential in order to achieve a just and permanent peace."

Lloyd George, an astute navigator on parliamentary seas, made much of Wilson's support. The opposition dropped its vote of censure.

When the newspapermen in Washington mobbed Tumulty for comment on the London cables, the President, suspicious in those days of the word "peace" in the mouth of a journalist; and perhaps, as a result of some suggestion of Edith's that House was getting too big for his boots, not unwilling to cut the colonel down to size, sent out a memorandum which caused consternation on both sides of the Atlantic: "Please tell the men that this must certainly have been built up merely upon my general attitude as known to everybody, and please beg that they will discount it and make no comment upon it. If they did, I would have to be constantly commenting upon similar reports."

Hearst's International News Service took these words to mean that the President denied having sent House a telegram backing a unified Allied command in Europe.

Le Tigre

Lloyd George's government almost fell a second time. European politicians began to think twice of leaning too hard on the confidential colonel. In Paris Painlevé had already met defeat in the Chamber. Clemenceau was Prime Minister in his stead.

Clemenceau, at seventysix, was the only survivor of the convention held in Bordeaux to form the Third Republic after the French defeat in

1871. As chairman of the permanent committee on the conduct of the war
of the Chamber of Deputies, the violent old man had raged and nagged
at every ministry's handling of affairs since the first battle of the Marne.
He was so free with his accusations of pacifism, defeatism and treason
that the editorials in his personal newspaper *L'Homme Libre* were
blanked out again and again by the censor. His answer was to change
the paper's name to *L'Homme Enchaîné*.

When Poincaré, who hated him, invited Clemenceau to form a cabinet
after Painlevé lost his vote in the Chamber, the President of the Republic
was reported to have said, "You have made it impossible for anyone else
to form a cabinet . . . See what you can do."

Georges Clemenceau's political monniker was the Tiger. He was a congenital republican and anticlerical from La Vendée, a region of France
notorious for the violence of its politics. His father was a country doctor
persecuted by Louis Napoleon's police for his liberal opinions. As a medical student Clemenceau served a jail sentence for being involved in a
political riot. He learned English early and published a translation of
John Stuart Mill's *Auguste Compte and Positivism*. The virulent political
journalism that played such a part in nineteenthcentury French politics
was more to his taste than the practice of medicine. He was an accomplished duellist. He made it so hot for himself in Paris that his father
sent him to America during the last years of the Civil War. He made his
living in New York by giving riding and fencing lessons, and by reporting
American events for Paris newspapers. He used to boast to American
callers in his quaint Yankee dialect that he had reported the fall of Rich-
mond for *Le Temps*.

He married a welloff American girl, one of his pupils at the Stamford
Seminary, and installed her in the small family château in La Vendée,
but he was nothing of a homebody. He promptly abandoned wife and
children to return to the fascinations of Parisian politics. When he was
accused of keeping mistresses he was said to have replied that his real
mistress was Marianne, *la troisième république*.

Impossible to live with, he was a continual broiler in the press and on
the duelling field. After seven years Madame Clemenceau left him and
took the children back to America. He was perennial mayor of the Commune of Montmartre, served in the Chamber of Deputies and in the Senate and, as an anticlerical and a friend of Zola, was swept into office as
Premier during the popular reaction to the Dreyfus case. It was then
that a bitter young Jew named Georges Mandel became his private secretary. For all his humanitarianism and his sympathy with the left his
political warcry remained revenge against Germany.

A solitary and illtempered old man, his only family was Mandel, his
inseparable secretary, and Albert, his valet, who both lived in worshipful
terror of his rages. His political friends used to point out whimsically that

some of the Huns were supposed to have settled in La Vendée after At-
tilla's defeat. He did have a mongol look with his high cheekbones over
the great mustaches, that the cartoonists liked to turn into the tusks of a
sabretoothed tiger, and the skullcap that covered his baldness, and the
lisle gloves that hid an eczema the doctors were unable to cure on his
small clawlike hands.

Clemenceau, working through Georges Mandel as *chef de cabinet* and
head of the censorship, had in a few days made himself virtual dictator
of France. It was from this unspoken eminence that he greeted the American delegates when they arrived in Paris from London, amid cheers
and bunting and flourishes of trumpets from the Garde Republicain.
Everybody in Paris was quoting his opening speech to the bedazzled
deputies: *"Mais moi, messieurs, je fais la guerre."*

Clemenceau only spoke English to his intimates, but he was good at
handling Americans. A practical realist House called him. At their first
meeting they agreed that the proceedings of the Interallied Conference
should be short and to the point. *Pas de discours.* House described him
in his diary as "one of the ablest men I have met in Europe, not only on
this trip but on any of the others."

At the first informal meeting with House and Bliss and Pershing it
came out that Clemenceau, like Pétain, wanted American doughboys to
beef up the French divisions. "He said if the Americans do not permit
the French to teach them, the Germans will at great cost." Pershing demurred. "He was of the opinion," noted House, "that if the American
troops went in very few would ever come out."

The American Commission was known to Americans in Paris as the
"house party." They put up at the Hotel Crillon where House occupied what was known as the Thomas Fortune Ryan suite. General Pershing and Harbord were invited there to meet them before they all went
together to the first ceremonial. The Crillon hummed with Americans.
Grasty of the New York *Times*, who was among the newspaper contingent, described the colonel as "busy as a squirrel in nutting time."

"I met the great little man," Harbord noted in his journal, "the man
who can be silent in several languages . . . He is one of the few men with
practically no chin, whom I have ever met, who were considered forceful.
He called the committee together and made them what I consider a
baldly cynical little speech . . . 'We are going to meet this morning. Nothing will be done more than to go through the form of an organization. No
speeches for someone might blunder onto the subject of Russia: and some
little fellows might ask disagreeable questions . . . It is our day to smile.
Just circulate around among the little fellows and listen to their stories.
Be kind and agreeable.' If that isn't giving a stone when they ask for
bread, then I dunno," added Harbord.

"Then we drove over to the French ministry of Foreign Affairs . . . A very large room with long tables with place cards, each delegation to itself. Seventeen Allied nations, such as U.S., Great Britain, Brazil, Liberia, Cuba, Japan, France, Serbia, Montenegro, Italy, Russia, Roumania, Argentine, Belgium, etc. from chrome yellow through brown and black back to clear white in color, a perfect polyglot of tongues . . . a gathering so little hopeful of unity, that as an investment I suspect the hardheaded Germans would have willingly paid the expenses of it."

Harbord described the new French Premier as "venerable." He had once taught school "in Massachusetts" and was reputed to know "the peculiar but amusing and sometimes efficient ways of the Americans. His personal manner is described as very direct and frank . . . Some months," Harbord added in the privacy of his journal, "of perfectly direct and frank intercourse with some Frenchmen, however, has shown us that however direct and frank, they are sometimes making mental reservations . . . So it probably was with the old Prime Minister." . . . Evidently the meeting was not quite as short as House and Clemenceau had planned. "I watched it for an hour," Harbord wrote, "and then left with my Chief." Colonel Dawes, who had stacks of money, had invited Harbord to lunch with him at the Tour d'Argent. There they ate pressed duck with oranges. Afterwards they went to Brentano's where Harbord helped his friend spend a hundred dollars on early editions. They were both fond of Napoleoniana.

The Supreme War Council, consisting of the prime ministers and military leaders and their aides, assembled at the Trianon Palace at Versailles. Its meetings proved hardly more productive than those of the Interallied Commission. "I can understand quite readily why Germany has been able to withstand the Allies," noted House. "Superior organization and method. Nothing is buttoned up with the Allies: it is all talk and no concerted action."

One thing came out clear. None of the belligerents was ready to make the sort of concessions necessary for a negotiated peace. The governments of each of the fighting nations had decided to try one more round. This was the information that House took home to the President.

PART FOUR

Force Without Stint

Let everything that we say, my fellow countrymen, everything that we henceforth plan and accomplish, ring true to
this response till the majesty and might of our concerted
power shall fill the thought and utterly defeat the force of
those who flout and misprize what we honor and hold dear.
Germany has once more said that force, and force alone, shall
decide whether justice and peace shall reign in the affairs of
men, whether Right as America conceives it or Dominion as
she conceives it, shall determine the destinies of mankind.
There is, therefore, but one response possible from us: Force,
Force to the utmost, Force without stint or limit, the righteous
and triumphant Force which shall make Right the law of the
world, and cast every selfish dominion down in the dust.

> —Woodrow Wilson on opening of
> Third Liberty Loan Drive
> in the Baltimore Armory,
> April 6, 1918

Chapter 16

TO MOBILIZE THE MIND

ON the afternoon of December 17 Colonel House's quiet tread was heard
again in the White House corridors. He had smuggled his mission out of
France so secretly that the correspondents were astonished. "Of all the
molelike activities of Colonel House," cabled the New York *Times* man,
Grasty, "the climax was his departure . . . Perhaps the Colonel had made
a quiet bet with himself on his ability to take the party of fifteen or twenty

persons out of the most conspicuous setting in Paris without anybody being the wiser."

House found the President waiting for him in his study. They talked privately for two hours. Though the colonel liked to cast an optimistic glow over reports of his operations as diplomat extraordinary, this time he made no effort to disguise the fact that little had been accomplished.

Due to the recalcitrance of the Italians, who still dreamed of turning the Adriatic into their mare nostrum, and to Clemenceau's lack of interest in anything but fighting the *boche,* the confidential colonel had failed to induce the Allied authorities to agree on the public statement of sane and liberal war aims which he and the President wanted. His arguments in favor of a central military command had met with evasive replies from Lloyd George, who ever since he had bet on the wrong horse with Nivelle was leery of the military. The hideous butcher's bill the British Prime Minister was confronted with from Haig's Flanders offensives made him suspicious of anything which would give that general or his associate General Robertson, the Imperial Chief of Staff, any added power of decision. He stalled and procrastinated. About all that House could report was that the meetings of the Supreme War Council had laid the foundation upon which unified command might, on some more auspicious occasion, be set up.

The President called in Secretary Baker and General Bliss for another conference with House next day. Then he sent him back to New York post haste to assemble the facts and figures the college professors were digging out of the libraries. He needed the peace inquiry bureau's research as the basis for a fresh statement of war aims.

Brest-Litovsk

The Bolshevik seizure of power in Petrograd drastically changed the course of the war of ideas which interested Woodrow Wilson far more than military strategy. One of Leon Trotsky's first acts in taking over the Ministry of Foreign Affairs, as commissar for the All Russian Congress of Soviets, was to publish the secret agreements among the Allies to carve up Turkey and Austro-Hungary and the various Balkan states for the satisfaction of "territorial ambitions."

The Manchester *Guardian* printed the first summary in English of these deals on December 13. They set the British nonconformist conscience to stirring.

Printed in America by Villard's New York *Evening Post,* they provided encouragement to the socialists and pacifists whose views Woodrow Wilson was coming to hold in low esteem. "What I am opposed to," he told an A.F. of L. convention in Buffalo, "is not the feeling of the pacifists, but their stupidity. My heart is with them, but my mind has contempt for them. I want peace but I know how to get it and they do not. You will notice that I sent a friend of mine, Colonel House, to Europe, who is as great a lover of peace as any man in the world, but I didn't send him on a peace mission yet. I sent him to take part in a conference on how the war was to be won, and he knows, as I know, that that is the way to get peace."

Wilson was not the only man in the world who thought he knew how to get peace. Lenin, spinning his webs behind the rifles and machine-guns of his partisans, in the humming dynamo of Smolny Institute, had announced that for the working class the war was at an end. Over the radio and through the propaganda organizations the Bolsheviks were feverishly constructing, they were telling the conscript armies that the way to get peace was to shoot their officers and go home.

To prove that they were as good as their word the Bolshevik leaders were already engaged in negotiations for an armistice with the Germans in the ruined Belorussian town of Brest-Litovsk. Comrades Kamenev and Joffe led the Bolshevik delegation.

Adolf Joffe, particularly, proved an adroit negotiator and propagandist. Like his friend Trotsky he came from a rural family of welltodo Jewish business people. After a somewhat dilettante education in various universities he became attracted by the idealism of the revolutionary movement and made over a considerable fortune to the Social Democratic Party. Lenin picked him for the delegation on account of his air of cosmopolitan culture. A workers' representative was included, as a matter of course, but it wasn't until the delegates were already on their way from Smolny to the railroad station that somebody remembered they had forgotten to bring along a peasant. "There's a peasant," said Joffe pointing to a broad bearded figure under a streetlamp. They stopped the car, and by threats and blandishments induced a confused and humble old countryman to come along. They never could break him of bowing and scraping and calling everybody "Barin," which meant "master"; so his collaboration was hardly considered a success.

The German representatives were Foreign Minister von Kuhlmann and Major General Max Hoffmann, Pershing's old acquaintance from Japanese War days who had won fame through his overall direction of the Riga offensive. Count Czernin represented the Austrian Emperor. There were contingents from Turkey and the Balkan states, four hundred delegates in all.

The proceedings started in an old theatre, one of the few buildings left standing in the town, in an atmosphere of unearthly reasonableness. Czernin, frightened by the strikes and foodriots spreading throughout his crumbling Austro-Hungarian empire, genuinely hoped to promote a general armistice. The Germans were biding their time. Possibly they did not want to upset the Bolshevist government which they were bolstering with millions of marks shipped into Petrograd for defeatist propaganda. They allowed Joffe to carry off an initial victory: the proceedings should be public, the participants could broadcast them to all the world. Then Joffe laid down two basic principles. There should be no annexations. Peoples should determine their own governments.

On Christmas Day the Germans produced their reply. They, too, were in favor of the principle of no annexations, particularly in relation to the German colonies the British had taken over, and were for selfdetermination, with some reservations in the case of these same German colonies.

Behind the scenes both sides were busy. The German generals were using the respite to consolidate their military positions and to sort out the units which could be spared for service at the western front. Nor were the Bolsheviks idle. Russian troops were fraternizing with the Germans along the whole length of the lines. Propaganda leaflets calling on the German workingclass to end the imperialist war were being hurried to the front from the printing shops of Petrograd and distributed by the hundreds of thousands.

The first talks ended with a ten day truce during which both sets of negotiators were to consult their governments. The German generals left dismayed. Somehow these despised Bolsheviks had managed to turn Brest-Litovsk into a sounding board for the preaching of their revolutionary apocalypse.

Von Hindenburg described the situation in his memoirs: "On December 15 an armistice had been concluded on the Russian front . . . Of course it would entirely have corresponded with our desires if the peace bells could have rung. The place of those bells was taken by the inflammatory wild speeches of revolutionary doctrinaires with which the conference room at Brest-Litovsk resounded . . . Peace on earth was to be assured by the wholesale massacre of the bourgeoisie . . . It seemed to me that Lenin and Trotzky behaved more like the victors than the vanquished, trying to sow the seeds of political dissolution in the rear as well as in the ranks of the army . . . I need hardly give any assurance," ruefully added the Prussian commander in chief, "that to negotiate with a Russian terrorist government was extremely disagreeable to a man of my political views."

Thawing Out the Railroads

With the coming of the holidays domestic problems piled up on the President's desk. The country was locked in one of the harshest cold spells on record. Blizzards in the west and zero weather on the eastern seaboard were disrupting railroad traffic, already disorganized by conflicting priorities issued by the commissions, purchasing bureaus and quartermaster's agencies which proliferated in Washington and around the thirtytwo camps where the draftees were in training. Every army paymaster was putting blue priority tags on the shipments he wanted with the result that priorities lost all meaning.

The railroads had come into the war in bad shape. Management was plagued by the results of past piratical financing, and held in a vice between the demands of skilled labor for wage increases, generally admitted to be long overdue, and the Interstate Commerce Commission's refusal to allow rates to be raised. The railroads were undermanned. High wages in munitions plants and shipyards were draining off their best employees. The draft boards depleted the rest. The growth of war exports, without compensating imports, tended to fill the railroad yards in the east with empty freightcars waiting for a westerly load. On top of that the prolonged cold spell froze up locomotives, trapped barges on rivers and canals and increased the nationwide demand for coal and petroleum products. The railroad war board appointed by the Council of National Defense tried to unsnarl the tangle through voluntary cooperation but to no avail.

As Christmas approached, news came to Washington daily of plants shutting down for lack of fuel, of finished goods essential to the war effort jammed into warehouses or deteriorating on open docks, of ships tied up in frozen harbors. New York City was facing a coal famine. A hundred and fifty ships were anchored in the bay waiting for coal. In two weeks no mails had left for Europe. Newspapers were claiming that within seven days there would be no coal at all on Manhattan. Criticism of the conduct of war production was mounting in Congress. Somebody had to be put in charge to keep transportation moving.

For the past month whenever the President and his Secretary of the Treasury had a moment together they had talked railroads. Where was the man who could organize the whole network and run it as a continental unit? Wilson's soninlaw already had the Treasury and four other fulltime jobs. "Mac I wonder if you would do it?" the President asked him one day. No man to underestimate his own powers, McAdoo answered that since he was already deep in railroad finance maybe he had better take the job himself rather than give it to someone he would have trouble cooperating with. Under the authority of a provision of the Army Appropriations Act, the President issued a proclamation taking possession of every railroad in the country and appointing William Gibbs McAdoo, with supreme powers over wages, rates, routing and financing, as director.

A Baneful Seething

In his address to the railroad executives gathered in at the White House the summer before when the President was trying to induce them to meet the railroad workers halfway and stave off a railroad strike, he spoke with emotion of the "baneful seething" he found beneath the surface of America. This baneful seething, if proper action were not taken, might express itself in radical action "the consequences of which no man can foresee."

Now he saw the possibilities of the sort of radical action he dreaded much enhanced by the flood of propaganda the Russian Bolsheviks were letting loose on the world. He saw Socialists, I.W.W.s, pacifists, anarchists of the Emma Goldman stripe all contributing in their separate ways to help enemy aliens and German agents impede the war effort. While he was a stickler for the forms of the constitutional process, he intended to use his powers under the espionage law and draft laws to the full.

His Attorney General was House's old Texas friend T. W. Gregory, a devout adherent since the days of the Texas delegation at the Baltimore convention. Gregory made his name as a lawyer by conducting the government case against the New York New Haven & Hartford in an antitrust prosecution. House described him as loyal as Caesar's legion. Now Gregory was zealously backing up the President by sending his assistants far and wide over the country to root out sedition.

Gregory's fellow Texan, Postmaster General Burleson, was already making life difficult for the hyphenated press. He banned the chief Irish newspapers *The Freeman's Journal, The Irish World* and *The Gaelic American* from the mails for statements disrespectful of the English ally. German and slavic language papers were continuously scrutinized for sedition. The Socialist *Leader,* published in Milwaukee, a city under suspicion as both a German-American and a Socialist center, was denied mailing privileges. Even the liberal *Metropolitan Magazine,* among whose contributors and editors were staunch adherents of the New Freedom, had an issue declared unmailable on account of an article by William Hard questioning the Administration's policy in the Caribbean. Organs of the angry young radicals, such as Max Eastman's *Masses,* were put out of business.

The Department of Justice even took action against a motion picture entitled *The Spirit of 1776* which was forbidden the screen on account of a scene showing redcoats committing atrocities against revolutionary civilians. The Attorney General was so pleased with the judge's decision in this case, tried in a federal court in California, that he had it published as a pamphlet.

Gregory's agents meanwhile were seeking indictments against the seditious and the disloyal. The notorious anarchists Emma Goldman and

Alexander Berkman were already in the toils of the law for their opposition to conscription. Enemy aliens were being weeded out of training camps and interned as fast as they could be apprehended. The disaffected were marked for deportation. Indictments were in the works against a college professor named Scott Nearing, who had been dismissed by the University of Pennsylvania for pacifist utterances; and against Rose Pastor Stokes, a Socialist from East Side New York, an old Wilson admirer, who was unable to stomach the Allied war aims as revealed by the secret treaties, and was saying so in public. Warrants were out for leaders of the Non-Partisan League who were too outspoken in their admiration for Senator La Follette. In Akely, Minnesota, a young Socialist let his fear of the Department of Justice so prey on his mind that he blew his head off by biting into a dynamite cap. In Chicago the federal District Attorneys were carefully laying the groundwork for the fulldress state trial of one-eyed William D. Haywood and a hundred and one members of the Industrial Workers of the World.

These "Wobblies" were easier game than the Socialists. The Socialists were respectable people. Their convictions about the sanctity of the democratic process were very near Woodrow Wilson's own. The Wobblies came from the bottom of the heap.

Their fundamental tenet, like that of the Russian Bolsheviks, was that the exploiting class, as they called the employers of the world, and the working class had nothing in common. Unlike the Russian Bolsheviks who were all for seizing government power, they would have nothing to do with the state, either theoretically or practically. They boasted of their belief in sabotage and direct action. They dreamed of the general strike which, by some mystical process they never got very far towards describing, would peacefully transform society so that the men who did the work would own the tools of production and retain the profits now being siphoned off into the money bags of parasite capitalists. It was a doctrine which appealed to the wild frontier fringe of American labor. It was a doctrine for tramps and freelivers. It smacked of talk around the campfire in hobo jungles and of the independence of the homesteader invading the wilderness with his axe and his gun. As Americans, they claimed, they were born with the right of free speech.

The Wobblies may well at that time have had a million and a half adherents. They encouraged draftdodging and denounced the war as a capitalist device to squeeze profits out of the blood of conscript workers. Their doctrines were prevalent among the lumbermen of the Northwest who were producing timbers for the shipyards and spruce for the airplanes which were so slow in coming into production. They were stirring up strikes and freespeech fights which, it was claimed, impeded the war effort. The trial and eventual conviction of the entire leadership and the

brutally long terms imposed by Judge Landis virtually removed the Wobblies' frontier syndicalism from the lexicon of American Labor.

While Gregory's federal agents, using what they called presidential
warrants when they could not get warrants duly issued by grand juries,
and even more zealous state officials, labored mightily to place critics of
the presidential policies behind bars, the general public joined in the hue
and cry.

Forty authors of standing petitioned the Senate for the expulsion of
that wilful man, La Follette. German courses were dropped from schools
and colleges. German dishes disappeared from bills of fare. Sauerkraut
became known as liberty cabbage, German measles was renamed. German clover appeared in the seed catalogues as crimson or liberty clover.
All manifestations of foreign culture became suspect. German operas were
dropped from the repertory. The drive against German music culminated
in the arrest of Dr. Carl Muck, the elderly and muchadmired conductor
of the Boston Symphony Orchestra.

The Opinions of Leviathan

"It is not an army that we must shape and train for war. It is a nation,"
Wilson wrote in his draft proclamation. "The whole nation must be a
team." To turn the whole nation into a team it was not enough to punish
the expression of the wrong opinions. It was necessary to disseminate the
right opinions.

During the first weeks after the declaration of war, at a time when Wilson was distracted by Congress's refusal to give him, along with his other
wartime powers, the censorship of the press, there appeared on the White
House desk the sort of document he most liked to peruse when he was
trying to make up his mind on some issue. The epistle summed up the
arguments for and against official wartime censorship and suggested that
what was needed was not suppression, but expression; in other words a
publicity campaign to sell the war to the nation.

This brief was the work of a Colorado journalist who had supported the
President with such vim, through a set of slashing editorials and a book
on the issues, during the 1916 campaign, that Tumulty had him down for
a post in one of the departments. The journalist's name was George Creel.

Creel was a little shrimp of a man with burning dark eyes set in an ugly
face under a shock of curly black hair. He came from an impoverished
family of Virginians who had moved to Missouri after the Civil War. He
had made his way up through Kansas City newspapers and muckraking
New York magazines by energy and brass to the position of Police Commissioner in Denver. He was a leader of the reform element among Colorado Democrats. He had graduated from the tubthumping Denver *Post*

to his own *Rocky Mountain News*. He was married to Blanche Bates, one of the reigning stars of the American stage.

A hardworking man with an inexhaustible selfconfidence, his failing was snap judgements. He was famous for his wise cracks. His remark that Senator Lodge, like the soil of New England, was carefully cultivated but naturally sterile, undoubtedly endeared him to the President.

"To Creel," wrote Mark Sullivan, the journalistic chronicler of the period, "there are only two classes of men. There are skunks and the greatest man that ever lived. The greatest man that ever lived is plural and includes everyone who is on Creel's side in whatever public issue he happens at the moment to be concerned with." "It must be admitted," Creel wrote of himself, "that an open mind is no part of my inheritance. I took in prejudices with mother's milk and was weaned on partisanship."

For years Creel, working his noisy way through single tax, socialism, muckraking, progressivism and reform to the New Freedom, had been proclaiming that Woodrow Wilson was the greatest man that ever lived. He certainly did not keep that opinion to himself when he appeared at the White House for consultation about the Committee on Public Information the President had decided to set up with Daniels, Baker and Secretary of State Lansing on the letterhead. The result of a single interview was that Creel was appointed chairman with full executive powers. It was understood that his instructions would come direct from the President.

As the wartime tensions increased around the President's desk, Creel, along with Baruch, Newton D. Baker and Colonel House were about the only men Tumulty was instructed to pass into the upstairs study. Creel was Wilson's link with the Censorship Board, with the Post Office and the Department of Justice. He cooperated with Military and Naval Intelligence. Through these he exercised the President's power to suppress. As head of the Committee for Public Information his function, so he liked to put it, was expression. He became the President's mouthpiece in the war of slogans.

Creel set up his office across the street from the White House in an old brick residence on Jackson Place. There he collected about him a staff of Wilson-minded journalists who, through subsidiary offices in the large cities, spread the doctrine from coast to coast.

The C.P.I. became the fountainhead of war news for the Washington press corps. The existence of an official press censorship was consistently denied but editors were safer if their material had passed through Creel's hands.

He developed a news bureau and a set of syndicated services giving the administration slant to events and explaining away false and damaging rumors. Special matter was prepared for the foreignlanguage press. A picture division was set up and a film division. A foreign division channelled propaganda into Germany and Russia. There was a speakers' bureau through which speakers for the various Liberty Loan drives were furnished with material. The seventyfive thousand volunteer orators groomed for four minute talks at street corners, in movie theatres and churches and at civic events, on topics prepared for them by Creel's bureaus, became known as "the stentorian guard."

C.P.I. posters were in every postoffice. C.P.I. information bulletins were on every bulletin board. Country weeklies and trade journals were nourished on Creel's boilerplate. In an astonishingly short time George Creel had the entire nation—except of course for the disreputable minority who insisted on forming their own opinions—repeating every slogan which emanated from the President's desk in the wordy war to "make the world safe for democracy."

Remaking the Map

Woodrow Wilson's birthday was on December 28. The group of White House intimates, that the President and Mrs. Wilson kept carefully insulated from any mention of the strains and anxieties of high office, conducted their jollifications in the small dining room because the larger White House rooms were closed off to conserve fuel. Mrs. Josephus Daniels baked the cake.

"The cake was perfectly beautiful and as palatable as it was good to look at," the President wrote her in his note of thanks. "The sixty one candles on the cake did not make so forbidding a multitude as I should have feared they would and our little family circle had a very jolly time blowing them out and celebrating." He allowed himself a professorial pun: "It was a regular blow-out."

Colonel House returned to the White House before Christmas bringing the documents his Inquiry had prepared on European populations and boundaries and on the pretensions of the various national leaderships. After New Years he came back with another mass of material including maps prepared by Dr. Bowman's assistants at the American Geographical Society. Wilson decided to give his statement the form of a message to be delivered soon after the opening of Congress. He had to answer the Bolshevik challenge that the Allies state their war aims. He hoped to stir the German socialists to the sort of pacifist demands he decried among the unruly at home, and to reassert his position as leader of liberal and idealist trends of thought in France and Great Britain.

House's train was late. McAdoo was giving coal shipments right of way even over crack passenger expresses. It was nine o'clock on January 4 before the colonel reached the White House. "They had saved dinner for me," he wrote in his diary, "but I touched it lightly and went into immediate conference with the President." Wilson who loved the number thirteen was trying to organize the points he wanted to make under thirteen headings.

Next morning they met again in the President's study. "Saturday was a remarkable day," wrote House. "I went over to the State Department just after breakfast to see Polk and the others, and returned to the White House at a quarter past ten in order to get to work with the President . . . We actually got down to work at half past ten and finished remaking the map of the world as we would have it, at half past twelve o'clock.

"We took it up systematically, first outlining general terms, such as open diplomacy, freedom of the seas, removing of economic barriers, establishment of equality of trade conditions, guarantees for the reduction of national armaments, adjustment of colonial claims, general association of nations for the conservation of peace."

They were still at work on a preliminary draft when the afternoon papers were brought in carrying a report of Lloyd George's speech the day before to the British Trade Union Congress. The unpredictable Welshman, pressed by the opposition in Parliament to answer the Bolshevik demands and by the laborleaders whose assistance he needed in his conduct of the war, had jumped the gun on the American President by declaring: "We are not fighting a war of aggression against Germany . . . We are not fighting to destroy Austro-Hungary or to deprive Turkey of its capital . . . The settlement of the new Europe must be based on such grounds of reason and justice as will give some promise of stability. Therefore it is that we feel that government with the consent of the governed must be the basis of any territorial settlement in this war."

The President was quite put out. He felt that Lloyd George had taken the wind out of his sails. It did not suit his idea of keeping the center of gravity of the war in Washington merely to parrot the views of the British Prime Minister. His first impulse was to pitch his whole speech in the wastebasket. It took all House's tactful persuasion to convince him that Lloyd George by "clearing the air" had prepared the way for Woodrow Wilson's more authoritative statement of war aims.

Sunday afternoon House was back in the President's study. The President read him the first draft of his speech. The colonel was delighted: "I felt it was the most important document he had ever penned."

House wanted immediate notice to be given in the press that an important declaration was coming, but Wilson insisted that to give advance notice would start a rash of editorials. "The President's argument was that . . . the newspapers invariably commented and speculated as to what he would say and that these forecasts were often taken for what was really said."

The President and the colonel lunched together Monday. Both men were anxious for fear the speech would be illreceived in the American press. House feared this sudden entrance into European affairs would stir up isolationist sentiment. ". . . The other points we were fearful of were Alsace Lorraine, the freedom of the seas, and the levelling of commercial barriers. However . . . there was not the slightest hesitation on his part in saying them . . . The President shows extraordinary courage in such things. The more I see of him, the more firmly I am convinced there is not a statesman in the world who is his equal."

That afternoon the meticulous Lansing was called in to dot the i's and cross the t's. For fear the Secretary of State might be offended by the scanty part he'd been allowed to play in drafting the document an occasional expression was changed to meet his approval.

After House and Lansing retired Creel came charging into the President's office with what he claimed was "cheering news from Petrograd." Edgar Sisson, his representative there, had managed to arrange the showing, at a large theatre on the Nevski Prospect, of a propaganda film extolling the American way of life entitled *All for Peace*.

At the very moment when President Wilson and his human megaphone were discussing their hopes for talking the Russians around to fighting a war for democracy, the Bolsheviks, wherever their armed men were in control, were seizing the banks and forcing the wealthy at the point of a gun to open up their safedeposit boxes. The result, if not the Wilsonian type of New Freedom, was a very substantial fund in gold rubles. To further their kind of peace the Council of People's commissars put two millions at Trotsky's disposal to spread the international revolutionary movement.

On the point of leaving Petrograd to take charge of the negotiations at Brest-Litovsk, Trotsky, while Wilson and his advisers were putting the final touches on the Fourteen Points speech, delivered himself of a blast at the Allied governments for not responding to his invitation to join in the peace conference. The sessions, so he put it, had been adjourned to give the Allied governments a chance to participate. Brest-Litovsk was their last chance: "Russia does not bind herself in these negotiations to the consent of the Allied governments. If they continue to sabotage the cause of general peace, the Russian delegation in any case will continue the negotiations . . . We at the same time promise our complete support to the laboring classes of any country which will rise against their national imperialists."

Among other "cheering news," Creel laid on the President's desk a report from Colonel W. B. Thompson of the American Red Cross, one of the many unofficial observers at large in Russia that winter, counselling friendly contact with the Bolsheviks who were not "the wildeyed rabble most of us consider them." Another item was the cabled rumor of a mutiny at the German Naval Base at Kiel. Perhaps the policy of the wedge was already beginning to take effect.

Creel gave place to a committee of the American Red Cross come to ask Wilson's assistance in their drive for contributions. When Tumulty got them out of the office the text of the President's message was hurried over to the Government Printing Office to be printed. The President dropped affairs of state for his usual family dinner. He retired early to be in form for his address to Congress on the morrow.

The Fourteen Points

January 8 turned out to be a fine cold winter's day. After breakfast the Wilsons went out to the country club to play a few holes of golf. It wasn't till his return to the White House at eleven thirty that morning that the President had Tumulty notify Vice President Marshall and Speaker Champ Clark that he would be arriving on Capitol Hill in half an hour to address a joint session of Congress. Since he had addressed Congress only the Friday before, asking for broader powers to deal with the breakdown in railroad transportation, this notification of a fresh message caught the leaders of both houses unprepared. There was a hubbub in the lobbies and a scramble to round up sufficient senators and representatives to fill the House.

Several cabinet members were not notified. The only ambassador seen in the diplomatic gallery was Sir Cecil Spring Rice who the week before had taken his leave of the President with the announcement that he was being replaced by Lloyd George's closest collaborator Lord Reading. A Serbian delegation waiting to be received by Congress had to be shunted off at the last moment.

Attendance was small in the visitors' galleries. Mrs. Wilson arrived at noon accompanied by her mother and sister and by two of the President's daughters. The ladies were discreetly joined by Colonel House. When the President was ushered into the speaker's stand the applause that greeted him was thinner than usual.

Woodrow Wilson spoke in low measured tones. He began by reminding his hearers of the breaking off of the negotiations at Brest-Litovsk and of the perfidy of the German proposals there. He spoke of the Bolsheviks with sympathy; the Russian representatives were sincere and in earnest: "They cannot entertain such proposals of conquest and domination . . . The Russian representatives have insisted, very justly, very wisely and in the true spirit of modern democracy that the conferences they have been holding with the Teutonic and Turkish statesmen should be held with open, not closed doors, and all the world has been audience . . .

"Mr. Lloyd George has spoken with admirable candor and in admirable spirit for the people and government of Great Britain."

Wilson went on to discuss in friendly tones the state of mind of the Russian people: "They call to us to say what it is that we desire, in what, if anything, our purpose and our spirit differ from theirs: and I believe that the people of the United States would wish me to respond with utter simplicity and frankness. Whether their present leaders believe it or not, it is our heartfelt desire and hope that some way may be opened whereby we may be privileged to assist the people of Russia to obtain their utmost hope of liberty and ordered peace."

At this point came the first applause. People were still filing into the galleries. Senators and representatives were sneaking into their seats.

"What we demand in this war, therefore is nothing peculiar to ourselves. It is that the world be made fit and safe to live in . . . All the peoples of the world are in effect partners in this interest, and for our own part we see very clearly that unless justice be done to others it will not be done to us."

The chamber was very silent when he began to enumerate the points of a program for a permanent peace: first open covenants openly arrived at; then freedom of the seas, the removal of economic barriers, the reduction of armaments; in the adjustment of colonial claims the interests of the subject populations must be considered equally with those of the colonizers; all conquered territory in Belgium and France and Russia must be evacuated and restored.

When he reached point VIII: the need to right the wrong done France by the seizure of Alsace and Lorraine in 1870, there was a burst of loud cheering. The galleries applauded. Senators and representatives jumped on chairs and waved their arms as if they were at a football game.

The President, smiling patiently, waited for the pandemonium to subside . . .

Point IX: The frontiers of Italy were to be adjusted along "clearly recognizable rights of nationality." (House and Wilson and Lansing, haunted by fears that the Italians might follow the Russian example in a separate peace, had struggled long over that phrase.)

Point X: This was another poser. The President hoped at that point to encourage the national minorities without breaking up the Austro-Hungarian empire; he announced that they should be "accorded the freest opportunity of autonomous development."

Point XI: Rumania, Serbia and Montenegro must be evacuated and restored.

Point XII called for free passage of the Dardanelles and autonomy and security for the various peoples making up the Turkish empire.

Point XIII demanded an independent Poland.

Point XIV called for a "general association of nations . . . formed under specific covenants for the purpose of affording mutual guarantees of political independence and territorial integrity to great and small states alike."

The President's peroration proclaimed this to be "the moral climax . . . of the culminating and final war for human liberty."

The response in America to the Fourteen Points speech was almost universal acclaim. Champ Clark wrote Wilson that it was clear as crystal: "Anybody that can't understand it, whether he agrees with it or not, is an incorrigible fool." Men of such diverse attitudes as Theodore Roosevelt and Senator Borah expressed their approval. Socialists applauded it. To the college professors whose thinking was shepherded by Herbert Croly's *New Republic* the Fourteen Points became holy writ. The Republican New York *Tribune* called the message a second Emancipation Proclamation.

In Great Britain the reception was cooler. Editorial writers were pleased to have President Wilson so loyally backing up Lloyd George, but the phrase "freedom of the seas" gave them chills. Even the liberals of the Quakerowned "cocoa" press were restrained in their enthusiasm. The London *Times* expressed some doubts that "the reign of righteousness was within our reach."

So slow was the transmission that a week went by before Creel's representatives in Petrograd had the complete message in their hands. When the translation into German and Russian was complete Sisson, who was a frantic journalist in the old tradition, hurried in a cab through snowy streets with a copy for Smolny. He was allowed to place it personally in Lenin's hands, and Lenin saw to it that it was immediately telegraphed to Trotsky at Brest-Litovsk.

Sisson described Lenin, whom he was seeing for the first time, as looking "like the bourgeois mayor of a French town, short, sparsely bearded, a bronze man in hair and whiskers, small shrewd eyes, round of face, smiling and genial when he desires to be." According to Sisson, Lenin was "joyous as a boy" when he read the President's words recognizing the honesty of purpose of the Bolsheviks.

Lenin recognized the value of Wilson's Fourteen Points in driving a wedge between the Germans and their government. He allowed the speech to be distributed to German prisoners and copied into the literature the Bolsheviks were spreading through the armies.

Sisson hired outofwork Russian soldiers to paste posters of the speech up all over Petrograd. He distributed three hundred thousand handbills and some million pamphlets. American consuls and representatives of the Y.M.C.A. and of the International Harvester Company handed it out wherever they could. The Fourteen Points made President Wilson a hero to eastern Europe.

To the members of the German High Command this talk about liberty and selfdetermination and the rights of peoples was dangerous nonsense. Their fear of its effect on softheaded civilians back home seems to have hardened their decision that they must, before it was too late, take the peace conference out of the hands of their diplomats and dictate iron terms to the Russians.

Chapter 17

THE FIRST BLOOD

In France the winter of 1917 settled in unusually early. Although the United States had been in the war seven months not an American soldier had come to grips with the enemy. By late October most of the elements to make up four large size divisions were training in Lorraine. The 1st Division, originally manned by regular army troops shipped straight to France from the Mexican border; the 2nd, which was half marines; the 26th based on the New England National Guard; and the 42nd, composed of militia outfits from twentysix states and the District of Columbia, were in the last stages of training.

These divisions amounted to something more than a hundred thousand men, a sizeable force, but not yet enough to count for much in the councils of the Allied commanders who were faced with the necessity of meeting the vast offensive which was expected on the western front as soon as the German High Command transferred its armies from the east.

The American doughboy was a changed man, in appearance at least, from the days of the Mexican border patrol. The broadbrimmed felt campaign hat had given way to the overseas cap and to steel helmets bought from the British. Rolled woolen puttees had replaced the canvas leggins left over from Philippine campaigns. Gasmasks were part of the regulation equipment.

Warm clothing was still scarce. Lucky were the men who had sweaters to wear under their tunics. Gloves were at a premium as were rubber boots to wade through the sleety muck of French barnyards. There were never enough blankets. Even woolen socks and proper footgear were in short supply. Flimsy shoes the doughboys called "chickenskins" disintegrated on the long hikes. Pershing's battalions sometimes left bloody prints behind them as they tramped through the snow.

Summer had been raw and rainy in the Lorraine sector and the foothills of the Vosges, but with the progress of fall the rain turned to sleet and snow. Americans, accustomed to warm houses at home, suffered agonies of cold in their chilly billets. Enlistedmen huddled in barns and haylofts often under shattered roofs of tiles or dilapidated thatch that let in the wind and the drizzle, or in hastily constructed Adrian barracks. So chary were the French of the wood from their national forests that fires were only allowed for cooking. Baths were unheard of. Even the officers, billeted in spare bedrooms and front parlors, felt lucky if they could scrape together a few damp twigs that produced more smoke than heat in the tiny fireplaces. It was a time of chilblains and frozen feet. The historically inclined reminded each other of Washington's winter at Valley Forge.

The Art of War

Drills and training continued in all weathers. Pershing was a stickler for drill. Dawes, one of the few men in the world who had real affection for John Pershing, told the story of how the Commander in Chief sent General Harbord across the street at some military function to button up Dawes' overcoat. Dawes had forgotten to button all the buttons. "A hell of a job for the Chief of Staff," muttered Harbord while he did it. An Englishspeaking French veteran of four years of war was heard to remark that the spit and polish at Pershing's headquarters at Chaumont made him feel like a Boy Scout.

Though many officers and noncoms were sent to learn trench warfare among the British most of the instruction was by French divisions drawn back for rest and recuperation. The French conducted their training with enthusiasm. It was a better life than fighting the boche.

Near Gondrecourt French engineers constructed a model sector with dugout shelters, line entrenchments and observation posts. There the Americans were put through gas attacks with real gas and taught the use of handgrenades and Very pistols for signalling and the vagaries of the heavy Chauchat automatic rifle and of the 37-millimeter gun and the trench mortar. Even their machineguns were the French Hotchkiss since Army Ordnance had lost so much time trying to decide on the best possible machinegun that it hadn't produced any.

Siege warfare had gone on so long that the French and British infantry instructors could hardly think of war except in terms of trenches and barbed wire entanglements and machinegun fire and riflegrenades for defense. For attack they relied on handgrenades. Shooting was the business of the artillery. The infantry's job was to occupy and hold a position after the barrage had made it uninhabitable for the enemy.

General Pershing had other ideas. He planned for open warfare and insisted on marksmanship on the rifle range. He planned for combat man to man.

Orders came down to indoctrinate the troops in hatred of the boche. Units were harangued on the atrocities the Huns had committed in Belgium and France. American troops must be taught to hate the sonsofbitches. The straw dummies at bayonet practice were named Hans or

Fritz. The troops got instruction in how to tear their guts out with proper zest.

In spite of swollen feet and frostbite, and exhaustion from the long quicktime hikes that were part of the weekly routine, the health and spirits of the men remained surprisingly good. Many were entranced by the picturebook prettiness of the countryside. Doughboys managed to squeeze a few pleasures out of the stony French villages. They got along famously with the children. Farmers' wives did a flourishing business selling the Americans omelettes and *vin chaud*. The Americans were free spenders. They were always ready to trade cans of bullybeef for wines and liquors or occasionally for complaisances on the part of the farmer's daughter. They helped the farmer with his chores. To the French they appeared not only as a protection from the boche but as a source of revenue. A whole language of Franco-American camaraderie grew up with French and English words interspersed. "Our *popote's* no damn good. Cook feeds us *beaucoup* slum."

On October 20 four battalions of infantry from the 1st Division were sent into the lines amid the undamaged scenery of a quiet sector along the Marne-Rhine canal between Lunéville and Nancy. The artillery, which had been learning the use of seventyfives and howitzers under French instructors at Le Valdahon, took up positions from which they could duplicate the fire of the guns of the French division which was holding that part of the front.

On October 23 the first American shell, out of a French seventyfive to be sure, was sent shrilling over the German lines. The boche replied in kind. The same day a few wounded were sent back to the new field hospital. Four days later a patrol out in nomansland managed to take a German prisoner.

By this time the Germans were alerted as to the positions of their new enemy. Since by mutual consent nothing ever happened on the Lorraine front the French had little aviation there. The A.E.F. did not yet have a plane fit to fly, so the men of the 1st Division had no air cover at all. The Germans bided their time until their observation planes reported that a relief of the American troops in advanced positions was in progress.

At 3 A.M. the morning of November 3 they let loose everything they had in a violent bombardment of an outpost which had just been occupied by a platoon of the 16th Infantry. It was the men's first moment at the front. They had been fumbling about in the dark trying to find their way in the maze of trenches. Before they knew what had happened they were boxed in by a barrage. A German raiding party blew a path through the barbed wire with bangalore torpedoes. Right away their handgrenades came lobbing over the parapet. Three men were killed. The sergeant and nine more were overpowered by bayonets and trenchknives and surrendered. The German radio had itself a time crowing over this easy victory over the green Americans.

The Fighting Engineers

The only other Americans to undergo their baptism of shrapnel that fall were some railroadmen from the 11th Engineers attached to the British under General Byng. Two companies of them helped unload the tanks brought up at night in camouflaged flatcars and hidden in the woods in preparation for the November attack in front of Cambrai. After the unexpectedly successful breakthrough they went up with the Canadians to repair the railroad line through Gouzeaucourt. When the Germans launched their sudden counteroffensive they dropped crowbars and shovels and gave a good account of themselves with their rifles. They reported two dead, thirteen wounded and fifteen missing, after falling back shoulder to shoulder with the British combat troops.

Another engineer outfit on similar duty, from the 12th, managed to hide out in a village during the high tide of the German advance. When the enemy was dislodged from the furthest point of his advance they reported back without the loss of a man at their post of command.

Tactical Command

The 1st Division, meanwhile, was pulled out of the lines for further training. Major General Sibert, who had made a name for himself superintending engineering work on the Panama Canal, but in whom G.H.Q. discovered a lack of combat initiative, was replaced by Robert Lee Bullard, a wiry Georgiaborn general with a twinkle in his eye, who had at least heard bullets sing as a young man in the pursuit of Geronimo and in the Philippines.

For many of the Americans that dank Christmas was the first they had ever spent away from home. The doughboys rigged up Christmas trees in every village where they were billeted and had a high time distributing candy and whatever toys they could get hold of to the sadeyed little French children. The Mayor of Gondrecourt was so touched that he wrote a letter of appreciation. It was like a *fête* of two large families he said. Never perhaps had such bonds of sympathy obtained between two nations.

A few days later the 1st Division floundered through a snowstorm to finish their training with five days of manoeuvres. "Worst weather in which I ever saw troops work," wrote General Bullard in his diary. He

described it as the fiercest strain to which he had ever seen troops sub-
jected outside of battle. The snow was four or five inches deep on the
open ground. The men in the practice trenches were over their shoetops
in slush. There were frozen fingers and ears and noses. Horses died from
cold and exhaustion. What saved the day, according to Bullard, were the
rolling kitchens which they had imitated from the French popotes. Hot
food kept up the men's spirits and strength. Only the horses died; the
doughboys held up, and the old army mules.

January 15 half of the 1st Division moved out of its billets in the training area to relieve the French on the eastern flank of the St. Mihiel sector.
This was the position which Pershing picked the summer before for the
eventual jumping off of an American drive into the vitals of industrial
Germany. Up to now the Americans had been nursed by French units
whenever they appeared. In the Toul sector they were on their own.

The weather was even more trying than during the five days manoeuvres. A cold night froze the snowy roads and a sleety rain smoothed them
to sheer ice where neither the horses' hoofs nor the wheels of trucks could
take hold. Men and animals fell in all directions in a tangle of harness
and ditched wagons. Upset wagons were continually having to be re-
loaded in the rain by men up to their knees in freezing slush. By night
the wagon train of the first detachment had only progressed a mile and
a half.

"I felt perfectly sure," wrote Bullard, "that these soldiers were never
afterward to encounter anything except death that would be harder to
face than the labors and exposure of this day."

Three days later the American battalions were filing into a five kilometer stretch of trenches on low and muddy ground in the vicinity of the
village of Seicheprey. The officers of the French Moroccan division they
relieved showed the Americans the lay of the land. The entire region was
overlooked by German positions on a high bare hill. In spite of miles of
camouflage every artillery position and every ammunition dump and
every daylight move of troops was clearly visible to the boche observers
looking through their glasses from safe observation posts on Montsec.

As harrowing as being under the enemy's eye, was the itching from
the cooties that swarmed in the dugouts and shelters. For most of the
Americans it was their first experience with lice.

For two weeks their officers fretted under the command of the French
corps headquarters. The French used the Toul area as a rest sector and
they wanted to keep it quiet. The Americans were rearing to go. At last
on February 10 Bullard could enter in his diary: "Received tactical command of my division on the fifth and began harrying the enemy at once
. . . Well we stirred him up and he came back at us . . . Of course I lost
men, but as we were the most active it seems probable that we made
him lose more."

The sector came to life in a series of raids and counterraids across the barbed wire and the muddy shellholes between the hostile positions. There was constant rifle and machinegun fire. Occasionally a highspirited doughboy who still felt war was a kind of a lark would poke his hat up on a stick above the trench just to see what Heinie would do. Heinie answered with minenwerfers. American detachments took losses but they struck back. The dead and wounded had to be carried two or three kilometers uphill through slippery access trenches where the mud never dried. Graves were always open in the little cemetery near headquarters at Mesnil la Tour. As signs of spring appeared on the ruined land the white crosses multiplied.

A Plan for the Knockout

The plight of the 1st Division wallowing in the muck of the Toul sector under observation from the Germans on Montsec was typical of the whole strategic scheme of the war that winter. The Germans had the inside lines. They had the advantage of position. The initiative was theirs.

The element they lacked was time. Although the German people were kept in ignorance, the inner circle of command was already aware of the failure of their submarine blockade of Great Britain. On the other hand the German people were all too conscious of the success of the British blockade of the Fatherland. They were hungry. Stories were going around of babies dying for lack of milk. Fats were hardly obtainable. Soap had ceased to exist. Breadstuffs were ersatz and strictly rationed. Industries were running down for lack of raw materials.

It was hoped that with the next harvest the Baltic provinces and Poland and the Ukraine, about to be denied to the Petrograd Bolsheviks by the peace terms at Brest-Litovsk, would be furnishing wheat and meat. For the moment the only way to provide sufficient food for the army was to starve the civilians.

Germany's allies were in a bad way. The Hapsburg empire was on the verge of emulating the collapse of the Romanoffs. In the Balkans victor and vanquished suffered equally from pestilence and famine. The Bulgarian Army was weakened by the strife of factions. The Turks lacked money and munitions and the will to fight. In the southern dominions the British had wiped out the shame of Kut el Amara by capturing Baghdad and Jerusalem. Arabian sheikhs were declaring their independence. Romantic British agents like Philby and Lawrence were lashing up the Bedouins to revolt. In the Aegean the Turkish rule was threatened by the Greeks whom the British were cautiously arming under Venizelos.

Erich von Ludendorff's successes in the East had won the Kaiser's devotion. Von Hindenburg relied on him completely. As Imperial Chief of

Staff, he was master of Germany. It was largely his decision that, before the untrained Americans should learn how to fight, and before the corrosion of Bolshevism and hunger and revolt should advance any further, the German armies must strike the Allies a knockout blow in the West.

As fast as the German divisions were pulled out of the eastern battle-fields they were put through courses of training in von Hutier's methods of open warfare which had proved so successful at Riga and Caporetto. The rank and file were thoroughly indoctrinated with the notion that one final blow would bring a victorious peace to the Fatherland. The staffs meanwhile were busy blueprinting every detail of a series of offensives which they believed would shatter the Allied armies. With immense pains alternative projects were drafted. If they made proper use of their new dominance in manpower they could not fail.

"St. George I" was the code name of an operation against Ypres, "St. George II" against Lys. These were to be under the group of armies commanded by Prince Rupert of Bavaria. Further south the German Crown Prince's headquarters would join the Bavarians in the conduct of operation "Michael" against the hinge between the British and the French in front of St. Quentin. The Kaiser's son would further assume command of operation "Roland" through the Chemin des Dames. If these went awry other plans dubbed "Castor and Pollux," "Hector and Achilles" were in readiness. There was preparation for diversions in Alsace and the Trou de Belfort. Dummy concentrations were to be used to confuse Allied intelligence as to where the real blows would fall. "It will be an immense struggle that will begin at one point, continue at another, and take a long time," Ludendorff told the Kaiser. "It is difficult but it will be victorious."

The information that came in from the camp of the enemy to the political observers attached to the German General Staff was not too discouraging. In America one of the first results of the war effort was the collapse of railroad transportation. American newspapers were full of the failure of the airplanebuilding program. Men were dying of influenza in the training camps. Ex-President Theodore Roosevelt—for whom the Germans had high respect—was stalking about the country denouncing the inefficiencies of the Administration. The War Department was said to have "ceased to function." So general was the disillusionment with the production of fighting equipment that a prominent Democrat, Senator Chamberlain of Oregon, was assailing Secretary Baker's management in a fulldress debate in the Senate.

More than a million draftees were in training, but no appreciable amount of ordnance was being produced. The shipbuilding program was still on the draftingboard and the British were proving unwilling to furnish enough of their own shipping to transport American troops to France in really large quantities.

On the western front, although the Allied Supreme War Council was functioning it was far from attaining unity of command. The French and British had to maintain twelve divisions in Italy to keep that country in the war. Pétain had managed to restore the morale of the French but only by his guarantee that no offensives would be attempted. His plan for a mobile reserve had been accepted by the Supreme War Council but Haig was proving reluctant to put British troops at his disposal. Lloyd George had not screwed up his courage to get rid of Haig whom he obviously distrusted, but he was retaining as a home guard in England the trained men Haig needed to replace the divisions he sent to Italy. Pétain and Haig were engaged in a dispute as to how much of the French lines the British should take over.

When Haig finally consented to relieve the French on a thirty mile stretch in front of St. Quentin he entrusted the new sector to Gough's Fifth Army which was far from recovered from the bloodletting at Ypres the autumn before. Gough's men manned the French positions so thinly and listlessly that this hinge between the French and British immediately became of paramount interest to Ludendorff's planners.

The High Command decided as early as January that operation "Michael" should come first. The concentration of troops and guns and ammunition was made at night and with extraordinary precautions for secrecy. At the same time trooptrains were allowed to be seen in Alsace to give the French the impression that something might be attempted from the direction of the Swiss border. Haig, though some of his staff-officers kept warning him that the attack would come through St. Quentin, was obsessed with the protection of the Channel ports.

He kept his strongest forces on his left. The various British army headquarters were full of talk about defense in depth: "let them come through and smash them from the flanks."

The Supreme War Council meanwhile was issuing neatly drawn maps showing the German armies poised for attack to the north of Cambrai and in the Champagne region between Rheims and Verdun. According to their prognostications the attack would come in June.

On March 10 the Kaiser signed the orders at Imperial General Staff Headquarters, the Hotel Brittanique, in the ancient wateringplace of Spa in Belgium, and, as the trees were beginning to bud on the wooded hills, moved forward in his court train to treeshaded Avesnes in the French department of Nord to animate his armies by his imperial presence.

March 20 all northern France was beaten by a storm of rain and mist. The weather was so bad Hindenburg almost postponed the attack set for the morrow. By night the rain had given place to dense fog.

At 3:30 A.M. the heaviest bombardment of the war with highly volatile gas mixed with shells from guns of all calibers overwhelmed the British positions on a forty mile front. After four hours the bombardment turned into a rolling barrage and the German infantry, in groups accompanied by field guns, trenchmortars, and heavy machineguns started to advance behind it through the fog.

Their instructions were to move ahead as fast as they could, leaving all mopping up of stubborn positions to the units that followed. By noon, when the sun burned through, the Germans found that they had broken the British Fifth Army defenses all along the front. Northward in the direction of Arras the British were holding firm.

For ten days the Germans kept advancing at the speed of about five miles a day through the region between the Somme and the Oise which they had devastated in their withdrawal the year before. The utter ruin of the land they crossed was more hindrance to them than the retreating British. By the time they had reached the flourishing farmlands and undamaged roads beyond Montdidier they had so far outrun their supply that they could advance no further. They had taken thousands of square kilometers of French soil. They had destroyed the British Fifth Army, capturing eighty thousand prisoners and nine hundred and seventyfive guns, but without the railroad junction of Amiens it would be hard to consolidate their victory.

The Sixth Engineers

Although the railroad line through Montdidier was lost to the enemy, General Byng's Third Army, the victors at Cambrai, dug in and held in front of Amiens with that British stubbornness that so often dismayed the German staff. A General Carey did a famous job of collecting stragglers from the broken divisions and throwing them into new trenches across the St. Quentin-Amiens road. These detachments became known as "Carey's chickens." Among the odds and ends of units he imbued with the will to fight was a group of American engineers.

Back in February some companies of the 6th Engineers had been detailed to join a British outfit near Peronne for instruction in military bridge building. They found the British engineers working an Italian labor battalion from the illfated army that broke and ran at Caporetto. The bridge work was absorbing.

The game was to construct a light bridge parallel to the river bank that could be swung around by a truck to span the river when needed. These Americans got along famously with the British who began to call them the Royal 6th.

The Americans were seeing the war at last. There were airraids every night. They watched with great interest the searchlights picking out attacking planes. Soon they could recognize the double whine and buzz of German bombers. The sound of the guns over the faraway front, so one of the officers entered in his diary, sounded to him like the engines of a large riversteamer in the distance. At night the gunflashes made a continual border of red along the northern horizon.

Their British friends frowned on all this activity. "'Uns are cookin' up something narsty." An offensive might come any day.

Gasmask drills were instituted.

Spring was early. There were flowers in the gardens of wrecked houses. Songbirds were singing in the trees along the sluggish green Doignt that flowed into the Somme at this point. The men were enjoying the mild presages of the first French spring any of them had ever seen.

On March 22 a Captain Davis, who had been ordered to return to their old billeting center to settle some claims of damage presented by the villagers, rejoined his unit. He had come through Paris without learning that anything particular was going on at the front, but when he stepped out from the train at Amiens he found the railroad station under heavy attack from the air. Getting out of Amiens as quick as he could he made it back to Peronne by road without too much difficulty, but there he found that the British had orders to burn all the fine bridges they had gone to so much trouble to build. The Americans' orders were to fall back on their dump of engineer equipment at Chaulnes, some fifteen kilometers to the south.

The roads were getting crowded. The sky was full of noise. Airraids were continuous.

They had hardly settled into their cantonments at Chaulnes when orders came to destroy all equipment, even field desks. With only the service records and the men's packs they were to retreat another twentyfive kilometers to Moreuil on the Amiens-Montdidier railroad. There they pitched shelter tents. The weather was pleasant.

On the morning of March 27 the 6th Engineers were informed that their colonel had volunteered them to join the British defense of Amiens. British lorries carried them out to a point on the road between Warfusse and Abancourt. Although they already had their Springfields and their bayonets, there they were issued British rifles too. The British rifle, they reported, was less accurate but handier for rough field work. The trenches to the right of the road had been wellbuilt, but to the left where the engineers were, they were barely started. The Americans were hard at work digging themselves funkholes, when they heard a lot of noise to the right of the road, shrapnel, machineguns, mortar fire; the rough field work had begun.

They were working engineers with little combat training. They were lying in an open field. Behind them was a small wood. In front of them was the advancing German Army. It gave them a lonesome feeling.

Hearts were thumping. Hands were cold on the riflestocks. Eyes were glued to the sights.

The Britishers in the trenches to the right of the road started, so Captain Davis put it, "retiring in some disorder and quite a hurry." An order came from the American colonel to hold and to close up with the troops to the right. At the same moment an excited British major appeared who ordered the Americans out of their trench. He told them to form a line, retire three paces and fire; and then to retire another three paces and fire again, just like at Waterloo. The order seemed rather humorous to the Americans because there weren't any Germans in sight to fire at.

A British general, maybe it was Carey himself, appeared on the scene and made a great outcry that the damned Yankees were running away. The damned Yankees went back into their trench and promptly helped repulse a German attack.

They spent all that day in the trenches without grub and with very little water.

Next day was fine. The Germans shelled. The blue sky filled with cotton blobs of shrapnel. The 6th Engineers stayed put. There were a few casualties. By this time they were getting regular British rations. Next day the Germans started shelling up and down the line. "It was like a *feu de joie* with guns," noted the captain in his journal. The shells sounded like a swarm of bees moving up and down the trenches. Jerry must be having trouble with supply because he was economizing on his ammunition. Eight casualties. Everybody was tense. German infantry was advancing in the shelter of a fold in the land.

All at once the Americans were amazed to see what looked like a haywagon coming towards them down the St. Quentin road. Couldn't be a farmer's haywagon, something funny about the wheels. A lieutenant pumped a few bullets from a Springfield into the haywagon and out popped a couple of jerries. They sure ran. When the hay fell away the thing turned out to be an eight inch howitzer.

Later the same day they captured a man who claimed to be an English sergeant. He'd been asking too many questions about whether the Americans had any machineguns. Of course they hadn't. He talked English all right. Next day the jerries came over in what looked like English planes, captured planes maybe, and machinegunned the trenches. This was the engineers' fourth day in the lines.

After dark that night the headquarters company was transferred to another line of trenches. These were better built and had barbed wire entanglements in front of them but they were full of water. The following night they were shifted again to a point north of the road. There a few Hun snipers bothered them but there was no other activity. Next night they were taken out of the line for good. The men were relieved in small groups. The Huns sent up starshells to see what was happening. The 6th

Engineers had lost two officers and twenty men killed and more than a hundred wounded or missing.

They were billeted at a place called Glissy for a rest. They slept all the first day. An Englishspeaking girl who came nosing around was arrested for a spy. The men were sent in batches into Abbeville for showers. After their showers they were served out British uniforms, the only fresh clothes available. Now they were Royal Engineers for fair.

A couple of days later they were back near Amiens working on the bridges again, this time on the Somme. From where they worked on a tubular bridge to be swung across the Somme they could see the shells taking bites out of the tall pinnacles of the Amiens cathedral in the distance. They worked quietly. No extra bloodpressure. The shelling was far away. They'd had their baptism of fire.

Luncheon at Doullens

The German thrust towards Amiens shocked the British and French leadership into taking one more reluctant step towards a unified command. Each meeting of the Supreme War Council was revealing more cross purposes among the Allies. Pétain's plan for assigning a few French and British divisions to a general reserve, which could be thrown into the line under a single commander wherever the need was greatest, was several times approved in principle but never put into effect. Only that naïve American, tonguetied old General Bliss, seemed wholeheartedly for it. His protests that it was the only logical plan were met by smiles and supercilious shrugs.

Clemenceau backed the general reserve for a while as an entering wedge for obtaining the supreme command for a Frenchman; but, so he told the story later, when he broached such a possibility to Sir Douglas Haig, the British Field Marshal jumped up with his hands over his head like a jackinthebox and cried, "Monsieur Clemenceau, I have only one chief, my king."

The latest meeting of the Supreme War Council in London on March 14 had proved particularly futile. The British produced so many arguments against the general reserve that even Clemenceau gave the impression of having been talked around to their way of thinking. Only Clemenceau's chief of staff, General Foch, stood his ground and insisted on putting himself on record with a long acidulous protest in writing. His stubbornness embroiled him with the grumpy old Tiger. The two Frenchmen left London on very bad terms indeed.

Ferdinand Foch, like Joffre, was a product of the Pyrenees. But unlike the anticlerical Joffre, he came of a devoutly Catholic family. His education was Jesuit. The Franco-Prussian war found him preparing for a military career at the Jesuit school of St. Clément in Metz. The taking over of the ancient French fortress city by the Prussians made an indelible impression on the ardent and studious youth of nineteen. As much as Clemenceau he dedicated his life to *la revanche,* but his career was among the old regime elements in the army and the clergy that never really accepted a French republic, neither the First, nor the Second, nor the Third. His father was an official of the Second Empire. His brother was a Jesuit priest. His silent hatred of democratic politics stood him in ill stead in the army. Though admittedly the artillery officer most learned in the classics of warfare, promotions came hard. In spite of their political differences Clemenceau, who appreciated brains, during his premiership in 1907 appointed Foch to be director of the Ecole de Guerre. As director of the French war college Foch made friends with his opposite number in England, the whimsical and slightly crackbrained Sir Henry Wilson, during the first interchanges of the *entente cordiale.* They became so congenial that he invited Sir Henry to his daughter's wedding.

When war broke out Foch was charged with the defense of Nancy. His son and his soninlaw were both killed during the first year. Foch made himself a brilliant reputation in command of the Ninth Army under Joffre in the first battle of the Marne, but after the disasters on the Somme in 1916 he shared Joffre's eclipse and was relegated to the post of inspector general on the Swiss border. Pétain brought him back as Chief of Staff, with offices in the Invalides, and ever since that day Foch had been stringing his wires towards eventual attainment of the supreme command. Since Robertson's retirement, Sir Henry Wilson, again Foch's opposite number as British Chief of Staff, had taken, in a chaffing sort of way, to promoting his French friend's qualifications for generalissimo.

The extent of the disaster before Amiens began to dawn on the British Government during the Palm Sunday weekend. Lloyd George, who was out of town, received a desperate wire from Haig begging him to do something to induce the French to get troops into the widening gap between the French and British armies. He called up Lord Milner, his Secretary of State for War, one of the few cabinet officers still in London, and told him to leave for France immediately. The Prime Minister had to have an on the spot report. Milner, he added hurriedly, had full authority to do anything necessary.

Milner picked up General Wilson at Versailles and all day Monday the twentyfifth the two of them went careening over the French roads in a staffcar from one inconclusive conference to another. Confusion everywhere. Recriminations. Haig complaining that the divisions Pétain had promised had failed to appear; Pétain accusing Haig of letting go strong points he had given his word to hold.

Haig was shaken. He had lost selfconfidence to the point that he admitted tremulously to Milner that if that was the only way of getting his flank covered he was willing to take orders from a Frenchman. To spare Haig's feelings Milner and Wilson were talking up Clemenceau as generalissimo with Foch as his technical adviser.

They found the Tiger at Compiègne, his eyes sunk behind his cheekbones, his mustache shaggier than usual. He told them gruffly that the only possible remedy was the immediate unification of command. Meanwhile Haig had sent word that he was too busy to come to Compiègne. A meeting was arranged for the following day with all the chief French and British commanders, at the little rural center of Doullens, about midway between Amiens and the sea, to come to a final decision.

Clemenceau spent Monday night in Paris. His sleep as usual was disturbed by airraids. A mysterious longrange gun, soon to be nicknamed Big Bertha, had started dropping shells at twenty minute intervals into the French capital. It was evidently the longest range gun ever fired.

The city, while not exactly panicky, was tense. Though outwardly the Premier gave an impression of confidence he was making secret arrangements for the evacuation of the most important government offices in case of need. The nervous and the rich were leaving already. Trains for Lyons and the Midi were full of standees. At the same time the gare du Nord was choking up pitifully with refugees arriving with their bundles and boxes from the invaded north.

The people who had decided to stick it out were in good spirits. Sunday afternoon the boulevards were unusually lively. The President of the Republic visited the sites of the explosions and brought the nation's condolences to the bereaved and the wounded. Holidaymakers were more curious than frightened about the projectiles from Big Bertha. The Parisians were pointing out to each other that they weren't doing much damage after all.

The appointment at Doullens was for eleven in the morning. Clemenceau and his military aide, General Mordacq, arrived on the dot. A second later President Poincaré and his military aide drove up. Along with them came Monsieur Loucheur, the minister for armaments and aviation. There was no love lost between the President of the Republic and the President of the Council of Ministers, particularly since the scheme for making Clemenceau generalissimo had been bruited about, but in this extremity they greeted each other cordially. Clemenceau, noted Mordacq, was in good spirits. He seemed almost gay.

Lord Milner and General Wilson were late. Since Haig and his staff had filled up the little town hall, the French leaders remained in the prettily gardened little square outside. The day was chilly with a raw wind off the Channel, so they had to walk briskly up and down to keep warm.

Townspeople crowded around them. They were asking if they were going to allow the Germans to come as far as Doullens. Should people pack up and leave? Bitter reproaches lurked under a polite demeanor. The Tiger growled one of his usual phrases about "they shall not pass" through his mustache.

From where he stood it was all too clear that the retreat was continuing. Refugees kept coming along the main road through the square. There were countrypeople in wagons piled high with household goods, lowing cows and flocks of sheep with their tinkling bells, now and then a protesting pig being dragged along, boys pushing handcarts, babycarriages full of prized possessions with the baby in among them, old women in bonnets, old men hobbling on sticks: a sickening repetition of roadside scenes in the tragic summer of 1914.

Among them, marching sedately in step, came pinkfaced detachments of retreating British troops. The Frenchmen were amazed at their expressionless faces. Whenever there was a moment of silence they could hear the German guns like heavy surf in the distance.

The President of the Council and the President of the Republic had only time to exchange a few anxious words before they were joined by General Foch. Foch at sixtyseven was a strutting gamecock of a man with gray blue eyes and an abundant grizzled mustache. He arrived, followed by his staff, with a great air of bustle and confidence. At last he was going to attain the command he'd so long desired. He greeted the heads of the French republic and made his famous gesture of brushing away cobwebs.

"My plan is not complicated," he exclaimed in harsh trenchant tones. "I want to fight. I'll fight in the North. I'll fight on the Somme. I'll fight on the Aisne, in Lorraine, in Alsace, I'll fight everywhere and blow after blow I'll end by knocking out the Boche; he's no smarter and no stronger than we are."

Mordacq noted in his journal that Foch seemed to bring a gust of victory with him.

Pétain's arrival was lugubrious. He came full of complaints. The British were not keeping him properly informed. How could they expect him to send in reinforcements if they wouldn't stop retreating? "That man," whispered Pétain to the group about him, when he caught sight of Haig's tall figure on the steps of the town hall, "will have to capitulate in two weeks."

The French were nervously comparing their watches with the town clock. Eleven fortyfive. Where the devil were the representatives of the British Government? The sound of the guns seemed to grow louder. Their pacing became nervous, almost feverish. Twelve o'clock struck. No sign of Milner and Wilson.

At twelve five, two British staffcars appeared at full tilt, scattering the refugees as they came. As soon as Lord Milner stepped out of his car, Clemenceau, who had the knack of putting people in the wrong, strode up to him savagely and asked if it were true that the British were planning to evacuate Amiens. Milner protested loudly that Marshal Haig intended no such thing.

He then asked if the French would excuse him for a few minutes so that he could talk to his generals in the mayor's office. They had had no chance to confer. Marshal Haig and Generals Plumer and Byng led the way into the building. After fifteen minutes they called in the French.

The conference of Doullens began with neatly bearded little Poincaré presiding.

The Tiger snarled at Haig: was he planning to give up Amiens? Haig said that was the last thing he was planning to do but that he must have French reinforcements to cover his flank. He had no reserves ready to fight.

It was Pétain's turn to say what he could do. Haig had already turned over to his command the elements of the Fifth Army nearest the French flank. "The Fifth Army," began Pétain, "has ceased to exist." He went into a long gloomy account of how for days he'd been trying to find divisions. He had found twentyfour, but most of them were tired and some frazzled from recent combat. The problems of transportation and redeployment would take a long time to solve. It would take time.

Pétain's words threw a chill over the group. For a while nobody spoke.

Clemenceau grabbed Milner's arm and backed him into a corner. "We must make an end of this," he whispered. "What do you propose?"

Milner had come all primed. He immediately proposed putting the French and British armies under the command of General Foch. To sweeten the pill for Pétain and Haig, Milner brought in the word "coordinate." Pétain announced loftily that indeed he would serve under General Foch. They all looked at Haig.

Mordacq noticed how lined and haggard Haig's face was. He'd lost the erect look of the wooden soldier perfectly painted and polished. He muttered something about doing everything necessary to serve the general interest.

Clemenceau insisted that the decision be put in writing. Foch's command must take effect from that moment. General Foch was charged with coordinating the British and French armies on the western front. All present signed the little document. Milner's signature committed the British cabinet.

Pétain went back gloomily to his train. Haig and his generals returned to their distracted headquarters. The staff officers felt something had been put over on their chief. Being forced under French command was the price he had to pay for reinforcements.

The French were rubbing their hands. The air was sharp. It was two and they were accustomed to their *déjeuner* at twelve. All present confessed to a good appetite. The President of the Republic, and General Foch and Monsieur Clemenceau and Monsieur Loucheur and their aides and secretaries walked around the corner to a highly recommended little country restaurant, L'Hôtel des Quatre Frères Aymon, where a bangup luncheon had been ordered for them.

As they sat down to table Clemenceau and Foch, who never agreed for more than a few minutes at a time, couldn't help a slight falling out. "Well," growled the Tiger glaring at Foch as he tucked his napkin under his chin, "you've got the position you wanted so much."

Foch snapped back, "You give me a lost battle and ask me to win it . . . I consent and you think you are making me a present. I am disregarding my own interest when I accept."

The others intervened. Like good Frenchmen they turned their attention to the food and the wine. According to Mordacq they were in as much of a glow as if they had won a victory over the Germans. He remembered the luncheon as being distinctly gay.

General Pershing Presses His Point

Newton D. Baker, mouselike as usual under a derby hat that looked too large for him, was in Europe during these days of tension. He had come, he explained modestly to Pershing and Bliss, to get the feel of the war. He was getting it. Long faces in London. Long faces in Paris. Refugees in the railroad stations. Airraid sirens wailing every moonlight night. The crunch of bombs in the distance. In Paris, during the Good Friday service, a shell from Big Bertha exploded in the church of St. Gervais. The Gothic vault fell. A hundred and fifty people, mostly women and children, were killed or badly hurt.

Wherever the Secretary of War went he was besieged with requests for American troops. The Italians wanted them. The French wanted them. The British wanted them so badly they were at last willing to forego a certain amount of lucrative commercial trade and to allot more shipping to overseas transport; but only for infantry and machinegunners, they insisted. None of the Allies wanted an independent American army; what they wanted was American cannonfodder.

Baker's report to Pershing was that the President was wavering on the question. Wilson had become convinced that everything must be sacrificed for unity of command. His cables strongly backed the appointment of Foch. Well and good, said Pershing, he was willing to serve under Foch, but they must never give up the plan for a separate American army.

Out of a total strength of just under three hundred and twenty thousand men under his command in the A.E.F. Pershing had already offered his 1st Division to Pétain. Now the 2nd, 26th and 42nd divisions were ready for service. Another soon would be.

After a long discussion at his Paris office with General Bliss and Secretary Baker on the bearing of the decision at Doullens, which they all applauded, on American plans, Pershing decided that the moment had come formally to put his troops at Foch's disposition. After lunch he set out with General Bliss to find Foch, who was reputed to be setting headquarters up in a little hillside town between Compiègne and Beauvais, called Clermont de l'Oise.

It was encouraging to the Americans to find the roads west of Paris encumbered by motor trucks loaded with supplies and troops heading towards the front. This confirmed the report that Foch was already filling the gap east of Amiens with French divisions. When they reached Clermont they drove around the town for a while before they could find anybody who would admit any knowledge of General Foch's whereabouts. At last Pershing's interpreter, Captain de Marenches, uncovered a friend at French Third Army Headquarters who detailed a poilu to guide them. He directed Pershing's chauffeur out through the truckgardens on the edges of town and down an avenue of tall poplars to a small picturesque farmhouse.

While they waited in the walled garden to be admitted, they admired the flowering shrubs. The place had a delicious air of quiet and seclusion. There was some pale spring sunshine. Leaving Bliss to admire a cherrytree in bloom in the middle of the lawn Pershing was ushered into the house. He had announced he wanted a private interview.

Pershing found Clemenceau, Loucheur and Generals Pétain and Foch deep in the study of a map laid out on the diningroom table. The French were counterattacking near Montdidier. Since the house was small, when Pershing repeated that he wanted to speak with Foch alone, the others went outside to admire the cherrytree.

"I have come to offer our American troops for the present battle," Pershing said. ". . . Artillery, infantry, aviation. Everything we have is yours. Dispose of it as you will . . . I have come especially to tell you that the American people will be proud to take part in the greatest battle in history."

Feeling that the occasion merited the effort, General Pershing addressed General Foch in French.

No man to underplay a dramatic moment, Foch seized Pershing's arm and rushed him out of the house to where the others were standing by the cherrytree. "Repeat what you said." Foch was radiant.

General Pershing repeated his carefully rehearsed speech with even greater emphasis. His aide, General Boyd, told him afterwards that his

French gushed out with unaccustomed fluency under the pressure of the great moment.

"We are here to be killed," blurted out General Bliss in English. "How do you want to use us?"

Pétain remarked dryly that he had already decided that with General Pershing. A spot had been picked where the American troops should go into the lines. Later Foch took credit for this decision. "I could only reply to their perfect comradeship," he wrote, "by at once placing the First American Division facing Montdidier in the very center of the German attack."

Pershing's chivalrous gesture was made much of in the French press. He was invited to accompany Bliss to the next meeting of the Supreme War Council, hurriedly called for April 3 at the town hall at Beauvais. The British were late again, so the American generals and their aides had leisure to admire the huge old cathedral left unfinished so many centuries ago. When they entered the town hall they found a certain assurance among the delegates. The German drive was petering out. Amiens was no longer in danger. The boche had outrun his supply. Foch's selfconfidence was catching. In the conference room Lloyd George, with his mane of white hair and his queasy smile, was very much in evidence.

As soon as Clemenceau called the meeting to order Foch rose to explain that now that the front was stabilized his instructions to coordinate the movements of the armies had been complied with. He wanted more specific powers. Lloyd George pointed out that after three years of war nothing had been accomplished . . . What had just happened, he added nervously, had stirred the British people very much and it mustn't be allowed to happen again or the people would start asking questions and somebody would be called to account. He threw the ball to the Americans.

General Bliss read out the Doullens resolution and said that Foch should be given broader powers. Pershing came out flatfootedly for a supreme commander and declared that commander should be Foch.

Lloyd George strode across the room to where Pershing was sitting and grabbed him by the hand. "I agree fully with General Pershing."

When Haig's turn came to speak he said that there had been unity of command right along. He saw no need for anything more.

It was decided to draft a resolution. Pershing pointed out when the draft was submitted to him that there was no mention of an American army.

Pétain said there wasn't such a thing. The American units were either in training or amalgamated with the British or the French.

Pershing stood his ground. He was not an eloquent man. He tended to start with "er er er" when he spoke. He managed to get across his message that if there wasn't an American army yet there damn soon would be. The resolution he subsequently approved granted Foch complete strategic direction of the Allied armies, but left tactical direction of the British, French and American forces in the hands of their national commanders. To mollify Haig a clause was added allowing these commanders to appeal to their home governments if in their opinion Foch's instructions placed their armies in danger.

Foch had to be satisfied with a qualified command, but Pershing had won his point; an American army was included on a par with the French and British.

Operation "Georgette"

It was the boche who conferred the supreme command on Foch. Hardly a week had elapsed after the conference at Beauvais, when, just as the various Allied headquarters were getting their breath and settling back into the old routine with the assurance that things were quieting down, on April 9 Ludendorff made his next move. Prince Rupert of Bavaria's group of armies attacked the British lines again, this time in the valley of the Lys south of Ypres.

This was operation "St. George," reduced in scope by Ludendorff's fear of risking too much of his reserve to the point where staff officers referred to it scornfully as operation "Georgette." The tactics were the same as in the first drive. The German command picked the moment when a Portuguese division that had been suffering miseries from insufficient clothing and poor supplies in the trenches was slated for relief. Seven carefully trained assault divisions converged in a surprise attack while the relief was being carried out. The Portuguese broke and ran. The relieving brigades became entangled in the rout. The thinly held British lines on either side melted away.

The success was greater than Ludendorff had dared hope. The movement he intended as a diversion to draw Allied reserves from his spearhead at Montdidier became a major offensive. On April 11 the British pulled out of Armentières, long famous in drunken singing and latrine talk as a rest center for British Tommies. The situation became so desperate that Haig issued the order: "Every position must be held to the last man. There must be no retirement. With our backs to the wall, and believing in the justice of our cause, each one of us must fight to the end."

Even so the retreat continued. All the ground so many British and Canadian lives were squandered to regain in front of Ypres was lost. As the spring had been unusually dry the German divisions were able to work their way across the swampy valley of the Lys to the high ground

to the westward. For a while it looked as if the British armies would be
driven back on Boulogne and Calais.

In spite of daily appeals to Pétain and Foch, French reinforcements
were slow in arriving. When they did appear their chief feat of arms
was to help the British lose their most important position on Mount
Kemmel to the southwest of Ypres. Still the British managed to hold
Ypres itself and the essential railroad center of Hazebrouck.

By the end of April the British could count around three hundred thousand casualties, dead, wounded and prisoners, since March 21. The German losses were almost as heavy. Ludendorff had extended his lines in
two huge salients, but in each case he had fallen short of his strategic
objective, which had been Amiens in the first offensive and Hazebrouck
in the second. Mordacq had been assuring Clemenceau that this would
happen. *"Les boches n'ont pas le cran,"* he said. The Germans haven't
the gall.

Foch was now firmly in the saddle. Brought up from boyhood in the
theory of *toujours l'offensif* he was collecting the mass of manoeuvre he'd
preached at the Ecole de Guerre and biding his time for a counterstroke.
He retained his confident swagger. When British officers begged him to
send more troops to their assistance he consistently refused. *"C'est la
bataille du nord,"* he would say with a shrug of his shoulders.

As the German pressure slackened, the French and British began to
become insistent again that American units should be incorporated in
their own armies as fast as they landed. At the conference of the Supreme
War Council at Abbeville they gave Pershing a bad quarter of an hour.

The plausible Lord Reading had been working on President Wilson in
Washington and had, so it seemed, brought him around to the belief that
the outcome of the war depended on merging the identity of the American troops in the British and French forces. Lloyd George had in his hands
a message from the White House acquiescing in the British plan to bring
over only American infantry and American machinegunners instead of
complete divisions. Lloyd George and Lord Milner, seconded by Clemenceau and Foch, started on Pershing and Bliss with arguments in favor
of this plan as soon as they showed their faces in the conference room.
Bliss had little stomach for debate, but Pershing held his ground.

He was fond of reminding the French that when they'd sent Rochambeau overseas to serve with the Americans in the Revolutionary War, it
had been with the understanding that he would have a separate command, but this time he answered in his halting way, wearing his grimmest
poker face, that since it looked as if the American Army was going to
have to bear the brunt of the war from now on it was essential for all con-

cerned that the Americans should fight the way they'd fight best, and
that was as a separate unit. The debate became so acrimonious that Clemenceau adjourned the conference, saying that Foch and Milner and
Pershing had better argue the matter out in private.

As soon as they were alone in a small room Foch turned on Pershing
and asked in his rasping voice, "You are willing to risk our being driven
back to the Loire?" Pershing answered yes it was a risk that had to be
taken. They argued so long that the three prime ministers became impatient and rapped on the door. Milner went to open the door and Pershing heard him whisper to Lloyd George, "You can't budge him an inch."

Pershing rose to his feet. "Gentlemen," he said, "I have thought this
program over very carefully and I will not be coerced."

In the end he agreed to follow the British plan for two months but no
longer. He overcame Italian opposition by promising Orlando to send a
complete American regiment to Italy. On the eventual autonomy of the
A.E.F. he would not yield an inch. "We parted with smiles," wrote Clemenceau, "that on both sides concealed gnashings of teeth."

After all this demand for infantry General Pershing was somewhat
amazed, upon arriving back at his headquarters at Chaumont, to receive
a letter from Marshal Haig asking for ten thousand artillerymen. Pershing
answered politely that the British had not yet furnished the howitzers
they had promised. If Haig would furnish the guns and the instructors
he would man six batteries for him. Haig withdrew his request.

"A year a month a week and a day . . ."

It was agreed that three more American divisions should immediately
be added to the three already holding quiet sectors and that the 1st
Division should be placed under orders of the VI Corps of the First
French Army in front of Montdidier. To carry out this arrangement the
1st was relieved on the St. Mihiel salient by the 26th or Yankee Division
under General Edwards. In the confusion that was spreading over the
rear of the French armies as a result of the German drives, the conduct
of the relief became thoroughly snarled up. As if to prove that it wasn't
only between allies that disagreements flourished, the staffs of the two
American divisions fell out among themselves. Valuable time was taken
up at Chaumont sorting out charges and countercharges until Pershing
called up both divisional commanders and told them sharply to drop it.

The boche added to the confusion by constant shelling and a crippling
gas attack. The Germans seemed bound to make the front as hot as they
could for their new enemy. The New Englanders of the 26th Division
had hardly learned to find their way through the labyrinth of old trenches
that led to an advanced post in the ruins of the village of Seicheprey

when the German artillery closed down on them with a box barrage which was followed by a raid in overwhelming force.

The garrison of Seicheprey was wiped out. When finally dislodged by a counterattack, in which the adjoining French division had to be called on for help, the boche carried off a hundred and eightyseven prisoners, including five officers. The casualties were heavy all around. The German radio exulted in the defeat of the Yankees and a corresponding gloom filled Allied headquarters.

A year, a month, a week and a day after the declaration of war the Americans scored their first victory.

Between April 7 and April 16 the 1st Division went through an intensive course in training in open warfare in a hilly region sprinkled with old Norman keeps around Gisors to the northwest of Paris. Pershing wanted to shake loose any trench warfare habits the men might have picked up from associating with the French in the eastern sectors. Then in three days the division was marched seventyfive kilometers up into the rear of the Sixth French Army. The night of the twentysecond the advanced brigade relieved the French division which was holding on by its eyelashes in front of the village of Cantigny.

It was a springtime landscape of long gently sloping green hills. The tileroofed houses of Cantigny clustered prettily around its chateau on the slope of a hill that hid the strategically important valley beyond, where a main line of railroad ran through Montdidier in the direction of Paris. Since the French had only fallen back into that region three weeks before they had not had time to construct their usual elaborate system of entrenchments and dugouts. The front was a line of occupied shellholes running through a wheat field. It wasn't a sector, the defensiveminded French officers told the Americans, but something that might be made into a sector.

Cantigny and the ridge behind it dominated the countryside. Its possession was essential for the counterattack Pétain's headquarters was planning in the direction of Montdidier. The French had recaptured Cantigny twice and had twice been driven out. The shallow valleys and the plain in front of the village was under continual shelling by the wellplaced German artillery. Ravines and patches of woodland were continually saturated with poison gas. The first weeks were spent by the Americans in counterbattery fire and in digging down into the soft chalk subsoil. The flimsy houses of the region were no protection at all. Lathe and mudplaster walls went up in dust with every shell's concussion. Headquarters and posts of command had to be established in the wine cellars and storage caves which luckily abounded under every farmhouse.

The boche had command of the air. His sausage balloons placidly directed the fire of his gunners. Since there was as yet no effective American airforce the division had to depend on French planes for protection and observation. At night the Germans bombed at will. The Americans' only experience with their British allies was a lone plane which appeared over their lines one day and resolutely strafed the trenches with machineguns. The Americans thought he must be a Heinie using a British plane for deception, but when a French aviator shot the stranger down he turned out to be a Britisher sure enough. He'd lost his way and thought he was machinegunning a boche position singlehanded. A few days later a British liaison officer appeared redfaced and profuse with apologies.

Life was sheer hell in the Cantigny sector. The Germans had plenty of gas and the American artillery had none. All movement had to be at night. Kitchencarts and watercarts drawn by a single mule could only be moved up after dark through the slimy chalk of the access trenches so the food was cold and the water muggy before it reached the men in the advanced positions. Watering horses and mules was a risky business as the boche knew the locations and no matter how often the hour was changed seemed to be always ready with a few wellplaced shells. Stretchercases had to be taken to the rear through long slippery cuts in the chalky hills. Field hospitals and ammunition dumps were often under fire. While their attack on Cantigny was being planned the Americans were suffering sixty casualties a day merely holding their defensive positions.

From buck private to General Bullard there was no difference in opinion: the Germans had to be driven out of Cantigny. While the staff, working in a deep stinking cellar under an old manor house back near the demolished railroad station, planned the attack, the men in the front lines executed small nightly patrols, and what they called silent raids, without artillery buildup, in the nomansland between the two armies. There the Americans rapidly gained the ascendant. Prisoners were brought in. Bits of information were picked up from which the staff could plot out the terrain to be covered in the coming attack.

The 28th Infantry was selected to make the assault. For several days they practiced in a position twenty kilometers to the rear where the topography of Cantigny was duplicated as nearly as possible. Meanwhile the French moved up a hundred and thirtytwo seventyfives, thirtysix one hundred and fiftyfive millimeter howitzers and thirtyfour trench mortars in addition to the regular divisional artillery. A dozen tanks and a contingent of flamethrowers were ready to support the infantry. The division was furnished with an unlimited supply of gas and high explosives. The French were as anxious as the Americans that there should be no slipup in the Cantigny operation.

May 27 in cooperation with the Crown Prince's offensive away to the east on the Chemin des Dames, the Germans in Cantigny put on a heavy bombardment with gas and explosives. This was followed by a number of

raids on the Americans and on the French to the right and to the left of
them. In repulsing one of these raids the French made a small advance.
They had already captured a wooded hill to the northwest. Though casualties were considerable the arrangements for the American attack were
in no way disrupted.

The night that followed was calm and clear. At 4:45 on the morning
of the twentyeighth, when the mist was rising out of the valleys, the artillerymen of the supporting batteries verified their adjustments by firing a
few rounds at their assigned targets. An hour later every gun behind the
1st Division broke loose. French airplanes took control of the air. Areas
where German troops were expected to be massed were heavily gassed.
At 6:45 the seventyfives changed their angle of fire to a rolling barrage
which moved at the rate of a hundred meters in two minutes. Behind it
the infantry advanced supported by machinegun units and mortars. The
French Renault tanks operated without a hitch. Flamethrowers followed
to clean out deep shelters and trenches. By 7:20, exactly on schedule, the
entire objective was gained.

Strong points were established in the cemetery and in a wood on the
ridge north of the town and in the shelter of the stone walls of the château. Every German in Cantigny was dead, wounded or captured.

Two hundred and twentyfive prisoners were marched to the rear to be
shown to General Pershing and members of the French Army Command
who had come up for the show. In the actual attack casualties were light
indeed. The success seemed almost too good to be true.

General Bullard remarked in his notes that his Commander in Chief
seemed unimpressed by the 1st Division's fine performance. Pershing was
worried for fear they might not hold their gains.

He had hardly left Bullard's command post when a written message
came from him emphasizing his orders that Cantigny must be held at any
cost. Some French general must have raised a doubt in his mind. Bullard
remembered Pershing's having asked him whether the French ever
patronized him. "Do they assume superior airs with you?"

Bullard answered no sir they did not; he'd been with them too long
and knew them too well.

"By God they've been trying it with me," said Pershing vehemently,
"and I don't intend to stand a bit of it."

"He inspires no enthusiasm, ever," Bullard noted of his Commander in
Chief; "respect, yes."

The 1st Division gave no Allied officer the opportunity to assume superior airs. Although the counterattacks were heavy; and, after the extra
French artillery was withdrawn, the German guns administered bitter
punishment, the Americans held on. When they were finally taken out of

the sector in early July they had suffered nearly five thousand casualties, killed, wounded, and gassed. Of prisoners they lost very few.

"A year, a month, a week and a day after we came into the war we took enemy ground and held it," the word spread like a flash through the A.E.F., to Chaumont, and down the line of communication to the ports where files of khakiclad men were shambling off the transports; to Washington, where sallow officeworkers struggled redeyed into the night with the problems of procurement and supply; to the mines and steelplants and the shipyards. The phrase went from mouth to mouth. "A year, a month, a week and a day."

Among the hardpressed French reeling back from the fresh German offensive the victory at Cantigny was exaggerated to almost miraculous proportions. The Americans Pétain had promised them the year before were in the war at last. The Americans had counterattacked and won.

Chapter 18

THE KAISER'S LAST VICTORY

THE 1st Division's feat of arms at Cantigny never got the play it deserved in the American press because it was overshadowed by frightening headlines reporting a new German breakthrough. Operation "Roland."

Ludendorff's generals managed to assemble fortytwo divisions and nearly four thousand guns in the neighborhood of Laon without the French command being any the wiser. These were poised against the Chemin des Dames front which was considered so impregnable it was lightly held by four French divisions and three English divisions sent there for a rest after the pounding they had taken in Flanders. Only Pershing's intelligence, studying such reports as were available of German troop movements, came to the conclusion that the boche was preparing an attack along the Aisne. When word was passed along to the French they paid no attention.

Foch, at his new headquarters in a small brick château named Bombon a good fifty kilometers to the rear of Paris, was busy with his plans for a counteroffensive between Montdidier and Noyon. He announced in his most oracular vein that no such attack was pending.

Von Hindenburg told in his memoirs of having visited Laon at the time of Nivelle's failure the spring before. It was a sunny morning. He found the views from the highset hill town delightful. Walking out on the terrace of the prefecture he carefully surveyed the landscape to the south. He described the ridge of the Chemin des Dames cutting across the green wellwatered plain like a wall that joined the hill masking Soissons to the southwest to the high land along the valley of the Aisne that sheltered Reims to the eastward. He remembered Napoleon's battle against the Prussians in that difficult terrain. Only with complete surprise would success be possible.

Ludendorff reassured him: even if the attack were only partly successful it would draw off French support from the British against whom the final knockout was being prepared. The German generals gloated a little over the prospect of mounting Krupp's new longrange guns, improved versions of the three Berthas that terrorized the Parisians, and bombarding England from the Channel ports.

The German Commander in Chief went on to repeat a humorous tale brought back to him from the front: the croaking of the frogs was so loud on the marshy little stream that for a ways separated the opposing armies that the German engineers were able to set up their portable bridges right under the noses of the French outposts. He remembered with pride how a captured Prussian noncom hoodwinked the French by telling them not to worry about the coming barrage because German morale had been so lowered by their losses in the Flanders offensive that they would refuse to advance.

Whether it was the croaking of the frogs or the fabrications of the Prussian noncom that lulled them, the French commanders took no precautions. It turned out later that the general in charge was in Paris that night visiting his light o' love. Surprise was complete.

At 1 A.M. the morning of May 27 the Germans began the heaviest bombardment they'd hitherto used in the war on the entire front from Soissons to Reims. Three and a half hours later seventeen divisions, preceded by the first German tanks to appear in force, attacked on a forty kilometer front.

The thinly strung French gave way. The British to the eastward managed to fall back in fair order in the direction of Reims. At noon the Germans were crossing the Aisne on bridges the Allies had neglected to blow up. By nightfall they had ploughed through a second range of defensible hills and were crossing the Vesle west of Fismes. Two days later they took the important supply centers of Soissons and Fère-en-Tardenois. By the end of the month they occupied most of the country between the Ourcq and the Marne.

As on the Somme and the Lys the very magnitude of the German victory threw Ludendorff's plans out of kilter. The Crown Prince's armies took sixtyfive thousand prisoners, scores of airplanes nested in their hangars and immense quantities of guns and ammunition. Discipline broke down when the German divisions found themselves unopposed in the rich unspoiled countryside.

The German soldiers were hungry. They were greedy for fats. Four years of wartime stringency had left them starved for every kind of goods. This was the champagne region. There were cellars stocked with wine in every village. While the more levelheaded officers were rounding up needed military equipment, the troops were slaughtering chickens and pigs in the barnyards and scattering to eat and drink and loot in the dwellinghouses. Re-establishing order became a major problem.

At the same time the advanced assault troops were moving so fast they outran their supply. The British, as ever stubborn in defeat, held with their backs to Reims. To the west of the Ourcq fresh French divisions, hastily entrenched in the wooded region of Villers-Cotterets, blocked advance down the Soissons-Paris railroad. The Germans found themselves squeezed into the wedgeshaped pocket between the Ourcq and the Marne. It was a rough farming region of low irregular hills, illprovided with highways and served only by a branch line of railroad. As they advanced towards Château-Thierry on the main road to Paris along the Marne the Crown Prince's armies found themselves stalled and squeezed between the two rivers.

In the rear of the defeated armies there was panic. More than a million people left Paris that spring. Big Bertha's bombardment redoubled. On the Bourse and in the Chamber of Deputies the word was Bordeaux. At Versailles the Supreme War Council went from one session of confused wrangling to another. It was as much as the grayfaced old Tiger could do, moving ceaselessly between the front and the rear, his mustache bristling and an old slouch hat pulled down on his head, to bully and cajole the politicians into staying put. While privately he speeded arrangements for removing the government departments, in public he repeated endless variations of Foch's declaration: they would fight in front of Paris and in Paris and behind Paris. They would fight on the Seine and they would fight on the Loire. For the present the battle was on the Marne.

Again on the Marne

On May 30, the day the American 2nd and 3rd Divisions received their orders to move up to the Marne, Pershing had eleven combat divisions under his command in the A.E.F. Three divisions, recently landed, were receiving hasty instruction between the British lines and the Channel coast. Another three were on inactive fronts in Lorraine and the Vosges mountains and the rest were billeted around in training areas. Elements of seven more were beginning to disembark in French and British ports.

The 2nd Division, going through final manoeuvres near Gisors, was being readied to relieve the 1st at Cantigny. The 3rd, made up mostly of regular army men, was waiting near Chaumont to move up to Lorraine when the orders came. Since this division had never been under fire, it was decided to parcel its units out among the French forces being marshalled to dispute a German crossing of the Marne. The 7th Machinegun Battalion, which was motorized, set out ahead and reached Château-Thierry late in the afternoon of May 31.

Château-Thierry, where la Fontaine was born, was a tranquil little town of seventeenthcentury French houses nestling among walled gardens between the slick green river and the mossy walls of Charles Martel's castle now landscaped as a park on the hill.

Caked with dust after twentyfour hours of travel in open trucks, the American machinegunners arrived on the stone bridge across the Marne

in time to be met with a wave of his kepi by the general commanding a
French colonial division which was advancing in the wrong direction.
The French were being dislodged by German gunfire. The arriving Americans were hailed with enthusiastic shouts, but there was little time for
cheering. Already the roofs and chimneypots of the town were being
knocked down about their heads. In the confused fighting while the Germans were held off long enough for the bridge to be blown up the
machinegunners gave a good account of themselves.

All along the placid Marne American doughboys, as fast as they piled
out of their trucks, were jogtrotting into position to oppose German crossings. The sector in front of Château-Thierry became known as the *"Pas
Fini"* sector, because the poilus there kept trying to tell the Americans as
they arrived: *"Guerre finie."* The Americans, most of whom had never
seen combat outside of the motion picture screen, roared them down.
"Pas finie. We've just begun our *guerre."*

While contingents of the 3rd were taking up positions on the south
bank of the Marne to the east of the German point of deepest penetration, the 2nd Division, under the command of General Omar Bundy,
leaving the tired 1st to hold on as best it could at Cantigny, was hurried
by truck and train towards Meaux.

Meaux, famous as a market for Brie cheeses, was a farming center
frequented by Sunday excursionists from Paris, who liked to row on the
quiet Marne and to picnic and eat fried gudgeons on its wooded banks. At
Meaux the Americans had their first experience with the backwash of
defeat. The place was in confusion. Shopkeepers were putting up their
shutters. The narrow streets were locked tight in a tangle of military vehicles headed to the rear and contesting the way with farmers' carts and
wagons loaded with household goods. Many houses had been wrecked by
an airraid the night before.

Decoration Day was sweltering hot. James S. Harbord, who had managed to get himself replaced as Chief of Staff and was now acting Brigadier General in command of the marine brigade of the 2nd Division, after
fighting his way from Paris through encumbered roads in his staffcar,
reached Meaux about noon. While he waited for the arrival of the officer
detailed to let him know his brigade's destination, he went into a hotel
for lunch.

The tables were crowded with hungry French officers rapping on their
plates for attention. The food was giving out. The waiters were rattled.
Nobody was getting served. Harbord fell to talking to a grayhaired American lady wearing the armband of the Y.M.C.A., who turned out to be
from Ohio and William Howard Taft's sisterinlaw. As soon as she'd
eaten she started pinch-hitting as a waitress. Before the general's meal
was over she had coolly taken over management of the kitchen and din-

ingroom. Everybody got fed. When the last plate was served the proprietors closed the hotel up and the whole staff departed.

By this time Harbord had his orders (of which details kept being changed in the course of the afternoon) to proceed some thirty or forty kilometers to the north into a region to the west of Château-Thierry where French detachments, that had been fighting a losing battle for six days without relief, were hard pressed by the Germans. Eventually during the night the divisional command was set up at Montreuil-aux-Lions on the main highway from Paris to Metz. The orders were to deploy one brigade to the north and another to the south of this arterial road. At French corps headquarters there was considerable doubt as to whether the raw American troops could hold. The French general was assured that these were American regulars and that in a hundred and fifty years they had never been beaten.

As they scoured the countryside for locations for bivouacs and billets the marines felt the full impact of the retreat. Every southbound road was crowded with a tangled mass of carts, trucks, barrows, artillery caissons, people on bicycles, flocks and herds, old and young fleeing as they could. The soldiers mingled with the civilians. Under roadside trees lay the untended wounded and the sick and helpless who could drag themselves no further. Every little gully was full of abandoned equipment, wrecked trucks, machineguns, rifles, coats, blankets, boots.

As the soldiers fled they plundered the villages, drank up the wines and liquors in the taverns, ate everything that could be eaten. They threw away ammunition belts and entrenching tools to load their knapsacks and musettebags with loot. Farmhouses were gutted, milk and wine spilled on the floor, drawers and cupboards ransacked for valuables, pictures torn off the walls, mirrors and windows smashed with riflebutts. What had been an army was a whimpering, sweating, drunken rabble spreading more terror than the advancing Germans, whose presence was made known by increasing shellfire at every crossroad, and by reconnaissance planes marked with the black German cross that skimmed unopposed overhead.

The weather continued fine. All night and during the morning of June 1 marine and infantry units of the 2nd Division kept arriving in the vicinity of Montreuil-aux-Lions. As fast as they arrived they were moved into positions facing the rolling wheatfields and the wooded knolls that formed the watershed of a small tributary of the Ourcq known as Clignon brook.

The first battalions were spread thin. One marine unit occupied so much of the line that their foxholes on the open hillside back of Les Mares farm had to be seven feet apart. The machinegun companies hadn't arrived. They had only their rifles, and a couple of batteries of French seventy-fives ensconced behind them. "Are you holding the line in depth?" asked a liaison officer from G.H.Q. "No, in width," the marine C.O. snapped back.

There the marines saw their first krauts, carefully spaced files of gray figures in coalscuttle helmets wading towards them through the wheat. A couple of heavy machineguns arrived in the nick of time. The marines were under shellfire. The village behind them was burning. They didn't start shooting till the krauts had approached to a hundred yards. Their shooting was good. The files hesitated. The dead and wounded dropped out of sight into the wheat. The first German line melted. Now the second line was taking punishment. Suddenly they broke and ran. The wheatfield was empty. Fingers scorched and blackened from the heat of their rifles, the marines stayed in their foxholes.

During the night of June 3 the rolling kitchens caught up. The men who had been living on bacon and hardtack and on what fowls and potatoes they could pilfer from abandoned farms, were served the first proper rations many of them had eaten since Chaumont.

There followed a few days breathing spell. It was a period of suspense. From dawn to dark and dark to dawn they lay in their positions waiting for the onrushing German army. Stragglers and refugees had drained away down the roads. A weird quiet gripped the countryside.

The French were still being pushed out of a string of small villages beyond the ridges that faced the 2nd Division. Occasional detachments of chasseurs in their black berets came through in fair order. Falling back was all they could think of. One French officer went so far as to order a marine battalion he came across to join in the retreat. Their captain made the retort that soon became legendary: "Retreat hell, we just got here."

Belleau Wood

By June 5 General Degoutte, who commanded the French corps to which the 2nd Division was attached, felt he had the situation well enough in hand to order some small advances to improve his defensive positions. He had enough artillery available to give support for a limited attack.

Part of the American lines was uncomfortably overlooked by a dense growth of hardwoods on the crest of the long smooth rise the boche occupied as soon as they ran the French out of the villages along Clignon brook in the valley beyond. This was Belleau Wood. General Bundy was ordered to take possession of it.

American staffwork was still rudimentary. Requests for topographical maps of the region met with shrugs at French headquarters. Maps could only be procured through certain army departments which were not in evidence on the battlefield. Billy Mitchell's airforce was promising observation planes but none had appeared. The Americans were utterly ignorant of the lay of the land. Maybe the way to find out what was in the wood was to go up there and look. The job fell to Harbord's marine brigade.

The morning of June 6 the Americans and the French on their flanks began a general advance to seize the higher ground. Most of the operation was successful. To the east of the Metz-Paris road elements of the 3rd Division helped capture at least part of the bare hill, marked 204 on the military maps, which dominated Château-Thierry and the road along the valley of the Marne.

At the same time the marines attacked the innocentlooking wood in front of them. Behind a brisk artillery barrage they deployed as they had been taught in manoeuvres, in four skirmish lines. When they reached the edges of the wood, fire from machineguns invisible amid the dense foliage cut them down like a scythe. The survivors kept on going and vanished among the trees.

The attack on either side of Belleau Wood moved with such dash that at the western end of the line some companies loped past the road where they were supposed to dig in and charged into the outskirts of Torcy in the valley beyond. There the krauts picked them off at their leisure. To the east the marines poured over the hill without too much loss and occupied the village of Bouresches. For hours there was no news from the battalion in the center which had disappeared into the wood.

The first reports to brigade headquarters were encouraging indeed. Harbord was in high spirits. "He is happy as a clam," a liaison officer wrote back to Chaumont, "even though he has about ten batteries so close to his p.c. that it sounds as if the guns were all in his bedroom."

During the afternoon Harbord's command posts began to piece together a picture of what was happening in Belleau Wood. The great trees that looked so harmless through the glasses extended much further than anybody had imagined. Under their shade was a nightmare of sudden ravines and boulders and mossy outcroppings masked in dense undergrowth. The enemy had the broken ground organized into a network of machinegun nests placed so that as soon as one machinegunner was overpowered others to the flank and rear could make the position untenable. Their mortars and minenwerfers were craftily hidden in hollows and behind jutting rocks. The artillery barrage had done them no harm.

The marines were suffering punishment. Their commander Colonel Albertus Catlin was severely wounded early in the day. Many companies lost officers and noncoms. One had only ten men left. The chain of command broke down. Isolated companies and isolated individuals roamed on as best they could without guide or chart among the trees and boulders, firing at an enemy they never could see. Men lost their sense of direction. Occasionally they strayed into their own machinegun fire. The nearer German machineguns were ringed with circles of dead marines. The lucky ones found spots of soft loam where they could dig themselves in among the rocks and the brambles. Wounded and bleeding men struggled ahead. If they were licked they did not know it.

Come nightfall the walking wounded started to trickle back, grimy ash-faced men with bandaged heads, men with arms in slings improvised out of web belts, men hobbling on rifles for crutches. Colonel Catlin was brought out on a stretcher. Lieutenant Colonel Lee took his place. Morale remained high. The machinegunning was tremendous, reported the marines, but if you got within bayonet range of a kraut the kraut would surrender. A little more time and they'd clean out that wood.

Reinforcements were sent into Bouresches under cover of darkness. A party of volunteers ran in a truckload of ammunition and rations through heavy German fire.

Next day the marines were encouraged by the sight of a real American airplane. From then on American pursuit and observation planes that had been training in French and British machines back of Toul became more common overhead. They continued to be outnumbered and outclassed by the Germans who had faster planes and more experienced pilots.

On June 8 the marines made another attempt to storm Belleau Wood. German machineguns too well placed. Casualties; but no results except for two minenwerfers and some machineguns captured. Harbord had to pull his marines back into a ravine on the edge of the wood so that the artillery could give the place a thorough shellacking.

June 10 after a stepped up barrage, the marines attacked again and reported optimistically as they had so often before that they held the entire wood. Still they had stopped short of the main German defense line in the northeast corner.

The marines were game. Next day another attack drove clean through to the north side but after the smoke cleared it was discovered the Germans hadn't budged. Still no accurate maps.

The men were wearing out. General Bundy telegraphed Pershing's headquarters asking for relief: "The Second Division has been marching, entrenching and fighting since May 30. During that time few of the men have had a night's rest . . . For the past five days it has been engaged in close combat, offensive and defensive. The division holds a front of ten kilometers. There are no troops to relieve them."

After a number of such messages, and one from Harbord pointing out that many of his men had not even taken their shoes off in two weeks, an infantry regiment from the 3rd Division was sent in to relieve the contingents that had suffered most casualties.

The usual confusion ensued. The officers were so green that they didn't know they had to keep their men out of sight of the sausage balloons that were directing the German artillery fire. The boche took the occasion to mount a brisk raid on Bouresches. A box barrage cut off the garrison for a while, and an officer fresh from the rear sent back word that Bouresches was overwhelmed. A little later a runner appeared with the message "Nothing but marines in Bouresches" and asking for hot coffee and drinking water.

By this time a little more than half of Belleau Wood was in American hands. Prisoners were accumulating, but still no one had an accurate idea of its topography. The marines sent in skirmish line after skirmish line of infantrymen to grope their way through ravines and underbrush into savage machinegun fire. By June 13 they were sure the wood was theirs.

That very day the boche, who had used little gas thus far, made a sudden and saturating bombardment with mustard gas. Eight hundred American casualties. Lines of blinded men came stumbling back to the dressing stations with their hands on eachother's shoulders, led by a wounded man who still had his sight. Though gasmasks gave good protection against the effect on the lungs, wherever there was moisture on the skin either from sweaty clothing or dew on the grass, the gas left painful burns. The mustard gas made Belleau Wood untenable. Next day Harbord had to pull his marines out to positions on the fringes of the thickets they had lost so many lives to conquer.

It wasn't until an Alsatian deserter was brought into headquarters during the night of June 21 and pointed out the German defenses on the map that Harbord's staff got a clear idea of their location. The garrison, they learned, was under the command of a Major Bischoff who had a reputation for the skill in bushfighting he had gained in colonial wars. He had suffered heavy losses from the fury of the marines' assault but his positions were impregnable to infantry.

Clearly this had been all along a job for the artillery. On June 25 the northern fringe of Belleau Wood was shelled for fourteen hours. In the late afternoon the marines advanced again behind a rolling barrage. "Come on you sonsofbitches do you expect to live forever?" the sergeants yelled. This time the losses weren't too heavy.

They found the great trees blasted to splinters, the German defenders stunned and helpless. By 9:30 that night Belleau Wood really was in American hands. Two hundred and fifty German prisoners and many machineguns. The Germans fell back on a defensive line along Clignon brook, and gave little more trouble in that sector.

The commanding officers of the 2nd Division had learned a great deal about warfare, at a cost as high, in proportion to the number engaged, as at Gettysburg or Chickamauga. During the month of June they lost roughly a third of their effectives in dead, wounded, and gassed.

The French lavished citations on the survivors. Since the American censorship deleted the identifying numbers of the infantry regiments, the American press gave the impression that a brigade of marines had stopped the German drive on Paris singlehanded. Actually two divisions had distinguished themselves. The French added to the misapprehension by courteously renaming le bois de Belleau, le bois de la Brigade de Marine.

Even the Germans were impressed. Ludendorff remarked that the Americans attacked bravely, "but they were unskillfully led, attacked in dense masses and failed." Hindenburg wrote with grudging admiration of the quality of the American troops which he described as being "clumsily but firmly led." A staff report described the 2nd Division as a very good one which might possibly be rated as a storm troop. "The moral effect of our gunfire cannot seriously impede the advance of the American infantry."

Pershing smiled his thinlipped smile. "Our first three divisions to participate in active operations had all distinguished themselves," he wrote. "The First at Cantigny, the Second at Belleau Wood, the Third at Château-Thierry." He started pressing Foch and Pétain for the formation of an American corps under which the divisions that had proved their mettle might be grouped in the neighborhood of Château-Thierry in preparation for the counterattack south of Soissons, which he was already talking up with Pétain's staff.

The warmhearted Harbord, closer than Pershing to the blood and guts of the fighting front, let himself go in notes he jotted down in the ramshackle fieldstone and mortar farmbuilding bedded between batteries of one hundred and fiftyfive millimeter-howitzers, where he made his brigade headquarters: "What shall I say of the gallantry with which these marines have fought? I cannot write of their splendid gallantry without tears coming to my eyes. There has never been anything better in the world . . . Literally scores of these men have refused to leave the field when wounded. Officers have individually captured German machine guns and killed their crews. Privates have led platoons when their officers have fallen . . . We are some 3400 fine officers and men less than we were a month ago . . . It is a dear price to pay for a bit of French territory but somewhat compensated for by the fact that the little bit of lovely France was at the very apex of the German push for Paris and that we exacted a toll from four German divisions that outbalanced our own losses . . . There are hundreds of cases of individual heroism and not one of misbehavior."

The American counterattacks were not the only factors that threw Ludendorff's plans into disarray but they surely helped. His new strategy, hastily improvised at a conference with von Hindenburg and the Kaiser in the first heady days of victory in the Chemin des Dames, was to encircle Paris with a pincers movement. He was meeting with increasing resistance from the French along the necks of his salients. The British were showing their usual obstinacy. The Americans cost him time and irreplaceable manpower. The dash and youthful recklessness of the American assaults, combined with news of the hardly believable speedup in the transportation of American troops to Europe, which the U-boats were proving helpless to hinder, had an impact on the German will to fight more far reaching than the results of a few tactical successes. Cantigny and Belleau Wood and the Marne bridges were seen by the German strategists as the first gusts of a coming storm. If the war were to be won it had to be won quickly.

Chapter 19

LUDENDORFF'S BLACK DAY

AMERICANS celebrated July 4, 1918, in various ways.

In Washington President Wilson, accompanied by Mrs. Wilson and the customary covey of relatives, by members of the cabinet and of the diplomatic corps and by a group of leaders of foreignlanguage societies, carefully picked by Creel and Tumulty in view of their usefulness in the forthcoming congressional elections, proceeded to Mount Vernon on the *Mayflower*.

The afternoon was a furnace. There was no air even on the river. The President showed his popular touch by moving among his sweating guests and urging them to doff their frockcoats and silk hats. Ferried ashore in launches they found a crowd of two thousand people trampling the shrubberies of George Washington's old plantation. Wilson addressed the throng from a stand set up beside Washington's tomb.

He spoke poetically of the quiet of the spot "serene and untouched by the hurry of the world." When he excoriated the central powers his eyes flashed with cold anger behind his noseglasses. There must be no peace of compromise. He proclaimed four more principles to reinforce his Fourteen Points:

"The destruction of every arbitrary power everywhere that can, separately, secretly and of its single choice, disturb the peace of the world."

The settlement of questions of territory and sovereignty "upon the basis of the free acceptance of that settlement by the people immediately concerned."

Government of nations "by the common law of civilized society."

The establishment of an international organization to preserve the peace.

". . . The blinded rulers of Prussia have aroused forces they know little of," —his voice rang through the little Virginia burying ground in the hollow among the trees by the riverbank—"forces which, once roused, can never be crushed to earth again."

"Four more nails in the coffin of German militarism," proclaimed Creel's propagandists.

The representatives of the European minorities, who had climbed back into their frockcoats to listen to the President's speech, expressed themselves as delighted: each man heard in those tolling words the call of his national aspirations.

Meanwhile the new shipyards, having applied massproduction methods to the construction of oceangoing freighters, were managing on that glorious Fourth to launch ninetyfive ships. "The great splash." Their target had been a hundred.

In the Amiens salient four companies of the recently disembarked 33rd Division, made up of Illinois militiamen, some of them wearing Australian uniforms in complete disregard of General Pershing's orders, joined the Aussies of General Richardson's Fourth Army in a successful *coup de main* against Hamel and were saluted by their allies as "fighting fools."

In Paris marines from the 2nd Division paraded down the Champs Elysées and were almost kissed to death by applauding crowds.

Back of Cantigny the 1st's artillery saluted the German positions with fortyeight salvos in patriotic bombardment. Later in the day, sheltered from German planes by the spreading oaks of the park that surrounded an ancient château, they put on, for the benefit of a superannuated French general who lived there and of a number of admiring ladies, a remarkably fine horse show.

The Drive for Peace

In Germany and Austria the early days of July were a time of scarcity, of explosions of pacifist sentiment in the Reichstag, and of open defiance of edicts of the Imperial Government. The Brest-Litovsk peace and resulting measures taken to include the old dominions of the Czar in the Mittel-Europa trading complex only resulted in spreading the Bolshevik contagion through the kingdoms, dukedoms and city states of the central empires. The imperial confederation that Bismarck cemented was shaking apart. Even Prussia, the cornerstone, was cracking.

The Kaiser had assured his subjects that Ludendorff's spring offensives would bring peace with victory, but all the German workingpeople could see was an immense new butcher's bill, and hunger and stringency. It was the turn of the Germans to get tired of being killed. They were beginning to listen to Bolshevik agitators whispering that peace lay in defeat.

Ludendorff's first three drives were smashing successes, but they only resulted in consolidating the Allies and in speeding the shipment of American troops. The fourth offensive, launched during the period of the bitter struggle for Belleau Wood, proved a failure.

The aim of this offensive, now known as "Project Gneisenau," was to capture Compiègne, and to take over the main trunk line of railroad between Paris and Cologne. It was to be the westward prong of the pincers around Paris. The operation was entrusted to General von Hutier himself. The attack was made at dawn on June 9 after the usual gas and artillery saturation on a twenty mile front between Noyon and Montdidier.

This time Foch correctly gauged Ludendorff's intentions. Seventyfives and howitzers were lined hub to hub behind his defenses. His troops escaped the initial bombardment by falling back from lightly held advance posts to entrenchments in the rear. The most the boche gained, after suffering crushing casualties, was six miles. The American operations on both banks of the Marne were part of a general French counterattack which stalled the enemy in his tracks.

Ludendorff was baffled. Indecision seized the High Command. Their strategists were torn between their original plan to drive the British into the Channel, and the tempting bait of Paris, Europe's capital city, lying at a mere fifty miles from their firing lines. While they prepared, with ever more meticulous care, for their final drive towards Paris, the Germans allowed the Allies a month's respite in which to regroup their armies according to Foch's ideas. Perhaps Ludendorff missed the keen mind of his adviser Max Hoffmann who was bogged down in the contradictions of his victory over the revolutionary Russians in the east. Ludendorff was picking his way cautiously. A new spirit of caution was spreading through his armies. This fifth offensive, which the General Staff named "the drive for peace," must not be allowed to fail.

The Midsummer Lull

Pershing now had twenty combat divisions under his command. Some of them were hampered in their effectiveness because, due to the British obsession that only infantry should be shipped, their artillery and other supporting services had not yet arrived. In spite of obstruction from both the British and French, who were still showing reluctance to give up their scheme to use American recruits as replacements for their own armies, a purely American service of supplies was functioning and beginning to function well. Twenty thousand tons of supplies were being unloaded daily in the American-managed ports. American railroadmen were reequipping the lines that led into Lorraine. American locomotives were pulling longer freights than had ever been seen on the continent. French railroad yards resounded with the root-to-toot-toot of their whistles. Tours, the hub of the S.O.S. was as much an American city as Chaumont.

On July 10 Pershing had a long conference with Foch at his château at Bombon. He wanted Foch to consent to pulling his American divisions out of the French and British sectors. He wanted them reorganized right away in an American army, at first on the Marne where they were needed in view of the coming German offensive, and later in Lorraine which was to be the point of departure for his drive planned for 1919 into the industrial heart of Germany. Already he was setting up American corps headquarters under which to group them. He urged on Foch his project for an American attack on the St. Mihiel salient.

Foch was keeping his own council. He was determined that this time there should be no leaks. He had no intention of letting either Pershing or Haig in on his real plans. He had grouped his mass of manoeuvre back of Compiègne and Soissons between the two German salients. He gave no inkling of where they would strike. He agreed vaguely with everything the American general said but he kept pushing back the date for independent American operations. He talked about a French drive to free the Marne in September. After that maybe.

The little Frenchman made up for his lack of candor by gusts of cordiality. Pétain would see to it that the American divisions would not lack for artillery, he said in his lordly way. "Today when there are a million Americans in France I am going to be still more American than any of you." He overwhelmed the tightlipped Pershing with staccato sentences. "America must have her place in the war . . . The American army must become an accomplished fact." By the end of July perhaps, or by September or certainly by the following year.

That afternoon General Pershing was up on the Marne at La Ferté-sous-Jouarre where the 2nd Division was recuperating behind the lines from Belleau Wood. The troops were paraded, citations read, decorations awarded. One marine gunner swam across the Marne to receive his.

A couple of days later the Commander in Chief lunched with Harbord at the headquarters of his marine brigade. Harbord boasted that one of his men had captured four German officers and seventyeight privates. Pershing retorted drily that no wonder Harbord was popular with the marines if he told such tall stories about them. At the same time he announced Harbord's promotion to Major General in command of the 2nd Division.

Behind the lines men kept listening for the roar of artillery that would announce an attack. "If the Germans do not bring off a very heavy offensive in the region between Château-Thierry and Reims within the next few hours our French allies are going to explode, blow up, disintegrate," wrote Harbord. "It has been announced daily for days, but the Boche must know how we are worrying about it for he has so far failed to produce either the heavy offensive or any visible usual preparations for it."

The streets of Paris had a feverish gaiety that July. Everybody who planned to leave had already left. The Bertha dropped in a shell every twenty minutes regular as clockwork. Except for a slight quickening of the pulse men and women laughed off the danger. When a shell exploded in the Seine, within minutes people were out in skiffs scooping up the fish killed by the concussion.

Appetites were good. When a shell burst in front of Foyot's sacred old restaurant across from the Senate Chamber, two American officials for whom an elderly waiter was pouring wine from a bottle of vintage burgundy noticed that his hand never quivered. "This wine is too good to shake up," he explained.

Nightlife was vivid. Venery reigned. All the women looked pretty in the dark streets. The boulevards were enchanting in the blackout. In shuttered halls entertainers sang to packed benches "Suis dans l'axe du gros canon."

The celebration of Bastille Day on July 14 was the climax. The morning shone bright and clear. French airplanes filled the sky over the city. The streets were full of flowers. There was a smell of strawberries in the air.

A brilliant military parade was deployed down the Champs Elysées. All Paris dressed in its best to crowd the wide sidewalks.

Preceded by the Garde Republicain in their gleaming helmets, riding their fine horses, detachments from all the Allies, carrying their national colors and led by bands playing their national airs, marched in dress uniforms from the Arc de Triomphe to the Place de la Concorde. There were French Chasseurs Alpins in bérets and black tunics, British Lifeguards, Italian Bersaglieri in roostertail hats, Portuguese, an anti-Bolshevik unit of cossacks in astrakhan, representatives of the Bohemian and Slovak regiments that had thrown off the Austrian yoke, Poles, Romanians, Serbs, Montenegrins, Greeks in their stiff white kilts. The United States was represented by units of the 1st Division.

Towards midnight American M.P.'s with a tense look on their faces darted out from their headquarters on the rue St. Anne. They went through hotels and nightspots rounding up officers and men on leave. All leaves were cancelled. The offensive had begun.

The Crossing of the Marne

Colonel Billy Mitchell was in Paris that afternoon trying to speed up the shipment of planes promised his brigade which was now attached to Hunter Liggett's I Corps. He was eating a late snack before hurrying back to his headquarters at Coulommiers about thirty miles to the eastward. In the restaurant he met a Red Cross man who was a friend of his and as they sat eating they speculated on the location of the coming offensive. It had to be against Reims because the Germans would not dare advance further south without having the use of the trunk line of the railroad to Paris.

As they talked they heard a rumbling sound. Guns to the north. Mitchell glanced at his wristwatch. It was 12:10 precisely.

Out on the street they could see a great flicker and glare in the northern sky. Mitchell told the Red Cross man to come along with him if he wanted to see the greatest battle in history.

They jumped into the air service colonel's fastest staffcar. A little before 3 A.M. they were at Mitchell's headquarters.

At the airdrome they could look about them. The flash of guns lit up the clouds. The colored signals from bursting rockets and the white glow of starshells hovered over the whole length of the lines. Searchlights dissected the sky. There was a continual buzz and whine of airplanes overhead. The thud of airplane bombs sounded out now and then against the pounding surflike roar of artillery.

Since few Americans as yet had training in night flying, Mitchell telephoned his pursuit and observation groups to be ready to operate with the first light. The news from his French liaison officers was disturbing. The French air division's orders had gone astray and their planes were not ready for combat. The Germans were attacking along the Marne. The only immediately available aviation on this part of the front consisted of American pursuit and observation groups, and a British brigade.

After a few winks of sleep Mitchell took up one of his pursuit planes and flew to the American lines beyond La Ferté-sous-Jouarre. The morning was overcast, the ceiling low. No German planes bothered him. Except for the artillery fire all along the lines he could see nothing particular going on.

Then he turned east and flew through low scudding clouds with occasional patches of clear sky up the valley of the Marne. Approaching the Jauglonne bend he met a few Fokkers but they paid no attention to him. To see anything he had to fly under the clouds. The river here was hemmed in by high hills. East of Dormans he found himself skimming above violent artillery fire. The Germans were crossing the river on five bridges. They were crossing in perfect order.

He was flying at about five hundred feet. There was no antiaircraft. "Looking down on the men marching so splendidly I thought to myself what a shame to spoil such fine troops."

He cruised a little further up the river, then swung north towards Reims. A terrific battle was going on in that vicinity. The air hummed with German planes. He spun around and headed back to the bridges. There seemed to be hand to hand fighting on the hill just south of a pontoon bridge swarming with boche.

"The opposing troops were almost together. This was the nearest to a hand-to-hand combat than anything I had seen so far. I thought they were Americans and later found it was our Third Division."

Mitchell had to duck into the clouds to escape a swarm of boche planes on the way back to his airdrome. He sent out his whole pursuit group to attack the bridges, and relayed the information to the nearest available French on the Champagne front east of Reims. They turned out in force, and, in spite of the distance they had to come, disturbed the perfect order of the Germans. By the end of the day American, French and British planes had dropped a recordbreaking fortyfour tons of explosives on the Marne bridges.

Defense in Depth

The Americans that Colonel Mitchell saw so heavily engaged were companies of Colonel Ulysses Grant McAlexander's 38th Infantry, from General Dickman's 3rd Division. Since the division's first precipitate appearance at Château-Thierry the combat units had had six weeks, under pretty continuous German shellfire from commanding positions on the northern bank, to dig into entrenchments along the river between Château-Thierry and the Jauglonne bend. They formed part of the French Sixth Army.

This time there was no surprise. In a raid across the river a couple of weeks before, the French had captured a German engineer officer with meticulous plans on him for two of the crossings, and the Americans had made prisoners of a boatload of patrolling krauts during the preceding night. The only unknown factors were the day and the hour of the attack.

McAlexander's men had been digging riflepits down to the water's edge, stringing barbed wire and making all the defensive preparations they had been taught by their French instructors. Due to a startling failure in liaison they had not understood the new tactics promulgated by Foch and Pétain by which the Germans were to be made to expend their artillery preparation on lightly held front positions while the real defense line was to be established several thousand yards to the rear. When the German attack came the Americans stayed put.

The boche managed to move up a stunning preponderance of artillery. Starting at midnight they shelled with high explosives. Then they drenched the whole countryside with gas and smoke bombs that smothered most of the French and American batteries. The gas and smoke mingled with the morning mist to form a dense fog so that the Germans could launch their pontoons, which had been hidden by the reeds and bushes, without being detected. They were halfway across the river before the Americans caught sight of them.

"Day was just breaking," wrote a lieutenant who was in one of the out-

2. *The Indispensable Destroyers*

33.

Sims of the Flotilla

34. *"Lafayette, here we come"*

35.

Weekending with Sir Douglas

36.

Through the Barbed Wire

37. The Loquacious Kerensky

38. Charles G. Dawes

39. Land Ironclads

40.

Discussion behind the Lines
(Albert Thomas, Haig, Joffre,
and Lloyd George)

41.

Clemenceau Had a Way
with Americans

The German Triumvirate

43. *Foch as Chief of Staff*

44. *The Service of Supply*

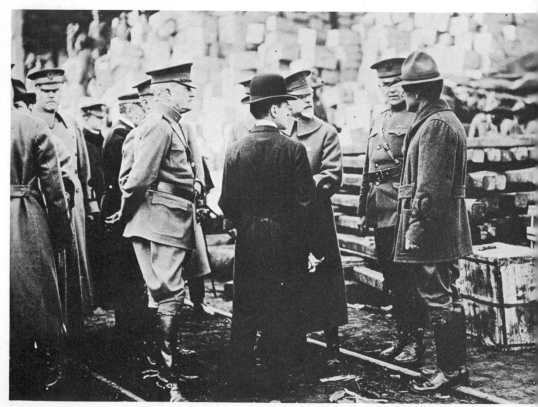

5.   *Château-Thierry*

6.   *The Ruined Forest*

47A. *Zero Hour*

47B. *Machinegunners*

C. *Antiaircraft*

D. *The High Command*

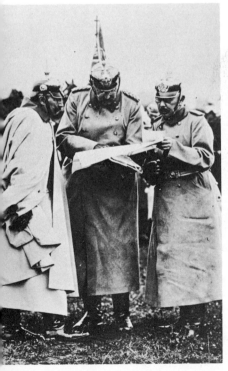

47E. *The Road Back*

48.   *Lenin in Red Square*

49.

Trotski of the Red Army

o. *The Tiger at the Front*

51.

The Savor of Victory

52. *The President on Parade*

53. *Under the Arch of Triumph*

54. *Reviewing the Troops*

55. *Among the Crowned Heads*

56. *Acclaim of the Crowd*

57.

The Formal Round

58. *The Only Man Who Came Out of the Peace Conference with Credit*

The Senator from Massachusetts

60. *Four Old Men*

61. *The General's Return*

posts, "and through the mist, fog and smoke one could see the boats and rafts loaded to the gunwales with enemy infantrymen and machinegunners set out for the southern bank . . . Men of the 38th, who had escaped the hours of shelling, met every attempt with rifle and automatic weapon fire. Scores of these boats were shattered or sunk or else disabled and sent drifting harmlessly down the river. Hundreds of Huns jumped into the water and were drowned. Those who reached our side by swimming were either killed or captured."

Soldiers wounded in the early morning remained in their riflepits firing as best they could until they were killed. One man was found dead with his rifle and pistol empty, and in front of him a heap of twelve dead Germans.

The advance posts along the riverbank were overwhelmed. The Germans swarmed up the hill and met the main line of American defense behind the embankment of the Paris-Metz railroad, which was the German objective for the first rush.

The Americans held their position while the French on their flanks fell back according to plan on a further line of hills. McAlexander's outfit found itself enfiladed by the boche on each flank.

The 38th did not budge. Their accurate riflefire caused heavy losses to enemy troops marching forward in formation on either side of them. Their most painful casualties came from a French barrage dropped between the railroad line and the river on the theory that all Allied troops had already fallen back. A lieutenant of the field artillery had several horses killed under him and was himself wounded in the numerous dashes he made back through the zone of fire to try to correct the range of the guns.

Costly as it was in lives, the 3rd Division's obstinate resistance managed to throw two crack German divisions into confusion. The Americans ended the day with a third of their number killed or wounded but holding their positions along the railroad and with three hundred kraut prisoners on their hands.

At the same time some companies of the 28th Division of the Pennsylvania National Guard were receiving their baptism of fire on the crest of a hill two miles south of the Marne to the eastward. Again there was a misunderstanding of the new French tactics. The four companies stayed in their positions instead of retiring with the French before the German assault and were killed or captured to a man, except for one small group, led by officers who had never seen combat in their lives, who managed to fight their way back to the new French entrenchments.

The German penetration south of the Marne amounted to five miles in some places, but their pontoon bridges took such punishment from Allied aviation that by July 16 their advance had lost momentum and by the seventeenth they were stalled.

This German crossing of the Marne was intended as the western prong of a new pincers operation directed at the railroad center of Reims and the high ground to the south of it. While the western prong was making great sacrifices for an initial success, the eastern prong was faring badly indeed.

The American 42nd, the Rainbow Division made up of a conglomeration of National Guard outfits under General Menoher, was turned over to onearmed Gouraud's French Fourth Army which was ordered to hold Reims at any cost. Here the liaison was good. Gouraud carefully instructed all the elements under his command as to the tactics about which he was particularly wellinformed.

In the Reims sector there was clear moonlight the night of July 14. Gouraud's artillery laid down a terrific barrage at ten minutes before the time they knew the German bombardment was scheduled to start. The boche troops were taking punishment long before their zero hour.

The French and Americans knew exactly what to expect. Every detail had been correctly predicted. When the German rolling barrage moved forward and the storm troops jumped off they retired, leaving sacrifice groups to signal the whereabouts of the attackers, to a rear defensive position. When the boche reached the Allied front lines, a curtain of fire descended on them from the Allied artillery. The attacking waves never reached Gouraud's fortified entrenchments. At ten in the morning the Germans were still trying to consolidate the gains that Gouraud had intentionally yielded to them. Next day a series of counterattacks pushed them back to their starting place. The 42nd Division's part in this most successful defensive operation in the entire war cost them fortythree officers and sixteen hundred and ten men in total casualties.

Three days after the jumpoff both Foch's headquarters and the German High Command knew that Ludendorff's fifth offensive had failed.

Foch's Mass of Manoeuvre

The hour had come that Ferdinand Foch had been waiting for. For a month he had worked to concentrate a striking force in the wooded region around Villers-Cotterets. From there he would be in a position, if the boche should continue to attack Reims in preparation for a drive against Paris, to hit them on the exposed flank of their salient between the Marne and the Ourcq. The very success of Ludendorff's drive south of the Marne, combined with his failure to budge Gouraud's force defending Reims, to throw him off balance and to make the western flank of his armies south of Soissons more vulnerable. This was the moment for Foch to risk an offensive.

Fending off interference from his British allies and from his own generals kept him even busier than planning the logistics of his troop movements. Versailles was in an uproar.

The success of three German drives threw Lloyd George into a case of jitters. He was desperate to stop the drain on British manpower. He kept advocating drastic changes in military policy. He dreamed of restoring the old stalemate in France and Flanders. He advocated moves against Germany through Austria or the Balkans. He wanted expeditions to Russia to keep the Germans from mobilizing Russian manpower. At the same time he was appalled by the prospect of a new German attack on Haig's shattered armies.

Every meeting of the Supreme War Council was angrier than the last. Backbiting and recrimination were the order of the day. Pershing was having to use all sorts of subterfuges to get the artillery and service troops he needed to complete his divisions shipped across the Atlantic. At Lloyd George's insistence cables were sent Woodrow Wilson making the completely impractical demand that a hundred divisions of American infantry be dispatched immediately. At the same time he was importuning Haig to take back his XXII Corps which, according to the Beauvais and Abbeville agreements, the British field marshal was placing at Foch's disposition.

Haig, who distrusted his own politicians even more than he distrusted the French, loyally stood by his commitments to Foch. When Lloyd George sent an emissary to try to make him change his mind, he wrote out his reply: "I take the risk, and I fully realize that if the dispositions prove to be wrong, the blame will rest on me. On the other hand, if they prove to be right the credit will lie with Foch. With this," he added bitterly, "the Government should be well satisfied."

In spite of continual private bickering between the two men, Foch had support from Clemenceau. Even so he was not yet master in his own camp. As late as the morning of July 15, when he was driving north to confer with Haig, he discovered, dropping in unannounced on the headquarters of his Tenth Army at Noailles, that Pétain, as commander of the French armies in the field, had issued orders to discontinue the concentrations of troops around Villers-Cotterets. Pétain, as always defensive-minded to the point of timidity, wanted to reinforce Gouraud at Reims.

"Let Gouraud take care of himself," said Foch with his arrogant gesture of brushing away the cobwebs of human stupidity. He countermanded Pétain's orders in the nick of time.

Possibly some rumor of Pétain's intended dispositions reached German Intelligence and encouraged Ludendorff to weaken his flank south of Soissons and throw everything he had against Reims. The High Command's strategic thinking seems to have been confused by the fact that the Germans had a double objective: to seize the Reims-Paris trunk line of railroad and at the same time to build up the reserves for Prince

Rupert's knockout blow against the British in the north which was set for two weeks after a German victory on the Marne.

Foch, always punctual, hurried from the Tenth Army to his meeting with Haig at nearby Monchy. That day he let the British commander in on just enough of his plan to keep him welldisposed. It wasn't until the morning of the seventeenth, when Foch knew that the German drive was stalled before Reims and at least slowed across the Marne, that he sent Haig a message fully disclosing his intentions: early next day General Mangin of the French Tenth Army would attack south of Soissons with twenty divisions.

The Forest of Retz

Charles Marie Emmanuel Mangin, a small jumpy sallow man with deep lines in his face and a jetblack mustache, was a veteran leader of colonial troops. Bullard described him as a little foxterrier with a bulldog jaw. He had made his reputation leading two successful counterattacks at Verdun in 1916. The plan of the move to cut off Soissons was his. The crux of the operation was intrusted to Berdoulat's corps which was to consist of the American 1st and 2nd and a Moroccan division famous for recklessness and dash.

The 1st, now under Major General Summerall who had been promoted for his conduct of the artillery at Cantigny, received orders on July 11. They were to start moving out of the Beauvais rest area for an undisclosed destination. Travel was to be by night and the troops were to hide from airplane observation in copses and villages during the day. The 1st's advance towards the front proved strenuous but was carried out with no more than the usual confusion.

The 2nd, notified three days later, had a rough time of it. The division was in the process of being relieved from the now fairly inactive Belleau Wood region to the west of Château-Thierry. General Edwards' Yankees were moving in to replace them. To add to the complications Major General Harbord had barely been notified that he was to take over divisional command from General Bundy.

Harbord was in Paris on two days leave, outfitting himself with new uniforms, and being wined and dined as the hero of Belleau Wood by his crony Charley Dawes, when he received orders to replace Bundy at once. Arriving at the rest area near La Ferté-sous-Jouarre where his division was supposed to be, he found that most of his troops were already on the move but nobody could tell him exactly where they were going.

On July 14, which was a nice quiet sunny day along the Marne, the marines of the first regiments to come out of the firing line were placidly swimming and washing their clothes in the green river or writing letters or dozing on the grass in anticipation of a few days of very much needed rest, when the sergeants began snapping out orders to fall in for a long march. They broke up camp in a hurry and hiked till long after dark.

Next day they hiked on through back roads of the beautiful green countryside between the Oise and the Ourcq. In the late afternoon their rolling kitchens caught up with them. They hurriedly swallowed some slum and hiked again. They hiked all night. After fifty hours of marching they reached their destination and were told to get ready to attack within twentyfour hours.

It wasn't till late in the night of July 16 that Harbord, after ramming his staffcar through an incredible tangle of military traffic moving up the main road into the woodlands around Villers-Cotterets, found General Berdoulat. The corps headquarters was in a village that proved to be a terrible bottleneck for traffic because the highway narrowed there to a single street hemmed between stone houses.

Berdoulat greeted Harbord cordially and served him some supper, but he could give him no idea of where the various units of the 2nd Division were at that moment. While they were eating he announced casually that Harbord's division was to take up positions along the edge of the woods and attack on the morning of the eighteenth in the direction of the Soissons-Château-Thierry road.

Nobody on Berdoulat's staff vouchsafed any further information as to where the regiments arriving by forced marches were expected to assemble or where such troops as were being transported by bus and truck would be unloaded. That was the business of the army, not of the corps the officers told him.

They did furnish him with maps and with copies of the general orders. A French general, who had fought over this countryside in 1914, hurriedly dictated a description of the terrain to Harbord's chief of staff, Colonel Brown.

Harbord and Brown spent the night writing up their divisional orders. The tactical problem, over ground as unknown to them as the face of the moon, was hard enough to put down on paper; the prospect of putting it into practice appalled them. They did the best they could, spurred to the work by a brief but vigorous bombing by boche planes which made them fear that perhaps the boche knew more about the plans of the French Army than they did. With the first streaks of day they were on the move.

"Just twentyfour hours before the coming attack," wrote Harbord, "we left Taillefontaine in my motor car to attempt to find the division, concentrate it, distribute the necessary orders, assure the supply of ammunition, rations, evacuation of the wounded, and to guarantee its assault at the prescribed hour."

Foch picked the ancient Forest of Retz as a concentration point because the enormous trees afforded considerable protection from boche observation planes. The highway to Soissons cut through the middle of this forest and from that highway narrow logging roads made tunnels of greenery to the right and left. Every road and woodland trail was packed with the troops and the mounts and the rolling equipment of twenty divisions converging for the attack.

The morning of the seventeenth dawned rainy but the day turned out hot. The rain from intermittent thundershowers was a relief for men hot and sweating from long marches. When the sun shone drenched uniforms steamed. The men suffered tortures of thirst. The roads became slippery and the ditches filled with mud.

Dogtired and footsore as they were, the arriving doughboys and marines were impressed by the majesty of their surroundings. Green on the fringes and dark almost to blackness within, great oaks and beeches towered on either hand ninety feet above the mossy forest floor.

It was midafternoon before the American units reached the depths of the forest. One regiment was late because the French major in charge of the trucks held them up for two hours while he haggled to have receipts signed for the transportation of the men. The Americans knew that the minute he had his receipts he would dump them out where they were instead of taking them to their destination. "Oh those frugal French!" exclaimed Harbord.

Men looked around wideeyed at the great concentration of troops. Picketlines of artillery and cavalry stretched out of sight among the trees. French infantrymen in faded blue lolling beside their stacked rifles seemed to the arriving Americans to be giving them appraising looks. Some thought they smiled approval through their wiry beards and droopy mustaches.

Tanks elbowed them to one side as they marched—along the right side of the road since the center had to be left open for heavy traffic. Many of the Americans were seeing tanks for the first time. There were big tanks and little tanks, weirdly camouflaged with splotches of green and brown and blue. They rattled and crunched and groaned and snorted along. Sometimes a man had to throw himself into a thicket to get out of their way. Plodding wearily along they passed piles and piles of small arm ammunition. There were rows of shells of every conceivable caliber, ranks of winged aerial bombs, enormous dumps of handgrenades and pyrotechnic equipment for signalling.

The center of the road was a jumble of howitzers propelled by lowslung caterpillars, graceful French seventyfives hauled by brisk sixhorse teams, larger fieldguns dragged by eight straining drayhorses. There were rolling kitchens and waterwagons behind their spans of mules, and troops of led horses of every color and shape: roan, sorrel, black, bay. Through the tangled mass wound neverending convoys of ammunition trucks, dispatch riders on motorcycles, officers in sidecars, the impatient crowded touring cars of some general's staff.

Through the trees on either side plugged weary files of mudcaked poilus, with their rifles that seemed much too long to the Americans, and all their paraphernalia of pots and pans for light housekeeping dangling and clattering from the knapsacks on their backs. Among them were dark Moroccans in khaki, black Senegalese, ruddy English in their welltailored uniforms. In the distance among the great treetrunks flitted shadows of mounted French grenadiers with plumes and lances.

As the long twilight faded into night the confusion was compounded. "Now it is night in the great Forest of Retz," wrote Private McCord in his diary, "and dark as a dungeon, and with the darkness comes rain. As we grope in single file we cling each man to a packstrap of the man in front, as blindly, doggedly on we go, in spite of the mud, the heavy packs and the rain that comes down in torrents . . . Blindly feeling our way, with the help of God and our own intuition, we the lousy infantry, s.o.l. as always, until they get us to where they need us, managed to miraculously accomplish the impossible by getting from the right to the left side of this dark, seething, confusing stream of traffic to follow other lousy troopers, men like ourselves, the other battalions and companies of our regiment, in single file off through the woods to our left . . ."

Wherever Harbord went, his men told the same story of a weary night ride or endless hike; no information, no maps, no guides, no orders.

The machineguns of the marine brigade were for some reason dumped off at an old château. "When finally located and told the mission of the division, these men," wrote Harbord, "carried their guns by hand on the long march across fields and muddy roads, getting into position at the last moment. No one can understand exactly what this means unless he has tried to carry a machinegun twelve miles through a ploughed field . . .

"Seven hours of darkness before the zero hour," wrote Harbord. "None of my units except the gunners were in place. It rained hard; the forest was plutonian in its darkness: the road, beyond words to describe: trucks, artillery, infantry columns, cavalry, wagons, caissons, mud, MUD, utter confusion . . . All realized that the task was almost superhuman, but that the honor not only of the division but of the American name was at stake. At 3 A.M. the 5th Marines and the 9th Infantry were forcing their way through the forest . . . they would be up with about five minutes to spare . . . The regiments got to the point designated for the assault at doubletime."

Towards the Soissons-Château-Thierry Road

The orders were for the Moroccan division to attack in the center with the American 1st on its left and the 2nd on its right. Many men of the 2nd had marched without sleep for two nights.

"The attack began at the appointed hour of 4:55 A.M.," Harbord jotted in his notes. "It was out of my hands when they went over the top and there was nothing to do but pray for victory and wait for news."

July 18: "Nearing dawn and stopped raining," noted Sergeant Carl Mc-Cune of the 5th Marines. His battalion halted on a hill about a half a mile from the front line where the men left their blankets and made up combat packs with reserve rations. Then the hike was resumed, the men very quiet and the artillery silent. A French machinegun outfit, bearded men muddy from the trenches, passed by towards the rear. The sergeant noted that they seemed tired and glad to see the marines. There were shellholes everywhere. Woods thinning out. At a farmhouse the men were issued two bandoliers of ammunition and two grenades each.

"A 75 barked suddenly and then began the most terrible barrage ever experienced up to this time. Every caliber of gun, large and small, firing as rapidly as possible, joined in throwing over a wall of steel and iron that was to drive the invader out of the land. The sky was becoming clearer. As we were late we began to double time into position, panting, stumbling, well-nigh exhausted; the men ran quickly through a counter-barrage thrown over by the Germans. Men fell now and then hit by shrapnel . . . A French sentinel posted at a wire strung across the road, opened it to let the Marines through; shells dropped closer, several men were hit. Big trees cut by artillery fire lay everywhere about the woods. Exhausted, the men dropped into holes constituting the line and paused for breath. Exhausted as they were, the men arose and went over the top to meet the enemy."

The Germans were taken by surprise. Some units were out in the fields taking in the wheatharvest the French farmers had abandoned in their flight. Their counterbarrage proved spotty. Outposts made little resistance.

The day turned out bright and clear. The sun was hot and men who had drunk up the water in their canteens during the night suffered agonies of thirst. When a man fell dead his comrades snatched for his canteen. Soon they were picking canteens off the fallen Germans.

"We went through barbed wire entanglements," continued Sergeant McCone. "In front of the advanced posts a machinegun opened up and the men who received the fire halted and lay on the ground, behind trees if possible; our units to the right and left advanced and forced the gun crew to withdraw. We advanced keenly on the alert from tree to tree.

Maxims lay scattered about with long belts of ammunition discarded by the Germans in their flight. The barrage roared steadily . . . The German artillery now dropped shells between the first and second wave which the men avoided by making an encircling movement around the shelled area and reforming when out of range. To the right of the company were captured a four inch gun, a telephone station and several prisoners. We found hot coffee and German warbread and butter which the men devoured after making the prisoners first sample it."

Marines of another detachment, after storming a ravine, found themselves the possessors of a barrel of sauerkraut. Parched with thirst and starving for food they broached it with a riflebutt. As they continued up through a wheatfield after the retreating Germans each man had his rifle in one hand and a dripping clutch of sauerkraut in the other.

At the same time infantry outfits were storming the village of Vierzy which commanded a heavily defended tunnel on the Soissons-Villers-Cotterets railroad.

"We emerged from the woods," wrote Lieutenant Marvin H. Taylor of the 23rd Infantry, "upon a broad stretch of wheatfields as flat as a table, which was bounded by a wide deep valley, in the bottom of which was the main position of the town of Vierzy. The houses were built in a series of terraces along the opposite side and each one offered excellent protection for Boche machine guns which opened up a murderous fire upon us, exposed as we were crossing the open fields. Our advance was a quick rush down the slope into the town, then a short delay caused by lurking snipers who were disposed of, after a bit of house to house fighting, and then the arduous climb up to the opposite slope again. There were fences and walls enclosing the grounds of each house and they were still intact. The destruction of war had apparently skipped that little town for some unaccountable reason, and all of these structures made progress extremely difficult. A formation of any sort was quite impossible, and we struggled forward in groups made up of men of all outfits, infantrymen, marines and Moroccans, in a strange hodgepodge . . .

"At the summit we came upon a strange scene. There on the very edge of the hill, somewhat concealed by shrubbery, a German machinegunner had been engaged in taking advantage of an unobstructed field of fire as we crossed through the wheat. But now retribution had been meted out and the German gunner was dead at his gun. Seated as in the act of firing, his finger on the trigger, his head bent forward on the breech, a bullet hole in the forehead and gaping bayonet wound in the throat. I never thought I would reach a point where I would glory in death but the sight of that fellow positively caused a thrill of exaltation to sweep over me and tired as I was I laughed aloud . . . When I laughed every man in the platoon caught the spirit of it and laughed a grim short laugh."

Night found the men of the 2nd Division scattered in exhausted disorder over a great segment of the battlefront. They had crossed the Soissons-Villers-Cotterets railroad and blocked off the northern end of the Vierzy tunnel and were occupying objectives which had been set for the third day, many of them in territory assigned to their allies.

Meanwhile the 1st Division to the north of the Moroccans advanced doggedly, with more order and less speed, against energetic German resistance, in a valley which sloped towards Soissons and the little river Crise, a tributary of the fateful Aisne. The hamlet of Missy-aux-Bois was fiercely contested. By night they had Missy and were among the gardenwalls of Breuil a short distance to the east.

For a brief respite exhausted marines and doughboys dug into funkholes. Lucky was the man who could catch an occasional catnap. "The night was cool and clear," wrote Sergeant McCone, "the stars shining. Wounded marines lay groaning in the fields because there were not enough stretchers to care for all."

"By night," noted Harbord, "we had three thousand prisoners; eleven batteries of German artillery, hundreds of machineguns and dozens of minenwerfers: had pushed the enemy before us six miles and were a mile ahead of the best shock troops in France, the fanatical Moslems from Morocco. But some of the best men America ever produced had watered with their blood those sunny slopes and wooded crests.

"At 10 P.M.," continued the general's diary, "I moved Division Headquarters forward to Beaurepaire farm . . . It was an advanced dressing station and a very distressing scene. The congestion on the one country road prevented ambulances from getting to the front and men had lain there in the yard of farm buildings all day, and were to continue to lie there twelve or fourteen hours longer. Water was unobtainable, the buildings were in ruins from shell fire, and the boche still dropped an occasional bomb from his airplanes as they circled over. But from these wounded there was no word of complaint, nothing but patience in suffering. There were wounded Germans, Americans and darkskinned Moroccans side by side on the ground, blood over everything, clothes cut away, some men dead, and a ceaseless stream of traffic still pouring to the front with ammunition and supplies for fighting . . . No sleep, of course, and at 2 A.M. of the 19th an order to push on the attack that day.

"The division had outrun its communications. There was no wire connection at all to the rear. The corps order was brought by a French officer who was very much surprised to find the division where it was."

That day German aviation turned out in force. Resistance stiffened, particularly in front of Berzy-le-Sec on a range of hills which dominated the Soissons-Château-Thierry road. All day, in liaison with the French on both flanks, units of the 1st Division advanced in short rushes against some of the best troops in the German Army.

By that night casualties of the 2nd Division had mounted so high and the men were so exhausted that Mangin decided to replace them by a rested French division. "The loss has been almost five thousand officers and men," noted General Bullard, now in command of the American corps which had supervision over the operation. "But what they did was worth any price to the Allied cause."

"The loss was heavy but the effect for the Allied cause was worth it all," wrote Harbord. "For over an hour this morning," he went on, "Brown and I stood by the roadside and watched the troops march back towards the Forêt de Retz. Battalions of only a couple of hundred men, companies of twenty-five or thirty, swinging by in the gray dawn, only a remnant, but a victorious remnant, thank God. No doubt in their minds as to their ability to whip the Germans. Their whole independent attitude, the very swagger of their march, the snatches of conversations we could hear as they swung past, proclaimed them a victorious division."

The First Sight of Soissons

Ever since the offensive began the French had been trying to take the upland village of Berzy-le-Sec and the little knolls to the south of it which dominated the outskirts of Soissons. Possession of this high ground would deny to the Germans the use of the Château-Thierry road in their retirement from the Marne. As well as being a railroad center, Soissons was the crossroads of six converging highways essential to the enemy's transport system.

The boche had placed his batteries and machinegun nests with his usual ingenuity. The French units were making no headway. On the morning of July 20 General Summerall received word from Mangin's headquarters that his 1st Division, which had been showing the same reckless dash as the 2nd during the past two days of fighting, should, as a reward for gallantry, have the honor of taking Berzy-le-Sec.

Take it they did.

The first attempt failed. A group of officers watching through field-glasses from a hill above the hamlet of Chaudun, which had been captured at heavy cost during the first day, saw the 2nd Brigade march out in column formation from the shade of the lines of lacerated poplars where the main road to Soissons emerged from the forest. At first the men's faces, shadowed by their helmets in the hot July sun, looked black. A French officer thought they were Algerians, but as they advanced, in perfect order at about the pace at which a barrage rolls, the observers on the hill began to make out the American box respirator hanging on each man's breast and the broad flash of American bayonets. As they advanced up over the bare hillside, dust and smoke rose from Allied shells pounding the village. There was as yet no sound from the German guns.

The formations went out of sight behind a fold in the land. Now the observers could see the leading ranks following their barrage across a ridge above the roofs and steeple of the village. Each individual soldier stood out against the grassy hillside. When the first rank, advancing in perfect order, reached the crest a few shells from large caliber howitzers exploded among them. The boche were testing the range.

"The accuracy of preparation of this fire was such that practically no adjustment was required, and almost immediately our infantry was shrouded in smoke and dust," the observer noted in his report. "Great gaps were left in the ranks as the shells crashed among them. Nevertheless the advance continued in the most orderly way . . . Many of our infantry passed out of sight over the ridge accompanied by the devastating fire of the enemy's artillery. Men struck by the enemy's fire either disappeared or ran aimlessly about and toppled over."

Now the observers were hearing the rattle of the enemy's machineguns. The lines of tiny figures dropped into shellholes. Files of wounded were seen hobbling painfully back. "Individual men and groups of twos or threes began to wander about all over the field. They were the unit leaders, reorganizing their groups against counterattack. The attack had met the resistance of a strong position occupied in great force by the enemy . . . Thus the afternoon passed and night fell."

Next morning at dawn the attack was renewed with Brigadier General B. B. Buck himself leading the first wave. Although depleted by three days of constant fighting the 1st Brigade, leapfrogging the survivors of the 3rd, crossed the deep gully of the Crise and planted itself on the heights clear across the Soissons-Château-Thierry road.

An hour later units of the 2nd Brigade swept through Berzy-le-Sec. They first had to capture a deadly battery of German 77s that had been firing on them at point blank range.

In the slanting light of late afternoon the Americans on the hills above the village could see the railroad yards of Soissons in the distance. That night as they lay in their positions awaiting a counterattack that never came they watched, in the misty valleys to the east and southeast, great fires rise from burning munitions dumps and villages put to the torch as the Crown Prince's armies retreated from the Marne.

The men were numb with the exhaustion of five days of fighting. It wasn't until dusk on July 22 that they heard the welcome bagpipes of a Scottish division marching in to relieve them.

When the soldiers of the 1st reassembled by companies around their rolling kitchens back in the forest out of range of the German guns, officers and men were aghast at what they saw.

Hardly a handful remained of each of the four regiments of infantry. Scarcely a company had an officer left to command it. A sergeant, a corporal, in one case a private was in command. Every battalion commander was a casualty. The 26th Infantry had lost all its field officers and came out commanded by a captain in his second year in the service. When the acting sergeants called the roll of their companies barely half of the enlisted men were there to answer Present.

Mangin was lavish in his congratulations to the two American divisions. "You rushed into the fight as though to a fête," he declaimed in his general orders . . . "91 guns, 7200 prisoners, immense booty, ten kilometers of country reconquered: this is your portion of the spoil of victory . . . I am proud to have commanded you during such days and to have fought with you for the deliverance of the world."

Once they recovered from the shock of defeat, the Germans carried out their retreat with coldblooded skill. It was not until August 2 that Soissons was actually reoccupied, though heavy artillery brought up to the heights round Berzy-le-Sec soon ruined its effectiveness as a transportation center for the boche.

To Clear the Railroads

The commanders in chief of the Allied armies, their spirits for once matching the glitter of gold braid on their caps, met on July 24 at Foch's headquarters at Bombon. Foch read a summary of the strategic situation. The Germans were in retreat. The Allied generals at last had more manpower at their disposal than did the German High Command. Two hundred and fifty thousand American troops arriving each month were tipping the scales. To meet this increased riflepower the Germans had a muchweakened defensive army holding their lines, and behind that front, a shock army of stormtroops still capable of delivering dangerous blows.

The Allies had seized the initiative, said Foch. His eyes flashed. He puffed out his bantam chest with an arrogant smile under his bristling gray mustache. They must never let it go.

He outlined three operations that must be completed in preparation for the great final offensive. He was taking it for granted that this final offensive would take place in the spring or summer of 1919. He had been steeped in war so long it was hard for him to imagine that it would ever end.

The first operation was already on: to drive the enemy off the Paris-Metz main line of railroad in the valley of the Marne.

Second operation: The northern trunk line through Amiens and Hasebrouck to the Channel coast must be cleared of enemy interference. This was up to Haig and the British forces north of Amiens. General Debeney's army in the southern part of the sector would cooperate.

Third operation: The eastern section of the Paris-Metz railroad must be restored to Allied use by the reduction of the Saint Mihiel salient east of Verdun. This would be the business of the Americans.

When Foch asked for comments from the Allied commanders—so the story was told at Chaumont—each spoke in his customary roles. Haig complained that his armies were not yet re-established after the shocking blows they had suffered in March and April. Pétain grumbled that the French were bled white. Pershing blurted out that his men asked nothing better than to get into the fight, but added, in a sour tone, that the only thing holding them up was that no American army had been formed for them to fight with.

Foch could be diplomatic when he wanted to be. He quieted their complaints with his confident smile. It was decided that the next move must be to disengage Amiens. That was the affair of the valiant British. It was hinted that the safety of the British Expeditionary Force might well lie in anticipating the offensive that was brewing against them in Prince Rupert's group of armies. Surprise, tirelessly repeated Foch; the watchword was surprise.

Again the Tanks

Haig entrusted the Amiens operation to General Sir Henry Rawlinson's Fourth Army.

Sir Henry, known as Rawly to his intimates in the upper echelons, was a British aristocrat brought up in the grand Victorian tradition. His father, as well as being an eminent servant of the empire, was a learned orientalist and one of the first students of Assyrian inscriptions. His mother was a Seymour of the great house of the Dukes of Somerset and a tolerable watercolorist besides. Rawly himself was no mean hand with a pencil and a man of some reading as well as of experience in the East. He served as aide to Lord Roberts in India. He was with Kitchener at Khartoum.

Though, as an old poloplayer, he couldn't bring himself quite to give up cavalry, he was one of the few British topdrawer generals who appreciated tanks. Furthermore he appreciated Anzacs. His army was made up of a corps of Australians, who were tough nuts to handle for officers who rubbed them the wrong way, a corps of Canadians and a corps of British. In reserve he had the American 33rd Division. He was broadminded enough even to like Americans.

The young men of Rawly's Intelligence had for some time been bringing in reports of warweariness among the German troops opposing him.

They were suffering from an epidemic of influenza. Their lines were thinly held. Long before the council of war at Bombon he had been prodding Haig to recapture the outer defenses of Amiens which the boche had held since March. He had attempted several tentative probes.

Rawly's Fourth of July operation was not only the first tryout of the Americans on the British front. It was the first tryout of the Mark V tank. Both experiments were successful. The Americans showed fight. The new tank proved faster and more easily manoeuverable than the old. The attack being planned would be led by Mark V tanks.

The battle of Amiens was purely a British show. French cooperation was secondary. Only a single regiment of Americans was involved. The staffwork could hardly have been better. The concentration of men and armament was carried out at night or in cloudy weather under air cover that kept German observation planes out of the area. Batteries were reinforced with new guns without showing any increased fire power. While the three hundred and sixty heavy tanks and ninetysix whippet tanks were being moved into position, masses of airplanes were used to create a sound barrage so that the enemy should not hear the rattling and clanking of the unwieldy vehicles.

Secrecy was so well maintained that not only Ludendorff's staff but the war cabinet and the Australian Labor Prime Minister, William Morris Hughes, who was in London raising a storm about the excessive casualties his Aussies were suffering at the front, were kept in ignorance of what was being planned. Canadian casualty stations were ostentatiously set up in Mount Kemmel area, with the result that the governor general of Canada protested publicly that his troops weren't being used as a unit as had been promised.

Everything led the Germans to expect an attack in the north. They were further lulled to security when the Australians extended their lines in front of Amiens to relieve part of a French division to the south of them. By zero hour the British had managed to move in unobserved not only the tanks, but a thousand extra guns and six fresh divisions. The final detailed orders were delayed to the last moment.

On the morning of August 8, Sir Douglas Haig made one of his customary placid entries in his diary: "Glass steady. Fine night and morning—a slight mist in the valley. An autumn feel in the morning air." He added that the Fourth Army reported a quiet night.

An hour before dawn, muffled by a thick ground mist made thicker by smoke bombs, the British tanks swarmed across the German lines. When they were well started a barrage dropped in front of them. The Aussies and Canadians followed in their trail. The big guns of the British artillery concentrated on knocking out enemy batteries. Whippets and armored cars broke through and romped about behind the German lines. The surprise was so great that one corps headquarters was caught at breakfast.

"Everywhere else the situation had developed more favorably for us than I, optimist though I am, dared to hope," Haig noted. "The enemy was completely surprised, two reliefs of Divisions were in progress, very little resistance was offered and our troops got their objectives quickly with little loss."

The Cruise of the Musical Box

"On August 8, 1918 I commanded Whippet tank 'Musical Box,'" reported Lieutenant C. B. Arnold. He told of crossing the railway at Villers-Bretonneux, a town hotly contested ever since the German March attack. His formation proceeded due east. "I found myself to be the leading machine, owing to the others having become ditched. To my immediate front I could see more Mark V tanks being followed very closely by Australian infantry . . . We came under direct shell fire from a four gun field battery of which I could see the flashes."

Shells exploded near. Two Mark V tanks a hundred and fifty yards on the right of him were knocked out. He saw clouds of smoke coming from the machines and the crews tumbling out of them. Men were dropping, among the infantry that tagged after. Lieutenant Arnold's whippet passed behind a screen of trees along the side of a road.

"I ran along this belt until level with the battery when I turned full right and engaged the battery in the rear . . . The gunners some thirty in number abandoned their guns and tried to get away. Gunner Ribbans and I accounted for the whole lot. I cruised forward making a detour to the left and shot a number of the enemy who appeared to be demoralized and were moving about the country in all directions."

He advanced through a railroad siding and found Australian infantrymen occupying a sunken road beyond the battery he'd knocked out. After asking their lieutenant if they needed any help he proceeded in an easterly direction along the railway embankment passing two British cavalry patrols which were taking punishment from a group of Germans in a wheatfield. He advanced on the Huns, scattered them and then proceeded along the railroad tracks, noting that a burning train was being towed away by its engine. He was searching for a spot marked on his map as a German cantonment.

"Many enemy were visible packing kits and others retiring. On our opening fire on the nearest many others appeared from huts making for the end of the valley, their object being to get over the embankment and so out of our sight. We accounted for many of these."

Then he cruised across country firing at retreating files of enemy infantry. As he was well ahead of his supporting troops the Musical Box was taking a lot of machinegun and rifle fire. Nine tins of gasoline for refueling carried on the roof of the tank were riddled. Gasoline dripped down over the cab.

"The fumes and the heat of the engine"—Lieut. Arnold noted that he had been in action for nine hours by this time—"made it necessary to breathe through the mouthpiece of the box respirator."

He shot up an airfield. He knocked out a truck crossing a bridge. He crossed the railway line and fired into a convoy of horsedrawn wagons with canvas tops. By this time he was under intense machinegun fire.

"The left hand port cover was shot away. Fumes and heat were very bad." Lieutenant Arnold was shouting to his driver to turn and discontinue the action when there were two heavy concussions and the cab burst into flames.

"Carney and Ribbans got to the door and collapsed. I was almost overcome but managed to get the door open and fell out onto the ground and was able to drag out the other two men. Burning petrol was running on to the ground where we were lying. The fresh air revived us and we all got up and made a short rush to get away from the burning petrol. We were all on fire. In this rush Carney was shot in the stomach and killed. We rolled over and over to try to extinguish the flames. I saw numbers of the enemy approaching from all around. The first arrival came for me with rifle and bayonet. I got hold of this and the point of the bayonet entered my right forearm. The second man struck at my head with the butt end of his rifle, hit my shoulder and neck and knocked me down. When I came to there were dozens all around me, and anyone who could reach me did so and I was well kicked: they were furious."

After a number of interrogations and a certain amount of face slapping Lieutenant Arnold was taken to a fieldhospital where he was given an antitetanus injection and his burns treated. When he refused to answer questions he was locked in a room with no window and kept there for five days with only a bowl of soup and a small piece of bread a day to eat. He still refused to answer questions and finally found himself at a camp for British officer prisoners at Freiburg. It wasn't until he was freed after the armistice that he was able to turn in his report.

"August 8 was the black day . . ."

"August 8 was the black day of the German army in the history of this war," wrote Ludendorff. German fear of tanks became obsessive. Crack units broke and ran. The Australians and Canadians carried their objectives in jig time. The British corps had trouble but advanced.

The French army to the south, which had few tanks, attacked after the usual artillery bombardment from Montdidier north to the Amiens sector. At first they had heavy going, but, as the confusion caused by the British penetration spread, they began to make headway.

Haig couldn't help recording the difficulties of the French: "I returned to my train for lunch," he noted, "and about 4 pm I called on H.Q. First French army at Conty. Debeney was much distressed and almost in tears because three batallions of his Colonial Infantry had bolted before a German machine gun. I told him that the British advance would automatically clear his front."

By night Rawlinson's army had advanced seven miles, had captured four hundred guns, among them a longrange weapon of the Bertha type that had been pounding the British rear back of Amiens, and taken thirteen thousand prisoners. The French caught up with them on the second day.

After the first twentyfour hours the tempo slacked. The waterlogged entrenchments of the old Somme battlefields proved a greater obstacle than the enemy. Tanks broke down and ran out of fuel. Tank crews were exhausted.

The British generals still relied on cavalry to exploit a breakthrough. The Germans proved again that with a very few machineguns they could make mincemeat of horses and riders. The whippets which had run far ahead of their units were handicapped by orders to stand by to help the cavalry. The advance petered out. By the third day the Germans were digging in tenaciously on a shortened line, but their hope of taking Amiens was gone.

Although in some ways a minor operation the German High Command heard the voice of doom in their defeat at Amiens. For the first time their armies had broken under assault. Officers had allowed themselves to be swept by panic. Divisional headquarters had allowed their records to be captured.

"We had to resign ourselves now," wrote Ludendorff, "to the prospect of the continuance of the enemy's offensive. Their success had been too easily gained. Their wireless was jubilant, and announced—and with truth —that the morale of the German army was no longer what it had been. The enemy had also captured many documents of inestimable value to them."

Ludendorff immediately called in divisional commanders and field officers to meet with him at his headquarters at Avesnes. "I was told of deeds of glorious valor, but also of behavior which, I openly confess, I should not have thought possible in the German army."

He laid the blame on pacifist propaganda. Prince Lichnowsky, who had been German ambassador in London in 1914, had allowed his account of British efforts to preserve the peace to be published in a pamphlet. The inference was that the German Imperial Government bore most of the guilt for provoking the war. The authorities were not interfering with its distribution, even to the troops. Wilson's Fourteen Points were in every hand. Soldiers who had been prisoners of war in Russia were re-enrolled under protest and spread the Bolshevik infection through their new regiments. Joffe, Bolshevik ambassador to Berlin, was making his embassy the center for the spreading of treason and defeatism. "The army," wrote Ludendorff, "was literally swamped with enemy propaganda."

"The failure of August 8," Hindenburg admitted in his memoirs, "was revealed to all eyes as the consequence of open weakness . . . The enemy had learned a good deal from us since the spring . . . he had employed against us those tactics with which we had soundly beaten him time after time."

So seriously did Ludendorff take the defeat before Amiens that he went to Hindenburg and offered to resign as Chief of Staff. Neither Hindenburg nor the Kaiser would accept his resignation.

At an imperial conference at the Hotel Britannique at Spa on August 13 Ludendorff announced brusquely that the war must be ended. The Kaiser instructed his Foreign Secretary to start immediately working for negotiations, if possible through the Queen of the Netherlands. Next day the Emperor Charles of Austria arrived with the news that the Austro-Hungarian Army could not be expected to resist through another winter. Although Hindenburg remained optimistic, Ludendorff repeated the facts as he saw them. The impression he gave to the conference at Spa was, in his own words, that "I no longer believed in a victorious issue of the war."

Chapter 20

IN Washington the summer of 1918 was unusually hot. Woodrow Wilson continued his relentless routine. At eight he presided, with Edith Wilson at the other end of the table, at his customary family breakfast. Visiting relatives from the large Wilson and Bolling connections were expected to appear with fresh morning faces. Through the windows Edith would point out the fourteen sheep and four lambs "doing their bit" cropping the White House lawns. After breakfast the President walked over to his office in the wing, and there dictated to his stenographer until a little before ten, when congressmen, cabinet members, or delegations that for some reason or another could not be shunted off on Tumulty, began to be admitted.

The President would listen to what his visitors had to say with cool affability. His replies were invariably noncommittal. He would ask for the problems to be put in writing so that he could decide on them later in the quiet of his study.

Lunch was at one but the President was often late. After lunch, if there were no cabinet meeting scheduled, would come formal calls from ambassadors and the like. If there were any of the afternoon left and the weather weren't too hot he would hurry with Grayson or sometimes with Edith to the country club for a little golf, coming back to the White House in time for a bath before dressing for dinner.

When he was dressed the great mass of letters and documents that had to be signed that day were brought to him. Sometimes he had time for a glass of scotch and soda before the formal evening meal. At table guests were discouraged from talking about politics or international affairs.

After dinner came consultations with close advisers such as Baker or Creel or with Colonel House if he were in town. Then the President would retire to his study, often helped by Edith, who liked to arrange his manuscripts for him, and would pore over the papers he'd collected during the day and make his shorthand notes or type out on his own typewriter the private memoranda from which his state papers or public speeches would gradually evolve. It was often long after midnight before he got to bed.

Saturday mornings he would try to play a full eighteen holes of golf, usually with Grayson, or with Edith if she felt up to it. Sundays he attended the Central Presbyterian Church. He always listened to the sermon with attention: he was a connoisseur of sermons as some men are of wines. In the afternoon he would collect the ladies of the family and take them motoring around one of his unchangeable itineraries in the White House car.

In Touch with World Movements

Woodrow Wilson's first wife's brother Stockton Axson, then serving as Secretary of the American Red Cross, was a frequent visitor that summer. "Stock," as he called him, was one of the men the President loved best. Their friendship was tinged perhaps by a certain nostalgia for academic days and for his lost life with Ellen whose death he still could not bear to think of.

Dr. Axson remembered a conversation they had one Sunday afternoon in late June of that year as so significant that, when Ray Stannard Baker asked him for anecdotes to include in his *Life and Letters* some years later, he told about it in detail. Axson came to lunch at the White House after church and found the President in "one of his most loveable talking moods." When Axson and the Wilsons were alone after the meal, Wilson suddenly asked him whom he would name for the next President.

Present company was excepted, they agreed. Axson suggested McAdoo. The President answered that he loved Mac as much as Stock did, but that the next President must have great powers of reflection as well as being a man of action. "Now nobody can do things better than Mac, but if Mac ever reflects, I never caught him in the act." He said Newton D. Baker was the best man but he could never be nominated. "The next President will have to be able to think in terms of the whole world," he went on. "He must be internationally minded . . . the only really internationally minded people"—Wilson was thinking aloud—"are the labor people. They are in touch with world movements."

After the war the world would change radically. Governments would have to do things now done by individuals and corporations. Waterpower, coalmines, oilfields would have to be government owned. "If I should say that outside," he exclaimed, "people would call me a socialist, but I am not a socialist. And it is because I'm not a socialist that I believe these things."

He added that he believed this was the only way communism could be prevented—Dr. Axson told Ray Baker he wasn't sure Wilson used the word communism, which wasn't yet in circulation, perhaps he said bolshevism—"the next President must be a man who is not only able to do things, but after having taken counsel and made a full survey, be able to retire alone, behind his own closed door, and think through the processes, step by step."

Thinking through the Processes

Woodrow Wilson, during those summer months, though brilliantly persuasive in his public appearances, was tortured by perplexities whenever he retired behind his own closed door, to think through the processes, step by step.

At home, now freshly stimulated by Bolshevik propaganda against capitalism and war, there was that "baneful seething" among the workingclass and the foreign born that never ceased to worry him.

The very Sunday Dr. Axson remembered as the date of their cosy afterluncheon talk, Eugene V. Debs, who proclaimed himself a socialist but whose basic notions of the democratic process were not too different from the President's, was arrested in Cleveland charged with making statements that violated the Espionage Act.

There was the troublesome agitation for the pardon of the syndicalist Tom Mooney convicted of bombing a preparedness parade in San Francisco, that would not down. There was the sedition of the now leaderless I.W.W., that was interfering with the cutting of timber in the forests of Oregon and Washington.

Strikes kept interrupting war production. The immediate problem on the President's desk was a strike being fomented against the Western Union Telegraph Company that threatened a tieup of communications inconceivable in wartime. The President's remedy for that was a bill being speeded through Congress to take over the telephone and telegraph services as the railroads had been taken over six months before.

Abroad, it was not the military problems that gave Wilson sleepless nights. Though he enjoyed thinking about the navy, he had little taste for the strategy and tactics of land warfare. He left that to the professionals. He recoiled from the thought of mass bloodshed. What few details of combat reached him came strained through the congenial mind of his Secretary of War. The problem that tortured him was political: whether or not to intervene in the ruined Romanoff empire that lay across the eastern third of the hemisphere, writhing in agony like a snake run over on the road.

Lloyd George's plausible friend, Lord Reading, the British ambassador, was at Wilson almost daily urging the British point of view, which was that Allied expeditions should be landed at Murmansk on the Arctic coast and at Vladivostok in the Far East to keep the stocks of war materials piled up in these two ports from falling into German hands. The bogy he kept presenting to the President was that the Brest-Litovsk peace, which was resulting in a seemingly friendly exchange of embassies between the Bolsheviks and the Imperial German Government, would produce an alliance from which the Germans could draw men and materials for the war in the West.

Various emissaries from Clemenceau, including the eminent philosopher Henri Bergson, sang to the same tune.

To add to these perplexities was a long dicker with the Japanese, whom the State Department felt were being encouraged by their British friends to invade Siberia on their own. The President's advisers agreed that the Japanese must be kept from taking advantage of the disintegration of Russia to build up their own empire, but there was difference of opinion as to how that should be done. Newton D. Baker was dead set against intervention of any kind. House pointed out that an invasion by the Japanese alone would throw the Russians into the arms of the Germans. In his opinion, if the Japanese insisted on going in it would be better to have an American force go along with them. In any case intervention should be preceded by largescale economic aid, administered by Herbert Hoover along the lines of Belgian Relief.

From Americans in Russia came conflicting reports. Some saw in the Bolshevik government merely a final phase of the revolutionary upheaval destined to pass away in a few months like the Jacobin terror that ended the French Revolution. Others saw in it the foundation of a new social order.

Woodrow Wilson was a tired man. His desk was stacked with more materials than he could cope with. House was already noting with alarm that he wasn't getting through as much work as he used to. Dr. Grayson remarked that his memory for names was failing. Ever since the Bolshevik seizure of power had shattered his dream of a democratic Russia he had been allowing the news from that revolutiontorn empire to pile up against some closed door in his mind.

He was becoming more and more reluctant to hear arguments about what action the United States should take in Russia. He balked at listening to the impressions of returned travellers. It was as if he felt that the data he had already absorbed were too difficult to resolve into the only terms his mind knew how to deal with. In early July he described to House, who had taken refuge from the extreme heat at Magnolia on the North Shore, in an intimate and affectionate letter, the desperation of his struggle to find the right words: "I have been sweating blood over the question of what is right and feasible"—"possible" he explained in parenthesis—"to do in Russia. It goes to pieces like quicksilver under my touch . . ."

The Closed Door

When people arrived fresh from the scene he refused to see them. He had listened distractedly to a few reports from Elihu Root's mission at the end of the preceding summer, but to the chagrin of that eminent and elderly Republican statesman, had paid no attention to his recommendations.

Returning members of the Red Cross Commission that followed fared no better.

Hard on the heels of the Root mission, transported by the same old worn imperial train rolling up the weary versts from Vladivostok, a fresh aggregation of Americans appeared in Petrograd. The engineers of the Railroad Mission, still loafing in uncomfortable hotels without being given any work to do, immediately dubbed the Red Cross people the Haitian army. Red Cross workers sent abroad were given assimilated military rank. There were colonels, majors, lieutenants, but not a single private.

This particular Red Cross mission differed from all others in that it was financed by a single individual. W. B. Thompson, who went along as business manager with the rank of colonel, paid all the bills.

W.B. was a legendary figure among Baruch's crowd on Wall Street. Born in Virginia City and raised in Butte, Montana, he struck it rich in copper. Coming east a millionaire, he applied an aptitude for poker and faro acquired in the mining camps of his boyhood, to such good account on the stock exchange that he became one of the country's wealthiest men.

With a war on, W.B., a big stout boisterous fellow in his late forties, was rearing to perform some patriotic service. His old friend Henry P. Davison of the Morgan bank, who headed the Red Cross, suggested that he go relieve the Russians. An expedition of about forty was collected. Though medical supplies and some doctors were taken along, the real purpose, as Edward N. Hurley of the Shipping Board hastened to explain to W.B. in behalf of the Administration, was to convince the Russians they should keep on fighting for the Allied cause. Copies of Woodrow Wilson's speeches took up more baggage space than gauze bandages.

W.B. arrived in Russia convinced he was the President's personal representative. In Petrograd he hired the largest suite in the famous Evropskaya Hotel, bought a wolfhound, had himself driven about in a glittering limousine by a French chauffeur, and with his lavish dinners and his skull cap and his big cigars appeared to the astonished inhabitants as almost a cartoon version of the American capitalist.

He developed a passion for icons and other Russian antiques. Taken to see Catharine Breshkovskaya, an old lady revered for her sufferings in the Czar's prisons as the "little grandmother of the Revolution," he became convinced that her friends, the Right Social Revolutionaries, were the people to back. When he found he could get no funds from the State Department he promptly drew a check of his own on the Morgan bank for a million dollars to spend in their behalf. This sudden financing of the Social Revolutionaries by the most flamboyant of Wall Street magnates gave the Bolsheviks an added talking point in their attacks on them. If anything more were needed to put the skids under Kerensky, W.B.'s million turned the trick.

After Kerensky's flight and the collapse of Kornilov's rebellion, W.B. made a sudden switch and decided that the Bolsheviks were the faction that had the organization and the ruthlessness to come out on top. In this decision he was much influenced by his second in command, Raymond Robins, who, travelling back and forth across the country buying wheat for relief purposes, had discovered in empirical American fashion that the Bolsheviks were the only people he could trust to get anything done. Leaving Robins in charge of Red Cross activities, which by now included a considerable and highly unreliable secret service, W.B. set out to carry the word to Washington.

On the way home he stopped in London to chum with his old school friend Tom Lamont, who as one of their leading sources of funds, was much listened to by British officials. He convinced Lamont that the Bolsheviks would fight the Germans if properly handled. Lamont took him to see various cabinet members. "Don't let Germany make 'em their Bolsheviks, made 'em our Bolsheviks," W.B. told them.

Lloyd George was so impressed he immediately instructed a Russian-speaking Scottish diplomat named Bruce Lockhart, who was acting British Consul General in Moscow, to establish contact with Lenin and Trotsky. The bait held out by Lloyd George was that if the Bolsheviks recognized Lockhart as unofficial representative, the British would similarly recognize their agent Litvinov, who was already in London.

Much encouraged, Thompson took the first boat and arrived in Washington in January 1918. Though Lamont went with him, eager to describe Lloyd George's reactions to W.B.'s tale, neither one of them got in to see the President. Wilson had just delivered himself of the Fourteen Points speech and felt that had settled the Bolsheviks for a while.

The Petrograd Intrigue

With Thompson gone the mantle of unofficial American representative in Russia fell on the shoulders of another mining prospector. Raymond Robins was an intensely emotional man, very much the thespian. He had

large smouldering black eyes and straight black hair. People noticed that
he looked like an Indian. Born in the Florida back country, he worked in
Appalachian coal mines as a boy, went west prospecting, and came back
rich from the Alaska gold rush. He was selfeducated, a devout Christian
and a practicing evangelist. After studying for the ministry, he picked
up some law and dedicated himself to settlementhouse work in Chicago.
In 1912 he joined the Bull Moose movement and ran for the Senate on
the Progressive-Republican ticket. A Progressive of the "Onward Christian
Soldiers" variety he was picked for the Red Cross Mission on Theodore
Roosevelt's recommendation.

Arriving in Petrograd with a vast desire to do good and no knowledge
of the language he picked up a young New York Jew for an interpreter.
Alexander Gumberg was born in Russia and remained a Russian citizen
but he grew up in the speculative intellectual life of the Jewish East
Side. As business manager of the Russian language paper *Novi Mir* he
struck up an acquaintance with Trotsky. Like so many others he returned
to Russia after the revolution hoping for the promised land. A brother
was a member of the Bolshevik party. Though a moderate socialist and
of a somewhat sceptical turn of mind Gumberg was trusted by the Bolshevik leaders.

Through his intelligent interpreting Robins was able to make closer
contact with Lenin and Trotsky than any other American. Though Robins
never pretended to share their dogmatic beliefs or to approve their
methods, he respected them for their dedication and their transparent
ability. There was a fervor about Robins that impressed even Lenin.

Robins became convinced that he could singlehandedly change the
course of history. Through Creel's representative, Edgar Sisson, and
through the Red Cross he sent home reports which he was confident would
be understood and appreciated by Woodrow Wilson, whom he greatly
admired.

The Bolsheviks were going to win in Russia, and they ought to win
because they were the only people capable of getting anything done.
During the Brest-Litovsk negotiations he reported that they were stringing the Germans along. When Trotsky refused to sign the German peace
terms and came back to Petrograd to broadcast his "Neither war nor
peace" statement, Robins' faith was confirmed. If he could get a promise
of immediate assistance from the Allies he believed he could induce the
Bolshevik leadership to turn on the Germans.

Their partners in the "dictatorship of the proletariat" the Left Social
Revolutionaries, whose support came from the peasantry and especially
from the prosperous peasants of the Ukraine, were all for waging guerrilla
war. Lenin was saying that peace was a necessity but Trotsky, through
Gumberg, was giving Robins intimations that if American recognition arrived soon enough and were followed by Allied aid, he would be for

continuing the war. Robins had fallen under Trotsky's spell. He felt kinship with Trotsky's dramatic oratory. He claimed that in his experience Trotsky had never failed to keep his word.

Trotsky, Robins told the sympathetic Lockhart, who was working against odds with his own government as Robins was with his, for Bolshevik recognition, "was a four kind son of a bitch, but the greatest Jew since Christ." The Bolsheviks were using the Germans more than the Germans were using them. By spending their money to back old regime elements against the Bolsheviks the Allies were doing the Germans' work for them. "If the German General Staff bought Trotsky they bought a lemon."

During the earlier part of the negotiations at Brest-Litovsk Sisson and Robins worked together in friendly fashion. They lived together and ate their meals together. It was through Gumberg's influence at Smolny that Robins helped Sisson get distribution of Wilson's Fourteen Points speech among the German troops.

Furthermore Robins, through connections which Thompson had set up, had contacts with the underworld of penniless and disinherited people who lived by catering to the various intelligence services. One group claimed to have tapped the telegraph wires into Smolny and was making hay selling the private communications of the Bolshevik command to the highest bidder.

Robins was using his connection with some of these connivers to get news of shipments of scarce war materials such as copper and nickel destined for the Germans. Then, through Gumberg, he would tip off the Bolsheviks at Smolny, who were only too glad to have them intercepted for their own purposes.

All through the Brest-Litovsk negotiations Petrograd teemed with undercover activities. Though the dictatorship of the proletariat was theoretically established the Bolsheviks had not had time to crush opposition. Free newspapers still appeared. The city was poorly policed. Selfstyled anarchists made free with the possessions of the rich. Secret agents swarmed. The German foreign office and general staff were spending buckets of money to foment pacifist and defeatist movements. French and British agents played hide and seek with them. Each secret agent was the center of a set of adventurers aiming to live high off inflated rubles while there was still time.

This gentry's chief stock in trade with the Allied missions was documents purporting to prove that the Bolsheviks were agents of the German secret service. The first batch seems to have been distributed quite widely and gratis as a comeon. This was a set of circulars supposed to have been issued by a branch of the High Command giving instructions to their Russian agents. The dragoman of the American Embassy had a copy.

Others were in the hands of the British and one set was published by a Cossack newspaper in anti-Bolshevik territory in the south.

One of the informers Robins was in touch with turned copies of these papers over to him early in February 1918. Though Robins himself took no stock in them, he felt the State Department should be informed of their existence and showed them to Sisson.

Right away Robins and Sisson disagreed as to what should be done. Both men were excited to the breaking point by the conspiratorial atmosphere of those wintry days of tension and suspense. Robins said the papers were worthless, but Sisson, a professional newspaperman and as fervent a Germanhater as could be found on Creel's staff, decided he'd hit on the most important scoop of the war. Their argument became so personal that at their last breakfast together neither man would speak.

Left on his own Sisson had to turn to the Embassy. As happens so often in American diplomatic history, none of the Wilson administration's agents were instructed to coordinate their activities with the others, and the last thing any of them thought of was to take the ambassador into their confidence. While Sisson was pondering how best to track down the clues he had in his hand he received a message from the Embassy that Mr. Francis would like to see him.

David R. Francis was a cigarsmoking whiskeydrinking old Kentuckian who had been Secretary of the Interior under Grover Cleveland, had served as Governor of Missouri and promoted the St. Louis World's Fair. When, as a deserving Democrat with a reputation for business acumen, he was offered the embassy in Petrograd he seems to have felt that with war threatening he could not refuse any service the President asked of him. Not wanting to subject his wife and family to the hazards of wartime Russia he set out accompanied only by a secretary and a faithful colored valet. He intrigued the Petrograd diplomatic corps during the last days of the Romanoffs by the simplicity of his establishment, his rough diamond frankness and his penchant for poker.

A further cause for comment was his relationship with a Madame de Cramm, a voluble lady suspected of being a German spy largely on account of her name. She was in and out of the Embassy at all hours, giving the ambassador lessons in French, so it was said; she accompanied him on walks through the broad Petrograd streets on the white nights of summer. The gossip about Madame de Cramm may account for some of the standoffish attitude of Robins and Sisson towards the Embassy staff.

Mr. Francis was no sooner established in the Romanoff capital than the imperial façade crumbled away disclosing a turmoil of ideologies and cutthroat factions which he was no better equipped to understand than any of the other Americans stumbling through the political nightmare. Being a man of some worldly knowledge he might have acquitted himself better if he hadn't been, intentionally he felt, kept in the dark as to the intentions of the Administration.

About the time of Sisson's quarrel with Robins the ambassador was approached by a Russian journalist, with a great black beard and a rather unsavory history, who showed him the photostat of a letter of Joffe's which he claimed proved under the table dealings with the enemy during the Brest-Litovsk talks. Much more interesting material, the journalist implied, could be had for a price. Mr. Francis called up Sisson and asked him to look at the photostat. Sisson brought along the material Robins had turned over to him. The two men put their heads together and decided that genuine or not the stuff should be cabled to Washington. Meanwhile Mr. Francis asked the State Department for twentyfive thousand dollars to spend for undisclosed purposes.

When Lansing showed Wilson the cable the President, who evidently blamed Ambassador Francis for Thompson's imprudence in so openly backing the wrong horse, noted: "our views and Francis' have not in the least agreed on the use which should be made of money in Russia." However he left the decision to Lansing.

The draft was honored and Francis, who probably felt that Creel's representative knew more about administration policy than he did, gave Sisson his head. Sisson got help from the British secret service and documents poured in. A few samples were cabled to the State Department in the diplomatic code. Secretary Lansing expressed interest, so with redoubled zeal Sisson bought every scrap of paper that was offered him.

Sisson's eager sleuthing was interrupted on February 18 when the German General Hoffmann announced that his patience was at an end and ordered his troops to advance into Russia. In two weeks his armies occupied the Baltic provinces. A German division marched into Narva, less than a hundred miles from Petrograd.

Panic struck the city. In Smolny, behind the rifles of their praetorian guard of Latvian troops, the Bolshevik leaders began packing their records for the move to Moscow.

Allied agents scattered in all directions. The embassy staffs crowded into special trains. The British managed to get through to Sweden before the civil war between Reds and Whites cut off communication across Finland. Monsieur Noulens the French ambassador was forced to turn back, an accident of war which greatly added to his distaste for the revolutionary Russians. Mr. Francis, insisting that since he was accredited to the Russian people and not to any particular government, his business was to remain on Russian soil as long as he could, retired in good order to Vologda.

Vologda was an ancient lumbering town, reported to have more churches than dwellinghouses, about three hundred miles east of Petrograd at the junction of the Trans-Siberian railroad with the line that led north to Archangel. From Vologda Mr. Francis was in a position to retreat either to Archangel or to Vladivostok, if retreat became necessary. The other embassies joined him there and for a few months Vologda became an Allied oasis from which the western diplomats looked out on the chaos about them. Nothing the Bolsheviks could do, not even the threats and blandishments of Karl Radek, their most disarming jokester and their most persuasive journalist, could lure the embassies to Moscow.

Sisson, a wiry dyspeptic waspish little man, by this time a bundle of nerves and selfrighteousness, entrusted his pack of incriminating documents to a friendly Norwegian diplomatic courier and set off in a crowd of refugees for Finland. Sticking to the Norwegian like a leech, after all sorts of hairbreadth escapes, he managed to make his way through the deadly skirmishing of the Finnish civil war and across the ice to Sweden. By early May, Sisson, who described himself as a nervous wreck, managed to reach Washington and to have his portentous package placed in the President's hands.

On March 3, 1918, at Lenin's insistence, the Bolshevik representatives had capitulated at Brest-Litovsk and signed a treaty with Germany by which Russia gave up any claim to Poland, Lithuania, Finland, the Baltic Provinces, the Ukraine and to the regions south of the Caucasus. Prisoners were to be turned loose. Diplomatic missions were to be exchanged and trade re-established. Trotsky's response was to resign his post as Foreign Minister. Immediately appointed Commissar for War, he started building a Red Army.

Robins, still hopeful of attaining Washington's recognition for Lenin's government, travelled back and forth between Moscow and Vologda. He too tried to induce Ambassador Francis to move his embassy to Moscow. Francis wouldn't budge.

Towards the end of April Count Mirbach-Harff, a German career diplomat, arrived in Moscow with a large delegation, and Adolf Joffe installed an equivalent crew of revolutionary propagandists in the old Imperial Russian Embassy in Berlin. Lansing and his counsellors at the State Department took this exchange to mean the complete penetration by German influence of such parts of Russia as were left under Bolshevik control. Robins was requested to come home immediately.

After final friendly interviews with the leading Bolsheviks, Raymond Robins' Red Cross car was attached to the Trans-Siberian express and started its long rumbling way to Vladivostok. His party was furnished with rifles and ammunition for their protection and also with a pass signed by Lenin himself. In his pocket Robins carried an appreciative personal letter from Trotsky and a document, drawn up under Lenin's direction, offering a rich bait of mineral concessions in Siberia to American capitalists consequent to American recognition.

The train stopped for fifty minutes at Vologda. Ambassador Francis went down to the station to pass the time of day. The two men walked up and down the platform chatting. Neither man told the other what was uppermost in his mind.

Ambassador Francis had just sent a cable to Washington announcing that he had at last come to the opinion that Allied intervention was necessary with or without the consent of the Moscow government.

Robins' thoughts were fervid with the hope that the document entrusted to him by Lenin would be the opening wedge for fresh relations between Washington and Moscow. He was planning a campaign of press releases and speeches. Perhaps Ambassador Robins would soon be succeeding Ambassador Francis.

"A private conversation of about twenty minutes," so Francis recalled the scene, "and I turned away from him or he turned away from me: I have forgotten which, not in any unfriendly spirit . . ."

Gumberg, who eventually found a business career in New York more congenial than life under the dictatorship of the proletariat, went along with Robins. He bore a commission from the Moscow government to set up a Russian press bureau in America.

In Vladivostok Robins received a curt message from Washington enjoining him not to talk for publication. In Seattle, at the request so it seems of Lansing himself, Robins and Gumberg were put to the indignity of being searched by the immigration officials. Already anyone who had even talked to a Bolshevik was suspect in America.

W. B. Thompson joined Robins in Chicago and rode with him to Washington to use what influence he could muster, but all he could achieve was a testy interview for Robins with the Secretary of State. The chief preoccupation of the Administration was that Robins should keep his mouth shut. This Robins loyally did. President Wilson's door remained closed to him.

It wasn't until the war was over and after Robins had had his say before a congressional committee that he was able to tell a businessman's luncheon what he'd intended to tell the President in the summer of 1918.

"You believe that private property has a great and useful mission in the world. So do I . . . That is why I am talking to you today. There is a bomb under this room and under every other room in the world; and it can blow our system—your system and my system—into the eternal past with the Bourbons and the Pharaohs . . . We are talking about something that can destroy the present social system. Riots and robberies and mobs and massacres cannot destroy the present social system or any social system. They can be stopped by force . . . The only thing that can destroy a social system is a rival social system—a real rival system—a system thought out and worked out and capable of making an organized orderly social life of its own."

The only communication that Robins was able to establish with Woodrow Wilson was through a short report setting forth the need for an American economic commission to work with the Bolshevik government in restoring Russian commerce and industry. The President read Robins' suggestions and noted for Lansing's benefit that: "they were certainly more sensible than I thought the author of them capable of. I differ from them only in practical details"; and that was the end of it.

The Commune Reborn

If Woodrow Wilson was having trouble finding the right words to deal with the riots and robberies and mobs and massacres daily reported to him from Russia, the German High Command, which had given up words for deeds, was not getting much better results. On the map their successes seemed staggering.

While their representatives were extorting peace terms that seemed to put the Russians at their mercy for ever, their troops were occupying the Aaland Islands to the north and getting ready to give Baron Mannerheim's White forces the backing which was to prove decisive against the Finnish Bolsheviks. In cooperation with the Turks their military missions were penetrating the Transcaucasian regions with the Baku oilfields as their objective.

At the same time mixed Austrian and German expeditions were pushing east along the railways from the old Galician front to occupy Kiev, the capital of the independent Ukraine with which they had signed a peace early in February.

Further south resistance had ceased in Romania and Moldavia. An armistice was in force and the German generals were drafting peace terms with King Ferdinand's government which would assure them a ninety year lease on the Romanian oilwells. With the wheat of the Ukraine and the oil of Romania the problem of supplying their armies on the western front seemed solved.

The Bolsheviks had managed during the winter since their seizure of power to achieve a certain amount of order. Up and down the Trans-Siberian, which was the spinal column of what was left of the old empire, the local soviets were controlled by Bolshevik agents. From Murmansk to Baku and from the Volga to Vladivostok, town and provincial governments were in the hands of sympathizers if not of party members. The nobility and the bourgeoisie were disfranchised. Decrees dividing the land among the working peasants, turning factories and industrial enterprises over to workers' committees, and outlawing the exploitation of one man's work by another, were being put into effect. The rundown machinery of czarist government fell without much struggle, from the hands of the professional people who had taken it over under Kerensky, into the hands of the Bolsheviks.

Except for a few centers of resistance in the south the dispossessed classes were hiding or in flight. Under the slogans of peace for the soldiers and land for the peasants the Bolshevik triumph seemed complete. Still Lenin hardly dared believe that his revolution was more than a fleeting affirmation of Karl Marx's immutable principles, doomed like the Paris Commune to extinction, unless help should come from revolutionary movements in Western Europe. Not a moment must be lost in consolidating state power.

At the Seventh Congress of the Bolshevik or Majority wing of the Russian Social Democratic party, the sense of continuity with the French Communards in 1871 was given new emphasis by changing the party's name. Henceforward it should be known as the Russian Communist Party.

Moscow was proclaimed as the seat of government and a Fourth All-Russian Congress of Soviets, made up of Communist-picked delegates, was hastily convened to ratify the Brest-Litovsk Treaty.

The Czechoslovak Legion

As fast as the brokendown railroads could carry them, German forces spread over southern Russia, opposed only occasionally by fleeting bands led by Social Revolutionaries or army officers from the old regime. On April 5 the Germans took Kharkov and a few days later the Black Sea port of Odessa.

The invasion did not succeed in adding much to the German food supply. Wherever the German economic missions appeared the countryside blew up into civil war in their faces. Other byproducts of the invasion were even more disastrous to the German cause.

The first result of the German takeover of the Ukraine was the appearance of a Czechoslovak army as a belligerent on the side of the Allies.

Among all the national aspirations of the various peoples of central Europe the demands of the Czechs for independence from Hapsburg rule had, since the beginning of the war, been looked on with particular sympathy by the French. The Slovaks, consisting mostly of slavicspeaking peasants in the hilly region that stretched east from Moravia to the Carpathian Mountains, who had long chafed under Hungarian rule, came to associate their demands for freedom with those of the more urban Czechs of Bohemia and Moravia. Under the Romanoffs panslavic circles in Petrograd assiduously cultivated these enthusiasms; backing the westernized Czechs took a little of the reactionary curse off Russian czarism.

The result was the formation of a Czechoslovak corps in the Russian Army. Czechs and Slovaks deserting from the Hapsburg armies were greeted as brothers. In 1916 a Czechoslovak national council was established in Paris with the blessing of the French and Russian governments. The Czechoslovak corps on the eastern front distinguished itself in Brusilov's last illfated offensive.

While the Russian armies disintegrated, the Czechoslovak corps, armed with material donated by the Russians and captured from the Austrians, remained intact. Discipline was good. Morale was high. All the Czechoslovak soldiers asked was to fight for the independence of their nation.

Professor Tomas Masaryk, one of their national leaders who had lived in the States and lectured at the University of Chicago, where he was the darling of the large Czech population—Chicago being the largest Czech city after Prague—and who had further friendly connections among university people in England, went to Petrograd. There he made himself welcome to the Soviet Government.

At the time of the German advance the Czechoslovakians, now amounting to more than two divisions, were billeted in the region of Kiev. They helped local Bolshevik elements obstruct the Germans until the signature of the peace. Then they fell back in good order towards Kursk and the Don River. Masaryk signed an agreement with the Bolsheviks for their evacuation across the Trans-Siberian to Vladivostok and set off for Washington to try to arrange for their transport across the Pacific and across the United States to the western front. There was tacit agreement with the French and the British that, in return for their help in the war, Czechoslovakia would be recognized in the final settlement.

When Trotsky arrived in Moscow as Commissar for War the Czechs were already moving east. Needing every scrap of armament he could lay his hands on, he began to revise the arrangement which his government had signed with Masaryk. The Czechoslovak Legion must give up their rifles and guns. They must dismiss counterrevolutionaries and officers who had served under the Czar.

Communist agitators were sent down to lure the rank and file into a Congress of Prisoners of War being arranged in Moscow for the indoctrination of Austrian, Hungarian and German soldiers being shipped back to their homelands.

The Czechoslovaks balked. Some detachments allowed themselves to be despoiled of their artillery, but most of them hid their rifles and machineguns. They retained their officers. As Bolshevik demands grew so did the suspicions of the Czechoslovaks.

Meanwhile the French recognized what began to be known in the Allied press as the Czechoslovak Legion as part of the Allied forces and with the consent of their national council appointed the French General Janin to command them. In Paris and London the idea dawned that forty thousand Czechoslovaks might well make the spearhead of a force which, by overthrowing the pro-German Bolsheviks, would reconstitute the eastern front. Maps emphasizing the importance of the Trans-Siberian Railroad began to appear at meetings of the Supreme War Council at Versailles. In Washington ever more urgent arguments in favor of intervention were poured into the ears of President Wilson's advisers.

Early in April the tense situation at Vladivostok, where the urban soviet was already operating under the guns of British, American and Japanese warships anchored in the harbor, broke out in violence. Some gunmen described as soldiers in uniform, held up a store and killed several Japanese. Claiming that he could get no satisfaction from the local authorities the Japanese admiral landed five hundred marines to protect the lives and property of his nationals. The British followed suit with fifty bluejackets. Under orders from Washington the American commander held off.

Chicherin, the shrewd little aristocratic bookworm who had taken Trotsky's place as Commissar for Foreign Affairs, published one of his first appeals to the opinion of mankind. An attack from the old enemy strengthened the Bolsheviks with the newspaper reading stratum of Russian society.

In Vladivostok itself the presence of the Japanese was overshadowed by the continual arrival of detachments of armed Czechs. Under a certain amount of suspicion and surveillance from the Communist-controlled committees that managed traffic on the railroad, but without too much friction, the long freights and trooptrains of the Czechoslovak Legion continued their slow uncomfortable progress across Siberia.

The Kremlin of the Ancient Czars

The stringing of detachments of foreign troops along the very backbone of their dominion immensely complicated the problems of the Communists. As Lenin's hopes of playing off the Allies against the Germans long enough to obtain the breathing spell he needed began to fade, a spirit of desperation permeated their leadership. They entrenched themselves behind the enormous walls, under the crushing painted vaults, and amid the tarnished splendors of the Kremlin of the ancient Moscow czars.

In their denunciations of those who disagreed with them, laden as they were with historical references to the French Revolution, terror began to be mentioned more and more as the rightful arm of the proletarian dic-

tatorship. The names of Robespierre, Saint-Just, Fouquier-Tinville began
to be pronounced in admiring tones. While Trotsky was training and
disciplining his Red Army, Dzerdzinsky developed the All-Russian Extraordinary Commission to Fight Counter-Revolution, Sabotage and Speculation into a powerful secret police.

Felix Dzerdzinsky was a cultivated Pole who had received the best
possible education in the German universities. As a Social Democrat he
had suffered much in czarist prisons. Stories were told of his strange self-
abnegation towards the other prisoners. In a cell he was always the one
to clean the latrine or wash the floor. He was a wanfaced man with long
white hands. Lockhart described the strange stare of his eyes between
their unblinking lids.

Dzerdzinsky threw himself into the work of repression with a total
abnegation of all human feelings that culminated in a mystique of massacre for its own sake, a monstrous aberration of the human mind unknown to Europe since the days of the Spanish inquisitors, when Philip II
could ask himself on his deathbed if he'd killed enough heretics for the
salvation of his soul. Dzerdzinsky made his extraordinary commission so
feared that people hardly dared pronounce the initials by which it was
known.

Dzerdzinsky's first public enterprise, after setting up his headquarters
in the office of an extinct insurance company at Lubianka, 11, won the
immediate approval of the foreign colony in Moscow. The American Red
Cross people, and the small group of foreign correspondents and the members of the French military mission and of the British agencies, that were
still carrying on partly aboveboard and partly undercover activities, were,
like the rest of the city's population, intimidated by marauding bands of
selfstyled anarchists who set themselves up in the mansions of wealthy
merchants, drinking up the winecellars, and sallying forth onto the streets
to rob and murder at will. One April night the Cheka, with the assistance
of Trotsky's Red Army, carried out a sudden raid on the anarchist dens,
shot down those that resisted and carted the rest off to prison.

Jacob Peters, Dzerdzinsky's Latvian assistant, who had learned English
working in a London office, was so proud of the job he took Lockhart
and Robins around to see the results of his work next morning. The dead
still lay among the silk hangings in pools of blood on the ruined Aubusson
carpets of the departed rich. In one diningroom, heaped with spilled
food and broken bottles, a young woman lay face downwards. "Peters
turned her over. Her hair was dishevelled. She had been shot through
the neck, and the blood had congealed in a sinister purple clump. She
could not have been more than twenty. Peters shrugged his shoulders.
'Prostitutka,' he said. 'Perhaps it is for the best.'"

By the time the German ambassador arrived with his suite at the end of April, law and order was perfect in the mediaeval streets of the ancient capital.

Though Count Mirbach-Harff came surrounded with German experts on Russian affairs, he seems to have been as unprepared as his British and French opponents in the diplomatic bout to deal with the revolutionary scene. He was housed in the insanely ornate mansion of a departed sugar magnate named Berg. One of his first experiences was to view from his automobile in the Red Square the May Day parade held to celebrate the proletarian triumph.

Lockhart watching Mirbach seated among his aides in an open car reported that the supercilious smirk left the German's face as he watched the ranks and ranks of illclad illfed illorganized working men march by. There was a look of strength about them. "He looked serious," wrote Lockhart.

The Poverty Committees

With the coming of summer the tensions reached the breaking point. In spite of the protests of their Social Revolutionary partners, the Communists were enforcing Lenin's policy of sending out "poverty committees," made up usually of the ne'erdowells of the villages, to requisition the stored grain and other possessions of their more prosperous and hardworking neighbors. Any successful farmer was a *kulak*.

To the cold social mathematics of Lenin's mind it was clear that he could never establish communism if he allowed a peasant bourgeoisie to grow up in the country. The kulaks must be eliminated.

But elimination of the best farmers would disrupt the production of food. Opposition grew among the most energetic and intelligent elements of the peasantry. In the mood pervading the villages it took only a small incident, like a match dropped in a ripe wheatfield, to set the whole of Russia blazing with civil war.

Civil War in Russia

On May 14 fighting breaks out at Chelyabinsk, just east of the Urals, between a trainload of Czechoslovaks headed east and a trainload of Hungarian prisoners of war headed west. A man is killed on each side.

Trotsky immediately gives orders to disarm the Czechoslovak Legion. The Legion refuses to be disarmed and continues on its way east, seizing the railroad as it goes. East of Lake Baikal their detachments have a clear track into Vladivostok, but the large forces still on the line to the west are trapped because the Communists keep control of Irkutsk, the railroad center at the southern end of the lake.

As if at a prearranged signal all Siberia shakes off the Moscow yoke. Communists on the governing committees melt away into hiding. Moderate elements, tending to favor the Allies against the Germans, take charge again. In Manchuria, with some support from the Japanese, czarist officers are organizing an army to restore the Romanoffs. In southern Russia wherever the Germans have penetrated reactionary movements come to life. In the Ukraine the parliamentary Rada has been overthrown by an old regime general giving orders as hetman. The Don Cossacks have their own government. Czarist groups with German support hold the Crimea and the towns on the Black Sea coast.

The remaining warmwater ports fall to the Allies. Vladivostok has become a Czechoslovak base. At the end of June the threat of invasion from Lapland by Mannerheim's Germanbacked Finns forces the soviet of the Murmansk region to submit to occupation by the British. When Chicherin remonstrates over the phone the president of the Murmansk soviet calls him a pro-German and says that the comrades in Moscow are in no position to understand the situation in the north.

Insurrections follow the spring thaw. "Green" armies of anarchist peasants, "White" armies dedicated to the old regime, dissident Reds of every socialist creed collect and fight and fade into the forests. Fleeting republics and governments rise and make proclamations and disintegrate into chaos again. Villages burn. Towns are pillaged. Granaries are raided, cattle driven off. Men kill and die fighting for causes they hardly know the names of.

The Last Rising of the Left

On July 4, 1918, the Fifth All-Russian Congress of Soviets meets in Moscow. The Left Social Revolutionaries, still represented in all the organs of the dictatorship, including the Cheka, have managed to elect a good third of the delegates. At a party caucus they decide that the parting of the ways has come. They will no longer submit to the despoiling of revolutionary peasants by the poverty committees, or to collaboration with the Germans who are shooting peasants in the Ukraine for resisting the requisition of their grain. Furthermore they demand the abolition of the death penalty.

The Congress is called to order in the old Bolshoy Theatre, where Muscovites of all factions still sit enthralled every night by the dancing of the nationalized imperial ballet which remains almost the only link to the culture of the old regime.

Lockhart, who is present in one of the boxes set aside for the Allied missions, describes the paladins of the Executive Committee seated on the stage. Sverdlov, its president, acts as chairman. At the end sits the leader of the Left Social Revolutionaries, Maria Spiridovna. Lockhart describes her as looking, with her pincenez and her dark hair pulled back smoothly on her head, for all the world like the rural schoolteacher in Tchekhov's *Three Sisters*.

Maria Spiridovna is revered by all factions of the revolution. As a girl at the time of the outbreak in 1905 she shot an unpopular czarist official, suffered nameless brutalities at the hands of the cossacks and served long years at hard labor in Siberia. She shows her nervousness by ceaselessly toying with her pincenez.

The sessions are stormy to the point of madness. On the second day Maria Spiridovna makes a personal attack on Lenin:

"I accuse you," she cries, "of betraying the peasants . . . of making use of them for your own ends, and of not serving their interests." Her voice rises to a shriek. "When the peasants, the Bolshevik peasants, the Left Social-Revolutionary peasants, the Bolshevik peasants, the non-party peasants are alike humiliated oppressed and crushed—crushed as peasants—in my hand you will find the same pistol, the same bomb which once forced me to defend . . ."

Her words are drowned in applause and in a roar of opposing shouts and yelps and screams. Trotsky tries to speak and is howled down. Sverdlov helplessly tinkles his bell.

"Then Lenin walks slowly to the front of the stage," writes Lockhart. "On the way he pats Sverdlov on the shoulder and tells him to put his bell away. Holding the lapels of his coat, he faces the audience—smiling, supremely self-confident. He is met with jeers and catcalls. He laughs good-humoredly. Then he holds up his hand and with a last rumble the tumult dies."

Lenin contends that the Left Social Revolutionaries are illogical. Renewed war with the Germans will only be to the advantage of the other imperialist faction, the Allies. The Russian proletariat must quietly consolidate its power, must patiently wait for the moment when warweariness shall cause the oppressed peoples of all the countries of Europe to rise in world revolution.

In spite of Lenin's calming speech the congress breaks out into a wild demonstration against members of the German mission seated in one of the boxes. Sverdlov adjourns the meeting.

The following afternoon, carrying identification cards signed by Dzerdzinsky and furnished them by Social Revolutionary members of the Cheka, two S.R.s call on Ambassador Mirbach on the pretext that the Cheka has discovered a conspiracy to assassinate him. He has papers says the first man. He puts his hand in his briefcase and draws out a pistol and shoots. The first shots go wild, but his companion takes careful aim and shoots Mirbach through the head. Both assassins escape through a window after exploding a couple of handgrenades in the embassy hall.

The assassination of Mirbach is the signal for a general rising of the Left Social Revolutionaries already planned against the Communists. They seize the office of the Cheka and hold Dzerdzinsky hostage. After a few hours Trotsky's troops and the disciplined chekists restore order. Almost before it begins the revolt is suppressed. The Left Social Revolutionaries are either dead or under lock and key. The survivors are expelled from all the organs of government. Lenin's Communists rule alone. Whoever is not for them is against them.

The End of the Romanoffs

The same day a rising was suppressed in Petrograd and a Green army, backed, so the story went, by the French military mission in Moscow, seized Yaroslavl, important strategically as the head of navigation on the upper Volga, and held out there for a month. Meanwhile the Czechoslovak troops blocked on the Trans-Siberian threw in their lot with the anticommunists, and started moving west with the objective of fighting their way north to Archangel and effecting a junction with the British forces in the Murmansk area. As they proceeded towards the Urals, town after town fell to them without resistance. Assorted anticommunists took over the local governments and proceeded to greet them as liberators.

Ekaterinburg was one of the towns in the path of the Czechoslovak Legion. The month before, as revolt spread through Siberia, the pitiful remnants of the Romanoff family had been brought to Ekaterinburg from internment at Tobolsk, and imprisoned in what had been the mansion of a local merchant. The party consisted of the Czar and Czarina and their daughters and thirteenyearold son. With them was the family doctor and three servants. Most of them were ill from poor food and harsh treatment.

In the middle of the night of July 16 they were awakened by a firing squad acting under orders from the Urals Regional Soviet and told to go down in the cellar. The Czar had to carry his son in his arms as the boy was too ill to walk. There they were lined up against a wall. The leader of the squad told them that they were going to die. The Czar did not understand him, and leaning forward to say "What?" was shot in the face with a revolver. Immediately the executioners emptied their revolvers into the huddled figures. Those who were still groaning were finished off with bayonets. The bodies were hastily covered with quicklime and thrown into an abandoned mineshaft.

A few days later the Czechoslovaks captured the city.

Masaryk at the White House

Professor Masaryk had arrived in Washington from Petrograd via
Vladivostok and Tokyo early that May. His arrival was eagerly looked
forward to by Lansing and his counsellors in the State Department. Here
at last was a returning Russian traveller in whose views the President
expressed lively interest. Everything Woodrow Wilson heard predisposed
him towards Masaryk. He was no arrogant millionaire or flybynight
placer miner but a college professor with academic standing. The fact
that he came from a small and oppressed country with a profound protestant tradition could not help but arouse the President's sympathy. The
Presbyterian in him was never far beneath the surface. Even so Masaryk
had to wait in Washington more than a month, after preparatory luncheons with Lansing and House who both reported favorably, before the
President could make up his mind to see him.

Their first interview was in late June. Masaryk, one of the most accomplished international lobbyists of the century, saw to it that he and the
President should hit it off.

Masaryk succeeded where the British and French embassies and the
Supreme War Council failed. He dramatized the plight of the poor
Czechs bravely fighting their way to freedom through hordes of Germans
and Hungarians armed by the Bolsheviks. Their occupation of Vladivostok, coming almost on the same day as the action of the Murmansk soviet
inviting British intervention "materially changed the situation," as Lansing cynically put it, "by introducing a sentimental element into the question of our duty."

The first result of Wilson's interview with Masaryk was that the cable
facilities of the State Department were placed at the disposal of the
Czechoslovak representative for a message to Chicherin protesting the
failure of the Soviet Government to live up to its guarantee of free and
unmolested passage to Vladivostok for the Czechoslovak Legion.

A few days later the President was confiding in House, in the same
letter in which he spoke of sweating blood over the Russian problem:
"I hope I see and can report some progress presently, along the double
line of economic assistance and aid to the Czechoslovaks."

Wilson had already made up his mind. Two days before he wrote
House he called in Secretary Baker and Lansing and Josephus Daniels
and General Peyton C. March, now Chief of Staff, to his quiet upstairs
study in the White House, ostensibly to consult them, but actually to
announce his decision after "thinking through the processes, alone, behind
his own closed door."

"It is the clear and fixed judgment of the Government of the United States," the President read off a small pad, "that military intervention there would add to the present sad confusion in Russia rather than cure it, injure her rather than help her, and that it would be of no advantage in the prosecution of our main design, to win the war against Germany."

After some cogent arguments against intervening in Russia's internal struggles, he delivered himself, possibly to the surprise of his hearers, of the proposition that military action was admissible after all: "only to help the Czechoslovaks consolidate their forces and get into successful cooperation with their Slavic kinsmen and to steady any efforts at self-government or self-defence in which the Russians themselves may be willing to accept assistance."

He itemized the sort of assistance he was thinking of: "Assistance by a commission of merchants, agricultural experts, labor advisers, Red Cross representatives, and agents of the Young Men's Christian Association." But military action must come first. "The execution of this plan will follow and not be permitted to embarrass the military assistance rendered in the rear of the westward moving forces of the Czechoslovaks."

What had started as a plan to help evacuate the Czechoslovaks had turned into a plan to secure their Siberian rear while they advanced into the heart of Russia west of the Urals. A discussion of details followed: the Japanese should be encouraged to furnish small arms, machineguns and ammunition to the Czechoslovaks besieged along the railroad. The Americans and Japanese should each furnish seven thousand men to protect the Legion's communications.

When the President was finished he asked for comments. According to March's notes Secretary Lansing commended the paper, Secretary Baker (who had argued himself blue in the face trying to talk the President out of it) merely nodded, Secretary Daniels approved and the general himself shook his head.

"Why are you shaking your head, General?" asked the President with some asperity. General March (noting for his private satisfaction that he had never been a yes-yes man) replied that he had already explained that he didn't think such an expedition was militarily feasible and that besides the Japanese would take advantage of it for territorial gains.

"We'll have to take that chance," said the President testily.

The document was circulated to the Allied chancelleries in the form of an *aide-memoire* but it wasn't till August 7 that public announcement was made that an American Expeditionary Force was being dispatched to Siberia. Masaryk immediately wrote the President an effusive note. "Your name Mr. President, as you have no doubt read, is openly cheered in the streets of Prague."

Once a decision was made on Siberia the decision to send a detachment to help the British hold Murmansk came easy. Some lingering doubt must have remained in the President's mind. In his answer to Masaryk he wrote that the professor's letter was particularly appreciated because "I have felt no confidence in my personal judgment about the complicated situation in Russia, and am reassured that you should approve what I have done."

Edgar Sisson's Scoop

As part of the campaign to arouse popular support for the President's decision to send troops to Russia the Committee for Public Information began directing towards Reds and Bolsheviks some of the hatred it had stirred up against the Germans. Press reports of the Moscow terror and of the murder of the Czar and his family made this not too hard an assignment.

When Sisson returned to Washington, still tense from his nervewracking escape from Petrograd, he resumed his position as second in command to George Creel at the old house on Jackson Place. Creel further put him in charge of the foreign desk. Sisson arrived big with portent over the globeshaking repercussions he expected from the publication of his documents on the German-Bolshevik Conspiracy.

Before leaving London, where he stopped over to consult with the British intelligence services, he prepared for the explosion by ordering all C.P.I. personnel out of those parts of Russia under Communist control. A man named Arthur Bullard, who seems to have been levelheaded and wellinformed on Russian affairs, was in charge of the Moscow office. Bullard protested that he was in no present danger. Lenin's government seemed reluctant to come to a final break with the American missions. Bullard cabled Sisson that he was getting considerable play for the President's statements in Russian newspapers and that he wanted to stay. Sisson answered that leave he must. In an aside to a friend Sisson explained his insistence on pulling his representatives out of soviet territory as a way of impressing the administration with the importance of his revelations.

According to Major Dansey of British Military Intelligence, the members of the secret services whom Sisson talked to in London were opposed to publishing the documents at all. British military and naval intelligence and the office of the postal censor had gone over a set of the same papers sent in by a British agent named Maclaren, whom Major Dansey described as "hipped on buying documents," and had decided that the so-called circulars were forgeries clumsily typed on the same Russian typewriter, and that such of the accompanying letters as seemed to be genuine had little propaganda value.

Though the full story of German financing of certain Russian revolutionary newspapers during the early part of the war did not come out till many years later, the British intelligence services were undoubtedly aware at that time that the Bolshevik leaders had been helped by German agencies to return to Russia and that they might have received subsidies in the period of antiwar propaganda before their seizure of power, but they saw no sense in trying to claim that Lenin and Trotsky were acting as German agents because it was untrue on the face of it. According to Major Dansey's account he explained to Sisson that many of the documents were forgeries and urged him to go slow with them.

All through the summer Sisson kept the documents in his safe. *Le Petit Parisien*, a sensational French daily, meanwhile published much the same series. Lansing was expressing the fear that their publication in America would endanger the lives of the considerable number of Americans still in soviet territory. Perhaps he smelled a rat.

The situation of the Moscow Communists seemed desperate. As fast as they shot down their opponents fresh opposition reared up against their rule. The Left Social Revolutionaries were continuing their campaign of assassination against Communists and Germans. In July S.R.s killed Field Marshal von Eichorn, the German commander in the Ukraine. In August the president of the Petrograd Cheka was assassinated and the same day young S.R. named Dora Kaplan just missed killing Lenin as he left a factory in Moscow where he had been addressing a workers' meeting. He was wounded in the neck and a bullet perforated one lung. He escaped death by a miracle.

In the wave of massacres that followed British representatives were arrested, a British officer was killed in a raid on the old Petrograd Embassy, and a state of war was declared to exist between the Soviet Government and the Allies. Even in the frenzy of repressions that continued long after Lenin was out of danger Americans were not molested.

As news of one hideous excess after another poured in from Russia, George Creel seems to have been of two minds as to whether to publish Sisson's papers or not. Lansing was still opposed and wrote the President to that effect. As was his wont Creel went over Lansing's head direct to Woodrow Wilson.

The President said to publish. Instalments were distributed to various newspapers. The New York *Times* started publication in the second section of its Sunday edition on September 15.

A few days later the New York *Evening Post* broke the story that the documents were forged. About the same day a worried cable reached the State Department from Ambassador Page in London. He had just talked to Major Dansey and Major Dansey expressed grave doubts. Furthermore Major Dansey said that he had told Sisson, when they had talked in London, that the British thought the documents were forgeries.

Page asked rather pointedly why Sisson hadn't informed his own government of these doubts.

Creel immediately called Sisson who was out of town on the long distance phone. Sisson denied "specifically and absolutely" having had any such conversation with Major Dansey, but he did admit having met him. A couple of college professors supposed to know Russian were induced to look over the documents and to declare in writing, in a guarded sort of way, that they were genuine. Publication continued.

Eggs Loaded with Dynamite

On the afternoon of August 2, William S. Graves, freshly appointed major general in the National Army, received a message in code from the Chief of Staff ordering him to take the first fast train to Kansas City. Graves, who had just taken over command of a division training in Palo Alto for service in France, had served for several years as secretary to the General Staff, and after pulling all the strings he knew, had finally gotten himself assigned to combat service. Worried for fear something had gone wrong with his plans, he sat up in a day coach all the way from San Francisco to Kansas City because the pullmans were full. His instructions were to proceed to the Hotel Biltmore and there to report to the Secretary of War.

When the much puzzled general stepped off the train in the Kansas City station, he was approached by a redcap who told him that the Secretary of War was waiting to see him in a private room.

His conversation with Mr. Baker was hasty because the little man was about to catch a train out.

The Secretary began by saying in a jocular tone that he was sorry but he had to send Graves to Siberia. He said he knew the general wanted to go to France and that Graves mustn't blame General March; March had tried to get him out of the assignment. Some day, Baker added mysteriously, he might tell Graves why he had to be the one to go. "If in future you want to cuss anybody for sending you to Siberia," he said, "I am the man."

He pulled a long sealed envelope out of his pocket and thrust it in the general's hand. "This contains the policy of the United States in Russia which you are to follow. Watch your step; you will be walking on eggs loaded with dynamite. God bless you and goodbye," and he was off to his train.

The general went to a hotel, locked himself in his room and read the document in the sealed envelope. It was President Wilson's aide memoire. So far as can be discovered, these were the only instructions he ever had from Washington.

"After carefully reading the document and feeling that I understood the policy," the general wrote in the account he published years later, "I went to bed but I could not sleep and kept wondering what other nations were doing and why I was not given some information about what was going on in Siberia."

If General Graves was a puzzled man reading President Wilson's aide memoire in that hotel room in Kansas City, he was an even more puzzled man when he arrived in Vladivostok. He disembarked from the transport *Thomas* with a force of about two thousand men, and found there two regiments awaiting his command, which had been shipped up from the Philippines with a field hospital and transport units. The morning he landed Graves discovered, on making what he thought was a courtesy call on the ranking Japanese general, that General Otani expected the American force to serve under his orders.

Instead of the seven thousand Japanese the War Department had informed Graves were to cooperate with his expedition, he found seventy-two thousand Japanese soldiers busily engaged in taking over the Chinese Eastern Railroad and preparing for Japanese colonization of the rich soyabean regions of Manchuria.

The Czechoslovaks, he discovered, instead of retiring to Vladivostok for evacuation to Europe, had taken Irkutsk and were being encouraged by the French and British to engage in a career of conquest along the Volga. Instead of being shipped out the Legion was being used to back anticommunist movements in the civil war.

General Graves' instructions were to help the Czechoslovaks consolidate their forces. The British and French were ahead of him on that.

As for "getting into successful cooperation with their slavic kinsmen," there were now twentyfour warring governments on Russian soil with little in common except hatred of the Communists.

As for "efforts at self-government" the only election to take place in Vladivostok, supervised by the Czechs and the Allied marines, had resulted, to everyone's chagrin, in a victory for the Communists.

As for assisting the Russians in "self-defense" the problem, as Lenin succinctly stated it, was: "What Russians?"

The Polar Bears

While, in consequence of President Wilson's "thinking through of the processes," General Graves and his puzzled doughboys were set to patrolling the eastern end of the Trans-Siberian Railroad in furtherance of international intrigues loaded with a sort of dynamite of which they were but dimly aware, another group of young Americans found themselves, with some astonishment, joining in the invasion of northwestern Russia.

At Stoney Castle in England the 339th Infantry, recruited from mechanics, clerks and factory workers mostly out of Milwaukee and Detroit, was training for service in France, when all at once the men were ordered to turn in their Enfields and instead were issued oddlooking long rifles which had been manufactured in the United States for the Imperial Russian Army. Before they had a chance to target these unfamiliar weapons they found themselves huddling in three small British transports, headed it was thought for Murmansk.

A few days out from Newcastle the violent influenza then epidemic broke out. There were no medical kits along. Without assistance from the army medics some recovered and many died. The colonel in command had orders to report to the British General Poole in Murmansk to assist in guarding stores. A few days out of Murmansk he received orders over the wireless to proceed instead to Archangel, four hundred miles to the southeast in the inner reaches of the White Sea.

Two days after Graves landed in Vladivostok the survivors and convalescents from the flu epidemic found themselves being disembarked under a chill drizzle in the outlandish arctic city, overtopped by the onion domes of its outlandish cathedral that had a huge vividly colored fresco of the Last Judgment emblazoned on its outside wall.

"The troopships *Somali, Tydeus* and *Nagoya* rubbed the Bakarita and Smolny quays sullenly and listed heavily to port," wrote an officer of the regiment. "The American doughboys grimly marched down the gangplanks and set their feet on the soil of Russia." The recollection stirred him to a certain eloquence: "The dark waters of the Dvina River were beaten into fury by the opposing north wind and ocean tide, and the lowering clouds of the Arctic sky added their dismal bit to this introduction to the dreadful conflict which the American sons of liberty were to wage with the Bolsheviki during the year's campaign."

One lucky battalion was detailed to patrol the town and at one point found themselves operating its streetcars. The other two were shipped immediately, one batch in boxcars and another in open barges towed up the Dvina, to the fighting front. General Poole, the British officer in command, found his French and British troops hardpressed in their scattered outposts where they were fighting to keep open communications up the Dvina and down the railroad to Vologda.

The Allied contingents, hitherto content with protecting Murmansk against the German and the Finnish Whites, had moved into Archangel, just a month before the arrival of the American infantry, in the wake of a revolution against the Communists carried out by a group calling themselves popular socialists. They were joined by the refugee embassies from Vologda, including American Ambassador Francis, who by this time had lashed himself into a holy frenzy of detestation of the Communists.

General Poole, their enthusiastic commander, with the support of the Allied diplomats, was implementing the plan which had first been formulated by the French: his forces would move down the railroad to Vologda to meet the Czechoslovaks advancing west from Ekaterinburg and the Urals. He laughed off the idea that the Red Army might interfere with this strategy of cutting European Russia in two. The Legion had just captured Kazan. The Reds seemed everywhere in flight. In mid August General Poole cabled the War Office: "I am quite cheerfully taking great risks."

General Poole was a sanguine man. The exploit of a bunch of American sailors made him particularly sanguine about the use of American troops.

One of the Allied flotilla anchored in the river off Murmansk was the ancient cruiser *Olympia*, which had been Admiral Dewey's flagship at the battle of Manila Bay. Tired of months cooped up on board under the leaden arctic sky, fifty gobs from the *Olympia* under an ensign volunteered to join in the landing at Archangel.

They wanted a chance to fight the Bolos. Among the rank and file of the Allied expedition there was no nonsense about helping "to steady any effort at self-government or self-defense" in Russia. The Tommies called the Communists Bolos and that was who they were there to fight.

Finding that instead of Bolo rifles, Archangel resounded with popular socialist speeches, the gobs decided to go look for the enemy. Searching among the ruined engines of the railroad yards, some of their number found an antique woodburning locomotive with a funnel stack that would run. They stoked it up, hitched it to a couple of flatcars and set off to see the country.

They went rattling off down the track in pursuit of the last Red train to pull out. They stoked so merrily that the Bolos didn't dare stop to burn the bridges until, about thirty miles south, the gobs had a hotbox. The time it took to repair the hotbox gave the Bolos time to burn the next bridge and to deploy their machinegun squad. They put up a lively resistance against any further advance. The ensign got a wound in the leg and the gobs dug themselves in around their train to wait for relief from General Poole's infantry.

This little incident made the gobs from the *Olympia* the heroes of the Allied command at Archangel, and when General Poole saw more Americans arriving, without consulting their commanding officer, a regular army colonel who seems to have been, to say the least, a retiring man, he immediately shipped them, sick or well, to his advanced posts, scattered in log huts among the swamps and stunted woodlands on the banks of the Dvina or along the railroad towards Vologda.

The fact that the Bolos had an organized army came as a shock to the

Allied command. General Poole's sanguine plans came to nothing. The Reds soon produced an armored train on the railroad and gunboats on the river. Red planes flew reconnaissance flights above American outposts. The officers particularly, most of them "ninety day wonders" who tried to get it all out of the book, were hard to convince that the Bolos had aviation. One day a somewhat unpopular major ran towards a plane that had crashlanded in a clearing. "Don't fire," he was shouting, "we are Americans!"

He was met by a machinegun burst and dove headfirst into the bog. By the time his troops had brushed the reindeer moss and lichen off him the Red aviators had disappeared into the forest.

"Don't fire" was the wisecrack that passed from mouth to mouth among the doughboys with the polarbear shoulderpatch, as they suffered through the arctic winter in bloody skirmishes with the Bolos. "We are Americans!"

Chapter 21

TOUT LE MONDE A LA BATAILLE

FAR from the sound of guns Ferdinand Foch pored over his maps in his tapestryhung château of stonetrimmed brick amid the quiet greenery of Bombon. The recapture of Soissons made him Marshal of France. After he had received the decorated baton one of his entourage caught him croaking "It is not a wreath of flowers on a grave."

Foch was a punctual man. Everything had to be on time. He always attended early Mass. Smoking a cheap stogy after his *petit déjeuner* he received the reports from the fighting fronts. Meals were sacred. *Déjeuner à la fourchette* was on the stroke of noon. Not even Weygand, his Chief of Staff, dared arrive a minute late. If he were unavoidably delayed, he'd wait to be served after the marshal had eaten. In the afternoon more conferences. Dinner was at seven sharp. *Le marechale est à table*. After dinner over the coffee visiting dignitaries shudderingly tried to smoke the marshal's cheap cigars. He didn't believe in wasting money on havanas. Early to bed. The members of his staff—known as *la famille Foch*—reported proudly that during the whole war the old fellow had only spent one night out of bed, during the first battle of the Marne when he had to stretch out on the floor of a small town hall. When he did have to travel, he complained jocosely that his *famille* wrapped him up like a package.

As summer advanced and the news from the armies improved, the marshal allowed his high spirits to express themselves sometimes at the table. "Oh ho, oh ho," a British brigadier reported him gloating over German reverses: "Where we made a single command, they made two . . . that of the Crown Prince and Prince Rupert of Bavaria. I wonder whether Ludendorff knows his business; I do not believe that he does."

As July advanced towards August, Foch began to promulgate his plan for a neverending series of attacks up and down the entire front: explaining his scheme to Colonel Repington, the most uppercrust of British war correspondents, at lunch one day the little man spluttered like a machinegun under his bristling mustache, *"Je les attaque! . . . Bon! . . . Je dis allez à la bataille! . . .* Everybody gets into the fight . . . God knows this is the time for the maximum effort . . . Let's go to work . . . *Bon!"*

This was the thesis he laid on the line for his staff: "The battle begins on one part of the front and the enemy is compelled to send there all his available reserves. Hardly has this been done when it begins again elsewhere and then again in a third place. The situation of the enemy is infernal."

Foch's watchword to all and sundry became: *"Tout le monde à la bataille."*

Prelude at St. Mihiel

When, at a general council of war at Bombon, Pershing set forth to the marshal his plans for his First American Army, both men still believed that the war would last into the following year. Pershing, with the ardent cooperation of General Bliss from Versailles, kept cabling the War Department that he wanted eighty divisions by April 1919, a hundred divisions (which would outnumber all the troops the French and British had in the field) by July.

Rumors of peace talks worried him. Peace would ruin his plans for an American army. "We must not let the people listen to rumors that the Germans are ready to make peace: there should be no peace until Germany is completely crushed," Pershing told the marshal earnestly. The marshal couldn't have agreed with him more. "We have pacifists who are lukewarm," Pershing complained, "too much inclined to accept any proposition to have the war stopped."

In their discussion of strategy for the autumn campaign the American Commander in Chief and the Marshal of France seem to have been talking at cross purposes. Pershing left Bombon believing he would be allowed to push through his longplanned drive through the St. Mihiel salient into the mining area of Briey.

His staff was already working out the details with Pétain's subordinates. The American Army lacked heavy tanks, artillery, aviation. Since the War Department was unable to supply these necessary items they had to be borrowed from the French, for a price.

There would be delays, particularly in the arrival of the heavy artillery. Mangin needed all the big howitzers he could line up for the operation he was conducting with the British against the German lines between Soissons and Arras. There were no heavy tanks available.

Pershing took personal command of his First American Army at the old American base of La Ferté-sous-Jouarre on the Marne on August 11 and immediately moved its headquarters to Neufchâteau in the rear of the St. Mihiel salient. In Neufchâteau and the surrounding villages the officers of the sundry newly formed corps worked overtime planning the moving up of munitions and troops for what was to be the first largescale American manoeuvre of the war. On August 30 General Pershing assumed command of all the Allied forces, American and French, in the St. Mihiel sector.

The same day Marshal Foch and Weygand arrived at Pershing's own private quarters at nearby Ligny-en-Barrois, and asked him to approve a completely new scheme of operations, which they claimed was the logical result of the unexpected speed of the British and French advance in Picardy.

The St. Mihiel operation was to be limited to pinching off the salient, and a number of Pershing's divisions were to be placed under French command for a completely new offensive which, instead of moving northeast into industrial Lorraine as had been planned, would push to the northwest, through the difficult terrain between the Meuse and the Aisne rivers. Thus it would form the eastern fang of a pincers of which the western jaw would be an Anglo-French drive for Cambrai.

Pershing immediately flared up: "Well Marshal, this is a very sudden change," he quoted himself as saying. "On the very day you turn over a sector to the American army you ask me to reduce the operation so that you can take away several of my divisions."

The discussion became heated indeed. Foch suggested, with his scornful snarl, that perhaps General Pershing didn't care to take part in the battle at all. Of course he did Pershing asserted doggedly "but as an American army and in no other way."

Foch insisted. Both men rose from the table where they were seated. "Marshal Foch you may insist all you please," Pershing remembered having said, "but I decline absolutely."

Pershing described Foch as picking up his maps and papers and leaving, "very pale and apparently exhausted," after placing a memorandum in Pershing's hands for further study.

Pershing was determined that Americans should no longer be used as cannonfodder to spare the troops of other Allied commanders. Though on the whole they got on better with the French than with the British, his doughboys he knew were fed up with being ordered about by the frogs. He was bound he would run his American sector as he saw fit.

The upshot of this irate discussion was that he consented to limit his St. Mihiel offensive to pinching off the German salient and promised that he would, immediately afterwards, in spite of the difficulty of changing his transport arrangements at that late date, join the French in a sweep down the valley of the Meuse starting to the west of Verdun.

"Plans for this second concentration," wrote Pershing, "involved the movement of some 600,000 men and 2700 guns, more than half of which would have to be transferred from the battlefield of St. Mihiel by only three roads, almost entirely during hours of darkness."

A million tons of supplies would have to be accumulated along the Voie Sacrée back of Verdun while American transport was busy in getting materials up to the Neufchâteau area for the St. Mihiel operation. "When viewed as a whole," wrote the general, "it is believed that history holds no parallel of such an undertaking."

For the St. Mihiel offensive some three thousand guns of all calibers were brought in, not one of them of American manufacture. A little less than half were manned by the French and the rest by American gunners. Forty thousand tons of ammunition were placed in readily accessible dumps.

Communications, consisting of telegraph and telephone lines, radio and a carrier pigeon corps, had to be connected with a central switchboard at Ligny-en-Barrois.

Convoys of trucks, some American but most of them French, moved back and forth from nineteen railheads, to bring up food, clothing and equipment which had been shipped from the American ports.

Nearly thirty thousand beds were ready in field hospitals provided by the Medical Corps.

Colonel Billy Mitchell for the first time commanded a really substantial airforce, some twelve hundred planes including French and British reinforcements.

There was still a total lack of heavy tanks and a shortage of light tanks. That meant that the doughboys would have to cut their own way through the barbed wire instead of having passages opened up for them by the tanks.

The total strength of the fighting forces under Pershing's command was 550,000 Americans and 110,000 French.

It had been hoped to attack on September 8. In spite of elaborate efforts to hoax the Germans by loud radio talk, and the setting up of a dummy headquarters to prepare an imaginary offensive in the Belfort region, the Germans were well aware of the American plans. The St. Mihiel offensive had for some time been the talk of the Paris cafés. Swiss and German newspapers started writing it up two weeks before it actually took place. The four day final delay gave the Germans a chance to pull a large number of their troops safely out of the salient.

This retirement had already begun when the American artillery barrage began an hour after midnight on September 12. A certain amount of shellfire was wasted on empty trenches. There'd been a heavy rain that night and at dawn the mist and drizzle shielded the movements both of the attacking Americans and of the retreating Germans.

Lacking tanks, teams of American engineers cut passages through the barbed wire with wirecutters. They laid down paths of chickenwire over the entanglements, a procedure which caused astonishment among the French, because nobody had thought of it before.

The attack, consisting of a twopronged operation, with more or less simultaneous assaults from the south and from the west, was carried out promptly and successfully. The Germans were outnumbered eight to one. In spite of spirited patches of resistance they were not able to get all their troops out before the mouth of the sack was closed on them.

In thirtysix hours two hundred square miles of French territory and a line of railroad were cleared of the enemy. The threatening height of Montsec, which had long terrorized the Allied entrenchments, fell with hardly a struggle. Something under sixteen thousand prisoners and four hundred and fifty guns of various calibers were taken at a cost of only seven thousand casualties.

On September 13 General Pershing, accompanied by General Pétain, made a triumphal entrance into the town of St. Mihiel which had suffered, by an odd fortune of war, very little damage. They were greeted by excited schoolchildren waving the tricolor and by the deputy mayor at the Hôtel de Ville. The inhabitants had been on the whole welltreated by the boche, they were told, except that all the ablebodied males had been carried off in the evacuation. News soon came that the Germans had to move so fast in their retreat that they had turned their prisoners loose ten miles out of town.

As the triumphant generals were leaving, they met Secretary Baker, who had a way of turning up when something important was going on, driving in unannounced with a bashful grin on his face. "I regretted," wrote Pershing, "he could not have gone in with General Pétain and me."

The following Sunday, Monsieur Clemenceau appeared at Pershing's headquarters. It was his custom to visit the frontline troops every Sunday. He demanded to be taken up to Thiaucourt, which was the recaptured town closest to Metz. Pershing, who thought the place was still being shelled, and knew the road would be blockaded with truck traffic, because the move to the Verdun sector was already beginning, said he was sorry, "We cannot take the chance of losing a Prime Minister." Clemenceau insisted. Pershing compressed his thin lips. When Pershing said no he meant no. The Tiger was furious. He made a try anyway and had to turn back.

To make things worse it turned out that President and Mrs. Poincaré, driving in a little later, had, in the course of a tour which included the ruined remains of a pleasant little country house they'd had on the heights overlooking the Meuse, been allowed to visit Thiaucourt.

At dinner at American headquarters Clemenceau bristled and would not be mollified. His distaste for Pershing turned into a fixed antipathy. All the way back to Paris he grumbled to his aides about the stupid way the Americans handled their military traffic. "They wanted an American army," he growled. "Anyone who saw, as I saw, the hopeless congestion at Thiaucourt will bear witness that they may congratulate themselves on not having had it earlier."

The Attack at the Pivot

The mopping up of the St. Mihiel triangle was hardly completed before Pershing moved his First Army Headquarters to Souilly on the Voie Sacrée between Verdun and Bar-le-Duc. The *mairie* at Souilly had been the chief French command post during the period of the great defense. The American officers felt a catch in their throats as they trooped up the worn steps. Their objectives lay to the northwest of the hills and fortresses that had been so drenched in blood during the battles of the previous years: Mort Homme, Hill 304, Vaux, Douaumont.

To mask the enormous movement of troops and munitions into the Meuse-Argonne sector, preparations for the dummy offensive through the Belfort Gap were ostentatiously stepped up. A phantom of Pershing's old plan for a drive into the Bassin de la Briey was projected into the press. Pershing's communiqué spoke of American doughboys as advancing on Metz.

At Belfort an army headquarters was established under command of General Bundy and bona fide preliminaries set in motion for an eastern drive to coincide with the imaginary movement against Metz from Thiaucourt. Twentyfive heavy tanks were brought up by night and went clanking in and out of patches of woodland where they would be heard by boche sentries across the lines. Preparatory raids and reconnaissances were made. An American Intelligence colonel was careful to drop a brand new wellmarked sheet of carbonpaper, from a letter to Pershing describing how all was in readiness for the offensive, in the scrapbasket in his room at a Belfort hotel where it was promptly scooped up by the German espionage.

Meanwhile correspondents were given false leads, a press bureau was set up in Nancy to cover the attack, and the Allied wireless, using an easily decipherable code, started talking about the formation of an American Tenth Army which was to spearhead the eastern offensive. Whether or not the Germans were completely taken in by this *ruse de guerre*, the threat was serious enough to cause Ludendorff to move several divisions into Alsace and Lorraine.

At dawn on September 26 nine American divisions, amounting to two hundred and forty thousand men, jumped off into the old nomansland of the defense of Verdun. They had quietly replaced the French holding troops during the night, while one of the heaviest artillery bombardments of the war combed the German positions. The front on which they were to advance extended twentyone miles from the Meuse to the western fringes of the plateau of the Argonne Forest where they were to keep contact with Gouraud's Fourth Army advancing through the plains of Champagne east of Reims.

Pershing's objective was to cut, in the vicinity of Sedan, the trunk line of railroad which furnished the Germans their chief lateral communication across their entire front from Metz to Valenciennes on the edge of Flanders. Giraud's objective was the same railroad a few miles further west at the important highway center of Mézières.

The staffs of the hastily improvised American corps had hardly two weeks to lay their plans for the sort of operation that usually took months to prepare. Since the three seasoned divisions had not had time to struggle out through the overloaded roads from the St. Mihiel sector, the initial attack had to be made mostly by raw troops who had not learned how to protect their lives on the battlefield. They were attacking one of the most defensible regions on the western front.

The day dawned clear. For a while it looked as if the Allied airplanes would have the sky to themselves. The correspondents were invited up to watch the opening moves. From the shellshattered hump of Mort Homme they looked north and west down the Meuse valley which tapered funnelwise towards Sedan thirtyone miles away behind the misted hills. The whole great funnel was dominated by the heights on the east bank of the Meuse, where the German artillery, once it recovered from the pounding of the first bombardment, was ready to do deadly work. To the west the treecrowned promontories of the Argonne Forest cut into the valley with a series of steep ridges culminating in an occasional height. In the distant foreground, overlooking the first day's objectives, was the ruined town of Montfaucon. Behind it was another ridge and behind that, fifteen miles away, was the hill village of Buzancy. Artillery in Buzancy would command the Meuse valley and the Sedan-Metz railroad.

At first everything seemed to go well. The Germans were almost as outnumbered as they had been at St. Mihiel. The main obstacle the American doughboys encountered was the mud in the shellchurned region of the old nomansland back of the heights that had defended Verdun. Roads had to be rebuilt foot by foot. Almost at once the infantry outran their field artillery and the tanks which were supposed to protect them.

The correspondents and the staffofficers up on Mort Homme watched with rapt interest through field glasses and telescopes olivedrab dots and lines moving forward according to schedule over the green land beyond the shellscarred area. The correspondents went back to Bar-le-Duc to write fanciful descriptions of a seven mile average penetration and of the taking of Montfaucon.

Some of them did have a qualm of suspicion before they left the observation post. A plane which they'd been admiring overhead as one of ours, made a sudden dive at them. When it opened up with its machineguns there was no more doubt that it was a boche. Staffofficers and newspapermen crawled for cover among the pebbly shellholes.

The truth came out gradually as night came on. The Americans had broken the first German defenses, but Montfaucon was still in German hands and the American divisions were scattered helter-skelter over a terrain perfect for defense by groups of machinegunners. They had insufficient artillery and almost no tank support. Their transport was mired in the nomansland behind them. Communications had to be by runner or carrier pigeon. From an observation post in Montfaucon the Germans continued to direct withering artillery fire on the advancing skirmish lines. To the left what the doughboys called the Oregon Forest turned out to be another Belleau Wood, only on a larger scale.

Next day the 313th Infantry, Marylanders from the 79th Division, did sure enough take Montfaucon, at very great cost, but it was late afternoon before the cellars and ruins of the town and the adjacent woods had been cleared of the enemy. Even then the German strong points turned out to be on the next ridge behind. The delay in getting up artillery, due to traffic snarls on the almost impassable roads, gave the German General von Gallwitz the chance he needed to deploy his reserve divisions and to reinforce his great guns which carried on an enfilading fire from the heights east of the Meuse. To make things worse the weather became rainy.

The days that followed were hideous for the Americans. German crack divisions were brought in to mount their usual skillful counterattacks. The troops were plagued with influenza, which throughout the army was killing almost as many men as machineguns and shrapnel. The roads up into the fighting areas were hopelessly inadequate. There were never enough tanks. Food and ammunition came up by fits and starts. The posts of command kept losing touch with their advance units. By the last day of September progress had stopped. General Bullard in command of the III Corps operating in the battlescarred regions along the River Meuse, remembered it bitterly as a time of "wavering and standstill."

Meanwhile Gouraud's Fourth French Army, which had made a good start the first day, was slowed to a crawl by a carefully fortified German position on a chalky hill known as Blanc Mont, which dominated the western fringes of the Argonne Forest, as Montfaucon had dominated its eastern defiles.

Further west French armies were beginning to make progress in the

Chemin des Dames section, the combined British and French moves towards St. Quentin and Cambrai were doing well, and in the extreme north the British and French and Belgians were meeting with light resistance as they advanced through the boggy lands in front of Ypres.

It began to be apparent that the German defenses, which the American divisions were battering themselves to pieces to break, were the pivot on which the whole German line from Sedan to the Channel was executing a gradual retirement. The manoeuvre was to pull back the armies step by step to a shorter line along the whole length of the Meuse as a door closes on its hinges.

The High Command was determined to hold the pivot at all costs.

The Wavering and the Standstill

Headquarters at Souilly was a grim place during the last days of September. A stream of orders that lashed like whips issued from the office of Pershing's Chief of Staff. Drive forward. Drive forward. There must be no yielding in the face of counterattacks. Brigade and divisional command posts must be continually moved up to keep in touch with the fighting lines. Woe to the officer who weakened at the task.

General Pershing himself gave no air of flurry. Bullard described him as visiting his corps headquarters and inquiring "about things in a very good-humored, agreeable, almost careless way; yet I knew that underneath his easy manner was inexorable ruin to the commander who did not have things right."

As the fighting dragged out from day to day, with little result but confusion and casualties, generals lost their commands; field officers or "ninety day wonders" who proved timorous or incapable of leadership were ordered to the rear. Constant dismissals and the high mortality among the firstrate officers and noncoms in the fighting meant that the command in all the units involved was constantly changing. This added to the difficulty of attaining the tight organization needed in such difficult country and against such a skillful enemy. Straggling and desertion became the problem of the day.

"The hardest work I did or saw done in France," noted Bullard, "was the holding of men to duty in service and battle. In the early days some of our military theorists who had been little at the front, desired to reduce the military police . . . As our fighting increased these military police had, on the contrary, to be augmented in every way possible. An unbroken line of them now followed our attacks."

Besides the difficulty of keeping an army, made up at least half of raw recruits, decently led and supplied, and headed in the direction of the enemy, Pershing had other battles on his hands.

By letter and cable he was carrying on a continual skirmish with the War Department in Washington for more trucks. He was in desperate need of horses. He didn't have enough locomotives. He was still dependent on his allies for tanks, for most of his airplanes and, except for a few naval guns, for ordnance. "After nearly eighteen months of war," he wrote, "it would be reasonable to expect that the organization at home would have been more nearly able to provide adequate equipment and supplies, and to handle shipments more systematically."

Besides the struggle with the War Department, where the high and mighty General March was not proving as much help as Pershing had hoped, he had his vendetta with Clemenceau.

On another of his Sunday jaunts the Tiger turned up at Souilly in his automobile and insisted on visiting Montfaucon. Pershing pointed out that the place was a target for German shells and spoke of the impassable roads. Clemenceau determined to try, and got caught in a road jam caused by the supply trains of a relieving division getting tangled with the division being relieved. It was worse than Thiaucourt. He went back to Paris more intent than ever to divest Pershing of his command.

A few days later Weygand arrived from Foch with the suggestion, which Pershing suspected of having originated with the President of the Council, that the French Second Army take over command of the Americans in the Argonne Forest. Pershing turned Weygand down cold.

Clemenceau never could understand why the Americans took so long in the Meuse-Argonne. The Tiger was in a hurry. He could see victory on the horizon. He was daily more impatient. He had flattering reports of advances from the western parts of the front. He blamed the stalemate in the Argonne on Pershing. He had long been intriguing against him through the French missions in Washington. In the end he wrote Foch a violent letter:

". . . You have watched at close range the development of General Pershing's exactions. Unfortunately, thanks to his invincible obstinacy, he has won out against you as well as against your immediate subordinates . . .The French Army and the British Army . . . are pressing back the enemy with an ardor that excites worldwide admiration; but our worthy American allies, who thirst to get into action and who are unanimously acknowledged to be great soldiers, have been marking time since their forward jump on the first day; and in spite of heavy losses, they have failed to conquer the ground assigned to them."

His solution was that, unless Pershing submitted to Foch's orders and accepted the advice of capable French generals, Foch should immediately appeal to President Wilson to have him removed. "It would then be certainly high time to tell President Wilson the truth and the whole truth concerning the situation of the American troops."

Foch did not respond directly to this outburst. He sent Monsieur Clemenceau an order of battle showing that out of thirty American divisions available for the front, ten were already with French or British armies, and only twenty under Pershing's direct command. He pointed out slyly that perhaps he might find ways to increase the ten and decrease the twenty. For the rest of their lives the topic remained a bone of contention between the marshal and the prime minister.

"Having a more comprehensive knowledge of the difficulties encountered by the American Army," Foch wrote in his official memoirs, "I could not acquiesce in the radical solution contemplated by Monsieur Clemenceau."

"The German People Shall Effectively Cooperate . . ."

While the raw Americans were slogging their way through the blasted woodlands and the ruined hillvillages of the Argonne and the Meuse against troops who used all the grim education of four years of fighting to make them pay dear for every step they gained, the political structure behind the German Army was breaking up.

The eastern alliance was the first to crumble.

In spite of the efforts of a German field marshal and of battalions of stormtroops the Turkish Army in Palestine allowed itself to be surprised and outmanoeuvred in mid September by Allenby's force of British colonials and rebellious Arabs, at Megiddo, north of Jerusalem. The Turkish Army was swept back in hopeless rout on Damascus. The remnants fled towards Aleppo.

Almost at the same time General Franchet d'Esperey's ramshackle coalition of French and British and Italians and Greeks and Serbs and Albanians defeated the Bulgarian Army in the Balkans. Communist orators started haranguing mobs in front of the royal palace in Sofia and gave the selfstyled Czar Ferdinand such a fright that on September 30 he concluded an armistice on terms of unconditional surrender. The Allies couldn't move in soon enough to protect him from a Red uprising. What was left of Mackensen's army had to retreat in a hurry across the Danube, leaving behind great quantities of rolling stock and the imperial hopes for a Berlin to Baghdad railroad and all that it implied.

Pro-Allied politicians took over in Bulgaria and a few days later Ferdinand abdicated in favor of his son. The loss of Bulgaria meant that communications between Germany and Turkey were cut off. Food riots and seditious strikes in Prague and Budapest disrupted the Hapsburg empire. Separatist movements came out into the open. In Vienna the Emperor Charles' government hung by a thread.

In Berlin the immediate result of the fall of Bulgaria was that the elderly chancellor, Count Hertling, resigned in despair. The voices of the Social Democrats in the Reichstag, and of such Independent Socialists as were still out of jail, were raised louder than ever in demanding an end to the war and democratic reforms at home. Criticism of the Hohenzollerns began to appear in the press.

Democrats and moderate liberals joined in the clamor which rose to such a pitch that the Kaiser Wilhelm, from his military headquarters at Spa, was constrained on that same September 30 to issue a proclamation that from now on "the German people shall effectively co-operate in deciding the destinies of the Fatherland."

As a successor to Hertling the Kaiser chose Prince Max of Baden. Prince Max, the heir to the throne of the Grand Duchy of Baden, had been long known as a moderate liberal. He had expressed opposition to *schrecklichheit* in general and to the submarine campaign in particular. He had announced his approval of the Reichstag resolution of July 19, 1917, calling for peace without annexations or indemnities. He immediately put forth the proposition that the interests of America and of Europe entire would best be served by a liberal coalition, in which a democratized Germany would play its part against the spread of Bolshevism.

In his first official address to the Reichstag he declared that Germany was ready to accept the Fourteen Points as a basis for peace. When Wilson, through Lansing, replied that Germany must first show good faith by evacuating all conquered territory, his answer was that Germany was prepared to do so. He suggested the appointment of a mixed commission to arrange the details.

The German note had hardly, through the good offices of the Swiss ambassador, reached President Wilson's desk, before the newspapers were full of the latest German atrocity. A submarine torpedoed the passenger steamer *Leinster* on the ferry service between England and Ireland.

The timid discussion of the desirability of a negotiated peace that had begun among the Allies and particularly in the English press, was drowned in a chorus of outrage. The news was crushing to the hopes of German liberals. Philipp Scheidemann, the Social Democratic leader, whom Prince Max had taken into the cabinet, declared to the Reichstag: "We must try to put ourselves in the enemy's place and view the state of affairs objectively . . . the frightful disaster of the torpedoing of a passenger steamer in which six hundred people, among them many women and children lost their lives . . . is terribly exasperating. The U-boat war should come to an end at once."

Although the armies in the field were still intact and disciplined, demoralization was spreading through the rear echelons. The High Com-

mand was in a panic. The story was being told that Ludendorff was so
upset by the news of the successes of Foch's general offensive that he
fell in a fit on the floor.

A wave of despair went through all the little courts of the kingdoms
and dukedoms and principalities that made up the hierarchy of the empire. The middle classes were bitterly disillusioned as it became clear
that the sacrifices of the war had gone for nothing. The working people,
who since the terrible "turnip winter" of 1916–17 had gone on working
long hours for low pay under conditions of undernourishment that occasionally reached the point of famine, began to turn towards the Russian example. The Russian masses had driven out their tormentors, why
not the Germans?

After all Germany was the cradle of socialism. The German Socialist
Party had for years been the largest and most respected in Europe. Split
into two wings in 1914 by the problem of whether or not to support the
war, the patriotic majority now became the mainstay of Prince Max's
hopes of rapidly improvising a liberal and selfgoverning Germany to meet
the specifications of a Wilsonian peace according to the Fourteen Points.
In all the German courts people of similar sympathies began to draft
reforms. As a gesture of conciliation towards the Independent Socialists,
who had opposed the war, the Chancellor amnestied their leaders sent to
jail by the old government.

The day Karl Liebknecht, one of the fieriest of the antiwar socialists,
was released he addressed an excited crowd to demand the Kaiser's abdication and a socialist workers' republic. From the workers in the Berlin
munitions factories and from the sailors of the fleet at Kiel came answering mutterings in premonition of revolt.

Germany teemed with agitators. Adolf Joffe had spent a busy summer
at the old Russian Embassy on the Unter den Linden. He had established
cordial relations with a group of welltodo radicals in Berlin. He helped
a number of Reichstag deputies from Independent Socialist constituencies
to subsidize newspapers. Moscow rubles paid the expenses of orators and
organizers who carried the Communist line to every corner of industrial Germany.

Carl Radek, fiery, humorous, resourceful, under the cloak of diplomatic
immunity, was fomenting a German revolution on the Communist model.
Lenin's paladins in the Kremlin, beset on every hand by counterrevolution, were pinning their hopes for safety in the workers' revolution they
believed could be provoked upon the collapse of German militarism.

The middleclass liberals and the soberer hierarchy of the trade unions
and the established officials of the Social Democratic Party saw a way to
peace and selfgovernment through President Wilson. The younger, wilder,
more reckless fringe of the German working class were calling for Lenin
and the red flag and for the total destruction of the existing order.

The Oregon Forest

While empires teetered to a fall, and rumors of peace flickered like heatlightning beyond the horizon, the American doughboys, struggling over ridge after ridge through thickets tangled with barbed wire, had no thought except to kill in order not to be killed. The weather was cold. Almost continuous rain increased the difficulties of supply. Gradually more and more American divisions became involved until, at the peak of the fortyseven day battle the First Army numbered more than a million men, and Ludendorff had thrown in forty of his shrunken divisions to oppose them.

Almost imperceptibly the tide was turning in the valley of the Meuse.

French forces drove the German artillery off the high ground on the east bank of the river. This enabled the 1st Division successfully to outflank the forest plateau from the east and thus relieve a battalion of the New York 77th cut off in the forest, when units on either side had failed to reach their objectives. Commanded by Charles Whittlesey, a New York lawyer in civilian life, the battalion, without food and almost without water, fought off German attacks from every side—including one polite request written in English inviting the major to surrender—for the better part of a week before the 1st Division's advance caused the Germans to quit the forest in a hurry. Five hundred and fifty officers and men of that battalion entered the woods. One hundred and ninetyfour walked out.

Two American divisions loaned to Gouraud managed to storm Blanc Mont from the rear. With that dangerous height in American hands the whole French line could move again.

Corporal John Aasland of the 5th Marines left notes of the assault in his diary: "October 3. At 4:30 A.M. the whistle blew and we packed up and stood by. The 6th Marines were to have the front the first day and we were to support them.

"The two regiments in the front line pulled a good stunt last night. At 11:00 P.M. they sneaked over into the German front line in the darkness and captured all the Germans there, then stayed there all night unbeknown to the Germans in the Second and Third lines, and used the German front as a jumping off place . . . The artillery opened up only five minutes before the attack started so by the time the Germans were half ready, the front line was . . . on their way to Blanc Mont ridge.

"We in support followed the 6th Marines by 600 yards . . . We advanced in line of combat groups. Crossed a creek and waded in water a foot deep, just enough to get wet. Broad daylight arrived, the sun shining brightly, and we had no fog to screen us. The enemy balloons behind the line were giving instructions to the artillery—which there was plenty of—

so they started to shell us for fair . . . When the fire was not quite so heavy we reached a narrow gauge railroad where we stopped again. On the barbed wire hung limbs of men who had been blown up before, around which lay blue cloth, the remains of the unsuccessful attacks of the French on this place.

"Up again and here comes machinegun fire from the left. We drop and lay perfectly still in the grass and weeds: someone from the extreme left will be sent after the machineguns. The firing stops. The whistle blows and we are up and start again. Sometimes when the whistle blew I got up real quick and looked around. Outside of the men right next to me I could see no one. Six inches of grass and the color of the army uniform made us invisible. If we could lay still all the time it would be soft. Looks funny when the whole line stands up and starts to move again: just like they came from nowhere.

"Now and then a man was killed and a wounded man called 'First Aid' . . . but this isn't bad yet . . . We are strung out in a trench with the Germans in the woods ahead of us. Every now and then machine gun fire comes our way. A heavy barrage began which plastered around us . . . On our way up the trench it was evident that other points in the woods had caught it also. Here and there were dead men lying in the trench. Soon we reached the top of Blanc Mont Ridge where the 6th Marines and 9th Infantry had been since yesterday noon. They were dug in in a shallow trench, right on top of the hill but with trees to screen them from the air."

Out of the welter of sudden death and hairbreadth escape, of men advancing in skirmish lines, pinned down in the muck of old trenches, scuttling out of harm's way among broken treetrunks, some deeds became legendary.

There was a solemn young man from the Tennessee mountains who, being an elder in his church, and pledged to the Ten Commandments, entered the army as a conscientious objector. An officer at the training camp, noticing that he was a remarkably good shot with a rifle, read the Bible with him and proved to him by chapter and verse that "Thou shalt not kill" did not apply to a just cause and that Jehovah was also the God of battles.

Corporal York was not only a crack shot but an accomplished woodsman. The Argonne was not too different from the Appalachian hills he'd been raised among.

Advancing through the woods with his squad he managed to get around behind a battalion field headquarters of the enemy.

The Germans were startled by the first American volley and threw up their hands and surrendered, but a German machinegunner in front of them slewed his gun around and shouting to the Germans to lie flat killed six doughboys and wounded the sergeant in command.

Taking charge, protected by a tree and a dead buddy on either side of him, Corporal York knocked off every man of the machinegun squad. When he ran out of ammunition for his rifle, he pulled out his automatic pistol and dropped a lieutenant and seven men who tried to rush him.

Then sticking his pistol in the German major's back he coolly started him towards the American lines. Flushing German machinegun nests from behind as they went the party trooped back to headquarters.

"Corporal York," he announced, with a precise salute to the startled battalion adjutant who thought it was a German raid when he saw them coming through the trees, "reports with prisoners, sir."

Asked how many prisoners he had he answered, "Honest, Lieutenant, I don't know."

The adjutant counted them as they filed by, headed for the rear. One hundred and two, including a major, two lieutenants, and twentyeight machineguns.

". . . In Deciding the Destinies of the Fatherland."

By the end of October the news that filtered through from the rear has begun to tell on even the most disciplined of the German troops.

On October 28 mutiny breaks out in the Kaiser's battle fleet. When orders come to put to sea the stokers on the battleship *Markgraf* drop their shovels and go trooping off the ship. When they are arrested by a squad of marines, the whole crew leaves the ship in protest. Other ships strike in sympathy. The sailors parade through the city and are met by red flags and orators telling them of the great part the sailors of the Baltic fleet played in the Russian Revolution. In a short time the whole naval base, almost without resistance from the officers, is in the mutineers' hands and the revolt is spreading to other ports, to war factories, to Berlin.

At Imperial Headquarters at Spa the Kaiser and von Hindenburg dismiss Ludendorff as Chief of Staff. Almost immediately word comes that as a result of the Italian victory at Vittorio Veneto the Austrian armies have disintegrated; that the Hapsburg government is begging President Wilson for an armistice; that mobs with red flags fill the streets of Vienna; that the Emperor Charles has abdicated and fled.

The Race for Sedan

Meanwhile the Belgians have taken Ghent and its U-boat pens. The British are past St. Quentin and Cambrai. The French have swept through the Chemin des Dames and taken Laon.

Along the Meuse the American First Army, having at last attained a smoothrunning organization under the direct command of a levelheaded oldtimer named Hunter Liggett, stands poised on the heights of the last ridge. Buzancy is behind them. There are American bridgeheads on the Meuse.

On to Sedan has been the watchword. At last the doughboys are ready to bear down on Sedan, but orders keep coming from Foch that send the American divisions slewing off to the east. Word goes around that they never will see the city they have shed so much blood to reach. The honor of taking Sedan will be reserved for the French 40th Division of Gouraud's army.

Late on November 7 a message is delivered to the commanding generals of the I and V Corps who are nearest to Sedan, at the far left of the American front. The reason they are nearest to Sedan is that Gouraud's army can't keep up with the mad pace of their advance. The doughboys are still full of ginger.

The message reads: "General Pershing desires that the honor of entering Sedan should fall to the First American Army . . . Your attention is invited to the favorable opportunity now existing for pressing our advance throughout the night. Boundaries will not be considered binding."

Immediately the advance becomes a race. The officers of the Rainbow Division of the I Corps lash up their tired men, their dying horses, their wornout transport and drive due north for Sedan. By morning they are on the heights overlooking the railroad yards and the historic plain, but in territory which Foch has assigned to Gouraud's army. Having run out of ammunition the 165th Infantry storms the last hill with cold bayonets.

General Summerall, in command of the V Corps, orders his 1st Division also to be in Sedan by morning. The men of the 1st, worn out by long fighting along the difficult fringes of the forest, footsore and short of food and ammunition, take him at his word and march all night at a desperate pace. So doing they tangle with advancing supply columns of the I Corps. With the dawn, more dead than alive, the men pour out on the heights above the city. In the confusion they have marched clean through the Rainbow Division's rear and come out even further to the left in territory reserved for the French. Everybody is lightheaded with fatigue.

In the course of their rush a 1st Division patrol has captured the dazzling young general just placed in command of the Rainbow, whose name is Douglas MacArthur. On account of his habit of taking the wire out of his cap they took him for a boche when they blundered into his small reconnaissance group studying out the road into Sedan.

At the same time Pétain is raising a storm at the headquarters of the French Fourth Army. The Americans are notified that the French 40th Division may find it necessary to open up with their artillery to clear the sector assigned to them for an advance.

For a few hours the situation is tense indeed.

MacArthur laughs off his capture. The Rainbow Division brings up its field kitchens to feed the men of the 1st who, although orders have come for them to retire, are pronounced too tired to move. Stiffly worded apologies go back and forth between the various staffs.

A French unit breaks the ice by asking an American unit to dinner and invites them to come along with the French into the city. The Americans are constrained to refuse.

Reluctantly Pershing has issued orders that no Americans shall enter Sedan. "Under normal conditions," he wrote later in his memoirs, "the action of the officer or officers responsible for this movement of the First Division directly across the zones of action of two other divisions could not have been overlooked, but the splendid record of that unit and the approach of the end of hostilities suggested leniency."

On the Siding in the Bois de l'Aigle

Early in the morning of November 8 on a siding in a tract of state forest known as the Wood of the Eagle near Compiègne, Marshal Foch waits in his headquarters train for the arrival of the German commission come to sue for an armistice.

At 7 A.M. the Germans, led by Matthias Erzberger, Prince Max's Secretary of State, arrive haggard and sleepless on the train which has brought them from the firing lines.

At nine they are received in his office car by Marshal Foch. He is accompanied by General Weygand, Admiral Sir Rosslyn Wemyss, British First Sea Lord of the Admiralty, and by British Admiral Hope, with their staffs. No other Allied delegates are present.

The Germans are stiffly greeted by General Weygand, representing the Allied armies and by Admiral Hope representing the navies.

Sphynxlike at the head of the table Foch asks the Germans why they have come. Cold hatred rings in every word. The Germans ask to know the conditions under which the Allies will agree to an armistice.

Foch's curt words are that he has no conditions.

The Germans ask leave to read President Wilson's latest note authorizing Marshal Foch to lay down the conditions. All Germany is waiting breathless for an armistice according to the Fourteen Points.

Foch insists that to have an armistice they must first ask for it.

The Germans request an armistice.

Then Weygand reads an outline of the conditions.

The conditions are:

"Immediate evacuation of all invaded countries within thirty days by German troops and of all of Germany west of the Rhine. The Rhineland to be occupied by Allied troops.

"Immediate repatriation without reciprocity of all prisoners of war.

"The delivery of an enormous list of various types of guns and of seventeen hundred airplanes.

"The delivery of five thousand locomotives and a hundred and fifty thousand cars and of five thousand motor trucks, all in good condition.

"The surrender of all submarines, of ten battleships and of a long list of other naval vessels."

The armistice is for thirtysix days, but renewable. Meanwhile the blockade of Germany is to continue.

The German delegates are so aghast they can hardly speak. Erzberger says hoarsely he cannot even discuss such conditions without communicating with his government.

Even while he is speaking his government is melting away. A workers' republic is proclaimed in Bavaria. Prince Max announces the Kaiser's abdication in Berlin and promptly resigns. A new Cabinet is formed of Social Democrats and Independent Socialists. Friedrich Ebert, as prime minister, proclaims a German republic.

Kings, princes and grand dukes go scuttling off in all directions. Leaving Hindenburg alone at Imperial Headquarters to struggle with the problems of the armies, the Kaiser and the Crown Prince board their imperial train and take refuge in Holland.

The commissioners make a play of communicating with their government but there is no government in Germany. Revolution roars through the land. All night of November 10 they argue for better terms.

Foch, who has only left the train long enough to attend Mass that Sunday morning, sits icily obdurate at the end of the table. He lets the others argue as they will.

It is the second night that the marshal has spent out of bed in the course of the war.

"We slept but little," he told one of his aides afterwards. "During the evening we had resumed our discussions. I lay down from eleven to one. Then we started arguing again till five fifteen that morning. At last they signed . . . and I saw Erzberger brandish his pen and grind his teeth when he signed the document. I was then glad that I had exerted my will, and employed the means of exerting it, for the business was settled."

Orders are immediately telegraphed out. At eleven in the morning firing ceases along the whole line from Switzerland to the sea.

At the Edge of the Arctic Dark

The very day and hour that the firing ceased on the western front, when the soldiers of the German and Allied armies were feeling themselves all over and crying out: By God I'm alive, three hundred Americans, supported by a company of Royal Scots and a few Canadians, were on the point of being overwhelmed by an assault of Russian Red Army troops in a group of log huts far upstream from Archangel on the Dvina River.

The village of Toulgas, under command of an American captain, was one of the fortified posts lost in the bogs and forests of north Russia left over from the sanguine British General Poole's ambitious plan to sweep south to join the Czechoslovak Legion. Now the Czechoslovaks had fallen back on the Trans-Siberian, and Poole had been replaced in command of the north Russian expedition by General Ironside, who saw at once that his problem was to consolidate his forces and so avoid another Gallipoli.

Ironside set the Allied troops to building blockhouses. On November 10 his second in command General Findlayson inspected the position at Toulgas and pronounced the village quite safe from attack. Winter was late setting in and the boggy forests had not frozen hard enough in his opinion to allow the passage of troops. At the same time, since the Allied gunboats had retired to Archangel to escape being caught in the ice when the river froze, he took it for granted that the Red Army gunboats were tied up at their base at Kotlas, a good hundred miles to the south.

On the morning of November 11 the garrison of Toulgas was startled at breakfast by riflefire up the river to the south of them and cries of "Urrah, Urrah" from an attacking force. Through darkness and freezing dawn mist the Bolos had crept up on a squad of Americans occupying a cluster of charcoalburners' huts at the upper end of the village.

Led by their lieutenant the Americans quickly fell back under fire across a little stream, past the church and the priest's house to the blockhouses in the central group of huts. At the same time the crash of riflefire and the ratatat of machineguns were heard from the log huts to the north of the village. The field hospital was in one of them. As no attack was expected from that quarter the field hospital was completely open and the only defense of the two Canadian fieldguns set in emplacements to shoot south was a few American rifles and a Lewis machinegun.

As luck would have it the Bolos, commanded by a great brigand of a man in an enormous black fur hat, took time off to loot the first huts they came to. The leader stalked into the hospital and ordered his soldiers to kill the sick men lying there. With great presence of mind the British noncom in charge offered the leader a bottle of rum and brought out everything he had in the way of rations. At the same moment what turned out to be a young woman, dressed in bundles of rags like the rest, burst into the hut with a rifle cocked and threatened to shoot any man who laid hands on the sick. This was the Bolo leader's girlfriend, a great strapping woman who had followed him through darkness and muck to the battlefront.

Food, drink and the lady's charms did their work. The Bolo countermanded his order and, leaving her in charge of the hospital, continued the assault.

The delay gave the Canadians time to pull their fieldpieces out of the slots and to swing them around and to load them with closerange shrapnel. They were expert gunners who had served on the western front. They allowed the yelling Bolos, attacking in a mass, to reach just the right distance and then touched off a blast point blank. The Bolos wavered, took a second blast and fell back on the huts and the edges of the forest, leaving the field littered with dead and wounded.

Meanwhile the main body of Americans, protected by log walls, were holding off the attack from the south. There were casualties on both sides but the Bolos' loss was much heavier. Clearing out snipers with a series of sorties the Americans and Britishers held off any further attack until early darkness fell.

During the night the American captain was cheered by blinker signals from a British post two miles across the river. When the message was decoded it turned out to be a demand that he account for six dozen Red Cross mufflers his outfit had been supplied with, and for which no receipt had been furnished. The night of Armistice Day when all the world was frenziedly celebrating an end to the war, the men of the little garrison at Toulgas slept on their guns.

Next morning five Red Army gunboats appeared around a bend in the river under the low arctic sun and started shelling. Rumor went around that Trotsky himself was aboard. This attack was no casual skirmish. The Russian guns outranged the Canadian fieldpieces so that they could lob shells at will into the long straggle of huts where the Americans and Britishers stood tense at their rifles and machineguns behind slits in the log walls.

The bombardment continued intermittently for three days. Though the attack to the north fizzled out with the death of the big Bolo leader in the black fur hat, repeated efforts to rush the little bridge that formed the northern entrance into Toulgas' one muddy street had to be beaten back. A shell wrecked the American blockhouse and the priest's house from which machinegun fire could be directed at the bridge. The church remained defensible.

The fourth morning before the late dawn an American company crept into the woods around the charcoalburners' huts where the Russian attackers were camping. The plan was to attack with as much noise as possible. It worked. The Bolos were surprised asleep. The hut where their ammunition was stored was set afire and made such a racket that the Bolos thought a whole division was on their trail and either ran off into the forest or surrendered.

The counterattack saved the day. That and the arctic winter. Zero temperatures froze the Dvina and drove the Red Army gunboats back to Kotlas.

When things quieted down the Russian woman, who had seen her Bolo lover breathe his last, turned out to have taken excellent care of the sick and wounded. Her story was that she had been a member of Kerensky's Women's Battalion and was following the war for the sport of it. She remained as a nurse in the Allied hospitals, and was revered by the doughboys under the title of Lady Olga.

To the American troops, who had lost twentyeight dead and seventy wounded, the siege of Toulgas became known as the Battle of Armistice Day.

PART FIVE

Mr. Wilson's Peace

It is to America that the whole world turns today, not only with its wrongs, but with its hopes and grievances. The hungry expect us to feed them, the homeless look to us for shelter, the sick of heart and body depend upon us for cure. All these expectations have in them the quality of terrible urgency. There must be no delay. It has been so always. People will endure their tyrants for years, but they tear their deliverers to pieces if a millenium is not created immediately. Yet you know and I know, that these ancient wrongs, these present unhappinesses, are not to be remedied in a day, or with the wave of the hand. What I seem to see—with all my heart I hope I am wrong—is a tragedy of disappointment.

—Woodrow Wilson to George Creel
as they paced back and forth
on the deck of the *George Washington*
bound for France

Chapter 22

THE PRESIDENT'S PLEDGE

On September 27, 1918, inaugurating the Fourth Liberty Loan drive at the Metropolitan Opera House in New York, Woodrow Wilson made a speech which did as much to bring the war to a speedy close as the mutual butchery of the armies contending along the Meuse and in the Argonne Forest.

". . . If it be in deed and in truth," he said, "the common object of the Governments associated against Germany and the nations whom they govern, as I believe it to be, to achieve by the coming settlements a secure and lasting peace, it will be necessary that all who sit down at the peace table shall come willing and ready to pay the price, the only price that will procure it . . . That price is impartial justice on every item of the settlement, no matter whose interest is crossed; and not only impartial justice, but also the satisfaction of the several peoples whose fortunes are dealt with. That indispensable instrumentality is a League of Nations formed under covenants . . ."

Colonel House, who was in attendance, noted in his diary that the opera house was beautifully decorated and crowded with the most important people in New York.

"The President read his address. Most of it seemed somewhat over the heads of the audience, the parts of it which were unimportant bringing the most vigorous applause. We are all wondering how the press will receive it. After speaking the President asked me to ride with him to the Waldorf . . . He was flushed with excitement and altogether pleased with the day's effort."

To Execute and Fulfill

The response to the President's speech was more favorable in the English newspapers than at home. American editorial writers were still befuddled by the theory, piped out of Washington by Creel's bureau, that the upheaval in Germany was a piece of sinister playacting staged by the High Command. London's "cocoa press" commented favorably. Cables of congratulation arrived from Grey and Lord Robert Cecil.

From Germany, the immediate response to Wilson's call for a peace of impartial justice was Prince Max of Baden's note, transmitted through the Swiss, asking for an armistice on the basis of the Fourteen Points.

The German note, coming on the heels of similar proposals from the Austrians, threw Capitol Hill into an uproar. Prince Max's suggestion of a mixed commission to arrange the details of the evacuation of occupied territory by the German armies was seen as a device to allow the Hun to regroup his forces for a defensive war on his own frontiers. "A trap"; clamored the newspapers. In the Senate Lodge marshalled the irreconcilables in a drive for unconditional surrender.

Meanwhile the President was consulting the members of his cabinet; and House, who was still in New York, over the longdistance telephone. House's suggestion was that he gain time by announcing that he was taking up the German request with the Allied Powers. "I would advise that you ask the Allies to confer with me in Paris at the earliest opportunity."

The confidential colonel hastened to Washington.

"I arrived at the White House as the clock was striking nine," wrote House . . . "The President met me and we went into his study." Lansing arrived. The President read the first draft of his reply to the two of them. Lansing sniffed and said the reply was an inquiry rather than an answer. House considered it too lenient. "He seemed much disturbed when I expressed decided disapproval of it. I did not believe the country would approve what he had written. He did not seem to realize . . . the nearly unanimous sentiment in this country against anything but unconditional surrender. He did not seem to realize how war-mad our people had become."

After Lansing went home to bed Wilson and House sat up till one in the morning reworking the President's reply to the German note. Their final version demanded, as preliminary to an armistice, the clearcut acceptance by the Germans of Wilson's Fourteen Points; the immediate evacuation of invaded territory without any dillydallying over a mixed commission; assurances that the government in Berlin spoke for the German people and not for the military clique.

The President's note of October 8 constituted the final wedge driven in between the Kaiser and his subjects. At the same time it was considered by neutrals and belligerents alike as a pledge by Woodrow Wilson that, if the Germans laid down their arms, they would be treated "with impartial justice" according to the principles of the Fourteen Points.

Comment in the American press was respectful but unenthusiastic.

On Columbus Day, renamed Liberty Day for the occasion, Woodrow Wilson marched at the head of a parade up Fifth Avenue and received, according to the New York *Times*, "an ovation such as no President has ever before encountered in this city . . . The Wilson smile was in evidence from start to finish, and his arm worked with the regularity of a piston doffing his tall hat to the cheering throngs."

That evening, while President and Mrs. Wilson were dining at the Waldorf before attending a benefit for Italian soldiers blinded in the war, again at the Metropolitan Opera House, Tumulty brought the news that the German Government had accepted the President's terms.

"There was an enormous crowd which cheered the President with much enthusiasm," noted House. "I was so stirred by the news that had come from Berlin I could not listen to the programme."

The President returned to Washington determined to lose no time. Every hour's delay meant an unnecessary sacrifice of human lives. House went with him on the train.

"Yesterday," noted House on October 15, "was one of the stirring days of my life. The President and I got together immediately after breakfast. I never saw him more disturbed . . . He wanted to make his reply final so that there would be no exchange of notes . . ."

Wilson's first demand, before an armistice could be considered, was the cessation of such atrocities as the sinking of the *Leinster* . . .

"Neither the President nor I desired to make a vengeful peace. Neither did he desire to have the Allied armies ravage Germany as Germany has ravaged the countries she has invaded . . . He is very fine in this feeling and I am sorry he is hampered in any way by the Allies and the vociferous outcry in this country. It is difficult to do the right thing in the right way with people like Roosevelt, Lodge, Poindexter and others clamoring for the undesirable and the impossible."

At this point it was essential that the President be personally represented on the Supreme War Council at Versailles, where the American representative, sturdy old General Bliss, had never been given any power to assume the initiative. Even before Wilson concluded his exchange of notes with Berlin, which cleared the way for an armistice, Colonel House was on the high seas headed for France.

Accompanied by Mrs. House, and by Miss Denton, who had furnished herself with a small pearlhandled pistol to protect the colonel's life if need be; and by Miss Denton's assistant, Miss Tomlinson; and by his soninlaw Gordon Auchincloss, on loan from the State Department, the confidential colonel boarded the U.S.S. *North Pacific* off Staten Island. On board he found Rear Admiral William S. Benson and his staff; Joseph C. Grew, onetime counsellor at the Berlin Embassy; a number of clerks and stenographers; and Frank Cobb of the New York *World*. That made up the party. They had a stormy crossing. They left in the fog and arrived in the fog. On October 26 the ship dropped anchor in the harbor at Brest.

In his pocket Colonel House carried a personal letter from the President which amounted to a power of attorney, and an impressively sealed document concocted at the State Department: ". . . Reposing special trust and confidence in the integrity and ability of William M. House of Texas, I do appoint him a special representative of the Government of the United States of America . . . and do authorize and empower him to execute and fulfill the duties of his mission with all the powers and privileges thereunto of right appertaining . . ."

To all concerned the moment seemed heavy with destiny. The President's farewells, and indeed those of Mrs. Wilson, were unusually affectionate. "As I was leaving," House noted in his diary, "he said 'I have not given you any instructions because I feel you will know what to do' . . . He knows that our minds are generally parallel and he also knows that where they diverge, I will follow his bent rather than my own."

The Republicans Take Congress

As the congressional elections approached, in spite of the vigor of the wellfinanced campaign led by Will Hays, newly appointed chairman of the Republican National Committee, administration leaders remained confident. The morning of election day the New York *Times* predicted a Democratic victory. When the results were tallied, Woodrow Wilson was confronted, not with a Republican landslide to be sure, but with a clear indication that the Republican trend, which had come near defeating him in 1916, was continuing.

Both campaigns were hampered by the calling off of public meetings in many parts of the country on account of the influenza epidemic. The Republicans claimed that more of their rallies were cancelled than of their opponents'. In spite of this, and of a certain wariness that the fear of the Department of Justice's interpretation of the Espionage Act instilled in antiadministration orators, the Republicans carried the House of Representatives by thirtythree seats and had a thin edge in the Senate. The cornbelt returned to the Republican fold.

In Illinois popular and pinkwhiskered J. Hamilton Lewis, who had tried to introduce a Senate resolution authorizing the President to conduct peace negotiations without senatorial consultation, lost to a Republican.

In Michigan, Lieutenant Commander Truman H. Newberry, industrialist and big navy enthusiast, had shown such zeal in his successful campaign against Henry Ford, who was induced to run for the Senate on a Wilson platform, that he had already become embroiled with a grand jury for the alleged misuse of campaign funds. If Newberry's election could be made to stick, the Republican regulars would organize the Senate and Henry Cabot Lodge would have the chair of the committee, allimportant at this juncture, on foreign affairs.

Political postmortems were almost unanimous in laying a large share of the blame for the administration's defeat on the President's appeal to the voters to show their support of his policies by electing a Democratic Congress.

"I have no thought of suggesting that any political party is paramount in matters of patriotism," Wilson wrote in a statement issued a few days before election. "I mean only that the difficulties and delicacies of our present task are of a sort that makes it imperatively necessary that the nation should give its undivided support to the government under a unified leadership, and that a Republican Congress would divide the leadership . . . I am asking your support not for my own sake, or the sake of a political party, but for the sake of the Nation itself."

In spite of its disarming phraseology, the President's appeal was greeted by an outpouring of righteous indignation from Republican orators. "An insult," shouted Will Hays, "to every loyal Republican in the land." In vain George Creel and Tumulty pointed out that similar appeals had been issued at electiontime by George Washington and Abraham Lincoln and that McKinley, Theodore Roosevelt and Taft had been far more partisan in their election day pronouncements.

The Democratic defense was lukewarm. Such administration leaders as had been consulted had advised against this sort of statement. Washington newspapermen claimed that McAdoo was "mad as a hornet" because the President hadn't asked his advice. Newton D. Baker was quoted as having pointed out wryly to a friend that of course it was wrong for a Democrat to ask people to vote for him; that was the prerogative of Republicans.

In the Senate lobby Henry Cabot Lodge, in behalf of his opposition group, handed the newspapermen an abusive rebuttal. "This is not the President's personal war" was its burden. Theodore Roosevelt made Wilson's appeal the theme of the final speech of his career.

Colonel Roosevelt's Last Charge

Ever since Wilson made him give up his scheme to lead troops in the European war, T.R. had been beating himself to pieces against a wall of frustration. He was fighting illhealth. His explorations in the Amazon basin had left him with an intermittent fever. The bullet lodged next his lung caused chronic bronchitis. "When I went to South America I had one captain's job left in me," he confided to Owen Wister. "Now I'm good only for a major's . . . It doesn't matter what the rest is," he added hastily, "I've had fun the whole time."

He showed occasional bursts of the old energy; like a fighting bull bemused by the capes of the *toreros*, he was still good for an occasional deadly charge. He'd see red in a Wilsonian phrase and show his old fire and dash for a while, but he would soon tire and trot back weakly to his wife, Edith, and to Sagamore Hill for a rest.

He was subject to fits of rage, as in his runin with Samuel Gompers in the summer of 1917, when they appeared on the same platform in Carnegie Hall to greet the democratic revolution in Petrograd.

The newspapers had been filled for three days with accounts of a murderous race riot in East St. Louis. Mobs, instigated, it was claimed, by union leaders, had attacked Negro families who had moved up from the south in search of work. Houses were set afire, men and women slaughtered as they ran out from the burning buildings; children died in the burning houses. The toll was twentynine dead, about ninety people badly hurt; three hundred shacks and houses and a large part of the business district burned to the ground.

T.R. could not shake off the horror of this attack on helpless people. When he was introduced, amid a storm of cheers, by Mayor Mitchel, he departed from his prepared speech to express his shame and grief that such a thing could happen in America.

Gompers asked for the floor and tried to explain that those really to blame for the race riots were the manufacturers, greedy for war profits, who had lured cheap Negro labor up to St. Louis to break down union wage scales.

T.R.'s face flamed red. He shook his fist under Gompers' nose. "Justice with me," he shouted, "isn't just a phrase or a form of words. How can we praise the people of Russia for doing justice to the men within their boundaries if we in any way apologize for a murder committed on the helpless?"

Gompers was ashy pale. He murmured something about an investigation being carried out by the A.F. of L.

"I'd put down the murders first and investigate afterwards," roared T.R., flailing with his arms.

Boos, hoots and occasional cheers rose from the audience. It was with difficulty that order was restored in Carnegie Hall.

The following winter T.R. spent several weeks in hospital with an abscessed leg. When the weather turned warm he was out again charging about the country, assailing the Administration's conduct of the war and lashing up patriotic fervor with his talks on Americanism. Wherever he went he shook men's faith in the Wilsonian rhetoric. His plain speaking on Negro rights helped alienate Negro voters in the northern cities from the Democrats.

The Colonel couldn't go to war himself but he gloried in being represented by his four sons. Archie and Theodore Jr. were officers in the A.E.F. Kermit had enlisted with the British and came down with malaria in the Mespot. Quentin, the youngest, was training for aviation. "I putter around with the other old frumps," T.R. wrote Quentin after getting out of hospital in the spring, "trying to help with the liberty loan and the Red Cross and such like."

As the summer of 1918 advanced, news from the fighting front warmed his heart. Theodore Jr. distinguished himself at Cantigny and was now a lieutenant colonel in his own right. Archie was badly smashed up by a burst of shrapnel. He came home on leave long enough to appear with his arm in a cast on the platform beside his father when T.R. addressed the erstwhile German-American Liederkranz Society in New York.

T.R. conducted two successful speaking tours through the middlewest. He staged a public reconciliation with Taft at a political dinner in Chicago. His re-entry into national politics seemed assured. Many elements in the Republican Party looked to his leadership to dislodge the Democrats from Washington in 1920. He was only sixtyone. If his health would mend he might be President once more.

Late in July news came that Quentin, the youngest, in some ways his father's favorite, had been shot down fighting a formation of German planes. At first he was listed as missing. Then the Germans reported his death and burial with full honors behind their lines near Cambrai.

It hurt more than T.R. had expected. He threw all his energies into keeping his wife's courage up. Unbowed he went to Saratoga, two days after the news came, to deliver the keynote address at the Republican state convention. All factions, even Boss Barnes whom he had lambasted in a libel suit, urged him to accept the Republican nomination for governor. Smiling he turned them down. He was out for bigger game.

On October 26, before a packed and cheering audience, he hauled the President over the coals for his call for a Democratic Congress. He denounced the arrogance of Wilson's conduct of the war. With his customary combination of wild inflammatory statements and commonsense reasoning he tore the Fourteen Points to pieces, crying out that they were shams and would not bring the peace with justice the American people wanted.

(T.R. hadn't been able to get Wilson's war away from him: maybe he could carry off the peace.)

That night in Carnegie Hall, flashing his eyeglasses and clacking his great teeth and waving his arms with the legendary zest, T.R. seemed to his listeners his old riproaring self. He admitted to no one that he felt feverish and sick. The abscess in his leg was acting up. When he got home to Sagamore Hill he confessed to Edith that he was really not well. The day of the armistice they took him to Roosevelt Hospital in New York. He was weak and running a temperature and in great pain, suffering from what he described as sciatica.

Roosevelt's old friend Henry White, a survivor from John Hay's diplomatic corps, who had represented Roosevelt at the Algeciras Conference during the great days of his presidency, came, along with Elihu Root, to call on him at the hospital. White had just been appointed, as a sop to the Republicans, one of Wilson's delegates to the Paris Peace Conference. White and Root wanted to consult T.R. on a program, but they found him too weak to talk.

He did pull himself together long enough to compose a few days later a careful denunciation of the President's peace plans: "Our Allies and our enemies and Mr. Wilson himself should all understand that Mr. Wilson has no authority to speak for the American people at this time. His leadership has just been emphatically repudiated by them . . . Mr. Wilson and his Fourteen Points and his four supplementary points and his five com-

plementary points and all his utterances every which way have ceased to
have any shadow of right to be accepted as expressive of the will of the
American people."

By Christmas T.R. was thought sufficiently recovered to go home. Two
weeks later he died, without a murmur, in his sleep in his own bed at
Sagamore Hill.

The Cause of Righteousness

Theodore Roosevelt intended his last blast as a warning to the world
that Woodrow Wilson's peace terms, even before they had been fully
elaborated, were likely to be repudiated by the voters back home.
Though blinded by personal bitterness the old campaigner had not lost
his political intuition. Somehow, while so skillfully driving a wedge between the populations of the central empires and their governments, the
President had allowed himself to become alienated from large and essential segments of the American people. The cleavage was not yet completely apparent.

In six years a change had come over the political landscape. The reform movements which had smoothed the way for Wilson's leadership
were losing their power or developing new aspects. During the years of
the century's youth the American people hungered and thirsted for
righteousness. T.R. and Bryan and Woodrow Wilson built their political
careers on popular faith in selfgoverning institutions, and on belief in the
eventual triumph of Christian ethics. Now many of the reforms had come
to pass. Senators were elected by popular vote. Woman's suffrage was a
fact. With many of the great aims attained the generous passion for civic
virtue was degenerating into a series of smallminded manias.

Backed by an effective and bigoted organization prohibition was
sweeping the country. Long before the war a good deal of reforming zeal
had spent itself in efforts to suppress gambling and prostitution. Now the
evils of drink became such an obsession that a man could hardly attain
the office of notary public without being endorsed by the Anti-Saloon
League.

In lashing the people up to a maximum war effort the Wilson administration unleashed blind hatreds and suspicions against foreigners and
foreign ideas, and in fact against any ideas at all, that could hardly be
controlled once their imagined usefulness, as a part of the psychology of
total war, was at an end.

Such enthusiasts for political reform as remained were estranged by
the prosecution of dissenting voices. As the suppressive measures weakened, movements like La Follette's Progressive Party and the Non-
Partisan League in Minnesota and the Dakotas, which were in many ways

the heirs of Bull Moose, would come back into the open, but as agrarian or farmer-labor groupings. Somehow they had lost their national character.

When their leaders would speak of the war it would be no longer in terms of the Wilsonian slogans. They would not find the world made safe for democracy. The recollection would be too fresh in their minds that while Wilson's Department of Justice conducted something like two thousand prosecutions of socialists, pacifists, syndicalists or alleged pro-Germans, hardly an effort was made to check the brutal profiteering that grew out of the cost-plus system. "Merchants of death" would be the reformers' theme.

The young radicals who, at an earlier day, followed the progressives in their hue and cry against malefactors of great wealth, and in practical efforts to refurbish the selfgoverning process, were turning to the Russian Revolution for inspiration. John Reed, whose *Ten Days that Shook the World* made the October days real to thousands of Americans, became an archetype of the indignant youth of the time who failed to find any idealism in massacres at the fighting fronts or in repression of workingclass movements by the Department of Justice.

In Soviet Russia they were finding the righteous cause their fathers sought in following Wilson and Roosevelt and Bryan. To them the soviets were spontaneous selfgoverning assemblies like New England town meetings. The Soviet Government had repudiated secret diplomacy and was fostering selfdetermination of national minorities. Lenin had brought peace to the soldiers and land to the peasants. The repressions and massacres conducted in the name of the proletariat were shrugged off as temporary phenomena in the war against a host of enemies financed by capitalist governments, or as capitalist fabrications on the order of the Sisson documents.

Obstreperous and nonconformist youth, which a generation before might have listened to Woodrow Wilson with respect, was now attracted to the various socialist and syndicalist ideologies which were already beginning to harden into the Communist dogma.

The bellwether of those disillusioned with democratic methods would be Lincoln Steffens. Steffens, the most influential writer of the muckraking era, had been T.R.'s personal friend. He had glorified in print the labors of Bob La Follette in Wisconsin and of Newton Baker in Cleveland. Now Steffens, who had been the guide and philosopher of a whole generation of indigenous muckrakers and of the reform movement from coast to coast, was suddenly to make public his loss of faith in the tradition he had served for a lifetime. Stopping in after a trip to the Soviet Union, to call on his friend the sculptor Jo Davidson—whom he found fingering the clay for a bust of Bernard Baruch—Steffens was heard portentously announcing: "I have been into the future and by God it works."

Organized labor was of two minds. Although Samuel Gompers kept the official leadership of the A.F. of L. in line behind the President, "a baneful seething," stimulated by the Bolshevik-inspired revolutions that were sweeping Europe, continued under the surface. The foreignborn, stung by discrimination and harassment in America, dreamed of joining the triumphant uprising of the world proletariat. Repression bred resentments even among native Americans. It was hard for working men and women to forget that Debs was serving time in Atlanta.

Superficially, in spite of the deep popular misgivings of which the Republican victory at the polls was an inconvenient symptom, everything was as it had been. With the news of the armistice a sense of reprieve swept over the country. There was hardly a family that didn't have men at the front or in training. Mothers, fathers, wives, sweethearts could take a deep breath and say to each other that their dear ones were safe. The elation of victory threw a certain halo about the figure of the President. His appeal to the crowd had never been greater. Yet mistrust was creeping in behind the cheers of the crowds.

Misgivings in the News

The Administration was losing its favorable press. Though in private, newspapermen had long been outspoken against George Creel's highhanded performances as presidential propagandist, the treatment of Woodrow Wilson himself, even by the opposition papers, remained respectful to the point of servility. He still had devoted adherents among the ablest journalists of the time. When the critical spirit began to express itself in the editorial columns, the tone was more of sorrow than of anger.

Three days after the armistice the President astonished the nation by using his wartime powers to seize the Atlantic cables. The move was ascribed to George Creel. Editorial writers explained sarcastically that Creel was planning to use his control of the cables to censor and distort the news of the Peace Conference as his "Committee of Public Misinformation" had censored and distorted the news from the fighting fronts. Hardly a voice was raised in the President's defense.

The flurry over the nationalization of the cables had hardly subsided before the story broke that McAdoo was resigning as Secretary of the Treasury and as Director of Railroads. The President's soninlaw was generally considered the strongest man in the Cabinet. Mac himself never did much to disguise the fact that he was of this opinion too; he snorted to House that the rest of the cabinet members were "nothing but clerks." Although White House intimates knew that Mac had suffered a couple of spells of illness attributed to overwork and had been discussing with the President and his confidential colonel the reasons that would soon impel him to return to private life, the news of his abrupt resignation at such a critical juncture aroused a storm of gossip.

As an apostle of free enterprise Mac was resigning in protest against the President's policy of nationalizing public utilities. He could no longer go along with Baker's inefficiency in the War Department as revealed by the Hughes report on the shortcomings of the airplane production program. He had thrown up his job in a peeve because the President wouldn't appoint him to serve at the Peace Conference.

McAdoo's resignation was the signal for a stampede of "dollar a year" men out of Washington. Business executives and industrial leaders who had been working themselves sick for no pay on the control and procurement agencies of the Washington leviathan, while out of the corner of an eye they could see their less patriotic and often less able colleagues getting rich on war profits, returned to private life in droves. Even Bernard Baruch, the President's dear Dr. Facts, announced he was leaving the Industrial War Board at the end of the year. The President wrote him immediately that he had further work in mind for him.

Though Wilson never had any idea of taking McAdoo to Europe, the resignation of his Secretary of the Treasury did force him to make a change in his list of delegates. With Mac gone, he would have to leave Secretary Baker, the only other cabinet member on whom he really relied, in Washington to keep the wheels of government moving during his absence. By mid November the story was in the headlines. The President was indeed planning to lead his delegation to the Peace Conference in person.

The news was received with dismay. At the State Department Lansing was quietly conducting his own canvass on the desirability of the President's going to Europe. From Cardinal Gibbons in Baltimore to obscure Democratic precinct leaders in upper New York State the answer was negative. Old friends wrote begging Lansing to talk the President out of the notion. Many referred approvingly to the tradition that no President should leave the territory of the United States.

When Lansing respectfully presented his arguments the President intimated that he hadn't yet quite made up his mind. Baruch was reported to be against the President's going. Baker was against it. Secretary of Agriculture Houston, who was passionately loyal, suggested at a cabinet meeting, that though it might be fitting for the President to open the conference in person, he should then come home and leave the details to his delegates. As his way was, Wilson listened politely to all this advice and kept his own counsel; then one night he appeared without warning at Lansing's house in the middle of a dinner party and brusquely announced to his Secretary of State that he'd made up his mind, he was going.

Echoes of these discussions and misgivings had been leaking into the nation's press through the Washington newspapermen, who, now that the fighting had stopped, were short of sensations to report. Even the New York *World*, the President's faithfulest supporter among bigcity newspapers, frowned on the idea. When the New York *Times* published a summary of editorials throughout the nation it was discovered that opinion was two to one against it.

His Bent Rather than My Own

From the moment House reached Paris on October 26 and set up his offices in a gray old mansion on the rue de l'Université on the Left Bank, the President and his confidential colonel exchanged incessant cables in their private code. Immediately House took his old chair on the Supreme War Council as the President's personal representative.

Clemenceau greeted him like a longlost brother. "He received me with open arms. We passed all sorts of compliments. He seems genuinely fond of me," noted House in his diary. "He thinks in the terms of the Second Empire," he added a little later. "He doesn't know what this new thought is about." In spite of the illtempered old Tiger's personal partiality, the colonel found the British more nearly in sympathy with the President's plans. Lord Milner and Marshal Haig feared bolshevism more than they feared a German revival, and were in favor of moderate treatment of the defeated nations. Lloyd George talked first one way, then the other. He gave the impression of being more than usually flighty and irresponsible. His mind was on the coming general election back home.

While the Supreme War Council sat at Versailles, working out, amid the stiff formalities of military protocol, ever more Carthaginian armistice terms for the defeated nations, the Allied civilian leaders took refuge from the exigencies of their generals at the Quai d'Orsay. The handsome offices of Monsieur Stéphane Pichon, the French Minister for Foreign Affairs, were among the few state apartments in Paris where the *chauffage centrale* really worked. There the prime ministers, Clemenceau, Lloyd George and Orlando, with House sitting in for President Wilson, could lounge in front of a fireplace around a large carved flattopped desk and carry on their debates in a more unbuttoned atmosphere.

House was shocked by the first meeting he attended: "Lloyd George and Clemenceau wrangled for an entire afternoon as to whether the British or the French should receive the Turks' surrender. They bandied words like fishwives, at least Lloyd George did . . . It would have been humorous if it hadn't been a tragic waste of time."

House's first task was to get the Fourteen Points firmly imbedded in the agenda of the peace talks which would follow. "If this is done the basis for peace will already have been made. Germany began negotiation on the basis of these terms, and the Allies have already tentatively accepted them . . . but it is becoming daily more apparent," he wrote, after he'd been two days in Paris, "that they desire to get from under the obligation these terms will impose upon them in the making of the peace. If we do not use care we shall place ourselves in some such dishonorable position as Germany did when she violated her treaty obligations as to Belgium."

There were two great sticking points. Lloyd George was skittish about freedom of the seas, and Orlando insisted upon assurances that Italy's Adriatic aspirations would be respected. After four days of argument House reached a compromise.

He promised that before the meaning of each debatable point was finally set down in definite and practical terms both the British and the Italians would be given the chance to argue out their exceptions in direct negotiations with the United States. Furthermore, with the President's full knowledge and consent, the colonel furnished the Allied leaders with a private and confidential document, drawn up under House's supervision, explaining away most of the features which the European statesmen found most objectionable in the Fourteen Points. The content was subject to negotiation, the ingratiating colonel assured them, if only they accepted the slogans in their outward form.

Just as House had reached this gratifying accord with the prime ministers, at a meeting this time in House's large parlor on the rue de l'Université, news was brought them that Austria had accepted the armistice terms. "There was great excitement," he noted, "and clasping of hands and embracing. I said to Orlando 'Bravo Italy' which brought him near to tears."

"This has been a red letter day," House cabled the President.

Sir William Wiseman was among the first to congratulate him. Wiseman, a slender active little man, hid a great deal of intrigue behind a frank and open countenance. Heading the British secret services in Washington during the better part of the war he had seen to it that he should become a familiar of the confidential colonel's. His usefulness as bosom friend to the President's chief adviser can hardly have been lost on his superiors at Whitehall. In Paris his function again was that of private British liaison man with Colonel House.

"Wiseman and my other friends," noted House exuberantly under the date of November 4, "have been trying to make me believe that I have won one of the greatest diplomatic triumphs in history. That is as it may be. The facts are I came to Europe for the purpose of getting the Entente to subscribe to the President's peace terms. I left a hostile and influential group in the United States frankly saying they did not approve the President's terms . . . On this side I found the Entente governments as distinctly hostile to the Fourteen Points as the people at home. The plain people generally are with the President . . . it is not with the plain people we have to deal . . . I have had to persuade, I have had to threaten." House's threat was that Wilson would ask Congress to make a separate peace—"but the result is worth all my endeavors . . . I am glad the exceptions were made, for it emphasizes the acceptance of the Fourteen Points."

House's cables caused jubilation at the White House. "Proud of the way you are handling the situation," cabled the President. Both the President and his confidential colonel felt they had taken the first step towards redeeming Woodrow Wilson's pledge to the peoples of the world.

The Tiger Takes a Trick

Leaving Foch to exercise his vindictiveness to the utmost, now that the rest of the central powers were *hors de combat*, in dictating an armistice to the Germans, the civilian leaders fell to discussing the location for the conference which was to impose a peace on Europe. Before House left for France he and the President had decided on Lausanne. They were taking it for granted that the conference must be held in a neutral country. Andrew Carnegie wrote Wilson suggesting The Hague, but when the Kaiser sought asylum in Holland that country was ruled out. Lloyd George started by suggesting the Spanish beachresort of San Sebastian. Orlando, the Italian prime minister, told House he would agree on any suitable city, preferably in Switzerland. House and Lloyd George settled on Geneva. All the while Clemenceau was quietly insisting on Versailles.

The day House cabled President Wilson for his approval of Geneva, the newspapers carried sensational news of a general strike in Switzerland. The Bolsheviks were repaying the hospitality of the Swiss during their years of exile by subsidizing revolutionary agitators there. Though the strike proved a flash in the pan Wilson took fright and cabled House that Switzerland was "saturated with every poisonous element." Clemenceau described the advantages of Paris hotels and of the stately huge buildings at Versailles. Allied statesmen were worn out from years of strain and effort, they were already in Paris: why move? They settled on Paris from sheer lassitude. To House's surprise Wilson readily agreed. Clemenceau had his way.

House confided his disappointment to his diary: "It will be difficult enough to make a just peace, and it will be almost impossible to do so while sitting in the atmosphere of a belligerent capital."

That left the final question to be decided between House and the President. On what terms should Wilson attend? Wilson had all along insisted that he must preside over the opening sessions. House's suggestion, like Houston's, was that the President should attend the preliminaries and then turn the detail work over to plenipotentiaries. It had been decided that the four victorious powers, Italy, France, Great Britain and the United States, should each be represented by a commission of five. House jotted down in private that he would like to be chairman of the American commission himself, with McAdoo and Herbert Hoover as his chief assistants.

Clemenceau's first thought when he heard that President Wilson was surely coming to Paris was that the arrival of another head of state would give Poincaré a chance to take the chair. That would never do; the Tiger intended to preside.

Lloyd George and Orlando were equally flustered. They feared Wilson would be hard to deal with. They dreaded the prospect of his appealing over their heads to their people back home. When they communicated their doubts to the colonel, House affably assured them that they would not find the President stiff and dictatorial in personal relations. Quite the contrary, House declared, he always found him amenable to advice.

The Americans whom House consulted in Paris were equally opposed to the President's trip, but for different reasons. Frank Cobb got up an impassioned memorandum on the subject:

"The moment President Wilson sits at the council table with these Prime Ministers and Foreign Secretaries he has lost all the power that comes from distance and detachment . . . In Washington President Wilson has the ear of the whole world. It is a commanding position, the position of a court of the last resort of world democracy . . . He can go before Congress and appeal to the conscience and hope of mankind . . . This is a mighty weapon, but if the President were to participate personally in the proceedings, it would be a broken stick."

Mindful of his determination "to follow his bent rather than my own" in representing Wilson in Paris, House, who knew how the President and Mrs. Wilson were looking forward to a state visit to Europe, felt he could not oppose the President's coming. He employed all his diplomatic finesse in wording a cable to the White House: "If the Peace Congress assembles in France Clemenceau will be presiding officer. If a neutral country had been chosen, you would have been asked to preside. Americans whose opinions are of value are practically unanimous in the belief it would be unwise of you to sit in the Peace Conference. They fear that it would involve a loss of dignity and your commanding position. Clemenceau has just told me that he hopes you will not sit in the Congress because no head of a state should sit there. The same feeling prevails in England. Cobb cables that Reading and Wiseman voice the same view. Everyone wants you to come over and take part in the preliminary conference."

When the President and Mrs. Wilson decoded House's cable in the privacy of the inner study they were not at all pleased. "It upset every plan we had made," Wilson cabled back waspishly. "I infer that the French and British leaders desire to exclude me from the conference for fear I might lead the weaker nations against them . . . I play the same part in my government that the prime ministers play in theirs. The fact that I am head of the state is of no practical consequence. No point of dignity must prevent our obtaining the results we have set our hearts upon and must have . . . I am thrown into complete confusion by the change of programme."

House's reply was soothing. "My judgment is that you should . . . determine upon your arrival what share it is wise for you to take in the proceedings."

Wilson had already intimated he was willing to yield the chairmanship to Clemenceau.

November 19, the morning after the President broke in on Lansing's dinner party to announce his final decision, he issued a formal announcement along the lines of House's suggestion: "The President will sail for France immediately after the opening of the regular session of Congress . . . It is not likely that it will be possible for him to remain throughout the sessions of the formal Peace Conference, but his presence at the outset is necessary . . . He will of course be accompanied by delegates who will sit as representatives of the United States throughout the Conference."

The announcement was sullenly received in Washington. In his recollections of those days Tumulty wrote that the President was profoundly distressed by the criticism "heaped upon him by his enemies on the Hill." Tumulty had never seen him look more weary or careworn: "Well Tumulty," he remembered Wilson's saying, "this trip will either be the greatest success or the supremest tragedy in all history; but I believe in a Divine Providence . . . it is my faith that no body of men, however they concert their power or their influence, can defeat this great world enterprise."

The choice of the commissioners was the subject of much correspondence. Lansing and Tumulty both backed up House in urging the President to appoint some leading Republicans such as Taft or Root or Senator Knox.

Wilson was very definite about not wanting Taft. Possibly he feared Taft might have his own ideas about how a League of Nations should be constituted. Root he wrote off as impossibly reactionary. For a while he toyed with the idea of taking Samuel W. McCall, the very Wilsonian Democratic governor of Massachusetts, or Justice Day of the Supreme Court. He was so firm in turning down Knox that none of his advisers dared suggest any other member of the Senate Committee for Foreign Affairs. Throughout the discussion Tumulty and the State Department were bombarded with names; everybody and his brother wanted to go to Paris. At last to quiet the rumormongering Tumulty gave out five names to the press.

Colonel House's choice was expected. He was already in Paris. Nobody objected to Mr. Lansing. After all he was Secretary of State. The idea of picking Henry White to represent the Republicans was received with scornful laughter. During that estimable gentleman's long diplomatic career, though nominally a Republican, he had hardly ever voted in an election. Nobody had anything against selfeffacing old General Bliss, but nobody had much to say in his favor either. The fifth name was Wilson's own.

Congress was still somewhat stunned by the fact that the list included neither a Republican nor a Democratic senator, when the President appeared before the two houses to wish them farewell. Secretary Houston sorrowfully noted the lack of enthusiasm among the legislators. The President's speech was received with unusual silence. He tried to explain that, although he was departing from precedent by sailing overseas, under modern conditions, through the use of the cables, he would be as near as if he had remained in Washington. "I shall be in close touch with you and you will know all that I do . . . I shall not be inaccessible." It was his duty to attend the Peace Conference in person to complete the good work so many brave boys had given their lives for, and to redeem America's pledge to mankind.

It was not one of Woodrow Wilson's most successful addresses. Houston described the scene: "Many Republicans and some Democrats looked as sullen and stolid as wooden men."

Aboard the George Washington

President and Mrs. Wilson sailed from New York on the old Hamburg-Amerika liner *George Washington*, long since converted into a troopship and operated by the navy. As the steamer warped out from the Hoboken dock into the turgid Hudson, full of tugs and launches packed to the gunwales with people come to see the President's departure, the presidential pennant was broken out from the mainmast. Five destroyers churning in midstream, fired a twentyone gun salute. Every steamship in the harbor let loose with its siren. The din was terrific.

Two army airplanes and a dirigible circled overhead. From every dock and from the glittering windows of Manhattan skyscrapers flags rippled under the wintry sky. When the guns ceased booming, the President and Mrs. Wilson, who were enjoying the scene from the captain's bridge, could hear faintly, fading into distance as the ship eased down the river, the cheers of an immense crowd, waving flags and handkerchiefs, that packed the Battery.

In the Narrows a gun on the old *Monitor*, of Civil War fame, anchored for her last sea duty at the opening of the submarine net, boomed a salute. A faint trilling could be heard, above the hiss of the wind through the rigging, of the voices of hundreds of schoolchildren singing "My Country, 'Tis of Thee" on the grassy slopes of Staten Island. The *George Washington* was joined by an escorting battleship in the Lower Bay and nosed out past Ambrose lightship into the heavy Atlantic swells in the center of a formation of destroyers.

Long before that the President and Edith Wilson had gone below to their quarters, where, amid what she described as "a wilderness of flowers," they were served, in their private diningroom, in the company only of Cary Grayson and of Edith Wilson's secretary, Miss Benham, a most delicious lunch. Edith noted that the luncheon was so surprisingly good because one of the best chefs from the Hotel Biltmore had been sent along to cater to the presidential party. When the President learned of it, detesting special privileges of this sort, he insisted that on his next trip he'd eat the same meals as the rest of the ship's company. Immediately after lunch the President, worn out by long days at his desk in Washington preparing for the trip, and by a bad night on the train down, went to his stateroom and slept for three hours.

Later in the afternoon, refreshed by his nap, and marshalling the air of crisp smiling charm he could assume when he felt like it, the President accompanied by Mrs. Wilson walked about the promenade deck greeting the members of their party.

There was the Secretary of State and Mrs. Lansing. Mrs. Lansing was already feeling the first qualms of seasickness, and the Secretary was hiding a torment of doubt under his huffy but deferential air. At this point he was conscientiously keeping his doubts to himself or entering them bit by bit in his private diary. He had misgivings about the entire enterprise. He was not reconciled to the President's attending the Peace Conference. His secret opinion of the Fourteen Points coincided with Theodore Roosevelt's. Particularly he could see misery and bloodshed arising out of clashing interpretations of "self-determination of nations."

There was the French Ambassador and Madame Jusserand. Monsieur Jusserand had just delivered to the President the Quai d'Orsay's proposals for the organization of a preliminary interallied conference. Any expectations Jusserand may have had that the President would confer with him on the subject during the Atlantic crossing were destined to be disappointed.

If the President gave this document any attention at all he thrust it aside without comment as another evidence of the reactionary tendencies he was going to have to combat. Neither Wilson nor his advisers seem to have given the French plan enough study to discover that it contained valuable suggestions as to procedure. Preliminary terms, including the federalization of the German empire, were to be imposed immediately. A general congress, modelled on the Congress of Vienna, where neutrals and enemy states would be represented, was to follow to take up the question of a League of Nations and the permanent pacification of the world. There was a sketch of a timetable according to which questions were to be brought up in order of their immediate importance; and, first of all—by a clause which, if it had been carried out, would have cleared up many difficulties—every secret treaty was to be cancelled.

Possibly it was some inkling of this memorandum, which threatened the Treaty of London so dear to the aspirations of Italia irredenta, that made the Italian ambassador decide all of a sudden that if Jusserand sailed on the *George Washington*, he had to go too. He threw a diplomatic tantrum in Frank Polk's office at the State Department and suitable accommodations were found at the last moment for him and for his countess and their four children and attendant servants.

Another passenger was the affable Henry White, who carried in his briefcase suggestions by Elihu Root and Henry Cabot Lodge, which were to get no more attention than the French proposals. There was the irrepressible George Creel, who still hoped, in spite of almost hysterical opposition against him building up in Congress and on newspaper row, to go on transmitting to the world the Wilsonian slogans as they fell from his master's lips. There was George W. Davis and his wife. The eminent New York lawyer was on his way to London to replace Walter Hines Page, who had come home to die in a New York hospital, as Ambassador to the Court of St. James.

Ray Stannard Baker was aboard, Wilson's fervent acolyte who was to handle the press bureau for the American commissioners, and a few other newspapermen picked as rightthinking. (The great mass of the working press had to follow on the less comfortable *Orizaba*.) Then there were the members of Colonel House's Inquiry, history professors, geographers, sociologists and experts in political economy, who were to furnish the President with the facts and figures he needed to back up his remaking of the map in accordance with principles of right and democratic justice. Along with three truckloads of printed matter the experts had been installed on the ship the night before she sailed.

In addition there was a group of highranking naval officers, two orchestras and a military band and operators and equipment for two motion picture theatres, and, below decks, a detachment of troops going as replacements to the A.E.F.

Although some of the secretservice men suffered from seasickness, the President and Edith Wilson found the trip delightful. Lifeboat drills and the threat of floating mines added a certain spice. The weather was mild.

Sunny afternoons they played shuffleboard. The President took daily naps. Sunday he attended divine service with the troops and in the evening, after another service of hymnsinging and choruses of "Over There," "Pack Up Your Troubles in Your Old Kit Bag" and "Keep the Home Fires Burning," in which the President joined with his fine tenor voice, the doughboys were allowed to file by and to shake the President's hand.

One day, when the *George Washington* was steaming past the green slopes and the misty violet cliffs of the Azores, the President called a meeting in his large parlor of the members of the Inquiry. They reported finding him relaxed, smiling, witty, and full of charm. According to Dr. Isaiah Bowman, who took notes, the President began by declaring that the Americans would be the only disinterested people at the Peace Conference.

"The men whom we were about to deal with did not represent their own people," noted Dr. Bowman. This was the first conference, the President emphasized, "that depended on the opinion of mankind." Unless the conference expressed the will of the people rather than of their leaders we would soon be involved in another breakup of the world . . . A League of Nations implied political independence and territorial integrity plus later alteration of terms and boundaries, if it could be shown that injustice had been done, or that conditions had changed. Matters could better be viewed in the light of justice when wartime passions had subsided . . . He didn't see how elasticity and security could be obtained except under a League of Nations. He envisioned a governing council selected from "the best men who could be found" and sitting in some neutral city such as The Hague or Berne. Whenever trouble occurred it could be called to the attention of the council. Boycott of trade, postal and cable facilities would be an alternative to war against offending nations.

The people of the world wanted a new world order. If it didn't work it must be made to work. The world readily accepted the poison of bolshevism because it was a protest against the way in which the world had worked. It was the business of the American delegation at the Peace Conference to fight for a new world order, "agreeably if we can, but disagreeably if necessary."

A friendly personal note entered his voice. He hoped to see his experts frequently. His smile sought out every face. They would work through the commissioners to be sure, but in case of emergency he wanted them not to fail to bring any critical matter to his personal attention. He wound up with a phrase that went straight to the hearts of the members of the Inquiry: "Tell me what's right and I'll fight for it."

Chapter 23

IT wasn't till December 13, amid the salutes of the French fleet and of six American battleships and of whole schools of destroyers, that the slow old *George Washington* steamed into the harbor of Brest. The date delighted the President. Thirteen was his lucky number. The rain held off. As they approached the shore the sky cleared and the sun shone through the smoke of the twentyone gun salutes. Mrs. Wilson found the day "radiant, just cold enough to be exhilarating."

While the Wilsons were snatching an early luncheon the ship dropped anchor. Immediately their staterooms swarmed with officials. There was Monsieur Pichon and the Minister of Marine and a flock of French generals and General Pershing and General Bliss and Admiral Sims and Admiral Benson. "After much kissing of my hand by the foreigners and clicking of heels and presenting of bouquets and general good humor," remembered Edith Wilson, "we left our good ship to go ashore in a tender called *The Gun.*"

They admired the gray stone harbor and the fishing boats with blue and tan sails hauled up on the rocks in the basin and the slatecolored town rising in terraces to the old castle of the dukes of Brittany. At the dock they found more officials, more gold braid, crack squads of French troops drawn up at attention, and the President's daughter Margaret, who had been dutifully singing for the doughboys in Y.M.C.A. huts. "Poor child," noted Edith Wilson, "the food or the climate had not agreed with her and she was really quite ill. We were glad to take her under our care."

After a round of speechmaking the presidential party climbed into open touring cars and was driven through narrow dank streets lined with men and women in their best Breton costumes. The khaki of crowds of American soldiers stood out against the dark clothing of the French. They passed through triumphal arches. The walls were placarded with signs in red: LE PRESIDENT WILSON A BIEN MERITE DE L'HUMANITE.

This was no programmed demonstration. Women in black had tears in their eyes. Wounded war veterans applauded with their stumps if they had no hands. The throngs were shouting themselves hoarse: *Vive Veelson.*

At the railroad station a crimson carpet led them to a *train de luxe* with the monogram RF painted on every dark blue coach. The President and Mrs. Wilson were ensconced in President Poincaré's own sleeping-car. Edith remarked that it was far from being modern or luxurious. The bunks were hard. "No part of the train was clean and the sheets felt damp as if just washed."

There was a long wait and a number of mixups about baggage. It was dusk before the train pulled out. At dinner in the state diningcar, where Edith Wilson noted privately that the service was terrible, she amused herself during the wait between courses, collecting on her menu card the autographs of all the important personages assembled.

Again the sun was shining when they reached Paris in midmorning on December 14. The train drew up at a rural looking station. As the President and Mrs. Wilson stepped down from their sleeper they were greeted by the President of the Republic, the entire Cabinet and the staff of the American Embassy. After a round of speechmaking and a fanfare from the Garde Republicain President Wilson and President Poincaré settled themselves in an open victoria, while the ladies, Madame Poincaré, Madame Jusserand, Mrs. Wilson and daughter Margaret were accommodated in a landau.

The brass of their helmets glinting under the horsetails in the wintry sun, the Garde Republicain, on their fine clanking horses, led the parade to the Champs Elysées. The great chains under the Arc de Triomphe were pulled away for the first time, it was whispered to Mrs. Wilson, since 1871, and the two Presidents passed under the arch.

Along the curbs of the great avenue were ranks of captured German cannon. Over them fluttered the tricolor and Old Glory endlessly alternated. Facing the narrow strip of pavement they kept open for the carriages stood files of poilus in horizon blue. Everything: guns, roofs, balconies, was crowded with cheering shouting people. "Even the stately horsechestnut trees," noticed Edith, "were peopled with men and boys perched like sparrows in their very tops . . . One grew giddy trying to greet the bursts of welcome that came like the surging of untamed waters. Flowers rained upon us until we were nearly buried."

Occasionally above the packed heads they could read on a kiosk or on a piece of bare wall the placarded words: WILSON LE JUSTE.

They were driven through the Place de la Concorde, more crowded, they were told, than even on the day of the armistice; and past the Vendôme column and the templeform church of the Madeleine; then out another boulevard where all they could see was swarming faces and cheering mouths, to a street blocked off by soldiers, where stood the mansion assigned them for a domicile. Great wroughtiron gates set in a high stucco wall opened between blue and red sentryboxes for the carriages to enter and closed behind.

In *My Memoir* Edith went to some length to describe the magnificence of the Hôtel de Mûrat; the gleaming parquet, the tall mirrors, the flame-colored brocades, the broad sweeping stairway. "Enchanting suites" were reserved for the President and herself. The hangings were embroidered in fiery gold with the Napoleonic eagle. There was a gold toilet set with the Mûrat crest in her marble bathroom and tall crystal bottles of orange-flower water.

In the President's bedroom the walls and draperies were of green damask studded with the gold bees of the Empire.

Edith Wilson hardly had time to glance into the cabinets full of *objets d'art* in her crimson and ivory parlor, before they had to change their clothes for the official luncheon at the Elysée Palace. The party was thrown into a dither by the announcement by a flustered young American liaison officer that everybody at the Elysée would be wearing a frock coat. These garments were already considered obsolete in America except by a few rural senators. The President was planning on striped pants and a cutaway. After a search through the trunks, Brooks, the President's colored valet, triumphantly produced not only one but two frock coats. He'd guessed they might be needed, he said, grinning. "One never knows different customs in different countries."

Idling the Days Away

So much of the afternoon was taken up by the luncheon, and the break-neck exchange of official visits demanded by protocol between President and Madame Poincaré and President and Mrs. Wilson, to the accompaniment of the rolling of drums from the guard of honor, that it was late before Wilson could get in a private word with his confidential colonel.

House found the President in a disgruntled mood. He seemed to be suffering a reaction from the exultation of his welcome. House, who may have suspected Wilson was a little miffed because his alter ego had not come to Brest to meet him, hastily explained that he hadn't yet recovered his strength after the bout of influenza that had kept him ten days in bed. Other members of American missions were dangerously ill. Willard Straight died of it. House's doctor had forbidden him to make the trip. House turned to pleasanter matters. He congratulated the President on having induced the British and French to lift the censorship of American press cables.

Wilson was inquiring with some bitterness why the conference on peace terms couldn't start immediately. He had planned on December 16. House pointed out that Lloyd George would not make a move until he knew the results of the general election in the United Kingdom. The French were quite content to wait while the Germans and Austrians starved a little more. All the Allies were sabotaging Herbert Hoover's efforts to get food and supplies moving towards populations in desperate need.

Wilson had already taken a dislike to Poincaré. He suspected the sawedoff little Président de la République of being behind the French Government's refusal to let workingclass delegations meet him at Brest. Permission was withdrawn at the last moment for the labor unions to lead a mammoth parade through Paris to greet the American President and to endorse the Fourteen Points. Wilson had planned to address them from the balcony of the Hôtel de Mûrat. The French Government was getting between him and the French people.

Then there was Lansing. The President complained that Lansing had tried to pack the *George Washington* with State Department people. "I found him in an ugly mood towards Lansing," House noted in his diary. House took advantage of that mood to put in a plug for his own organization by telling the President how favorably impressed the specialists of the Inquiry were by his frank chat with them on the boat.

House admitted that Lansing was tactless. Still the President must remember that Lansing was playing a minor part and playing it without complaint. Jealousies between the State Department crowd and the Inquiry were inevitable. "I am sure Lansing does not mean to be brusque and impolite but he has an unfortunate manner."

During the days that followed, President and Mrs. Wilson had every moment taken as they hurried from formal luncheons to formal dinners. They were always changing their clothes. They visited hospitals, they laid a wreath on Lafayette's tomb, they listened to interminable speeches at the Hôtel de Ville, where the President was presented by the city authorities of Paris with a handsome gold pen to sign the treaty with, and Edith Wilson with "a beautiful Lalique box containing a most unusual pin composed of six doves of peace made of rose quartz."

Whenever Wilson wasn't delivering speeches or listening to speeches he was kept busy receiving callers: Clemenceau, Foch, Pershing, Venizelos with a pair of bodyguards in starched white kilts; military and civilian leaders from countries great and small. "Each day brought more interesting people," Edith Wilson wrote, "and every hour was parcelled out."

House meanwhile was trying to build a fire under the Allied statesmen. He got hold of Northcliffe, the selfrighteous lord of a large section of the British press, and tried to scare him with Herbert Hoover's documented reports that the most fearful famine since the Thirty Years War impended in Europe. Famine threatened the defeated nations and the newborn republics with disintegration and chaos. The heirs of chaos would be the Communists.

House urged Northcliffe to use the power of his great press to bring some sense of urgency to the politicians.

"Northcliffe and I agreed that the President should visit England at once and receive the reception there which we knew awaited him." According to House's notes Northcliffe further agreed with him that Wilson's reception by the Paris populace had already changed the attitude of the French politicians. "We believe that if he goes to England and gets such an endorsement from the English people, Lloyd George and his colleagues will not dare oppose his policies at the Peace Conference."

It was clear by this time that it would be the middle of January before the interallied conference, still thought of as preliminary to the real Peace Conference, could get started. In the interval House advised the President to make state visits to England and to Italy.

The colonel, who had moved his organization to the Crillon when that handsome old hostelry became the headquarters of the American commissioners, chaperoned some preliminary meetings between the President and Clemenceau. House considered the first meeting a success. "Neither said anything that was particularly misleading. They simply did not touch upon topics which would breed discussion."

A few days later, when Clemenceau called on the President for a second time at the Hôtel de Mûrat, House noted that in the hour and a half they were together the President did nearly all the talking. "Clemenceau expressed himself in a mild way in agreement . . . He thought a League of Nations should be attempted, but he was not confident of success either of forming it or of its being workable after it was formed."

A meeting, carefully stagemanaged by House, between the President and bland Premier Orlando and avid hawkfaced Sonnino, the redheaded Italian Minister of Foreign Affairs, was similarly ineffectual. "The President talked well but he did not convince the Italians that they should lessen their hold on the Pact of London."

The French presidential train was brought out once more to take the Wilsons to Chaumont to spend Christmas with the A.E.F. Edith Wilson found it more uncomfortable than ever. The heat didn't work. "The sheets in the icy beds felt damp and dangerous." She wondered how they lived through the miserable night without catching pneumonia. They reached Pershing's general headquarters in a snowstorm and toured the barns and farmyards where the doughboys were billeted. Edith Wilson found touching their efforts at Christmas decorations with green sprays and bits of red paper. Both she and her husband were impressed by the discomforts the doughboys were undergoing through the French winter.

Deep mud and driving sleet took some of the sparkle out of the military show put on for them by the 77th Division. Even mules bogged in the mire. They ate Christmas dinner in a cantonment with the soldiers.

The only warm place they found in Lorraine was General Pershing's chateau where a welcoming fire roared in the hearth and hot tea was ready for them. There was a dreary train ride back to Paris and next day they started for England.

Colonel House failed to accompany the President. He was husbanding his health, and he felt he was more useful in Paris trying to talk Clemenceau around to the Fourteen Points than appearing in short pants at the Court of St. James. In his place he sent his soninlaw Gordon Auchincloss. Auchincloss, an uppety young man to begin with, was becoming a little too conscious of the importance of his position. The President's secretaries blamed him for not getting them invited to the state banquets. He officiously made daily reports to House over the longdistance telephone and managed to give Mrs. Wilson and Cary Grayson the impression that the colonel had sent him along to spy on their doings. They promptly infected the President with their suspicions.

From Auchincloss's phone calls House heard the details of the British election. It was the first election since woman's suffrage, and there was a large soldier vote. Lloyd George ran scared. Though he began his campaign with a number of speeches advocating a peace of justice and a League of Nations in Wilsonian style, the wily Welshman soon found that the three topics that appealed to his listeners were immediate demobilization of conscripted men, making the Germans pay the whole cost of the war and trying the German leaders as warcriminals. "Make the 'uns pay to the last farthing" and "'ang the Kaiser" became the slogans of his campaign. The result was a landslide victory for Lloyd George and for his coalition government. The khaki election, it came to be called.

House had hardly digested the results of the khaki election when he learned of the overwhelming four to one vote of confidence Clemenceau won in the Chamber of Deputies the night of December 29. The Tiger spoke sarcastically of Woodrow Wilson's plans. He described what he called *"la noble candeur"* of the American President. All Paris fell to discussing the exact shade of meaning in the French phrase. *"Candeur"* could be translated as candor but it could also be translated as the simplicity of the village idiot. When Clemenceau told the chamber that he preferred firm treaties and alliances to preserve the balance of power to some chancy League of Nations the deputies rose in a stormy ovation.

House noted that this was about as poor an augury as could be for the success of progressive principles. The facts were exactly the opposite of Wilson's highflown declaration to the specialists on the *George Washington:* "The men whom we are about to deal with do not represent their own people." Of the four national leaders on whom the main decisions would rest at the Peace Conference, Woodrow Wilson was the only one who had been repudiated at the polls.

"Coming on the heels of the English elections," noted House dismally in his diary on the last day of the old year, "and taking into consideration the result of recent elections in the United States, the situation strategically could not be worse."

Edith Wilson's Grand Tour

The royal train that picked up President and Mrs. Wilson at Calais was "luxuriously comfortable." King George and Queen Mary met them at Charing Cross Station at the end of a red carpet lined with potted palms. They were driven to Buckingham Palace in the cumbersome old royal coaches by coachmen in periwigs. Footmen in crimson liveries perched behind. The day turned out sunny. In spite of Boxing Day being a bank holiday, the streets of downtown London were packed with people shouting "We want Wilson." When they passed Marlborough House the dowager Queen Alexandra was seen leaning out of a window, kissing her hand and waving a small American flag. In every open space troops were drawn up at attention and brass bands played.

The courtyard of the palace was massed with American doughboys, with hospital cases, on crutches or in wheelchairs, in the front rank. A great shout went up as, with his silk hat in his hand, Woodrow Wilson stepped from the coach to greet them.

The President and Mrs. Wilson had hardly settled in their state apartments, which they found stacked with baskets of roses from members of the Cabinet and thoroughly chilly from the lack of steam heat, when the President was asked to address the crowd from the balcony. His speech aroused prolonged cheering and the waving of English and American flags.

The King and Queen could not have been more considerate. Through the days that followed the Wilson party moved in the complicated evolutions of court etiquette. Edith performed the ceremonial acts with rapture. The President caused some sartorial confusion by appearing in plain evening clothes, which meant that all the gentlemen-in-waiting had to do likewise. Cary Grayson preened himself in a fulldress admiral's uniform.

In the houses of the politicians conversation was freer than at the state banquets, where they ate under the stern gaze of beefeaters with halberds. While the President was meeting the past, present and future prime ministers at a luncheon tendered him by Lloyd George at 10 Downing Street, Mrs. Wilson was entertained by Lady Reading. Next her at table sat Margot Asquith, whom Edith described as smoking incessantly and scratching her matches, as some men did on their pants, on the seat of her tailored dress. She announced she was dying to meet the President because she had never yet met an American with brains.

After the traditional receptions at Guild Hall by the Lord Mayor of London, and turtle soup at the Mansion House, the royal train with the royal sleepingcar attached carried the presidential party up into the North to Carlisle. According to House's diary, he and Northcliffe cooked up this visit of the President to his mother's English birthplace as sure to appeal to English middleclass sentiments.

On a rainy Sunday morning the Wilsons attended the service in his grandfather Woodrow's church and in the afternoon their train took them to Manchester, the capital of the nineteenthcentury liberalism Woodrow Wilson was brought up in. There after accepting the freedom of the city at a municipal banquet, he delivered in Free Trade Hall a speech which he and House had prayerfully concocted in Paris a few days before.

He touched on the immense complexity of the problems, petitions, demands irreconcilable each with the other, that had poured in on him since he had landed in Europe. "I am not hopeful," he admitted, "that the terms of the settlement will be altogether satisfactory . . . Interest does not bind men together, interest separates men," he exclaimed. "There is only one thing that can bind people together, and that is a common devotion to right . . . We are not obeying the mandate of party or politics, we are obeying the mandate of humanity."

Only a League of Nations would "provide the machinery of readjustment" to right whatever wrongs might be perpetuated in the tugging and hauling he was anticipating at the Peace Conference. His frankness was wellreceived. His idealistic phrases stirred the Midlands crowd. He came away feeling that in Manchester he had met one of his most understanding audiences.

Returning to the Continent on New Year's Day of 1919 the Wilsons spent only a few hours in Paris. The President found time for a long talk with House. They discussed the economic commission on which Baruch and Vance McCormick, who were sailing from New York that day, would serve with Herbert Hoover to try to formulate an American policy towards the Allied demands on Germany for reparations, which were getting more exorbitant every day. House was to be chairman.

The President gave House a lively account of the British political figures he had hobnobbed with in London. Wilson did not feel at home in the fashionable club atmosphere of British politics. House remarked maliciously that Wilson's trip had robbed the British statesmen of their Christmas vacations on the Riviera. They had all stayed home to welcome him. House pronounced himself delighted with the popular response to the President's visit to England.

House then brought up the ticklish question of getting cooperation out of the Republican Congress. He wanted the President to tell the Republicans that legislation was now their affair. His advice was to follow the policy of give and take. House could note the familiar stiffening of the President's jaw at that suggestion.

"He had grown so accustomed to almost dictatorial powers," House confided in his diary, "it will go hard to give them up."

After accomplishing a series of official chores the President drove with Mrs. Wilson in the evening to the Gare de Lyon, where the Italian royal train awaited them. "To my surprise," wrote Edith, "the Italian train was the most magnificent of all. I had never seen anything like it: servants in livery of royal scarlet; plate, china and glassware bearing the Italian arms; table linen and bed linen beautifully embroidered."

The Italian ambassador to Washington and a "tall lugubrious-looking individual wearing a longtailed frock coat and looking like the undertaker at an important funeral" who represented the King of Italy were hosts on the train. Margaret Wilson and Miss Benham were of the party and, of course, the indispensable Dr. Grayson who cared for two of the ladies who were taken with travellers' ills on the journey.

Next morning the American ambassador to Rome met them at the frontier. They stopped in Genoa long enough for the President to visit the house Columbus was reputed to have been born in. The journey south was lovely. "Our arrival in Rome," wrote Edith Wilson, "will always be the most brilliant canvas in all the rich pictures in my memory." No more rain. The sky was sapphire blue. Golden sand had been spread on the streets traversed by the state *cortège*. Brocades and velvets embroidered with coats of arms in tarnished gold hung from the balconies.

The Quirinal Palace, where they were lodged, was still used as a military hospital, but one wing had been furnished with tapestries and rugs and museum pieces of statuary and of Renaissance furniture. The pictures were a collector's dream. Every window of their suite of rooms looked out on a garden full of flowers. Edith Wilson was told that a hundred thousand people packed the streets and squares around the palace waiting for her husband to show himself on the balcony.

During all the state dinners and the mummery and the toasts of his visit to Rome, Woodrow Wilson was tortured by the prospect of having to call on the Pope. Various State Department advisers and members of the diplomatic corps had been insisting that such a visit was essential. Protestant missionaries were bitterly protesting. All the President's Presbyterian hackles rose at the thought. He had consented to go to the Vatican with the proviso that he should spend the same amount of time calling on his friend the Reverend Mr. Lowry, the rector of the American Episcopal Church.

The President's ride across Rome to the Vatican, standing up in an open touring car, developed into a triumphal procession. The crowd was so great His Holiness was kept waiting fortyfive minutes.

The President had let it be known that on his return from the Vatican he would address, from the window of the Quirinal, the enormous crowd that had gathered in the square outside. He was intending to undercut Orlando and Sonnino through a direct appeal to the Italian people to back the Fourteen Points. When he returned from his papal audience he found that squads of police had dispersed the crowd.

This discourtesy threw the President into a cold rage. He let loose to the newspapermen gathered about him in no uncertain terms. The incident threw a chill over the rest of the Italian trip, although the enthusiasm of the crowds in Milan surpassed that of the crowds in Rome.

In Milan the President's presence had been advertised for a gala performance of *Aïda* at La Scala. It was a Sunday. The President declared he never went to the theatre on Sunday. The Italian chief of protocol smoothly explained that this was a "sacred concert," and the President allowed himself to be placed in a box where he listened solemnly while choruses sang the national anthems and soloists caroled out some arias from church music. Right after, the curtain rose and *Aïda* was performed in its entirety.

In Turin the President harangued a thousand mayors from the cities and towns of the Piedmont region who had gathered to greet him. They represented men of every walk of life, bankers, merchants, farmers, storekeepers, blacksmiths. When he shook hands with them all after his address a few of the more rustic mayors bent over and kissed his hand. The President was deeply touched.

At the university an honorary degree was bestowed on him. Edith felt her husband was at his best in the simple friendly speech of appreciation he addressed to the students. He brought down the house by putting on a blue student cap. "How young and virile he looked as he stood there," she exclaimed.

These stately progresses seemed to Edith Wilson the consummation of her girlhood dreams. "Fate having chosen me," she wrote in *My Memoir*, "for such a Cinderella role, I have tried to picture it for others, in an endeavor to make a return for this great privilege which was mine."

Colonel House's Predicament

When the Wilsons arrived back in Paris on January 7, fagged by many functions and long trainrides, the President was determined that ceremonial engagements should no longer be allowed to interfere with the work of peacemaking. He instructed his secretary to accept no more invitations.

As soon as he was settled at the Hôtel de Mûrat, he called his confidential colonel on the private telephone line he'd had installed between his study and House's room at the Crillon, to be brought up to date on the news. The formal opening of the Peace Conference was set for January 18.

The American commissioners were meeting that afternoon at House's rooms at the Crillon. Much to Lansing's chagrin, House—who with innocent vanity noted in his diary that he had more rooms than all the other commissioners put together—usually managed to have them meet in his suite. The President, whose familiars were already dropping hints that the confidential colonel was taking too much the center of the stage during his absences, sent word that he would be there at five to preside over this meeting in person. Almost at the same moment a message arrived from Clemenceau that he too was calling on House at five P.M. for a private talk.

The colonel faced a dilemma. Even his worldfamous tact was strained to meet this test.

"The President came first," House noted. "I brought him to my reception room and had the other commissioners meet him." The President of the United States had just started a lively discussion with Lansing and Bliss and White on the difficulties they were facing, when Monsieur le Président du Conseil de Ministres was announced. "I asked President Wilson to excuse me and took Clemenceau into another room, where we had one of our heart to heart talks."

Clemenceau, one of the most malicious of men, who liked House, but was already complaining that Wilson thought he was Jesus Christ, undoubtedly appreciated the possibilities for mischief. Keeping the President of the United States waiting in the anteroom was as much fun as putting something over on Poincaré. He dawdled over his conversation with House.

House was preoccupied with his task: "I convinced him," House dictated to the faithful Miss Denton when she typed out his diary, "I think, for the first time that a League of Nations was for the best interests of France . . . I called his attention to the fact that today there was only one great military power on the Continent of Europe and that was France . . . There was no balance of power so far as the Continent was concerned, because Russia had disappeared and both Germany and Austria had gone under . . . I asked whether or not in the circumstances France would not feel safer if England and America were in a position where they would be compelled to come to the aid of France in the event another nation like Germany should try to crush her . . . If she lost this chance which the United States offered through the League of Nations it would never come again . . . Wilson could force it through because, with all the brag and bluster of the Senate, they would not dare defeat a treaty made in agreement with the Allies, and thereby continue alone the war with Germany or make a separate peace."

Clemenceau in his *Splendeur et Misère de la Victoire* described House with approval as "a supercivilized person escaped from the wilds of Texas, who sees everything, understands everything, and while never doing anything but what he thinks fit, knew how to gain the ear and the respect of everybody." Certainly he wanted House to think well of him.

Maybe he really was convinced, for the moment. "The old man seemed to see it all," noted House, "and became enthusiastic. He placed both hands on my shoulders and said, 'You are right. I am for the League of Nations as you have it in mind and you may count upon me to work with you.'"

House took advantage of the Tiger's enthusiasm to bring up the troublesome matter of reparations. Certain sections of the French press, known to be "inspired" by the government, were beginning to call for the cancellation of American war debts, at the same time demanding incredible billions in reparations from Germany. The Germans must not only be made to pay the whole cost of the war and repair all the damage the war had done, but they must furnish pensions for Allied veterans. "I urged him to use his influence to discourage such schemes. They were doing harm to France and would eventually prejudice the Americans against her."

When House finally ushered Clemenceau into the meeting of the commissioners, it was obvious that the colonel's absence had lasted too long. The President had been left to mark time with what he'd come to consider a group of dunderheads. Observers noted the chill in Wilson's manner. Some dated from that moment the President's alienation from his confidential colonel.

Paris under the Flood

During the first days of January all Paris tingled with expectation. The city had never been more crowded. The population awaited the opening of the Peace Conference as they would await the opening of the season of horseracing or a world's fair. People resorted to every conceivable intrigue to obtain admission to the opening session set for the Salon de l'Orloge at the Quai d'Orsay.

Every great hostelry flaunted the flag of some foreign potentate. The less expensive *hôtels meublés* were packed with humbler representatives of every nation, tribe, enclave, minority on the Eurasian continent. In uniform and out of uniform Greeks, Macedonians, Serbs, Montenegrins,

Croats, Slovenes, Czechs and Slovaks, Transylvanians, Ukrainians, Galicians, Poles, Lithuanians, Esthonians, Latvians milled in the lobbies. There were robed Arabs of the Hedjaz chaperoned by legendary young Colonel Lawrence.

There were Palestine Arabs and Arabs of the Mespot, Persians, Kurds, Syrians, Christian Lebanese and Moslem Lebanese; representatives of Armenia and Azerbaidjan and Caucasian Georgia. There were Jewish Zionists, and contesting factions of Poles and Silesians and an envoy from the Duchy of Teschen.

Luxemburg had its mission, and Lichtenstein. A Swedish committee had come to ask for the Aaland Islands. Danish diplomats arrived to demand Schleswig-Holstein. Each group wanted something at the expense of its neighbors.

The American Commissioners Plenipotentiary had their offices at 4 Place de la Concorde in a rambling suite which included the old *cabinets particuliers* upstairs from Maxims, with their memories of the grand dukes and the superannuated whoopee of the Second Empire. Navy yeomen were in charge: Harold Nicolson remarked that the place smelled like a battleship. There security was rigorous. Marines scrutinized passes so sharply that many an important personage was left kicking his heels in the guardroom while clerks scuttled about looking for his identification. At the entrance swarthy delegations stormed around the tall immovable sentries begging for appointments with *"Monsieur le Président Veelson."*

Disappointed there they would troop up the Champs Elysées to the Hotel Astoria near the Arc de Triomphe, where the British delegations had their offices. Every province of the empire on which the sun never set had its representative, with attendant bevies of experts and specialists. The entrance was barred to foreign inroads by a cordon of Tommies resplendent with brasspolish and pipeclay.

Around the edges of the recognized delegations hovered all sorts of adventurers peddling oil concessions or manganese mines, pretenders to dukedoms and thrones, cranks with shortcuts to Utopia in their briefcases, secret agents, art dealers, rug salesmen, procurers and pimps. *Petites femmes* solicited strangers on the boulevards with scraps of all the languages of Europe. Restaurants and nightclubs were packed to the last table. Taxis were at a premium. Business boomed at the Maison des Nations.

Even the Seine was in flood. The autumn rains had turned to intermittent slushy snow. The quais and lowlying streets were awash and the brown water swirled as high as the carved keystones of the bridges.

He Didn't Want Any Lawyers

Excited by the carnival atmosphere, thrilled by the hope of humane and rational solutions, the younger men among the British and American delegations got along famously. They swapped back copies of *The Nation* and *The New Republic* for *The Spectator* or *The Round Table*. They exchanged luncheons at the Crillon for luncheons at the Hotel Majestic, where the British had imported an entire London staff, from headwaiter to dishwasher, so that their tabletalk should not be reported to foreign ears.

At the Crillon the eager young men might be rewarded with a glimpse of Colonel House's receding chin as he slipped with silent tread down a corridor, but the important personages among the Americans kept out of sight.

At the Majestic the British leaders ate in full view. While you talked of the League the tall figure of its fosterfather, Lord Robert Cecil of the bulging forehead and bushy hair, might be seen unfolding like a jackknife from behind a table.

For any world problem you could find an expert with the facts at his fingertips. A great number of dedicated and wellintentioned and wellprepared people were putting all they had into solving the world's ills. The American specialists were encouraged to find such likemindedness among the British. Such of them as could get through the language barrier found occasional young Frenchmen unexpectedly in accord. Full of hope they compared their plans to fashion a just peace and a League of Nations that would work.

Left in a certain isolation by the fact that the livelier spirits tended to foregather in Colonel House's anterooms, the Secretary of State kept his nose to the grindstone. Lansing was a conscientious man. He liked precision. He was convinced that careful agenda must be prepared for the coming meetings. Over the Christmas period he suffered agonies from an ulcerated tooth. Mrs. Lansing was not a bit well. Illness in the family did not keep him from carefully elaborating a skeleton plan for a treaty for the President's use, or from cooperating with House's specialists in drawing up a tentative formula for a League of Nations. When he tried to explain his schemes to the President, he discovered, to his mortification, that the President was not in the least interested.

Wilson had his own ideas. According to House, he was still trying to fit his own sketch of a covenant for a League of Nations into thirteen headings. His constitution for the league was based on the draft House had presented the summer before. House's assistants were sitting up nights harmonizing this document with Cecil's reworking of the British Phillimore Committee's plan, which had just been flown over from London, after some final touches by the energetic hand of the South African representative, Jan Christiaan Smuts. The President let Lansing know in no uncertain terms that he didn't want him to meddle in the business. He didn't want any lawyers, he told him in the tone he knew how to make so disagreeable. Problems of procedure did not interest him.

Lansing like House was a careful diarist. He made his entries in a small precise hand. On January 10 he recalled the hour's conference with the President and the commissioners in General Bliss's room, at which he presented his memorandum. "A very unsatisfactory session," wrote Lansing. "Pres't apparently resents anybody offering suggestions or doing anything in the way of drafting a treaty for a league of nations except himself . . . He said he did not want lawyers to engage in that."

Lansing was proud of his knowledge of international law. It was his whole career. This remark of the President's cut him to the quick. Years later, when he published his apologia for his part in the drama he wrote a whole chapter about it. From that moment he made no further suggestions about the covenant or the league.

He unburdened himself to his diary. "Auchincloss has shown me the President's draft. It is most inartistically drawn and I believe will be riddled in its present form."

Secretary Lansing had disagreed with the President once too often. From now on he was held at arm's length. "Lansing is a man one cannot grow enthusiastic over," House noted, "but I do think the President should treat him with more consideration."

Two days later House was taken ill with a kidney ailment. He had a high fever and was in great pain. He had two nurses in attendance. The story got about that he was dying. Obituaries were actually published in the American press.

With Lansing mortally offended and his confidential colonel incapacitated, Wilson, who paid scant attention to the prolixities of General Bliss or to Henry White's diplomatic anecdotes, and who didn't even have a competent secretary, was left to struggle singlehanded in his initial bout with a group of the most astute political operators in Europe and Asia.

The Council of X

The leaders of the British delegation arrived in Paris on January 11. Lloyd George, fresh from his smashing victory at the polls, came surrounded by some of the ablest men in the United Kingdom. All political factions were represented except for Asquith's Liberals. Arthur Balfour embodied the philosophy of the Conservative gentry in its most rarified form. Bonar Law could speak for the financial and manufacturing and mercantile interests, George Barnes for the trade unions. Cecil and Smuts, who were to be the godfathers of the British Commonwealth of Nations, stood for an international idealism as radical as Woodrow Wilson's.

As a second string, Lloyd George, who was as skilled, as Wilson was deficient, in the art of using other men for his own purposes, had the premiers of the selfgoverning dominions: Hughes from Australia, Massey from New Zealand, Sir Robert Borden from Canada. Each of them represented the majority parties of their respective electorates. Smuts and Botha, at that moment, had all factions in South Africa behind them. In the background was a bevy of emirs and maharajahs, each animated by a knowledgeable Foreign Office adviser, from India and the Oriental protectorates. To organize and synchronize the work of the delegations came the accomplished Sir Maurice Hankey, fresh from a similar job for the Imperial War Cabinet. Largely because the Americans could not present anyone equally competent, Hankey became confidential secretary of the inner circle of the Peace Conference, and the only reporter of the most secret meetings of the Allied leaders.

The British prime minister arrived in Paris at the head of one of the most formidable groups of negotiators ever assembled. "On the other hand," as Winston Churchill, who was then serving as Secretary of State for War put it, "he reached the Conference somewhat dishevelled by the vulgarities and blatancies of the recent general election. Pinned to his coat tails were the posters 'Hang the Kaiser,' 'Search their pockets,' 'Make them pay'; and this sensibly detracted from the dignity of his entrance on the scene."

The French, as hosts of the British and American delegations, had the advantage of being on their home ground. The Quai d'Orsay was almost as wellfurnished with brains as the Foreign Office. Clemenceau had the Chamber of Deputies under his thumb. Through Mandel's alternating censorship and subsidy, he could play like an organist on all the varied political pipes, right, left and center, of the French press.

Though the Tiger found Foch and his generals even more troublesome in victory than they had been in defeat, he could give them their heads from time to time when he needed a *fait accompli*.

British observers noticed how much slower the Americans were than the Europeans in the give and take of repartee in committee work.

Although the prime ministers had been meeting right along in the guise of the Supreme War Council or at less formal interallied conferences, and had already established a set of rules by which they hoped to keep control of proceedings, the British and French looked forward with misgivings to the first plenary meetings of the representatives of all the Allied and Associated Powers. They knew that Lansing's project was for the United States to marshal the smaller nations against what the Americans

considered the evil designs of the Europeans, and they feared that, in
the absence of the understanding Colonel House, he might carry President Wilson along with him.

Since Lansing's crowd from the State Department commandeered all
the tickets available for Americans, the members of House's Inquiry, temporarily bereft of their guardian, had to content themselves on January 18
with watching the arrival of the dignitaries from the courtyard of the
Foreign Office. Each arrival was greeted by a fanfare and a roll of drums
as the plenipotentiary descended from his automobile or carriage. President Wilson removed his silk hat and bared his horseteeth in a good long
smile for the benefit of the motionpicture cameras.

The arrival of the plenipotentiaries was a lengthy parade. The United
States, Great Britain and France each had five delegates and, to the surprise of the bystanders, so had Japan. The Japanese diplomats had taken
advantage of the Americans neglecting to attend a somewhat surreptitious meeting of the interallied council held in London before Christmas,
while House was laid up with the flu, to insist that the British stand by
their alliance. At a period in the war when Japanese torpedoboats were
desperately needed for convoy service in the Mediterranean, the British
had made further promises. So now five Japanese delegates, smiling and
bowing and hissing through their teeth, filed in towards the seats allotted
to the great powers. Without anybody's knowing exactly how it happened
the Big Four had become the Big Five.

Next in importance came Belgium, and Brazil, which had also furnished
a few torpedoboats; and the Kingdom of the Serbs, Croats and Slovenes,
with three delegates each. Then came China, Greece, the Hedjaz, Poland, Portugal, Rumania, Siam and the brandnew Czechoslovak Republic,
with two. A crowd of nations that had been merely "technical belligerents"
followed: Cuba, Guatemala, Haiti, Honduras, Liberia, Nicaragua, Panama, Bolivia, Uruguay, Ecuador and Peru had one delegate apiece.

The confirmation of Japan's admission to the inner circle, during the
confused skirmishing of the final week before the Peace Conference
opened, was a defeat for Woodrow Wilson. Another was the admission
of five British dominions, which were also represented on the British Empire delegation, to the sessions in their own right. That afternoon at the
Quai d'Orsay, two delegates were seated for Canada, Australia, South
Africa and India, and one for New Zealand. As balm for President Wilson's hurt feelings, he was allowed to remove Costa Rica, ruled by a dictator of whom he disapproved, from the list of technical belligerents.

When all the delegates were seated in the splendor of diplomatic uniforms or the gravity of frock coats amid the scarlet damask and the
ormoulu, under the glittering chandeliers reflected in the long mirrors,
amid the smell of furniture polish and musty hangings and pomade and

cologne, President Poincaré arrived with a welcoming speech. Amid the applause that followed he waddled from delegate to delegate until he had shaken every hand. Some of the British amused themselves by noting that Mr. Wilson wore oldfashioned highbuttoned shoes.

Monsieur Clemenceau, in black skull cap and lisle gloves, hastened to assume the chair, provisionally it was announced. President Wilson gracefully proposed him for permanent chairman and he was duly elected. He proceeded expeditiously to conduct the election of vice presidents, a secretary, commissions to deal with this and that.

The first two items of the agenda were no surprise to anybody. (1) Responsibility of the authors of the war, (2) Responsibility for the crimes committed in the war. The third created quite a hubbub: legislation with regard to international labor. This was a tribute to the Communist threat.

Clemenceau allowed nobody to catch his breath. He raced through the items. The powers were requested to submit memoranda on these questions. In compliment to Mr. Wilson it was announced that at the next plenary meeting a society of nations would come first in the order of the day. Before anybody had put in a word the Tiger declared the meeting adjourned.

Harold Nicolson who attended as a young Foreign Office brain described Clemenceau as "highhanded with the smaller powers . . . 'Y-a-t-il d'objections . . . ? Non . . . adopté' . . . like a machine gun."

As they were getting their coats in the lobby, a friend of Nicolson's found himself next to the veteran French diplomat Jules Cambon. "*Mon cher,*" he said, "*savez-vous ce qui va resulter de cette conference?*" He dragged out his vowels for emphasis: "*Une impro-vis-a-tion.*"

"Cynic" young Nicolson called him in his diary.

It was obvious to all concerned that the plenary conference was too unwieldy a body to accomplish anything. Even before it was organized two delegates from each of the five powers had been meeting regularly in Monsieur Pichon's room. Now formally named, the Council of Ten proceeded to take up, in somewhat helterskelter fashion, all the questions which had been neglected since the signing of the armistice.

During the two months that had gone by since fighting ceased on the western front, none of the problems the plenipotentiaries had to deal with had stood still. The situations described on neat white papers in the briefcases of the specialists changed continually, and always for the worse.

The class war was overflowing the boundaries of Europe. In spite of column after column in the Allied press to the contrary, Lenin was stabilizing the merciless Communist regime. British detachments were seizing the oilwells throughout the Middle East and clear up to Baku, but they controlled very little beyond the range of their sentries' rifles. In spite of all the French generals could do to stir up reaction and nationalism around the fringes of Bolshevism, Trotsky's Red Army was regaining lost ground. The people starved, the people died, but the soviet organization remained.

In the borderlands of Europe and the Near East national selfdetermination was becoming a scourge. Amid famine, cholera and typhus newly hatched republics showed their mettle by attacking their weaker neighbors. In Paris the representatives of all these ethnic groups were tireless in their demands. Outlets to the sea; strategic frontiers, racial frontiers, linguistic frontiers; none of them coincided. Greedy hands were tearing the map of Europe to pieces.

As Tasker Bliss put it in a letter to his wife: "The submerged nations are coming to the surface and as soon as they appear they fly at somebody's throat. They are like mosquitos, vicious from the moment of birth."

No one man could keep the details in his head.

The three worst problems that continuously buzzed about President Wilson's ears were: first the Japanese contention that the concessions which the Germans had wrung from China in the Shantung area be turned over to them instead of being given back to China; second the Italian demands (somewhat encouraged by House, who in return for Italian backing of the League, had promised Orlando that he would make the President see reason on strategic frontiers for Italy); and third, the disposition of the German colonies.

Harold Nicolson in his *Peacemaking* told of being called all of a sudden as an expert on Italian boundaries to attend Arthur Balfour at a conference at the Hôtel de Mûrat. He quoted from his diary:

"On arrival pickets of police, troops, much saluting. Wilson is much guarded. We are taken up to an upper gallery which contains a glass roof and a statue of Napoleon in Egypt . . . Balfour is ushered into a room on the right. We others wait outside for two and a half hours, while the drone of voices comes from the next room. Mrs. Wilson passes, her high heels tocking on the parquet, a mass of mimosa in her arms. The old butler enters and puts on the lights one by one. I read *The Irish Times*."

Suddenly the door opened and out came Lloyd George, followed by Bonar Law, Balfour and President Wilson.

Balfour introduced Nicolson as a young friend who knew all about Italian boundaries. "Now let me see what was it we wanted? Ah yes, Fiume."

"No not Fiume, we had all that," said Wilson. Nicolson noticed his southern drawl.

President Wilson wanted to know the exact number of Germans who would be annexed to Italy if the frontier were set at the Brenner Pass.

Nicolson estimated the number at two hundred and forty or maybe two hundred and fortyfive thousand.

"Well a matter of thousands anyway," said the President airily.

"Yes and anti-Italian thousands," spoke up Nicolson, who at that moment was an enthusiast for selfdetermination and for every one of the Fourteen Points.

"You mean they are pro-German?"

Nicolson contended that they were pro-Tyrol.

The President then asked for statistics on Fiume. What was the dividing line between Fiume and Susak? Ashak, corrected Nicolson tactfully; that was the Yugoslav suburb. A mere rivulet divided them.

The President said the Italians had told him that if you tried to pass from Fiume to Ashak you were certain to be murdered. Nicolson demurred.

"I guessed he was talking through his hat," said the President cheerfully. "Well good night to you gentlemen. Good night Mr. Balfour."

"We withdrew," noted Nicolson. "This is called giving expert advice."

Nicolson found the President younger than his photographs. "One does not see the teeth except when he smiles which is an awful gesture." He described the President's shoulders as broad and his waist narrow, the face very large in proportion to his height. His clothes "those of a tailor's block, very neat and black and tidy; striped trousers; high collar; pink pin."

As they walked downstairs Balfour, who was a courteous man, apologized for having kept Nicolson waiting so long. "To tell the truth the last half hour we have only been discussing whether Napoleon or Frederick the Great could be called disinterested patriots." Nicolson asked what conclusion they reached. Balfour could not remember.

At Colonel House's Oval Table

It was a relief to Wilson to turn from the illtempered wrangling over geographical and ethnological details that went on in the Council of Ten to the academic calm of the commission, which he was appointed to head at the second plenary meeting of the Peace Conference on January 25, to draw up the constitution for a League of Nations. Drawing up constitutions had been his hobby since he was a college student. This was the sort of thing he had been looking forward to, so House put it, "as an intellectual treat."

The meetings took place around a large oval table in Colonel House's comfortable salon at the Crillon. House stagemanaged the proceedings with his usual selfeffacing hospitality. Wilson and House represented the United States. Cecil and rugged General Smuts—who spoke from experience, nourished not only from books, but from the rude personal vicissitudes of a life studded with victories and defeats in war and in politics —represented the British Empire. Longwinded Léon Bourgeois and a fellow international lawyer represented France, Orlando and a colleague from the Italian Senate, Italy. The Japanese had two and the Belgians, Czechoslovaks, Chinese, Portuguese, Serbians and Brazilians one member each.

The committeemen were interested and cooperative. The work, based on a draft drawn up by British and American experts who had tried to cull the best out of Smuts' and Cecil's and Wilson's plans, proceeded so smoothly that at the end of ten meetings the document was ready to be presented to the plenary assembly.

The American secretaries and attendant specialists noted with pleasure the skill and tact with which their President dealt with thorny problems and with some of the thorny characters at the committee table. On February 7 House noted, after a particularly successful session: "Many important articles adopted. Practically everything originates from our end of the table, that is with Lord Rob't Cecil and the Pres, and I acting as adviser. The P. excels in such work. He seems to like it and his short talks in explanation of his views are admirable. I have never known anyone to do such work so well."

The Presentation of the Covenant

As the drafting progressed the idea of the covenant more and more assumed a mystical significance to Woodrow Wilson: through all the deep tunnels of his memory the word resounded. It carried him back to the religious dedication of his boyhood, through his father's sacred stories of the Scots Covenanters who were their forebears, to the Old Testament pact between Almighty God and His chosen people. It irked him that there were people in the world who did not appreciate the divine appointment of his dedication to the great task.

The French press, which most of the Americans scorned as flippant and venal, was shifting from the reverential treatment accorded "Meester Veelson" during his first days in Paris. Squibs and cartoons were appearing. Wilson's patience broke down completely when a leading article that he considered scurrilous appeared in the respectable *Figaro*.

"President Wilson," the article read, "has lightly assumed a responsibility such as few men have ever borne. Success in his idealistic efforts will undoubtedly place him among the greatest characters of history. But let us admit frankly that if he should fail, he would plunge the world into a chaos of which Russian Bolshevism is but the feeble image; and

his responsibility before the conscience of the world would be heavier
than any simple mortal could support."

In theory Wilson was all for freedom of the press but this was going
too far. Although the signature was "Capus," he suspected that the voice
was the voice of Clemenceau. Edith Wilson led the outraged chorus in
the little family party at the Hôtel de Mûrat. The President sent Grayson
running to Ray Baker to instruct him to release a story that if the propaganda against the assembled governments were not curbed immediately
President Wilson would propose moving the conference to a neutral city.
On his way Grayson confided in House.

House expostulated. "To my mind it was a stupid blunder," the colonel
noted angrily in his diary. Although Mandel refused to allow his newspapers to print any report of President Wilson's threat, he did tone down,
for a while, the gibes of the Paris press.

On the surface everything was splendor and serenity at the plenary
session of the Peace Conference which took place on Valentine's Day in
the Salon de l'Orloge. The fact that the President was leaving that night
for Brest in order to reach Washington in time for the closing of the Sixtyfifth Congress added to the air of drama. Monsieur Clemenceau opened
the meeting and immediately gave President Wilson the floor. Wilson
seemed to his friends to be in unusually fine form when he reported, his
fine voice thrilling with pride, the unanimous agreement of the committee
representing fourteen nations on the text he was about to read.

With careful enunciation he read the preamble:

"In order to secure international peace and security by the acceptance
of obligations not to resort to the use of armed force, by the prescription
of open, just and honorable relations between nations, by the firm establishment of the understandings of international law as the actual rule
of conduct among governments, and by the maintenance of justice and
a scrupulous respect for all treaty obligations in the dealings of organized
peoples with one another, and in order to promote international cooperation, the Powers signatory to this Covenant adopt this constitution of the
League of Nations."

He went on to read the twentytwo articles, establishing an executive
council in which the United States, Great Britain, France, Italy and Japan
should have the leadership, a body of delegates of the lesser states, a
secretariat, the machinery for consultation and arbitration . . . The High
Contracting Parties agreed "to respect and preserve . . . the territorial
integrity and existing political independence" of all member states . . .
An international court of justice, reduction of armaments. Sanctions
against transgressors, the abrogation of all treaties inconsistent with the
covenant . . .

The words "High Contracting Parties" resounded like a refrain from article to article. To many of the men listening in the airless hall it seemed the consummation of twentyfive years of effort to secure a world polity. The President's speech was received with profound emotion. Tears were streaming down House's face when he shook the President's hand in the ovation that followed.

Although delegates' wives were categorically excluded, Edith Wilson had induced Clemenceau to get her and Cary Grayson smuggled in. They sat on stiff chairs in a tiny alcove behind a red brocaded curtain.

"It was a great moment in history and as he stood there—slender, calm and powerful in his argument—I seemed to see the people of all depressed countries—men and women and little children crowding round and waiting upon his words."

The covenant was unanimously accepted and Edith Wilson had the pleasure, peering through a crack in the curtains, of seeing the delegates crowding around to press her husband's hand. The Tiger had been insistent that she should not let herself be seen or else "he'd have all the other wives on his neck." The hall cleared fast. When the last coattail had disappeared out of the door Edith Wilson and Cary Grayson tiptoed out of their hiding place. The presidential limousine was waiting for them in the courtyard below. Woodrow Wilson took off his silk hat and leaned back against the cushions. She asked him if he were tired. "Yes I suppose I am, but how little one man means when such vital things are at stake."

The President had a last conference with House before setting off for the train. "I outlined my plan of procedure during his absence," noted the colonel. "I told him I thought we could button up everything during the next four weeks. He seemed startled and even alarmed by the statement. I therefore explained that my plan was not to actually bring these matters to a final conclusion but to have them ready for him to do so when he returned. This pleased him." House drove with the Wilsons to the station.

There were the usual palms and flags and red carpets, President and Madame Poincaré, Clemenceau patient behind his mustaches, the Cabinet in frock coats, ambassadors, attachés. Just before the President stepped on the train he sought out his confidential colonel, who as usual was allowing himself to melt into the background. He was seen to place his hand on House's shoulders and whisper, "Heavy work before you, House." "He looked happy," wrote House, "as well indeed he should."

The Round Robin

President Wilson's trip home was an indifferent success. Landing in Boston he was greeted amiably by a sourfaced little man named Calvin Coolidge, who was the new Republican governor of Massachusetts, and by a crowd that packed Mechanics' Hall and spread out along Huntington Avenue. They cheered him till the rafters rang. Henry Cabot Lodge, who was already excoriating the League on the Senate floor, took fresh umbrage at the President's having addressed a Boston crowd. Wilson was trying to undercut him in his own bailiwick.

The President arrived in Washington in time to preside at a White House dinner of thirtysix covers for the members of the Senate and House committees on foreign affairs. He told stories and answered questions with his most disarming smile.

"I never saw Mr. Wilson appear so human or so attractive as that night," Congressman J. J. Rogers wrote Henry White, who was keeping up a busy correspondence from Paris with his Republican friends in an effort to cozen them into going along with the League idea.

Lodge himself admitted that the dinner had been pleasant, that the President "was civil and showed no temper," but claimed that he seemed illinformed about the constitution of the League of Nations, particularly on the subject of mandates. "We went away as wise as we came."

The President's few days in Washington were largely spent signing his name. However, he found time to review, amid exuberant crowds, a parade of returned soldiers. Newton Baker's War Department was bringing the doughboys home almost as fast as it got them transported overseas. Every move towards demobilization received universal acclaim. It was remarked that the American public thought war was like baseball. "We won; let's go home."

The immediate results of the President's dinnerparty were unfortunate. Senator Frank Brandegee of Connecticut and Senator Lodge and a group of kindred spirits, alarmed at the influence they feared the President's declarations might have with the public, immediately introduced a resolution to the effect that the Senate opposed the League of Nations, as at present constituted, and demanded the immediate negotiation of peace with Germany on terms favorable to the United States.

The Wilson Democrats managed to block their resolution. Brandagee and Lodge gave the document to the press in the form of a "round robin." They secured the signatures of thirtynine senators, enough to prevent ratification of any treaty under the twothirds rule.

When Wilson appeared at the President's room in the Senate wing to sign the last bills, he found the Sixtyfifth Congress expiring in turmoil and confusion. A Republican filibuster, largely animated by that willful man, La Follette, prevented the passage of essential appropriation bills. The President would be forced almost immediately to call a special session of the new Sixtysixth Congress which was safely in Republican hands.

It was in a defiant mood that the President arrived in New York to go aboard the *George Washington*. He met some encouragement there. When he went through the streets, protected, so the newspapers said, by the largest contingent of police ever seen in the city, he was greeted by cheering crowds estimated as nearly as large as the crowds on Armistice Day. Al Smith presided over a monster audience gathered in the Metropolitan Opera House to hear the President. Caruso sang "The Star-Spangled Banner." Ex-President Taft, who had been wearing out his health on a speaking tour in behalf of the League of Nations, made the introductory address. The two men appeared on the stage arm in arm as the band played "Over There" and the platform committee tried to whoop up an ovation.

"The first thing I am going to tell the people on the other side of the water," declared Woodrow Wilson, "is that an overwhelming majority of the American people is in favor of the League of Nations."

The New York *Times* reporter discerned no overwhelming applause. Certain expressions aroused "short nervous moments of clapping." He described the audience as intent, attentive to every word.

A large part of the speech was an attack on the President's critics. "The men who utter the criticisms have never felt the great pulse of the heart of the world."

Wilson announced for the hundredth time his dedication to the cause the soldiers had given their lives for. He was determined there would be no peace without the covenant: "When that treaty comes back, gentlemen on this side will find the covenant not only in it, but so many threads of the treaty tied to the covenant, that you cannot dissect the covenant from the treaty without destroying the whole vital structure."

Colonel House at the Helm

Freed, for a while, from the sermonizings of the American president, the negotiators in Paris turned eagerly to House. Lip service had been paid to the "*noble candeur*" of Wilson's aspirations for a league to abolish war. The time had come to get down to practical business. The colonel expressed understanding of everybody's problems. Orlando called him "my dear friend." He was Clemenceau's chum.

When Lloyd George, facing an uprising in Parliament and suffering daily tonguelashings from the Northcliffe press, went home to trim his fences, he left the absentminded and philosophic Balfour in command. Though skeptical of the perfectability of human affairs, Balfour was a thoroughly humane man. House and Balfour became thick as thieves.

They agreed that before bolshevism made any further inroads the German peace terms must be settled. A bad peace today might be better than a good peace three months later. The League of Nations must temporarily be shelved in favor of a preliminary treaty.

The American and British plenipotentiaries had an appointment for a meeting with Clemenceau on this very topic at House's office at the Crillon at ten the morning of February 19. The Tiger, so House explained, with perhaps a touch of fatuity, in his diary, "had come around to my way of thinking that it was best to make a quick and early peace with Germany."

House and Balfour were waiting for him when news came that the French Premier had been assassinated as he left his house on his way to the meeting.

Stephen Bonsal, House's interpreter in French, reported that Balfour exclaimed "Dear, dear" in his dreamy way, as if someone had spilled a cup of tea; "I wonder what that portends."

They were soon reassured. Clemenceau was seriously wounded but he was far from dead. A demented young man named Cottin, shouting that he was a Frenchman and an anarchist, had jumped on the runningboard of Clemenceau's car and shot seven bullets at him with a revolver. Only one took effect but it lodged much too near the lung for safety. The Tiger remained unruffled. He insisted that the madman's sentence should not be too severe and kept making jokes about how it disgusted him to find that, after four years of war, any Frenchman could be such a bad shot.

The doctors ordered quiet. Clemenceau laughed at the doctors. He was a doctor himself. Three days after the attempt on his life, he was sending Mandel to ask House to call on him. House found him in his apartment, out near Passy, sitting up in an armchair, wrapped in an old army blanket with a soiled silk muffler around his neck. A Sister of Mercy in a big butterfly cap, whom Clemenceau kept teasing unmercifully, hovered over him for a nurse.

"The poor old fellow," wrote House, "has not been able to leave his chair since he was shot"—when he tried to lie down he started to choke. "He speaks of it as 'the accident.' He should not be permitted to see visitors but I suppose he is so insistent that they think it is best to humor him. I was surprised to see the very humble apartment where he lives."

Bonsal, who went along, found the Tiger "gay as a cricket"; he quoted him as telling House in his quaint fluent English, "As I cannot lie down since that madman shot me I naturally will not let anyone else lie down. I shall insist on a little speed being turned on. I am confident that if we Americans"—he grinned through his mustache. It amused him to think of himself as an American—"and the British and French could only get together we could push through the peace treaty with Germany in a very few days and then we would be at liberty to take up arrangements with Austria, Turkey, and the Bulgars—and those fellows should not detain us for long."

Speed was essential. Behind the blockade Germany was starving. The

Spartacist revolt seemed on the verge of success. Although Joffe and his propagandists had been forcibly expelled from the Russian Embassy in Berlin by the Social Democratic Government, Communist rubles and Communist agitators remained behind. Although the Social Democrats were firmly backed by the rank and file of returning soldiers, they were desperately put to it to preserve order. Only in January a Spartacist revolt had been suppressed with great loss of life. Karl Liebknecht and Rosa Luxemburg, the most eloquent of the revolutionists, were killed at that time. News came daily of further uprisings. Kurt Eisner, on whom all German moderates depended, was assassinated in Munich. A Communist coup threatened in Bavaria.

In Russia Trotsky was using the winter breathingspace to improve the organization and rifle power of his Red Army. At the same time on the anti-Bolshevik frontier the Czechs were fighting the Poles for Vilna. Other Polish contingents were trying to take Lemburg from the Ukrainians. Where they weren't fighting their neighbors the liberated Poles fought among themselves. As fast as the Supreme War Council furnished them arms they turned them on each other.

The French military were busy everywhere. Foch had the bit in his teeth. His agents were stimulating a movement for an independent Rhineland. His plans were Napoleonic. He was airily telling the Supreme War Council that if they would give him a hundred thousand Americans he'd solve the bolshevik problem once and for all. He'd raise an army of Poles, Lithuanians, Ukrainians and Balts and, with the Americans as a solid core, he would mop up the Reds to the Urals.

Bliss, representing the United States, sat stoneyfaced. He called it a program for a new Thirty Years War. He exploded in a private letter to Mrs. Bliss: "We ought to get out of Europe, horse, foot and dragoons."

Lloyd George came back to Paris full of new zest for reparations. He had to bring home something tangible for his electorate. The British experts had settled on a sum amounting to a hundred and forty billion dollars. The French went them one better by demanding two hundred billion. Most of the Americans agreed with Baruch that it didn't make sense to even talk of anything more than twenty billions. Both Lloyd George and Clemenceau admitted to House in private that the Germans would not be able to pay these astronomic sums, but talk of big sums was what the people wanted. "I was amused and struck," House noted, "by the cynical way they discussed their people."

In order to hurry a preliminary treaty through, House was making concessions right and left. He was getting concessions in return. "It is now evident," he wrote, "that the peace will not be such a peace as I had hoped."

On the first day of March, Clemenceau was back in his chair presiding over the meetings in Monsieur Pichon's parlor. At his best he was lively as ever, but people noted that he tended to drowse off during discussions. Often he was in pain. The old ivory of his eyelids would drop over his strangely animal-like eyes, and he'd sleep gently as a baby; except when something came up pertaining to French demands. Then he would be awake in a moment.

March 2, House noted in his diary, was Texan independence day. "I wish I was home to celebrate it."

Though stimulated by the free hand the President's absence gave him to model history as he'd dreamed of doing, House was far from encouraged by the prospect ahead. "There is scarcely a man here in authority, outside of the President, who has a full and detached understanding of the situation . . . The President himself lacks a certain executive quality which in some measure unfits him for the supreme task . . . If the President should exert his influence among the liberals and laboring classes, he might possibly overthrow the governments of Great Britain, France and Italy, but if he did he might bring the whole world into chaos . . ."

House felt the weight of the world on his shoulders. "It is Archangel and Murmansk at one moment, the left bank of the Rhine the next, next Asia Minor, the African Colonies, the Chinese-Japanese difference, the economic situation as to raw materials, the food situation . . . No one can ever know how hardpressed I have been during the past month."

March 6 he had a cosy lunch along with Lloyd George at the prime minister's apartment off from the *Place des États-Unis*. The Welshman made a clean breast of it to the confidential colonel. He had to bring home the bacon. The British electorate dreamed of reparations to cut down their taxes, to pay war pensions, to float new industries. The colonials wanted repayment for their sacrifices out of the German colonies.

"It always amused me to have George say in his naïve way that he has done this or that or the other for political effect but that he really knew better," noted House musingly. "He doesn't seem to have any ingrown sense of right and wrong, but only looks at things from the standpoint of expediency . . . with all his faults," the colonel concluded, "he is by birth, instinct and upbringing a liberal."

Decisions had to be made. Problems had been postponed too long to be settled properly. Lloyd George was beginning to promise Clemenceau a separate treaty guaranteeing France from attack in return for French complaisance to British demands. He would even build a tunnel under the Channel to bring British troops over faster.

"When the President was away," wrote House of these informal meetings, "I never hesitated to act and take as much responsibility as either of the others."

By the time Wilson arrived back in Paris the three Europeans, plus House, had managed to freeze out the Japanese delegation. The reiter-

ated request of the little yellow brethren that racial equality be written
into the covenant was as embarrassing to the British colonials as it was
to President Wilson. In the strictest secrecy, at meetings which, as soon
as Wilson arrived were to be given official status as the Council of Four,
they were at work on a preliminary treaty with Germany.

President's Return

The President arrived at Brest on March 13 too late to leave for Paris
the same night. He had insisted on the *George Washington* making port
on his lucky thirteenth. He was recovering his equanimity after the dis-
appointments of his trip back to America. The sea voyage did him a world
of good. Edith and Dr. Grayson thought him in fine fettle.

He arrived in an ugly mood towards House. The confidential colonel's
plan for a preliminary treaty conflicted with his decision not to sign any
treaty that didn't have the covenant imbedded in it. He was worried,
and with reason, for fear Lodge's round robin would serve as an excuse
to shelve the whole plan for a League of Nations. Reports from the British
and American newspapers gave him reason to believe a rumor was being
circulated that the League was dead.

Edith Wilson never had liked House any better than she liked McAdoo.
Now she saw a chance to get rid of him. "A regular jellyfish," she called
him. She kept telling her husband that House was weakkneed; and, besides, he got too much publicity. He was no longer the anonymous adviser. Last spring the President had had to write personally to Doubleday
Page, the publishers, suggesting that they quietly drop Arthur Howden
Smith's book called *The Real Colonel House*. Now House was being written up in the British and American press as the brains of the Peace Conference. His photographs were everywhere. Wickham Stead, one of the
foremost British advocates of a League of Nations, was giving House all
the credit.

Grayson agreed with Mrs. Wilson. A "yes man," he called the confidential colonel. The whole presidential party was up in arms against Colonel
House. Even the secretservice men were indignant about how he had
sold out the President.

House rode down to Brest on Poincaré's train to meet his affectionate
friend. Although House states in his journal for March 14: "I did not
go out to the *George Washington* to meet President and Mrs. Wilson,
but met them at the landing stage," both Mrs. Wilson and E. W. Starling,
one of the secretservice men, describe in their recollections a scene in
the President's stateroom aboard the ship.

Starling described, to the journalist who wrote up his story, the President and Colonel House being closeted that night in the President's cabin.

". . . After what seemed like a long time Colonel House emerged from the suite, looking disturbed and walking rapidly. As I stepped inside to close the door I saw the President standing, his eyes fixed on me but showing no recognition . . . His face was pale and seemed drawn and tired. The whole figure expressed dejection. I closed the door, mentally cursing Colonel House."

Edith Wilson remembered the scene even more dramatically. "I look back at that moment," she wrote in *My Memoir,* "as a crisis in his life, and feel that from it dated the long years of illness, due to overwork, and that with the wreckage of his plans and his life have come these tragic years that have demoralized the world."

Her account of the scene was vivid: "It was after midnight and very still aboard, when I heard my husband's door open and the Colonel take his leave . . . Woodrow was standing. The change in his appearance shocked me. He seemed to have aged ten years, and his jaw was set in that way it had when he was making a superhuman effort to control himself. Silently he held out his hand, which I grasped, crying 'What is the matter? What has happened?'

"He smiled bitterly. 'House has given away everything I had won before I left Paris. He has compromised on every side, and so I have to start all over again, and this time it will be harder.'"

Wherever the interview took place—Ray Baker writes of it as taking place on the train—it was tense. The President blamed House for having induced him to set the senators up to that dinner; "Your dinner . . . was a failure as far as getting together was concerned," House remembered his saying. The senators had been intransigent. The President would have no part of a preliminary peace with Germany. If they forced him he'd insist on a preliminary peace with every one of the belligerents.

House summed up the conversation: "The President comes back very militant and determined to put League of Nations into treaty."

This time the President and his party put up in the newer quarter of Paris, near the apartment house where Lloyd George and Balfour were lodged. The President didn't want to be beholden to the French for his residence; the Hôtel de Mûrat was too napoleonic to be comfortable and, besides, he was convinced the French flunkies there were all spies. Eleven Place des Etats-Unis was an *art nouveau* mansion belonging to a banker named Bischoffsheim. It contained a fine collection of paintings. Edith Wilson's bathroom was ornamented with enamelled appleblossoms. The lighting fixture was a tangle of birds and butterflies. There were gold faucets at the washstand. On the square outside rose Bartholdi's sculptured group of Lafayette being received by George Washington.

The President immediately ordered the cluttered parlors cleared for office space. His first act was to have Ray Baker issue a statement to the press:

"The President said today that the decision made at the Peace Conference at its plenary session, January 25, 1919, to the effect that the establishment of a League of Nations should be made an integral part of the Treaty of Peace, is of final force and that there is no basis whatever for the reports that a change in this decision was contemplated."

The Council of Four

The work of the Council of Four became an unremitting grind. Wilson's insistence on scrapping plans for a preliminary peace meant that many things had to be taken up all over again. It wasn't long before Clemenceau and Lloyd George and Orlando, each in his particular way, discovered how to handle President Wilson. If they threatened the League of Nations he would make concessions. He would give up anything for the covenant.

The detail work was punishing to everyone concerned. The Council of Four did not suffer from a lack of information. It suffered from the excess of it.

Hordes of specialists, and good ones, were ready to produce statistics on every conceivable subject. Their difficulty was in finding out what use the Big Four were making of their reports. The proceedings, except when some one of the olympians leaked a story to the press for some particular purpose, were shrouded in the blackest secrecy.

The British delegations had the advantage of a discreet summary of developments distributed daily by Sir Maurice Hankey. Wilson never saw fit to inform his various teams of what was going on. Lansing's men didn't know what House's men were up to. Neither group had any consistent contact with Baruch's commission.

Herbert Hoover, schooled in the troubled waters of international intrigue by his experience in Belgium, went doggedly ahead with Quaker tenacity organizing his relief work where it was most needed; but, although he knew more than anybody about what actually went on among the populations whose fate was being so arbitrarily decided, he was hardly consulted; and his only information about what was being decided upstairs came from occasional chats with Colonel House.

The Secretary of State was reduced to sitting in glum idleness in sessions of the various councils, which went on revolving as a series of fifth wheels after the Big Four had gone into their inner sanctum. Lansing amused himself making sketches of the delegates on his pad. As for Henry White and Tasker Bliss their opinions were never asked. They were reduced to tagging after House's soninlaw, Auchincloss, for any little hints

of news he would vouchsafe them. House was still consulted, but Edith
Wilson and Grayson were busy behind the scenes whittling away what
little influence he had left.

The President had rolled up his sleeves. There was no one he could
trust. He would have to take the whole business on singlehanded. At
first he put up a stubborn battle to reduce French demands for the left
bank of the Rhine, for a Rhenish republic and for the coalfields of the
Saar. None of this could be made to jibe with the pledge of selfdetermination in the Fourteen Points. By the end of March the discussion culminated in a personal row with Clemenceau. Unless France had the Saar,
growled the Tiger, he would not sign the peace treaty. "In that event do
you want me to return home?" asked the President in the tone he could
make like a whip. Clemenceau lost his temper. "I do not wish you to go
home, but I intend to do so myself." He stamped out of the room.

The peacemaking was at a deadlock. Lloyd George confided in House
that he was impressed by the President's show of spirit. House tried to
rub it in about how terrible the President was in his rages.

On April 3 Mrs. Wilson telephoned House that the President was sick
with a cold and that he was requesting that House take his place at the
Council of Four. The President was in bed with what Dr. Grayson described as influenza. He had a high fever and a cough that kept him from
sleeping.

It is probable that along with the grippe Wilson suffered a minor cerebral hemorrhage. When he got to his feet Ray Baker noticed a taut look
on one side of his face. The eye twitched constantly.

Ike Hoover, the White House usher, who now officiated in striped
pants and a cutaway in the waiting room to the President's suite, dated
a drastic change in the President's personality from this bout of illness.

From his sickbed Wilson made good his threat to Clemenceau by letting Ray Baker leak to the press the fact that he'd cabled the skipper of
the *George Washington* to get the ship ready to bring him home.

The Broken Stick

When the President returns to the council meetings he finds everybody more conciliatory. His colleagues are in a flurry to get the business
over with. A gruff reminder that there is reason for haste comes to the
Big Four when the liberal Count Karolyi, failing of support by the western powers, gives up in despair his effort to reorganize Hungary and is
replaced in Budapest by the Communist Bela Kun.

Concessions become the order of the day. President Wilson himself
makes the sort of concessions he blamed House for even suggesting. He
concedes the Saar and the left bank of the Rhine to France, but for fifteen

years only. The Tiger agrees to the time limit. The President makes Clemenceau even happier by joining with Lloyd George in the promise of a separate treaty guaranteeing France from attack. He accepts the exaction of unlimited reparations from Germany.

Through Smuts' influence mandates under the League are substituted for outright possession of the German colonies. The Poles are given the chance of a plebiscite in Silesia. The Japanese are assured that if they drop their untimely insistence on racial equality, justification will be found for their exploitation of the Shantung peninsula. Everybody is happy except the Italians.

On April 13 the Four decide they are ready to invite the German representatives to Versailles to hear their fate. The Austrians will come to St. Germain a little later. The Turks and Bulgars can wait. All idea of a Congress of Versailles where victor and vanquished would meet with the neutral states to establish the reign of justice and commonsense has long since been abandoned.

The Italians are raising a storm about Fiume. The subtle Venizelos is getting concessions for the Greeks that conflict with Italian plans in the Aegean. Wilson has given the Italians sovereignty over the German-speaking Tyrol so that they may have their strategic frontier. He feels that should satisfy them. Clemenceau and Lloyd George back him up.

On April 22, amid distressed entries about Italian intrigue, House notes in his diary that it is San Jacinto day. Again he wishes he were home in Texas.

Next day Orlando announces that without Fiume, Italy will never sign the peace treaty. The Council of Four is deadlocked again.

The President is on his high horse. He types out a statement on his own typewriter appealing to the Italian people, pointing out that they have been given the Brenner Pass. They have Trieste. Adjacent Fiume must be a free port serving the new nations of the Balkans and the Danube Valley. He begs the Italians "to exhibit to the newly liberated peoples across the Adriatic that noblest quality of greatness, magnanimity, friendly generosity, the preference of justice over interests."

Grayson hurries the statement to Ray Baker who broadcasts it to the press.

The result is that crowds march about Rome crying "*Abasso Veelson*." Humble Italians who had pasted up the President's photograph on their walls beside the effigies of *la santissima* tear them down. The streets of Fiume are decorated with posters showing President Wilson in a German helmet. Orlando and Sonnino depart for Rome in a huff.

Lloyd George, though he doesn't want the Italians to have Fiume, keeps on suggesting soothing compensations in the carving up of the Turkish dominions. Not many days elapse before Sonnino and Orlando are back in Paris as if nothing has happened.

What is now the Council of Three is cosier without Orlando. Compensation for everybody is the watchword now. They meet at Lloyd George's flat or in President Wilson's study on the Place des Etats-Unis. They pore over maps. They trace out railroads, rivervalleys, ethnographic boundaries, spot coalmines. Details, details. Complication on complication. They keep forgetting the strange names, the location of tunnels, the ports. They are tired. The facts slip through their fingers, details blur. Both Clemenceau and Wilson are severely shaken in health. Lloyd George, though a well man, is easily distracted as a sparrow.

Harold Nicolson, who as a Foreign Office specialist has been detailed to the olympians, jots down glimpses of them at work. First, one May morning at Lloyd George's flat: "We are still discussing when the flabby Orlando and the sturdy Sonnino are shown into the dining-room. They all sit around the map. The appearance of a pie about to be distributed is thus enhanced. Ll.G. shows them what he suggests. They ask for Scala Nova as well. 'Oh no,' says Ll.G., 'you can't have that. It's full of Greeks.' He goes on to point out that there are further Greeks at Marki, and a whole wedge of them along the coast towards Alexandretta. 'Oh no,' I whisper to him, 'there are not many Greeks there.' 'But yes,' he answers, 'don't you see it's colored green?' I then realize that he mistakes my map for an ethnological map, and thinks the green means Greeks instead of valleys, and the brown means Turks instead of mountains. Ll.G. takes this correction with great good humor. He is quick as a kingfisher."

That afternoon Nicolson is called into a meeting of the Three to President Wilson's study. He thinks of them as the witches in *Macbeth*.

"The door opens and Hankey tells me to come in. A heavily furnished study with my huge map on the carpet. Bending over it (bubble, bubble, toil and trouble) are Clemenceau, Ll.G. and P.W. They have pulled up armchairs and crouch low over the map . . . I was there about a half an hour talking and objecting. The President was extremely nice and so was Ll.G. Clemenceau was cantankerous . . . *'Mais voyez vous, jeune homme, que voulez-vous qu'on fasse? Il faut aboutir.'*

"It is appalling," Nicolson adds, "that these ignorant and irresponsible men should be cutting Asia Minor to bits as if they were dividing a cake . . . The happiness of millions being decided that way . . . Their decisions are immoral and impracticable . . . But I obey my orders." *Il faut aboutir.*

April 29 the German plenipotentiaries arrive at Versailles. The French shut them up in a small house inside a barbed wire enclosure as if they were prisoners.

May 7, which the Allied newspapers make much of as the anniversary of the sinking of the *Lusitania*, the Germans are summoned to the Trianon at Versailles. It is a fine spring day. The sunlight pours in through the tall windows as the German plenipotentiaries walk in to meet the victorious powers. Clemenceau presides. Count Brockdorff-Rantzau, a skinny man in black who with tremulous steps has led in the German envoys, doesn't glance at the document. Without rising—his friends claim he is so nervous he can't trust his legs to support him—he launches into a speech defending the German people from full responsibility for the war. He accuses the Allies bitterly of having caused the death of thousands of noncombatants by continuing the blockade after the armistice. He declares the principles of President Wilson to be binding on victor and vanquished. He announces that the German people are ready to cooperate wholeheartedly in putting into effect the principles enunciated in the Fourteen Points.

His speech, translated sentence by sentence, is received with cold hostility, aggravated by the seeming discourtesy of the man's not rising to his feet. "Any more observations?" growls Clemenceau. "If not the meeting is closed."

The German Government promptly complies with the Fourteen Points by making public the terms of the treaty. Many of the American delegates in Paris first read it when a clandestine translation is hawked about the streets. At home in the States the members of the Senate and House committees for foreign affairs are thrown into a fury because nobody has thought to furnish them with an official text. They have to read the details in the newspapers.

The more farseeing Americans in Paris receive the treaty with almost as much dismay as the Germans. Herbert Hoover writes in his memoirs of being waked up at four in the morning of May 7 by a messenger bringing him the text. In this Hoover is one of the favored few. He sits up in bed and reads it through. "I was greatly disturbed . . . It seemed to me the economic consequences alone would pull down all Europe and thus injure the United States."

Hoover is so disturbed he has to get up. He dresses and goes out on the street to try to walk off his agitation. The sun is rising. The streets are deserted. "In a few blocks I met General Smuts and John Maynard Keynes . . . It flashed in all our minds why the others were walking about at that time of day . . . We agreed that it was terrible, and we would do what we could . . . to make the dangers clear."

At the eleventh hour Lloyd George has an attack of conscience. He tries to get Wilson, Clemenceau and Orlando to agree to modifications and adjustments suggested by the saner men in all the delegations. Nicolson describes him as fighting "like a little Welsh terrier" in the Council of Four to set a limit to reparations, to revise the eastern frontiers, and to assure Germany of admission into the League. To the surprise of the specialists it is Wilson this time who refuses to budge. *Litera scripta manet.*

The day the new batch of German envoys arrives at Versailles with instructions from the Weimar Government to sign the treaty at any cost, the news comes out that the crews have scuttled the entire German fleet, interned, according to the armistice terms, under the eyes of the British, at Scapa Flow.

La Journée de Versailles

The French have spared no effort to make the signing of the peace treaty a mighty show. Above the heads of the crowd at Versailles the blue and white pennants on the lances of the cavalrymen lining the long avenue flutter in the sun of a fine summer's day. The tallest of the Garde Republicain stand like statues in their horsehair helmets on either side of Louis XIV's grand stairway as the plenipotentiaries and their delegations and their wives and families climb the steps to the Hall of Mirrors. Their sabers are at the salute.

At one end of the enormous gaudy hall the world press is packed in a motley throng. At the other the plenipotentiaries sit at a horseshoe table. Around them are all the uniforms of the Allied armies, embossed with every conceivable decoration. Between the tall mirrors and the tall windows shine the gilded curlycues and the encrusted capitals of the *grand siècle.* Overhead stretch painted ceilings in a whirligig of colors and shapes.

At the center of the table sit Wilson and Lloyd George, almost lost, in all the splendor, in their somber frock coats. Squat Clemenceau is hunched between them. Harold Nicolson, who likes to describe Clemenceau as looking like a gorilla carved out of ivory, notices that over the Tiger's head on the flamboyant ceiling is a scroll which reads: LE ROI GOUVERNE PAR LUIMÊME.

When Clemenceau gestures for silence a sharp clank resounds through the thronged hall as the guards thrust their sabers back into their scabbards.

In the silence that follows Clemenceau's voice croaks harshly: *"Faites entrer les Allemands."*

Two ushers hung with silver chains enter from a door at the end of the hall. They are followed by four officers, one American, one English, one French, one Italian. After them totter two small civilians in glasses. Their feet plunk miserably on the strip of parquet between the carpets, as, in the heavy silence, under the stare of two thousand eyes, they walk the length of the hall to the little table where the texts of the treaty have been laid out for signature.

They sign. At that moment the guns start to roar outside. The crowds cheer. The sky is aflutter with frightened pigeons. Amid the ancient trees along the green prospects of the park spurt the legendary fountains.

In the hall the tension has snapped. People move about and crane their necks to see. The plenipotentiaries form a queue to sign like men buying tickets at a railroad station. President Wilson leads the Americans, next comes Colonel House.

From her seat Edith Wilson, who is wearing a gray picture hat, a gray gown and orchids, and carrying a gray and blue beaded bag her husband has just presented her to match her dress, can hear the whir of the motionpicture cameras that press about the plenipotentiaries.

From behind her she catches the apologetic Texas drawl of Loulie House who has jumped to her feet. "Please let me stand long enough to see my lamb sign."

That night President and Mrs. Wilson undergo the final longdrawn ceremonies of a dinner at the Elysée Palace.

(When the invitation came from Poincaré Wilson flew off the handle. He vowed he would not sit down at table with the swine. It was as if all his resentment of the frustrations suffered in Paris were focussed into hatred of the stubby little President of the French Republic. It was all House and Henry White could do to convince him that not to accept the invitation would cause an international incident. Perhaps Mrs. Wilson had already clinched the matter by getting a special dress for the occasion designed for her by Worth.)

She describes it, with feeling, in *My Memoir* as a closefitting black *charmeuse* gown with a fishtail train, encrusted from the knees up with sequins shading in color from black through tints of gray "to glittering white at the bust and shoulders." She carries a large ostrichfeather fan and, having been impressed by the diamond tiaras the court ladies wore in England, wears a special tiaralike headdress made up by Worth out of sequins and rhinestones.

From the banquet they hurry to the station.

"Everyone was in a holiday mood and happy, though a note of sadness too was felt . . . For one last time we found the red carpet stretched, the lines of soldiers to be inspected, the palms waving, and the French officers lined up to bid us bon voyage."

Next day they are aboard the *George Washington* bound for home.

Chapter 24

THE SUPREMEST TRAGEDY

On July 10, in the noonday glare of the Washington summer heat, Woodrow Wilson appeared in solemn mood before the Senate and saw the great bound volume of the Treaty of Versailles placed upon the clerk's desk. Grayson, who was watching him carefully, found his step elastic, his eyes bright, his color good. His attitude was challenging:

"The united power of free nations must put a stop to aggression and the world must be given peace . . . Shall we or any other free people hesitate to accept this great duty? Dare we reject it and break the heart of the world? . . . The stage is set, the destiny disclosed. It has come about by no plan of our conceiving but by the hand of God who led us into this way."

He urged immediate ratification.

The document was rushed to the printers. That night copies were distributed throughout the Senate office building so that at last the senators could read the actual text of the commitments which the President had made in the name of the United States.

By the end of the month Henry Cabot Lodge was ready, as chairman of the Committee for Foreign Affairs, to inaugurate public hearings on the question of ratification. The Republicans, perhaps in somewhat mischievous deference to the President's call for open covenants, openly arrived at, insisted on these hearings being open to the reporters and to the public. Sensationally reported in the press, the hearings brought dismay to the White House.

The Heart of the Covenant

August 19 the President invited the entire Senate committee to a private conference in the East Room. He greeted the senators amiably. He had taken the liberty, he said, of writing out a little statement on the points of controversy which had so far come up. This he proceeded to read.

He repeated his arguments for ratification of the treaty at the earliest practicable moment. At home and abroad the revival of trade and commerce and industry, and reconstruction, and every sort of plan for the orderly life of the world, waited on the peace. He reminded the senators that he had already introduced revisions on points which some of them had brought up.

He spoke vigorously in defense of Article X, "the heart of the covenant," by which the United States joined the Allied powers in undertaking to "preserve as against external aggression the territorial integrity and existing political independence" of all members of the League; but he pointed out, in a disarming tone, that this obligation was moral, rather than legal.

The senators presented their questions. They asked about the disposition of the Pacific Islands under the mandate system. How would that affect American control of the Pacific cables? The President's answers did not satisfy them.

The chief stumbling block was Article X. The conference became involved in a tangled argument on the difference between a moral and a legal obligation. The argument became heated.

The Democratic senators had little to say.

The President seemed reluctant to reveal how decisions had been reached at the Peace Conference. He was particularly evasive on the subject of Shantung. Had the Japanese been offered Shantung in return for their signature?

Senator Hiram Johnson of California read the minutes of his examination of Secretary Lansing a few days before. After some squirming, the Secretary of State had admitted that in his opinion the Japanese would have signed even without Shantung.

Johnson read out his question: "So that the result of the Shantung decision was simply to lose China's signature, rather than to gain Japan's?

"Secretary Lansing: 'That is my personal view, but I may be wrong about it.'"

The President exclaimed testily that his conclusion was different from Mr. Lansing's.

The discussion continued until one of the Democrats suggested that maybe they'd better recess. The President graciously invited the senators to lunch with him. While waiting for the lunch hour Senator Brandegee in acid tones summarized the points at issue.

Senator Johnson asked to be informed on the practical details. Would American troops be expected to help the French garrison on the Rhine? Would they be expected to enforce every provision of the treaty in Europe, Asia and Africa? The President admitted American troops might have to be stationed for the next fifteen years on the Rhine.

The senator brought up the paragraph on ratification.

President Wilson seemed a little vague as to how many signatures, besides Germany's, it would take to put the treaty in force. Senator Hitchcock came to the President's rescue by reading a paragraph to the effect that the treaty would be binding on a nation only from the date of that nation's signature.

Senator Moses of New Hampshire came back to the mandates: "Mr. President, under the terms of the treaty, Germany cedes to the principal allied and associated powers all her overseas possessions?

"The President: Yes.

"Senator Moses: We hereby, as I view it, become possessed in fee of an undivided fifth part of those possessions.

"The President: Only as one of five trustees, Senator. There is no thought in any mind of sovereignty.

"Senator Moses: Such possessions as we acquire by means of that cession would have to be disposed of by congressional action.

"The President: I have not thought about that at all.

"Senator Moses: You have no plan to suggest or recommendation to make to Congress?

"The President: Not yet, sir, I am waiting until the treaty is disposed of."

At that point Senator Lodge remarked that it was thirtyfive minutes past one. They had been talking for three hours and a half. The conference adjourned and the senators followed the President into the diningroom.

Though he managed to keep his temper the conference left Wilson in angry turmoil. It was now clear that without modifications the Senate would never ratify the treaty. He was determined to appeal to the people. The voice of the people would cry down these crabbed criticisms. Already he was planning with Tumulty a swing around the country that would bring his great League plan home to the people. The Republicans in the Senate would never dare face a popular uprising.

Tumulty was all for it. As a practical politician the President's secretary was appalled by the disrepair into which the Democratic Party had fallen during the President's absence abroad. In bringing the League home to the people, the President, in whose gifts as a campaign orator Tumulty had childlike faith, would revive the party machinery at the grassroots. Enthusiastically he went to work to plan a speaking tour through the middlewest and down the Pacific coast. The President would meet the erstwhile Progressives like Johnson and Borah, who were the most fervent opponents of the treaty, on their home ground.

Although Wilson intended to urge the people to insist on ratification of every word of the treaty as he had laid it before the Senate, without dotting an i or crossing a t, at that moment he was admitting to himself that he might have to consent to some modifications. Late in August he drew up a document on his own typewriter for the information of Senator Hitchcock.

Gilbert M. Hitchcock was a wellmeaning smalltown publisher from Nebraska who, with little parliamentary experience, found himself, through the illness of the aged minority leader, Senator Martin of Virginia, in the position of minority leader pro tem in the Senate. Consequently it was upon Hitchcock that devolved the task of sponsoring the Versailles treaty. What he lacked in knowhow he made up in loyalty to the President as head of the Democratic Party.

Wilson noted, for Hitchcock's private information, that he was willing, if absolutely necessary, to agree to four reservations. More emphasis could be placed on the provision that any state could withdraw from the League at any time. States could use their own judgement as to whether they would use armed force to carry out the League's decisions. It should be specified that the League might not meddle in questions of immigration, naturalization or tariffs; and he was willing to restate in stronger terms his original reservation as to the Monroe Doctrine.

Hitchcock told the President he was convinced that these concessions would go far towards meeting the views of all but the most irreconcilable of the Republicans. In his opinion a twothirds majority would not be too hard to obtain.

Wilson hated the senators and all they stood for. He would arouse the people. He hoped to lash public opinion to such a pitch of enthusiasm for the League that the senators would not dare oppose him. Even so, at that moment, he was willing to go along with those Republican and Democratic senators who were in favor of moderate reservations.

As the day for the President's departure approached, Grayson and Edith Wilson grew more and more uneasy about the possible effect on his health of such a gruelling trip. He had not really recovered from his illness in Paris in April. The summer heat had been unusually hard on him. Although he took long periods of rest each day he did not seem able to throw off fatigue as he used to. Edith Wilson urged Grayson to assert himself as the President's personal physician. They both begged him to call the trip off.

The President's answer—as Edith quoted it—was, that as Commander in Chief he had been responsible for sending American soldiers into battle. "If I don't do all in my power to put that treaty into effect, I will be a slacker and never able to look those boys in the eye. I must go."

Tumulty added his plea. He had been argued around to the conclusion that the President's health was even more important than the Democratic Party. "I know that I'm at the end of my tether," Tumulty remembered Wilson's telling him. ". . . Even though, in my condition it might mean giving up my life, I will gladly make the sacrifice to save the treaty."

The Appeal to the People

The Washington streets were hot and muggy and airless on the evening of September 3 when the President and Mrs. Wilson drove to Union Station. The President arrived jaunty in a straw hat.

Tumulty had thrown everything he had into the preparations for the trip. A private clubcar named Mayflower was specially arranged for the presidential party. There were staterooms for the President and Mrs. Wilson and for Dr. Grayson and for Mrs. Wilson's Swedish maid. Brooks the valet was to sleep on the couch in the drawingroom. An office had been installed. On the foldup table was one of the President's favorite Hammond portable typewriters.

Tumulty and the White House staff and the secretservice men rode in pullmans ahead. There were accommodations for more than a hundred newspapermen and reporters.

The first stop was Columbus. The meeting there was thinly attended. After the President had finished speaking a Chinese student called out from the gallery, "What about Shantung, Mr. President?"

At Indianapolis there was a parade to the state fair. Dust and heat and yelling crowds. An enormous turnout; but when the President spoke people seemed more interested in the fat cattle and the exhibits of prizewinning pickles than in the League of Nations.

At St. Louis, the bailiwick of knownothing Senator Reed, who was raging up and down the country denouncing the treaty, the crowds were unexpectedly cordial. Wilson was introduced as "The Father of World Democracy." Shouts of approval and storms of handclapping capped every sentence.

Kansas City was even better.

The presidential train avoided Chicago where anglophobe "Big Bill" Thompson was mayor and where Senator Medill McCormick's excoriation of the treaty had been frantically applauded and Wilson's name booed, amid shouts of "Impeach him, impeach him."

Wherever Wilson talked people seemed to leave the halls convinced. He threatened them with doom. "I can predict with absolute certainty," he said in Omaha, "that within another generation there will be another world war if the nations of the world do not concert the method by which to prevent it." He was thrilled by the response he got. "I am catching the imagination of the people," he told his wife. "I don't care if I die the minute after the League is ratified."

At Mandan he spoke from the rear platform to a throng collected in the station. Billings and Helena turned out excited crowds. He met with an ovation at Coeur d'Alene in Senator Borah's home state. Spokane, the hated Poindexter's home town, seemed to have gone mad for Wilson.

Tumulty was in his element. He had democratic committees aboard the train at every stop to wring the President's hand. The President smiled and smiled. Good humor reigned in the presidential party. Grayson and Tumulty carried on a sort of minstrel show that kept everybody in stitches. Edith Wilson put up a brave front though she knew that her husband was suffering blinding headaches, that he hardly ate or slept.

Wilson was agreeable to everybody. He told stories and shook hands and tirelessly stood up in open touring cars, waving at the crowds through the dusty broiling western towns. At night he'd ask the newspapermen in for sandwiches. He'd never been more affable. When people suggested that he was pushing himself too hard he had a wisecrack for them. "My constitution may be exhausted, but I still have my bylaws."

The reception in Seattle was overwhelming. The President made three speeches in a day and reviewed the Pacific fleet in Puget Sound from the deck of the famous old *Oregon*, back from overawing the Russians off Vladivostok. On the way to the armory singing schoolchildren waved red white and blue flags. When he appeared on the platform he was greeted like a presidential candidate with confetti and balloons and a prolonged demonstration.

The only sour note was the young Wobblies standing with folded arms along the curb on the downtown streets with PARDON DEBS on their hatbands and banners reading RELEASE THE POLITICAL PRISONERS. Wilson had repeatedly refused even to consider a pardon for any of them.

The baneful seething that had worried Wilson in past years was rising hourly to the surface in the news that came to the presidential train. The President wracked his brains for solutions. While one secretary was kept busy typing out fresh speeches another had to pound away on the day to day work of the presidency.

From coast to coast came complaints about wartime profiteering and the high cost of living. War industries were shutting down. There was unemployment everywhere. Wages were cut. There were bloody race riots where Negro laborers had moved north. Steelworkers were on strike. Coal miners were walking out. Employers were fighting strikes with injunctions and hired gunmen. The New York theatres closed because the actors refused to perform until they got fair contracts. In Boston a strike of the police force turned the streets over to hoodlums and thugs.

To quiet the unrest of labor the President was calling an industrial conference to meet in Washington.

Overseas hotspots kept exploding on the map like popcorn in a skillet. French and British plans to establish some respectable capitalist regime in Russia went continually awry. The leaders they backed, though they massacred the Reds that fell into their hands as tirelessly as the Reds massacred the Whites, seemed to face invariable defeat. In China echoes of the Fourteen Points had set the young students' ears to tingling. The blind revolt against foreign exploitation of Boxer days was taking new forms. Students were learning the language of European politics from Wilson and Lenin and from the democratic idealism of American missionaries. Voices calling for Chinese selfdetermination and Chinese selfgovernment were reaching the American press. On the Adriatic a baldheaded poet named Gabriele d'Annunzio was defying the dictates of Versailles by lashing up an Italian mob to seize Fiume. The President could hardly control his indignation.

As a final aggravation wires from Washington detailed the testimony of a rich and earnest young man named William C. Bullitt before the Senate Committee for Foreign Affairs. Bullitt had resigned from a Peace Conference job in protest against the treaty and against the Allied policy of backing every outbreak in Russia of partisans of the old regime against the soviet power. Now he revealed some private conversations with Secretary Lansing. Lansing not only disapproved of the Shantung agreement, but of the covenant. The Secretary of State had said the American people would unquestionably defeat the treaty if they ever understood what it let them in for.

"My God," Wilson cried out to Tumulty, "I did not think it was possible for Lansing to act in this way."

The train was rushing on to the next speaking engagement. There was no time to deal with Lansing now. Lansing would get what was coming to him later.

Back in Paris the story tickled Clemenceau. His *bon mot* was going the rounds. "I got my bullet during the conference; Lansing got his after."

In Portland the crowds were sedate, but three times as many people stood outside the armory as could get in to hear the President. When the presidential cortege took a fast tour of the scenic drives up the Columbia River, one of the most popular of the newscorrespondents was killed in a car crash. The President and Edith Wilson were immensely saddened. People noticed that the President couldn't seem to throw off the sense of shock. "It made us jittery," said one of the secretservice men. "From then on nothing seemed to go right."

San Francisco was a success in spite of efforts of the Irish societies to cause trouble. Berkeley and the bay towns were delirious. A special stop was made in Sacramento to boost the League in Hiram Johnson's back yard.

The newspapermen declared that San Diego was the high point of the trip. Through a recently installed loudspeaker system the President addressed fifty thousand wildly enthusiastic people. "The war we have just been through," he told them, "though it was shot through with terror, is not to be compared with the war we would have to face next time." They shouted approval of the League. Los Angeles tried to go San Diego one better.

Wilson and Tumulty were so elated they talked of carrying the campaign into Massachusetts and lighting a fire under Senator Lodge back where his voters lived.

In Salt Lake City the Mormon Tabernacle was packed to suffocation. The heat was insufferable. Edith said she felt sick and blind from the lack of air and would have fainted if her maid hadn't handed her a bottle of lavender smelling salts. She sent a handkerchief drenched with the salts by a secretservice man up to her husband. After his speech the President came back dripping with sweat. He changed his clothes, but Edith noticed he couldn't seem to stop sweating.

At Cheyenne and Denver there were more parades, more delegations, more hands to shake. Wilson's headache was continuous now, blinding. He suffered nerve pains in his arms.

In Pueblo he suddenly announced that he wouldn't go to greet fifty thousand people waiting at the fairgrounds. He'd never said he would. When Tumulty showed him the itinerary with his okeh on it he lost his temper. Entering the new city auditorium Starling, the secretservice man who was right behind him, noticed that he couldn't seem to see where he was going. The President stumbled on a step. Starling almost had to lift him up the steps to the platform.

Many of the reporters spoke of it as the best speech of the whole tour, but Starling, who stood right behind him to catch him if he fell, thought he seemed to lose the thread, to repeat himself. His enunciation was thick. At one point he broke down and cried.

"What of our pledges," he cried, "to the men that lie dead in France . . . There seems to me to stand between us and the rejection or qualification of this treaty the serried ranks of those boys in khaki, not only those boys who came home, but those dear ghosts that still deploy upon the fields of France."

With tears streaming down his face he told of Decoration Day at a cemetery for the war dead . . . French women putting flowers on the graves . . . "There was a little group of French women who had adopted these graves, had made themselves mothers of these dear ghosts by putting flowers every day on these dear graves" . . . He wished the men in public life who opposed the covenant could visit such a spot. "I wish that the thought that comes out of those graves could penetrate their consciousness . . . the moral obligation . . . to see . . . the thing through . . . and make good their redemption of the world."

His peroration was in the old style: "Now that the mists of this great

question have cleared away . . . we have accepted the truth and it is
going to lead us and through us the world, out into pastures of quietness
and peace such as the world never dreamed of before."

Tumulty was deeply moved. He saw tears in every eye. Edith Wilson
was crying. The hardboiled newspapermen sniffled. "Down in the amphi-
theatre I saw men sneak their handkerchiefs out of their pockets . . . The
President," Tumulty wrote, "was like a great organist playing upon the
heart emotions of the thousands of people who were held spellbound
by what he said."

Woodrow Wilson had covered something like eight thousand miles in
less than a month. He had delivered thirtysix set speeches and all sorts of
short addresses from the rear platform of his train. He had sat in on
countless political meetings and exerted himself to the utmost in a dozen
parades.

The night after the Pueblo speech, while his train was speeding towards Wichita, President Wilson, shortly after he had turned in, was
stricken with unbearable pain. Grayson could do nothing to alleviate it.
The President couldn't lie down. He couldn't stay still. He dressed himself and tried sitting up. There seemed no way of making him comfortable.

"It's a stroke," Brooks told Starling. "It's all over now."

"The Doctor and I," Edith wrote, "kept the vigil while the train dashed
on and on through the darkness . . . About five in the morning a blessed
release came and sitting upright on the stiff seat my husband fell asleep
. . . The dear face opposite me was worn and lined; and as I sat there
watching the dawn break slowly I felt that life would never be the same
. . . and from that hour on I would have to wear a mask, not only to the
public but to the one I loved best in the world: for he must never know
how ill he was and I must carry on."

In the morning Wilson protested that he must continue his tour but
Edith Wilson and Grayson and Tumulty took things into their own hands
and ordered the train to head straight back to Washington. The special
train sped across the countryside with blinds drawn as if there were a
dead man aboard. When the train arrived in Washington the President
had recovered sufficiently to be able to walk from the train to the car.

Three days later President Wilson was stricken down by cerebral
thrombosis.

The first the White House staff knew was when early one morning Ike
Hoover got a sudden call from Mrs. Wilson to send for Dr. Grayson. "The
President is very sick." The chief usher sent a car for Grayson to his house.
When they went up to the President's suite Hoover found every door
locked. The door was opened just enough to let the doctor in and closed

in Hoover's face. When Grayson came back he was terribly shaken. "My God," he told Hoover, "the President is paralyzed."

The White House Circle

For weeks Wilson lies desperately ill. His left side is paralyzed. His speech is affected. His condition is complicated by acute inflammation of the prostate gland. Edith is convinced an operation is too risky. A stricture almost causes his death. Showing the extraordinary powers of recuperation he has shown in similar but less drastic attacks, gradually he begins to recover.

Edith Wilson is determined that "he must never know how ill he was . . . I must carry on."

Without hesitation she takes upon herself complete charge of the sickroom and of such duties of the presidency as cannot be postponed. Ever since their marriage she has been giving him advice, and arranging his papers for him, and helping decipher messages in the private code he had with Colonel House.

Now Edith Wilson becomes *de facto* the President. Grayson collaborates humbly. He brings in trained nurses, consulting physicians. He rigs up the presidential suite as a small hospital. They both take extraordinary precautions that no word of the President's real condition shall reach the world outside. A nervous breakdown, Tumulty is told to report to the press. With rest and seclusion the President is recovering.

A few days after the President's stroke, Lansing, profoundly disturbed, seeks out Tumulty in the cabinet room. In default of any real information the wildest rumors are current in Washington. The President is dead. He has lost his mind and is confined in a straitjacket.

Something must be done to cope with the situation. Lansing has a copy of Jefferson's *Manual* in his hand. If the President really is incapacitated, he tells Tumulty, his powers and duties should devolve on Vice President Marshall. He points out the pertinent paragraph in the Constitution.

Tumulty flies up in his face. "Mr. Lansing," he quotes himself as declaiming, "the Constitution is not a dead letter in the White House." He needs no tutoring from Lansing about the Constitution. Whose business will it be to certify to the disability of the President, he asks hotly.

Lansing says it would be up to him and Dr. Grayson.

"You may rest assured," shouts Tumulty, dropping into brogue in his excitement, "that while Woodrow Wilson is lying in the White House on the broad of his back I'll not be a party to ousting him."

He adds, almost in tears, "The President has been too kind, too loyal, too wonderful to me to receive such treatment at my hands."

At that moment Dr. Grayson appears.

Tumulty turns to him. "And I am sure Dr. Grayson will never testify as to his disability. Will you, Grayson?"

Grayson will do no such thing.

"I then notified Mr. Lansing that if anyone outside of the White House circle attempted to certify to the President's disability, that Grayson and I would stand together and repudiate it."

Lansing retires crestfallen to the Department of State.

With Edith Wilson in command from behind the locked doors, such White House business as is essential is carried on. Through Grayson, Tumulty informs her of the problems of each day. She decides which items won't worry the President too much and makes a show of consulting him and sends back a scribbled note for Tumulty to act on. When the time comes for a Thanksgiving proclamation, Swem, the private secretary to whom the Wilsonian style has become second nature, drafts it. This time Mrs. Wilson manages to get the President to sign his name. The document comes back with the signature barely decipherable, at the top instead of the bottom of the sheet.

To Break the Heart of the World

The news that the treaty may fail in the Senate has been received with consternation in England. When, in the cool light of afterthought, the British statesmen read over the Treaty of Versailles they find themselves in agreement with President Wilson that only a series of rational readjustments under a league of nations can save Europe from disaster. Smuts, who signed under protest, is aghast at the document he put his name to. John Maynard Keynes has resigned his job with the British treasury and is preparing his famous blast against the treaty's iniquities.

House, in London, on his way home from fulfilling the pleasant task of helping pick Geneva for the League's capital, has been busy stirring up the English. He wants them to let the American Senate know that the British Government will accept almost any reservations the senators feel necessary.

Sir Edward Grey, now Viscount Grey of Falloden, though ill and discouraged and nearly blind, is prevailed upon to accept a special embassy to Washington to make such agreements as are urgently needed to avoid a naval armament race and to get ratification for the League of Nations. The British Cabinet thinks of him as an eminent liberal almost certain to be congenial to President Wilson. He arrives in Washington the day Wilson is stricken on the train to Wichita.

A few days later House reaches New York from England so weak from an attack of gallstones he has to be carried off the boat on a stretcher. Hopelessly incapacitated himself, he sends his friend and erstwhile in-

terpreter Stephen Bonsal to Washington. He knows that Bonsal, a school-
mate of the senator's soninlaw, is on good terms with Lodge. They
have in common a passion for the writings of George Borrow. If any man
can talk the senator around it is Bonsal. At a couple of friendly interviews
Bonsal fills the senator in on the gossip of the Peace Conference. He
wheedles him into admitting that his reservations might be modified.
Lodge pencils some suggestions, particularly certain changes in wording
that might make him accept Article X, on a printed copy of the covenant
which Bonsal just happens to have in his pocket. Bonsal rushes this copy
to the post office and mails it to House in New York. House promptly
dispatches it to President Wilson at the White House.

No reply. Edith Wilson has ceased to deliver House's letters to the
President. She hates House and undoubtedly she feels that anything
connected with the hated Lodge may upset her husband and bring about
a relapse. Nothing is ever heard of Lodge's modification of his reservations.

Senator Lodge, who knows of Bonsal's intimacy with House, and who
still considers the confidential colonel the quickest channel to the President's ear, being touchy as a bear, is insulted by what he considers a
direct rebuff from the White House. A few days later he reintroduces his
reservations, in their original form, on the Senate floor.

Edith Wilson has cut all channels of communication with the President.
When Sir William Wiseman, whom the Foreign Office sent ahead of the
new ambassador, trusting in his intimacy with the confidential colonel
to smooth the way, calls at the White House, Mrs. Wilson tells him the
President is too ill to see him. "I had never liked this plausible little man."
Besides she knows he's a crony of House's. The eminent Viscount Grey
suffers the same fate as Wiseman. Not even Tumulty has the courtesy to
give him an interview. Without being received by the President he can't
function as an ambassador. After cooling his heels dismally for three
months at the British Embassy he goes home in despair.

Edith Wilson, however, does consider the President well enough during
this period to receive a visit from the King and Queen of Belgium. Like
many another Virginian, Mrs. Wilson has a soft spot for royalty. She lets
them in to see her husband in his bed and allows them to show him a
beautiful set of china they have brought the Wilsons for a present. When
the young Prince of Wales arrives in Washingon he is dutifully taken up
to the sick man's bedside.

Meanwhile the fulldress debate on the peace treaty resounds through
the Senate chamber. Twice during November Edith Wilson allows Senator Hitchcock to see the President. He finds a tremulous whitebearded old
man propped up with pillows. The paralyzed arm is hidden under the
covers. Hitchcock still believes moderate reservations may win. When

Hitchcock brings up Wilson's own suggestions as a basis for compromise Wilson tells him, "Let Lodge compromise."

As the day of the Senate vote draws near, the pressure for a compromise builds up in Washington. Herbert Hoover is using all the influence he has with the members of Wilson's cabinet. Baruch, whom Edith likes, and who is a cordial friend of Grayson's, urges them both to try to convince the President that enough senators are ready to vote for the treaty with moderate reservations if he will only give his consent. Half a loaf is better than no bread.

"For my sake," says Edith, "won't you accept these reservations and get this awful thing settled."

He pats her hand. "Little girl don't you desert me. That I cannot stand." Grayson puts in his two cents' worth.

Wilson shakes his head. "Better a thousand times to go down fighting," Edith quotes him as saying.

The day before the vote he dictates a letter to Hitchcock: "I sincerely hope that the friends and supporters of the treaty will vote against the Lodge resolution of ratification."

Lodge uses all his parliamentary skill to set a trap for the Democrats. He arranges for the treaty to be brought to a vote first with his own reservations attached. Following the President's instructions the southern Democrats join the diehard Republicans to vote it down. Then Hitchcock moves that the treaty be reconsidered with his moderate reservations attached. He is voted down by the Republicans voting solid. Lodge, to prove to the world that the Democrats are defeating their own treaty, now allows a new resolution to consider the treaty with his own reservations to be presented. In a rollcall vote, it is defeated by fortyone ayes to fiftyone nays, with the President's Democrats voting against.

Senator Swanson of Virginia rushes across the aisle to Senator Lodge's desk. "For God's sake, can't something be done to save the treaty?"

"Senator, the door is closed," replies Lodge. "You have done it yourselves."

By the end of December the President is well enough to dress himself and to hobble about a little with a cane. "He had changed from a giant to a pygmy in every wise," wrote the White House usher. "It was so sad that those of us about him, who almost without exception admired him, would turn our heads away when he came along, or when we went near him."

For another fourteen months Woodrow Wilson lives on at the White House, immured in a sickroom. Every message, every newspaper passes through Edith Wilson's hands.

"He must never know how ill he was; and I must carry on."

When he is well enough to go out for drives in the White House motor car he sits covered by a cape in front with the driver, because it's too painful for him to try to sit up in the back seat. He takes pathetic pleasure in the motion pictures that are shown him almost every afternoon, propped in his wheel chair in one of the large upstairs rooms.

By early February Wilson is well enough to settle with Lansing. Secretary Lansing has been calling informal meetings of the members of the Cabinet to keep the government rolling during the President's illness. This is the last straw. He dictates a stiff letter asking for the Secretary's immediate resignation.

Bainbridge Colby, erstwhile Progressive who became a devoted Wilsonian, and who has the reputation of writing a very good speech, is appointed in Lansing's stead.

Illusions flourish in the sickroom world.

Wilson is convinced that the American people, the people who cheered him in Omaha and Seattle and Coeur d'Alene and Pueblo, Colorado, are for him and for his covenant almost to a man. Only the reactionary senators stand in their way.

He propounds a strange scheme: he will challenge the senators who are against the treaty to resign and seek re-election. He will promise that if they are re-elected he will induce the Vice President to resign and, after appointing a Republican Secretary of State he will resign himself; the Secretary of State will thus become President. Hasn't he always believed in party government in the English style?

When the Senate reconsiders the Versailles Treaty, and the possibility arises that ratification may still be secured, with reservations tempered by compromise, Wilson again insists that Hitchcock's obedient Democrats cast their votes against any treaty with reservations of any kind. So strong is the clamor for compromise that, even so, the treaty almost passes with the necessary twothirds vote. Only strict orders from the White House keep the Democrats in line for rejection. "We can always depend on Mr. Wilson," says Brandegee to Lodge.

The theory is abroad that Wilson has insisted on rejection of the amended treaty because he wants a campaign issue for 1920. Can it be that he dreams of a third term?

When the Democrats convene in San Francisco in June the candidates are William Gibbs McAdoo and A. Mitchell Palmer. Wilson won't let Tumulty give his endorsement either to his soninlaw or to his Attorney General. Newspaper articles are inspired about the President's very good health. Photographs are broadcast taken from his good side. Colby is dispatched to San Francisco as bearer of a message from the White House: in case of a deadlock; why not Wilson?

The scheme goes awry. On the fortyfourth ballot a harmless Ohio poli-

tician named James M. Cox receives the nomination. His runningmate is
the Assistant Secretary of the Navy, Franklin Delano Roosevelt.

Cox is to run against another Ohio politician, considered equally harmless, Warren Gamaliel Harding, whose candidacy is the product of a similar deadlock in the Republican convention. Senator Harding's qualifications are that he's a strong reservationist on the treaty and that he comes
from Canton which was William McKinley's home town. Perhaps there is
something that reminds people of McKinley about the way Harding wears
his frock coat.

Wilson calls the Democratic candidates to the White House for his
blessing. From his wheel chair he receives their assurance that they will
treat the campaign as a solemn referendum on the Covenant of the
League of Nations.

When the American people go to the polls in November to decide this
solemn referendum Harding wins by seven million votes.

On Inauguration Day Woodrow Wilson drives to the Capitol from the
White House with President-elect Harding. While Harding walks with
swinging stride up the broad steps of the Capitol, Wilson is smuggled in
a wheel chair through a side door and up by a private elevator to the
President's room in the Senate wing. There the traditional congressional
committee waits upon the retiring President to ask if he has any further
communications to make to the retiring Congress. The man whose duty it
is to ask that question as committee chairman is Henry Cabot Lodge.

"I have no communication to make," says ex-President Wilson; "I appreciate your courtesy, good morning, sir."

No crowds packed the empty sidewalks of the avenues when Woodrow
Wilson was driven from the Capitol to the house on S Street which Edith
Wilson had readied to receive him. The sickroom life went on. A querulous invalid, sometimes he surprised his family by a burst of high spirits.
He liked to spring a limerick on them. For a while his health seemed to
improve. He would speak of his plan to write a book on the philosophy of
government, but he got no further than a dedication to his wife.

When he sat up he liked to wear an old gray sweater he had worn as a
young professor. When occasionally an old friend, or a delegation, was
admitted to see him, they found him seated by the fire in his library, always in the same worn brown leather armchair that had come with him
from Princeton. Visitors deferred to him as titular head of the Democratic
Party.

Each Armistice Day a small nostalgic crowd would gather on the quiet
street and a few extra policemen would be assigned to the beat and Edith
Wilson would arrange for him to say a few words urging all good men to
come to the aid of the League, and the lost peace. He enjoyed the afternoon rides in their motor car. Though the day was excessively hot, he

22

was well enough, when President Harding, whose administration was beset with storms and scandals, died of poisoning attributed to an Alaskan crab, to attend the funeral.

There was no real recovery. In the fall of 1923 the sight began to fail in Wilson's good eye. Glasses brought no relief. His digestion failed. Dr. Grayson remembered him whispering, "The machinery is worn out . . . I am ready."

He died on February 3, 1924, about churchtime on a Sunday morning. When he was interred in the crypt of the unfinished Episcopal cathedral up on St. Alban's Hill, President and Mrs. Calvin Coolidge were present at the ceremony.

There is more material on World War I than any man can possibly cope with. The reader who tries to thread his way through the currents and crosscurrents of the period is faced by astronomical quantities of printed matter. Everyone remotely connected with even the most distant aspects of the conflict managed to get some volume printed celebrating his exploits. Persons in authority, with the help of journalists, ghostwriters, and rewrite men, produced a flood of memoirs, almost always selfserving, and often inaccurate. The official records are monumental. The patient reader has to wade through shelf after shelf of flatulent verbiage in pursuit of that tiny flicker of truth which makes a page worthwhile.

My method was to try to relate the experiences of the assorted personalities and their assorted justifications to my own recollections of childhood and youth during those years; and to seek out, wherever possible, the private letter, the unguarded entry in the diary, the newsreport made on the spur of the moment.

For the period from 1900 to 1910 (and the two decades before) Theodore Roosevelt's letters make fine reading. T.R. improves with acquaintance. Though the history of the first decade of the twentieth century in the United States is still unwritten, you can gather some of its elements from such personal narratives of the time as Lincoln Steffens' and Max Eastman's autobiographies, and from biographies like Robert La Follette's life by his wife and daughter, Pusey's work on Hughes, Pringle's lives of Theodore Roosevelt and Taft, and Hermann Hagedorn's *Leonard Wood*.

It was the era of the two-volume life. The chief value of the "life and letters" type of biography lies in the accompanying documents. A blight infests the whole literature: the authors and editors shamelessly expunged from the record any items or expressions which they fancied might reflect adversely on their heroes. Their writing tends towards the bland inexpressiveness of a retouched cabinet photograph.

It was in some ways a golden age of American journalism. Much of the newspaper reporting was excellent. Magazines like *McClure's* and *Everybody's* are readable today. Lyman Abbott's *Outlook* from week to week gives you the picture of the aspirations and obsessions of the "better element."

For Woodrow Wilson, the early volumes of Ray Stannard Baker's *Life and Letters* offer copious documentation. Baker was a heroworshipper and careless about dates and details, but he had access to an immense amount of material when it was still fresh; and, on the whole, up to the difficult years of the presidency, handled it well. Perhaps Professor Arthur S. Link's careful volumes on Wilson, of which three have already appeared, will prove the necessary corrective.

Among family narratives Eleanor Wilson McAdoo's *The Woodrow Wilsons*, Margaret Elliott's *My Aunt Louisa and Woodrow Wilson* and Stockton Axson's *Private Life* are all essential.

James Kerney's *The Political Education of Woodrow Wilson* is probably the most revealing book written about him by a contemporary. The editor of the Trenton *Evening Times* wrote freshly and with rare candor.

Tumulty's and McAdoo's books, though both gentlemen leave out more than they put in, are useable; as are David F. Houston's *Eight Years with Wilson's Cabinet* and Franklin K. Lane's letters.

Among manuscript sources I struck paydirt in Robert Lansing's diaries at the Library of Congress and, for wartime Britain, in the Walter Hines Page papers at Harvard. Outside of the vast aggregation of Wilson papers at the Library of Congress, and the Bryan papers and the other collections under the care of the Division of Manuscripts there, the supreme source of information on Wilson's waging of peace and war is to be found in his confidential colonel's day to day comments preserved in the Edward M. House papers at Yale.

On Colonel House himself there is Arthur Howden Smith's *Mr. House of Texas* and a somewhat sensation-mongering work, not without its insights, by George Sylvester Vierick called *The Strangest Friendship in History*.

W. F. McComb's *Making Woodrow Wilson President*, R. E. Annin's *Woodrow Wilson, A Character Study* and *Wilson the Unknown*, by someone writing under the name of Wells Wells, offer, if taken with the proper grains of salt, valuable sidelights.

For the shooting side of the war John J. Pershing's *My Experiences in the World War* remains surprisingly good. I don't know whether the general wrote it all himself or not, but it shows the impress of his character in every line. Admiral Sims' book is good. Robert Lee Bullard's *Personalities and Reminiscences of the War* is the frank report of a combat officer. Harbord's *Leaves from a War Diary*, William Mitchell's *Memories of World War I* and Charles G. Dawes' *A Journal of the Great War* deal with things actually experienced.

There is shelf after shelf of combat narratives, many of them either spiced or expurgated for publication. These works are best read in con-

nection with the records of command posts and divisional and corps headquarters which are to be found in the publications of the American Battle
Monuments Commission.

The regimental and divisional histories range from Creel-style journalism to sober recitals of facts in the good military tradition. *The History
of the Second Division* is irreplaceable for its quotations from soldiers'
diaries.

The Russian imbroglio is excellently covered by George F. Kennan's
two volumes on *Soviet American Relations 1917–20.* Raymond Robins'
farsighted appraisal of Lenin's government can be found in William
Hard's *Raymond Robins' Own Story.* Edgar Sisson's *100 Red Days* is not
without interest as a document of the time. R. H. Bruce Lockhart's *British
Agent* makes good reading, as of course does John Reed's account of the
coup d'état. General William S. Graves wrote a useful book: *America's
Siberian Adventure;* and three lieutenants named Moore, Mead and Jahns
collaborated in *The History of the American Expedition Fighting the
Bolsheviki in Northern Russia,* privately published in Detroit by what
they called "The Polar Bear Press," which constitutes one of the few
original American sources for that campaign. The Murmansk and Archangel story has recently been well recapitulated by E. M. Halliday in
The Ignorant Armies.

The best account of the Peace Conference remains, for my money,
Harold Nicolson's *Peacemaking.* James T. Shotwell's published diary
comes a close second. Winston Churchill's *Aftermath* is enlivening in connection with R. S. Baker's *Woodrow Wilson and World Settlement,* which
the eminent statesman excoriates in good Churchillian style. John Maynard Keynes' enumeration of Wilson's faults and weaknesses in *The Economic Consequences of the Peace* is historical vituperation in the grand
manner.

Edith Bolling Wilson's *My Memoir* throws, with a cogency perhaps
unintended, the pathetic light of feminine egotism and affection on the
tragic figure of her husband, as he went about performing, with the ritual
determinism of a hero of Sophocles, act after act to bring about his own
destruction.

The last phase is well described by Thomas A. Bailey in *Woodrow
Wilson and the Lost Peace* and *Woodrow Wilson and the Great Betrayal.*
The record of the final ironical twist to the tragic drama is to be found
in Stephen Bonsal's *Unfinished Business* where Bonsal tells of the near
success of his mission from Colonel House to Senator Lodge, which might,
had Mrs. Wilson not stood in the way, have opened up the possibility of a
compromise on the Covenant.

I want to thank Mr. Mearns and his assistants of the Manuscript Division of the Library of Congress for their help in making available the
Wilson, Lansing, and Bliss papers and other sections of the vast hoard of

material under their jurisdiction. Colonel E. G. Bliss has given me permission to use two short quotations from his father, General Bliss's letters. Excerpts from the Walter Hines Page papers are quoted by permission of the Harvard College Library. Mrs. Richard Fell is allowing me to quote a paragraph from her uncle's diary on deposit at the University of Virginia. I want to thank Professor Seymour and his assistant Mr. Gotlieb, for their unfailing hospitality and to acknowledge the permission given me by the Yale University Library to study and utilize unpublished papers in the Edward M. House collection. I owe many thanks, as often before, to the Peabody and Enoch Pratt Libraries in Baltimore.

INDEX

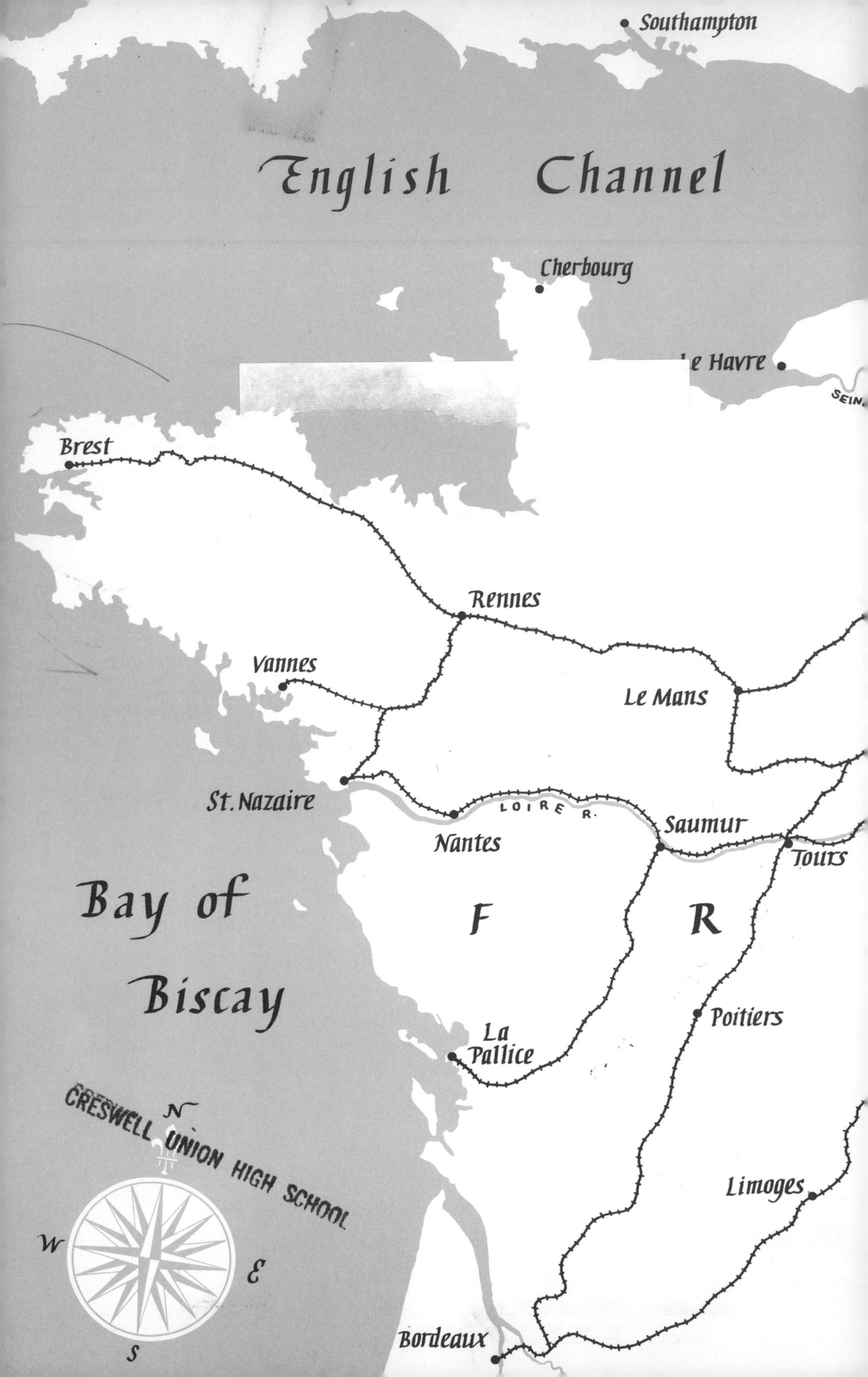
Southampton
English Channel
Cherbourg
Le Havre
SEIN
Brest
Rennes
Vannes
Le Mans
St. Nazaire
LOIRE R.
Nantes
Saumur
Tours
Bay of
Biscay
F
R
Poitiers
La
Pallice
N
W
E
S
Limoges
Bordeaux